CASES IN OPERATIONS MANAGEMENT

THE IVEY CASEBOOK SERIES
A SAGE Publications Series

Series Editor
Paul W. Beamish
Richard Ivey School of Business
The University of Western Ontario

Books in This Series

CASES IN BUSINESS ETHICS
Edited by David J. Sharp

CASES IN ENTREPRENEURSHIP
The Venture Creation Process
Edited by Eric A. Morse and Ronald K. Mitchell

CASES IN OPERATIONS MANAGEMENT
Building Customer Value Through World-Class Operations
Edited by Robert D. Klassen and Larry J. Menor

CASES IN ORGANIZATIONAL BEHAVIOR
Edited by Gerard H. Seijts

CASES IN THE ENVIRONMENT OF BUSINESS
International Perspectives
Edited by David W. Conklin

Forthcoming

CASES IN GENDER AND DIVERSITY IN ORGANIZATIONS
Edited by Alison M. Konrad

ROBERT D. KLASSEN
The University of Western Ontario

LARRY J. MENOR
The University of Western Ontario

CASES IN OPERATIONS MANAGEMENT

Building Customer Value Through World-Class Operations

SAGE Publications
Thousand Oaks ■ London ■ New Delhi

One time permission to reproduce granted by Ivey Management Services on December 14, 2004.

The Ivey cases have been prepared solely to provide material for class discussion. The authors do not intend to illustrate either effective or ineffective handling of managerial situations. The authors may have disguised certain names and other identifying information to protect confidentiality.

Ivey Management Services prohibits any form of reproduction, storage, or transmittal without its written permission. Ivey case material is not covered under authorization from CanCopy or any reproduction rights organization. To order copies or request permission to reproduce Ivey materials, contact Ivey Publishing, Ivey Management Services, c/o Richard Ivey School of Business, The University of Western Ontario, London, Ontario, Canada, N6A 3K7; phone (519) 661-3208, fax (519) 661-3882, e-mail cases@ivey.uwo.ca

For information:

Sage Publications, Inc.
2455 Teller Road
Thousand Oaks, California 91320
E-mail: order@sagepub.com

Sage Publications Ltd.
1 Oliver's Yard
55 City Road
London EC1Y 1SP
United Kingdom

Sage Publications India Pvt. Ltd.
B-42, Panchsheel Enclave
Post Box 4109
New Delhi 110 017 India

Printed in the United States of America.

Library of Congress Cataloging-in-Publication Data

Cases in operations management: Building customer value through world-class operations / edited by Robert D. Klassen, Larry J. Menor.
    p. cm.—(The Ivey Casebook Series)
Includes bibliographical references.
ISBN 1-4129-1371-3 (pbk.)
   1. Production management—Case studies. 2. Industrial management—Case studies.
I. Klassen, Robert David. II. Menor, Larry J. III. Series.
TS155.C31582 2006
658.5—dc22   2005003580

This book is printed on acid-free paper.

05 06 07 08 09 10 9 8 7 6 5 4 3 2 1

Acquisitions Editor:	Al Bruckner
Editorial Assistant:	MaryAnn Vail
Production Editor:	Laureen A. Shea
Copy Editor:	Gillian Dickens
Typesetter:	C&M Digitals (P) Ltd.
Proofreader:	Scott Oney
Cover Designer:	Edgar Abarca

CONTENTS

INTRODUCTION TO THE
IVEY CASEBOOK SERIES

As the title of this series suggests, these books all draw from the Ivey Business School's case collection. Ivey has long had the world's second largest collection of decision-oriented, field-based business cases. Well more than a million copies of Ivey cases are studied every year. There are more than 2,000 cases in Ivey's current collection, with more than 6,000 in the total collection. Each year approximately 200 new titles are registered at Ivey Publishing (www.ivey.uwo.ca/cases), and a similar number are retired. Nearly all Ivey cases have teaching notes available to qualified instructors. The cases included in this volume are all from the current collection.

The vision for the series was a result of conversations I had with Sage's Senior Editor, Al Bruckner, starting in September 2002. Over the subsequent months, we were able to shape a model for the books in the series that we felt would meet a market need.

Each volume in the series contains text and cases. "Some" text was deemed essential in order to provide a basic overview of the particular field and to place the selected cases in an appropriate context. We made a conscious decision to not include hundreds of pages of text material in each volume in recognition of the fact that many professors prefer to supplement basic text material with readings or lectures customized to their interests and to those of their students.

The editors of the books in this series are all highly qualified experts in their respective fields. I was delighted when each agreed to prepare a volume. We very much welcome your comments on this casebook.

—Paul W. Beamish
Series Editor

PREFACE

This book was developed to address the growing demand in business schools for a casebook that has strong coverage of critical concepts that collectively contribute to building world-class operations. To address this need, we have selected a diverse, yet foundational, set of cases from which to cover a number of major topics that are central to an introductory operations management course.

Overall, the chapters and cases are arranged to develop two central messages that are crucial for every manager to understand about operations: the contribution of process management to customer value and building world-class competitiveness through operations. The first message emphasizes how customer value is defined from an operational perspective, and the second stresses how excellence can be developed through improvement across multiple dimensions of operations.

We would like to point out that the cases included in this casebook, for the most part, are somewhat longer and more complex than the typical short cases included at the ends of chapters in many introductory operations management textbooks. As such, this casebook is designed for faculty and students who use cases in at least half their classes. Why at least half? We truly believe that both faculty and students experience a learning curve effect when it comes to any particular pedagogical approach, whether lectures, simulations, or cases. Longer, more complex cases are easier to integrate into core operations courses if students have made the shift from merely looking at symptoms of problems to exploring the underlying issues that cause these problems. However, this shift takes repeated exposure and practice. Thus, it also takes a fair amount of experience with cases for students to become comfortable with a discussion-oriented, Socratic style of learning.

This casebook is well suited for MBAs or advanced undergraduates because of its managerial decision orientation and strong coverage of process management. Business students need to understand the interrelated processes of a firm, which connect operations with all other functional areas of an organization. They also must explore how each part of an organization, not just the operations function, must design and manage processes and deal with such critical areas as quality, supply chain management, and operations strategy.

After introducing a framework for world-class operations and its six basic components in the first chapter, the casebook considers each area in greater detail in the following chapters. In a nutshell, we view the foundational areas of process design, planning and control, and project management as critical underpinnings for the systems-oriented aspects of quality and supply chain management. At the top, operations strategy provides the integration necessary for developing and implementing world-class operations.

A short overview is provided at the beginning of each chapter, and half the chapters also include several experiential exercises for use in the classroom. Collectively, approximately 40 cases, simulations, and exercises address the six main topic areas. However, despite our efforts to position each case in a single chapter, it will quickly become apparent that cases, like real-world problems, are rarely confined to a single topic. This is one of the true merits of using cases; they allow both students and faculty to cross topical boundaries, integrate learnings from earlier discussions, and expand opportunities for improvement.

Given that most managers will need to function effectively in an international context, many of the cases draw from challenges faced by experienced managers in such diverse settings as Japan, India, the Caribbean, and China, in addition to the United States and Canada. It is our hope that the settings of these cases, while continuing to illustrate basic concepts, also will expand students' understanding of cultural concerns that must be interwoven into such classic areas as process design, quality, and supply chain management.

ACKNOWLEDGMENTS

We wish to thank the people at Sage Publications and Ivey Publishing who inspired this project and supported us as authors. Specifically, we offer our thanks to Al Bruckner, Senior Editor at Sage, and Paul Beamish, our colleague at Ivey and Director of Ivey Publishing. We are also indebted to the Ivey faculty, past and present, who have contributed cases included in this volume. In addition to the senior operations management faculty noted earlier, we thank Paul Beamish, Deborah Compeau, Elizabeth Grasby, Neil Jones, Carol Prahinski, Lynn Purdy, Scott Schneberger, Bert Wood, and Mark Vandenbosch. We would like to extend our gratitude to the many case writers who worked with the faculty to produce these case materials. Finally, we appreciate the very helpful assistance of Penni Pring and Diana Lee in compiling the material included in this casebook.

—*Robert D. Klassen and Larry J. Menor*

This book is dedicated to our senior colleagues at Ivey who have been instrumental in our development as case teachers: Michiel Leenders, James Erskine, John Haywood-Farmer, Chris Piper, and Fraser Johnson. Each has helped us develop and refine our approach to both writing and teaching cases in so many ways. Their thoughtful and constructive feedback has changed the way we personally think about operations—and business—management.

1

DEVELOPING WORLD-CLASS OPERATIONS

O perations management is integral to the development and delivery of goods and services throughout the global economy. In essence, operations management is about the creation of customer value through the effective and efficient management of processes. Whether we purchase a new automobile, visit a medical clinic, or converse with friends in other parts of the world via the Internet, processes in the public and private sectors underpin our daily lives. In a nutshell, processes transform inputs into value-added outputs using a variety of resources. For example, your presence in Chicago, an input, might be transformed using such inputs as a mobile phone, fiber-optic cable, customer service personnel, and billing systems into your virtual presence a continent away in London, an output.

For managers, several immediate concerns spring to mind from this general definition of operations management. How do we define value? How should processes be configured to be both efficient and effective? Which resources are most critical, and how should they be managed? How might operations contribute a competitive advantage for the organization? In fact, it is these pivotal questions that this casebook seeks to explore through decisions that confronted real managers.

CUSTOMER VALUE

To begin, it is important to identify what we mean by customer value from an operations management perspective. Customers are interested in a product, which is usually a bundle of goods and services. At the simplest level, a product might include a physical asset, such as an automobile, and a straightforward service, such as peace of mind provided by a five-year warranty. However, increasingly complex product offerings, such as the mobile phone service described earlier, must synthesize a diverse array of goods and services into a final product. Thus, value can be defined in terms of what is offered, as well as how well particular attributes are delivered.

1

Operations management contributes to four general dimensions of customer value: time, quality, flexibility, and cost. Each of these is considered in multiple case settings throughout this book. Time captures aspects related to speed, reliability of delivery, and rapid product and service development. Quality incorporates both the tangible and intangible characteristics related to product or service design and consistency. Like quality, flexibility also captures elements that are seen by customers, such as the ability to customize products and services, as well as those that remain unseen, such as the capacity to accommodate significant changes in demand. Finally, the last dimension, cost, is not measured directly by customers but instead is translated by competitive forces into price.

BUILDING BLOCKS OF OPERATIONS MANAGEMENT

Six basic building blocks provide a structured approach for describing, diagnosing, and improving an organization's operations (see Figure 1.1). At the foundational level, understanding basic drivers of process effectiveness and efficiency explores three critical elements: process design, planning and control, and project management. At the immediate level, managers must develop broader systems that transcend and integrate individual process elements. Two primary systems that deserve much management attention are quality and supply chain management systems. Finally, the pattern of decisions and actions at both the process and systems levels must be integrated into a coherent operations strategy, which in turn is linked to corporate strategy.

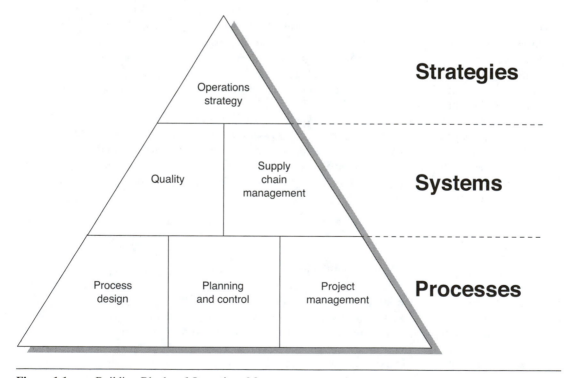

Figure 1.1   Building Blocks of Operations Management

Drawing on this model, the cases at the end of this chapter overview the basic challenges and decisions that are explored in much greater detail later in the book. Chapter 2, "Process Design," provides more insight into the fundamental structure and management of processes. Using the conceptual relationship between product volume and customization as a starting point, the cases in this chapter explore how process-related decisions often involve trade-offs between two or more dimensions of customer value. The cases illustrate a conceptual framework that links the concepts of process capacity, inventory, and variability.

Chapter 3, "Planning and Control," considers how customer demand drives much of the planning process for operations resources. Forecasts must be developed, often with very limited information, and data can then be translated into a plan to accommodate that demand and/or a set of management actions to influence that demand. Once long-term aggregate plans are in place, management must actively coordinate the use of resources to meet demand and budget.

Chapter 4, "Project Management," captures both strategic planning and practical tools that collectively contribute to effective project management. Understanding these issues is important for all managers throughout their careers, as much time is usually devoted to coordinating short-term, team-based projects.

Chapter 5, "Quality," focuses on defining and controlling quality. In addition, this chapter emphasizes the importance of the systematic improvement of products (including both goods and services) and processes. Improvement is undertaken through the adoption and implementation of a total quality management (TQM) system, which involves aligning the entire organization around delivering customer value. Although the definition of quality may differ between manufacturers and services, the strategic elements and quality tools of TQM are the same in both operational contexts.

Chapter 6, "Supply Chain Management," concentrates, from a total systems perspective, on the efficient and effective flow of information, materials, and services from raw materials suppliers, to production facilities, to distributors, to end customers. Supply chain management requires the timely coordination of upstream and downstream activities, and many organizations have achieved significant strategic, financial, and operational advantages through better configuring and managing their supply chains. Some of these operational advantages have included reductions in inventory levels and investment, as well as increased delivery reliability and responsiveness.

The final chapter, "Operations Strategy," involves the combination and synthesis of operating processes and systems to gain a competitive advantage. Managers in manufacturing and service organizations have recognized the criticality of developing effective operations, as well as the need to actively manage many of the process and system elements introduced in earlier chapters. Operations strategy also bridges between systems and the broader corporate strategy. Organizations that successfully develop and manage their operating resources in an integrated manner are likely to achieve an enviable strategic advantage and, in some cases, world-class status.

WORLD-CLASS OPERATIONS

World-class operations is more than simply understanding the six building blocks of operations. And it is more than developing and maintaining a reputation for offering solid customer value. Organizations also must assess the business setting with their operational

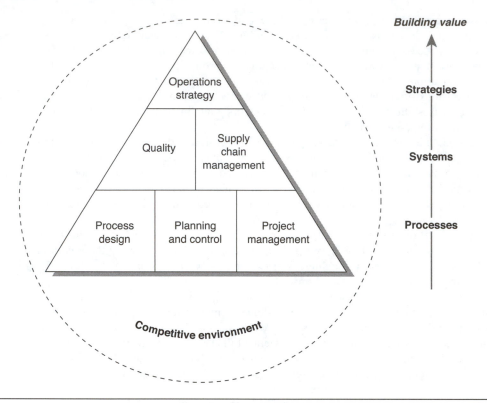

Figure 1.2   Building Value With World-Class Operations

capabilities to identify emerging and unfilled market opportunities that leverage existing strengths. Moreover, it is critical to recognize when competitive forces dictate the adaptation of existing operational capabilities or the development of new ones.

Thus, world-class operations demonstrate industry leadership. New operational capabilities must be developed ahead of the competitors, and operations must be leveraged to deliver superior value over the long term (see Figure 1.2). This emphasis on operations is a key opportunity to build a strong competitive advantage. For example, organizations described in later cases, including Spin Master Toys, Electrosteel Castings, ASIMCO, and the Atlanta Symphony Orchestra, are making great strides toward building such capabilities.

As you move through the initial introductory cases in this chapter and the six chapters that follow, two central concepts will emerge and continue to be reinforced. Both concepts are crucial for every manager to understand about operations. First, operations must be actively designed and managed to deliver and enhance customer value. Identifying important managerial levers helps us to do this. Second, building world-class competitiveness is possible through operations; however, it is not a static competence focused on a single dimension, but rather a dynamic set of capabilities that improve and evolve over time across multiple dimensions.

INDUSTRIE PININFARINA: THE NEW CUSTOMER DECISION

Pininfarina SpA, a renowned Italian manufacturer and designer of niche vehicles for major automobile companies, has traditionally competed on flexibility using a highly skilled design and manufacturing workforce and low levels of automation. However, the European auto market is threatened with a shakeout. Renato Bertrandi, manager of operations, must decide whether to accept an offer from Mitsubishi to become the exclusive European manufacturer of a sport utility vehicle. The order would more than double the company's manufacturing volume and relieve pressure to replace models currently in production. However, the fit of the order with existing manufacturing strategy is poor, and major changes in facilities and equipment as well as people and systems would be required.

Learning objectives: introduce the basic concepts underlying operations strategy, examine industry-level evolution, and explore the dynamic nature of operations capabilities.

FELL-FAB PRODUCTS (A)

Fell-Fab Products is a Canadian manufacturer of interior coverings for airlines, bus companies, and passenger rail services. Glen Fell, president of Fell-Fab Products, was recently approached by a key customer with a request for the company to expand its product offerings into servicing all aspects of the interior coverings business. However, Fell was unsure whether this new service dimension fit, if at all, with existing capabilities, what the financial returns might be, or how to best leverage this opportunity.

Learning objectives: examine product, process, and strategy differences for manufacturing and service operations; identify strategic opportunities for product bundles of goods and service; and understand the rationale for business process outsourcing.

UNICON CONCRETE PRODUCTS (H.K.) LTD.

Unicon supplies precast concrete products to the flourishing construction market in Hong Kong. Herman Li, deputy managing director, is evaluating an opportunity to pursue a "blanket" regulatory approval for Unicon's custom-designed concrete products with its largest customer, the Hong Kong Housing Authority. This opportunity promises to offer cost savings to both Unicon and this customer, although questions remain about the broader implications for Unicon's manufacturing operations and other customers. At the same time, Li must develop a plan to expand Unicon's manufacturing capacity if Unicon hopes to capitalize on the rapidly expanding market and fend off new competitors from mainland China.

Learning objectives: compete on dimensions of customer value, understand product and process relationships in operations, develop congruence between operations and marketing, and adapt to low-cost competition.

MANAGEMENT QUESTIONS ADDRESSED IN DEVELOPING WORLD-CLASS OPERATIONS CHAPTER

1. How is customer value defined? How does customer value prioritize price, quality, time, and flexibility?

2. What operational decisions must managers typically make, and what is the operations challenge? What are the real problems, opportunities, and issues, and what are merely the symptoms?

3. What are the basic elements of an operations strategy? How is it linked to corporate strategy? To the competitive setting?

4. What forces push management to change an organization's operational capabilities? How quickly can these capabilities be changed?

5. What drives the cost structure for operations? Which costs are fixed? Which costs are variable?

6. How important are labor versus material versus capital costs?

7. What criteria should be used to make a decision? Along what dimensions of customer value are trade-offs necessary?

INDUSTRIE PININFARINA: THE NEW CUSTOMER DECISION

Prepared by Professor Neil Jones

Version: (A) 2001-05-17

The 25th of April is a national holiday in Italy, but it was not for Industrie Pininfarina (Pininfarina) top management in 1996. A meeting between Pininfarina and high level Mitsubishi executives lasted the entire day. The following day, a Friday, Renato Bertrandi, manager of operations at Pininfarina, sat in his office at the Pininfarina plant at Grugliasco, in the Piedmont region of Italy. In a rare quiet moment, he reflected on the challenges that lay ahead for the manufacturing operations. On Monday, he would recommend whether Pininfarina should accept European manufacturing responsibility for a new vehicle, the Mitsubishi Pajero. The vehicle presented both a major opportunity and a significant commitment, which would impact Pininfarina's fortunes through the year 2004 and beyond and it would require major changes in manufacturing. The contract would virtually double Pininfarina's output.

Once again, Bertrandi thought through the company's options and tried to evaluate the near-term benefits and challenges to manufacturing as well as the longer-term consequences. He thought with satisfaction about the many achievements in manufacturing since the 1980s. An active triathlete, he wondered where the next phase of the competitive race in the changing global automotive industry would leave the company.

PININFARINA BACKGROUND

In 1904, at the age of eleven, Battista "Pinin" Farina began work in his brother's coach-making business—which also specialized in making seats for racecars. After long experience in the emerging and rapidly expanding Turin automobile industry, he founded his own company in 1930. Farina specialized in the design and production of custom and small series automobiles. While he expected to build relatively few "special" cars and was rooted in a tradition of highly skilled craftworkers, he was much impressed with the Ford system, which he had seen on a plant tour in the United States in 1920. The visit contributed to his conclusion that he had to draw on the strengths of Ford's method to be successful. As he would later say,

> I was looking for a third state, between the craft we had to leave behind and industry. The state had to have industrial norms and structures but it must not suffocate that individual reality, which can be defined as style. There was no tradition to which we could appeal, our occupation was brand new and we paid for any mistakes we made in person.

The company soon earned a reputation for the quality and beauty of its designs. By 1939, Farina Industrie employed over 500 workers and manufactured close to 800 automobiles. For a period of time during World War II, the company product line included ambulances, airline seats, and stoves, but it returned to a focus on automobiles after the war ended. And it was in automobiles where it continued to find its greatest success—producing revered designs such as the Ferrari Berlinetta Dino and the Alfa Romeo Spider Duetto (Exhibit 1). Farina's Cistalia automobile, designed in 1947, was celebrated in a collection of mobile sculptures at New York's Museum of Modern Art.

In 1954, after the great success of the Alfa Romeo Spider, the company added facilities to manufacture lower volume cars for major automobile manufacturers. To handle an increasing demand, in 1958 the company moved from Turin to a manufacturing plant in Grugliasco, a nearby suburb. Upon Farina's death in 1966, management of the business was taken over by his son, Sergio, and his son-in-law, Renzo Carli. The family name and that of the business

were changed from Farina to Pininfarina by presidential decree.

Throughout the 1960s and 1970s Pininfarina continued to design and produce unique automobiles such as the Ferrari Berlinetta, the Lancia Flaminia, the Austin A 40, and the Morris 1100. By 1972, the company employed about 1,900 people and was producing more than 23,000 cars per year. In 1979, Pininfarina split its design and manufacture divisions into Pininfarina Studi E Ricerche and Industrie Pininfarina (IPF), under the holding company Pininfarina S.p.A. In 1986, 30 per cent of the company's shares were listed and sold on the Italian stock market, and a further three per cent of shares were sold to Mediobanca. However, the company remained closely held by the Pininfarina family who retained 67 per cent.

THE NICHE MANUFACTURER

Pininfarina was considered a niche car manufacturer. Niche manufacturers were chiefly distinguished by their low production volumes, which were often sub-contracted from a volume manufacturer. In Pininfarina's case, typical production volumes ranged from only one or two cars per day (for example, the Bentley cabriolet) to perhaps 50 to 60 cars per day for "special" sedans such as the Fiat coupe (Exhibit 2). In contrast, volume manufacturers might produce a thousand cars per day or more at a factory dedicated to just a few models or even one model.

However, not all volume manufacturers were the same. In the early 1990s, Japanese manufacturers on average produced around 70,000 cars per model per year, while an average European or American manufacturer produced around 200,000 per model per year. Japanese producers also had shorter model lives at around three years, while European producers had been averaging four to seven years of model life. Bertrandi felt that the best Japanese volume producers were profitable on very much lower production volume per model than even the Japanese average. One Japanese producer had

Alfa Romeo Spider Duetto

Ferrari Berlinetta Dino

Exhibit 1

Fiat Coupé

Bentley Azure

Exhibit 2

told him that it would not consider outsourcing production volumes of greater than 5,000 cars per year. In contrast, Pininfarina had produced over 17,000 Fiat Coupes in 1994.

Volume producers could apply considerable pressure to niche producers to keep prices low. Usually, they had detailed knowledge of the product and production processes associated with a model and often had their own experience with part of the process. Further, a given volume producer was usually a vastly larger company and represented a high percentage of the niche manufacturer's total business. Volume producer bargaining power was, therefore, high and niche manufacturer margins were narrow, especially during industry downturns. In general, margins were higher for fully assembled vehicles, and these offered more scope for production cost reductions to be achieved and captured by niche manufacturers. Profit margins for niche manufacturers were typically in the range of two to four per cent of the target unit manufacturing cost.

Advantages of Niche Production

Niche manufacturers provided three principal advantages to the volume producers who performed their own assembly for the vast majority of their production: niche manufacturers had lower total costs for cars made at low volumes, they could accept higher levels of volume uncertainty and their product designers brought both superior designs and famous brand names to volume producer models.

First, niche manufacturer costs for small-volume products were lower than those usually achieved by volume assemblers. At low daily production rates, typical volume producer process designs were too expensive to implement. A typical volume producer might have capital and other fixed costs that were more than twice the level of a niche manufacturer. Niche manufacturers were forced to limit capital investments that were specialized to a particular model because the costs had to be amortized over fewer cars. As a result, niche manufacturers designed

production processes that used general purpose equipment and required fewer dies, jigs and other specialized tools. Usually they had fewer mechanically performed operations and lower levels of automation.

To achieve lower capital costs, a niche producer was also skilled in making tradeoffs between what could be accomplished by machine and what could be done by hand. Bertrandi explained:

> It is mainly our engineering that provides an advantage. We get the product to 90 per cent with our process and compensate with skilled labor to provide the last 10 per cent. For example, we might decide to stamp a door in three stages instead of the four a volume producer would use. This can result in some small waves in the door metal, but we can correct this by adding five minutes of additional handwork. This can work at a production of 30 cars per day, but it would be suicide at 1,500 cars per day.

A more highly skilled workforce than that typically found at a volume producer was used to assemble parts and ensure quality in fit, finish and function. Many niche producers did not use a continuously moving assembly line. The variety of work performed at each station led Pininfarina, for example, to design a stop and go process, with a time between moves that might vary from about 10 minutes to about half an hour, and even up to eight hours, depending on the volumes needed.

Niche manufacturers sometimes based their product and process designs on modifications to a higher volume design that was being produced at a major automobile assembler. Often, such modifications required more skill of the workforce than would be required if a similar product had been designed from scratch. For example, Pininfarina production of the Peugeot 406 coupe was based on a sedan model produced at Peugeot. Pininfarina took bodies supplied by Peugeot and inserted a stamped part that altered the slope from the roof to the trunk lid in the rear. This alteration demanded a critical hand weld at the intersection of the mass-produced and niche-produced metal parts. Achieving proper part position and a strong, flat weld, which could be properly finished, was essential to ensure quality in this operation. The higher proportion of labor required imposed an additional cost of some four to eight labor hours per car for a niche manufacturer.

The second advantage of niche manufacturers was flexibility. Consequently, they were often given contracts on models that had higher than usual volume uncertainty and larger seasonal fluctuations in sales. For example, a convertible or cabriolet might have sales in the spring that were 150 per cent of the low sales in winter. Lifetime sales and the model life of highly specialized niche vehicles were also highly uncertain, as such products were aimed at narrow consumer segments that were difficult to specify and had rapidly shifting tastes. Some of the risks associated with such products could be shifted to niche producers. Contracts typically did not fully compensate niche producers for the costs of unanticipated volume fluctuations on a seasonal or overall basis. Uncertainty over model life complicated niche manufacturer planning for new model introductions, as, for example, models with low sales might be discontinued.

Niche manufacturers coped by configuring their facilities to be flexible and by developing elaborate contingency plans. Contingency planning allowed the niche producers to rapidly shift workers from one line to another as demands fluctuated. For example, work at a given station, which might be carried out by a team of five during high volume periods, could be reduced to a team of two when volumes were low. Fewer people at a station meant that each worker had to perform a greater number and variety of the operations needed, and it usually increased station time so that the line moved more slowly. The line also had to be rebalanced so that each work station's output rate was matched to keep worker idle time to a minimum. A line that needed a higher output rate would have more workers at a station and would assign fewer and narrower tasks to each worker. When

necessary, workers could be temporarily laid off or could be asked to work overtime.

The third benefit provided by niche manufacturers was highly competent and often renowned design skills in product and process. Design services were an independent source of revenue for some niche manufacturers. At Pininfarina in 1994, design and engineering revenue totalled nearly £90 billion[1] and was growing rapidly. Work might be performed for a production model or for prototype cars, which might never go into production. Although manufacturing contracts were not always awarded for suitable models that had been completed by niche manufacturers, participation in design significantly increased the chance of winning manufacturing business.

Close links and effective joint problem-solving between design and manufacturing were considered a major advantage in the success of a new car model. Some designers, such as Pininfarina and Bertone, had widely recognized brand names. These brands were believed to command premiums and suggest luxury, fashion and high performance. Although Pininfarina's major customers, Fiat and Peugeot, reported that they made little, if any, money on niche models, Bertrandi suspected their calculations excluded the positive impact of image and the attraction of niche cars in pulling potential buyers of other cars to showrooms.

PININFARINA POSITION IN THE 1990S

After relatively high profits in the late 1980s, the European auto market became less hospitable in the 1990s. Industry returns on net assets fell from their 1980s high of 10 per cent to 15 per cent to below five per cent on average in the 1990s. In the view of many, the primary problem was capacity utilization, which had averaged below 75 per cent from 1990 to 1995.

Over-capacity was partly the result of low underlying growth in the Western European consumer base and partly due to the addition of new factories by globalizing competitors. The spread of more efficient manufacturing practices, which had been pioneered by Japanese firms, also contributed to capacity growth. Although shares had been relatively stable overall, "voluntary" Japanese restraints on European market share were due to expire by the year 2000 in many large markets and Korean firms had begun to build a large European presence. In markets without restraints, Japanese producer shares were considerably higher than in markets with them. Exhibit 3 shows industry sales and share in Western Europe in the 1990s, and Exhibit 4 shows data on customer satisfaction. At the beginning of the 1990s, European producers had lagged behind other global competitors in some key areas of performance, and despite improvements were not believed to have fully closed the gap. Exhibit 5 shows comparative regional data.

Manufacturing Operations at Pininfarina

As it entered the 1990s, Pininfarina produced both bodies and fully assembled cars at two major production facilities, one in Grugliasco and the other at San Giorgio, about 40 kilometres away. The Grugliasco complex housed a full-scale wind tunnel test facility, which had been one of the first of its kind in the world. Production at Grugliasco was divided among three major buildings. In one, parts stamped by Pininfarina's suppliers were welded together to form the basic "Body in White" (BIW), so named because the completed bodies were not yet painted. Suppliers made stamped parts to specifications set by the designing firm—often, but not always Pininfarina Studi E Ricerche. The stamping process itself—the sequence of steps whereby the metal was formed—was typically specified by Pininfarina process design engineers.

A second building contained the paint shop, which painted all production models. The paint shop performed six major steps, some separated by drying phases. In the paint shop, the bare steel was first galvanized, then phosphate-coated and given an electrostatic treatment. Next, a primer was applied and then a base coat, before a final clear coating completed the process. The paint shop had been upgraded in stages beginning in 1985 at a total cost of some £100 billion. It was initially designed for a capacity of 100 cars per shift, but its capacity had been increased to 140 cars per shift and then 160 cars per shift. Throughput time was about seven hours.

The limited number of models produced by Pininfarina came in a total of 52 possible colors. The paint shop could change colors in about one minute, but required some manual setup to paint a specific model. At each arrival, the paint shop changed colors and set up for the appropriate model. Some cars, which needed special painting processes, were painted in a special area. The Rolls-Royce Bentley model, for example, required multiple steps of coating and surface preparation to achieve an adequate finish. About 100 hours of labor were required.

The last step—the trim facility—installed all the rest of the parts needed to form the complete automobile. Here, engines, suspension and other mechanical parts from suppliers were installed, as were details of interior and exterior finish—from door seals, seats and instrument panels to exterior mirrors and bumpers. Trim steps were greatly complicated by the wide variety of options that were supplied to customers. For example, each Fiat model came with a choice of five different engines, and each was configured slightly differently in the engine compartment. Interior options and other options also increased the complexity of process control in assembly and resulted in inventory levels higher than comparable higher volume facilities. At San Giorgio, a more modern trim facility had been built in 1985 primarily for the Cadillac Allante business. Pininfarina's test track was also located at San Giorgio.

Improvements in the 1990s

In 1992, Pininfarina faced a crisis. Production of bodies for the Cadillac Allante and Peugeot 205 and assembly for the Alfa Romeo Spider

Manufacturer	1990	1991	1992	1993	1994	1995
VW Group	15.6	16.4	17.5	16.4	15.8	16.7
General Motors Group	11.3	12.1	12.4	13.0	13.1	13.1
Opel/Saab/GM	11.3	12.1	12.4	13.0	13.1	13.1
Lotus	0.01	0.01				
Peugeot-Citroen	12.9	12.1	12.2	12.3	12.8	12.0
Peugeot	8.2	7.6	7.4	7.4	7.7	7.0
Ford Group	11.6	11.7	11.3	11.3	11.9	11.9
Ford	11.4	11.7	11.2	11.2	11.8	11.7
Jaguar	0.1	0.1	0.1	0.1	0.1	0.1
Fiat Group	14.2	12.8	11.9	11.1	10.8	11.1
Fiat*	10.3	9.3	8.8	8.3	8.6	8.7
Lancia	2.3	2.0	1.7	1.6	1.4	1.4
Alfa Romeo	1.5	1.4	1.2	1.1	0.8	1.1
Innocenti	0.06	0.11	0.10	0.11		
Ferrari**	0.019	0.021	0.023	0.018		
Maserati	0.015	0.011				
Renault	9.8	10.0	10.6	10.5	11.0	10.3
Mercedes	3.3	3.3	3.0	3.1	3.5	3.4
BMW	2.8	3.1	3.3	3.2	3.3	3.3
Rover***	2.9	2.6	2.5	3.2	3.3	3.1
Nissan	2.9	3.3	3.2	3.5	3.2	3.0
Toyota/Lexus	2.7	2.7	2.5	2.7	2.6	2.5
Mazda	2.1	2.1	2.0	1.7	1.5	1.4
Volvo	1.8	1.5	1.5	1.5	1.7	1.8
Mitsubishi/DMS	1.3	1.4	1.2	1.2	1.0	1.1
Honda	1.2	1.3	1.3	1.4	1.4	1.5
Hyundai	0.1	0.3	0.6	0.7	0.7	0.8
Suzuki/Maruti	0.7	0.7	0.9	0.9	0.7	0.8
Chrysler	0.3	0.3	0.3	0.5	0.5	0.6
Subaru	0.4	0.4	0.3	0.4	0.3	0.3
Porsche	0.1	0.1	0.1	0.1	0.1	0.1
Others	2.0	1.8	1.5	1.2	0.9	1.4
Total	100	100	100	100	100	100
As Per Cent of 1990	100	102	102	86	90	91
Total Vehicles	13,258,807	13,504,345	13,497,536	11,428,352	11,910,952	12,012,415

Exhibit 3   Western European Manufacturer Share of Total Number of Vehicles (in per cent)

Source: Company files.

*Includes Innocenti, Ferrari, and Maserati after 1993.

**Includes Maserati after 1991.

***Part of BMW Group after 1991.

	Overall Index	Parts/Service	Problem Incidence/ Resolution
Subaru	142	145	150
Honda	141	151	145
Daewo	140	134	89
Mazda	137	136	145
Toyota	137	142	141
Jaguar	136	158	118
Nissan	136	127	138
BMW	132	157	121
Daihatsu	130	129	137
Mercedes	128	159	131
Mitsubishi	124	117	129
Saab	124	139	112
Audi	119	109	118
Suzuki	116	101	122
Volvo	115	116	103
Hyundai	111	102	95
Renault	106	107	109
Volkswagen	105	104	105
Citroen	100	97	96
Rover	100	108	95
Peugeot	99	96	98
Fiat	95	88	94
Alfa Romeo	94	74	80
Ford	78	72	79
Lada	62	81	28
Total Industry	100	100	97

Exhibit 4   Customer Satisfaction Survey Sample Results by Make (United Kingdom data)

Source: Company files.

	Japanese in Japan	Japanese in North America	American in North America	All Europe
Performance				
Productivity (hours/vehicle)*	16.8	21.2	25.1	36.2
Quality (assembly defects/100 vehicles)	60	65	82.3	97
Layout				
Space sq. ft./vehicle/year	5.7	9.1	7.8	7.8
Size of repair area (as % of assembly space)	4.1	4.9	12.9	14.4
Inventories (days)	0.2	1.6	2.9	2
Workforce				
% of workforce in teams	69.3	71.3	17.3	0.6
Job rotation (0 = none, 4 = frequent)	3	2.7	0.9	1.9
Suggestions/employee	61.6	1.4	0.4	0.4
Number of job classes	11.9	8.7	67.1	14.8
Training of new production workers (hrs)	380.3	370.0	46.4	173.3
Absenteeism	5	4.8	11.7	12.1
Automation				
Welding (% of steps)	86.2	85	76.2	76.6
Painting (% of direct steps)	54.6	40.7	33.6	38.2
Assembly (% of direct steps)	1.7	1.1	1.2	3.1

Exhibit 5   Summary of Assembly Plant Characteristics: Volume Producers (1989)

Source: Womack, J. P., D. T. Jones, et al. (1990). *The Machine That Changed the World*. New York, Rawson Associates.

*Includes all labor within factory walls.

were being rapidly phased out, while volume replacement sufficient to maintain existing production levels had not yet been committed for new models (Exhibit 7, see p. 17). The shortfall eventually left 1993 production at less than 50 per cent of the average level for the 1990s to that point. Margins were also squeezed as European prices fell. Customers had begun to press for operational improvements in quality, cost and deliverability.

Further, the company had by now concluded that despite some recent operational improvements, more fundamental and far-reaching changes to improve its manufacturing performance would be necessary to ensure future viability. Faced with deteriorating financial results, Pininfarina laboriously negotiated with its unions. The resulting accord, signed on July 28, 1992, was viewed by many as a new model for Italian labor relations. It called for the early retirement and "temporary" layoff[2] of some 435 blue-collar employees—50 per cent of the total workforce.

Workforce and Quality Initiatives

Two major changes were introduced with the new accord, designed to allow Pininfarina to improve its operations to near Japanese levels, while adapting to Italian conditions. First, Pininfarina introduced a work team system modelled on the Toyota NUMMI plant in California, including systems to track morale and elicit suggestions for improvement. Second, a program of training for shop-floor workers was instituted. The training program had two major components. First, skills were built in specific operations and techniques (for example, statistical process control and problem-solving techniques). Second, workers were given interpersonal skills training intended to develop the capability of the workforce to work in teams (doubts had been expressed about the potential for Italian workers to submerge a pride in individuality to the constraints of teamwork). A training program for new workers was also instituted.

The training programs were a complement to an expansion of the quality initiative that had

been underway since the middle 1980s. Renato Bertrandi had originally joined the company in 1986 as a manager of quality control, reporting to the general manager. After the accord of 1992, the quality control function reported to Bertrandi himself at the operations manager level.

Pininfarina, while adopting some of the methods and practices of the quality movement, decided to adapt the philosophy to Italian and niche producer conditions. Renato Bertrandi explained:

> As a first step in our situation, it is better not to stop the line for most types of problems. Stopping the line lowers our production and costs us more. It is better for us to have highly skilled people at the end of the line fixing problems after they have occurred. Of course, we also ask workers to identify problems they can't fix on the line and work to remove the source of some problems. I realize this violates the philosophy of lean production, but it doesn't pay to fix the root causes of all of our problems now. This will be our next step.

Supplier Development

At about the same time, and in concert with the quality program, major programs were also initiated in supplier relations. In 1991, Pininfarina had about 650 suppliers. Typically, competitive bids were held among suppliers who were asked to meet Pininfarina's predetermined design specifications. Volumes were then split among several suppliers. By 1993, the number of suppliers had been reduced to 350, despite a major decision to outsource the stamping operations, which had been lagging in the capital investment required to keep them competitive. This reduction was achieved by concentrating volumes in fewer, more capable suppliers, with whom Pininfarina worked more closely—even doing joint design work and parts planning.

Major efforts had been made with the reduced number of suppliers to increase the frequency of deliveries, to correspondingly reduce their size, and to increase quality while decreasing the total amount of combined inspection. In the 1980s, incoming parts inspection employed 70 people to inspect all incoming supplier parts. In 1993, 30 people inspected only about 20 per cent of the incoming parts. Pininfarina also believed purchase prices and inventory levels had been improved.

By 1996, the number of suppliers had increased again to 450, driven by the new production models and a shift in mix toward the assembly of complete vehicles. This trend had been offset slightly because new business was with existing customers who had substantial carryover of existing suppliers and similar needs. About 25 people were needed to manage these suppliers. Pininfarina could control the choice of supplier for about half of its purchase monetary volume and could negotiate freely on price for about two-thirds of its volume. The other one-third came mostly from major customers, who were also major parts suppliers.

The progress of Pininfarina in achieving improvements in some key operating parameters is shown in Exhibit 6, and financial results and operating statistics are shown in Exhibit 7. Bertrandi was pleased with the fact that of the 20 per cent of cars produced that did not go immediately to a buyer, only 10 per cent of these were due to quality problems. The remaining 90 per cent were due to parts shortages of one type or another, typically the result of last-minute changes in option mixes in the production schedule and a consequent shortage of the correct part.

Search for a New Customer

Budgeted improvements called for further increases in the productivity of direct labor of three per cent annually. To utilize the extra capacity created by productivity improvements, to

	1992	1996
Performance		
Productivity* (hours/vehicle)	60	42.5
Rework Cost** (% of Total)	12–15	9
Layout		
Space sq. ft./vehicle/year		380.25
Size of repair area (as % of assembly space)		N/A
Inventories (days)		.5–3
Workforce		
% of workforce in teams	0.25	95
Job rotation (0 = none, 4 = frequent)	3	2.7
Suggestions/employee	0	0.1
Number of job classes		4
Training of new production workers (hrs)		N/A
Absenteeism	7.7	6
Automation		
Welding (% of steps)	5	5–34
Painting (% of direct steps)	35	40
Assembly (% of direct steps)	5	5

Exhibit 6   Pininfarina Assembly Characteristics

Source: Company files.

*Includes all labor within factory walls.

**Includes cost of rework labor and materials only.

	1989	1990	1991	1992	1993	1994	1995
Sales (group total in billion lira)	372.0	479.5	501.9	412.4	417.2	731.4	670.0
Expenses:							
Purchases & Services		270.7	258.7	175.2	201.0	556.6	410.4
Labor Cost		77.6	89.4	97.4	93.5	83.6	116.6
Depreciation		14.6	13.6	16.2	13.5	16.2	18.2
SG&A		92.7	113.4	121.8	98.0	72.5	117.1
Total Expenses	357.6	455.6	475.0	410.6	406.0	728.9	662.3
Operating Income	14.4	24.0	27.1	1.8	11.2	2.5	7.7
Production Model Mix	**1989**	**1990**	**1991**	**1992**	**1993**	**1994**	**1995**
Assembled Vehicles							
Lancia Thema SW/K SW	3,010	3,456	2,536	1,894	1,310	806	0
Alfa Romeo Spider	3,978	7,106	9,073	3,640	1,956		
Fiat Coupe					276	17,332	12,500
Bentley Azure					3	170	250
Peugeot Coupe							
Total Assembled Vehicles (units)	6,988	10,562	11,609	5,534	3,545	18,308	12,750
Total Revenue—Assembled Vehicles (billion lira)	153	237	252	142	104	426	312
Revenue per Assembled Vehicle (million lira)	21.9	22.4	21.7	25.7	29.3	23.3	24.5
Bodies							
Ferrari (Testa Rossa, 512TR, 456GT)	1,207	1,312	1,565	870	306	625	600
Cadillac	3	3,775	2,495	2,660	1,978		
Peugeot 205 Cabriolet	9,303	11,051	12,982	11,718	3,450	784	
Peugeot 306 Cabriolet					414	11,154	11,600
Total Bodies	13,565	16,138	17,042	15,248	6,148	12,563	12,200
Total Revenue—Bodies (billion lira)	157	172	167	160	85	143	153
Workforce	**1989**	**1990**	**1991**	**1992**	**1993**	**1994**	**1995**
Direct Workers	803	964	889	846	824	927	864
Indirect Workers	443	444	431	408	352	351	344
Total Workers	1,246	1,498	1,320	1,254	1,176	1,278	1,208

Exhibit 7   Pininfarina Data

Source: Company files.

Note: US$1 = £1,600 (approximately).

leverage its newly achieved production skills, and to diversify its risk of lower future volumes from current customers, Pininfarina decided to seek a third major customer in late 1994. Although some production of new models from existing customers would begin in 1996, these volumes would be insufficient to replace the production that would be phased out by the year 2000. The typical lead-time from the beginning of design until the first production vehicle was 38 months.

Pininfarina actively marketed itself in the auto industry for new business in product design and manufacture, sometimes proposing joint development of prototype design projects for niche vehicles to volume manufacturers. Such projects were a source of profit to Pininfarina's design division and could result in new manufacturing work for vehicles that were to go into production. Although at present, only the Peugeot 406 had been wholly designed at Pininfarina, the interior of the Fiat coupe had been a Pininfarina design, and Pininfarina had competed with Fiat's internal designers for the exterior as well. Bertrandi felt that the present low level of relationship between manufacturing and design projects at Pininfarina was unusual and did not represent a trend among volume manufacturers to make the two functions more independent of one another.

Pininfarina had worked with Peugeot's styling centre to create all of its major models since the middle 1950s and had regularly performed work for Fiat for an even longer time. In addition, General Motors had been a large customer. While the identity of niche manufacturers' design customers was a closely guarded secret, outside investment analysts' reports stated that Mercedes, BMW, Porsche, and Honda were among Pininfarina's current design and development customers. Analysts had anticipated the announcement of a major new manufacturing customer in 1995, but, as yet, no firm commitments from those prototyping and developing cars with Pininfarina had been received. Pininfarina's prospects for a new niche vehicle-manufacturing customer remained good, however.

THE NEW CUSTOMER DECISION

Following a marketing contact with Mitsubishi proposing a niche vehicle product design project, in July 1995 Pininfarina was surprised to receive a counterproposal from Mitsubishi. Mitsubishi proposed that Pininfarina be the manufacturer of one of their sport utility vehicles, the Mini Pajero, which was to be marketed in Europe and Asia. A Pajero built in Japan was being successfully sold in Europe. A new model was already designed to the prototype stage and would be introduced first in Japan, in 1998. Vehicles for Asian sales would be manufactured by Mitsubishi; however, Mitsubishi proposed that Pininfarina adapt the design and manufacture in Italy for all of Europe. The major design work would be in adding a left-hand drive model and in adapting the process design to Pininfarina's capabilities. Bertrandi was particularly surprised at this offer since to that point, Mitsubishi had not asked to visit or inspect Pininfarina's factories—a common practice of volume manufacturers, who wished to verify Pininfarina's manufacturing capabilities. Beyond the excellence of Pininfarina's reputation and recent performance improvements, Bertrandi suspected that Mitsubishi had factored Italy's relatively low automotive labor costs into their choice. Bertrandi believed these were one-half Germany's levels (see Exhibit 8).

The details of the Mitsubishi proposal had not been fully specified, but the basic characteristics of the proposal were clear. Based on previous experience Bertrandi believed any decision to proceed would be taken with many details not completely specified. Mitsubishi proposed that by no later than May 1999, Pininfarina should begin volume production in Europe of the new model, after a three-month trial and debugging

Germany	62.44
Belgium	44.6
Sweden	41.8
Japan	41.56
United States	38.52
Netherlands	34.75
France	33.08
Spain	28.06
Italy	27.79
United Kingdom	27.08

Exhibit 8   1996 Labor Costs in the Auto Industry (DM per hour)

period. Production would be at a rate of about 150 vehicles per day. Mitsubishi would pay Pininfarina a standard margin on a target cost that would be based on Mitsubishi's own experience in producing the model in Japan and correction for differing process, parts and transportation costs. The standard margin had not been set, but it was clear it would be low—perhaps one-half of the two to four per cent margins Pininfarina earned on its current production contracts. Bertrandi believed that if Pininfarina could achieve production costs below Mitsubishi's target, Pininfarina would be able to keep the additional profit.

Mitsubishi would guarantee that total volumes would be at least sufficient for Pininfarina to recoup any model-specific capital costs. However, Pininfarina would have to bear the risk of investment in general purpose equipment such as the basic facilities themselves or robots, which could be used for other purposes. The exact guaranteed volume would be calculated on the basis of the standard margin that was allowed Pininfarina by the production contract. Total investments were expected to be £300 billion. General purpose capital equipment for a new model was usually in the range of 10 to 15 per cent of total investment. As Mitsubishi had roughly a three per cent share of the global automobile market, and over US$20 billion in worldwide sales, Pininfarina management had few doubts as to Mitsubishi's ability to meet its commitments.

The term of the production phase would be five years, expiring in 2003, with no obligations on either side to continue the arrangement with other models or services, beyond those which might be part of the Pajero contract such as warranty obligations or spare parts production. Revenues to be collected by Pininfarina each year on average over the life of the project were expected to be £900 billion.

Some design changes would be needed for Europe. These were well within Pininfarina's capabilities, although the model development time would be less than the approximately three years needed for a typical design project. As long as the Japanese schedule was kept, Bertrandi felt product and process design changes could be made in time easily, since the model was already in the prototype phase. In process design, Mitsubishi would design much of the process. Pininfarina had only to adapt the process to its facility—designing an appropriate flow and layout—and to adapt certain processes to a somewhat more labor-intensive system. Bertrandi felt such differences would mainly be in the BIW area where Japanese producers had a tendency to place more robots than American or European producers.

Capital Investment

As a result, new production facilities would have to be acquired and equipped for Mitsubishi production. Bertrandi felt confident such facilities could be built or acquired in time since potential expansion sites had already been identified near Grugliasco. Basic facilities were expected to cost somewhat in excess of £4 billion, including land, the trim facility and adequate parking for workers. Mitsubishi would not cover these expenses. Pininfarina would not invest in welding automation for the Pajero.

The paint shop, which was currently running at capacity, would have to be run for an additional shift. To supply it, the logistics for transporting BIW from the Mitsubishi facility to the Grugliasco paint shop and back would have to be set up, but this posed no problem in principle since BIWs were already being painted at Grugliasco and transported to San Giorgio for trim. There would be additional expenses with the paint shop, however, associated with the Mitsubishi production. Currently, the necessity of cleaning the painting system with solvent to change paint color after each car placed Pininfarina near the limits of what would be acceptable under Italian pollution control regulations. Additional volumes for the Mini Pajero would force a switch to a water-based system. The Pajero would offer a two-tone painting option, and this also posed some problems for the paint shop. Two-tone painting required additional space to dry and store vehicles in between painting stages, and this space would also have to be created.

Quality

Although they had not yet been definitively set, Bertrandi knew that Mitsubishi considered its own quality standards to be very high and that its focus would differ substantially from those of Pininfarina's existing customers. Some in the company believed Mitsubishi might demand defect levels of one-fourth the level of Pininfarina's current customers, although what would be considered a defect was not clear. Experience had shown different customers considered different things in deciding what was a defect. For example, some customers closely specified the routes and positions of electrical harnesses and hoses in the engine compartment, while for other manufacturers, only the functionality was considered, aside from ensuring no basic hazards such as a plastic hose resting on a hot running part existed.

Parts Supply and Logistics

Major mechanical parts, including engines, would be supplied by production in Japan—either from Mitsubishi itself or one of its suppliers. Other parts would be sourced from Europe, predominantly from suppliers who Mitsubishi qualified. Parts supply and logistics from Japan would have to be established jointly with Mitsubishi. Mitsubishi agreed to own the inventory until it arrived at Pininfarina, but it would be shipped at Pininfarina's request. Pininfarina would be responsible for having sufficient parts on hand to meet its production obligations.

Pininfarina had some experience in long distance supply chains. In the 1980s and early 1990s, it had shipped BIW Cadillac Allantes to Detroit for final assembly. However, the supply chain to Japan was even longer and Mitsubishi and Pininfarina calculated that some 13 days shipping would be required, and a further three days of inventory at port in Italy would be needed, in addition to the normal supply of inventory at the plant. Pininfarina logistics staff believed these inventories would be adequate to ensure supply even in the event of strikes. During a strike or port closure, contingency plans would be established to divert production to a free port and to ship to Turin overland.

Many parts from within Europe would also be shipped further than was usual for Pininfarina operations. At present, the most distant supplier was 900 kilometres away for Peugeots and 65 per cent were within 60 kilometres. However, Mitsubishi, which had production in Holland, wanted to retain many suppliers with which it had familiarity. Many of these suppliers were outside Italy, with the most distant being in the United Kingdom—a three-day shipping distance.

Many of the new suppliers would be unfamiliar to Pininfarina and would present challenges. Despite the presence of Mitsubishi, Pininfarina was responsible for parts supply and negotiation of price. The volumes needed were much less than those usual for volume manufacturers, and this made negotiations of price and delivery difficult compared with what could be accomplished by larger firms. Suppliers often incurred extra costs in overhead and packaging and shipping costs, as well as additional set-up costs to supply smaller orders. Many of the suppliers would be unfamiliar to Pininfarina and might increase the number of Pininfarina's suppliers by 150 or so.

Outgoing logistics would also be more complex than usual since Pininfarina would be shipping greater volumes to dealers in major European markets, but this was not expected to present insurmountable problems. It would also be necessary to forecast sales further in advance since the interval from parts order to arrival would be about 46 days—considerably longer than for the current models. For example, for Peugeot, the current standard for orders was about 10 days in advance of production.

Workforce

While Mitsubishi would pay for tooling and fixtures under the volume guarantees at standard margins, the workforce needed was another matter. Bertrandi felt some 600 additional direct workers (inside the factory) would be needed to meet the Mitsubishi volume needs. At traditional ratios of direct to indirect workers, this would imply some 200 to 240 indirect workers. However, Bertrandi felt that while some classes of indirect workers could not be reduced from usual levels, other classes could. For example, purchasing might not need a fully proportional addition to staff because some suppliers would still be in common, some additional capacity could be added in information systems and present resources were not fully utilized. Bertrandi estimated that only one-half the historical number of additional indirect workers might be needed.

Increasing productivity would free some direct labor capacity by 1999. Further, by the year 2000, existing contract business would be ramped down so that some of the current direct labor force could be freed to work on the Mitsubishi vehicle.

The Pajero might also present Pininfarina with a learning opportunity. Bertrandi anticipated that work methods, jigs and tools would be refined in Japan prior to beginning production in Italy. Using Japanese designs and production tools and processes, Bertrandi was excited by the prospect of being able to compare his operations with world-class volume manufacturers. Pininfarina would need to learn fast. After the initial test and ramp-up phase, which would last two to three months, Pininfarina would have to meet the agreed target costs or else pay for any overages itself. Bertrandi wondered if he should accept the contract and the challenge.

NOTES

1. US$1 was equal to approximately £1,600.
2. Under Italian law, the government would, under certain circumstances, use a fund created by Italian companies to pay 80 per cent of a laid off worker's salary for up to two years.

FELL-FAB PRODUCTS (A)

*Prepared by John MacDonald
under the supervision of Professors
John Haywood-Farmer and Larry Menor*

Version: (A) 2001-02-09

In December 1998, Glen Fell, president of Fell-Fab Products of Hamilton, Ontario, knew it was time to respond to North American Airlines (NAA), one of Fell-Fab Products' important aircraft interiors customers. Two months earlier, NAA had asked Fell-Fab

Products whether it was interested in taking over complete management of NAA's aircraft interiors business. Although the proposal was financially promising, it represented a significant departure from Fell-Fab Products' traditional business of interiors manufacturing. Now, after considerable study and discussions with NAA, Glen Fell had to decide whether Fell-Fab Products should accept the offer and, if so, how to implement it.

FELL-FAB PRODUCTS

Fell-Fab Products was a family firm that the current chairman, Don Fell, had founded in 1952. The company described itself as a manufacturer of engineered textile products, all of which required cutting and sewing (or welding[1]) textiles according to a specified pattern. Its main business (75 per cent) was the manufacture of interior coverings such as seat covers, carpeting, drapes, curtains, galley furnishings and magazine pouches for the transportation industry. Airlines accounted for 80 per cent of this business; railways and bus lines accounted for the remaining 20 per cent. The company's remaining revenues (25 per cent) came from a diverse line of products such as tents and vests for the Canadian military, carrier bags for newspaper and mail delivery, liners for shipping containers and elevators, sofa beds for recreational vehicles, microwave receiver dishes,[2] thermal insulation blankets for aerospace applications, custom-designed covers and the overhaul of airline seat assemblies. Its customers for these products included organizations in the aerospace, material handling, packaging, industrial and government sectors. The company's customer base and product mix had remained reasonably stable. Among its core competencies, Fell-Fab Products counted its ability to react quickly through manufacturing flexibility, materials management and constant communication with the customer.

Exhibit 1 shows an organizational chart. The company's head office and main manufacturing facility were in Hamilton, where about 20 head office and 180 manufacturing staff worked. The Hamilton plant, which was ISO 9001 certified and included a Class 100,000 clean room essential for aerospace products, produced Fell-Fab Products' full product line. FELLFAB, L.L.C. near Atlanta, Georgia, employed about 60 people

and was devoted entirely to manufacturing parts for transportation interiors. The company's annual revenues were about $27 million; about $15 million of this amount originated from the Hamilton plant and about $12 million from the Atlanta plant. About $7 million came from non-transportation products.

COMPETITORS

The North American aircraft interiors business had many relatively small producers. John MacDonald, Fell-Fab Products' director of sales and marketing, and a recent EMBA graduate, believed that Fell-Fab Products' Canadian market share was about 20 per cent. The various active companies tended to carve out roles with different degrees of vertical and horizontal integration. One Canadian competitor was a subsidiary of a textile mill. One United States company made complete seats. Other companies were involved in interiors replacement and cleaning. According to MacDonald, Fell-Fab Products' experience, consistent product quality, design capability, two manufacturing sites and ability to transfer design specifications between them electronically made it competitive. Transportation customers preferred to avoid the risks of single sources and to deal with suppliers near their major aircraft refurbishment sites. In North America, those sites included Toronto and Vancouver in Canada, and Atlanta, Chicago, Dallas and Los Angeles in the United States.

THE SEAT COVER PRODUCTION PROCESS

Although making interior covers for an airplane was not difficult, some salient features complicated the process. There was a considerable degree of asymmetry and variation in airline seats. Each aircraft type had its own seats, often in several configurations. Even for a single aircraft type, each airline had its own seat needs. Naturally, the larger seats in business and first

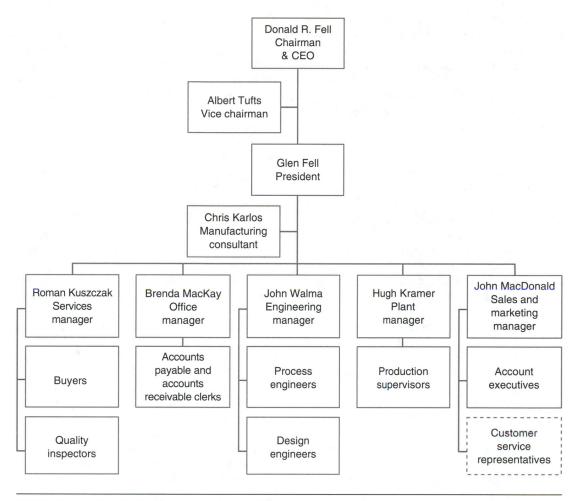

Exhibit 1   Fell-Fab Products' Organizational Chart

class required different covers than the standard economy class seats. However, left side seats could differ from right side seats, and aisle, centre and window seats could all differ. Consequently, a row of seven seats might have seven different covers. Special features of the aircraft, such as the presence of bulkheads and seats for each crew member, created yet more cover designs and/or materials. Carpeting was also complex. For example, the carpet kit for a Dash 8, a short-haul commuter aircraft, had a total of 23 pieces in 12 separate designs with up to six pieces per design. And, because some

newer Dash 8-400s had custom interiors, all kits for that series were different.

Aircraft interior manufacturing began with a contract between the airline and a small number of textile mills, typically from overseas, to supply material to certain specifications. The airline then informed interiors manufacturers such as Fell-Fab Products of the names of acceptable suppliers and the product numbers and prices of the proper materials. Fell-Fab Products purchased fabric according to this list with lead times of about 12 weeks. Advance planning was crucial for Fell-Fab Products. When an airline needed interior coverings, it informed Fell-Fab Products, typically requesting delivery in about four weeks.

Fell-Fab Products drew the purchased material from raw materials inventory (which averaged about 60 days' worth) and spread it in layers on a large cutting table. The company stored designs for the interiors electronically in a computer aided design (CAD) and computer aided manufacturing (CAM) system, which was able to optimize a cutting pattern and cut up to 40 layers of material. In addition to order size, the number of layers cut depended on the thickness and composition of the material. Once cut, the material continued to be handled in batches based on the number of layers cut. It then passed through about six sewing operations and was labelled and bar coded. The final product was inspected, gathered into kits and boxed ready for shipping.

Sewing and inspection were labour intensive operations and it was more labour intensive to process leather than man-made textiles. Although it took only a few minutes to complete each step for a single interior covering, from cutting to shipping it took about a week to process a typical order for a large commercial aircraft. In common with other batching operations, queue time before, during and after production was significant.

Fell-Fab Products' transportation product customers included 10 major airlines that, in general, demanded high quality, prompt and on-time delivery, and excellent customer service. Occasionally, in the past, Fell-Fab Products had lost business because it had failed to deliver on time. All products had to be certified to particular safety specifications. Late shipments or other problems with an order could result in lost revenues for the airline as they would not fly with even a single seat cover missing. For Fell-Fab Products, the term "aircraft on ground" (AOG) was a panic signal. In such cases the company gathered the necessary materials and processed them as quickly as possible using the regular equipment and operators. Although the result might satisfy the AOG-affected customer, the practice could significantly disrupt the flow of other orders.

NORTH AMERICAN AIRLINES

North American Airlines (NAA) was a full service airline offering scheduled passenger, charter and air cargo transportation services. In 1998, NAA flew more than 10 million passengers to more than 200 destinations in North America and 30 destinations in Asia, Europe and Latin America. It was a founding member of a leading industry alliance and was also affiliated on a code-sharing basis with smaller regional carriers that served shorter flights, often as feeders. NAA was among the five largest passenger carriers between North America and Asia in terms of total flights. NAA had benefited significantly from its partnerships.

NAA prided itself on the quality of its service. In recent years, it had undertaken a variety of changes to its products and services based on extensive benchmarking against its competitors and partners along with customer surveys encompassing check-in, boarding, in-flight, and baggage retrieval. In evaluating NAA's airline equipment, facilities and uniforms, customers believed that the airline was "friendly but tired." Customer research identified comfort and flexibility as the important factors passengers considered when measuring a pleasant in-flight experience. Among the most visible of NAA's improvements was a complete overhaul of the aircraft fleet's interiors and change in colour schemes planned for early 1999. NAA's fleet, including those of its affiliated regional carriers, consisted of about 130 aircraft in eight different makes or models (see Exhibit 2).

Like its competitors, NAA spent a great deal of money managing its fleet's interior coverings. As part of its interiors management program, the buyers assigned to this product class were responsible for inventory management and servicing, as well as purchasing the coverings. Approximately every three months, while the aircraft was on the ground for scheduled servicing and mechanical upkeep at one of NAA's major service centres, an NAA crew stripped the interior coverings from the aircraft and replaced them with others from inventory. It sent the removed coverings to an independent

Aircraft		Typical Economy Seats		Typical Business Seats	
Type	Number	Number per Aircraft	Total	Number per Aircraft	Total
Boeing 747-400	4	379	1,516	42	168
DC10-30	10	228	2,280	24	240
Boeing 767-300ER	11	180	1,980	25	275
Airbus 320	12	108	1,296	24	288
Boeing 737	44	88	3,872	12	528
Fokker 28	27	85	2,295		
Dash 8-100	10	37	370		
Dash 8-300	14	50	700		
Total	132		14,309		1,419

Exhibit 2   NAA's Fleet[1]

1. Although the number of aircraft of each type and the seating configuration varied from time to time, they were reasonably stable.

cleaner who dry cleaned all of them, regardless of their condition. After cleaning, the dry cleaner returned the coverings to NAA for storage. NAA's coverings inventory was thus found in use on the NAA fleet, in stock in NAA's warehouse, in transit to or from the cleaners, and at the cleaners for service. Although colour or design modifications could prompt an earlier change, the lifetime of a seat cover was approximately one year. Wear was the most common reason for cover changes. It was important to keep track of the number of dry cleaning cycles for each seat cover because flammability specifications were typically compromised after 10 to 20 cleanings, depending on the fabric used.

NAA stored the covers in large bins, with one complete set for a given aircraft per bin. It identified the bins by aircraft type. To reduce the risk of being out of stock, NAA and other airlines often stored extra coverings for emergencies. When they came to put a cleaned set of covers on, the replacement crew might also discover that some covers had been damaged and needed replacing. The crew discarded covers it identified as damaged at the time of installation; if NAA could not

find adequate replacements in inventory, it placed a rush order, under AOG conditions, with Fell-Fab Products. As soon as possible after replacing an aircraft's interior coverings, the replacement crew supplied NAA's purchasing personnel with scrappage reports. Purchasing, in turn, prepared monthly scrappage reports to help forecast future coverings purchasing requirements.

THE NAA PROPOSAL

In October 1998, NAA asked Fell-Fab Products if it was interested in widening its business relationship beyond the manufacture of interior coverings. Fell-Fab Products was one of a few airline interior manufacturers upon which NAA relied. Since becoming a producer of these products for NAA in 1965, Fell-Fab Products had seen its sales to NAA increase steadily; currently it accounted for 35 per cent of NAA's purchases of cabin interiors. Exhibit 3 shows NAA's history of purchases from Fell-Fab Products.

In October 1998, MacDonald and a Fell-Fab Products account executive met a purchasing

	1996	*1997*	*1998*
January	12.0	11.5	21.7
February	18.5	21.3	15.1
March	4.9	14.6	11.2
April	9.1	18.1	19.7
May	21.8	12.2	23.6
June	7.6	11.9	16.9
July	17.8	21.9	15.6
August	10.9	8.0	23.0
September	10.3	18.5	15.0
October	14.6	20.0	21.2
November	13.0	15.1	19.4
December	9.2	13.8	19.0
Total	**149.7**	**186.9**	**185.5**

Exhibit 3   Fell-Fab Products' Recent Sales to NAA[1]

1. Figures are in thousands of dollars.

manager and two buyers from NAA to discuss the NAA proposal. The meeting focused on one aspect of NAA's interiors management program—the management of aircraft interior coverings. MacDonald described his impressions:

> NAA approached us to express their intent to withdraw from the interior coverings management business and offer it to an external, though reputable company like us. It makes sense: NAA is in the flight business, we are in the cabin interiors business. And, effective interior coverings management is extremely important. A single missing seat cover is enough to ground a plane. By purchasing the complete management of interior coverings from one or more external service providers, NAA would realize four benefits:
>
> - reduced costs,
> - reduced interior coverings inventory,
> - better use of their existing service crew, and
> - a simpler interior coverings management process.

Since a bin of coverings is typically unsorted and the seat covers aren't even identified by seat type, the replacement crew spends a lot of time sorting through the clean bin trying to fit seat covers by trial and error. Besides dealing with interior coverings, the crew is also involved with other servicing and mechanical tasks such as maintenance of telephones, the entertainment system, seats, lighting, the heating and air conditioning system, galleys and lavatories. Because NAA has a high overhead structure and its interiors coverings replacement crew is highly paid, NAA wants them to work more on these higher-value-added tasks. NAA officials believe that lower-waged, unskilled workers could be employed to replace coverings. However, NAA's employees are unionized and the union has objected to using unskilled workers in the past.

NAA's current process is complex because of its many logistical difficulties related to tracking the location and levels of interior coverings inventory, the choice of independent cleaners, and the sorting of cleaned covers. NAA is interested in withdrawing from the interior coverings management business if it can't simplify its process internally.

To date, no North American firm offers a service as comprehensive as the one NAA envisages. This opportunity deserves further study.

NAA's Interior Coverings Management Business

Over the following weeks, MacDonald gathered as much information as he could from NAA and other sources. NAA seemed to know little about its interior coverings management process. The officials found it difficult to provide immediate responses to basic questions such as: "How many seat covers do you own?" and, "How long does it take to change a cover?"

Interior Covering Replacements, Inventory and Cleaning

NAA restricted interior covering replacement on its Boeing 737, Boeing 767, DC-10 and Airbus A300 aircraft to two North American centres, one in the east and one in the west. In total, these sites changed an average of 1,350 seat covers per week. NAA changed the interior coverings on its Boeing 747s during layovers in a city in southeast Asia at a rate of 50 covers during each layover with four layovers per week. NAA changed the interior coverings on its DC-10s once annually. NAA's affiliated regional airlines changed their interior coverings at their major centres of operation.

On average, a seat cover was inspected every 300 flying hours. NAA carried up to six spare seat covers per aircraft aboard for emergencies to eliminate the need to carry stock at each of its line stations. NAA did not currently account for the number of dry cleaning cycles by seat type.

Interior Covering Management Responsibilities and Expenses

Replacing a seat cover required approximately 19 worker minutes per seat at an average cost of $20 per worker hour. The most recent scrappage report indicated that for the preceding 12-month period, NAA discarded approximately 4,500 seat covers. The total number of seat covers cleaned for 1998 numbered 48,000 at its western centre and 27,000 at its eastern centre for an estimated total cost of cleaning of Cdn$75,000, not including transportation, repairs, sorting, or cover replacement.

The more Glen Fell and MacDonald investigated this business opportunity, the more they became intrigued by it. They estimated that it would substantially increase Fell-Fab Products' revenues and profits as the service offered a potentially high contribution. Margins in the interiors manufacturing business were 20 per cent to 60 per cent, with almost all of them at the low end of that range. The two estimated that a contract with NAA would provide annual revenues of $1.2 million with costs of $475,000 per year for labour, transportation, cleaning and storage.

They were also able to confirm that the airline industry was moving towards buying such services. Further, NAA's offer to Fell-Fab Products had not gone unnoticed; several of NAA's alliance partners as well as NAA's primary competitor were interested in the outcome of the proposal.

MacDonald was concerned that the NAA offer was too great a departure from Fell-Fab Products' traditional business. He described his views:

Fell-Fab Products has an established reputation as a quality-conscious manufacturer of engineered textile products. Over the years, we have made efforts to improve our production processes as well. For example, we have incorporated CAD/CAM technology to ensure the most economical use of materials. This has improved our fabric yield and further eliminated human error. Our computerized cutting equipment ensures a high degree of accuracy in cut parts and permits us to work within tight tolerances and our full electronic data exchange capability and product bar coding provides more efficient materials management and inventory control. Companies do business with us because we're good at making things. We probably made the carrier bags like those there on the wall used to deliver your newspaper and mail today.

NAA's proposal would require us to invest about $250,000 to acquire a crew experienced in dressing aircraft, suitable cleaning equipment, and a fleet of service vehicles to transport the crew and covers to airport locations. Operating costs would be extra.

Accepting NAA's offer would require us to be more of a service-based business. Service organizations make money by being good in executing activities, not through making things. Fell-Fab Products currently provides some auxiliary services to its air interiors customers. We have an in-house staff of design engineers that can assist in the design stages of particular products. Covers for the Canadarm and robots and nuclear reactor insulation are examples. Also, although we are able to provide our customers with historical information regarding inventory, consumption and other reports as needed, these services are not our principal order winners.

What kind of service would NAA expect? Cleaning, inventory management, and repair are the obvious ones. But others are also possible. The actual service would depend on just what NAA wants. The quality of any service we provide to NAA would rest on our ability to respond and be reliable. At a minimum, the interior coverings management business would necessitate greater interaction with the customer. Would our sales staff be able to provide the levels of assurance and empathy required when dealing with an airline executive forced to ground an aircraft because we were not able to service all his or her aircraft interior needs? Value for Fell-Fab Products would have to include issues related to customer allegiance too.

GLEN FELL'S DILEMMA

Glen Fell had decidedly mixed feelings concerning this decision. Before committing to NAA's interior coverings management proposal, he was mulling over a list of issues that he had to address. He contemplated his vision for the future of his company's involvement in the airline industry. He described his thoughts:

> This could be a very attractive business for us. It is a natural extension that complements our core business of manufacturing aircraft interiors. We already know this market. We also know NAA and many of the other players in it. We understand them well and have good relations with them. In fact, a move like this should strengthen our relations with NAA. In addition, it wouldn't involve adding facilities as we could use our existing ones, except for space for dry cleaning. We already have a building lined up near our Hamilton plant for dry cleaning. And, we could use this as an opportunity to learn about running a service operation. That would be a real asset if we decided to extend our non-core businesses into service too.

> The demand for such a service seems to be there, although the picture is not entirely clear. Lots of airlines are making noises about outsourcing interiors management. One claims to have saved some $5 million per year by doing so.

> There are really two types of airlines. One is already outsourcing a certain amount of business. In those cases, our job would be to convince them to switch suppliers. The other type does it in-house. Our job would be to convince them that we can do a better job than they can do themselves. But, many of them have strong labour unions who recognize outsourcing as a real threat to their jobs. It would be tough to get them to go to the wall with their workers over outsourcing refurbishment services.

> The possibility of a deal with NAA is intriguing. They seem to want to help us by sharing what they know. It was clear from our meeting that they are going to go with someone. If we wait, they will go with someone else, and we will find ourselves very much behind.

> Despite its potential, this deal makes me nervous. Extending beyond our core competence in interior coverings production is potentially risky. We don't have the logistical expertise at the centre of NAA's problems so we would have to develop our own or get assistance. Over the years, we have grown by diversifying. It is always risky to put all your eggs in one basket. This diversification has taken two routes. Don [Fell] is always looking for opportunities to use our core strengths in sewing fabric. Whenever he sees a possibility, we investigate it. This has led to our wide range of small volume products, which really share only one thing—they involve sewn or welded fabric. But,

we miss out because we don't understand the industries to which we sell the products. They don't have much in common at all.

The second route in our diversification has been the acquisition of companies that make products involving sewing or welding. Over the years, we have made at least 10 of them. And yet, not one of them is still operating. We have tended to focus on the sewing and welding while ignoring other aspects of the production process. In some cases, we have not had the management skills to handle those differences. In other cases, production has been no problem, but we have had trouble growing sales because of our inexperience in those markets. We have been reluctant either to leave our acquisitions alone or to develop the necessary skills inside the company to deal with them. Would the NAA opportunity be a success or would it simply be one more failed attempt to diversify?

If we were to go ahead, what would be the impact on our manufacturing business? With our failures in the past, we have been protected from major effects because the part in trouble has been relatively small. But this time, it would be different. I am sure that if we were to fail to adequately serve airlines through a logistics or cleaning mistake, we could hold up an aircraft. Not only would that cost us money, but the whole company would get a bad reputation. And, we think that the airlines currently buy about 20 per cent more interiors than they actually need because they don't maintain them very well. Even if we were to succeed in service, it might hurt our interiors sales.

We would also have to find, hire and train the right people. We don't quite know what service people would be like, but we do know that our current staff probably wouldn't be right. And, we would need new management systems for a service arm. The whole logistics area would be quite different. Managing aircraft interiors involves a lot of inventory control that we don't have experience in. Our main inventory task right now is handling a small amount of raw materials. In this business, we would have to handle large numbers of finished goods and make quality calls for our customers. It would be our decision whether a seat cover was torn or worn badly enough to need replacement. And, of course, we know nothing about dry cleaning. We wouldn't

want to have a problem and have seat covers last only half as long as they should because we made an error in the mix of solvents in the dry cleaning process that affected fire retardation.

The Atlanta plant certainly adds to administrative load and costs. Aircraft interior refurbishment might mean a large number of additional sites, and fairly quickly. A large carrier like NAA probably wouldn't want to wait too long while we expand to other centres to serve them.

In our current business, we have a pretty good idea what quality is and how to manage it. We have a set of benchmarks to go on and well described standards set out in product specifications. When we produce a new seat cover, the first two units we produce become test standards. We send them to our customer for checking. If the customer is satisfied, it signs off on them and returns one sample to us as a reference that we can always refer to if we have to. But how do you do that on the service side? There are no benchmarks and certainly no reference standards. And, almost everything would be done by people. Their work is not nearly as reproducible as a machine's. Of course, maybe each customer would want it different each time. We would have to develop some comfort in dealing with quality in such an environment and some systems to handle it. These factors all point to developing a high level of communication with customers.

It probably sounds odd for a manufacturer in the just-in-time and zero inventory age to say it, but services present a problem because they don't involve inventory. Although we try to cut inventory wherever possible, the penalty we pay is that inventory isn't there to buffer the business from fluctuations in the market. You wind up with a very different capacity management task. We don't have any experience managing capacity in an inventory-free environment. I am not sure we are up to it.

On the bidding side, we have limited experience in estimating service contract costs. If we were to get a fairly long-term contract below cost, we could lose our shirt.

It seems to me that there are several key success factors in implementing such a service. First, communication between the customer and service provider is vital, especially during the early stages of developing the service relationship. The customer must communicate its needs to the service provider, while the provider must communicate its capabilities to the customer. Second, both parties must be committed to the long-term success of the venture. Third, a successful external aircraft interiors management business rests on developing a partnership between the customer and the service provider.

So, my decision comes down to heading off in a new direction with an attractive set of benefits but also significant costs, or continuing to work on improving our existing core manufacturing business, which, as you can appreciate, is far from perfect. NAA plans to introduce a new colour scheme in March 1999, so I have to decide quickly.

NOTES

1. Welding two pieces of synthetic textile together was very similar to welding two pieces of metal, except that the source of heat was radiofrequency radiation rather than an electric arc or acetylene combustion. Like metal welding, the two pieces of textile had to be of similar composition.

2. The heart of a microwave receiver was a small electronic device, typically located at the focal point of a curved reflecting surface where the radiation was concentrated. The curved surfaces of some dishes were made from fabric supported by a rigid frame. Fell-Fab Products made the reflecting fabric surface rather than the supporting frame or the electronic components.

UNICON CONCRETE PRODUCTS (H.K.) LTD.

Prepared by Professors
Fraser Johnson and Rob Klassen

Version: (A) 2000-09-25

Herman Li, deputy managing director of Unicon Concrete Products (H.K.) Ltd. (Unicon), was considering what action he should take to address the growing demand for two of his company's products, precast concrete facades and slabs. It was now November 1997, and the construction industry in Hong Kong was flourishing. Mr. Li felt that an opportunity existed for Unicon to make changes to the current process of submitting structural design drawings to the Hong Kong Housing Authority for approval. He believed that streamlining this process would both reduce lead times and eliminate unnecessary costs. Because of the long lead time associated with such a change, Mr. Li felt compelled to finalize his strategy quickly. He was concerned, however, about the implications of this change on Unicon's operations and competitive position.

HONG KONG

Hong Kong was an important centre of economic activity in southeast Asia. Located on the South China Sea, Hong Kong was the economic gateway to the People's Republic of China (PRC). In fact, 60 per cent of all of China's exports passed through Hong Kong, while the Territory accounted for approximately 70 per cent of the direct foreign investment in the PRC. Hong Kong had the world's largest container port, where exports of electronic products, clothing and textiles passed through to North America and Europe.

Hong Kong reverted back to China from the British on July 1, 1997, under the "one country, two systems" approach to government. Although the per capita income of Hong Kong was second in Asia only to that of Japan, the Special Administrative Region (SAR) faced certain problems. With over six million people on only 1,076 square kilometers (415 square miles), affordable housing was one of the most critical problems facing the Hong Kong government.

Needless to say, housing in Hong Kong was among the most expensive in the world. A typical 800 to 1,500 square foot apartment in Hong Kong with two or three bedrooms ranged in price from HK$15 to HK$35 per square foot per month for rental and between HK$5,500 to HK$8,000 per square foot to purchase.[1] Even apartments at the low end of the market, with only two bedrooms and 500 to 800 square feet, cost about HK$10 per square foot per month to rent and between HK$3,200 to HK$5,500 per square foot to purchase.

CONCRETE CONSTRUCTION MARKET

As a supplier to the construction industry, Unicon sold its precast concrete products to general contractors in Hong Kong. General contractors were large firms capable of co-ordinating the construction of large, expensive building projects. These firms had expertise in building construction and design, together with the capabilities to finance such ventures. Although there were many general contractors in Hong Kong, the largest of these, numbering approximately 12, controlled an estimated 80 per cent of the market. Unicon had historically worked with all 12 of these organizations.

While seasonal variations were relatively small, construction activity followed a cyclical pattern, with infrastructure and superstructure developments peaking at different times. A developer interested in constructing a superstructure complex would secure the services of an architectural firm to coordinate the design and build the project. The architectural firm would provide engineering support, dealing with both the substructure (the foundation below ground) and superstructure (the building complex above ground).

The typical process called for the architect to engineer both the substructure and superstructure concurrently. Under the existing superstructure submission procedure for private development, detailed design calculations and drawings had to be prepared by a Registered Architect and a Registered Structural Engineer (RSE) jointly and submitted to the Government Building Department for approval. The submission could be approved, minor changes requested, or rejected. This submission and review process could take up to two months.

In Hong Kong, tender offers for the superstructure were requested just prior to completion of the substructure. General contractors then were expected to be capable of immediately commencing construction of the superstructure following formal review of the tenders. This placed considerable pressure on the bidder to have subcontractors and suppliers that could meet very tight schedules on time.

When constructing superstructures, the general contractor used either the traditional method of pouring concrete walls and floors on-site, using forms built in place, or alternatively, assembled precast concrete facades and slabs, which were produced elsewhere. Facades were the exterior walls of the superstructure, and slabs were the interior floors. The use of either method was determined in advance from the architect's specifications during the design phase. With either method, the general contractor typically used subcontractors to complete this phase of the construction project.

Unicon's products were used in all three primary categories of superstructures in Hong Kong (industrial, residential and office buildings). Although the cost of the precast materials was generally three to four per cent more than the traditional, pouring on-site method, other advantages favored its use. First, precast systems provided opportunities to reduce total costs in the construction project. Building assembly time could be shortened, site construction simplified and site congestion reduced.

Second, reliance on skilled tradespeople, such as carpenters and steel-fixers, was reduced. Skilled tradespeople were in short supply in Hong Kong, and these workers typically commanded salaries of HK$1,500 per day, although during peak times they could reach as high as double that. Furthermore, the reduction of on-site workers decreased the need for supervisory personnel and administration.

Third, because precast products were produced in a controlled environment, production was not affected by the traditional problems that beset the construction industry. For example, bad weather and unscheduled shortages of labour and equipment were not problems that affected precast production. Consequently, availability of products could be assured. Fourth, for related reasons, precast products offered quality advantages. The exterior finish was regarded as superior to on-site construction, and the window frames could be cast in the concrete so as to avoid water seepage.

Notwithstanding these advantages, there were several factors that continued to favor the use of the traditional construction method. If the super-structures were not initially designed with precast materials in mind, and precast materials were then considered, the general contractor was required to resubmit revised designs for approval. This resubmission could result in substantial delays. Since the expectation was that construction of the superstructure would begin immediately follow-ing the formal review of the tenders, opportunities to redesign the project to accommodate precast components usually did not exist. Consequently, precast systems had to be specified by the archi-tect at the outset of the design process. In addition, precast systems had to conform to standard dimensions in order to be economically viable. Such requirements placed restrictions on the cre-ativity and originality that an architect could apply to overall building design.

Finally, construction activities differed sub-stantially when precast systems were used com-pared to traditional methods. There was less reliance on skilled labor and increased depen-dence on equipment, such as tower cranes. As a result, general contractors had to be capable of supporting this particular method of superstruc-ture construction.

HONG KONG HOUSING AUTHORITY

The Hong Kong Housing Authority (HKHA) was a government agency responsible for pro-viding affordable housing for local residents. The HKHA provided both rental "blocks" and home ownership scheme (HOS) "blocks." The approximate number of apartments in a residen-tial block was 640; a typical block consisted of a 41-floor superstructure, which required 1,120 facades and 3,400 slabs. A typical floor plan for a residential block is provided in Exhibit 1.

The rental blocks offered apartments at below market rates, while the home ownership schemes provided Hong Kong residents with an opportu-nity to acquire units at discounted prices. In order to qualify for either the rental or ownership properties, residents had to meet certain income restrictions and not own other property. From a design standpoint, each block, whether rental or HOS, had the same structural layout. However, the HOS building had a different finish that was slightly more stylish.

Current regulations restricted the manufac-ture of facades and slabs for HKHA projects to production facilities located in Hong Kong. However, the regulations were being revised to permit firms in the PRC to supply these. This revision was expected to take place by 1998.

For HKHA projects, the approval process was quite similar to other superstructures. Detailed design calculations and drawings had to be prepared by an RSE employed by the general contractor, who had successfully tendered for the contract. These drawings were submitted to the project architect, who was the supervising officer representing the HKHA, for approval. The archi-tect was obliged to issue his comments within 28 days.

HKHA construction projects represented the largest segment of Unicon's sales. Mr. Li expected that approximately 80 per cent of the company's sales would be supported by HKHA projects, while the balance would be split between industrial and office projects. Under present market conditions, Unicon expected to receive HK$11.3 million per block, HK$4.8 million for facades and HK$6.5 million for slabs.

The Hong Kong government had recently announced an ambitious four-year program for the construction of new residential blocks. The most recent forecast provided to Unicon by the HKHA indicted that contracts for a total of 179 blocks would be tendered in just the next year alone. It was expected that approximately 50 per cent of these would require precast mate-rials for construction. Under present conditions, Mr. Li felt that Unicon had the capacity to man-ufacture sets of facades and slabs for seven

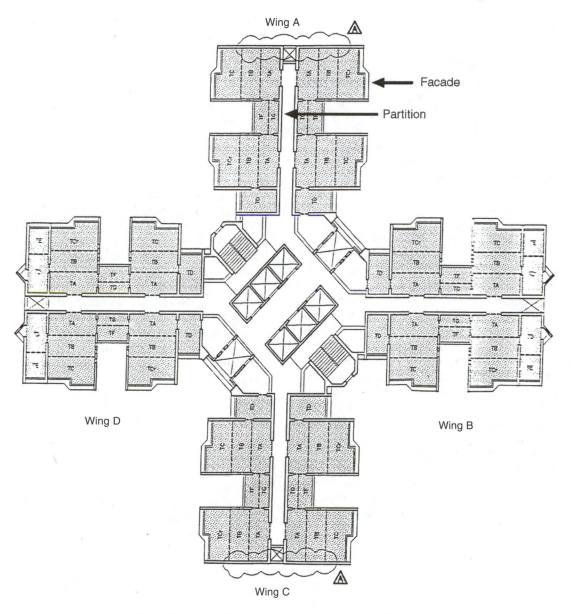

Precast Facade and Partitioning Location for Typical Floor Plan

Exhibit 1   Residential Block Diagram

blocks per year. Total current industry capacity was estimated at only 20 blocks per year.

UNICON CONCRETE PRODUCTS (H.K.) LTD.

Unicon was part of International Tak Cheung Holdings Limited (ITC), a multi-billion dollar holding company with interests mainly in Hong Kong. The 1997 ITC financial report listed 44 subsidiary and associated companies, with activities in a wide range of areas, including property development, construction, petroleum trading and sales, and electronic products.

A primary business activity of ITC was real estate development and construction. In addition to Unicon, ITC also owned Paul Y.—ITC Construction Holdings Limited (Paul Y.). Paul Y. was a major general contractor in Hong Kong with annual sales of HK$7.5 billion in fiscal 1997. Approximately one-third of Unicon's sales were to this affiliated company.

Unicon manufactured precast concrete products, consisting of four principal product lines: facades, slabs, stairs and partitioning walls (Exhibit 2). Each of these products was used in the construction of large, high-rise residential, office and industrial complexes. Company sales for fiscal year 1997 were HK$88 million, and next year's revenue was expected to continue to grow substantially for fiscal 1997–98. Similar growth was forecast for the following year (1998–99), after which sales were expected to stabilize.

Company Products

Partitioning walls, the interior wall used in the construction of superstructures, was the only product manufactured by Unicon when it was founded in 1992. Mr. Li described the company's evolution into other precast concrete products:

Our factory was originally built for producing partitioning walls. Unfortunately, we were unable to support our operations with only that one product. Eventually, we ventured into precast facades. This led to the development of our process for precast slabs as well.

In general, we are shifting our production process from a reliance on skilled trades-people, which are in short supply in Hong Kong these days, to a more standardized product, which is machine-dependent. This strategy has been enormously successful for us. Of course, with the current high level of demand, three other firms have entered the market, and we expect to see two more before the end of this year.

Although partitioning walls were a proprietary design, they came in a variety of standard sizes, with the typical product measuring approximately eight feet (2.44 metres) high, two feet (0.6 m) wide and three inches (0.075 m) thick. This product was engineered to meet certain performance requirements, such as fire resistance, structural support and sound dampening. It was up to the company to provide engineering certificates demonstrating the quality of its partitioning walls. In fiscal 1997, this product represented 40 per cent of company sales. Growth in this market segment was expected to correlate with the overall level of activity in the residential construction industry.

The other two major product lines were facades and slabs. Sales of these two products were interrelated. Since designs were not standardized among the four Hong Kong manufacturers, customer orders tended to require corresponding commitments for both products. Consequently, production of slabs and facades were make-to-order only. In contrast, sales of partitioning walls, because of their modular design, were independent of facades and slabs. Thus, production of partitioning walls could be make-to-stock.

Sales of facades represented 20 per cent of total sales in 1997, while slabs were 34 per cent for the same period. Management predicted that sales of these product lines would grow much faster than partitioning walls as general contractors and architects became more familiar with the advantages of their use. Mr. Li considered profit margins on both facades and slabs to be very good—significantly higher than the margin on partitioning walls.

Stairs were the smallest of Unicon's product lines, accounting for only six per cent of sales in fiscal 1997. Profit margins on the stairs business

Precast concrete facades ready to be assembled and installed onto the floor slab

Precast concrete slab being hoisted into position

Exhibit 2   Unicon Products

was comparable to that of the facades, which was somewhat less than that of slabs. Roger Cheung, sales director at Unicon, described the situation as follows:

> Stairs are a fairly standardized product, with no engineering approvals required. Design is standardized. Customers that buy our facades and slabs do not necessarily have to use our stairs. Usually, we can't justify contracts for producing stairs based on industry pricing. However, if I can pick up the business at a good margin, we will take it.

Facade and Slab Manufacturing

Unicon operated a 7,500 square metre facility in Yuen Long, in the New Territories. All shipments into and out of the plant were made by highway transport. The plant layout is depicted in Exhibit 3. Partitioning walls were produced at one end of the plant, labeled "drywall production area," while slabs, facades and stairs were produced at the other end.

Currently, Unicon employed 64 people, including 46 in the production department and 18 staff. The production department included supervision, quality control, maintenance and 14 production workers. These production workers were dedicated exclusively to the manufacture of partitioning walls.

In contrast, subcontractors were used for facade, slab and stair production. One subcontractor provided two teams of four workers for facade production, another provided three teams of four for slab production, and a single team of three workers was provided by a third contractor for stair production. Finally, another 14 production workers in the bending area prepared the reinforcing bar. These workers also were provided by a subcontractor.

The company operated a single shift that ran between 8:00 a.m. and 6:00 p.m., with a one-hour lunch break from noon till 1:00 p.m. The average production worker at Unicon was paid HK$15,000 per month, including benefits, but not including overtime. The plant operated a regular production schedule from Monday to Saturday, plus overtime every other Sunday. Over

the course of the year, employees were entitled to 14 statutory paid holidays, in addition to regular paid vacation days. Mr. Li estimated that labor costs were 30 per cent of total revenue, while material costs were approximately 40 per cent. The balance was for plant overhead and profit.

The plant had 25 facade moulds and 64 slab moulds, and some slab moulds were capable of producing two slabs. Consequently, the production of slabs could range from as low as 64 per day to as high as 101 units per day, depending on the design of the building under construction. The production process for both facades and slabs was identical, involving four groups of activities (a detailed process flow diagram for facades is provided in Exhibit 4).

Mould Setup

Mould setup, the first group of activities, began each morning at about 8:30 a.m. First, the steel moulds were cleaned with a high-pressure air gun to remove loose debris. Oil was then applied to the metal moulds in order to avoid bonding between the mould and the concrete. Cast-in items were then added to the mould. In the case of facades, this included windows, sockets and electrical boxes. In the case of slabs, areas were "boxed-out" for electrical conduits. Steel reinforcing bar was then placed into the mould. This material was included to provide structural support to the finished product, and was prepared earlier in another dedicated area. Finally, a quality control audit was performed before the mould was "closed" and ready for pouring. Mould setup activities were typically completed by 11 a.m.

Pouring

Concrete was added to the mould during the pouring stage. Concrete, which was comprised of a mixture of cement, aggregate (e.g., stone or gravel) and water, was mixed off-line by three Unicon employees in the batching plant and delivered to the moulds via an overhead crane. Pouring commenced at 10:30 a.m. and concluded at approximately 2 p.m. This operation was suspended during the lunch break.

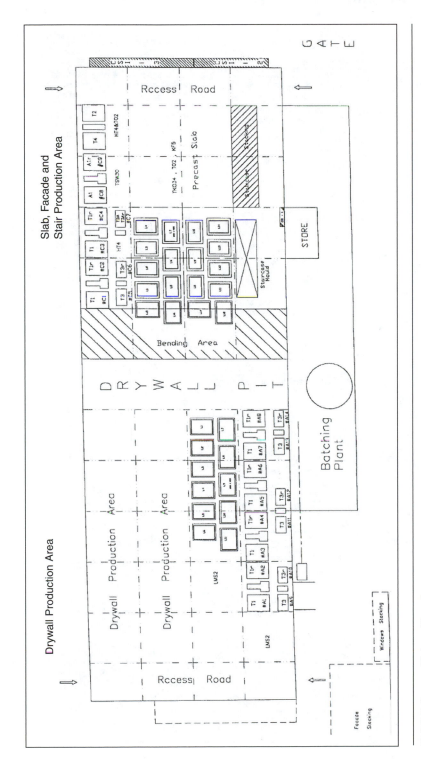

Exhibit 3   Unicon Plant Layout

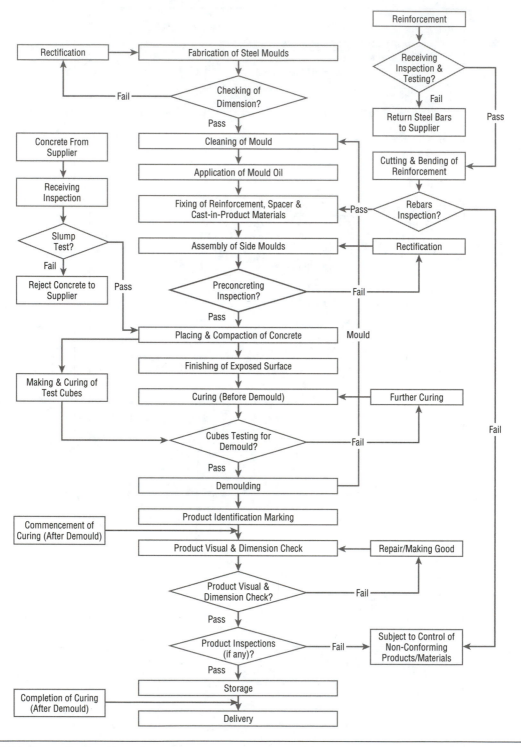

Exhibit 4   Process Flow Diagram

Finishing

Finishing commenced at about 11:00 a.m. Each product was specified as requiring either a smooth or rough finish. Finishing was completed in two phases. The first phase started immediately after the pouring operation, while the second occurred approximately 90 minutes later, because the concrete finish deteriorated as it settled. Finishing concluded at approximately 4:30 p.m. in the summer months. However, in the winter months, steam curing was required, which extended this process till about 6:30 p.m. Finally, the mould was then covered with a canvas overnight. Each mould was required to cure for 14 hours following the second finishing phase, before stripping the next morning. If accelerated steam curing was applied, the curing period could be reduced to eight hours.

Mould Stripping

The last group of activities was performed the next morning after curing was completed. Starting at 8 a.m., the steel mould was vibrated to separate the mould from the finished precast slab or facade. The mould and the precast product was then rotated 90 degrees, after which the mould was returned to its normal position on the plant floor. An overhead crane was used to remove the precast product to the finished storage area where "remedial" work was performed to repair any visual defects. Stripping was usually complete by 10:30 a.m.

Teams often worked on different activities concurrently. For example, as part of the team finished the stripping operation, other members of the team would start the mould setup operation.

Quality was an important element of Unicon's operations. The company was first ISO 9002 certified in 1994. As part of the company's quality plan, samples were taken from products throughout the manufacturing cycle to test for conformance to material specifications.

Capacity Expansion

The current demand for Unicon's product lines, facades and slabs in particular, had forced Mr. Li to evaluate possible options to expand capacity. Mr. Li was considering the expansion of the plant by 5,000 square metres in an effort to double capacity. However, he did not expect that the expansion could be completed before August 1998.

The market was in the middle of a boom and Mr. Li did not want to miss this opportunity. He was considering two alternatives to expand capacity in the short-term. First, he could add a second shift. Mr. Li wondered how this would affect quality and customer responsiveness. Furthermore, he was concerned about how his organization would cope with such a change and what the additional costs of such a plan would be.

The second alternative was to re-allocate plant space. Plant space currently dedicated to the production of stairs and partitioning walls could be converted to slabs and facades. The difficulty of this strategy was that Unicon would be abandoning two products, and Mr. Li was concerned that such a move was short-sighted. However, with the plant expansion, the opportunity existed to re-enter the partitioning wall and stairs markets in the future.

STRATEGY TO
PURSUE A BLANKET APPROVAL

Mr. Li was considering a strategy whereby approved technical submissions for HKHA projects could be resubmitted for future projects and would not require review and approval by an RSE or government authority. Mr. Li explained his logic:

> Despite the fact that the design has been used for 10 previous projects, you still have to submit it for approval. This costs both time and money.

> We want to get approval for future contracts if the design has been previously approved by the HKHA. Of course, we would still have to submit our plans for record purposes, and the general contractor would still expect to see our quality plan and method statement.

If his plan was accepted, the use of facades and slabs in superstructure construction would be similar to that for partitioning walls and stairs. Unicon would still be required to submit technical drawings for record purposes, but avoid the long, expensive review process. Mr. Li anticipated that on a typical contract, cost savings for one housing block would be about HK$150,000.

Mr. Li could see additional opportunities for savings if his plan was implemented. For example, lead times could be reduced by approximately one month. This represented the delays Unicon experienced as part of the approval process. Furthermore, the company could extend its product standardization. Minor changes to moulds based on individual comments from engineers would no longer be a concern. From Mr. Li's perspective, the decision regarding his efforts to establish a blanket approval process was obvious:

> This will reduce our costs as the engagement of a RSE incurs expenses in the form of professional fees. Another big advantage is that I won't have to wait for an order to support production. There are no significant disadvantages that I can see.

THE FUTURE

Mr. Li was concerned with the matter of establishing the blanket approval process with the HKHA. He wondered if this was an appropriate move for the company; there were still several lingering issues in his mind. What implications would it have for his manufacturing operations? How would such a move impact Unicon's competitive position in the marketplace? In the short-term, his order book was full. However, Mr. Li knew that the marketplace would adjust, and he wondered about the long-term implications.

He felt that two issues had to be resolved. First, should he continue with his plans to establish a blanket approval? When he contacted others in the precast industry, no one seemed interested in working to develop industry-wide standards. Second, if so, how could he convince the HKHA to accept his recommendation? The chief architect of the Design and Standard Section at the HKHA had the authority to approve such a proposal. However, he would need to demonstrate the mutual advantages of his plan.

Mr. Li expected that it would take approximately four months to negotiate a blanket approval arrangement with the HKHA. He knew that the process would have to be initiated quickly, if this arrangement was to be in place in time to take full advantage of the booming market expected next year.

NOTE

1. In November 1997, HK$1 was equivalent to US$0.1290 and C$0.1818.

2

PROCESS DESIGN

All organizations have business processes, whether manufacturing goods or providing services, whether part of the private or public sector, whether located domestically or international. Processes encompass any sequenced set of activities and operations that transform inputs, including materials, energy, people, capital, and knowledge, into outputs. The output of any process, termed a *product,* frequently comprises a bundle of goods and services (see Figure 2.1).

Although we risk stating the obvious, it is worth stressing that the product must, in turn, offer customers value. Customers can be external to an organization, such as passengers of a taxi service or the purchaser of an automobile, or internal, such as users of a market analysis for a new product launch. Yet, too often, managers focus on how value has been defined historically, with little attention being paid to the changing competitive landscape or customer needs. Ultimately, it is the customer's—not management's—definition of value that determines whether a process is effective. Recall from Chapter 1 that customer value is defined as the combination of cost, quality, delivery, and flexibility inherent in the bundle of goods and services.

Designing effective, customer-driven processes involves many different choices in selecting human resources, equipment, and materials. Process *design* is strategic in nature and can either improve or hamper an organization's ability to compete over the long run. For example, managers at a radiology clinic can improve their ability to compete on the basis of time by examining each step of their patient process and identifying steps that unnecessarily cause customers (i.e., patients) to wait. Moreover, operating efficiency tends to be constrained by many choices made early on during design, which later drives operating costs. Thus, managers at the previously mentioned radiology clinic might assess accounting and billing processes with a view toward eliminating activities that require extraneous information or duplicate data entry. Doing so will reduce cost through improved worker productivity.

In contrast to design, process *management* is an ongoing activity. Processes used by companies are never static; instead, they must change as customer demands evolve, competitive opportunities emerge, and new technologies improve. Process improvement is critical to redesigning processes and adapting to change. Both quality management

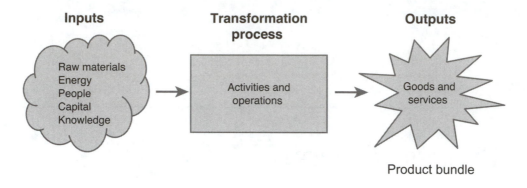

Figure 2.1   Process Overview

(Chapter 5) and supply chain management (Chapter 6) further build on this dynamic view of processes to foster improved competitiveness.

Process design and subsequent improvement is one of the three basic foundational blocks that support world-class operations (see Figure 2.2). Consider the following observations, paraphrased from a leading thinker in operations management:

> The firm now demands a great deal more of managers. The assignment becomes—"Make an increasing variety of goods and offer an increasing array of services, with faster responsiveness and greater customization, but with flawless quality. Improve our return on investment by automating and introducing new technology in processes and materials so that we can cut prices to meet local and foreign competition. Mechanize—but keep your schedules flexible, your inventories low, your capital costs minimal, and your work force contented."
>
> The firm whose managers master these apparently conflicting demands commands a strategic position of enviable advantage. An operations system that can quickly adjust schedules, get innovative offerings out fast, take advantage of new technology, and produce a wider variety of products and services from limited facilities has forged a formidable competitive weapon. (Skinner, 1966, p. 140)

Although initially penned almost four decades ago, these challenges remain no less relevant and vital today. Managers are faced with a complex set of operating issues and concerns that oftentimes necessitates trade-offs. Moreover, internal and external sources of variability related to the design and operation of processes, such as changing customer needs, supplier disruptions, new competitors, and evolving worker demands, further complicate process management.

PROCESS CHOICE

Process design, first and foremost, involves a basic choice about how resources are organized around the production of goods and the provision of services, and it is explicitly linked to a clear definition of customer value. However, given that most firms have many processes spread out across multiple facilities, processes can be tailored to fit particular customer needs in specific market segments.

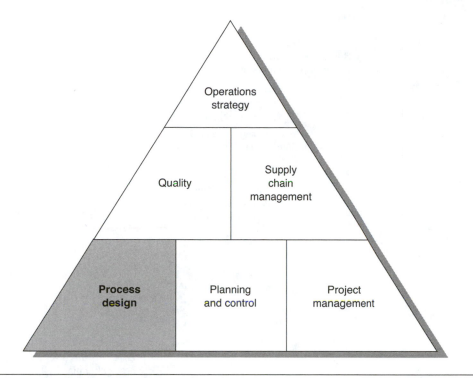

Figure 2.2   Process Design Is Foundational

In general, two major customer-related factors drive process selection: the degree of product customization needed and the relative volume of the good or service demanded. The manager has five basic process types that form a continuum to choose from:

1. project;
2. job (e.g., Quinte MRI);
3. batch (e.g., Earth Buddy, ING Direct Canada, Red Cross Blood Mobile Clinics, McLeod Motors);
4. line (e.g., Greaves Brewery, Celestica Inc., Thera-Aid Medical Devices, VBF Tubing); and
5. continuous (e.g., Iron Ore Company of Ontario).

These two dimensions, along with several examples of these five process types, are depicted in Figure 2.3. With the exception of project management, which is considered in greater detail in Chapter 4, all basic process types are presented in cases in this chapter.

Process choice—whether a project, job, batch, line, or continuous process—implicitly combines three process dimensions that management must balance and control: capacity, inventory, and variability (see Figure 2.4). Collectively, these three management levers determine the overall output yielded by the process and form a central challenge for each

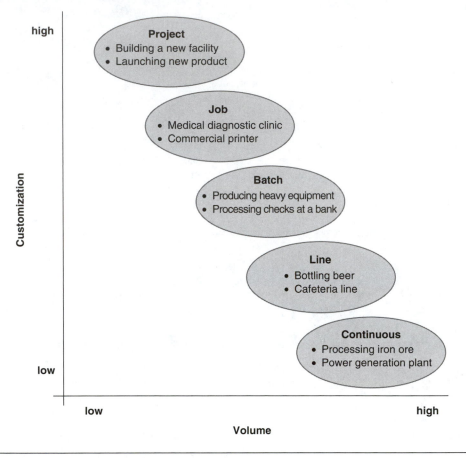

Figure 2.3   Process Choice

Source: Adapted from Ritzman, Krajewski, and Klassen (2004).

of the cases offered in this chapter. More generally, understanding the trade-offs inherent among these factors is critical to building world-class operations.

These three levers must be viewed as interrelated, as suggested by the triangle; a change in any one factor has managerial implications for the other two (Lovejoy, 1998). In a very practical sense, greater capacity, greater inventory, and lower variability can be substitutes for each other in achieving an overall output volume (or flow) through a process (see Figure 2.4).

CAPACITY

Capacity is often challenging to specify for particular activities and operations, and even more so for the entire process. In general, capacity captures the maximum rate of items processed per unit time (either explicitly or implicitly). Unfortunately, no single capacity measure is applicable to all types of situations, as is evident in the cases later in this chapter.

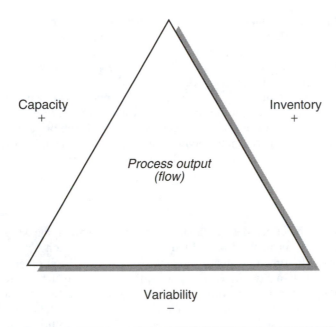

Figure 2.4   Process Management Triangle

For example, check-scanning equipment, one of several activities in ING Direct's operations, might report a capacity of 30 checks per hour. Yet, this does not account for moving batches of checks in and out of this processing step. By way of comparison, a machining shop such as McLeod Motors might consider the number of machine-hours available, with management attention focused on one or two critical machines.

At a very basic level, the overall process output is limited by the activity or operation with the lowest capacity, otherwise known as the *bottleneck*. A bottleneck is the activity or operation that has the lowest capacity in the process. Thus, a critical first step in designing or analyzing a process is to identify the bottleneck.

INVENTORY

Inventory is any stock of items used to support the production of goods and services or satisfy customer demand. These items include any materials, orders, and information. In some service processes, people flowing through the process might be considered inventory.

For purposes of process choice, inventory has two critical implications: cost and time. First, increasing the amount of inventory adds to the cost of producing goods and services. For example, if VBF Tubing receives shipments of steel coils (raw material) weekly from a supplier, the firm must pay for working capital and warehouse space. Even people waiting in line at the Red Cross clinic have a cost—for the physical space, customer aggravation, and potentially lost goodwill.

Second, the amount of inventory in the process is an important driver of the time that customers or products take to move through the entire process. A waiting line at the Quinte MRI clinic offers a simple example; as the average number of patients waiting in line ahead of the MRI scanner increases, the average overall service time increases for patient care. The same principle applies to both manufacturing and services, and items typically must wait ahead of several operations, further slowing responsiveness. The total time that a typical item spends in any process, termed *throughput time,* increases as the average level of inventory in that process increases.

Thus, having greater inventory tends to hurt two important dimensions of customer value: cost and delivery time or responsiveness. So why have inventory? This critical question is partly answered by the process management triangle. Inventory can smooth the flow of customers, parts, or materials into and through the process, which, in turn, either allows managers to invest in less capacity or to buffer against greater variability, discussed next.

VARIABILITY

Unfortunately, in practice, designing and evaluating process capacity is rarely as straightforward as it is in the Earth Buddy case, in which each activity is precisely defined and exactly timed. Instead, products, people, and equipment change from minute to minute, day to day, and year to year. Variation is really a measure of how much something changes and is often difficult to get a good sense of. By way of contrast, many managers have a general intuition about the average production or demand rates for a process, usually based on personal observation. Yet, variability is just as critical as capacity.

For example, a quick look at daily volume of mail received by ING Direct from its banking customers shows huge day-to-day fluctuations. Moreover, the volume of mail received on any specific day is very difficult to predict—at least until it arrives on the doorstep. Management must accommodate these changes, possibly by adding additional staff "just in case," by working overtime, or by allowing customer mail to be carried over from one day to the next. The first two actions are examples of an increase in capacity; the last action illustrates an increase in inventory. If management could smooth the day-to-day arrival of mail even to a moderate degree by leveling direct-mail advertising campaigns, then fewer just-in-case workers would be needed, or managers could ensure that all mail was processed the same day without carryover. Costs would fall, *and* responsiveness would improve!

ING Direct's process variability is primarily driven by external factors, here customer behavior. But for other firms, such as Iron Ore Company, variability comes from internal sources within the process. Here, both random equipment breakdowns and planned preventive maintenance create challenges that force managers to add excess capacity at upstream or downstream operations or build inventory around a critical, bottleneck operation. Ultimately, much of the variability within any process must be reduced using quality management tools (see Chapter 5).

In summary, managers make process design choices at the organization level, as well as at the level of individual activities and operations that collectively form a process. Moreover, processes are not confined to one particular functional area but instead are present in marketing, operations, human resources, information systems, and finance, to name several. Finally, process design involves trade-offs, first, in the general configuration of the process and its effective contribution to customer value and, second, in the combination of capacity, inventory, and variability embodied in any design.

Earth Buddy®

Earth Buddies were rapidly becoming a hit novelty product of the summer. Ben Vardi, production director, was faced with a need to expand quickly, yet remain flexible with little inventory for this small start-up firm. With about 15 operators, Earth Buddies were produced using a simple batch-flow process. Vardi must assess the bottleneck, process capacity, throughput time, and other performance characteristics as he plans for process improvement and firm expansion.

Learning objectives: process analysis, definition of bottlenecks and process performance measures, and process start-up in entrepreneurial venture.

Greaves Brewery

Lesley Simpson was completing the design on a new bottling line for this brewery in Trinidad. At the time, the company was using manual labor to palletize cases of beer, and the ongoing bottling expansion had led to a reassessment of this operation, as well as the downstream warehouse operations. More automated equipment, available from two equipment suppliers, offered several potential advantages. Simpson wanted the best system possible for handling finished goods in this highly seasonal business.

Learning objectives: understand process flexibility trade-offs, explore linkages between operations, assess operational and technological risks, and conduct a financial assessment of process technology.

Quinte MRI

This small service provider offers medical diagnostic technologies to patients who need a fast turnaround. After just 6 weeks in operation at a medical center, the company had developed an extensive waiting list, and physicians had already begun referring patients to competing facilities. David Wright and Kevin Saskiw, Quinte's business development coordinators, must provide recommendations and an action plan to deal with this process and productivity problem in a setting with extreme variability.

Learning objectives: identify process bottlenecks and system capacity in a service setting, determine alternative work designs and allocation, and reduce growing backlogs.

ING Direct Canada

This retail banking operation is the Canadian subsidiary of one of the top global providers of integrated financial services, ING Group of the Netherlands. Growth has been phenomenal, and Basil Bell, senior vice president of operations, must meet the demands of a growing client base while maintaining its current staffing levels, physical space, and commitment to same-day processing of accounts. Any changes to procedures must address the immediate challenges of the company's growth, as well as develop a long-term strategy. Options to consider included new technology, increased efficiencies, or relaxing the same-day processing requirements.

Learning objectives: matching process capacity to demand, workforce scheduling, and implications of and planning for product variety and demand variability.

CELESTICA, INC.—MEMORY BUSINESS UNIT

Celestica, a major player in the electronics contract manufacturing industry, is considering relocating or reconfiguring its production facilities for the Memory Products group. Tim Jacobs, chair of the task force, is considering options for redesign that include moving toward a cellular layout. Both moving and reorganizing have attractive benefits as well as significant risks and costs.

Learning objectives: identifying the benefits and risks of cellular layouts, management of change, and facilities planning.

THERA-AID MEDICAL DEVICES

Sean Graham must estimate the production cost of a therapeutic wrist exerciser prototype. Automated assembly was possible long term, but a manual assembly and test procedure was necessary until the product was firmly established. As a member of a team and using hands-on observations, you must develop an assembly process for the new product using either an assembly line or a single-operator configuration. Job design and work measurement methods are used to estimate overall product cost and propose alternative prototype designs that might reduce assembly costs.

Learning objectives: comparison of process choices, work design, productivity and cost estimation.

INTRODUCTION TO PROCESS SIMULATION

Simulation is commonly used as a decision tool by managers in marketing, engineering, production, finance, and many other disciplines. Managers simulate processes to gain a better understanding of their processes, diagnose problems, train new employees, and explore possibilities. Both the advent of powerful personal computers and the development of graphically driven simulation packages have contributed to this greater adoption. This note presents a brief overview and illustrates the techniques with a tutorial model of a deli operation using Extend. (Note: Student and free Player [i.e., runtime] versions of the software are available from Imagine That Inc. at www.imaginethatinc.com.)

Learning objectives: overview of the critical aspects of process simulation, application of simulation tools to service, and manufacturing process analysis and improvement.

RED CROSS MOBILE BLOOD CLINICS—IMPROVING DONOR SERVICE

Peggy Ladowski, regional director of donor services for the American Red Cross, was wondering how to improve services to blood donors. Faced with an increasing number of complaints that donors were being held up in long lines at Red Cross mobile blood collection operations—commonly termed *bloodmobiles*—she was considering several design alternatives for the blood collection process. For each alternative, a comparison is possible along a number of performance dimensions. (Note: An Extend runtime model, data file, and structured assignment are available to help you explore changes in staffing assignments, donor registration, and donor-bed configurations.)

Learning objectives: manage performance objectives in not-for-profit service organizations, compare operational and demand variability, assess service quality, and model and assess process changes.

Introduction to Inventory Control and Independent Demand

Inventories exist in virtually every organization and can serve any number of purposes. However, they can also represent a significant investment. Consequently, an important challenge facing managers is balancing the economic benefits of less frequent orders or setups versus the costs of holding inventory. This note provides an introduction to managing independent demand inventory items. It reviews the basic techniques associated with independent demand items, including fixed order quantity and fixed time period systems, and the ABC inventory classification system. The note is intended to address the questions of how much to order (the lot size issue) and when to order (the reorder point issue).

Learning objectives: identify the forms and functions of inventory; assess how much to order (the lot size issue) and when to order (the reorder point issue).

McLeod Motors Ltd.

McLeod Motors recently rationalized a number of motor end shields to reduce manufacturing costs, improve service, and reduce inventories. However, rather than seeing less inventory, overall levels have risen. Sue Reynolds must identify why the level is so high and what could be done to reduce inventory levels. The economic order (or production) quantity can also be calculated and compared against an estimate of the minimum level possible through process redesign.

Learning objectives: identify the causes and implications of inventory buildup, assess inventory policies, and estimate the costs associated with inventory.

Iron Ore Company of Ontario

A large, open-pit iron ore mine is plagued with crusher delays. Information has been gathered on the relevant capacities and costs, as well as statistical data on the frequency and duration of crusher stoppages. George Sharp, mine superintendent, must choose from holding trucks idle during crusher delays, reassigning the truck-shovel teams to waste removal, or dumping ore at an ore stockpile for later consumption at the crusher.

Learning objectives: bottleneck management; resource policies and scheduling as a source of variability in a continuous process.

VBF Tubing (Abridged)

VBF Tubing, a Dutch firm, is facing increased demand for its products. Unfortunately, inventory costs also are high because of significant setup costs. In light of these problems, the logistics manager, Rob Smit, must decide how to respond to a proposal that longer production runs be scheduled. The production, cost, and market data supplied allow him to explore the necessity for and implications of changing production batch sizes on these competing priorities. (Note: A short video is available that illustrates the operations of VBF Tubing.)

Learning objectives: match capacity to market demand; identify the impact of setup time, preventive maintenance, and product scheduling; and estimate economic order quantity based on facility operating practices.

MANAGEMENT QUESTIONS ADDRESSED IN PROCESS DESIGN CHAPTER

1. What level of capacity is needed from the process to serve market demand?

2. How should capacity be measured for each process operation or step? What is the capacity of each operation?

3. Which factors or operations limit the output rate of the process? Where is (are) the bottleneck(s)?

4. Do upstream or downstream operations interfere with the capacity of the bottleneck? If so, after what length of time?

5. How much time do customers or materials spend in the process?

6. How much inventory is needed to maintain the required process output? Where should it be located in the process and why? How low can we reduce the overall inventory level?

7. What are the effects of changing batch sizes on time characteristics?

8. What aspects of the system are highly variable?

9. How does this variability affect our need for capacity? How does this variability affect required inventory levels?

10. Can variability be reduced? What are the options to improve our ability to predict variability? How do the options to reduce variability differ if the source is primarily from inputs, the process itself, or output requirements?

11. How might new process equipment contribute to customer value, and how much will it cost? What are any benefits, in such areas as flexibility, quality, reliability, capacity, safety, performance characteristics, speed, initial cost, operating cost, compatibility, or maintenance, to name a few?

12. Have the right people been hired and trained for our process? How will any proposed changes to the process affect them?

13. How should performance standards be set for our workforce, including such areas as productivity, quality, and customer service?

REFERENCES

Lovejoy, W. S. (1998). Integrated operations: A proposal for operations management teaching and research. *Production and Operations Management, 7*(2), 106–124.

Ritzman, L. P., Krajewski, L. J., & Klassen, R. D. (2004). *Foundations of operations management.* Toronto: Pearson Education.

Skinner, W. (1966). Production under pressure. *Harvard Business Review, 44*(6), 139–146.

EARTH BUDDY®

Prepared by Professor Chris Piper

Earth Buddy® was rapidly becoming the hit novelty item of the summer. Although it was only mid-July, Seiger Marketing had already moved and expanded its Earth Buddy division's factory and warehouse twice since production began in mid-April. Even so, current production levels were straining the physical limits of its latest facility in Toronto, Ontario.

Nothing was certain, however, and Anton Rabie and Ronnen Harary, recent Ivey Business School graduates and Earth Buddy's co-owners, were reluctant to give their production director and business school classmate, Ben Varadi, any production advice except: "Remain flexible. We could get an order for 100,000 units, but if the order doesn't arrive, we would have to put the workforce on hold. We can't afford to carry large inventories." Against this background of uncertainty, Ben was looking for ways to increase his capacity and stay flexible at a minimum of expense.

THE PRODUCT

When the Earth Buddies' owners removed them from their boxes, they found a bald, but cute, humanlike head about eight centimetres in diameter. After soaking in water and sitting in a moist environment for a few days, the Earth Buddy sprouted a beautiful head of green hair. See Exhibit 1 for the before and after look. The

Care for your Earth Buddy®

Submerge your Earth Buddy® in a bowl until he sinks (approx. 2 -3 min.)

Place Earth Buddy® in a dish, and put in a warm, sunny place

Keep water in the dish at all times, and Earth Buddy's grass hair will sprout after 7 to 10 days

Trim Earth Buddy's hair, style, carefully mold the face and treat your Earth Buddy® with love and care

Have fun!

Exhibit 1   The Earth Buddy

Source: Company files.

owner's creativity could be expressed through the hair's styling. Earth Buddy sales had originally been through Toronto-area flower shops and gift stores, but as the product's wide appeal began to be realized, distribution spread nationally through stores such as K-Mart, Toys R Us, and Wal-Mart. By mid-July, over 100,000 units had been sold in Canada, and exports had begun to the United States.

THE PROCESS

Earth Buddies were produced in a hybrid batch-flow process illustrated in Exhibit 2. Six filling-machine operators working in parallel produced the basic rounded shapes by filling pieces of nylon stocking with sawdust and grass seed. The operators placed the heads in plastic tote boxes that held batches of about 25 heads. In another batch operation, an operator shaped the Earth Buddies' eye glasses by wrapping plastic-coated wire around a simple jig composed of two short, vertically-mounted dowels.

The remainder of the process was a worker-paced flow. Three moulding operators removed the heads from the tote boxes, and formed the nose and ears with the help of elastic bands. Next, two people working between the moulders placed the previously-formed eye glasses over the nose, and glued small plastic eyes inside the rims. Each shaped and assembled Earth Buddy was placed in a bin for the painter, who fashioned a red mouth with fabric paint before placing the head on shelving to dry. Drying usually took about five hours, but could take as long as seven hours during humid summer days. After drying, two packers placed the Earth Buddies in boxes, and then into cartons ready for shipment.

Work in process inventory (WIP) prior to drying was not large. Typically about 250 heads were at various stages of completion between filling and painting, but sometimes WIP seemed to grow much larger.

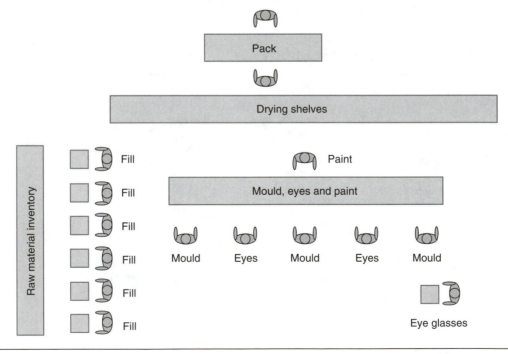

Exhibit 2   The Earth Buddy

In an effort to analyse his capacities, Ben and his day supervisor, Bob Wakelam, estimated the time it took an operator to process and move an Earth Buddy through each step. The times were: filling—1.5 minutes; moulding—0.8 minutes; eyes—0.4 minutes; eye glass fabrication—0.2 minutes; painting—0.25 minutes; and packing—0.33 minutes. After allowing for unavoidable delays and rest periods, Ben figured that he could count on seven hours of production from each eight-hour shift.

With weather forecasts calling for more hot, humid summer days, Ben wondered how his production capacity and WIP levels might be affected.

GREAVES BREWERY

Prepared by Professors
M. R. Leenders and J. A. Erskine

Copyright © 1991, Ivey Management Services

Version: (A) 2002-12-23

In February 1991, Lesley Simpson, chief engineer at Greaves Brewery, Trinidad, was completing the design of a new bottling line. The last remaining major issue dealt with the materials handling situation at the end of the line. Currently, the company was using manual labor to put the full cases of beer on pallets. Lesley was considering the possibility of using automatic equipment.

COMPANY BACKGROUND

Greaves Brewery was located on the southern Caribbean island of Trinidad. Founded by John Greaves in 1924, the company had established an excellent reputation. Greaves beer had also become a favorite with tourists and, as a result, a modest export business to the United States had started a few years ago. In February, sales reached the highest level in the company's history.

Four sales peaks occurred during the year: Carnival in February; Easter—six weeks later; Independence Day at the end of August; and the December Christmas season. Carnival was the highest sales period, but each peak caused the company to operate on tight schedules during which Greaves hired more labor and scheduled extra shifts.

BREWING PROCESS

Beer brewing started with extraction of sugar from malt by an enzymic process. This sugar was boiled with hops, producing a sterilized and concentrated solution. The resins extracted from the hops during boiling acted as a preservation and gave the beer its bitter flavor. The hops were then removed, and the solution was cooled to a temperature of 50 degrees F for bottom fermentation lasting seven days, during which yeast converted the sugar to alcohol and carbon dioxide. After fermentation the beer was cooled to 30 degrees F and stored for 10 days (during which the yeast separated out) and then roughly filtered through diatomaceous earth. After 24 hours of storage it was put through a polish filtration process, was artificially carbonated and was ready for bottling. After bottling and case packing, the beer was stored in the finished goods warehouse ready for delivery to retail outlets.

CURRENT OPERATIONS IN
BOTTLING AND WAREHOUSING

The bottling department and warehouse were part of the same building, but were separated by a wire fence (see Exhibit 1). The current bottling line had a capacity of 400 bottles per minute and usually operated two eight-hour shifts, five days a week. Periodic interruptions resulted in the line operating about 85 per cent of the time. For the past three months it had run at three shifts per day. This had meant that maintenance, previously done at night, had begun to interfere with production time. The third shift was difficult to staff and supervise, but the expanded bottling capacity would eliminate this need. At 1,000 bottles per minute, demand could be met by a one-shift operation with occasional overtime.

The last operation on the current bottling line was performed by two operators who manually stacked the full cases of 24 bottles per case on wooden pallets. Each case weighed 32.7 pounds. Each pallet held 40 cases (five layers high of eight cases per layer). See Exhibit 2 for the stacking patterns of the first two layers. Operators, who were paid $360.00 per week each, worked

independently on separate pallets. On average, it took seven and a half seconds per case to load the pallet.

Two fork lifts carried the full pallets to the warehouse, where they were stacked three high. The company owned 12 forklifts, and usually had at least two in the repair shop at any one time. The warehouse (ceiling height 15½ feet) had four storage bays in total. Usually two were being unloaded while the other two were being loaded. Space was reasonably plentiful except before peak sale periods when extra pallets were stacked in the aisles for inventory build-up.

NEW BOTTLING LINE

The new bottling line called for major changes in the bottling shop. Line capacity was to be increased by 600 bottles per minute with the addition of twin packers which would unload onto

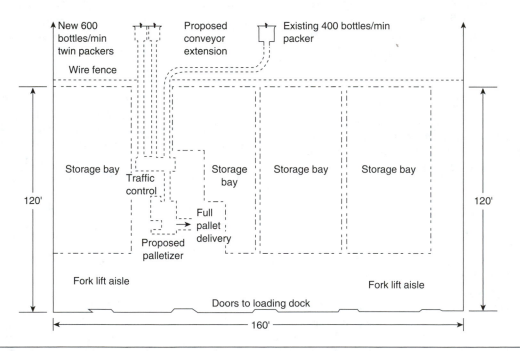

Exhibit 1   Warehouse Layout Showing Proposed Automatic Palletizing System

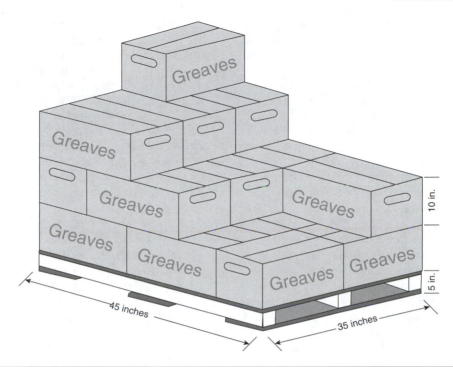

Exhibit 2   Pallet Stacking Pattern

two exit conveyors. Aside from this, a new empty bottle conveyor feed-in system was planned and would occupy all existing space between the bottling shop and the warehouse. As a result, it would be necessary to move the unloading and palletizing operation into the warehouse (see Exhibit 1). The required conveyor system from the three bottling lines to the warehouse for hand loading of pallets would cost $108,000 including installation. One advantage of the move to the warehouse, however, was the shortening of the fork lift route. Lesley calculated that turnaround time from the new location would range from 35 seconds to three minutes and would probably average one minute.

AUTOMATIC PALLETIZER

Lesley was considering the possibility of substituting an automatic palletizer for the hand loading operation in the new location. The machine's operation was similar in concept to the manual loading procedure. It would take eight cases at a time and feed them onto the pallet in a predetermined pattern. The pallet was then lowered for the next layer. The full pallet was put onto the discharge conveyor which could hold up to three full pallets. The machine required one operator whose primary function was to make sure the machine shut off in case of trouble and to clear jams if they occurred at the feed-in point. The operator would probably be paid $450.00 per week. The palletizer would require a different feed-in system from manual loading because of the counting operation and machine height.

Lesley was considering two different makes of equipment, Perrin and Clark. Lesley had received literature on both, had talked with sales representatives and also with executives in North American breweries. Lesley wanted a palletizer which could handle 45 cases per minute, operate on a 50-Hz electrical supply, load at least

40 cases per pallet and have a stacking pattern identical to the present system. Both Perrin and Clark sales representatives said they could produce satisfactory equipment.

Perrin Conveyors, Ltd. was a Canadian subsidiary of an American firm. It handled all Canadian and Commonwealth sales and operated relatively autonomously from its parent. For over 50 years Perrin had enjoyed a top reputation for its conveyor systems which were light, easy to install, durable, and efficient. An additional feature was the ready convertibility of all conveyors to any of three basic types—live roller, gravity, or belt. Perrin had designed and manufactured many of the conveyor systems for Canadian grain handling and mineral processing installations. Perrin manufactured a variety of materials handling equipment including palletizers, although it had never built one which met all of Lesley's specifications. Maximum capacity was determined by the number of cases the machine could handle in a given amount of time, and Perrin had never manufactured a unit faster than 40 cases per minute. In answer to Simpson's request, Perrin had said it would design a machine especially for Greaves, which could handle 45 cases per minute and stack five, six, or seven layers high with eight cases per layer. The machine would be strictly mechanical, consisting of gears, belts, etc., and would not require a foundation of any sort. It would require an air line at a pressure of 120 pounds per square inch (psi) which exceeded the 90 psi in the current general shop lines. Therefore, a separate small compressor would have to be added at a cost of about $2,400. Perrin would supply a skilled technician for ten days to help with installation after delivery. The equipment would carry a standard guarantee of one year. Greaves Brewery had purchased Perrin conveyors in the past and had been fully satisfied. Perrin's quotation for the palletizer was $324,000,[1] including the air compressor.

Clark Loading Systems was an American company with a top reputation in the palletizer field. It could supply a standard model which met all of the specifications and could stack five, six, or seven layers high. The Clark palletizer would be hydraulic, with few mechanical parts, but required a 12-foot hole in the floor for the piston in the pallet lift. The general shop air line pressure would be sufficient for the machine. Service and guarantee terms would be the same as Perrin's. Clark also manufactured conveyors which tended to be heavier, bulkier, and more difficult to install than Perrin's, but which also enjoyed an excellent reputation for quality and durability. Clark quoted a price of $408,000 for the palletizer.

If Lesley decided to use an automatic loader, the three exit lines would have to be combined into one line for delivery into the loader. Both Perrin and Clark were asked to quote on a traffic control system to join the lines. This system would have to jockey the cases into the single line and automatically count eight cases for delivery to the loader for each layer on the pallet.

Clark indicated that a traffic control unit would cost $72,000, plus $60,000 for conveyors leading from the end of the bottling lines to the control unit and from the unit to the loader. Perrin quoted $72,000 for the control and $48,000 for the conveyors.

Two mechanics would have to be trained to service the loader, and Lesley felt training could be done when one of the supplier's technicians was at Greaves for installation and start-up. A palletizer was not a complex machine and servicing should not be difficult for a skilled mechanic. Spare parts would be available from the makers, but with normal maintenance, costs would be negligible. Lesley felt that two of the mechanics already employed to service the bottling shop at about $540.00 per week could be trained to handle a palletizer as part of their regular duties.

Both palletizers under consideration would require electric power from lines extended into the warehouse from the bottling department. Each palletizer had a 12.75 horsepower motor, whose power consumption would probably cost $4,500 per year.

Installation costs would be substantial for either palletizer-conveyor system. Lesley estimated that a total Perrin System with traffic control could be installed by a local engineering contractor for $90,000. A complete Clark system would require $108,000.

Lesley wondered if Greaves should change to a seven-layer pallet if an automatic palletizer were purchased, but was not sure how to quantify the advantages and disadvantages of such a move. In any case, Lesley wanted to find the best system possible for handling finished goods. Lesley lacked familiarity with this kind of equipment, but realized that help was not easily available elsewhere. It had been standard practice at Greaves Brewery to justify certain investments on the basis of meeting future demand. These investments would also have to show a reasonable return in the long run.

NOTE

1. All prices quoted represent landed cost to Greaves, including freight and duty but not including installation.

QUINTE MRI

Prepared by David Wright and Kevin Saskiw under the supervision of Professors Carol Prahinski and John Haywood-Farmer

   Version: (A) 2003-06-16

On June 12, 2002, David Wright and his colleague, Kevin Saskiw, business development co-ordinators at Quinte MRI in Belleville, Ontario, were trying to decide what to propose regarding the magnetic resonance imaging (MRI) facility at Benton-Cooper Medical Center (BCMC) in Palmer, New York. Both men were frustrated and confused. Although the BCMC facility was only six weeks old, it already had a waiting list of 14 days for MRI scans. Because of this backlog, physicians had begun to refer their patients to competing MRI clinics. Dr. Syed Haider, Quinte MRI's chief executive officer, expected Wright's and Saskiw's recommendations and action plan in two days.

QUINTE MRI

Quinte MRI, Inc. was a small (annual revenues of $1.5 million),[1] but growing, international service provider specializing in medical diagnostic technologies, including MRI, nuclear medicine, ultrasound, computerized tomography (CT) scanning, bone densitometry, mammography and teleradiology services. The company helped design, install and operate scanning centres, and provided continued training and support for data interpretation. It maintained a variety of exclusive or partnership business arrangements with both fixed-site and mobile service turnkey operations. Quinte MRI's equipment and components were from many leading manufacturers.

Quinte MRI's founder, Dr. Syed Haider, received his PhD in electron spin resonance and nuclear magnetic resonance from the University of Wales. After a short time as professor at the University of Guelph, he became a physics and chemistry teacher at Centennial Secondary School in Belleville, Ontario, in 1968. When he retired 30 years later, he started Quinte MRI. Haider firmly believed that the residents of small communities deserved the same level of health services as residents of large urban centres. However, MRI systems in small communities were rare. Haider's first attempt to establish an MRI facility (in Belleville) was unsuccessful because Canadian regulations prohibited private-sector MRI. Thus, he turned to the Caribbean and the United States.

Quinte MRI had established facilities in five locations: the company headquarters in Belleville; a partnership arrangement with a radiologist in Laval, Quebec; and private MRI clinics in St. Louis, Missouri, the Cayman Islands, and Palmer, New York. With the exception of the Palmer facility, Quinte MRI held an interest of less than 20 per cent in each clinic. In June 2002, the company employed a total of about 20 people.

Quinte MRI served three distinct client groups:

1. Hospitals seeking to outsource their diagnostic imaging services were particularly interested in service reliability, access to the diagnostic equipment 24 hours per day, seven days per week and reasonable cost.

2. Physicians wanting to be partners in an independent diagnostic imaging centre saw cash flow, accessibility to the equipment and the strength of the relationship with their diagnostic imaging partner as major criteria.

3. Individuals wanting to operate their own diagnostic imaging centre, using Quinte MRI as a consultant in developing and carrying out the necessary steps to establish the clinic, wanted freedom from the hassles involved with establishing the business and were willing to pay a 10 per cent project development fee.

SCANNING TECHNOLOGY[2]

Various scanning technologies produced high quality images of the human body. The most obvious imaging technique was to use a camera to capture a visual image on photographic film. Although this technology was simple, it could be invasive, as surgery or probes were required for images of internal tissues, and it was normally limited to the wavelength range of visible light.

Modern scanning began in 1895 with the discovery that tissues absorbed X-rays. Although X-ray technology was relatively easy to use and gave high-resolution scans, the rays were penetrating and potentially dangerous,[3] and gave unclear images of some body features. They were particularly suited for examining tissue abnormalities, such as fractures, malignant tumors and respiratory diseases.

The 1970s saw the first of an explosion in imaging techniques, all of which relied on computers to help gather and analyse scanning data in electronic form. Computerized tomography (CT) relied on a series of X-rays from various angles that were combined to provide a three-dimensional picture from which two-dimensional images from any angle and at any depth could be derived. In positron emission tomography (PET), the patient ingested a positron-emitting radioactive substance that could be monitored as it proceeded through the body. In the closely related technique known as single-photon emission computed tomography (SPECT), the ingested active component emitted high-energy photons. In ultrasound (US), sound waves were bounced off tissues or objects inside the body; the reflected sound waves were converted into an image.

MRI relied on the fact that diamagnetic nuclei (those with magnetic moments) interacted with strong magnetic fields to create their own small magnetic fields. The induced fields were studied using variable frequency electromagnetic signals. At a certain frequency, the induced field resonated with the electromagnetic signal; this resonance was measured. Water comprised some 70 per cent of the human body, making hydrogen, which was diamagnetic and thus gave an MRI signal, the most common atom in living tissue. Although MRI did not involve the radiation danger of many other scanning techniques, it could heat up the tissues if the radio frequency was too intense. Also, because ferromagnetic materials—those containing iron, nickel or cobalt—interacted strongly with magnetic fields, people with screws, plates or other ferromagnetic materials such as pacemakers or metal fragments in their bodies could not be scanned with MRI. Doing so gave poor resolution scans and could be dangerous to the patient.

The many types of scans were valuable and complementary because they relied on different physical phenomena and gave different information. Although X-ray scans differentiated among tissues based on their density, MRI differentiated based on the tissues' water content. Whereas

X-rays and MRI gave information about internal structures, PET, SPECT and US could be used to observe biochemical processes, such as metabolism and fluid flow, as they occurred.

Active research continued in scanning technology and techniques. Although conventional MR machines were multi-purpose and expensive, many newer ones were smaller, cheaper, tailored for a particular part of the body and more patient-friendly, with reduced noise and open on one side to reduce the patient's feelings of claustrophobia. Other research streams aimed to (1) improve the MRI image and scanning depth capabilities by modulating the frequency of the electromagnetic signal; (2) broaden the scanning technique to other diamagnetic atoms, such as carbon, sodium and phosphorus; (3) develop ways to monitor body processes with MRI; (4) combine two or more scanning techniques; and (5) expand the ways in which these technologies could be applied.

Image quality depended critically on the strength of the magnet and the time required to produce the image. In 2002, the newest generations of magnets approved for clinical use were 3.0 Tesla, whereas the previous standard had been 1.5 Tesla and 0.7 Tesla for the closed and open MRI unit, respectively.[4] Exhibit 1 shows a photograph of a 1.5 Tesla short-bore MRI system. A typical exam took from 30 to 45 minutes, although some exams could be completed in 10 minutes.

MRI had become increasingly popular within the medical profession. In 1998, an estimated 11.9 million MRI procedures had been performed in the United States; by 2001, this number had risen to 18 million procedures. In addition to growth in the number of scans, the number of hospital and non-hospital scanning sites had risen from 4,490 in 1998 to 5,550 in 2001.[5]

MRI equipment represented a significant investment. In 2002, the approximate cost of an MR machine was $1.5 million to $3.5 million. In addition, the facility required space[6] and the equipment required shielding from magnetic fields. Installation, including shielding, cost

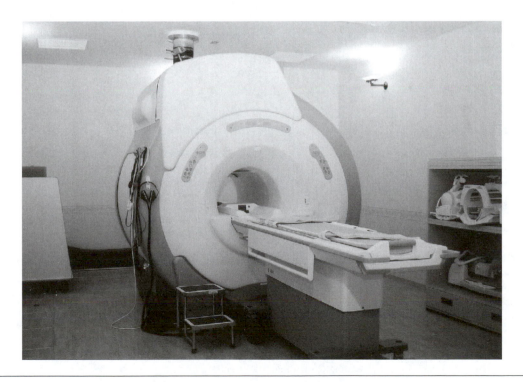

Exhibit 1   An Image of a 1.5-Tesla Short-Bore, High-Speed MRI System

$250,000 to $500,000 depending on the extent of renovations required. The typical reimbursement from United States insurance companies was $700 per scan. Exhibit 2 shows operating costs, which Quinte MRI's managers believed were conservative, for a typical MRI facility.

BENTON-COOPER MEDICAL CENTER

Benton-Cooper Medical Center was a private, not-for-profit, 144-bed community hospital and regional cancer centre that provided primary care to the nearly 16,000 residents of Palmer and regional services to the 118,000 people in Adelaide County, which was in a largely rural area. BCMC had an active medical staff of more than 40 physicians, representing over 20 specialties.

Although Creston, another Adelaide County community of 19,000, about 40 kilometres from Palmer, had two 200-bed hospital facilities with MR machines, BCMC's administrators believed that there was an opportunity to compete successfully with a third MR machine. The primary reason for this view was that there appeared to be enough demand—in the United States the annual scan rate was approximately 68 per 1,000 people and the cancer rate in Adelaide County was somewhat higher than the national average. Second, the administrators anticipated that overall demand for MRI scans in Adelaide County would continue to grow at approximately 15 per cent per year. However, they recognized that the number of scans depended critically on the number of doctors practising various specialties. Because the MRI centre would get referrals from

Leases		
Equipment	$240,000	
Building	50,000	
Salaries and wages		
Radiologists	140	per scan
MR technologist	60,000	
Support staff	30,000	
Office manager	45,000	
Other		
Medical supplies	50	per scan
Insurance	15,000	
Leasehold improvements	10,000	
Utilities	15,000	
Advertising	15,000	
Maintenance	110,000	
Miscellaneous unforeseen expenses	100,000	
Total annual operating expenses	**$690,000**	plus variable costs per scan
Assumptions		
Revenue per scan	$700	
Number of referred scans per year	1,600	
Number of walk-in scans per year	600	
Operating days per year	250	
Effective tax rate	25%	

Exhibit 2 Typical Annual Operating Costs of an MRI Centre

Source: Quinte MRI files.

the hospital doctors and promotional support for advertisements with the local print and radio stations, the administrators believed that they would be able to generate sufficient volumes for their own fixed MR systems. In conjunction with the hospital administrators, Quinte MRI staff developed the monthly demand forecasts shown in Exhibit 3, which reflect seasonality owing to doctor vacation schedules and statutory holidays. And finally, the administrators were concerned that if they did not have an MR machine, BCMC would become a second-rate hospital.

During the winter of 2001–02, BCMC decided to replace its MRI service provider because the medical centre wanted to increase the number of days of operation beyond the current two days per week. As they searched for a replacement, the administrators became aware of Quinte MRI's impressive capabilities, such as availability for 24 hours per day and seven days per week, and Haider's integrity and personal attentiveness.

In February 2002, BCMC's chief executive and board approved the outsourcing of MRI services to Quinte MRI. The agreement specified that Quinte MRI would own 100 per cent of the MRI centre, including imaging equipment, and would be responsible for most of its operation and management, including the hiring and salary of MR technologists to conduct the actual

procedures. Quinte MRI would bill the hospital on a fee per scan basis. In the negotiation process, the anticipated average revenue was adjusted based on the expenses that would be covered by BCMC. The hospital would pay the salary and expenses of the radiologist, who would analyse the MRI scan and report the results. The hospital would also schedule the MRI clinic. It would charge Quinte MRI $140 and $5 per scan, respectively, for these two activities. The imaging suite was housed in a trailer connected to a hospital corridor. The other required functions were housed inside the hospital, some distance from the scanning suite. Exhibit 4 shows a layout of the radiology department. The MRI clinic began operations on May 1, 2002.

At the hospital's request, Quinte MRI leased one 1.5-Tesla General Electric (GE) short-bore high-speed MRI system, as shown in Exhibit 1. Although the rated capacity of the machine was two patients per hour, the actual number of scans in any period of time would depend on the types of exams being performed. For example, as shown in Exhibit 5, an abdominal MRI scan without contrast was projected to take 30 minutes, whereas an abdominal scan with contrast was projected to take 45 minutes. Contrast, which provided a more detailed image, was usually required in about 25 per cent of scans.

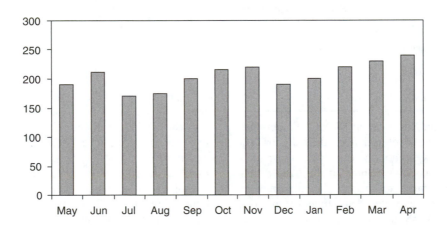

Exhibit 3   Forecast of Sustainable Demand for MRI Scans at Benton-Cooper Medical Center

Source: Quinte MRI files.

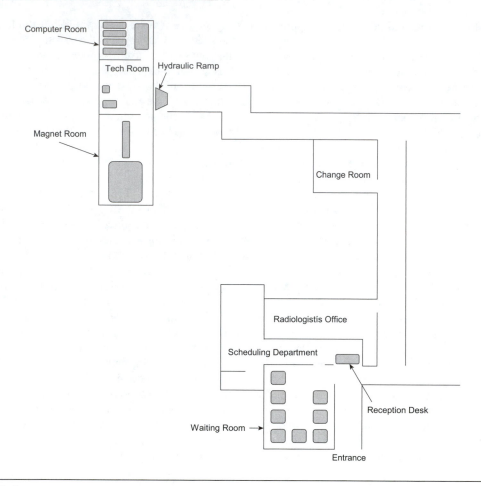

Exhibit 4   Layout of the Radiology Department

Source: Hospital files.

Note: This diagram is approximately to scale.

THE SCANNING PROCESS

To receive an MRI scan at BCMC, patients first had to receive a referral from their doctor. The scanning process commenced when the patient or doctor's assistant contacted the MRI scheduling department to arrange an appointment. Although the expected lead time for referred patients was 48 hours, some patients, called "walk-ins," required a scan that day.

When the scheduling department received a call, the receptionist wrote the patient's name and type of procedure on a form with eight time slots, each for a one-hour increment. Exhibit 6 gives the schedule for June 12.

Upon arrival at the MRI clinic for their appointment, patients checked in with the receptionist at the front desk and waited for the MR technologist to escort them to the MR machine in the magnet room. Some patients had difficulty walking or were confined to stretchers or wheel chairs. As the patients were escorted, the MR technologist asked questions to determine whether there were any health reasons that would prevent

Procedure	Time	Procedure	Time
Abdomen with contrast	45	Lumbar spine with contrast	30
Abdomen without contrast	30	Lumbar spine without contrast	30
Abdomen with and without contrast	45	Lumbar spine with and without contrast	60
Bone marrow	60	Magnetic resonance angiogram (MRA), chest	60
Brain with contrast	60	MRA, abdomen	60
Brain without contrast	30	MRA, head with contrast	30
Brain with and without contrast	60	MRA, head without contrast	30
Breast, bilateral	60	MRA, head with and without contrast	45
Breast, unilateral	60	MRA, lower extremity	90
Heart	60	MRA, neck with contrast	30
Chest-mediast with contrast	60	MRA, neck without contrast	30
Chest-mediast without contrast	30	MRA, neck with and without contrast	45
Chest-mediast with and without contrast	60	MRA, pelvis	60
Cervical spine with contrast	60	MRA, upper extremity	90
Cervical spine without contrast	30	3-D reconstruction	15
Cervical spine with and without contrast	60	Orb, face, neck with contrast	60
Lower joint extremity with contrast	30	Orb, face, neck without contrast	30
Lower joint extremity without contrast	30	Orb, face, neck with and without contrast	60
Lower joint extremity with and without contrast	60	Pelvis with contrast	30
Lower extremity with contrast	30	Pelvis without contrast	30
Lower extremity without contrast	30	Pelvis with and without contrast	45
Lower extremity with and without contrast	60	Temporomandibular joint	60
Upper joint extremity with contrast	30	Thoracic spine with contrast	30
Upper joint extremity without contrast	30	Thoracic spine without contrast	30
Upper joint extremity with and without contrast	60	Thoracic spine with and without contrast	45
Upper extremity with contrast	30		
Upper extremity without contrast	30		
Upper extremity with and without contrast	60		

Exhibit 5   Time Scheduled for Typical Procedures, in Minutes

Source: Jeff Sinclair's estimates.

the patients from having an MRI. Patients who indicated possible health risks were further tested. The technologist took approximately five minutes to pick up the patient and determine if there were health conflicts. Patients not fit for the MR test were sent home. In such cases, the machine sat idle. During the first month of operation, an average of 1.2 patients per day were rejected for these reasons. In addition to checking possible health risks, the MR technologist ensured that patients were not wearing clothes with metal components. If the clothes had metal, the patient was required to change into a hospital gown at the change room, which took an additional four minutes, on average. Approximately 25 per cent of patients were in this category.

Once in the magnet room, the MR technologist took one minute to provide a brief orientation and verify the paperwork. Patients would lie on a movable bench protruding from the bore, or tunnel, of the MR machine. A surface coil was positioned around the part of the patients' anatomy of interest, such as the head, and the patients were then moved into the bore where the scanning began. It took approximately four minutes to position the coil and move the patient into the bore. The MR tunnel was relatively small, dark and noisy, which caused a feeling of claustrophobia in some patients. In addition, during scans it was important for patients to remain as motionless as possible. The MR technologist was responsible for conducting

MRI

DATE: June 12 Wed.

BLUECROSS/BLUESHEILD INS. CK FOR PHYSICIAN AUTH. PRIOR TO REGISTRATION

Schedule / Time	Patient Name	Procedure (Exam)	Doctor	Diagnosis (Reason)	D.O.B.	Telephone #	Insurance	Radiology Number	IP/OP
8:00		~~(crossed out)~~							
9:00	Patient A	C-spine		pain	8/3/63		Work Comp.	208970-2	
10:00	Patient B	℞ Knee		pain	1/9/59		GHI	83745-02	
10:30	Patient C			the Pymphono Pain	8/15/60		MR	32377-1	
11:00	Patient D	Cervical + thoracic		pain in legs	6/30/65				
11:30									
12:00	Lunch								
1:00	Patient E	℞ foot		arthritis	155-5-21		B/BS	1320-02 #EX3946	
1:30	Patient F	MRI neck brain		Synupe	5923			2055CL	
2:00									
2:30	Patient G	LSP		bulging disc	13-27-55		Comp.	3558-DI	

* Pt. Should come 15 min. Early to Register.

* Pt. Should have clothes that have No Metal – If possible.

Exhibit 6 The Schedule for Wednesday, June 12

Source: Company files.

Note: The patients' names, phone numbers and doctors have been omitted for reasons of confidentiality.

a set number of procedures to obtain the images requested by the referring physician. These procedures took a specific amount of time that was easily measured and consistent. For a 30-minute scheduled MRI scan, the actual time in the MR tunnel was 16.5 minutes. While the scans were in progress, the MR technologist sat in the tech room and entered the patients' information into the hospital information system so that the patients could be tracked. Data entry took one minute, on average.

Upon finishing the MRI scan, the MR technologist printed the MRI films and removed the patient from the machine. The technologist then took two minutes to escort the patient back to the front desk, stopping at the change room, if needed, for approximately four minutes. At the receptionist's desk, the MR technologist checked off the patient's name on the log to confirm that the task had been completed. Then, the technologist greeted the next patient. Throughout the day, the receptionist printed the confirmations and reports for billing purposes.

Because each patient required between four and 16 sheets of film per MRI scan, averaging eight sheets, and it usually took 45 seconds to print each sheet, the MR technologist waited until after the fifth or sixth patient before collecting, sorting, labelling and then transferring the film to the radiologist's office on his or her way to pick up another patient. The radiologist took approximately five minutes to read the patient's film and dictate a diagnosis into a recorder. The dictation was transferred electronically to the transcription department, where it was typed. The transcription department was located in a building adjacent to the hospital. One to three hours after they received the transcription, the transcription department returned the typed diagnosis to the radiologist for final approval.

About every two hours, the radiologist verified and signed a group of transcriptions as a break from reading images. Once approved, the signed transcriptions and MRI films were transferred to the scheduling department, where a copy of the signed diagnosis was printed. The original transcript report and the MRI films were attached to the patient's files, and together they were sent to the basement for filing and storage. The copy of the transcription report was sent to the referring physician.

IMPLEMENTATION ISSUES

Now that the BCMC MRI clinic had been in operation for six weeks, Haider was becoming increasingly concerned about its performance. The MRI clinic was not meeting promises made by Haider and GE to scan patients at a rate of two per hour. The hospital's administrators continued to complain about the MR machine's low productivity, the strain resulting from the MR technologist's heavy overtime schedule, and the loss of patient referrals from doctors within the hospital and in the surrounding community. Doctors expected to receive the transcription report within two days of their request. BCMC, Quinte MRI's customer, was dissatisfied because the backlog had exceeded 14 days by early June and doctors had begun to refer patients to competing clinics to obtain more timely MRI scan results.

On June 11, 2002, Haider asked Wright and Saskiw to address the problems. Wright and Saskiw were halfway through the two-year honors business program at the Richard Ivey School of Business, at The University of Western Ontario, London, Ontario. Both of them were seeking challenges in entrepreneurial environments and wanted to avoid positions in large corporate environments, which limited business exposure and responsibility. They viewed the opportunity of summer jobs at Quinte MRI not only as being consistent with this career goal, but also as an opportunity to assist Wright's long-time family friend, Haider, by applying some of the tools they had learned. Although none of Quinte MRI's employees had a job description, Wright and Saskiw understood that, as business development co-ordinators, their job was to establish new relationships with doctors and investors, review existing operations and make and implement recommendations to improve operations.

MR Technologist

Before operating an MRI machine, most MR technologists had earned a two-year degree in radiological technology. If the technologist planned to work solely with MRI, the minimum education requirement was a one-year MR technician diploma. In upstate New York, MR technologists earned approximately $32 per hour; MR technicians earned about $25 per hour.[7] Employee benefits typically added an additional 20 per cent to salary figures. After earning a degree and finding employment, new MRI technologists were typically trained by their employer on its MR systems for about three weeks.

Jeff Sinclair, BCMC's sole MR technologist, was scheduled to work 40 hours per week, Monday through Friday, 7:30 a.m. to 4:30 p.m. The first half hour of each day was occupied with setup and debugging of the equipment, called "phantom scanning." During May, Sinclair had worked an additional 40 hours at a rate of 1.5 times his regular hourly wage. Although the MR machine was scheduled for one scan per hour, it was not meeting that rate (see Exhibit 7). When Wright asked Sinclair about his productivity, Sinclair responded:

> Due to poor communication between the patient and the scheduling department, many patients fail to show up on time or cancel their appointment at the last minute. At the other extreme, patients experience frequent delays at the clinic. Some wait as long as an hour before I can start the MRI scan. I alternate between sitting on my butt for an hour or two to running around frantically attempting to placate angry and impatient customers.

> I've got to deal with a lot of mistakes in the scheduling department. Patients are booked at the wrong times and they aren't being screened properly. I'm getting patients that shouldn't receive an MRI—but they are scheduled and I have to deal with them. Since they had to take a day off work, they get angry when I send them home. And I'm sitting here twiddling my thumbs! The scheduling department really causes me a lot of headaches. They write down that I'm supposed to do scan A, but when the patient gets here, the form says do A and B. Another time there were only three appointments scheduled for a day, and the scheduling department thought the day was

full because they couldn't understand what other people had written on the form. The previous MRI provider handled all of the scheduling. Now, however, the scheduling department is expected to buck up and cope with the additional workload.

> In addition to the scheduling department, I've got to put up with the radiologist. He wants the images right after each patient is scanned. There is no way I can do that. It takes way too much time. I do it when I have a slow moment.

> I've been putting in a lot of overtime since I started here and, to be frank, I am getting sick of it. The money is nice, but I have a family and my son is experiencing some medical problems. I need to be there for him. I really don't want any more hours.

> Things are improving a bit, though. I was originally trained on equipment from GE, but during May, the clinic used a Siemens unit. It took me a while to get used to it. Now, we've got our GE equipment and I'm much happier with it.

Monica Zimmerman, manager of the radiology department, was concerned that Sinclair was working too hard and for too long. She was pressuring Wright and Saskiw to hire another MR technologist to alleviate Sinclair's load and improve the lead-time. She believed that the most appropriate move would be to add a partial second shift in the late afternoon and early evening hours.

In considering this option, Saskiw said:

> Hiring another MR technologist is a big decision for Quinte MRI. While Jeff worked a lot of overtime in May, he hasn't worked much overtime yet in June—even though we are doing more scans. Hiring another MR technologist would increase our costs, since we would have to pay $38 per hour plus benefits for someone to come in for the second shift, and it might mean more idle time. It would alleviate the problem of allowing Jeff vacation time, or leave for illness or other extenuating circumstances. As it is now, it would take a while to get an MR technologist through a temporary employment agency specializing in medical personnel, and we would have to pay at least $60 per hour. In addition, using that source would eliminate our control of quality. The bottom line, though, is that we lose over $6,000 in revenue for every day we are down. Whatever the decision, two things need to be considered—Quinte's relationship with BCMC, which is getting fragile due to

Date			Number of Scans	Number of Patients Rejected	Hours Worked[1]
May	1	(Wednesday)[2]	2		8.0
	2	(Thursday)[2]	5	2	10.0
	3	(Friday)[2]	5		8.0
	4	(Saturday)	0		5.0
	5	(Sunday)			
	6	(Monday)	8		14.0
	7	(Tuesday)	4	4	9.0
	8	(Wednesday)	10		11.0
	9	(Thursday)	6	2	9.0
	10	(Friday)	4	2	7.5
	11	(Saturday)			
	12	(Sunday)			
	13	(Monday)	7	2	9.5
	14	(Tuesday)	9		9.0
	15	(Wednesday)	11	1	11.5
	16	(Thursday)	9	2	7.5
	17	(Friday)	6	1	8.0
	18	(Saturday)			
	19	(Sunday)			
	20	(Monday)	10	2	9.0
	21	(Tuesday)	12	1	11.5
	22	(Wednesday)	11	1	10.0
	23	(Thursday)	13	2	11.0
	24	(Friday)	10	2	9.5
	25	(Saturday)			
	26	(Sunday)			
	27	(Monday)[3]			
	28	(Tuesday)	10		8.0
	29	(Wednesday)	16		12.0
	30	(Thursday)	7		6.0
	31	(Friday)	10	2	12.0
June	1	(Saturday)			
	2	(Sunday)			
	3	(Monday)[4]			0.0
	4	(Tuesday)	7	3	7.5
	5	(Wednesday)	12		12.0
	6	(Thursday)	12	2	12.0
	7	(Friday)	6		5.5
	8	(Saturday)			
	9	(Sunday)			
	10	(Monday)	14	1	8.5
	11	(Tuesday)	14		11.0

Exhibit 7   Data on Performance Since Start-Up on May 1, 2002

Source: Company files.

1. Overtime was calculated based on weekly, not daily, hours worked.
2. From May 1 to May 4, Sinclair was conducting application and hospital safety training, in addition to his MRI duties.
3. May 27 was Memorial Day, a national holiday.
4. On June 3, the clinic was closed to allow for the removal of the Siemens MRI equipment and the installation, testing and training on GE MRI equipment.

the backlog, and providing quality patient care. There is a shortage of good MR technologists, especially in rural areas, so I think it will be virtually impossible to find someone competent enough who would be willing to work part time.

In attempting to solve the problems at BCMC, Wright was focused on trying to find the bottleneck. From his reading of *The Goal,* he remembered a boy named Herbie, who hindered his boy scout troop's ability to reach its destination quickly during a hike. Wright commented:

Finding Herbie is our first order of business. I know that if we can find out where he is, then we can take the appropriate action and make him more efficient. We are committed to keeping things simple and moving quickly because we are working within such a short time frame. I know decisions have to be made and action taken, and we can't sit around waiting for Herbie to find us. We need to hunt him down. But, where is he?

We are tossing around the idea of developing a pay-for-performance system for Jeff so that he has an incentive to work harder and faster. Jeff is our most valuable asset at the clinic and he needs to be treated that way. We need to find a way to maximize his consistency so we are able to maximize the number of scans performed. I know we can grow the number of patients that we can handle in an eight-hour shift. But, if we continue to follow the same process, we won't be able to continue to grow.

I am worried since we have only two days to provide a detailed action plan on how to solve the problem. Haider expects us to identify the problem and outline, in detail, the steps that should be taken to solve the capacity issues. He also expects us to make any additional recommendations to improve the performance of the MRI clinic. I wonder what would make sense here.

NOTES

1. All currency in this case is expressed in United States dollars. In June 2002, the Canadian dollar traded at about US$0.63.

2. Much of the material in this section was adapted from the Web site: www.whitaker.org/94_annual_report/over.html, September 20, 2002.

3. Although X-rays were potentially dangerous, the low intensity of the radiation and the short duration of typical scans had effectively eliminated the danger to patients. However, medical personnel faced a much higher risk, as they received repeated exposure to this radiation.

4. By way of comparison, a 1.0 Tesla magnet had a magnetic field about 20,000 times stronger than the Earth's natural magnetic field.

5. Van Houten, Ben, IMV Census Shows MRI Growth, Decisions in Imaging Economics, **15** (8), August 2002, page 8.

6. For example, a model facility proposed by General Electric occupied 167 square metres gross and 154 square metres net.

7. As a comparison, in 2002, the United States Department of Labor established the minimum wage rate at $5.15 per hour. In upstate New York, an assistant for an MR technologist would earn about $10 per hour.

ING DIRECT CANADA

Prepared by Natasha Ebanks under the supervision of Professors Michiel R. Leenders and Robert D. Klassen

Copyright © 2002, Ivey Management Services   Version: (A) 2002-10-08

On March 6, 2000, Basil Bell, senior vice-president of operations at ING Direct in Toronto, Canada, was reviewing the processing of new accounts. He believed that back office processing capacity had reached its limit and had, therefore, recently requested the transfer of Hadley MacDonald from the credit area to head up the department and address staffing level concerns in back-office operations. Major space, budget and headcount constraints made it impossible to increase staffing levels to cope with the bank's rapidly growing client base. In Bell's opinion, it was critical that ING Direct develop and implement long-term solutions for coping with the immediate challenges of growth. Moreover, Bell recognized that within the next two years a more technologically, sophisticated solution would have to be found. Bell and MacDonald had selected the processing of new accounts as the first set of operations to review and had documented the procedures currently in use. The processing of new accounts by the mailroom staff represented a significant part of the tasks performed by back office personnel, and was required to be completed on a same-day basis.

THE CANADIAN BANKING INDUSTRY

Since the opening of the first Canadian bank in 1817, banks had played a vital role in Canada's economic development. Not only were they deposit-taking institutions and the primary financial intermediaries but they facilitated the process of payments and exchange. On an annual basis, the national clearing and settlement system cleared over three billion items valued at over $16 trillion.[1] By the end of 1999, there were 53 federally regulated banks operating in Canada. Eight of these were domestic Schedule I banks, three were domestic Schedule II banks, and the remaining 42 were foreign Schedule II banks. Of the eight domestic Schedule I banks, six held approximately 90 per cent of the industry's assets.

Until 1980, Canadian banks were the only competitors in the banking sector. In 1980, new legislation allowed foreign banks to open Canadian subsidiaries, though significant size restrictions were initially applied. These restrictions were gradually lifted with successive amendments to the Bank Act, and by 1995, all such restrictions had been removed. In 1999, further revisions to Canada's Bank Act gave foreign banks permission to establish full-service branches or lending branches in Canada, but they were unable to take deposits

under $150,000. Those banks wishing to accept retail deposits under $150,000 could do so only through the establishment of a separate Canadian subsidiary.

INTERNATIONAL NETHERLANDS GROUP (ING GROUP)

ING Group's headquarters were located in Amsterdam where the company served seven million customers through direct-response banking. The Group's success in its home market had resulted in the company's standing as one of the five largest companies in the Netherlands. Active in more than 60 countries, ING Group was also among the top 10 global providers of integrated financial services with banking and insurance assets totalling more than US$800 billion. In 1998, ING Group employed over 82,000 people worldwide and experienced a 21 per cent growth in net profit. The Group's activities included insurance operations, banking, and asset management, and part of its international strategy was to build strong markets for these activities worldwide.

ING DIRECT CANADA

ING Bank of Canada was licensed as a Schedule II bank and was officially launched on April 22, 1997, under the trade name of "ING Direct." ING Group's strategy was to develop a retail banking operation in Canada using a "low cost" platform, offering a savings account as its initial product. ING Direct operated from three floors of an office building located on Gordon Baker Road on the outskirts of Toronto. Customers were served seven days a week, 24 hours a day, through a call centre and by Internet.

The corporate mandate was to provide a superior value proposition through the use of cost-effective products, processes and distribution channels. ING Direct offered only a limited line of standard products and services with high interest rates on deposits, low rates on loans, simple and easy enrollment processes, and no service charges or fees. By March of 2000,

ING Direct was offering its customers a small selection of saving, mutual fund and loan accounts (see Exhibit 1). The company's low infrastructure costs (only one location, no branch network) allowed it to offer very competitive rates. For example, the investment savings account (ISA) carried one rate of daily interest, regardless of the amount on deposit, and withdrawals could be made from and to an existing Canadian bank account only.

Over the past three years, management had emphasized new account growth. The corporate plan for 2000 called for 50 per cent client growth from about 220,000 accounts in December 1999, with a further 30 per cent growth in each of the next two years.

As part of its efforts to maintain low infrastructure costs, management also stressed tight budgetary controls, with strict restrictions on staffing levels. In March 2000, staff numbers at ING Direct totalled 242 people. Of these, 94 were full-time call centre employees with the title Direct

Associate (DA). To provide peak-time support, 75 per cent of ING Direct's remaining employees, including mailroom employees, were trained to answer phones in the call centre at peak times.

OPENING AN ING DIRECT ACCOUNT

To open an account with ING Direct, customers had to provide their address, postal code, social insurance number (SIN) and a cheque from their chequing account with any major Canadian bank. There were four ways in which a client could open an account with ING Direct.

1. Telephone the 24-hour call centre and request an application (otherwise known as a fulfilment package). Approximately 60 per cent of these requests resulted in account openings.

2. Fill in an online application, or download the application from the Internet and mail it to ING Direct.

Products	Rates as at March 1, 2000
Savings	
Investment Savings Account (ISA)	
Canadian Dollar	4.5%
U.S. Dollar	5.0%
Guaranteed Investment Confirmation (GIC)	
• One year	5.4%
• Five year	6.1%
Registered Savings Plan (RSP)	
• RSP ISA	4.5%
• RSP GIC	6.1%
Mutual Funds	
ING Canadian Fund	
ING American Fund	
ING Global Brand Names Fund	
Loans	
Loan Account	8.1%
Mortgages	
• One year	7.0%
• Five year	7.6%
RSP Loans	5.5%

Exhibit 1   Products Offered by ING Direct

3. Enroll in person at one of the ING cafés in Toronto or Vancouver.

4. Fill out an application sent through the mail as part of the company's direct mail campaign.

If a customer telephoned the 24-hour call centre, DAs responded with either a standard or express fulfilment package. For a standard fulfilment package, a DA would answer the call and take down the customer's name, address, postal code and telephone number. Twice daily, an electronic file of customer requests was generated and sent to a letter house subcontracted by ING Direct to mail out standard fulfilment packages to prospective clients. Each client was requested to complete an enclosed application form and return it with an initial deposit.

Alternatively, about 20 per cent of all new clients called the 24-hour hotline to open an account immediately using an express fulfilment package. In order to be sent this package, these clients also supplied the DA with their date of birth and SIN, in addition to the information noted earlier. The DA would immediately assign a client number, which created a customer information file (CIF), and instruct the customer to mail their initial deposit cheque to ING Direct. The account would be opened when the cheque was received, and interest would begin accruing at that time. Legal regulations also required a client to send in an application form; upon receipt by ING Direct, the client could withdraw funds from the account.

Periodically, direct mail was sent to potential clients to attract new customers. In 1999, two million ISA application forms were sent to potential clients as part of five direct mail campaigns. The direct mail requested clients to send in an application form along with a cheque for their first deposit.

THE OPERATIONS GROUP

The operations group, headed by Basil Bell, senior vice-president of operations, consisted of 41 operational associates (OAs) and managers. The prime task of the operations group was to provide back office support to the call centre and the other functions in the bank. The group was responsible for various processing activities such as new accounts, deposits on existing accounts, service requests, client statements and tax receipts, and automated outbound correspondence.

Staffing Challenge

Bell found the challenge of coping with the bank's growth while maintaining minimum staffing levels particularly difficult. No forecasting or benchmark measurements existed on any of the processing activities to determine appropriate staffing levels. Also, space limitations prevented a massive growth in operations personnel as the number of clients and product offerings increased. In February 2000, he requested the assistance of Hadley MacDonald, who had worked in the credit area, to review all functions and activities in the operations department.

Bell and MacDonald decided to focus their initial efforts on the processes associated with new clients. New client applications currently received the highest priority for processing in the mailroom. These were also considered good candidates for review because they accounted for the majority of mailroom data entry. Any improvement in the relatively simple and repetitive steps for processing new applications was expected to significantly reduce the total workload. Later, a similar process of review and analysis would eventually have to be performed on all operations.

A normal workweek in the mailroom consisted of five eight-hour shifts. However, employees generally worked only 6.5 hours per shift after allowing time for lunch and breaks. If an employee worked more than 44 hours during a week, government regulations required overtime payment of time and a half. The normal hourly rate for employees was $12 per hour, and fringe benefits combined with unemployment premiums increased the cost per employee to $15.60 per hour.

Recent Mailroom Improvements

ING Direct's mailroom operations were almost exclusively paper-based. In the last two years however, two steps had been taken to move the company towards automation in order to speed the flow of mail through the system. The first investment was a mail extractor. The purchase of the Agissar R/V5 had reduced the time required to open daily mail by approximately four hours. The second investment was a new machine, the NCR 7731, which encoded, scanned and endorsed cheques. This machine was equipped with the software necessary to hold the image of each cheque for later posting and clearing.

MAILROOM OPERATIONS

The majority of new account applications were received as a result of a direct mail campaign or call centre inquiry. During 1999, processing relating exclusively to new accounts engaged approximately 50 per cent to 60 per cent of mailroom capacity. A further 20 per cent to 25 per cent of mailroom capacity was required for preparation activities for processing of new and existing accounts. Preparation activities involved opening and extracting the mail, sorting and checking document quality, and scanning and encoding all cheques.

Once an account was set up, a client could conduct any further business with ING Direct through the call centre, the Internet, Web site, interactive telephone system or Canada Post. Clients would complete the transaction through the desired channel and, if necessary, mail in the related cheque for processing. Processing of cheques for existing accounts engaged 15 per cent to 20 per cent of mailroom capacity.

The mail was received Monday to Friday at 8:30 a.m. from Canada Post through a contract courier. The mail was received at reception on the ninth floor and directed immediately to the mailroom (see Exhibit 2) on the eighth floor.

Mail Extraction

Once the mail was received in the mailroom, an operations associate (OA) fed the mail into

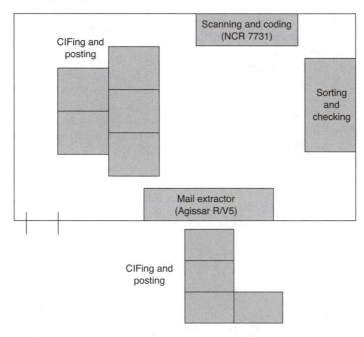

CIFing and posting was performed in space adjacent to the mailroom

Exhibit 2   Floor Plan of Mailroom

the extractor and pre-sorted the mail into the following six categories.

1. Applications and cheques from standard fulfilment and direct mail clients,
2. Cheques from express enrolment clients,
3. Cheques from existing clients,
4. Free-standing inserts from other promotional efforts,
5. Marketing surveys, and
6. Loans.

The same OA also performed a preliminary verification on all cheques and applications to ensure that there was no missing or obviously incorrect information. The first category, standard fulfilment and direct mail clients, represented about 70 per cent of new clients and did not already have a customer information file (CIF); therefore, their applications would take longer to process. The second category was customers who had a CIF, which was created following a call to the 24-hour call centre or through the Internet. About one-third of the new applications with a CIF were Internet-generated. The last three categories were set aside to be handled by different groups. This process of mail extraction and preliminary verification took approximately 50 minutes per 1,000 pieces of mail.

Sorting and Checking

Shortly after the extraction process was started, the applications and cheques (i.e., first three categories) were passed to OAs for further sorting and quality checking. Up to five OAs performed these tasks simultaneously. As many as two OAs dealt with the applications and cheques for fulfilment of new clients, while up to three others processed cheques for existing clients. All cheques were sorted according to account type.

New client applications within the first two categories were further sorted according to whether or not they were single or joint accounts. Joint accounts took longer to process, as the OA would have to enter information for the secondary or joint account holder who might or might not have a CIF. Applications were grouped into batches of 50, and two calculator tapes of each batch were made to verify totals.

During this additional sorting, applications underwent quality checking. OAs checked for the client's SIN, telephone number, date of birth and deposit amount. They further checked the body and figure of all cheques and the information relating specifically to the various account types (e.g., customers opening a GIC account had to include the term of investment). The mailroom supervisor also completed signature verification by matching the signature on the cheque with the signature on the application. The entire process of sorting and checking took six person-hours per 1,000 mail pieces.

Exceptions were separated during the Q&A process, prior to batching. All applications and cheques not received in good order (IGO)—e.g., no signature on application, cheques stale-dated, or travellers' cheque instead of personalized cheque—were set aside. All not in good order (NIGO) items had to be returned to the client by mail. The number of exceptions was not tracked.

Scanning and Encoding of Cheques

Cheques were next sent to an OA at the NCR 7731 image transport machine for imaging and encoding. The OA sent the cheque through the scanner but had to enter the deposit amount of each cheque manually in order to encode it. The capacity of the NCR 7731 machine was 30 cheques per minute, although it took the OA about 7.5 minutes to process one batch of 50 checks. Software that cost about $100,000 was available to fully automate the scanning and encoding step by the NCR 7731 using intelligent character recognition.

Manual verification of totals was also performed on the cheques. Running batch totals were taken from the scanning machine and compared against the calculator totals run during sorting and checking. If the totals balanced, the cheques were taken to the stamping bin for deposit.

The cheques were sent to the bank for deposit, even though posting usually occurred much later in the day (posting occurred when a particular cheque was credited to that particular client's account). The NCR 7731 machine hosted a software program called INQUIRE, that held the cheque image, and therefore allowed it to be posted later the same day. The OA simply had to sequence the batch number to retain the information for posting purposes. Batches of applications were logged and placed in a tray for CIFing and posting.

CIFing of New Applications

CIFing was the process of either creating or updating the CIF; this process required the manual entry of all client data into the contact management system, called EDGE. If the client already had a CIF, then the OA would go to the look-up screen and enter the client's first and last name and update the primary account holder's data. If the account was a joint account, the OA would enter the secondary account holder's first and last name to ensure that no duplicates had already been entered in the system. New or updated client relevant data was also entered. Once the data entry was complete, the "setup" code was indicated to instruct all DA's that the client's account was active and ready for personal identification (PIN and password).

If the client did not have a CIF, then one had to be created prior to data entry. First, the OA would input the client's first and last name to verify that no duplicates had already been entered into the system. Joint account information was also entered, if applicable. Once the data had been entered, the OA would switch to the "Profile" system (a generic banking system used worldwide) to create the new account. The OA would then enter the client's new CIF, the product type, the currency code, Canadian or U.S. dollars, the relationship code (single, joint), and the branch code. Once completed, the OA would transfer the application to another OA for posting of the cheque.

Process times for CIFing varied, depending on whether or not the creation of a CIF was required and further on the type of account requested by the client. For single accounts requiring the creation of a CIF (about 30 per cent of all new accounts), processing took 1.75 person-hours per batch of 50 applications. For joint accounts requiring the creation of a CIF, about 40 per cent of all new accounts, processing times equalled 2.5 person-hours per batch of 50. Single accounts that already had a CIF (about 10 per cent of all new accounts) took 1.40 person-hours per batch of 50. Joint accounts with a CIF (about 20 per cent of all new accounts) took 1.75 person-hours per batch of 50.

Posting of Cheques

After completion of all CIFing, the OA's would use the INQUIRE system to post the cheques. The posting of cheques required three primary steps: (1) open the CIF on the contact management system, (2) set up deposit details— term, amount, interest management and maturity and (3) post transactions to client's accounts.

To post a cheque, the OA had to access the appropriate screen and then enter the cheque amount and the account number of the client. For new clients, external bank information held in the INQUIRE system was also linked to the account holder. This step for new clients took approximately 1.25 person-hours per batch of 50, double the time it took to process deposits for existing clients. Posting for existing clients was much simpler, as the client's external bank information was already linked. Thus, deposits for existing clients took half the time.

STAFFING LEVELS AND BATCH SIZES

In total, nine OA's were involved in the mailroom operations process at various times during the day. One OA was responsible for opening the mail, up to five OA's were responsible for sorting and checking, and an additional OA was responsible for the scanning. Once these tasks were complete, these seven OA's would join the other two in the CIFing and posting part of the process.

Hadley MacDonald had tried to estimate the mailroom capacity for preparation and processing of new and existing accounts. He knew that delays were not currently tracked, although there was a factor built into average process times to account for delays at each step. As a result, total available staff hours were an approximation based on the following calculations.

> Nine OAs worked 6.5 hours, for a total of 58.5 hours per day. However, only five of these associates worked in the preparation, including extracting, sorting and checking, and scanning and encoding. The remaining four OAs worked in another area of the operations group until some applications were ready for CIFing and posting. Mail was received at 8:30 a.m., and CIFing and posting were scheduled to begin at 10:30 a.m. As a result, eight hours were subtracted from 58.5 hours, giving an approximate total of 50.5 hours available for preparation and processing of new and existing accounts.

Hadley MacDonald learned that the batch size for the various mailroom processes had been set by a previous mailroom supervisor and had not been changed since 1997.

PROBLEMS WITH THE
CURRENT MAILROOM OPERATIONS

In the last year, the number of new accounts and the number of deposits associated with existing accounts had increased dramatically. During 1999, 110,000 new accounts had been created and there had been 185,000 deposits associated with existing accounts. By the end of 1999, ING Direct's client base had grown to more than 220,000 accounts. Similar growth was expected for 2000, with a projection for 320,000 accounts by yearend. ING Direct's commitment to same-day processing of both new accounts and deposits to existing accounts was becoming increasingly difficult, given the volume of new accounts. Moreover, there were deposits and maintenance associated with these accounts once they became active.

Another operations challenge was the variability in daily processing volume. Typical daily mail volume ranged from 500 to 1,500 pieces, with about 35 per cent of receipts being for new accounts. As a result, heavier volume days required the use of some overtime to maintain same-day processing. However, if the marketing department was conducting a direct mail campaign, mail receipts could spike to over 2,000 pieces of mail per day (see Exhibit 3). These campaigns entailed sending a total of 400,000 pieces of mail over a 16-day period (i.e., 25,000 pieces per day). The total promotion and advertising budget ran well over $10 million annually.

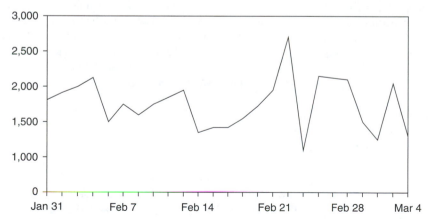

February data for mail volumes were considered fairly typical in terms of daily variations during a time when a January 12 to February 3 major mail campaign was under way.

Exhibit 3   Daily Mail Volumes for the Month of February 2000

Mailroom processes had evolved piecemeal in response to needs. Performance goals and benchmarks were difficult to measure accurately. The need to optimize mailroom operations was further compounded by the possibility that an additional $5 million could be added to the total marketing budget.

Bell was concerned about the current practice of using overtime. In addition to the extra costs, it was believed that excessive overtime and the subsequent staff burnout led to increased error rates—although no hard data were available. In 1999, overtime paid to the OAs in the mailroom totalled approximately $61,000, an increase from $40,000 and $21,000 in 1998 and 1997, respectively. The operations group was already at the maximum head count, according to corporate budgeted staffing levels. Therefore, current staff covered any excess processing through overtime.

POTENTIAL ALTERNATIVES

Bell was aware that at least three alternatives existed for dealing with workload challenges, although all had significant drawbacks. Outsourcing was one option. ING Direct had experimented with the outsourcing of its mutual fund accounts with a reasonable amount of success. The issue with outsourcing, besides the ongoing service fees and the loss of control, was a potential restriction by the Office of the Superintendent of Financial Institutions regarding the outsourcing of core business activities in the banking sector.

Increasing staff levels was a second option but not likely to improve the efficiency of the system. The prime purpose of the current review was to seek ways and means of avoiding this alternative.

Relaxing the same-day processing requirements was a third option, because customers were generally not aware whether processing took place the same day. However, same-day processing was an integral part of ING Direct's customer service mandate. Given the clients' sophistication and the competition in the marketplace, ING Direct had to maintain a high standard of service. It was also unclear as to whether this option would solve the long-term volume problems.

CONCLUSION

Bell's operations review had two main objectives. The first was to find ways and means of coping with the short-term challenge of avoiding staff level increases while meeting the operations demands of a rapidly growing client base. He hoped that a careful review of each operations process might reveal improved ways of carrying out current operations tasks. To this end, Bell believed the processing of new accounts could possibly be improved. He also knew that once all operations processes had been reviewed, a long-term solution might involve major investments.

Bell and MacDonald had decided to work closely together on the operations review. The previous week, they had agreed to analyse new account processing separately and to share their insights on March 9. Bell was, therefore, anxious to complete his review of new account processing within the next few days in order to reduce overtime and begin examining other operations.

NOTE

1. All values are in Canadian dollars unless otherwise noted. In 2000, Cdn$1 = US$0.65 approximately.

CELESTICA, INC.—MEMORY BUSINESS UNIT

Prepared by Professors
John Haywood-Farmer and Lyn Purdy

Version: (A) 2002-11-08

In February 1996, Tim Jacobs, a process control engineer and chair of the Phase One Task Force, was preparing for the group's forthcoming meeting. He expected that the group would finally settle on the location and organization of the Memory manufacturing facility at Celestica, Inc. The task force faced two decisions: should Memory Business Unit relocate its facilities to some space on the ground floor that had recently become available? And, if it did decide to move, should it change the way it organized the process flow? Each of the various options had a number of advantages and disadvantages and Mr. Jacobs wanted to be sure he had evaluated them thoroughly before the meeting. He knew that Celestica's senior managers were not satisfied with the current production costs. The fact that any move would have to be made without shutting down production complicated the decision.

THE ELECTRONICS CONTRACT MANUFACTURING INDUSTRY[1]

Celestica participated in the electronics contract manufacturing industry. According to industry sources, the 1994 worldwide contract manufacturing market had been nearly US$18 billion. Contractors were located primarily in North America, Europe, East Asia and Japan, with growth being fastest in East Asia and Europe. Because many of Japan's original equipment manufacturers (OEMs) were vertically-integrated, its contract manufacturing industry was smaller than might otherwise be expected. Over 1,000 contract manufacturers served the market; however, the 29 with annual revenues of over US$100 million each made up almost two-thirds of the total.[2]

The industry sold to seven market segments: computers, communications, automotive, consumer, industrial, instrumentation, and military and avionics. The consumer market segment was relatively small for contract manufacturers because its members tended to focus on making their own components rather than contracting them out. Computers and communications were both the largest and the fastest growing segments; combined, they accounted for almost three-quarters of all contract manufacturing work. These segments were particularly important to the large contract manufacturers, accounting for over 80 per cent of their revenues. This dominance reflected the high-volume, low-mix nature of products in these segments.

Industry observers expected a number of industry trends to continue. Although memory product prices had rapidly decreased, the number of units sold, their capacity (in megabytes) and revenues had grown rapidly. Sales for the large companies were forecasted to continue to increase through 1999 at an average compounded annual rate of 18.0 per cent compared to the small and medium companies at 7.7 per cent. A number of mergers and acquisitions had occurred, resulting in rapid growth among large companies and threatening the independent survival of small companies. Part of the industry's growth had come from an increasing acceptance by OEM customers of the notion of contracting out their manufacturing activities. Indeed, there was a trend, particularly pronounced for large contract manufacturers, for the contract manufacturer to become the manufacturing arm of one or more OEMs. Technological advances had led to increased miniaturization, density, efficiency, and throughput, and decreased cost in high-volume applications. These moves gave an advantage to large contract manufacturers and were particularly important for the computer and communications market segments. Reducing product life cycles placed additional pressure on contract manufacturers to be flexible and innovative.

There was also a trend towards contract manufacturers adding increasing amounts of value by becoming full-service providers—advanced design, development, testing, repair, box-build[3] and delivery. The make-buy decision for components depended on several factors. An OEM might buy components or use outside manufacturing services (contract manufacturers) to:

- allow it to focus on its own core competencies in designing and marketing new products, rather than manufacturing them. In such a case, the contract manufacturer might become a full-fledged partner of the OEM;
- achieve a higher level of quality than it could achieve itself;
- reduce variability;
- get a product to market faster;
- reduce costs, often by 10 to 20 per cent, through exploiting manufacturing scale economies;
- benefit from shared innovation, a factor of increasing importance as the speed of change in the technology increased. In this regard, OEMs allowed, and even expected, contract manufacturers to test new technologies.

Despite these advantages, the use of contract manufacturers was not problem-free. Industry surveys indicated problems with:

- communication of manufacturing expectations and needs surrounding design, quality, cost and delivery;
- poor responsiveness owing to high capacity use and many customers;
- long lead times, lack of schedule flexibility, and delays;
- remote management; and,
- lack of flexibility owing to reliance on a single contract manufacturer.

Memory Modules

Celestica's Memory Business Unit focused on contract manufacturing for memory module

customers and also sold its own line of branded memory products. Memory modules contained memory devices that a computer used when working on an application. They were distinct from long-term storage memory, normally in the form of hard drives or floppy discs. Most were dynamic[4] random access memory (DRAM). There were 11 families of DRAM products with different physical dimensions, memory capacity and data path width. They were physically small—a typical unit measured 10.8 by 2.5 by 0.8 centimetres and weighed about 30 grams—ranged in memory capacity from one to 128 million bytes, and in data path width from 32 to 72 megabytes. In use, DRAM chips were mounted on a printed circuit board in various configurations such as single in-line memory modules (SIMMs) or double in-line memory modules (DIMMs). Memory devices were sensitive to temperature, humidity and electrostatic discharges.

Celestica, Inc.

Until 1994, when IBM formed Celestica, Inc. as a wholly-owned subsidiary, Celestica had been one of IBM's prime manufacturing sites. The company manufactured, assembled and tested computer electronics, such as custom memory products, power supplies, printed circuit cards, system boards, communications products, and integrated contract manufacturing services. Celestica, with revenues of about US$2.0 billion in 1994 and US$2.85 billion in 1995, was one of North America's largest full-service contract electronics manufacturers selling around the world to OEMs in the computer, communications and related industries, including IBM. Its expertise was in design, miniaturization, development, proto-typing, testing, failure analysis, quality assurance, component procurement, supplier management, manufacturing, warehousing, distribution and after-sales service.

The company was organized into six customer-focused business units, each equipped to handle the needs of its customers and products, coupled with 13 functional units whose functions cut across the business units. Exhibit 1

Business Units

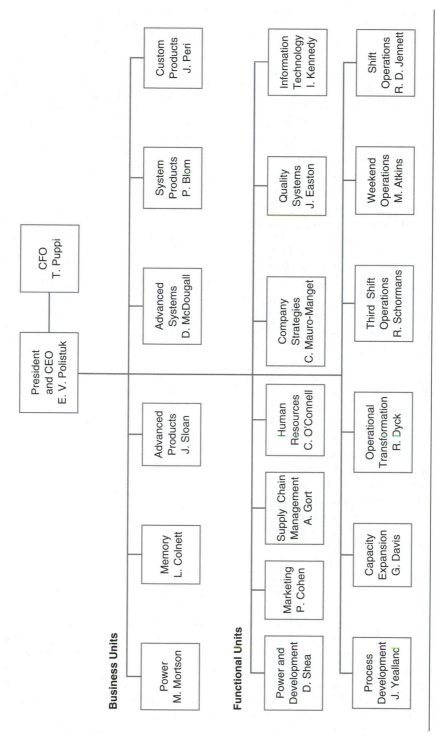

Functional Units

Exhibit 1 Organizational Chart for Celestica, Inc.

Source: Company files.

79

shows an organizational chart. The company had earned many prestigious awards for business excellence, including ISO 9001 certification and accreditation as a national testing laboratory capable of meeting standards set by the Canadian Standards Association and the British Approvals Board for Telecommunications. Celestica prided itself on its environmental friendliness.

CELESTICA'S MEMORY BUSINESS UNIT

About 300 of Celestica's 2,500 employees worked for the Memory Business Unit, which was devoted to manufacturing memory products. It operated 24 hours per day, seven days per week and produced a total of about 200,000 units per week. Its annual revenues of about US$1.25 billion in 1994 and US$1.6 billion in 1995 placed it among the industry leaders. All memory units in its two product lines were made using the same facilities and to the same quality standards. Although most of its approximately 100 memory products competitors were relatively small, some were comparable in size to Celestica. Many, particularly the major ones, were also growing rapidly.

About 20 per cent of the business unit's revenues came from a branded line of lower-margin standard memory modules. Demand for this product line was forecastable; consequently, they could be made to stock in batches. Its major competitors in the standard line were Kingston Technology Corp. and PNY Electronics, Inc.

The remaining 80 per cent of revenues came from higher-margin contract memory manufacturing services for OEMs and other technology customers. For this line of business Celestica invested a considerable amount in design and engineering, manufactured in small to large batches to order, and required longer lead times, at least initially. Celestica added most of its value in this product line in the design and engineering steps as well as through its capability in surface mount technology (SMT). Celestica's main competitor in this segment was SMART Modular which was somewhat smaller. Lisa Colnett, head of the Memory Business Unit, described the unit's competitive environment:

Our focus is competing on service and quality. We charge a slight premium and sell to large OEMs. We also sell to resellers and distributors which serve the smaller OEMs. Unlike us, Kingston does no manufacturing at all—it subcontracts everything out to organizations that specialize in manufacturing. It charges a 20-per-cent price premium and goes after channel development, targeting end customers. It's a real pull strategy. The company bundles its products with software, but doesn't sell at all at the retail level. PNY, like us, manufactures its products and competes on service, selling mainly to the retail market. SMART Modular, unlike PNY and us, is largely a contract manufacturer. It produces a limited line of its own branded products.

Celestica had recently received a report from a market research firm concerning the memory upgrade market. Some of its findings are shown in Exhibit 2. The market research firm believed that the memory upgrade market (see Exhibit 2) represented an opportunity for memory manufacturers such as Celestica. It believed that memory manufacturers which were also OEMs had been somewhat reluctant to move actively into this market because it required new sales channels and responsiveness in manufacturing that they could not easily achieve. It commented that the memory market was subject to wide swings in supply and demand, and prices, and that a supply shortage was expected in 1998 to 1999 because:

- prices would allow significant increases in OEM equipment memory;
- new, memory-rich video uses and operating systems would emerge; and,
- the industry would correct its production plans in 1997.

It further noted that the OEM and aftermarket markets were strongly inter-related. When DRAM prices were dropping, OEM demand weakened as OEMs constrained inventory and restricted the growth of their systems' memory content. Under the same conditions, aftermarket sales exploded because aftermarket companies had to sell more product at lower margins to break even. When supply was tight, the OEMs enjoyed a larger market share as they restricted supply to aftermarket channels. It concluded that in periods of excess demand, memory manufacturers should

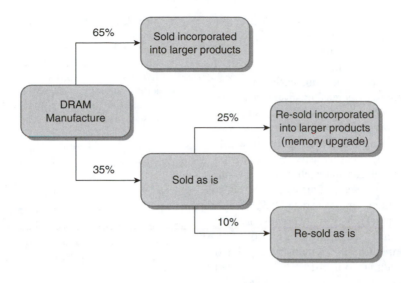

Market size			1996	2000
Capacity (millions of megabytes)			679	3,300
Value (billions of US$)			7.1	12.5
Relative prices		1995	1996	2000
		1	0.35	0.25
Benchmarking survey of manufacturers[1]	1994	1995		
Inventory turns per month	4.3	6.4		
Finished goods inventory (days)	8.1	5.1		
Forecasting accuracy	65%	76%		
Build time (hours)[2]	3.7	4.6		
Scrap	2.1%	2.0%		
Rework	2.2%	2.2%		
Number of part numbers	400	670		
Number of daily shipments	1,148	1,882		
Number of customers per month	282	325		
Share of top five customers	44%	33%		
Delivery to customer commitment date	93%	94%		
Delivery to customer request date	82%	89%		

Exhibit 2   Market Research Results (data and forecasts)

Source: Company files.

1. The figures are averages. For most categories, the ranges were large.

2. The time to make a batch of 1,000 SIMMs of a specific configuration.

focus on increasing flexibility and DRAM buffer inventories. In contrast, during excess supply, they should focus on reducing turnaround time, increasing throughput and efficiency, reducing work-in-process inventories, increasing the frequency of forecasts, increasing inventory turns, minimizing DRAM inventories, and increasing printed circuit board inventories.

The market research firm's price forecasts assumed that the DRAM industry would have to stimulate demand at least to match average bit supply growth and that the cost of the memory content in personal computers must average US$200.

The market research firm surveyed a sample of manufacturers (see Exhibit 2) and commented on competition in the industry. It pointed out that the leading competitors had exceeded industry average growth rates substantially by focusing on a selected set of markets, marshalling resources to strengthen their relationships with those markets, and erecting competitive barriers. The market research firm noted that Kingston Technology focused on the larger traditional channels, PNY on the retail channel, and SMART Modular on the OEM market.

PRODUCTION

Production at Celestica's plant continued to evolve. In 1990, manufacturing was process oriented with the equipment arranged by type and the manufacturing organization and space structured into sectors: surface mount, pin-through-hole, wave, inspection, and test. Each sector had its own staff and operated independently. Products requiring those operations were transported to the appropriate sector in batches in a sequence determined by engineers. To handle the variety of products and routes, this operation required much material handling equipment, such as carts, conveyors and magazines. Plant personnel believed that this layout resulted in:

- high work-in-process levels,
- slow, inefficient and costly material handling,
- a continual challenge to manage routing and scheduling,

- slow detection of defects from quality feedback loops,
- high supervision costs,
- high costs owing to the special attention required for each product or customer,
- a throughput time of five weeks, and
- protection from equipment breakdown or absenteeism.

In the early 1990s, business units were made responsible for specific product families. To improve overall plant efficiency and to separate the resources used by each business unit, the plant was reorganized into multiple, focused factories-within-a-factory based on type of customer. One focused factory subsequently became the Memory Business Unit. The resulting improvements in efficiency and effectiveness were dramatic; for example, in SIMM products, Celestica's most common class of products at the time, throughput times dropped from about three weeks to two days and work-in-process inventory levels reduced accordingly.

The creation of Celestica as a separate entity in 1994 was followed by significant growth in revenues. From time to time, as sectors became bottlenecks, the plant installed additional capital equipment next to the existing equipment. The results were shifts in the plant's bottlenecks and a *de facto* return to the functional layout of the early 1990s within each focused business unit. By early 1996, the Memory Business Unit's manufacturing facilities occupied about 1,500 square metres in an area of about 5,880 square metres on the third floor. Celestica's total plant area was about 84,000 square metres. Other business units used most of the larger area; the Memory Business Unit shared some areas, such as washrooms, lunch rooms, storerooms, offices, and areas devoted to parts kitting, holding and remarket, with these units. Exhibit 3 shows a floor layout. The roof of the building was supported by pillars in a rectangular pattern separated by 9.75 metres in one direction and 7.6 metres in the other. The unit used additional space on another floor to make workstation memory controller cards which were larger subassemblies incorporating memory products.

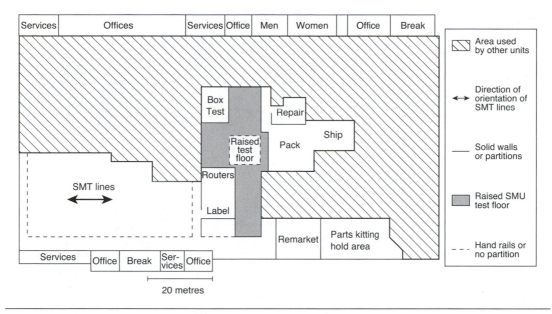

Exhibit 3   Existing Layout of the Memory Business Unit's Production Facility

Source: Company files.

Memory board production involved six basic stages or sectors: mounting memory chips onto panels, labelling, separating panels into individual memory units or modules, inspecting visually and mechanically, electrical testing, and packaging. Although material flowed in a standard route between sectors, the machines in each sector were treated as being equivalent. Thus, flow between machines was jumbled and controlled by a scheduler, upon whom the sectors relied to make priority calls, schedule flow and expedite parts. The process was typical of batch manufacturing. Production planning and scheduling staff, basing their decisions on customer orders and projected inventory needs, released orders for specific products to the shop floor. Batches tended to be large to take advantage of scale economies. An order occupied the complete resources of each sector as it progressed through the process. Orders remained in inventory between sectors; the scheduler controlled progression from sector to sector. Batches were frequently bumped as priorities shifted. Batches

of panels were moved between sectors using hand carts.

Exhibit 4 outlines the process for making memory products. The initial steps used SMT, which relied on an advancement in design from the 1980s. Printed circuit boards were made up of circuits sandwiched between layers of insulating material. In the older pin-through-hole technology, electronic devices, such as memory chips, were inserted into holes drilled completely through the boards and held in place by solder that penetrated the holes. This technique connected the appropriate circuit layers in the board at each hole. In SMT, electronic devices were applied to one or both surfaces of the board and held in place by solder applied to the surface. The surface devices were connected to inner layers by circuits that were connected to the surface of the board. In preparation for mounting memory chips, solder paste was applied to purchased printed circuit board panels using a screening machine. The appropriate screening template or stencil was selected and

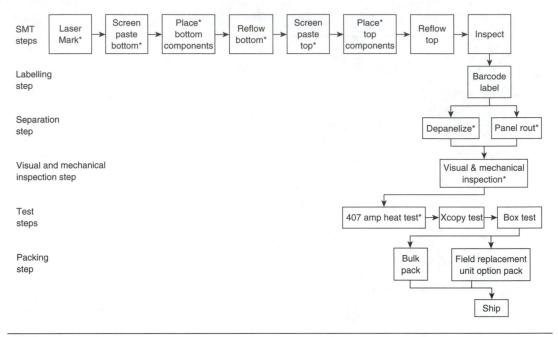

Exhibit 4   Diagram of Celestica's Memory Products Process Flow

Source: Company files.

*Steps that lead to rework loops for failed products.

placed into the screening machine. The 28.4 by 15.3 by 0.1 centimetre panels were then fed into the screening machine, which applied solder paste to a thickness of 0.2 millimetres. After the panels were prepared, they moved by conveyor to the SMT machine where the required chips were applied. The panels were then baked in an oven which operated at 210 degrees Celsius, about 25 degrees above the melting point of solder, to ensure that the chips were securely bonded. The panels then sat for a short period to cool.

The panels were moved from the insertion area to labelling where identifying labels were manually applied to the individual memory units or modules. From this point, the panels moved to depanelization where they were separated into units; a panel contained seven to 20 units.

Individual units then proceeded to visual and mechanical inspection. The operators inspected them for obvious errors, such as poorly placed chips or excess solder. Simple errors were corrected by hand; more complex errors, such as those involving many solder joints, were corrected by an automated repair machine. Once repaired, units were passed on to the next process step.

The next step was electrical testing of the product. The time required to test each product was different; the longest test took about 15 times as much time as the shortest test. Scheduling this bottleneck operation was a key to efficient utilization of the plant's resources. Each unit was functionally tested to ensure that all connections and chips were operating properly.

The inspected final product was then sent to packing where it was wrapped, boxed, and cased for delivery to the appropriate customer.

PROBLEMS

Mr. Jacobs was not entirely happy with the process and space used by the Memory Business Unit. He described his feelings:

Although this area allows us to do the job, it does have some undesirable features. Right now, it is somewhat cramped, especially in our packing area. This has led to some problems for us in improper labelling, boxing, and packaging. Even though these sorts of problems don't directly affect the quality of the memory products themselves, they do concern customers and really leave a bad impression. And, as shown in this graph [see Exhibit 5], in the short to intermediate term we expect a significant growth in DRAM capacity but a decrease in the number of units we produce. With us working 168 hours per week now, it is going to get rather tight if demand goes up very much. Right now, the throughput time for one of our orders is about two to three days. Even though that figure is a fraction of what it was before we adopted our business unit organization, we want to reduce it to about one day to cut work-in-process inventory and give better service to our customers. Celestica

expects a two-year payback on capital investments, so inventory is quite expensive for us to carry, although bank loans are a lot cheaper than that. Memory products are easy to hide and they have a high street value—I am told that, per gram, they have about the same retail value as gold, although our direct costs of labor and materials to make them amount to almost 85 per cent of the selling price.

THE OPPORTUNITY TO MOVE

In late 1995, a reorganization of the Celestica factory freed up some space which was subsequently offered to the Memory Business Unit. Ms. Colnett commented on the opportunity:

In many ways this new space is ideal for us and would address many of our current problems. First of all, although it includes some common staff areas, such as washrooms and lunch rooms, it is still big. It is over 4,100 square metres, which would allow us lots of space to expand. Although we currently have enough space, any addition to our demand will have to involve adding test equipment because that is our bottleneck. And, with

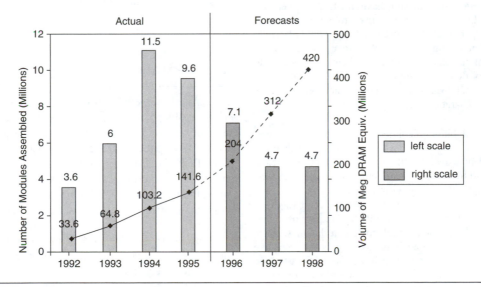

Exhibit 5   Celestica's Memory Module Manufacturing Experience and Forecasts

Source: Company files.

rapidly increasing DRAM capacity in each unit we produce, that bottleneck is getting more severe. Within about a year it will be even worse when a new type of memory—synchronous DRAM—begins to replace our current extended data output products. This new generation of products will require not only new test equipment which will be much larger, require special cooling on a raised floor, and be more expensive—US$3 million per unit, three times the value of our current test equipment—but also specially trained people to operate it. Synchronous DRAM comes in 66 megahertz and 100 megahertz versions. We can adapt our current test equipment for the 66 megahertz products but the 100 megahertz ones will require an upgrade. And, we expect that we will need significant new manufacturing technology by about 1999.

The new space is also on the ground floor and has its own receiving and shipping docks. Now, we have to send our products down two floors and over to Central Shipping where they are likely to have to wait in a queue. That hurts our ability to get product out to customers quickly. The new space is surrounded by outside walls so it is more secure than other parts of the building. It is largely open space, too, so we can get away from the walls that we have to live with now. Although it has pillars like our existing facility, we won't get space in this building that doesn't have them. However, we would be better able to plan around the pillars in a larger area. New space like that would also help our marketing efforts. We frequently get visits from customers and it would help us to be able to show them a secure area. Also, a dedicated space like that makes it easier to isolate services and, thus, charge for them appropriately.

Like all things, of course, it has some disadvantages. First of all, the ceiling is quite a bit lower than our current space. The floor of our current test area is raised by 20 to 30 centimetres to allow for machine cooling. Those systems are well established and work very effectively. Because we can't raise the floor of the new area, moving will require us to find or develop some novel cooling techniques. Also, some of the test equipment we use is very sensitive and might get damaged if we move it. Lastly, we wouldn't be able to shut down production at all during a move. With our short lead times and high volume production, we can't build inventory to tide us over during a move. We could buy more

equipment though, but we don't want a huge investment hanging over our heads. Floor space is a consideration as Celestica charges us rent of US$140 per square metre for the area we occupy. Like any business investment decision, the rate of return is a key factor. We estimate that it will cost some US$4.5-million to refurbish the new space, but Corporate will pay for that. However, it would cost my unit another US$0.5-million to move and an additional US$250,000 per year in extra operating expenses.

But what if we don't move? Can we continue where we are? Would it make more sense to divide production up by getting more space somewhere else and keeping our current space as well? Could we get more space where we are by getting one of our neighbors to move? Although we are cramped, we are getting by now. Our revenue growth has come largely from increases in the memory capacity of our products rather than from increases in the number of units we sell. That might change, of course. However, contract manufacturing also needs more physical space. The question for me is: should we let them have the new space or should we take it ourselves and let contract manufacturing have our existing space? So, what might look like a pretty easy decision, isn't so easy and will need some careful evaluation and a thorough implementation plan.

THE OPPORTUNITY TO REORGANIZE

As part of her evaluation, Ms. Colnett asked Tim Jacobs to investigate ways of organizing memory board production if the unit did move to the new space. Mr. Jacobs formed the Phase One Task Force to help him with this activity. Its members comprised eight people from manufacturing and engineering, including a student intern. Celestica actively promoted internships for business and engineering students to spend a period of up to 16 months during their studies working at Celestica to gain practical experience.

The task force initially assumed that there would be no substantial change in the basic methodology the plant used to make memory products; that is, areas of the plant would be devoted to various production operations. Thus, the task force focused on the layout of the new facility and the logistics of moving. It spent considerable time developing a novel means of cooling so that it would not need to raise the test floor. Exhibit 6 shows the proposed layout.

Near the end of its work, a sub-group of the task force proposed a radical realignment of the production flow into cells. The notion was that a cell, including all the necessary equipment and staff, would be responsible for the complete production of a product batch from start to finish. In contrast, production staff in the current layout were responsible only for the processes in their sector; they handed off responsibility when they transferred a batch to another sector.

The proposed cellular layout, shown in Exhibit 7, offered a number of advantages and disadvantages. Mr. Jacobs commented:

The cell notion has a number of quite attractive features. Because of the different dimensions of this potential new space, no matter what we do, we will have to reconfigure our equipment. So, if we are going to reorganize, we might as well think radically. With the pillars, it might be easier to reconfigure into cells than to retain our traditional process orientation.

A cellular manufacturing layout is only a start, of course. The real change comes in the way the organization functions. I think cells will allow us to focus more on orders for customers, which should help us increase our on-time deliveries. Cells will encourage more teamwork as the whole cell will be responsible for getting good product out the door, on time, at a low cost.

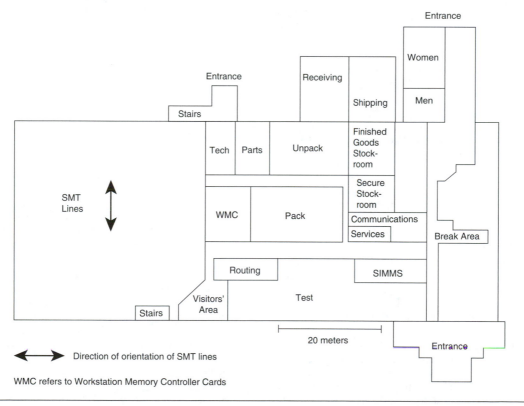

Exhibit 6   Proposed Process-Oriented Layout for Potential New Production Facility

Source: Company files.

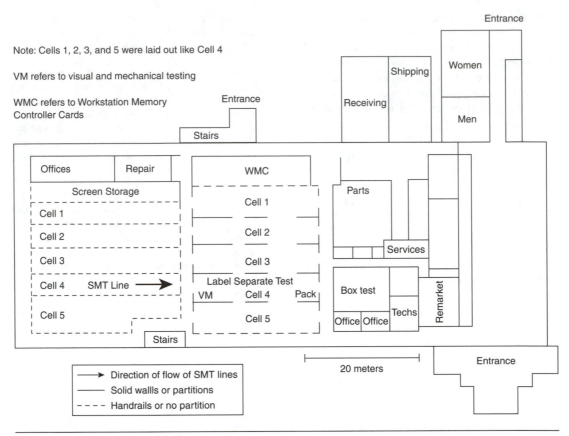

Exhibit 7 Proposed Cell Layout for Potential New Production Facility

Source: Company files.

Cells should also help us to reduce work-in-process inventory levels—we are always trying to save here—and improve our control of parts. Under a cellular arrangement, a cell would be issued a certain number of parts and be held responsible for any discrepancies at the end of the process. Now, communication between sectors is minimal and each worker tries to utilize his or her own workstation well without optimizing the job as a whole.

Cells could also make for easier scheduling. Essentially, we could schedule cells around customers or groups of customers and hold the cells responsible for moving the material through on schedule from start to finish. Now, there is continual shuffling as orders are always competing for

resources. You could argue, I guess, that better scheduling is the best way to deal with our problems. However, it seems to me that scheduling works best when you have high volumes of a few products. In contrast, we have high volumes of many products, so maybe we need a different approach. The production scheduler, who now establishes priorities for production starts and the order of testing and packing, would have most of those decisions taken over by the cells. Cells should also enable us to improve quality and, thus, produce less scrap and reduce problems in packing. A recent study concluded that 78 per cent of our quality errors are information driven. With hundreds of product codes and part numbers, and four different packing requirements, shipping good products comes down to minimizing human error. Operators need information that is both accurate and fast. In a cell arrangement, the proximity of people and the shorter expected throughput times should enable us to do that and discover errors faster.

The sub-group that studied the cell possibility simulated a number of scenarios. For this exercise, they generated demand levels for over 100 product codes based on experience and then grouped them according to the test times required. They assumed that down-time would be 16 per cent to allow for lunches, breaks and shift overlap. They also assumed that, initially, 98 per cent of the products would pass the electrical test, our current bottleneck. They ignored such problems as parts shortages, equipment failures, absenteeism and stop-build orders that affect production. Their main goal was to compare various scenarios rather than to study absolute numbers. They were specifically interested in the following questions:

- Is the simulation model realistic?
- Would it be better to retain the process-oriented layout but use generic instead of product-specific testers?
- Would it be better to retain the process-oriented layout but increase SMT and testing capacity?
- Would it be better to retain the process-oriented layout or use cells, possibly with some sharing of testing capacity among cells?

They simulated operations for a week and got these results [see Exhibit 8]. I am not completely familiar with their model, but their assumptions look reasonable to me and I trust them to do a good job. As part of their study, they simulated the performance of cells laid out in straight lines instead of squares and found that we should still get something like 80 per cent of the advantages.

These are attractive benefits; however, cells are a radical departure for us. We are organized by sector and there is somewhat of a pecking order among them. Some sectors, for better or worse, have more status than others. For example, placement is seen as a challenging and important job while packing is less attractive work. Cells will require people to cross-train and be flexible to do all the jobs. There may be some resistance to this

change. One of the basic ideas behind cells is that staff will be cross-trained to work anywhere in the cell. Although that will add to our flexibility and is something that we are trying to encourage anyway, we might face some resistance when we ask people in high status jobs to do low status tasks and they see their current jobs done by others, for whom they might not have much respect. We have discussed the notion of cells with quite a few of the workers. Many of them are sceptical. They figure that we could achieve many of the apparent gains from cells simply by reducing our batch sizes.

The training required to get everyone multi-skilled will cost quite a lot, about US$100,000, and it is not as if we have lots of extra time to do it; however, we are committed to quite a bit of it anyway. We don't envisage multiskilling as adding to our labor costs. Instead, we think that it will enrich jobs by allowing workers at one skill level to do several jobs at that level. For example, there are several relatively low skill jobs in testing, labelling and packing; workers could rotate among them but not do the skilled jobs in repair and debugging. In reality, what we envisage would be better described as multitasking rather than multiskilling. Although, because of cross-training, cells should not increase our staffing, they would mean adding some extra equipment as each cell would be, in effect, a small customer-focused factory. Right now, we have four sets of SMT equipment, three separation lines, eight visual and mechanical checking stations, eight electrical testing stations, and six packing stations. With cells, we would need extra equipment of some types to create completely self-contained, independently-operating cells. Of course, we could avoid some of those by sharing some equipment between cells, such as the simulation model assumed.

Cells also imply autonomy—the staff in the cell would take responsibility for quality and productivity. That has implications for our current supervisors and other managers. Planning personnel would assign orders to cells based on capacity and possibly some specialization within cells for specific products. However, once a cell has an order, it is up to the cell to get it filled.

Whatever we do, we have to remember that we can't afford to shut down, or even to slow down. Consequently, we will have no chance to test any

	Run 1	Run 2	Run 3	Run 4
Purpose	Verify and validate simulation model	Generic versus Product-specific testers	Increased surface mount and testing capacity	Cell versus Process layout
Layout	Process	Process	Process	Cell[1]
Surface mount equipment lines	4	4	6	6
Test equipment	8, product specific	8, generic	13, generic	13, generic
Capital required (millions[2])	$6.4	$6.4	$9.9	$10.2
Capacity (millions[2]) during week-long test	$15.6	$16.1	$25.9	$28.8
Work-in-process inventory (millions[2])	$12.6	$12.2	$20.1	$13.5
Throughput time (days)	2.2	2.2	2.4	1.2

Number of pieces of equipment allocated to each cell:

	Cell 1	Cell 2	Cell 3	Cell 4
SMT	2	2	1	1
Label	3	3	2	2
Separate	2	2	1	1
Visual & mechanical	4	4	3	3
Test	4	4	2	3
Pack	3	3	2	2
Final assembly repair	2	2	2	2

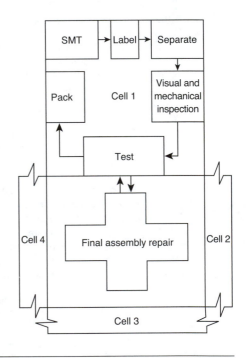

Exhibit 8   Conditions and Results of Simulation Studies

Source: Company files.

1. The cell layout suggested was as follows (Cells 2, 3 and 4 were similar to Cell 1).

2. Figures are in U.S. currency.

layout off-line before committing to it. And, if we get it wrong, we want something that we can easily revise to what we know works. In terms of costs, moving would cost the same, no matter which layout we choose.

CONCLUSION

As Mr. Jacobs pondered his various options, he began to realize how difficult it would be to make the right decisions. Both alternatives offered attractive benefits but also had significant risks.

NOTES

1. The material in this section is based largely on: R. Sherman, The Worldwide PCB Contract Manufacturing Market, Electronic Trend Publications, San Jose, California, 1995.

2. For this dominant group, profits averaged 2.5 per cent of revenues and the revenues of US$164,000 per employee were less than twice asset value.

3. Box-build activities involved assembling memory products into subassemblies or end products.

4. The term "dynamic" meant that information was lost when the computer was turned off.

THERA-AID MEDICAL DEVICES

Prepared by Professor Robert Klassen

Version: (A) 2002-02-27

Sean Graham, manufacturing manager, was reviewing the design specifications for a prototype of a new product. The firm, Thera-Aid Medical Devices, was a small, private firm in the growing therapeutic devices industry. Denise Miller, Thera-Aid's president and owner, wanted to offer a new product, the Therapeutic Wrist Exerciser, to assist patients recovering from hand and wrist injuries by rehabilitating these muscles.

PRODUCT DESIGN

The latest prototype of the Therapeutic Wrist Exerciser is shown in Exhibit 1 (Model 2, revision 3). The Exerciser was designed to be held with one hand, with the fingers across the turnbuckle and the thumb over the expansion spring. The thumb would then be repeatedly squeezed toward the turnbuckle, with the spring providing a modest amount of resistance.

Consumer research had indicated that one critical specification for quality was the spring resistance, determined by the distance between the two carriage bolts. The distance between the

centers of the two carriage bolts at the top must be *exactly four inches* (expansion spring will be under mild tension). In addition, the turnbuckle must be one inch from the end of the carriage bolt. Ideally, both the spring and turnbuckles are oriented at 90 degrees to the carriage bolts.

DIRECT PRODUCTION COST

Sean had been asked to develop an estimate of the production cost of this prototype (Model 2, revision 3). While automated assembly was possible in the long term, Sean needed to develop a manual assembly and test procedure for the Exerciser until the product was firmly established in the market place. At that point, an estimate of long-term volumes could be made, providing justification for additional capital investment.

Material was to be purchased from neighbouring suppliers at the discounted costs noted in Exhibit 2. Ignoring manufacturing overhead, Sean needed to estimate the direct cost of producing the Exerciser using a labor rate of $9.50 per hour, including benefits.

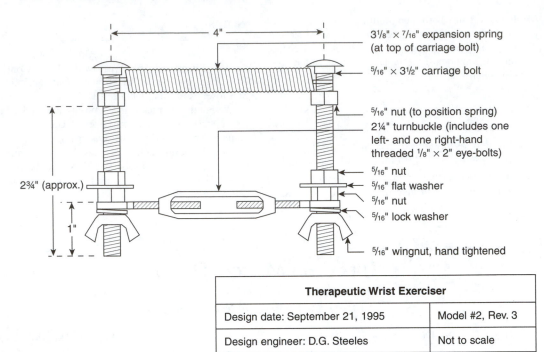

Exhibit 1   Prototype Design for Therapeutic Wrist Exerciser

No.	Part Specification	Cost ($/part)
2	$5/16$" × $3½$" carriage bolts	0.40
6	$5/16$" nuts	0.04
2	$5/16$" wingnuts	0.20
2	$5/16$" flat washers	0.03
2	$5/16$" lock washers	0.12
1	$3⅛$" × $7/16$" expansion spring	1.20
1	$⅛$" × $2¼$" turnbuckle	0.60
1	$⅛$" × 2" eye-bolt, right-hand thread	0.05
1	$⅛$" × 2" eye-bolt, left-hand thread	0.05

Exhibit 2   Parts List for Therapeutic Wrist Exerciser

INTRODUCTION TO PROCESS SIMULATION

*Prepared by Fraser Johnson under
the supervision of Professor Robert Klassen*

Version: (B) 1999-09-01

INTRODUCTION

Simulation is now commonly used as a decision tool by managers in marketing, engineering, production, finance, and many other disciplines. Managers simulate their processes to gain a better understanding of their processes, diagnose problems, train new employees, and explore possibilities. Both the advent of powerful personal computers and the development of graphically driven simulation packages have contributed to this greater adoption.

Fundamentally, a simulation has two elements. First, a model is constructed to represent a particular system or activity. This model can take many forms, including physical exercises, board games or computer-based representation. The model may represent a physical flow, such as a checkout line in a grocery store, or a concept, such as plans for a new office complex. Second, simulations provide information by running the model through a series of iterations. As the model passes through time, data can be collected about the system's performance. Simulation is not an optimization tool; instead it reflects reality as it currently is, or could potentially be. For example, a restaurant manager can simulate the flow of customers through her deli operation to predict the effects of changes in customer volume and employee scheduling on customer service times.

In a business context, simulation often refers to the use of computer-based software to model a real-world activity. As noted for the deli, managers can develop a model to test the impact of changes, both controllable, such as employee scheduling, and uncontrollable, such as customer volume, to the system on its performance. Models need not be constructed that simply reflect a current process but instead can be used effectively at the design phase to test design logic and sensitivity to changes. Moreover, simulation is often helpful in situations where the flow of items or information is complex and the utilization of individual resources is uncertain. Simulation can then help clarify trade-offs to improve the performance of the system. Other examples of applications where simulation can be applied include:

- market research to predict consumer buying behaviour to determine brand market share and consumer price sensitivity;[1]
- facility design, system development and design;[2]
- scheduling and process analysis to predict lead-times, inventories, downtime and capacity utilization; and
- process re-engineering.

WHY SIMULATION IS IMPORTANT

Simulation is a powerful tool that can save managers both time and money, while improving the quality of the decision-making process. A recent survey indicates that simulation modelling is most often used for design, research and scheduling.[3] To that end, simulation models can:

- test system changes without disrupting the actual system;
- develop a better understanding of the actual system;
- answer "what if" questions;

- predict the course and results of certain actions;
- understand why observed events occur;
- identify problem areas before implementation;
- explore the effects of modifications;
- confirm that all variables are known;
- evaluate ideas and identify inefficiencies;
- gain insight and stimulate creative thinking; and
- communicate the integrity and feasibility of your plans.

Simulation offers several potential benefits. First, models enable you to test hypotheses at a fraction of the cost and time of actually undertaking the activities which the model simulates. This activity can save both time and costs when either implementing a new process or adjusting an existing process. Studies can be conducted using "what if" scenarios to examine the potential impact of system design changes.

A second benefit of simulation is the knowledge and familiarity with the operating system gained by managers and designers of a new process. Both the resources needed and relationships among the various activities in a system must be explicitly identified. Simply constructing a model of a system often requires management to significantly re-think the logic of the process and document the relationships among the variables. A natural outcome is often process re-engineering.

Simulation is not without disadvantages. First, simulation tests do not guarantee success; the actual system is the real measure of how the items in the system will interact. Second, simulation techniques lack standardisation. A single system can potentially be simulated in a number of different fashions, depending on how an individual conceptualises the system.

DISCRETE AND CONTINUOUS EVENT MODELLING

A system is the object of a study or interest. When you simulate, you model the performance of a system over time. Models of systems are classified as either discrete event or continuous. Discrete event models track individual and unique items. Continuous modelling is used to describe a smooth flow of homogenous values. In both types of simulations, what is of concern are changes in the state of the model.

In discrete event models, discrete items change state as events occur in the simulation. The state of the model changes only when those events occur. For a discrete event model, simulated time advances from one event to the next and does not have to be equal. A factory that assembles parts or a deli that serves customers is a good example of a discrete event system. The individual items (parts or customers) are processed based on specific events for each item (receipt of an order or arrival of a customer).

Continuous models are analogous to a constant stream of fluid passing through a pipe. The volume may increase or decrease, but the flow is continuous. In continuous models, values change based directly on changes in time, and time changes in equal increments. These values reflect the state of the modelled system at any particular time, and simulated time advances evenly from one time step to the next. For example, an automobile travelling on cruise control represents a continuous system since changes in state, such as speed, change continuously with respect to time.

Here, we focus primarily on models that use discrete events.

THE SIMULATION PROCESS

Developing and using a simulation model to make managerial decisions can be separated into four steps:

- problem definition and description;
- model development;
- running of the simulation, analysis of results, and model validation; and
- experimentation.

The following tutorial will introduce the application of simulation to the operation of a small restaurant, Betty's Deli, during a typical lunch hour. The model used in this example can be found in the directory as "DELI.MOX" and can be run in the simulation package *Extend*. Other sources provide a more detailed treatment of the theoretical aspects of the simulation.[4,5]

Betty's Deli is a small restaurant operation that is located in a large office tower. The Deli serves sandwiches, drinks and other foods to customers over the lunch hour. Customers enter the food area through a single entrance, where they place an order for a sandwich at the sandwich counter, and gather additional food items from nearby service counters. There is a drink counter, snack food display rack, a dairy refrigerator, and pre-packaged dessert counter. Customers can move through these counters in any order, but spend an average total time of four minutes assembling their

complete order. The capacity of this area is 25 customers. Customers then move to the payment area. Here, they wait in a single line, with the first person in the line being served by the first of two available cashiers. Up to 20 people can wait in this line. After paying for their food, the customers exit through a single door (see Exhibit 1).

1. Problem Definition and Description

Of the four steps, this first step has been identified as the most difficult by users of simulation.[6] Defining the problem requires you to identify the relevant variables and specify the objectives of the simulation. In the case of the tutorial, Betty operates a deli and is concerned about her current staffing levels. Specifically, she is concerned that she is unable to process customers in the food ordering area and cashier stations in a timely fashion.

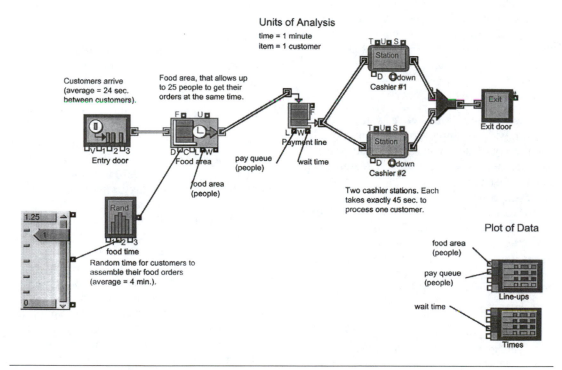

Exhibit 1   Process Simulation: Betty's Deli

By defining the area of concern, in this case customer processing, Betty is able to construct a model which explores how she will manage this concern. Other possible concerns could have been order processing costs, the potential introduction of an "express lane" or the effect of menu variation.

2. Develop Model

Model development is both an art and a science. In terms of art, the model must reflect enough detail to capture the essential elements to meet the problem objectives. However, too much detail obscures the important relationships and performance implications. As a science, measurable variables, probability distributions and systems architecture also must be realistically specified. Before constructing the model, there are a few additional questions: What is the scope of the system and what items should be incorporated? What are the components of the system and how do items flow among them? How much detail do I need to address the basic problem? What rules determine the use of resources, such as equipment and people?

a. The Process

When building a model, it is always easiest to start with a simple process and expand its complexity. Once you have established the basic process, you can then add features, such as customer mix, "express lanes," and different processing routes to any model.

To focus only on the problem that Betty identified, the "real world" can be simplified to only a few critical steps in the customer process. Each step can then be identified by one or more blocks when the model is constructed. For this simplified view of the world, the important steps are:

- customer entry;
- getting the food at the deli counter;
- a single waiting line ahead of the cashiers;
- two cashier stations; and
- customer exit.

b. Unit of Analysis

The tutorial model has been created to represent the flow of customers through Betty's Deli. Each step in this simplified view of the world is represented by a block. Additional blocks perform functions such as merging output lines, inputting random numbers and graphing performance over time. Two critical decisions about the basic model design must be made:

- what and how big is an item (e.g., individual customers or busloads of customers; individual parts or batch of 500 parts; etc.)
- what unit of time should be used (e.g., months, days, seconds, etc.)

If too large a unit of time or item is used, critical information is lost; alternatively, if too small an item or unit of time is used, the simulation will generate excessive detail, and require too much time to run. The choice is somewhat arbitrary: any units will work; however, some work better than others to address your problem objectives.

Generally, the time unit should be chosen based on the total length of time over which you would like to study your system. Thus, if your operations change each eight-hour shift, and you would like to model several days, hours or minutes might be appropriate. However, if you want to observe seasonal changes over the year, time units of days or weeks are likely to be more reasonable. For Betty's Deli, minutes are appropriate because she is only trying to manage the system over a lunch hour period.

Once the time unit has been identified, units for items can be set accordingly in each block where time is relevant. Time units also are set globally as a default for the entire model. A general rule is to have processing times at any station, machine or operation of between 1–10 time units. This is not necessary, but simplifies the output and interpretation of data. For Betty's Deli, treating each customer as an "item" is appropriate because the processing time is four minutes in the food area and 0.75 minutes for the cashier.

c. Block Diagramming

A Generator block has been used to schedule customer arrivals on a random basis. Here, Betty has previously found that customers arrive, on average, every 24 seconds (e.g., 0.4 minutes between each arrival). This block is identified in the model as "Entry Door." Double clicking this block calls up a dialog window that allows you to access and change this setting. This dialog window also has a Help button that provides a detailed description of the general function of the block, the meaning of each parameter, and the function of each connector to the block.

An Activity Multiple block is used to represent food preparation. Once again, double clicking this block allows you to examine its parameters. Recall that space limitations in the food area allow a maximum of only 25 people in this area at one time, and Betty estimates that each customer spends an average of four minutes in the food area, selecting their food, placing their sandwich order and receiving their food. Although the customers spend an average of four minutes in the food area, she knows that there is some variation, approximated by the normal distribution with a mean of four and a standard deviation of one minute.

After collecting their meal, customers wait in the "payment line" preceding the two cashiers. The payment line is a Queue FIFO block, which holds the customers, on a first-in first-out (first-come first-served) basis until they can be processed by one of two cashiers. Based on space constraints in front of the cashier stations, the maximum queue length is 20 customers. Again, this setting can be adjusted by double clicking on this block.

Customers are processed at one of two equivalent cashiers, who accept the first waiting customer from the single line. Each cashier is represented by a Station block. Here, each cashier takes exactly 45 seconds to process each customer (variability can be added later).

After paying for their food, each customer leaves through the exit door. Here an Exit block has been used. This block counts the number of items (i.e. customers) that pass through.

d. Item Flow and Data Input/Output

Two Plotter blocks have also been incorporated into the model to display the flow and timing of customers at several points throughout their time in Betty's Deli. The plotters track the number of people in the food area and the length of the line ahead of the cashiers. A separate plotter is used to track the length of time a customer must wait in line ahead of the cashiers.

Blocks have two basic types of input and output connectors: item or value. As noted earlier, a customer moving through Betty's Deli is an item. Thus, an item output connector (dark large square) on the "Food Area" block is connected to an item input connector (large square) on the "Payment line" block.

Values are information used to change or record the way an item is processed. A value output connector (dark small square) on the "food time" block is connected to a value input connector (small square) on the "Food area" block. The "food time" block is a Random Input block that generates normally distributed, random numbers with a mean of 4.0 and standard deviation of 1.0. Double clicking on this block allows you to change the type of probability distribution and the average service time. The standard deviation can be adjusted easily by moving the slider control over the range from 0 to 1.25 minutes.

Similarly, the "L" connector (a value output connector) on the "Payment line" block allows you to monitor the length of the queue ahead of the cashiers. It is connected to a label, "pay queue (people)," entered by clicking on the text "T" tool below the menu bar. This label is also connected to one of the "Line-up" Plotter block value input connectors to provide information for graphing.

3. Run Simulation, Analyse Results and Validate Model

You are now ready to run this model by simply clicking "Run Simulation" under the Run menu. The plotters display summary data on the screen with respect to the items processed. The individual blocks also provide data. For example, double clicking the "Food Area" block will allow you to examine key data such as the number of arrivals and departures, average delay, utilization, average wait time and average queue length.

At this point, the model may need some adjustment. For example, you may feel that the real time to serve the customer in the Food area is less than an average of 4.0 minutes, and should be reduced. The objective is to ensure that the model approximately reflects the real-world system. You are, in fact, verifying the model by ensuring that you can account for each activity.

4. Experiment

Satisfied that your model is valid, you can conduct experiments. For example, you might want to add another cashier to examine how such a change in the process affects the number of customers processed through the deli. Alternatively, you might want to make improvements to the Food Area, which appears to be the bottleneck, in order to increase the volume of traffic that could be served over a typical lunch hour at the deli.

Any number of experiments could be conducted in order to establish a better design for Betty's Deli. Sensitivity analysis can be conducted to see what happens if key variables change. For example, what happens if a new cashier is hired, and the processing time is lengthened?

This tutorial has been designed to illustrate a possible application for simulation and to familiarise you with certain aspects of the Extend software. You are now prepared to start running your own simulation.

SIMULATION TERMINOLOGY[7]

Listed below are certain terms used in the simulation field.

Animation: Using computer graphics to dynamically display items and their activities as represented in the model.

Attributes: Data values that characterise the items used in the model.

Queue: A line of items waiting to be served.

Resource: An item in a simulation that has limited capacity.

System: A set of components or elements that are related to each other and collectively form a network.

Validation: The process of making sure the simulation model accurately represents the "real world" system being modelled.

USING EXTEND

Extend is an easy-to-use advanced simulation tool for decision support. Using Extend, you can develop dynamic models of real-life processes in a wide variety of fields: create models from building blocks, explore the processes involved and see how they relate, then change assumptions to arrive at an optimal solution.

With Extend, you create a block diagram of a complex process where each block describes one part of the process. You can create a model quickly because Extend comes with all the blocks you need for most simulations and relies on simple graphical interface.

1. What Extend Can Do

With Extend, you get all the ease-of-use and capability you need to quickly model any system or process:

- A full array of building blocks that allow you to build models rapidly
- Animation of the model for enhanced presentation
- A customised graphical interface showing the relationships in the system you are modelling
- Hierarchical modelling to make even complex systems easy to build and understand
- Dialogs and Notebooks for changing model values, so that you can quickly try out assumptions and test your model

- A full-featured authoring environment for simplifying interaction with models
- The ability to adjust settings while the simulation is running
- Monte Carlo, batch-mode, and sensitivity analysis for optimising systems
- Customizable reports for presentations and in-depth analysis
- Full connectivity with other programs

2. General Concepts

a. Blocks

A block in Extend is like a block in a process flow or logic diagram. It is used to represent a portion of the model. A block specifies an action or process. Items or data come into the block and are then processed by the block. The block then passes the item (possibly altered) and data along one or more other blocks in the model. Some blocks, such as the Input Random Number block, generate data that are passed to other blocks to control their activities. Other blocks may modify data as they pass through them.

b. Libraries

Libraries are repositories for blocks. Standardised blocks can simply be "dragged" from any library to use in a new or existing model (click on the block in a Library window and "drag" the block onto a model worksheet). Alternatively, individual blocks can be added by selecting a block from a hierarchical menu command at the bottom of the Library menu.

When you include a block in a model, the block itself is not copied to the model; instead, a reference to the library is included. Extend also stores the data that you entered in the block's dialog in the model.

There are two ways to open a library. First, Extend automatically opens libraries when you open existing models, such as the DELI.MOX model. Second, you can also open any library by choosing Open Library from the Library menu. Five libraries are typically used: Generic; DE (Discrete Event); Manufacturing; Plotter; and Stats. After any library is opened,

a new hierarchical menu command will be added to the Library. Then select a block from the open library and it will be placed on your worksheet.

Discrete event models must have an Executive block from the Discrete Event library at the far left on the model worksheet.

c. Building and Editing a Model

Start with a New Model from the File menu. Individual blocks that are appropriate for your model can be added to the blank worksheet as described in the previous section. To move a block, click once on the block with the mouse to highlight the block, and then drag the block where desired on the worksheet. To remove a block from the worksheet, click once on the block to select it, and then press the Delete or Backspace key.

Parameters in any individual block can be modified by double-clicking on that block. The dialog window also provides data on its performance during the last simulation run, if any. Information about any block's operation, along with an explanation of each input and output connector, can be accessed by double clicking on any block, and then clicking the Help button located at the bottom of the dialog window.

Connect blocks by clicking on one of the block's small rectangular output connectors, and then "dragging" the mouse to another block's input connector. (Output connectors are darker than input connectors.) Connections can be removed by clicking on the connection and choosing Clear from the Edit menu or using the backspace or delete key.

As noted in the "Using Simulation" section, blocks have two basic types of input and output connectors: item or value. Item output connectors (dark large square) on a block generally must be connected to item input connectors (large square) on a block. Similarly, a value output connector (dark small square) on a block generally must be connected to a value input connector (small square) on a block. An error message will inform you if an illegal connection is attempted.

To enter text on the worksheet for either data labels or general description, click on the text tool (A) in the toolbar below the menu bar. Alternatively, double-click on the worksheet and type. To delete a block, select the block and choose Clear from the Edit menu or use the backspace or delete key. You can copy and paste blocks from one part of the model to another; copying includes the values entered in the block's dialog.

Save your model worksheet using "Save" under the "File" menu.

d. Running a Model

Load a model file using "Open . . ." in the "File" menu if it is not already loaded.

You are now ready to run this model. Simply click Run Simulation under the "Run" menu. The "Simulation Set-up ¼" command on this menu controls the general characteristics of the simulation run. Of particular importance is the run length. If any data are being plotted, one or more Plotter windows will appear.

When you start a simulation, Extend displays some initial start-up information in the form of messages that appear momentarily on your monitor screen. Depending on the speed of your computer, you may see the following messages: "Please Wait," "Checking Data," or "Initialising Data." On fast computers the message may appear too quickly for you to read.

Once the simulation run begins, Extend shows a small Status Bar at the bottom of your screen. The numbers after the hourglass are an estimate of the actual time left in the simulation (expressed as "minutes:seconds") so that you can determine how long it will actually run. The clock shows the current time of the simulation in simulation time units. Steps is the total number of steps or simulated messages in the simulation, and Run is the number of the simulation if you are running multiple simulations (simulation runs start at 0). These values are determined by your entries in the "Simulation Setup" dialog.

To stop a simulation in progress, click the "Stop" button in the Status bar or press Ctrl-period at any time.

e. Plotters

Extend comes with flexible charts and graphs that can be used to capture data or information from any block in the model. Plotters show both a graphical representation of the numbers fed to them as well as a table of the numerical values. If a plotter is connected to your model, using the same point and click as with any block, Extend will show the plotter on the screen when you run a simulation. A new plot is generated each time you run the model.

Extend's plotter remembers the pictures from the last four plots. You can see the other plots by clicking on the small turned-up page symbol at the bottom left of the graph part of the plot window.

To change axis values in a plotter block: click on the axis limit values and titles on the plot pane, or use the autoscale tools at the top of the plot pane.

NOTES

1. Burke, R.R., "Testing the Virtual Store," Harvard Business Review, 1996, vol. 74, no. 2, p. 128–129.

2. Cochrane, J.K., G.T. Mackulak and P.A. Savory, "Simulation Project Characteristics in Industrial Settings," Interfaces, 1995, vol. 25, no. 4, p. 104–113.

3. Ibid.

4. Law, A.M. and D.W. Kelton, Simulation Modeling and Analysis, second edition, New York: McGraw-Hill, 1991.

5. Khoshnevis, B., Discrete Event Simulation, New York: McGraw-Hill, 1994.

6. Cochrane, J.K., G.T. Mackulak and P.A. Savory, "Simulation Project Characteristics in Industrial Settings," Interfaces, 1995, vol. 25, no. 4, p. 104–113.

7. McHaney, R., Computer Simulation a Practical Perspective, San Diego: Academic Press, 1991.

RED CROSS MOBILE BLOOD CLINICS—IMPROVING DONOR SERVICE[1]

Prepared by Professors Robert Klassen and John Haywood-Farmer

Version: (A) 2000-12-05

Peggy Ladowski, a regional director of donor services for the American Red Cross, was wondering how to improve services to blood donors. She knew that donor satisfaction was one important factor in the American Red Cross's ability to attract a continuing stream of blood donors. Recently she had heard an increasing number of complaints that donors were being held up in long lines at the organization's mobile blood collection operations, commonly termed bloodmobiles. Ladowski was considering several design alternatives to reduce these complaints.

THE RED CROSS

The Red Cross could trace its history back to 1863 when it was formed to provide care to those wounded in warfare. The national Red Cross societies were allied under the International Federation of Red Cross and Red Crescent Societies, founded in 1919 and based in Geneva, Switzerland. The Red Cross's mission was to improve the lives of vulnerable people by mobilizing the power of humanity. It considered vulnerable people to include victims of natural disasters and health emergencies, poverty brought about by socio-economic crises and refugees.

One of the Red Cross's prominent activities was management of blood services; this vital fluid was used, for example, to replace blood lost in accidents, during surgery or as a result of haemophilia or damaged through treatment for cancer. Some 60 per cent of blood collected worldwide was donated either directly to the Red Cross or indirectly to organizations supported by the Red Cross. It was Red Cross policy that its blood always be donated voluntarily and without remuneration.

Since the inception of its national civilian blood services program in about 1950, the American Red Cross had helped to satisfy the changing national health care needs by making several important contributions in the health care field, making major improvements to blood safety and developing new blood products and technologies.[2] American Red Cross Blood Services provided nearly half the nation's blood for transfusion and therapeutics, receiving nearly six million volunteer blood donations a year and serving over 3,000 hospitals nationwide. In the United States, someone needed blood approximately every two seconds. Approximately 95 per cent of the collected blood was processed into plasma, platelets, red blood cells, albumin, clotting factors and other components. In 1991, the American Red Cross launched a comprehensive program to modernize and standardize its systems to collect, test, process and distribute blood.

However, Ladowski knew that support for the Red Cross could be fragile. For example, in Canada in the 1990s, it came to light that during the previous decade many innocent people had become infected with hepatitis C and human immunodeficiency virus (HIV) because the Canadian blood supply had become corrupted by these deadly pathogens. The Canadian Red Cross had been significantly criticized both for this contamination and, equally importantly, how it had handled the crisis. As a result, the agency lost substantial public trust and, ultimately, the right to manage blood supplies in Canada.[3]

AMERICAN RED CROSS

The American Red Cross operated over 400 fixed and mobile collection sites in 38 regions, such as the one for which Ladowski worked.[4] Fixed sites were permanently established locations open during regular hours. In contrast, mobile sites were usually operations set up using portable equipment at a temporary site provided by a sponsor, often for a few days during a blood drive. Mobile sites accounted for about 80 per cent of the collected blood.[5]

The American Red Cross depended heavily on regular repeat donors; recruiting and retaining them was a challenge. Surveys of donors indicated that time spent at the clinic and time spent waiting in line were important determinants of their level of satisfaction and significantly influenced their decision to return. Donor service time was also important to sponsors, especially employers who gave employees time off to donate blood. Although the American Red Cross told donors and sponsors that donation required about one hour, for many, it took one and a half to two hours.

Several factors contributed to the delay. Because the American Red Cross did not use an appointment system for its blood clinics, arrival at blood donation clinics was essentially random. In addition, the recent increase in awareness that blood could transmit some serious diseases had affected the collection process in two ways. Donors had to read more material, answer more questions and complete a confidential self-exclusion step. Second, the threat of disease transmission had forced staff to use gloves, needle guards and other devices and procedures to reduce their exposure to blood.

Despite an increase in the complaints from sponsors and donors about the time spent at blood clinics, unfortunately, the American Red Cross had been able to dedicate few additional resources to alleviate the problem as its budgets were limited and nurses were in short supply.

THE BLOOD COLLECTION PROCESS

Although many American Red Cross regions had developed their own specific variations, all had to perform the same basic procedures as described in Figure 1. First, a registrar asked all arriving prospective donors for certain demographic information, wrote this on a donor registration form, gave prospective donors reading material and directed them to the waiting area. Prospective donors then read the information provided and answered the questions on a self-administered health history (SAHH) form with yes-no answers.

Third, a collections staff member recorded the prospective donor's temperature, blood pressure and pulse rate, took a blood sample and tested it for haemoglobin level. A second iron level test was given those who failed the haemoglobin test. Prospective donors whose vital signs fell outside standard limits were rejected.

Fourth, a collections staff member clarified the prospective donor's responses to the SAHH, if necessary, and asked him or her a series of health history questions. The purpose of this step was to ascertain the likelihood that the prospective donor carried HIV or hepatitis virus. If any of this information indicated that the prospective donor should not donate blood, he or she was rejected. To accepted donors, the staff member issued and explained the confidential unit exclusion (CUE) form that allowed any donor to indicate confidentially whether his or her blood should be used. This procedure allowed a donation resulting from peer pressure to be quarantined and later discarded.

Next, a staff member issued a blood bag set to the donor. The bag set, the registration form

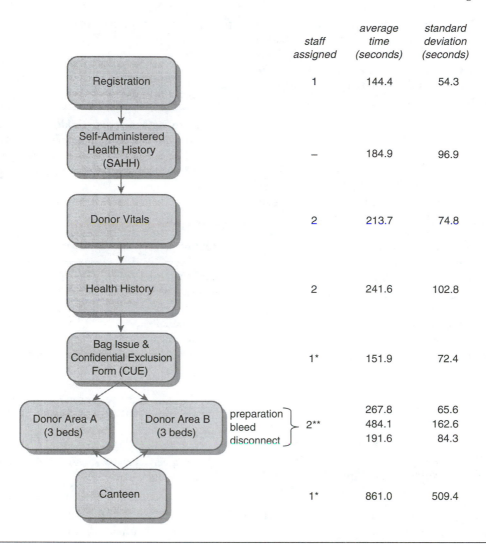

	staff assigned	average time (seconds)	standard deviation (seconds)
Registration	1	144.4	54.3
Self-Administered Health History (SAHH)	–	184.9	96.9
Donor Vitals	2	213.7	74.8
Health History	2	241.6	102.8
Bag Issue & Confidential Exclusion Form (CUE)	1*	151.9	72.4
Donor Area A/B — preparation	2**	267.8	65.6
bleed		484.1	162.6
disconnect		191.6	84.3
Canteen	1*	861.0	509.4

Figure 1[1] Mobile Blood Clinic Donor Process and Observed Average Service Times

* Staff are involved for only a small fraction of this time.

** Phlebotomists need to monitor the donor only periodically during the bleed step.

1. Adapted from: Brennan, B.E., B.L. Golden and H.K. Rappoport, "Go with the Flow: Improving Red Cross Bloodmobiles Using Simulation Analysis," *Interfaces,* 1992, 22(5), 1–13.

and the CUE form were all bar coded. The donor then completed the CUE form in a private area.

For the donation itself, the donor lay on a bed while a phlebotomist disinfected his or her arm, inserted a needle and drew the blood. After about 450 ml of blood had been drawn, the phlebotomist withdrew the needle and applied a bandage to the donor's arm. Each phlebotomist was assigned to serve several donor beds.

Finally, following donation, the donor sat and recovered in the canteen, which provided some liquid refreshment and a snack. This step allowed staff to monitor donors to make sure they had no immediate post-donation reactions.

DATA COLLECTION

To better understand the problem, Ladowski commissioned the collection of certain data using a six-bed clinic model, which was the most common one used. Such a clinic typically served 50 to 75 donors over a six-hour period. She believed that understanding it thoroughly would also help her deal with other models. Historical records and standard operating procedures gave data on donor flow, percentages and locations of donor deferrals. Data were also collected at several clinics on the frequency of donor arrivals and the time required for each major step.

RESULTS

The observed service times and standard deviations for the various stages of the donor process are summarized in Figure 1. The data revealed several interesting patterns for the arrivals of potential donors. The vast majority of the clinics, approximately 91 per cent, experienced one of three basic arrival patterns, as shown in Figure 2. Approximately 22 per cent of the clinics—dominated by open, community drives in which donors must come in their own time—showed one steep peak near midday (Figure 2[a]). Thirty-six per cent of the clinics displayed both mid-morning and mid-afternoon peaks (Figure 2[b]). This distribution was most prevalent in employer-sponsored clinics in which employees got time off work to donate. The remaining one-third of the clinics showed a single large peak during the morning hours of the clinic, followed by a gradual decline in the arrival rate (Figure 2[c]). This

pattern was most common in colleges or facilities with shift work.

CONCLUSION

With these data in hand, Ladowski set about trying to identify possible options for improved service. She decided to begin her work by examining arrivals that displayed the midday peak.

ANALYSIS OF DONOR SERVICES USING SIMULATION

Unzip the *Bloodmobile.exe* file into a new directory. The self-extracting zip file contains the Extend Player™ simulation software, libraries, and the model file.

Questions to consider before exploring the simulation of service at Red Cross mobile clinics:

1. How should the performance of the system be assessed—what constitutes good performance?

2. What is a reasonable length of time for a potential donor to spend in the system (actually being served and waiting)? What is a reasonable waiting time?

3. What is a reasonable time for a rejected potential donor to spend in the system?

4. Where do you think the longest lines will form?

5. What general changes to the current arrangement are possible to reduce donor frustration and concerns?

Start Extend Player (*extend.exe*) software and open the model (*blood.mox*).

General Description

To view the entire model, choose *Reduce to Fit* from the model menu. Although the model may appear complex, after donor arrival there are really only seven basic steps, as listed on the left

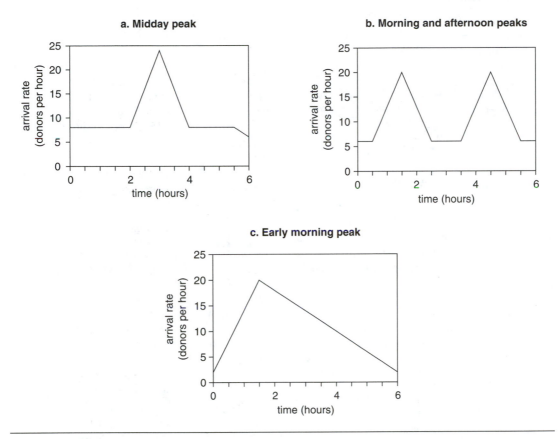

a. Midday peak

b. Morning and afternoon peaks

c. Early morning peak

Figure 2[1]   Typical Donor Arrival Patterns

1. Brennan, B.E., B.L. Golden and H.K. Rappoport, "Go with the Flow: Improving Red Cross Bloodmobiles Using Simulation Analysis," *Interfaces,* 1992, 22(5), 1–13k.

side of the worksheet and depicted in Figure 1. However, the model is slightly more complex as the donor bed area has three substeps: preparation, bleed and disconnect.

In general, each step is depicted with a labelled transaction block icon and a queue block upstream (e.g., Registration).

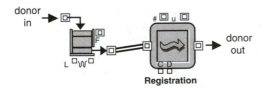

Registration

The transaction block controls the number of donors that can be served simultaneously based on the number of staff assigned to each step (e.g., Registration is one, Vitals is two). The queue block allows a line of customers to form ahead of each transaction. The transaction time of each job is determined by the "D" input, and the length of the queue that forms ahead of that job can be monitored using the "L" output.

Several steps require multiple resources, such as the donor area that requires both phlebotomists and beds to be present for some or all of the steps. For these, the necessary resource must be assigned to a donor before he or she can leave the queue.

As a result, a different queue (resource) icon is used to assign the resource (i.e., phlebotomist) and an extra icon is used to release the resource.

Monitoring Donor Service Performance

The simulation worksheet summarizes the results in two forms: tabular, on the model worksheet; and graphic, in separate windows. The tabular performance measures are listed to the right of the model in the *Performance statistics* region, and include:

- average total donor time in the bloodmobile (i.e., processing and waiting time) (minutes);
- average total process time for all seven donor steps (minutes);
- average wait time (minutes);
- percentage of donors that do not experience any wait time before: i) registration; and ii) donor bed area; and
- total number of donors served.

As the model runs, these statistics are updated continuously.

Three graphical windows are generated as the simulation runs, and these are listed in the *Graphical Output* region. The first graph window tracks the service times of individual donors and cumulative average, in minutes:

- average total donor time in the bloodmobile [red];
- individual donor total time in the bloodmobile [blue];
- individual donor process time [yellow]; and
- individual donor wait time [green].

The second graph window tracks the queue lengths ahead of four steps in the bloodmobile, in number of donors:

- registration [yellow];
- vitals [green];

- health history review [blue]; and
- donor bed area [red].

Both these graph windows open and update automatically as the simulation runs. The last graphic window opens at the end of the simulation and reports the total number of donors simultaneously in the bloodmobile, i.e., those currently being served and those waiting anywhere in the clinic. All open windows are listed under the *Window* menu. Clicking the "Auto Scale XY" icon either during or after a simulation run can rescale all graphs.

Resources

Below the *Performance statistics* region is the *Resources (people and beds)* region, which contains six resource icons that correspond to the two phlebotomists, two donor bed areas (each with three beds), a staff pool and a floater. The current donor process did not use a staff pool or floater.

There are two other shaded regions on the far right of the worksheet: *Data* and *Calculations*. The *Data* region contains all the descriptive statistical data that Ladowski has compiled. The *Calculations* region contains blocks that automatically monitor the simulated donor service times and queue lengths.

SIMULATE THE BASIC PROCESS

The model is set to simulate ten days of Red Cross mobile blood clinic service—each day comprises seven hours (the last hour allows the clinic to clear any remaining donors in the mobile blood clinic). Movement of individual donors and changing queue lengths can be viewed by selecting *Show Animation* from the Run menu. (*Show Animation* also dramatically lengthens the real time that is required to simulate the model.) To turn off animation, select (uncheck) *Show Animation* again.

To run the simulation, select *Run Simulation* from the Run menu. Unfortunately, Extend Player does not allow you to print or save the revised models and you must manually record the results from the *Performance statistics* region and the three Graph windows for future reference.

1. Based on the tabular output, what was the total average time in the system for all donors? Based on the graphical output, what is the range of times in the system for individual donors?

2. On average, how long does a donor wait in a queue? What fraction is this of the total time in the system? What is the maximum time that a donor waited?

3. Based on the graphical output, where in the bloodmobile is the queue the longest? What is the maximum queue length? How much does this maximum vary from day to day?

POOLING STAFF (COMBINING TWO STEPS)

One alternative is to change from a series of individual steps with individual staff assigned to each step to a pool of staff that process donors through both steps. Thus, the two staff formerly assigned to Donor Vitals and the two staff formerly assigned to Health History form a staff pool of four. Each staff member then completes both steps for each donor.

To make this change:

- For the donor process, increase the maximum number of transactions for the Vitals step from 2 to 4 by editing the box next to the Vitals transaction block (Figure 3) (i.e., the four staff from the pool could be working simultaneously on this step with four separate donors).

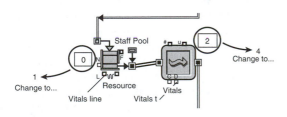

Figure 3

- Change the number of staff allocated from the Staff Pool to each donor from 0 to 1 by editing the box next to the queue block ahead of Vitals transaction block (Figure 3) (i.e., one staff member is needed per donor for both steps).
- Finally, increase the maximum number of transactions for the History step in a similar fashion from 2 to 4.

The Staff Pool, which has four staff, limits the number of donors being simultaneously served in both the Vitals and History steps (to confirm this, double-click on the Staff Pool icon in the *Resources* region and note that the initial number is four). Run this modified model.

1. On average, how much has the wait time changed for each donor?

2. Why did combining these two steps using a staff pool alter the donors' average wait time?

COMBINING THE DONOR BED AREAS

Rather than have each phlebotomist focus on a designated bed area (i.e., three beds), another option is to have a single donor bed area with six beds served by both phlebotomists.

To make this change:

- Retrieve the basic model *(blood.mox)*.
- For the donor process, double-click on the queue (resource) icon that has the label "Beds B" (in the orange highlighted area, also as shown in Figure 4).

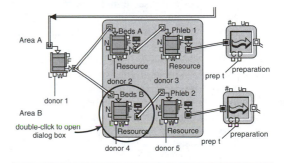

Figure 4

- Now change the first pop-up menu from "Beds B" to "Beds A" (Figure 5). Close the dialog box.

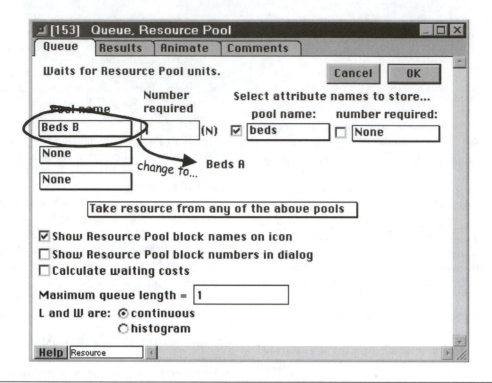

Figure 5

- In an identical fashion, change the adjacent queue (resource) icon, which is labelled Phleb 2 (also in the orange highlighted area) to Phleb 1.
- Repeat this step with the second queue (resource) icon that is labelled Phleb 2 (in the *pink* highlighted area) to Phleb 1 to allow both phlebotomists to serve these donors for the disconnect step.
- Finally, both the number of beds and phlebotomists available in this combined donor area needs to be entered. Double-click the Beds A pool icon in the *Resources* region. In the dialog box, increase the initial number from 3 to 6, and then close the dialog. Similarly, increase the initial number of phlebotomists in Phleb 1 from 1 to 2. The Bed B and Phleb 2 resource pools are no longer used.

All beds and donors are now available to all phlebotomists. Run this simulation.

1. On average, how much wait time has been eliminated for each donor? What is the maximum wait time now?

2. What fraction of time does a donor spend waiting in a queue?

3. Why was this change (c) so much larger than combining two steps (b)?

SELF-REGISTRATION

A last alternative was to change the process to require the donors, most of whom were repeat customers, to register themselves and then complete the self-administered health history (SAHH) form on their own immediately after arrival. Doing so frees that staff member to be a "floater" who could assist where the help is most needed.

To test this alternative:

- Retrieve the basic model *(blood.mox)*.
- Similar to the changes made for (b), increase the maximum number of transactions for the Vitals step from 2 to 5 by editing the box next to the Vitals transaction block (similar to that shown in Figure 3) (i.e., the four staff from the pool and the floater might be working on this step simultaneously).
- Increase the maximum number of transactions for the History step in a similar fashion from 2 to 5.
- Next, remove any limitation in the Registration step by editing the text box next to the Registration transaction block to increase capacity from 1 to 100 (i.e., self-registration).
- Then double-click on the resource queue icon ahead of the Vitals step (where Staff Pool is listed). Change the *second* pop-up menu from "None" to "Floater." This allows *either* one of the four Staff Pool members or the Floater to serve a donor. Close the dialog box.
- As in Figure 3, change the number of staff allocated to each donor from 0 to 1 by editing the box next to the queue block ahead of Vitals transaction block.
- Next, double-click on the queue (resource) icon which has Phleb 1 listed (in the orange highlighted area). Change the *second* pop-up menu from "None" to "Floater." Close the dialog box.
- In an identical way, double-click on the queue (resource) icon that has Phleb 2 listed in the orange highlighted area. Change the *second* pop-up menu from "None" to "Floater." Close the dialog box.
- Finally, change the last two phlebotomist queue (resource) icons in the pink highlighted area to allow for a Floater to serve these donors, too.

Now a single Floater staff can assist donors in the Vitals, Health History, Preparation and Disconnect steps. However, the Floater can be in only one place at any given time serving a single donor (to confirm this, double-click on the Floater icon in the *Resources* region and note that the initial number is 1). Run this simulation.

1. On average, how much wait time has been eliminated for individual donors? What is the range of wait times observed now?
2. What fraction of time does a donor spend waiting in a queue?
3. Why was this change (d) so much larger than any of the previous changes in (a), (b) or (c)?
4. Could you expect to see further improvement if all three alternatives were combined (i.e., pooling staff, combining bed areas, using self-registration and a floater)?
5. What implementation concerns will likely surface with each of these alternatives?

Notes

1. This case has been written on the basis of published sources only. Consequently, the interpretation and perspectives presented in this case are not necessarily those of the American Red Cross or any of its employees.
2. http://www.redcross.org/biomed/who/whobs.html; American Red Cross, November 23, 2000.
3. "It's official: Red Cross gets the pink slip. Agency formally dropped as head of country's blood system." *Toronto Star,* July 31, 1997, p. A3.
4. http://www.redcross.org/biomed/who/index.html; November 23, 2000.
5. This data and the following description is drawn from Brennan, B.E., B.L. Golden and H.K. Rappoport, "Go with the Flow: Improving Red Cross Bloodmobiles Using Simulation Analysis," *Interfaces,* 1992, 22(5), 1–13.

AN INTRODUCTION TO INVENTORY CONTROL AND INDEPENDENT DEMAND

Prepared by Professor P. Fraser Johnson

     Version: (A) 2002-11-08

Inventories exist in virtually every organization, and can serve any number of purposes: provide customer service, decouple operations to maximize manufacturing efficiencies, provide an ongoing supply of a seasonal product, and take advantage of volume discounts, to name only a few. However, inventories can also represent a significant investment. The costs of holding, ordering and storing inventories can be substantial. Inventories tie up working capital, require plant and warehouse space, and they must be counted, handled and insured, and there are risks of loss, damage and obsolescence. Consequently, an important challenge facing operations managers is balancing the economic benefits of less frequent orders or setups versus the costs of holding inventory.

This note provides an introduction to managing independent demand inventory items. The objective is to review the basic techniques associated with independent demand items, including fixed order quantity and fixed time period systems. In doing so, this note is intended to address the questions of how much to order (the lot size issue) and when to order (the reorder point issue).

INDEPENDENT VERSUS DEPENDENT DEMAND

Inventory management necessitates making a distinction between independent and dependent demand items. Very simply, *independent demand items* are unrelated to each other and are directly determined by customer orders, whereas *dependent demand items* are related to the demand for some other item. Dependent demand items are typically the components that make up higher level (independent demand) products. Independent demand items are the assembled products, demand for which is determined by external customers. This relationship is represented in Figure 1, a product structure for a chair assembly, which consists of one back, two armrests and one seat with four legs attached.

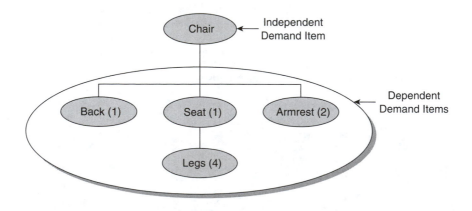

Figure 1   A Representative Product Structure

Understanding this distinction is important. Demand for independent demand items is forecasted based on a range of possible factors, such as previous sales patterns and economic forecasts. Demand for dependent demand items is better calculated from the forecasts of the higher level independent demand items. Consequently, dependent demand items are said to have a *derived demand.* For example, in Figure 1, the demand for armrests is a direct function of the demand for chairs. For each chair, the company must make one back, one seat, two armrests and four legs.

The nature of the demand patterns for independent and dependent demand items can be very different. The demand for independent demand items is more continuous than the demand for dependent items. Consequently, demand for dependent items is determined by factors within the control of the firm, such as the master production schedule. For example, although the demand for chairs may average 100 units per day, assembly of chairs may occur weekly, say each Friday, in order to take advantage of economical lot sizes. The demand for armrests is influenced by the lot sizing decision for chairs. Therefore, demand for armrests may be 1,000 units each Wednesday.

INVENTORY CONTROL SYSTEMS

When addressing issues associated with independent demand items, managers are faced with two fundamental questions: How much do I order? and, When do I order? The issue of how much to order is referred to as a lot sizing decision. The issue of when to order is referred to as a reorder point decision. The following discussion addresses these two issues.

There are two basic types of inventory control systems: fixed order quantity systems (sometimes called continuous inventory systems or Q models) and fixed time period systems (sometimes called periodic systems or P models).

Fixed Order Quantity Systems

Fixed order quantity models maintain a perpetual record of the inventory for each item. When the inventory on hand reaches a predetermined point, an order is placed for a specified number of units (Q^*). The inventory level at which a new order is placed is referred to as the reorder point (R). A representation of a simple fixed order quantity model is provided in Figure 2. In this example, Q^* is 200 units and R is 20.

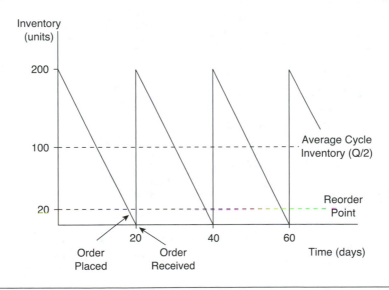

Figure 2   The Basic Fixed Order Quantity Model

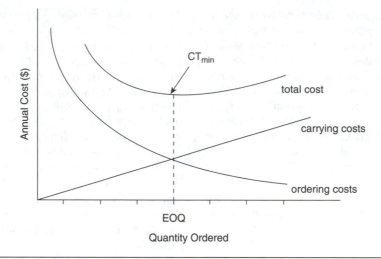

Figure 3   The Economic Order Quantity Model

The critical questions when using fixed order quantity systems, therefore, become how to determine Q* and R. The reorder quantity, Q*, can be determined by calculating the amount that will minimize total inventory costs. This can be calculated using the *economic order quantity* (EOQ) model. Although there are several variations of the EOQ model, this discussion will focus on the basic EOQ model.

The economic order quantity is the amount that minimizes the sum of the ordering or set-up costs and holding costs. These two costs are inversely related as presented in Figure 3. For example, the more inventory that is ordered, the higher the average inventory levels, which increases holding costs. However, increasing the order size reduces the number of orders and, therefore, the ordering costs. The EOQ model determines Q* by calculating the minimum total cost point on the total cost curve.

The EOQ model is represented by the following:

$$EOQ = \sqrt{\frac{2DS}{Ci}}$$

Where,
  D = annual demand
  S = set-up or order costs per order
  C = unit cost
  i = annual holding cost rate

Therefore,

  Ci = unit holding cost (H)

Example:
  The purchasing manager for the Calgary General Hospital was reviewing the hospital's inventory management policies. He learned from the controller that annual inventory holding costs were 25 per cent and the cost of placing an order was $60. The hospital was currently paying $28 per box for #3 hypodermic syringes. Total annual usage was estimated at 100,000 boxes. How many boxes should be ordered each time an order is placed for this product?

The *EOQ* can be calculated as follows:

$$EOQ = \sqrt{\frac{2DS}{Ci}}$$

Where,
  D = 100,000 boxes
  S = $60
  C = $28
  i = 25%

$$EOQ = \sqrt{\frac{2 \times 100,000 \times 60}{28 \times 0.25}}$$

$$EOQ = 1,309 \text{ boxes}$$

Note that the annual holding costs and the ordering costs are equal. For example, the annual holding costs can be determined by:

$$(1{,}309 \text{ boxes} \div 2) \times \$28 \times 0.25 = \$4{,}581.50$$

The annual ordering costs can be determined by:

$$(100{,}000 \text{ boxes} \div 1{,}309 \text{ boxes per order}) \times \\ \$60 \text{ per order} = \$4{,}583.65$$

In this example, it is most likely unrealistic to expect the supplier to deliver in lots of 1,309 units. For example, order quantities would most likely be limited to convenient units, such as 1,300 or 1,320 units. Because the EOQ curve has a flat bottom, small deviations from the EOQ quantity do not result in substantial cost penalties, as illustrated by the total cost (TC) calculations below:

$$\text{TC} = \text{annual holding costs} + \text{annual ordering} \\ \text{costs}$$

$$\text{TC}_{1{,}309} = \$4{,}581.50 + \$4{,}583.65 = \$9{,}165.15$$

$$= \$4{,}550.00 + \$4{,}615.38 = \$9{,}165.38$$

$$= \$4{,}620.00 + \$4{,}545.45 = \$9{,}165.45$$

EOQ Assumptions

The EOQ model is derived based on several unrealistic assumptions:

- Product demand, lead times, product price, and ordering or set-up costs are constant, uniform and known with certainty.
- Inventory holding costs are based on average inventory and are proportional to value.
- Supply is unlimited.
- No back orders or shortages allowed.
- The entire order quantity is received simultaneously (no partial shipments).

Despite these limiting assumptions the EOQ model is fairly robust. There are also ways of dealing with certain assumption violations. However, for the purposes of this Note, appreciate that the EOQ formula is a good starting point for determining optimal order quantities.

Lead Time and Safety Stock

When using a fixed order quantity inventory system, the reorder point (R) is the inventory level at which the new order should be placed. The basic EOQ model addresses the issue of how much to order. To determine when to order, the lead time of the product must be considered. If no safety stock is necessary, the reorder point can be calculated as:

$$R = \bar{d}L$$

Where,
R = reorder point
$\bar{d}$ = average daily demand
L = lead time

Example:

The delivery lead time from Calgary General Hospital's hypodermic syringe supplier is three days. Assuming that the hospital operates 365 days per year, the reorder point can be calculated as follows:

$$R = \bar{d}\,L$$

$$= (100{,}000 \text{ boxes per year}/ \\ 365 \text{ days per year}) \times 3 \text{ days}$$

$$= 822 \text{ boxes}$$

Therefore, the purchasing manager at the Calgary General Hospital should place a new order for hypodermic syringes when inventory is depleted to 822 boxes.

In many situations, however, demand is not constant and totally predictable. Inventory might be depleted at either a slower or faster rate during the lead time (L). If demand during the lead time is higher than expected, the result is a *stockout*. In order to help avoid stockouts, *safety stock* (sometimes also called buffer stock) can be held. Safety stock is added to the reorder point (R) to provide coverage for unexpected demand during the lead time (L). Figure 4 illustrates this relationship.

Safety stock is added to ensure that appropriate service levels are maintained. Service level refers to the ability to meet customer demand and is measured as a percentage of orders filled on time. For example, if annual demand is 100 units and 95 units are supplied from stock as required by the

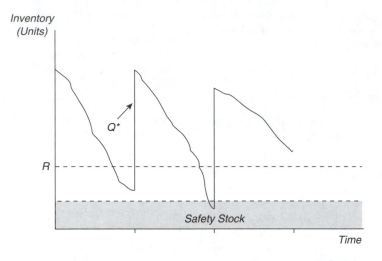

Figure 4 The Fixed Order Quantity Model With Safety Stock

customer, the service level is 95 per cent. To compute the reorder point in situations where demand is uncertain, the following formula can be used:

$$R = \bar{d}L + z\sigma_d \sqrt{L}$$

Where,

R = reorder point
$\bar{d}$ = average daily demand
L = lead time
z = number of standard deviations corresponding to the service level probability
σ_d = standard deviation of usage during lead time

Example:

The standard deviation of demand for hypodermic syringes at the Calgary General Hospital is 25 boxes per day. What is the reorder point and safety stock if the hospital wants to maintain a 95 per cent customer service level?

$$\bar{d} = 100,000 \text{ boxes per year}/$$
$$365 \text{ days per year}$$

$$= 274 \text{ boxes}$$

$$L = 3 \text{ days}$$

$$\sigma_d = 25 \text{ boxes per day}$$

The value of z can be determined from Table 1. Using a value of 0.4505 (for a 95 per cent service level), we can estimate the value of z to be 1.65. Therefore, the reorder point and safety stock can be calculated as:

$$R = \bar{d}L + z\sigma_d \sqrt{L}$$
$$= (274 \times 3) + (1.65 \times 25 \times \sqrt{3})$$
$$= 822 + 71$$
$$= 893 \text{ boxes}$$

The reorder point of 893 boxes consists of 822 boxes for coverage during the lead time and 71 boxes for safety stock due to variation in demand.

Fixed Time Period Systems

During the preceding discussion, the main characteristics of the fixed order quantity inventory system were covered. This system held the order quantity constant, while the time between orders was permitted to vary. Another commonly used method is to hold the time between orders constant while varying the order size. One example is the grocery store industry where vendors restock their products on a weekly schedule. Such systems are referred to as fixed time period inventory systems.

Table 1   Normal Curve Areas

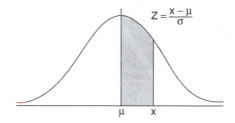

Normal Curve Areas

Z	0.00	0.01	0.02	0.03	0.04	0.05	0.06	0.07	0.08	0.09
0.0	0.0000	0.0040	0.0080	0.0120	0.0160	0.0199	0.0239	0.0279	0.0319	0.0359
0.1	0.0398	0.0438	0.0478	0.0517	0.0557	0.0596	0.0636	0.0675	0.0714	0.0753
0.2	0.0793	0.0832	0.0871	0.0910	0.0948	0.0987	0.1026	0.1064	0.1103	0.1141
0.3	0.1179	0.1217	0.1255	0.1293	0.1331	0.1368	0.1406	0.1443	0.1480	0.1517
0.4	0.1554	0.1591	0.1628	0.1664	0.1700	0.1736	0.1772	0.1808	0.1844	0.1879
0.5	0.1915	0.1950	0.1985	0.2019	0.2054	0.2088	0.2123	0.2157	0.2190	0.2224
0.6	0.2257	0.2291	0.2324	0.2357	0.2389	0.2422	0.2454	0.2486	0.2517	0.2549
0.7	0.2580	0.2611	0.2642	0.2673	0.2704	0.2734	0.2764	0.2794	0.2823	0.2852
0.8	0.2881	0.2910	0.2939	0.2967	0.2995	0.3023	0.3051	0.3078	0.3106	0.3133
0.9	0.3159	0.3186	0.3212	0.3238	0.3264	0.3289	0.3315	0.3340	0.3365	0.3389
1.0	0.3413	0.3438	0.3461	0.3485	0.3508	0.3531	0.3554	0.3577	0.3599	0.3621
1.1	0.3643	0.3665	0.3686	0.3708	0.3729	0.3749	0.3770	0.3790	0.3810	0.3830
1.2	0.3849	0.3869	0.3888	0.3907	0.3925	0.3944	0.3962	0.3980	0.3997	0.4015
1.3	0.4032	0.4049	0.4066	0.4082	0.4099	0.4115	0.4131	0.4147	0.4162	0.4177
1.4	0.4192	0.4207	0.4222	0.4236	0.4251	0.4265	0.4279	0.4292	0.4306	0.4319
1.5	0.4332	0.4345	0.4357	0.4370	0.4382	0.4394	0.4406	0.4418	0.4429	0.4441
1.6	0.4452	0.4463	0.4474	0.4484	0.4495	0.4505	0.4515	0.4525	0.4535	0.4545
1.7	0.4554	0.4564	0.4573	0.4582	0.4591	0.4599	0.4608	0.4616	0.4625	0.4633
1.8	0.4641	0.4649	0.4656	0.4664	0.4671	0.4678	0.4686	0.4693	0.4699	0.4706
1.9	0.4713	0.4719	0.4726	0.4732	0.4738	0.4744	0.4750	0.4756	0.4761	0.4767
2.0	0.4772	0.4778	0.4783	0.4788	0.4793	0.4798	0.4803	0.4808	0.4812	0.4817
2.1	0.4821	0.4826	0.4830	0.4834	0.4838	0.4842	0.4846	0.4850	0.4854	0.4857
2.2	0.4861	0.4864	0.4868	0.4871	0.4875	0.4878	0.4881	0.4884	0.4887	0.4890
2.3	0.4893	0.4896	0.4898	0.4901	0.4904	0.4906	0.4909	0.4911	0.4913	0.4916
2.4	0.4918	0.4920	0.4922	0.4925	0.4927	0.4929	0.4931	0.4933	0.4934	0.4936
2.5	0.4938	0.4940	0.4941	0.4943	0.4945	0.4946	0.4948	0.4949	0.4951	0.4952
2.6	0.4953	0.4955	0.4956	0.4957	0.4959	0.4960	0.4961	0.4962	0.4963	0.4964
2.7	0.4965	0.4966	0.4967	0.4968	0.4969	0.4970	0.4971	0.4972	0.4973	0.4974
2.8	0.4974	0.4975	0.4976	0.4977	0.4977	0.4978	0.4979	0.4979	0.4980	0.4981
2.9	0.4981	0.4982	0.4982	0.4983	0.4984	0.4984	0.4985	0.4985	0.4986	0.4986
3.0	0.4987	0.4987	0.4987	0.4988	0.4988	0.4989	0.4989	0.4989	0.4990	0.4990

Source: Russell, R.S. and Bernard, W.T., *Operations Management: Focusing on Quality and Competitiveness,* Second Edition, Prentice Hall Inc.: Upper Saddle River, N.J., 1998.

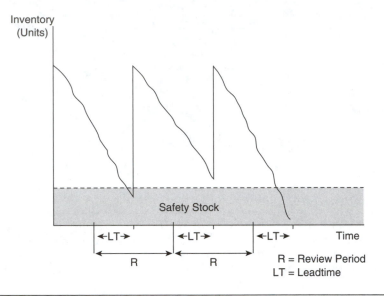

Figure 5   Fixed Time Period System With Safety Stock

Fixed time period systems count inventory at regular time intervals, such as every week or month, and place orders for new stock at that time. Depending on the usage rate over the time period, the quantity ordered can vary. Figure 5 illustrates a fixed time period inventory system.

Fixed time period inventory systems set the review period, but the order quantity must still be calculated. Assuming demand is variable (but with a normal distribution), the following formula can be used:

$$Q = \bar{d}\,(t_b + L) + z\sigma_d\,\sqrt{t_b + L} - I$$

Where,

$\bar{d}$ = average daily demand
t_b = review period
L = lead time
Z = number of standard deviations corresponding to the service level probability
σ_d = standard deviation of usage during lead time
I = inventory on hand

This formula consists of three components. The first, $(t_b + L)$, represents the amount required to cover demand during the review period and the lead time. The second, $z\sigma_d\sqrt{t_b + L}$, is the amount of safety stock required based on variable demand. The final component, I, is an adjustment for the inventory on hand when the order is placed.

Example:

The aspirin supplier for Dresden Drug Store checks the inventory levels for her product every 30 days. The average demand for aspirins at Dresden Drug Store is eight bottles per day, with a standard deviation of 1.2 bottles. The lead time to receive an order is four days. During the last visit the supplier counted seven bottles in stock. How much should be ordered to meet a 95 per cent service level?

$\bar{d}$ = 8 bottles per day
t_b = 30 days
L = 4 days
σ_d = 1.2 bottles
I = 7 bottles

The value of z can be determined from Table 1. Using a value of 0.4505 (for a 95 per cent service level), we can estimate the value of z to be 1.65. Therefore, the reorder point and safety stock can be calculated as:

$$Q = \bar{d} \, (t_b + L) + z\sigma_d \sqrt{t_b + L} - I$$

$$Q = 8 \, (30 + 4) + 1.65 \times 1.2 \times \sqrt{30 + 4} - 7$$

$$Q = 272 + 11.5 - 7$$

$$Q = 276.5 = 277 \text{ bottles}$$

The reorder point of 277 bottles consists of 272 bottles for coverage during the lead time and the review period, 11.5 bottles for safety stock due to variation in demand, and an inventory adjustment of seven bottles for the existing inventory.

ABC Inventory Classification

Controlling and managing inventories can be expensive, requiring dedication of information systems, staff and physical resources. The potential exists in many organizations where there may be several thousand separate inventory items, but the costs of tight control of many of the items exceed the benefits.

The objective of the ABC inventory classification system is to segregate inventory items based on their level of importance to the firm in order to address the issue of concentrating resources on those items that are most critical. ABC analysis has been around for many years, and was originally credited to Vilfredo Pareto in the 19th century. It is commonly referred to as the "80-20 rule," and has applications in a number of areas other than inventory control.

The ABC classification system segregates inventory items on the basis of their total annual value into one of three categories:

- A Items: These are the five to 15 per cent of the items that account for 70 to 80 percent of the total dollar value in inventory activity.
- B Items: These are the 30 to 35 per cent of the items that account for approximately 20 to 25 per cent of the total dollar value in inventory activity.
- C Items: These are the 50 to 60 per cent of the items that account for only five to 10 per cent of the total dollar value in inventory activity.

The percentages described above are only guidelines, and differences may exist between firms. Furthermore, it is possible for low value C or B items to be treated like A category items if they are deemed to be critical.

The implications are that management resources are focused on the A items. Inventory levels of these items are closely monitored and controlled. For example, regular cycle counting might be used to ensure inventory records are accurate and orders might be placed weekly. Such activities allow safety stocks to be minimized while helping to avoid stockouts.

Inventories for the B and C items require less stringent control. Because of their low total value, safety stocks can be expanded and review periods lengthened. For example, inventories for B items might be checked every month and C items reviewed once every two months.

WHICH SYSTEM IS BETTER?

The answer to this question is, of course, it depends. Each system has its strengths and weaknesses. Understanding the advantages and disadvantages of these systems is useful in appreciating how and where they can be used.

An important feature of fixed order quantity systems is that inventory levels are constantly monitored. Fixed time period systems can go long periods of time without checking inventory levels. The result is that fixed time period systems carry larger safety stocks, and, therefore, incur higher inventory carrying charges than are normally incurred when using fixed order quantity systems. For this reason, fixed order quantity systems are best suited for expensive high volume items, which require substantial investments in inventory.

Constant monitoring of inventory levels has other advantages as well. For example, important products with high penalties for stockouts should be controlled through the use of fixed order quantity systems.

The tradeoff is the cost of operating a fixed order quantity system. Monitoring inventory levels continuously and recording each transaction have associated costs. Fixed time period systems reduce such operating costs. Consequently, fixed time period models are best suited for less critical, low volume, low cost items.

Finally, seasonality of demand should be considered when selecting an inventory management system. Products that are characterized by wide, sudden changes in demand patterns should be monitored using a fixed order quantity system. A fixed time period system could be used, but only if the review period is adjusted to reflect the seasonal demand pattern.

McLeod Motors Ltd.

Prepared by Professor John Haywood-Farmer

Copyright © 1995, Ivey Management Services

Version: (A) 2002-12-02

Sue, I just got the fourth quarter inventory reports. When we standardized those end shields last September you told me it would cut both our manufacturing costs and our inventories. Manufacturing costs are down all right, although not as much as I would like, but our inventory has gone up. It costs us 25 per cent to keep that stuff around for a year, you know, Sue, and the warehouse guys are really cramped for space. I want you to look into it and let me know what is going on and what we should do about it by Monday. I leave on Tuesday and won't be back until early February.

Sue Reynolds, plant manager at the McLeod Motors Ltd factory in Chilliwack, British Columbia, put down the phone and thought back to the decision implemented four months earlier in September and to which John Ingram, vice president of manufacturing, had referred.

McLeod Motors

The Market

In its plant McLeod made over 40 models of electric motors ranging from one-quarter to 10 horsepower. The plant was divided into three parts. One half was devoted to production; the other half was divided into a small office, and a warehouse used to store raw materials, work in process, and finished goods inventories and supplies. Production was in small batches. The production area of the plant was laid out by process; that is, the machines were grouped together by function into departments (drilling, milling, turning, assembly, etc.). The plant operated five eight-hour days per week.

The company had a number of customers in the original equipment manufacturer (OEM) market, who used the motors as components in larger products, and also in the replacement market. Naturally, McLeod's product mix changed over time as its OEM customers phased products in and out and made annual supply decisions. In general, however, the size of the OEM market was known well in advance through the annual order process and was fairly easy to forecast beyond that. In contrast, the replacement market was less stable and harder to forecast, especially for relatively short time periods. McLeod had recently experienced a welcome sales boom which was affecting all areas of the company. Warehouse space was scarce and the machines were usually busy. Consequently, company personnel would be certain to question any change that would take machines "out of circulation."

As a start to the bidding process for new contracts, the company calculated the direct costs of its products, added overhead based on direct labour hours (at 300 per cent), and added a 20 per cent profit margin. The recent sales boom had led to profits which management considered to be "decent for a change," but the business tended to be boom or bust. In addition, labour negotiations, that management thought might be difficult, were scheduled to begin within a few months. Consequently, control of costs was important to the company.

The BN-88-55 End Shield

During the previous year, a McLeod engineer had suggested that the company could reduce the number of different end shields (see Exhibit 1) it made and used as motor components from 36 to about five by making minor modifications. Ms. Reynolds decided to propose a test with BN-88-55, a new end shield for the shaft end of some motors (see Exhibit 1). It would replace 15 others in one motor product line accounting for about 20 per cent of McLeod's sales. Ms. Reynolds expected that this move would allow longer production runs, lower inventories, and better service to and by the manufacturers, wholesalers, retailers, and repair shops that used and carried McLeod products.

The BN-88-55 was machined from an aluminum die casting which came complete with several indentations and holes, including one to accommodate the shaft, and a hardened steel ring

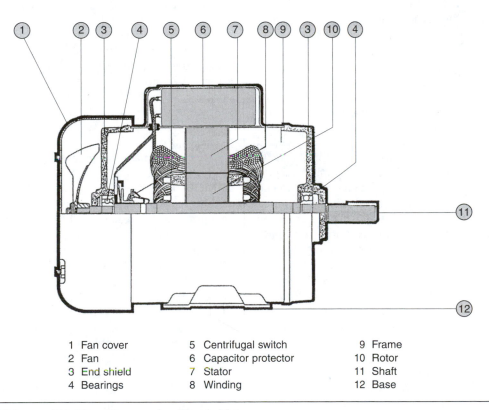

1 Fan cover	5 Centrifugal switch	9 Frame
2 Fan	6 Capacitor protector	10 Rotor
3 End shield	7 Stator	11 Shaft
4 Bearings	8 Winding	12 Base

Exhibit 1   Side View Diagram of an Electric Motor

in the centre which acted as a bearing housing. The BN-88-55's inner surface had various ribs to add strength, particularly around the holes and indentations. McLeod had to thread (tap) eight of the holes (two sizes), and finish the surfaces in contact with the bearings and the frame (see Exhibit 1) and the convex (outer) face which abutted on machines using the motors. When finished, the BN-88-55 was bowl-shaped (16.6 centimetres in diameter, 4.8 centimetres deep, and 0.5 centimetres thick) and weighed about 800 grams. Because of its function, almost all of the BN-88-55s were sold as part of complete motors to either the OEM or the replacement market. Each BN-88-55 casting cost $5.28 (net of recovered scrap) and took a total of 3.1 minutes ($0.77) of direct labour time to process. With the added overhead allocation of $2.31, the total cost of a BN-88-55 was $8.36. McLeod sold them for $10 to replacement market customers but, as noted above, usually sold them in completed motors priced at $150 to $300.

The Production Line

All production in the plant was in lots; parts were carried in standard bins by forklift trucks. The standard bins held a maximum of 1,248 BN-88-55s. Demand for the 15 end shields replaced by BN-88-55 had totalled 2,500 units per week, ranging from 58 to 375 per week with an average of 165. BN-88-55 was very similar to the 15 end shields it replaced and their production required the same basic steps. The differences were in the structural features of the casting, particularly hole size and location. Before production of BN-88-55 had begun, the end shields had been made in batches of about two weeks' demand. Although there had been some variation between products, the direct labour processing time for the 15 original end shields had also averaged 3.1 minutes.

Each machine had space for only two bins near it. On one side was a supply bin from which the worker took parts as he or she worked on a batch; on the other was a receiving bin into which the worker placed completed parts.

Although the batches could not be divided (that is, only a single machine could work on a given batch at any one time), if necessary, more than one machine in a department could be scheduled for BN-88-55 production simultaneously. For each operation the inventory in a supply bin slowly decreased and that in a receiving bin slowly increased as work on the batch progressed. Each of the production operations (milling, drilling, etc.) involved a number of small steps (locating a piece in the supply bin, picking it up, inspecting it, aligning it in the machine, activating the machine, inspecting the part, putting it in the receiving bin, etc.). When working on a batch, a production worker carried out these steps on each part in the batch. After the worker finished the batch, he or she informed the supervisor, the supervisor informed the production control department, and the production control department issued a move order. Subsequently, a materials handler moved the full receiving bin to a work-in-process storage area in the warehouse, a materials handler brought a new supply bin of parts, and the two-person set-up crew set the machine up to do the next operation. A materials handler later moved the full receiving bin to the next operation in the sequence where it then became a supply bin for the next stage.

After this series of activities had been completed, production could continue. It took only about 10 minutes to move a batch to or from the warehouse, and about 30 minutes on average to set-up and test a machine. However, based on their experience, the production control staff knew that, on average, a batch spent a total of 17 working days between operations: three working days in the warehouse between each pair of operations, and an additional working day for each operation waiting while the material handling and set-up personnel became available and completed their work, and moving between the work centres and the warehouse.

After McLeod's executive committee approved Ms. Reynolds' proposal, the engineering and production control staff drew up manufacturing plans for BN-88-55. The company would require about 2,500 BN-88-55s per week to meet motor assembly and replacement part demand. This demand was the same as the total for the 15 end shields it replaced. BN-88-55 would require five separate operations normally performed in the sequence shown in Exhibit 2. Although tapping had to precede turning, the two tapping operations and/or the two turning operations could be interchanged. The production control staff decided on a lot size of 1,248 to maximize run length using full standard bins.

Operation	Department	Machine	Pieces per Machine Hour[1]	Machines Available in Department
1. Tap four holes, concave face	Drilling	Drill press	75	9
2. Tap four holes, convex face	Drilling	Drill press	75	9
3. Turn convex face	Turning	Lathe	100	5
4. Turn concave face	Turning	Lathe	120	5
5. Inspect and finish	Inspection	Work bench & hand tools	150	3[2]

Exhibit 2 Operations Sheet for Motor End Shield BN-88-55

1. Assuming a 40-hour week, an output of 2,500 units per week requires 62.5 units per hour on average, or just under 20 hours per work centre for each batch of 1,248. McLeod could vary the output rate by assigning two machines and/or workers in a department to work on more than one batch at a time. However, because each department also worked on jobs for other motor lines and for other parts of motors in addition to end shields, it was extremely unlikely that all of a department's capacity would be working on BN-88-55s at any one time.

2. The number of inspectors—no machinery involved.

IRON ORE COMPANY OF ONTARIO

Prepared by Professors
C. J. Piper and A .R. Wood

Version: (A) 2000-07-21

In April 1990, George Sharp, the mine superintendent of Iron Ore Company of Ontario (IOCO), was preparing for a meeting with the company's general superintendent of operations, Tom Smith. Both Sharp and Smith were concerned about the question of handling loaded ore trucks during operating delays of the ore crushers at the mine. This was a problem that had plagued mine supervisors for several years. Sharp knew that some action was urgently required and that he would be asked for his recommendation at the forthcoming meeting.

COMPANY BACKGROUND

The Iron Ore Company of Ontario (IOCO) operated a large open-pit iron-ore mine in Northern

Ontario. Besides the mine itself, the company operated an ore-handling facility on Lake Superior, loading ocean-going ships, and lake freighters. The mine was accessible by aircraft, railroad and by a 40 kilometre[1] road from the Trans-Canada Highway. The region had a cool climate with snow beginning in November and disappearing in June.

The mine was located in a crescent-shaped ore deposit which is shown in Exhibit 1. Exhibit 2 shows a cross-section of the deposit and indicates how the waste was removed in order to expose the deposit itself. As excavation of the pit progressed, the principal waste-removal operations were located further and further from the actual ore deposit. As shown in the cross-section, waste removal could occur at left benches 3 and 4, plus right bench 2. Ore removal, on the other hand, could only occur at bench 4 and right bench 3. An overall view of the mine is shown in Exhibit 4.

Production was scheduled on a year-round, 24-hour-per-day basis to produce over 46 million tonnes of crude ore per year, yielding about 21 million tonnes of high-grade concentrate. To accommodate this production, a concentrator was built with an input capacity of about 1,760 cubic metres of crude ore per hour. It was the policy of the mine to operate the concentrator at capacity at all times.

THE PRODUCTION PROCESS

The production process (Exhibit 3) began with large drills cutting 12-metre holes into the solid rock along the face of a bench. These holes were filled with an explosive slurry of ammonium nitrate and fuel oil. When the explosive charge was detonated, the solid rock shattered into 12-metre-high piles of loose material known as "muck."

After a blast, large electric shovels moved into position to load diesel-powered trucks (Exhibit 5). These hauling units carried waste material to a waste dump outside the mine, while ore was hauled to the crushers. Every day, about 128,000 tonnes of ore and about 80,000 tonnes of waste rock were hauled to the crushers and waste dumps, respectively.[2]

The ore, containing about 30 per cent iron, entered the crushers, where large rocks were reduced in size by jaw and gyratory crushers. After being crushed, the material passed by conveyor to the concentrator where it was further ground and separated into waste tailings and 66 per cent iron concentrate.

The concentrate thus produced was collected and loaded aboard railroad trains. After a one-hour trip to the port facility, the train was unloaded automatically, and the ore was loaded

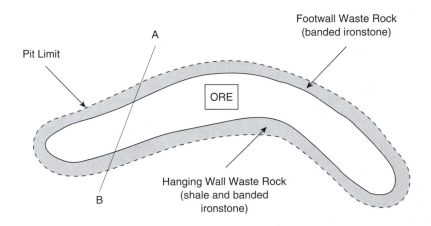

Exhibit 1   Plan of Ore Deposit, Overhead View

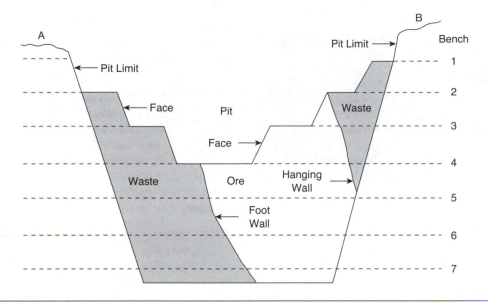

Exhibit 2   A–B Cross Section of the Pit

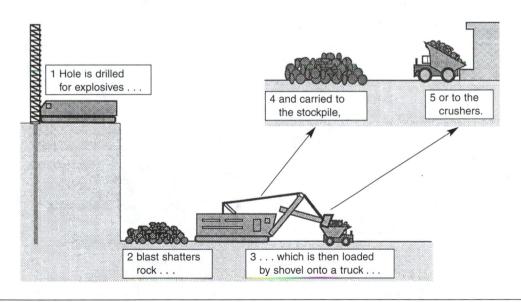

Exhibit 3   Schematic Diagram of Production Process

Exhibit 4   Overall View of the Mine

Exhibit 5   The Loading Operations

aboard ships bound for European and North American customers.

Shovels

In 1990, IOCO operated electric-powered shovels at various bench faces in the mine, with one unit assigned full-time to the crude-ore stockpile. Average operating costs and capacities appear in Exhibit 7. All shovels were equipped with 11.5 cubic metre capacity buckets. Recent time studies indicated that shovels loaded an average of 480 cubic metres per hour. While all shovels were located in active ore or waste

locations in the mine, there were normally only seven shovels available on any given shift. The remaining shovels were usually undergoing scheduled maintenance. This maintenance rarely required more than one shift to complete. An eighth available shovel, located at the crude-ore stockpile, was an older unit with a very weak undercarriage. Mine operators had resolved to retire the unit, but then decided to use it on the stockpile where very little moving about was required.

Tractors

Tractors were assigned to operating shovels for the purpose of smoothing the loading area to reduce truck-tire wear. The tractor cleared loose rock from the loading area while the shovel was waiting for trucks. (See Exhibit 6.) One tractor was also assigned to the stockpile shovel. IOCO's accounting department assumed that this tractor worked one hour for each hour worked by the stockpile shovel, plus 1.5 minutes per load dumped on the stockpile. Appropriate hourly operating costs appear in Exhibit 7.

Trucks

IOCO moved the ore and waste with a fleet of off-highway rear-dump trucks. Average costs,

Exhibit 6   Tractor Clearing Loose—"Muck" Around The Shovel

Costs ($ per hour)	Shovels		Tractors		Trucks	
	Operating	Idling	Operating	Idling	Operating	Idling
Labour	$24.10	$24.10	$15.44	$15.44	$15.44	$15.44
Maintenance	126.90	25.38	24.50	4.90	24.52	4.90
Fuel/Electricity	10.68	10.68	11.00	1.10	13.00	1.30
Supplies	32.00	6.40	6.50	1.30	23.00	4.60
Overhead	6.32	—	4.04	—	4.04	—
Total	**$200.00**	**$66.56**	**$61.48**	**$22.74**	**$80.00**	**$26.24**

Capacities	Shovels	Trucks
Number owned	11	41
Number available at any given time	7	28
Cubic metres per load per unit	11.5	36
Cubic metres per hour per unit	480	128

Exhibit 7   Average Mining Costs and Capacities

availabilities, and carrying capacities appear in Exhibit 7. Usually, four trucks were assigned to each shovel, with the remaining units undergoing preventive maintenance or repairs.

During a typical operating cycle, a truck assigned to a shovel working in ore began by travelling about 1.5 kilometres from the crushers to the shovel-loading area at a bench face in the mine. The truck would turn at the shovel, wait for any trucks being loaded to leave, and then "spot" or back into position beside the shovel, which would then load the truck. Once the truck was loaded, it would leave the shovel area, turn onto the haul road and drive up out of the mine to the crushers. On arrival, it would turn, back up to a crusher, dump, and return to the mine.

The Crusher

There were two crushers. Together they were capable of handling a maximum of 9,420 tonnes per hour. Trucks took an average of 1.7 minutes to dump. Two trucks could dump simultaneously into each crusher. The ore subsequently entered a series of jaw crushers, screens, and gyratory crushers. Because of the weight and hardness of the rock, there was considerable wear and tear on the machinery in the crushers. This deterioration was rectified by a continuing program of repairs and preventive maintenance. To this end, one crusher was closed throughout the day shift, reducing the intake capacity of the crushers from 9,420 to 4,710 tonnes per hour. During the afternoon and night shifts, both crushers remained open.

In addition to the daily 8-hour shutdown for repairs and maintenance on one of the crushers, the crushers were prone to brief holdups caused by "bridging" and other operating delays. Bridging occurred when a large rock jammed between the jaws of the jaw crusher, blocking the crusher completely. Once a crusher was blocked, it would remain closed until the rock was removed or shaken loose. Delays of this nature could last from one minute to over an hour, and sometimes (very rarely) continued throughout a complete shift. During the afternoon and evening shifts, it was rare for both crushers to be "down" (closed) simultaneously, but during the day shift, when one crusher was down for maintenance, it was not uncommon to have a complete temporary shut-down, while blockage of the one serviceable crusher was removed. Exhibit 8 shows a distribution of the duration of crusher delays during the day shift.

The Stockpile

When the mine began operations in 1985, Sharp's predecessor noted that trucks often arrived from the mine with a full load of ore only to find both crushers closed. Trucks then turned around and returned to the mine and dumped the ore beside the shovel which had originally loaded it. The entire shovel-truck crew then moved from their ore zone to a waste zone until the crusher was re-opened. About 15 minutes of production was lost each time a shovel changed location to move from an ore zone to a waste zone.

Recognizing the inefficiency of this type of operation, the superintendent started a stockpile about 120 metres from the crushers. Loaded ore trucks dumped at the stockpile, instead of returning loaded to the mine when both crushers were down. It was thought to be cheaper to station a shovel, which would otherwise be "spare," at the stockpile, and move the ore from the stockpile to the crushers later, than to send loaded ore trucks back to the mine.

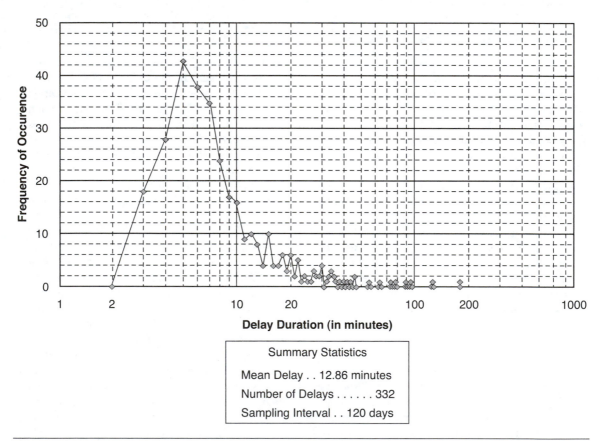

Summary Statistics

Mean Delay . . 12.86 minutes

Number of Delays 332

Sampling Interval . . 120 days

Exhibit 8   Distribution Showing the Duration of Crusher Delays During the Day Shift

The time required for a loaded truck to come from a shovel in the mine, turn, and dump on the stockpile was effectively the same as the time needed to carry ore to one of the crushers, turn, and dump. Therefore, the cost of ore reaching the stockpile was the same as the cost of ore entering the crushers.

Any ore dumped on the stockpile, however, would ultimately have to be moved from the stockpile to the crushers. For this purpose, the electric shovel mentioned previously was stationed at the stockpile. When this shovel was not in use, it stood idle at the stockpile. Trucks could haul 252 cubic metres per hour over the short distance to the crushers. Time was spent reducing the stockpile during periods of blasting when all production trucks were moved out of the mine, and during shovel breakdowns which freed trucks. When necessary, stockpile removal could be carried out during the afternoon and night shifts.

OPERATING OPINIONS

Sharp felt that once a shovel-truck "team" began to produce, it was important that the team remain on the go. He believed that a rhythmic cycle was set up which was undesirable to break. Workers in the mine might conceivably feel frustrated and lose enthusiasm for their work, if their cycle were periodically disrupted. Long periods of waiting at the crushers, he believed, might break the rhythm, causing a considerable reduction in efficiency and productivity in the mine. However, Sharp knew that the cost of the resulting inefficiency could not be measured accurately.

Accountants had suggested, however, that the fuel consumption of waiting trucks or bulldozers would only be about 10 per cent of the normal amount. Also, their maintenance and supplies expenses were about 20 per cent of the normal amount. A temporarily idle shovel consumed electricity at its normal rate, and

incurred maintenance and supplies expenses at about 20 per cent of normal rates. Costs of idle time are summarized in Exhibit 7.

On the other hand, Sharp wanted to use the stockpile as little as possible because of the additional cost of re-handling ore. He was aware that the mine general foreman might be tempted to use the stock-pile during *any* crusher delay, since the foreman was motivated to produce as many truck-trips per shift as possible. Sharp thought that the stockpile was not necessary for providing an in-process inventory because the concentrator was equipped with 12 silos for storing crushed crude ore. These silos, which held about six hours live storage of crude ore production, could continue to supply the concentrator during long mine delays or slow-downs.

It had also been suggested that the stockpile be used for storing various grades of ore, ranging from 27 per cent Fe to 35 per cent Fe. The varying grades of ore could then be used for blending to maintain constant grade control of the finished concentrate. Such a practice was considered impractical because of the lag between the input of crude ore and the production of finished concentrate. However, the stockpile was useful for ensuring a continuous flow of ore to the crushers during the 30 minutes each day that the mine was cleared for blasting, as well as during poor road conditions and shovel breakdowns.

Sharp had to evaluate the courses of action open to him. He and Smith had agreed that there was an optimum point at which total waiting and stockpile re-handling costs would be minimized, and further agreed that the current rule failed to minimize these costs. He knew he would be called on to recommend a new plan to Smith.

NOTES

1. One kilometre = 0.6214 miles. One tonne = 1.102 tons. One cubic metre = 1.308 cubic yards.
2. One cubic metre of waste weighs 2.37 tonnes. One cubic metre of ore weighs 3.03 tonnes.

VBF Tubing (Abridged)

Prepared by Professors
C. J. Piper and R. D. Klassen

Version: (A) 2004-03-24

Rob Smit, logistics manager for VBF Tubing, knew the problems all too well. VBF's inventory investment of over \$4.5 million was turning over only seven times per year (Exhibit 1). This slow turnover was a major burden on the financial resources of VBF, whose required return on capital was about 13 per cent per year. Smit knew that changes would have to be made quickly if VBF were to survive in the competitive European tubing market.

COMPANY BACKGROUND

VBF Tubing, whose full name Verenigde Buizen Fabrieken can be roughly translated from Dutch as United Tube Works, was a wholly-owned subsidiary of Hoogovens, the largest steel producer in the Netherlands. VBF produced welded steel tubing in three plants, and although Rob Smit was responsible for logistics management at all of the plants, it was the thick-walled product line made at the Oosterhout mill that was of immediate concern. Smit expected, however, that solutions to the problems there could be applied to the other operations as well.

VBF's thick-walled tube products were sold in about 10 diameters and 15 wall thicknesses. Most tubes were six metres long, although other lengths were available. VBF's customers used its tubing (or pipe, as it was called in the plumbing trade) in a wide variety of applications ranging from structural components to gas, steam and liquid transmission.

THE MANUFACTURING PROCESS

Tube production can be broken into four stages:

- raw material preparation;
- tube formation;
- stretch-reduction; and
- finishing operations.

An overview of the processes used by VBF is shown in Exhibit 2.

Stage in Processing	Tonnes	Value
Raw material	4,000	\$1,280,000
Semi-finished tubes	3,600	1,444,000
Tubes in finishing	700	317,000
Finished goods	3,000	1,650,000
Totals	**11,300**	**\$4,691,000**

Exhibit 1   Current Inventory Position

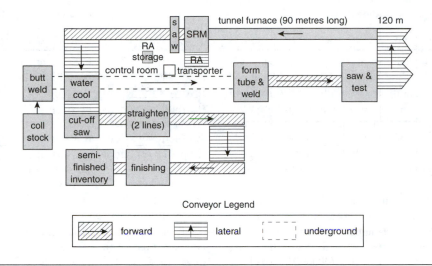

Exhibit 2 Overview of the Thick-Walled Tube Production Process

Raw Material Preparation

VBF's principal raw material was flat-rolled steel. Steel of appropriate thicknesses (four millimetres was typical) was slit to the required width and wound into rolls (or "coils" as they were called in the steel industry) at Hoogovens' primary steelmaking facility. The coils arrived at the Oosterhout mill by barge.

When the steel arrived at Oosterhout, it was unloaded by a dockside crane and placed in an outside storage yard, from where it moved by forklift truck and overhead crane into the factory. A two-man team placed the coils on an unwinder and straightener, and then butt-welded the start of one coil against the end of the previous coil. The continuous steel strip was then fed about 200 metres under the floor to the tube forming and welding operations.

Tube Formation

The Oosterhout plant produced all of its tubes from two basic sizes called "mother tubes." One was four inches in diameter and accounted for about 90 per cent of production. The other was three inches in diameter. The three-inch mother tube was produced over a five-day period, only three times a year because it required a major changeover. The remainder of the case describes the production and scheduling of the four-inch mother tube and its derivatives.

A series of rollers progressively curved the incoming flat ribbon of steel into a tubular shape. Immediately after the steel had passed through the forming rollers, a welding station tended by a single operator welded the butted edges into a tube at a continuous rate of about 36 tonnes per hour.

The next operator monitored the tube's progress as it passed through a set of calibration rollers that ensured that the wall of the tube was uniformly round. At this point the tube was sawed into 120-metre lengths. Each length was cleaned and pressure-tested by flowing water through the tube. At the same time a small sample that had been cut from the end of each piece was tested to ensure that the weld was stronger than the steel it bonded. Tubes that successfully completed testing were moved on to a conveyor-accumulator capable of holding 170 tubes, equivalent to approximately 190 tonnes.

Stretch-Reduction

The vast majority of the four-inch tubes were next sent to the Stretch Reduction Machine (SRM) where they were stretched and reduced into smaller diameter (one-half inch to two and one-half inch) tubes. The remaining tubes were cut into six metre lengths for sale in their original diameter. The SRM was not able to operate during the 10 days in which the four-inch tubes were being cut. Combining this lost production with the 15 days a year that the plant used to produce the three-inch tubes meant that only 211 days were available for producing the one-half inch to two and one-half inch tubes.

An operator prepared the tube for stretching by feeding it into one end of a 90-metre long tunnel furnace. When the tube began to emerge from the tunnel about one and a half minutes later, the 950 degrees centigrade oven temperature had given it a plastic-like consistency. From here, the tube entered the SRM.

The working elements of the SRM consisted of up to 19 roller assemblies (RAs) of progressively smaller diameter. Each RA consisted of three steel rollers mounted in a housing at 120-degree angles to one another, as shown in Exhibit 3. The spacing of the three rollers, the contour of the grooves in the rollers' surfaces, and the RA's speed were set so that the tube would be smoothly stretched-reduced and uniformly accelerated as it passed through the SRM. Exhibit 4 provides the various production rates. The smaller diameter tubes were processed more slowly due to the extra forces involved in the more extreme size reductions in the mother tube.

As the resized tube left the SRM, the first 1.5 metres was cut off and dropped into a scrap heap. The remainder was cut into 12- to 13-metre lengths by a high speed rotary saw. Because the tubing was still quite flexible at this stage, an operator ensured that each length of tube dropped correctly on to a take-away conveyor. Short or bent pieces were removed by the operator and placed on a scrap pile. About once an hour, the operator also took a 15-centimetre sample to the control room, where the sample's dimensions and weight were compared against standard and were then recorded.

From here, the tubes were carried under a water cooling station. A saw operator watched as the cooled tube, which by now had shrunk to its cold size, was squared up and then cut into two final (possibly unequal) lengths. The two pieces then travelled along two parallel, but separate, conveyors where a final operator supervised a number of automatic operations, including straightening, end-finishing, pressure-testing, and electro-magnetic testing.

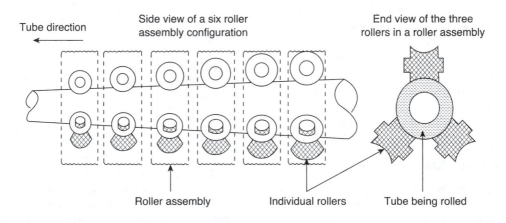

Exhibit 3   Configuration of the Typical Roller Assembly

Tube Diameter	½″	¾″	1″	1¼″	1½″	2″	2½″
Standard production rate[2]	20.7	25.1	27.9	27.9	27.9	27.9	27.9
Observed production rate[3]	20.7	25.1	33.5	33.5	33.5	33.5	33.5

Exhibit 4   SRM Production Rates[1]

1. In tonnes per hour.
2. The standard rates were the speeds used in the plant's internal documentation.
3. The observed rates were the speeds at which the SRM currently operated.

Finishing Operations

The semi-finished tube, which had cost about $400 per tonne to produce, was stored in racks. VBF performed a number of standard finishing operations, including zinc plating, painting, plastic coating, threading tube ends, and adding caps, before placing the tubing in finished goods inventory or shipping it to customers.

SRM Maintenance

The stretch-reduction process subjected each RA to extreme temperatures and pressures. After a period of use the grooves in the rolls became worn and the RAs had to be replaced. The frequency of RA replacement depended upon the location of the RA in the SRM. RAs in the front and middle sections were changed after rolling 1,000 tonnes and 750 tonnes, respectively.

RAs in the last or "end set" section, specifically the last four to six RAs that the tube passed through prior to leaving the SRM, were changed more frequently since they determined the quality of the tube. The time between these changes depended upon tube size, as well as tonnes rolled. Last year's experience with RA end set changes for replacement of worn RAs, as well as the quantity of tube produced, is summarized in Exhibit 5. The SRM was stopped for about 15 minutes during these RA set changes. In general, replacement of worn RAs, unscheduled problems and planned maintenance, caused the SRM to be unavailable for about 450 hours per year.

PRODUCTION PLANNING

Scheduling Production

The planner provided the production department with the quantity and sequence in which each diameter tube was to be made. The schedule specified:

- production starting and ending dates;
- quantities to be made;
- quantities ordered by customers; and
- quantities to be made for anticipated future needs.

The planner tried to maintain a fixed six-week production cycle, so that enough of each tube size was made to last for the next six weeks. The exact quantities of tubing scheduled depended upon the planner's assessment of several factors, including past demand, customer orders, expected orders, tube inventory, and coil availability.

A proposed schedule for the next two weeks was distributed weekly. Although the planner worked with a three month horizon, only the two days prior to production were not subject to change. The production foreman kept himself informed by daily visits to the planner's office in the building adjacent to the factory. On rare occasions rush orders were accepted

Tube Diameter	½″	¾″	1″	1¼″	1½″	2″	2½″	Total
Number of RA end set changes for:								
Replacement of worn RAs	38	30	30	14	22	16	3	153
Size changes	9	7	7	7	10	6	7	53
Time to change from the next smaller size (in minutes)	45[1]	15	15	45	15	15	15	165
Tonnes produced	7,540	9,127	11,925	8,047	11,902	9,165	3,187	60,893

Exhibit 5 SRM Roller Assembly (RA) End-Set Changes and Production Levels During the Last Year

1. The ½″ tubes were produced after the 2½″ tubes.

that required schedule changes within the two days.

Estimating Delivery Dates

The planner broke the month into three parts—start, middle and end—for specifying expected delivery times. Delivery lead time depended upon the availability of semi-finished stock and the amount of finishing required. Orders that could be filled from inventory were promised delivery in about one week if zinc plating was not required; otherwise, they were given a date according to the zinc schedule. Promised delivery dates for orders that could not be filled from semi-finished stock were obtained by adding the above times to the date the required size was expected from the SRM.

ECONOMICAL BATCH SIZES

In addition to ensuring that sufficient raw material was available, and that the required tube was produced by the promised delivery dates, the planner tried to request production batch sizes that were economical to produce. Factory accounting valued the loss in contribution caused by changeovers at $800 per hour.

SRM Setups

One objective in scheduling the SRM was to select a sequence of tube diameters with the fewest number of RA changes. Setup time was minimized by producing the smallest diameter tubing first, and then progressing through each diameter until the largest was attained. The smaller tube sizes (one-half inch to one inch) required one set of RAs while the largest sizes (one and one-quarter inch to two and one-half inches) required a totally different set. Switches between small and large sizes took 45 minutes. Size changes within either group required only a few RA changes in the end set and could be performed in about 15 minutes. As noted previously, the SRM was scheduled to cycle through the entire range of sizes once every six weeks, although in practice the actual number of setups for each size varied somewhat. Exhibit 5 indicates the experience last year.

As soon as the SRM had been shut down, a special RA transporter was moved under the RAs in the SRM. After the coolant hoses had been disconnected, a pin was inserted through the base of each RA that was to be removed and into matching holes in the transporter. The transporter then pulled the RA back to a position about three metres in front of the SRM. See Exhibit 6 for a photograph of the SRM, the RAs, the coolant hoses, the pins and the RA transporter.

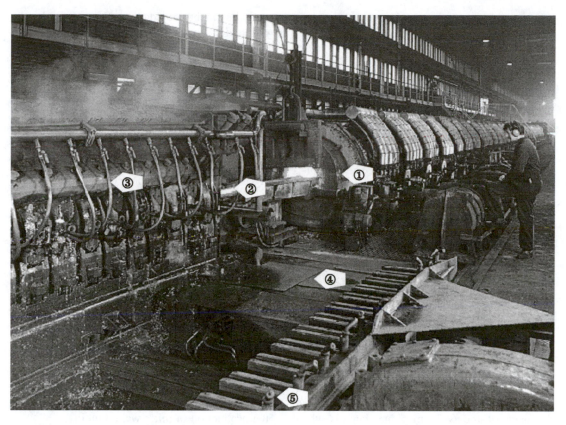

1 Furnace   4 RA transporter
2 White-hot mother tube   5 RA removal pin
3 Coolant hose

Exhibit 6   View of the SRM and Furnace From the Control Room

Each RA was handled in the same way. Two workers stood on each side of the RA they wished to remove, and the overhead crane was positioned above them. Each worker then inserted a carrying pin into the side of the RA, looped the ends of the crane's pickup cable over the pins, and guided the RA as the crane hoisted it clear of the transporter. The workers and crane moved the RA approximately 15 metres to a carrying device in the area marked RA storage in Exhibit 2. The workers positioned themselves on each side of where the RA would be placed, guided the RA into position on the carrying device, and released it from the crane by removing the two carrying pins. The crane and workers then reversed the process and moved a new RA into position on the transporter. This process was repeated until the SRM was completely reconfigured for the new size.

Several other tasks were performed by the crew leader, including adjusting the saw, changing its blade, cleaning its scrap discharge chute, and setting the speed of the RA drive motors. Although standard operating speeds were provided by engineering, motor speeds were "tuned" by experience.

There were also several small adjustments required in the operations tended by the two operators after the tube had passed through the water cooling station. Many involved the material handling equipment, which was changed by loosening appropriate fasteners, sliding a sample tube of the new diameter under the mechanism to provide the correct adjustment, and retightening the bolts at the new setting. In addition, a couple of minutes were required to set the electromagnetic tester for the new size.

Wall Thickness Adjustments

During production of a given tube diameter it was possible that the tube would be made in two or three wall thicknesses. This variation was achieved by changing the thickness of the input coil. About 75 per cent of all tubing of a given diameter was produced from one thickness, while another 15 per cent came from a second. Thickness changes required a 20- to 30-minute stoppage of the weld machine, but elsewhere

the adjustments could be made with no loss of production time.

The Current Situation

Far from shrinking, the inventory problem threatened to become even greater. VBF's thick-walled tube was experiencing a resurgence in demand. Last year's sales (Exhibit 5) had increased 15 per cent over the previous year, and a further 10 per cent growth was forecast for next year. Sales at this higher level were expected to place a severe strain on capacity, and local custom precluded prolonged use of overtime or adding a third shift to the current two shift operations. One particularly worrying proposal involved a substantial increase in the length of production runs. Larger batch sizes, it was argued, would reduce the number of hours lost to size changeovers.

Although Rob did not have the final say on production batch quantities, he knew that he would be responsible for any extra inventory that was produced. Given the current situation, he wondered what position he should take regarding the production of thick-walled tubing.

3

Planning and Control

Offering desirable customer service at a reasonable cost requires an efficient flow of materials and services while simultaneously managing the organization's resources that direct and transform these flows. Effective planning and coordination ensures that all resources required to deliver services or produce goods are available in the right quantity and quality at the right time. Such planning and coordination, however, is often very complex. For example, a typical manufacturer is required to track hundreds or thousands of raw materials, components, and subassemblies for effective production. In a similar way, a service provider must ensure that the appropriate employees and range of necessary materials are available to fill the needs of multiple market segments, often on very short notice. Effective internal planning and control represents the fundamental "block and tackling" underlying an organization's efficient and effective operations.

Operations planning and control is the second of the foundational blocks that contribute to the management of broader operational systems (see Figure 3.1). Forecasting customer demand based on a wide range of business factors is one critical input. Planning for operations then must cover both the long-term planning horizon for overall capacity and process-related resources, such as facilities, equipment, and personnel, as well as detailed schedules to match these to customer needs. And once plans are in place, management must actively control the use of resources to meet customer demands and to stay within budgets.

In practice, planning and control is a multistage process, often with iteration to refine the development or acquisition of particular resources (see Figure 3.2) (Vollmann, Berry, & Whybark, 1992). Although long-term forecasts and plans can stretch out over a number of years, a great deal of management attention is often focused on some form of annual plan. The medium-term, annual plan is then further broken down into detailed, short-term schedules for specific customer orders, equipment, and employees.

Demand Management

A critical input for much of the planning process is the challenge of forecasting customer demand. It is a difficult task because the demand for goods and services can vary greatly from year to year, month to month, and even hour to hour. For example, customer demand

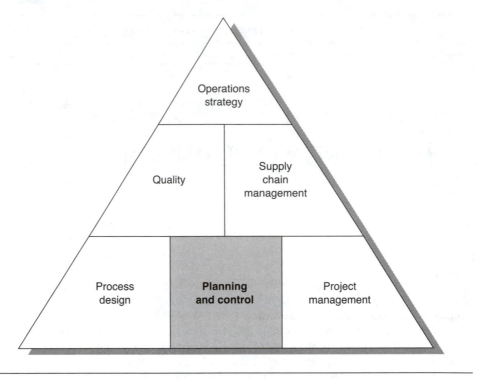

Figure 3.1   Operations Planning and Control

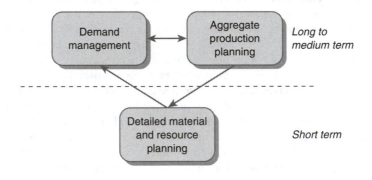

Figure 3.2   Basic Components of Planning and Control Systems

for snow skis predictably increases in the autumn and early winter months; however, the particular demand in any particular region of the country varies to some extent based on the snowfall experienced.

Sometimes, changes in demand are reasonably predictable. For example, in the fast-food industry, customer purchases are likely to be highest on days late in the week, such as Friday or Saturday. Moreover, demand at mealtime also routinely exceeds that during midafternoon. However, even here, it is much harder to predict how particular dietary factors, such as low-carbohydrate diets and food scares, affect overall demand for fast food from year to year. These large-scale trends, combined with the actions of competitors, our own new product introductions, and other process changes, only add to the complexity of forecasting. A number of these issues are central to the Greaves Brewery case.

For short-term fluctuations in demand, managers might be tempted to simply respond to this variability by rescheduling resources. However, in many situations, proactive actions can be taken to either encourage or attenuate demand. Customer buying patterns can also be shifted through prices or waiting time information, thereby smoothing demand. Reservation systems, promotional marketing, and price increases all affect both timing and quantity of demand. For example, as we experience firsthand in the American Airlines case, adjusting price as time passes can help to better match demand with available capacity.

AGGREGATE PLANNING

Given the anticipated demand and overall capacity levels, management develops an aggregate plan for its resources, which is a formal document describing future production rates, workforce levels, and inventory holdings, if any. An aggregate plan is developed before detailed material and resource plans, as it provides the general direction of the organization over the longer term, and it is usually more accurate to develop a forecast for a group of product lines than for individual goods or services. Thus, the aggregated plan offers projections for several periods, often with a time horizon extending up to a year.

A manufacturing firm's aggregate plan, called a production plan, generally focuses on production rates and inventory holdings, whereas a service firm's aggregate plan, called a staffing plan, centers on staffing and other labor-related factors. Clearly, holding inventory may not be possible if the customer is the item being served within operations, and so a flexible workforce, material delivery, or facility configuration may be essential. For example, an auto repair center might carry a wide range of parts inventory and have quick distributor delivery and/or flexible employee skill sets to accommodate a diverse array of customer problems and vehicle models—all planned around offering same-day service. For both manufacturing and services, the plan must balance conflicting objectives involving customer service, workforce stability, cost, and profit (Ritzman, Krajewski, & Klassen, 2004).

The cases in this chapter address multiple challenges faced in developing and implementing an aggregate production plan. MacPherson Refrigeration must access the pros and cons of three different alternatives that collectively illustrate the three basic archetype plans available to many manufacturing firms: chase, level, and mixed plans. However, improvement is possible, and any plan must always address multiple objectives that transcend individual functional concerns. In contrast, Lamson Corp. requires you, as the operations manager, to develop, live with, and change a plan for the coming production season. Over the course of 12 decision periods, you are able to see the strengths and weaknesses of your evolving plan, as well as how well your corrective actions performed.

MATERIAL AND RESOURCE PLANNING

Materials requirements planning (MRP) and resource (i.e., capacity) planning collectively form the bridge between large-scale, aggregate plans and day-to-day scheduling and fulfillment of particular customer orders. Much of this planning is enabled by the concept of *dependent* demand, where the need for particular items and/or associated resources is exactly related to the production or delivery of a specific final service or end item.

For example, changing and balancing a new set of tires for an automobile at the repair center, described on the previous page, might require the use of a single service bay, 1.5 hours of a mechanic's time, four tires, and four valve stems. If a customer phones several days in advance to make a service appointment, the resources (i.e., mechanic and service bay) can be immediately booked for the needed time, and appropriate-sized tires can be ordered from a distributor. Scheduling the pickup of the used tires for recycling is also possible.

These concepts are developed further in the final two cases in this chapter. Martin Trailers considers both the complications surrounding the development of an aggregate production plan and its translation into materials and resources plans. However, the seasonal nature of the business, multiple product lines, and the necessity of hiring and laying off temporary workers compound the challenge. Illustrious Corp. moves down one level and focuses specifically on developing a detailed, though basic, MRP schedule for a product and a few of its component parts.

In summary, by considering the integration of demand management, aggregate planning, and material and resource planning, managers encounter operational elements that are foundational for the effective and efficient delivery of goods and services.

GREAVES BREWERY: BOTTLE REPLENISHMENT

Early in 2004, Alex Benson was trying to determine how many returnable beer bottles to purchase in the coming year. During 2003, the market had leveled off, and sales for 2004 were proving very challenging to predict. Moreover, there was a possibility that the bottle's design would change, in which case all bottle supplies would be scrapped. On one hand, Benson wished to be sure sufficient bottles were available to meet this year's sales, yet he also wanted to minimize year-end inventories. Benson needed to forecast beer sales, estimate bottle replenishment needs, and recommend how many bottles to purchase.

Learning objectives: application of demand forecasting methodologies, such as moving averages and exponential smoothing, modeling dependent demand, order timing, and order quantities.

YIELD MANAGEMENT AT AMERICAN AIRLINES

American Airlines is a widely cited leader in the development and implementation of yield (or revenue) management practices. This case is based on a training exercise used at American Airlines to introduce managers to their yield management system. You are given the responsibility for a single flight from Dallas–Fort Worth, Texas, to Miami, Florida, and are required to make a series of sequential booking decisions in real time in class. The objective of the exercise is to maximize total revenue for the flight, after taking into account no-shows and penalties.

Learning objectives: background theory underpinning yield management, key inputs needed and expected benefits, and linkages between demand forecasting and capacity utilization.

MacPherson Refrigeration Limited

Linda Metzler, newly appointed production planning manager, is drafting an aggregate production plan for the company's refrigerators, freezers, and air conditioners for the next year. She has considered three plans, each of which must be evaluated from both a quantitative and qualitative perspective. In the end, Metzler is unsure of whether she might be missing a better alternative.

Learning objectives: identify the key inputs to an aggregate production planning, explore the inputs from and uses by different functions within the organization, and have quantitative approaches for improving the planning process.

Lamson Corporation (R)

This business game puts you in the position of Mr. Marino, who must develop and execute a plan for the coming production season. Your group of 3 to 5 participants must make 12 scheduling decisions under conditions of demand uncertainty, with an opportunity to revise future period plans as the season progresses.

Learning objectives: aggregate production planning with uncertain demand, rescheduling, and managing trade-offs between capacity and inventory.

Martin Trailers Limited

Martin Trailers, which is experiencing rapid growth, produces a line of camping trailers, which have a pronounced seasonal sales pattern. Details for the previous year's planning process, staffing levels, production outputs, and costs are being reviewed by the owner, Kim Martin, with the objective of improving the management of materials in the year ahead. Based on this information, Martin is trying to assess how best to plan for the growth predicted for the coming year.

Learning objectives: develop an aggregate production plan in a highly uncertain, seasonal industry; understand the impact of productivity; and have a conceptual introduction to materials requirements planning.

Illustrious Corporation

This exercise briefly describes the assembly of a fictional product, X500. You must construct a structured bill of materials and an MRP plan for 10 weeks for a single product, X500, and seven components in four levels. Based on the results of this analysis, you must develop an action plan to deal with any shortcomings.

Learning objectives: define bill of materials, work through a basic materials requirements plan, and understand the managerial inputs for and implications of building and using an MRP system.

MANAGEMENT QUESTIONS ADDRESSED IN PLANNING AND CONTROL CHAPTER

1. What factors determine the customer demand? Do these factors interact?

2. How might demand forecasts be generated? What are the advantages and disadvantages of each approach?

3. What are the benefits of developing an aggregate plan, from the perspective of operations, marketing, finance, and human resources?

4. How are chase, level, and mixed production plans defined?

5. What are the cost and productivity implications of various approaches to production planning, including chase, level, and mixed production plans?

6. How are inventory and capacity related for production planning purposes?

7. What is a master production schedule (MPS)?

8. What is materials requirements planning (MRP)? How can MRP be used to help improve operations performance?

9. How are operations controlled? What could be done to make planning and control systems more responsive?

REFERENCES

Ritzman, L. P., Krajewski, L. J., & Klassen, R. D. (2004). *Foundations of operations management.* Toronto: Pearson Education.

Vollmann, T. E., Berry, W. L., & Whybark, D. C. (1992). *Manufacturing planning and control systems* (3rd ed.). Homewood, IL: Irwin.

GREAVES BREWERY: BOTTLE REPLENISHMENT

Prepared by Professors Jim Erskine, Michiel Leenders and Chris Piper

Copyright © 2004, Ivey Management Services

Version: (A) 2004-10-01

THE BOTTLE REPLENISHMENT DECISION

Early in 2004, Alex Benson, purchasing manager for Greaves Brewery, Trinidad, was trying to determine how many bottles to purchase in the coming year. During 2003, the market had levelled off, and 2004 sales predictions were difficult. On the one hand, Benson wanted to be sure sufficient bottles were available to supply 2004 sales levels, yet also wanted to minimize year-end inventories. Covered storage space for empty bottles was tight, and a bottle design change seemed possible in 2005 or 2006.

COMPANY BACKGROUND

Greaves Brewery was located in the southern Caribbean Island of Trinidad. Founded by John Greaves in 1924, the company had established an excellent reputation. Greaves beer had become a favorite with tourists, and as a result, a modest export business to the United States had started in 2000. In February 2004, sales reached the highest level in the company's history. However, in 2003, the sales increase had been well below the trend average (see Exhibits 1 and 2).

Four sales peaks occurred during the year: Carnival,[1] Christmas, Easter and Independence.[2] Carnival was the highest sales period but each peak caused the company to operate on tight schedules and Greaves hired more labor and scheduled extra shifts.

BREWING PROCESS

Beer brewing started with extraction of sugar from malt by an enzymic process. This sugar was then boiled with hops, producing a sterilized and concentrated solution. The resins extracted from the hops during boiling acted as a preservative and gave the beer its bitter flavor. The hops were then removed and the solution was cooled to optimum temperature $(10C)^3$ for bottom fermentation lasting seven days, during which time the yeast converted the sugar to alcohol and carbon dioxide. After fermentation, the beer was cooled to $(-1C)$ and stored for 10 days (during which time the yeast dropped out) and was then roughly filtered through diatomaceous earth. After 24 hours' storage, the mixture was put through a polish-filtration process. By this time, the beer had been artificially carbonated, ready for bottling. After bottling and case packing, the beer was stored in the finished goods warehouse ready for delivery to retail outlets.

SALES PROJECTIONS FOR 2004

Benson had difficulty forecasting sales for 2004, particularly because of the 2003 slump, government excise taxes and other factors such as the number of tourists and U.S. sales.

In November 1997, the government had placed an additional excise tax of $0.60[4] on each case of beer. The company passed this tax on to the consumer, raising the retail price from $9.90 to $10.50 per case, plus a bottle deposit of

Month \ Year	Jan	Feb	Mar	Apr	May	Jun	Jul	Aug	Sep	Oct	Nov	Dec	Total
1999	211	338	191	192	138	148	205	244	164	200	205	229	2,465
2000	244	403	213	244	153	195	231	327	337	247	234	438	3,266
2001	291	386	335	278	159	209	205	364	263	280	282	273	3,325
2002	323	478	327	327	211	342	288	374	304	337	304	357	3,972
2003	328	512	310	346	261	296	394	331	305	305	321	369	4,078
2004	342	535											

Exhibit 1   Monthly Sales January 1999 to February 2004 (in thousands of cases)

Source: Company files.

Year	Annual Sales	"Full Goods"	"Warehouse Empties"	"New Bottle Inventory"	"New Bottles Ordered in March"
1995	1,845	—	5.2	N/A	96.0
1996	2,088	11.7	10.4	N/A	70.0
1997	2,345	19.5	10.4	N/A	123.0
1998	2,876	18.2	18.2	N/A	71.0
1999	2,465	40.3	9.1	0.4	73.0
2000	3,266	23.4	7.8	0.7	66.0
2001	3,325	0.7	0.1	0.1	182.0
2002	3,972	23.4	29.9	16.9	195.0
2003	4,078	13.0	62.4	53.3	122.0
2004		28.6	33.8	38.0	To be decided

Exhibit 2   Sales and Inventory Position Ending February (in thousands of cases)

Source: Company files.

Note: New bottle inventory equals inventory at beginning of February, plus deliveries, minus breakage, minus transfers to warehouse.

$0.90. During 1999, sales slumped 13 per cent below the 1997 level. Again, in July 2001, a further tax of $0.90 per case was levied, and the company raised the retail price to $11.40. Sales growth slumped to a 2.0 per cent increase. In July 2003, another tax of $1.20 raised the retail price to $12.60 per case. Benson was reasonably certain that the government would not levy additional taxes during 2005, but wondered whether the full effect of the tax had been reflected in 2003 sales.

BEER BOTTLE PURCHASES

Benson had joined the company in 1999 as purchasing manager. Benson was responsible for all goods and materials used in the company's production processes, including the purchasing of new bottles and the scheduling of deliveries. Local bottle producers were equipped to manufacture only clear glass bottles. Greaves, therefore, had to import its standard 10 oz. dark amber, long-necked bottle. The company's brand name was etched in the glass, which eliminated replacing the label after each filling.

For many years, Greaves had imported bottles from a German manufacturer. Benson had continued buying from this supplier and had found the service excellent. The German company was one of the largest glass companies in Europe and Greaves' purchases represented less than two per cent of the supplier's 30 per cent export sales. The supplier allowed a minimum order quantity of 15,000 cases per year, with minimum deliveries of 5,000 cases per month. Prices were always quoted cost, insurance and freight (CIF). The CIF price included transportation and insurance, but excluded import duties and local handling. The CIF price gave the supplier the option of shipping the deliveries by any number of freighters in any one month. Ownership passed to Greaves as soon as the shipment left the factory. Quantity discounts were not given on orders below 300,000 cases. Benson had always found the German company's price to be competitive compared to quotes received from South American companies.

Benson was responsible for setting the delivery schedule, and the supplier was quite reliable in this regard. "If new bottle stocks are too low," Benson said, "it's my fault for not ordering in sufficient quantities or not scheduling properly." When the freighters arrived at the docks in Port-of-Spain, Greaves was responsible for wharfage charges plus transportation costs of the four-mile trip to the company premises. Wharfage charges varied based on space used and time held on the dock. Under normal circumstances, stock remained at the dock for three to four days while the company's broker cleared the goods through customs. When the shipment needed to be expedited, the broker could clear the papers in less than a day if they arrived ahead of the shipment. For transportation from the port to Greaves, Benson used a local delivery service that charged $15 per truckload of 400 cases.

To prepare for shipment, the supplier stacked the cartons on pallets and wrapped them with a plastic cover. The cover gave added protection in transit and during outside storage at Greaves. New bottle breakage prior to filling was less than one per cent per year.

EMPTY BOTTLE FLOW

Empty bottles were either returns from the trade or new bottles. The warehouse superintendent was responsible for control and storage of all returned bottles. Every day, truckloads of empty cases returned from retailers. The printed, corrugated and reusable cardboard cases used by Greaves were imported from the United States. Each case contained 24 bottles. The warehouse crew ensured that each case was in reusable condition and contained 24 unbroken bottles. They then loaded 40 cases of empties on each pallet and delivered the loaded pallets to the covered warehouse. The printed cartons could deteriorate when exposed to the weather, so empty returns received priority over new bottles for covered space. Normally, space in the warehouse was barely sufficient to store the returned empties.

Benson found it very difficult to determine the turnaround time for bottles (i.e., the elapsed time from being removed from storage through processing, finished goods, retailer, consumer, retailer again, and back to storage). The warehouse superintendent estimated turnaround time as being between two and three months. Empty bottle stocks were lowest just after Carnival, and did not build up to normal levels until late April or early May. One executive estimated that, every eight years, the total stock of in-service bottles was completely replaced with new bottles, but another thought that at least 80 per cent of the bottles were replaced in two to three years.

The warehouse superintendent sent empty bottles into the bottling shop as production demanded. When the empty stocks were low and returns not sufficient to meet production requirements, the warehouse superintendent requested new bottles from Benson. When Benson received the warehouse order, a five-person crew "picked" the new bottles. Picking consisted of removing the plastic cover from the pallets, unpacking the new bottles from their plain cardboard shipping containers, and repacking the bottles in the printed company cases. The men placed the cases on pallets again, and a forklift truck transported the pallets to the warehouse.

ORDER PROCEDURE

Each year at the end of February, Benson reviewed the stock control sheets showing empty bottle stocks, finished goods stocks, new bottle purchases and delivery records (see Exhibits 2, 3 and 4). Benson then compared these stocks with the sales trends and projected the new bottle order quantities for the next year. Benson had to order four months ahead to allow for supplier and transportation lead times. Cancellation charges were high, thus it was not practical to try to reduce the order once it had been placed. Increases were possible, however, provided minimum order quantities and lead time were met. It had been standard practice to order 75 per cent of yearly requirements in March followed by another order in August.

The situation would be different when Greaves requested a change in the bottle design.

Month \ Year	Jan	Feb	Mar	Apr	May	Jun	Jul	Aug	Sep	Oct	Nov	Dec	Total
2001	N/A	N/A	—	—	—	—	18	18	13	61	36	18	164
2002	17	—	—	—	—	—	8	20	15	26	58	18	162
2003	48	—	—	—	—	—	21	—	17	12	9	35	142
2004	—	28											

Exhibit 3   Monthly Deliveries of New Bottle Purchases (in thousands of cases)

Source: Company files.

Note: Deliveries over 20,000 cases occurred in two to four shipments.

Month \ Year	Jan	Feb	Mar	Apr	May	Jun	Jul	Aug	Sep	Oct	Nov	Dec	Total
2002	N/A	N/A	5	—	—	—	10	8	19	32	18	9	101
2003	32	16	—	—	—	—	27	16	18	—	—	18	127
2004	35	22											

Exhibit 4   Monthly New Bottle Warehouse Transfers (in thousands of cases)

Source: Company files.

In this case mold design costs increased, and the supplier would require a minimum of six months' notice. Benson was aware that there was a 50 per cent possibility the company would change the bottle design at the end of 2005, and if not, it certainly would change in 2006. At change-over time, all remaining old-type bottles, new or used, would be scrapped.

PAST BOTTLE PURCHASES

Prior to 1999, because of a tight working capital situation, the plant manager controlled expenditures for new bottles closely so that just enough were available to meet demand. In 2000, extra funds became available and this policy was relaxed. Because of an unexpectedly large increase in sales during 2001, however, Benson's

new bottle order of 66,000 cases in 2000 was barely large enough. By mid-February of 2001, the company ran out of finished goods and empty bottles in the warehouse. Bottling operations were cut back in the plant, and capacity depended on the speed at which daily empty returns were washed. Delivery salesmen waited for the finished goods to load their trucks. February sales suffered with this bottle shortage crisis and were 17,000 cases less than in February of 2000. In 2001, Benson made sure sufficient bottles would be available and ordered 182,000 cases; in 2002, 195,000 cases were ordered. Empty bottle stocks at the end of February 2003 were the highest in the company's history, and Benson reduced the 2003 order to 122,000 cases.

Benson always met with the plant manager and the sales manager before placing the bottle order. The forecast problem had already been informally discussed with both, and neither was confident in Benson's predictions. Benson wanted to suggest a buying strategy that made sense to both production and sales, but could not delay ordering past March 4, 2004. Benson had, therefore, requested a meeting with both executives for March 2, 2004. Regardless of the uncertainties, the proposals would have to be ready by then.

NOTES

1. Carnival took place two days before Ash Wednesday, which normally occurred during February or occasionally in early March.

2. Trinidad gained its Independence from Britain on August 31, 1962.

3. The temperatures in Fahrenheit corresponding to Celsius temperatures of 10C and −1C are about 50F and 30F, respectively.

4. All monies in US$ unless otherwise specified.

YIELD MANAGEMENT AT AMERICAN AIRLINES

*Prepared by Professors P. Fraser Johnson,
Robert Klassen and John Haywood-Farmer*

Version: (B) 2002-01-29

AMERICAN AIRLINES

One of the largest passenger airlines in the world, with sales of $15 billion in 1998, American Airlines provided scheduled service to destinations throughout North America, the Caribbean, Latin America, Europe and the Pacific. Each day the company's employees processed more than 340,000 reservation calls, and operated over 2,200 flights carrying approximately 200,000 passengers.

Faced with an expanding service network, a costly fleet of aircraft and an increasingly diverse group of customers, American Airlines began research in the 1960s on how to improve its reservation system to ensure greater capacity utilization. Natural seasonal fluctuations in demand could be partially offset by altering ticket prices. Moreover, some customer groups could plan trips well in advance, while others often booked days, or even hours, before a flight. Combined, management recognized that both supply and demand could be actively changed to alter dynamic competitive markets and to improve business performance.

American Airlines' yield management system, sometimes termed revenue management, attempted simultaneously to combine demand management, by changing fares, and supply management, by controlling availability. It took into account aircraft capacity, historical customer bookings, pricing, cancellations and no-show rates, costs of oversales and costs of spoilage. Its purpose was to fill seats on each flight with the highest paying passengers by determining the optimal mix of fares to sell on each flight to obtain the highest possible revenue. By the late 1990s, the company, through its Sabre division, used its expertise in a variety of service industries, such as hotels and car rental agencies.

The following exercise is based on the training program used at American Airlines to introduce managers to their yield management system.

HOW TO PLAY THE EXERCISE

In the Yield Management Exercise, your team will take on the role of a yield management analyst responsible for a single flight from Dallas-Fort Worth, Texas (DFW) to Miami, Florida (MIA). Over the course of the exercise, you will be making the actual booking decisions for the flight as customers make travel inquiries and decisions. Your objective is to maximize the flight's total revenue, taking into account penalties. Under normal circumstances, these decisions are made using American Airlines' yield management system.

The objective of the exercise is to maximize revenue on your flight (prorated fares paid, less spoilage or oversales penalties). You are scheduled to use a Super 80 jet for your flight, with a capacity of 125 seats.

Over the course of the exercise, you will be given 20 to 25 booking opportunities. To simplify this exercise, all tickets are fully refundable. Before each booking opportunity, you will have a chance to set a new *bid price*. After all groups have set their bids for the next booking, the instructor will announce the actual passenger booking price and the number of passengers (pax) for the booking.

Your bid price is used only to trigger accepting or rejecting the booking. If the passenger-requested booking price (*prorated fare*) for the DFW to MIA flight is *equal to or greater than your bid price,* you must accept the entire number of passengers at the prorated fare requested by the customer.

For example, if your bid price is $100 and you receive a request for booking for 10 passengers with a prorated fare of $110, then you must take all 10 passengers at a price of $110. If the prorated fare is less than $100, then you cannot accept the booking. Consequently, final revenue is calculated based on the prorated fare, not on your bid price.

You are responsible for setting the bid price before each bidding opportunity through whatever means you wish. Historically, fares for this flight have ranged from $170 to $750 per seat. As you might expect, there is far more demand at the lower end of the price range than the top end. As the flight starts to fill up, you normally increase your bid price to hold for more lucrative bookings. If the flight is lightly booked, you can lower your bid price to allow for more bookings. Exhibit 1 shows average historical data for the Dallas to Miami flight.

The final part of the exercise is the day of departure (*DOD*). Not every passenger that books a flight will show up on the day of departure.

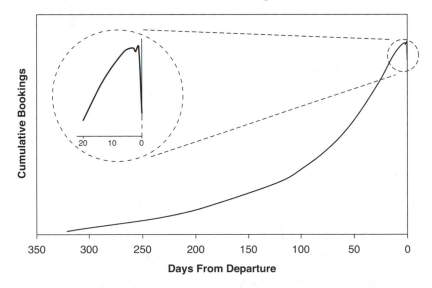

Historical Cumlative Booking: DFW-MIA

Exhibit 1   Historical Cumulative Bookings: Dallas-Fort Worth (DFW) to Miami (MIA)

Historically, the no-show rate for local passengers has been 15 per cent. This figure has been 20 per cent for flow passengers (those with connecting flights). At the conclusion of the exercise, the instructor will identify the passengers that arrive for the flight, after which you will be asked to calculate your total revenues and penalties for this Dallas to Miami flight. If passengers fail to show up for the flight, no revenue is obtained for their booking.

Costs Involved

Two additional costs are normally incurred: spoilage and oversales. The penalty for unsold seats (spoilage) is $150 each, which is an estimate of the opportunity cost of the lost contribution on this flight as well as on connecting flights from flow passengers.

Penalties for oversales escalate as the number of disappointed passengers increases. If five or fewer passengers are oversold, the cost is $100 per passenger. Costs increase to $250 per passenger for six to 10 oversales, and to $500 per passenger for 11 or more oversales. All oversales penalty costs are calculated on a per seat basis (e.g., for seven oversales the penalty would be $1,750). These amounts are to cover out-of-pocket costs for passengers and subsequent rebooking, as well as the inevitable "badwill" incurred when a passenger is disappointed.

A glossary of terms that you might find useful is provided in Exhibit 2 and a list of airport codes is provided in Exhibit 3. A Yield Management Exercise Score Sheet to be used by you to keep track of your progress during the exercise is provided in Exhibit 4.

Bid Price: The minimum acceptable fare for a reservation to be accommodated on a flight. The prorated fare value must equal or exceed the bid price in order for the passenger-requested booking to be accepted.

Cancellation: A passenger who makes a booking for a flight and later cancels the reservation (before departure).

Capacity: The physical number of seats on the aircraft. Coach capacity is often referred to as Y capacity (as Y is the code for the coach cabin).

DOD: Day of departure.

Fare: The price the customer pays for the flight. Typically, the fare refers to the ticket price only, and does not include taxes, departure fees or passenger facility charges (PFCs).

Flow Passenger: A passenger travelling behind or beyond the city pair. In this example, boarding in DEN, connecting in DFW and then deplaning in MIA. Or, boarding in DFW, connecting in MIA and then travelling to GRU.

Itinerary: The complete trip taken by a passenger, including all flights.

Local Passenger: A passenger travelling only between the city pair. In this example, a passenger boarding in DFW and deplaning in MIA.

Market: Any given pair of cities between which a flight operates.

No Show: A passenger who does not show up for the flight in which he or she was holding a reservation.

No Show Factor: The percentage of passengers who do not show up for their flight as a percentage of total reservations at departure.

Oversales: Occurs when the airline has to deny boarding to a revenue passenger because too many seats have been sold for the flight. This does not include revenue passengers booked on earlier/later flights but standing by for a different flight.

Pax: Passenger(s).

Prorated Fare: The portion of the fare for a complete itinerary that is attributed to a particular flight within the itinerary.

Spoilage: Occurs when a flight departs with empty seats and **at any point prior to departure**, the flight was closed for sale or a booking was turned away. This would indicate sub-optimal yield management of the flight.

Voucher: Also known as denied boarding compensation. This is a future travel credit in some amount that is compensation for having been an oversale on a previous flight.

Exhibit 2   Glossary of Terms

START OF EXERCISE

The only decision that you will be asked to make during the class is setting the bid price for each booking opportunity. In preparation for the class, you should develop a bid-price strategy for the exercise and decide on your opening bid price.

ABQ	—	Albuquerque, New Mexico
ANU	—	Antigua, West Indies
AUS	—	Austin, Texas
DEN	—	Denver, Colorado
DFW	—	Dallas/Fort Worth, Texas
EYW	—	Key West, Florida
GIG	—	Rio de Janeiro, Brazil
GRU	—	Sao Paulo, Brazil
HNL	—	Honolulu, Hawaii
LAS	—	Las Vegas, Nevada
LAX	—	Los Angeles, California
LIM	—	Lima, Peru
MAD	—	Madrid, Spain
MCO	—	Orlando, Florida
MIA	—	Miami, Florida
MSP	—	Minneapolis/St. Paul, Minnesota
NAS	—	Nassau, Bahamas
NRT	—	Tokyo, Japan (Narita Airport)
PDX	—	Portland, Oregon
SCL	—	Santiago, Chile
SFO	—	San Francisco, California
SJO	—	San Jose, Costa Rica
SJU	—	San Juan, Puerto Rico
TUS	—	Tucson, Arizona
YYC	—	Calgary, Alberta
YYZ	—	Toronto

Exhibit 3   Airport Codes Used in Exercise

Bid Price?	Booking Code	Prorated Fare	Pax	Running Total Pax		DOD Show-Up	Revenue Value
_____	_____	_____	_____	_____		_____	_____
_____	_____	_____	_____	_____		_____	_____
_____	_____	_____	_____	_____		_____	_____
_____	_____	_____	_____	_____		_____	_____
_____	_____	_____	_____	_____		_____	_____
_____	_____	_____	_____	_____		_____	_____
_____	_____	_____	_____	_____		_____	_____
_____	_____	_____	_____	_____		_____	_____
_____	_____	_____	_____	_____		_____	_____
_____	_____	_____	_____	_____		_____	_____
_____	_____	_____	_____	_____		_____	_____
_____	_____	_____	_____	_____		_____	_____
_____	_____	_____	_____	_____		_____	_____
_____	_____	_____	_____	_____		_____	_____
_____	_____	_____	_____	_____		_____	_____
_____	_____	_____	_____	_____		_____	_____
_____	_____	_____	_____	_____		_____	_____
_____	_____	_____	_____	_____		_____	_____
_____	_____	_____	_____	_____		_____	_____
_____	_____	_____	_____	_____		_____	_____
_____	_____	_____	_____	_____		_____	_____
_____	_____	_____	_____	_____		_____	_____
_____	_____	_____	_____	_____		_____	_____
_____	_____	_____	_____	_____		_____	_____
_____	_____	_____	_____	_____		_____	_____
_____	_____	_____	_____	_____		_____	_____

Total Booked Passengers: _____

Enter total in "Total DOD Pax" at lower left — Enter total in "Total Revenue" below

Total DOD Pax: _____

Final Capacity: _____

Oversales? _____ × penalty _____

or

Spoilage? _____ × $150/pax _____

Total Revenue: _____

⟶ _____

Total Flight _____

Exhibit 4 Yield Management Exercise Score Sheet

MacPherson Refrigeration Limited

*Prepared by Bill Rankin under the
supervision of Professor John Haywood-Farmer*

Version: (A) 2002-12-16

In October, Linda Metzler, newly appointed production planning manager of MacPherson Refrigeration Limited (MRL) of Stratford, Ontario, was formulating the production plan for the year beginning on January 1. She had to submit the plan to the plant's general manager by the end of the month.

Background

MRL had sales of about $28.5 million. The company began in Stratford almost 30 years ago, specializing in commercial refrigeration. Ten years ago the company opened a new 300,000 square foot plant in Stratford and diversified into consumer refrigeration. Subsequently, MRL added air conditioners to its freezer and refrigerator lines. The company sold its Hercules brand appliances through independent furniture and appliance stores in southern Ontario.

The Stratford Plant

In the past 20 years, manufacturing efficiency at the plant had increased dramatically through changes in both process design and assembly technology. During this time, annual output per worker had increased from about 240 to 450 appliances; it was expected to be about 480 appliances next year. Although the Canadian market was too small to allow the productivity levels of American appliance manufacturers, MRL was considered to be relatively efficient by Canadian standards.

The Planning Process

Each year in September the marketing and sales department produced a forecast of appliances by month for the next year. The production planning department used these forecasts to plan production for the next year. The first step in the planning process was to construct an aggregate production plan. This plan consisted of planned gross production by month for the year and did not indicate numbers of specific appliance types, sizes, or models to be made each month but, as the name indicates, was an aggregate. Linda Metzler's task in October was to construct this aggregate plan. As the production periods approached later in the year, master production plans would be formulated which would be specific regarding appliance type, model number, etc.

Exhibits 1–4 present the September forecast showing the expected seasonal fluctuations and the aggregate number of appliances to be shipped each month. Linda knew that, although there would be significant variation of specific appliance types within each month, each type of appliance required roughly similar materials and labour resources. Thus, for aggregate planning purposes, the number of appliances to be shipped would be sufficient.

The Aggregate Plan

In preparation for her decision, Linda gathered the following information:

1. The Stratford plant had the physical capacity to make only 13,000 appliances per month.

(Text continues on page 155)

Month	Dec	Jan	Feb	Mar	Apr	May	June	July	Aug	Sept	Oct	Nov	Dec	Totals
Production Plan														
Shipment Forecast		4,400	4,400	6,000	8,000	6,600	11,800	13,000	11,200	10,800	7,600	6,000	5,600	95,400
Production Plan		8,440	8,440	8,440	8,440	8,440	8,440	8,440	8,440	8,440	8,440	8,440	8,440	101,280
Shipments		4,400	4,400	6,000	8,000	6,600	11,800	13,000	11,200	10,800	7,600	6,000	5,600	95,400
Inventory[1]	240	4,280	8,320	10,760	11,200	13,040	9,680	5,120	2,360	0	840	3,280	6,120	75,000
Extraordinary Labour Costs														
Number of Workers[2]	160	211	211	211	211	211	211	211	211	211	211	211	211	2,532
Hirings		51	0	0	0	0	0	0	0	0	0	0	0	51
Layoffs		0	0	0	0	0	0	0	0	0	0	0	0	0
Worker Months Overtime		0	0	0	0	0	0	0	0	0	0	0	0	0

Cost of Alternative 1

Hiring Costs	$51 \times 1,800 =$	91,800
Layoff Costs	$0 \times =$	0
Inventory Holding Costs	$75,000 \times 8 =$	600,000
Labour Costs		
Regular	$2,532 \times 2,400 =$	6,076,800
Overtime	$0 \times =$	0
Total Costs		**$6,768,600**

Exhibit 1   Level Production to Meet Peak Demand

1. On December 31, finished goods inventory was predicted to be 240 units.

2. On December 31, the workforce was predicted to be 160 workers.

Month	Dec	Jan	Feb	Mar	Apr	May	June	July	Aug	Sept	Oct	Nov	Dec	Totals
Production Plan														
Shipment Forecast		4,400	4,400	6,000	8,000	6,600	11,800	13,000	11,200	10,800	7,600	6,000	5,600	95,400
Production Plan		4,160	4,400	6,000	8,000	6,600	11,800	13,000	11,200	10,800	7,600	6,000	5,600	95,160
Shipments		4,400	4,400	6,000	8,000	6,600	11,800	13,000	11,200	10,800	7,600	6,000	5,600	95,400
Inventory[1]	240	0	0	0	0	0	0	0	0	0	0	0	0	0
Extraordinary Labour Costs														
Number of Workers[2]	160	199	199	199	199	199	199	199	199	199	199	199	199	2,388
Hirings		39	0	0	0	0	0	0	0	0	0	0	0	39
Layoffs		0	0	0	0	0	0	0	0	0	0	0	0	0
Worker Months Overtime		0	0	0	1	0	96	126	81	71	0	0	0	375

Cost of Alternative 2

Hiring Costs	$39 \times 1,800$	=	70,200
Layoff Costs	0	=	0
Inventory Holding Costs	0	=	0
Labour Costs			
Regular	$2,388 \times 2,400$	=	5,731,200
Overtime	$375 \times 3,300$	=	1,237,500
Total Costs			**$7,038,900**

Exhibit 2   Chase Production Plan With Constant Workforce and Overtime

1. On December 31, finished goods inventory was predicted to be 240 units.

2. On December 31, the workforce was predicted to be 160 workers.

Month	Dec	Jan	Feb	Mar	Apr	May	June	July	Aug	Sept	Oct	Nov	Dec	Totals
Production Plan														
Shipment Forecast		4,400	4,400	6,000	8,000	6,600	11,800	13,000	11,200	10,800	7,600	6,000	5,600	95,400
Production Plan		4,160	4,400	6,000	8,000	6,600	11,800	13,000	11,200	10,800	7,600	6,000	5,600	95,160
Shipments		4,400	4,400	6,000	8,000	6,600	11,800	13,000	11,200	10,800	7,600	6,000	5,600	95,400
Inventory[1]	240	0	0	0	0	0	0	0	0	0	0	0	0	0
Extraordinary Labour Costs														
Number of Workers[2]	160	104	110	150	200	165	295	325	280	270	190	150	140	2,379
Hirings		0	6	40	50	0	130	30	0	0	0	0	0	256
Layoffs		56	0	0	0	35	0	0	45	10	80	40	10	276
Worker Months Overtime		0	0	0	0	0	0	0	0	0	0	0	0	0

Cost of Alternative 3

Hiring Costs	$256 \times 1,800 =$	460,800
Layoff Costs	$276 \times 1,200 =$	331,200
Inventory Holding Costs	$0 =$	0
Labour Costs		
Regular	$2,379 \times 2,400 =$	5,709,600
Overtime	$0 =$	0
Total Costs		**$6,501,600**

Exhibit 3   Chase Production Plan With Varying Workforce

1. On December 31, finished goods inventory was predicted to be 240 units.

2. On December 31, the workforce was predicted to be 160 workers.

Month	Dec	Jan	Feb	Mar	Apr	May	June	July	Aug	Sept	Oct	Nov	Dec	Totals
Production Plan														
Shipment Forecast		4,400	4,400	6,000	8,000	6,600	11,800	13,000	11,200	10,800	7,600	6,000	5,600	95,400
Production Plan		—	—	—	—	—	—	—	—	—	—	—	—	—
Shipments		—	—	—	—	—	—	—	—	—	—	—	—	—
Inventory[1]	240	—	—	—	—	—	—	—	—	—	—	—	—	
Extraordinary Labour Costs														
Number of Workers[2]	160	—	—	—	—	—	—	—	—	—	—	—	—	
Hirings		—	—	—	—	—	—	—	—	—	—	—	—	
Layoffs		—	—	—	—	—	—	—	—	—	—	—	—	
Worker Months Overtime		—	—	—	—	—	—	—	—	—	—	—	—	

Cost of Alternative 4

Hiring Costs	____	× 1,800 =	____
Layoff Costs	____	× 1,200 =	____
Inventory Holding Costs	____	× 8 =	____
Labour Costs			
Regular	____	× 2,400 =	____
Overtime	____	× 3,300 =	____
Total Costs			$ ____

Exhibit 4   Aggregate Plan for MacPherson Refrigeration Limited

1. On December 31, finished goods inventory was predicted to be 240 units.

2. On December 31, the workforce was predicted to be 160 workers.

2. On October 1, MRL employed 160 hourly paid unionized production workers. Their two year contract, signed in February of last year, called for an increase of $0.75 per hour effective next January 1, bringing the average hourly rate to $10.50. With fringe benefits, the monthly cost to MRL would be about $2,400 per worker. Under the agreement, overtime was 1.5 times the regular hourly rate but, because not all fringes were affected, a worker-month of overtime cost about $3,300. The standard work week was 40 hours. The aggregate plan in effect until December 31 called for a total production workforce of 160 at that time.

3. The personnel department estimated that hiring, training, and related expenses would amount to $1,800 per worker. It also estimated that severance and other layoff expenses would cost a total of $1,200 per worker.

4. The accounting department predicted that it would cost about $8 to hold an appliance in inventory for a month during the next year. Raw materials were readily available from regional sources on short notice. The current aggregate plan, supported by marketing's most recent revised forecasts and the master production schedule, predicted an inventory of 240 finished units on December 31.

5. Although MRL manufactured some parts and subassemblies, the plant was primarily a final assembly operation with a throughput time of about three days. The company used an MRP-based planning system. For aggregate planning purposes, management had found that it was adequate to assume that all worker hours scheduled in a particular month would contribute directly to output in the same month. Similarly, they had learned from experience that they would not have to consider any special allowances for learning.

6. There appeared to be three basic tools available to meet demand fluctuations, each of which involved both quantitative and qualitative tradeoffs:

   - building inventory to meet peaks
   - using overtime
   - hiring and laying off workers

THE ALTERNATIVES

Linda identified three alternatives the company could follow to meet forecasted demand:

1. The production level and the workforce could be held constant throughout the year at a level sufficient to meet the peak demand period. In periods of low demand inventory would be accumulated and would be drawn down during peak demand periods. Linda was attracted by the protection this plan offered against unforeseen demand changes. This plan is one example of a level strategy and is shown in Exhibit 1.

2. The production level could vary to meet demand with a constant workforce by the use of overtime in peak months and restricted output in slow months; it is an example of a chase strategy and is shown in Exhibit 2. The workforce would be held at just the number to meet average monthly requirements. MRL would incur no inventory carrying costs with such a scheme. However, Linda wondered if excessive overtime might lead to lower efficiency, or if restricted production might promote poor work habits and low morale.

3. Some of these potential problems could be overcome by a strategy that met demand by varying workforce levels. Linda's calculations showed this to be the cheapest of the three alternatives (see Exhibit 3). However, she was well aware that union relations and employee morale could be adversely affected by frequent layoffs. As well, hiring and training new employees brought their own headaches, especially in a limited labour market such as existed in Stratford.

THE DECISION

Linda knew that these three very different plans were by no means the only feasible ones available. She realized that her decision on an aggregate plan would involve both quantitative and qualitative trade-offs. One thought nagged in the back of her mind: no matter which plan she chose, how would she know if a better one existed? She decided to start by filling out her blank form (Exhibit 4) one more time.

LAMSON CORPORATION (R)

Prepared by Professor M. R. Leenders

Version: (A) 2001-07-20

In this game you will have the chance to try your skill at inventory and operations planning using the information similar in type to that available to Mr. Marino, the operations manager of Lamson Corporation, a large multi-plant manufacturer of sewer pipes. Every two weeks in the summer sales period, Mr. Marino had to decide how many tiles of each type and size should be produced during the coming two weeks. In doing this planning, he took into account sales trends, the time of the year, the capacity of Lamson's tile making machinery, the stock of the various sizes of tiles on hand, the cost of overtime production and the cost of missed deliveries. In this game you will be able to make similar decisions, although the game will be a simplified version of the actual situation. The most important feature of this simplification is that you will be dealing with only two sizes of sewer tile—the 18" diameter size and the 36" diameter size. Mr. Marino, in contrast, had to decide on production levels for 13 different sizes of tile and which plants would produce what mix.

SALES PATTERNS

Company sales, and industry sales in general, were very much influenced by general economic and seasonal factors. Since weather affected tile laying conditions and the number of construction starts, sales of sewer tiles exhibited a yearly sales trend of the following general shape (Figure 1). Sales were low for six months, from October to April 1, and rose rapidly in the spring to a summer peak and then tapered off again. About one-third of all annual sales were made in the two middle months of the year, while about three-quarters were made in the summer sales season. However, there was not necessarily a smooth rise and fall in

sales in any particular year. The curve shown is only the average of the experiences of many years. In any given year, biweekly sales might vary ± 25 per cent from levels they would assume if a smooth sales curve existed. Last year, the maximum number of 18" tiles sold in any two week period between April and October was 4,500.

The similar figure for 36" tiles was 2,000. Major fluctuations in annual sales and mix levels were caused by economic conditions.

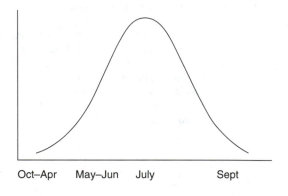

| Oct–Apr | May–Jun | July | Sept |

Figure 1

In the game you are about to play, Period 1 refers to the first two weeks in April. Thus, company sales are just leaving the low part of the annual swing. The game culminates in Period 12, the last two weeks in September, when sales are reentering the low winter period. Between Periods 1 and 12, sales follow the general shape of the curve shown in Figure 1.

All sales made by Lamson are booked for delivery within the period being considered.

That is, there is no advance ordering. Mr. Marino has no idea what the sales for any coming period will be other than from judgement of the sales level of prior periods and from consideration of the general shape of the sales trend curve.

PRODUCTION CONSTRAINTS

The most popular sizes of concrete tile sold by Lamson were the 18" diameter and the 36" diameter sizes. Mr. Marino had found that together, these tiles accounted for a large part of tile sales; in fact, roughly one half of each period's production was devoted to one or other of these sizes. The other half of each period's production was used to manufacture the other sizes of tile produced by Lamson. In order to simplify the game, it has been assumed that Mr. Marino will continue to schedule the production of the less popular 11 tile sizes and that he will use half the production time each period for these sizes. Each participating group will be asked to schedule the number of 18" and 36" tiles to be produced during each period. Thus, each group will, in fact, schedule the production of a summer season's supply of 18" and 36" diameter tiles.

There were nine possible volume combinations of 18" and 36" tiles. Four of these output values were based on the normal capacity output of the plants. The other five values represented the maximum output possible at Lamson, which required 50 per cent overtime.

The nine production levels possible for 18" and 36" tiles in each two week period are shown in Exhibit 1.

COST INVOLVED

Inventory Costs

In deciding on production alternatives, Mr. Marino bore in mind several costs which he knew were fairly accurate. For instance, storage costs of an 18" tile for one period were an average of $2. This amount took into account interest on tied-up capital, insurance against breakage, and direct handling expense. The inventory carrying costs of each 36" tile were higher and averaged $6 per tile per period. Mr. Marino had found that, over the period of a season, inventory carrying charges could be reasonably calculated on the basis of inventory on hand at the end of each period.

	Normal Capacity			50% Overtime	
Option	18" Tiles	36" Tiles	Option	18" Tiles	36" Tiles
1	6,000	0	5	9,000	0
2	4,000	600	6	7,000	600
3	2,000	1,200	7	5,000	1,200
4	0	1,800	8	3,000	1,800
			9	1,000	2,400

Exhibit 1   The Nine Possible Production Choices Open to Mr. Marino Each Two Week Period

Please notice that trade-offs are involved in choosing a production level for a period. If the number of 18" tiles to be produced is increased, the number of 36" tiles that can be produced will necessarily decrease unless overtime is used.

Stock-Out Costs

Stock-out costs also had to be considered by Mr. Marino. A stock-out occurred whenever sales in a particular period could not be filled because there were insufficient tiles of the required diameter on hand or in production during that period. For instance, if 100 tiles were on hand at the beginning of a period, 2,000 tiles were produced during the period, and sales during the period totalled 2,200, then a stock-out of 100 tiles would occur. When such a stock-out occurred, there was a chance that a future customer of Lamson would be lost. Furthermore, Lamson lost the profit potential on the missed order. Mr. Marino had assessed the risks and costs involved and thought that a stock-out cost Lamson $20 for each 18" tile and $60 for each 36" tile. These figures took into account the fact that the larger the number of tiles that could not be delivered, the more apt the customer was to take future business elsewhere. Stock-outs could not be made up in subsequent periods. If a stock-out occurred, the sale was lost forever to the firm and the above costs were incurred.

Overtime Costs

If overtime was used in any period, a fixed charge of $20,000 was incurred, mainly to pay extra wages to the employees. The amount was fixed because the employees had been guaranteed a minimum amount each period overtime was used.

How to Play the Game

In the actual conduct of this game, teams will make the production decisions normally made by Mr. Marino regarding the 18" and 36" diameter tiles. Before each period, each team will be required to decide on the production level that will be used in the plant. This decision will be made by the team by whatever means it chooses. Thus, a prediction from a plot of past period sales might be used by some teams, a pure guess by others. In making the decision, teams should consider both the possibilities of future sales and the inventories of tiles now on hand.

After each team has decided on the production level it desires for the coming period, the instructor will announce the actual sales levels for the period. Given this information, teams will then be able to calculate inventory on hand, and inventory, stock-out, and overtime costs. These costs will be added to a total period cost which will then be added to a cumulative total of costs.

The objective of the game is to keep the total costs incurred over 12 periods to a minimum. This objective means that teams will have to decide whether it would be cheaper in the long run to incur overtime costs, inventory carrying costs, or stock-out costs. It is impossible to avoid all three. At the end of Period 12 the game will be stopped and final costs calculated. Your team's results will be compared to those of other teams. During subsequent discussions the merits of various inventory and production policies can be evaluated. Teams will probably find it advantageous to split the work of making sales estimates, calculating costs and keeping records among the various members. To make the keeping of results easier for all teams, Exhibit 2 will be used.

The Early Season

Each team member should carefully trace the steps Mr. Marino followed already this year to understand fully all of the steps involved in playing and recording the game.

Mr. Marino has already used the form to record the operating results of the two periods prior to the first period for which you will be required to decide the production level (Period 1). Lamson started Period –1 with 400 – 18" tiles (Column B) and 100 – 36" tiles on hand (Column K). Because he knew that a special, large order for 18" tiles would be placed in Period –1 (a most unusual size of order at this time of year), Mr. Marino decided to go to overtime and to produce 7,000 – 18" tiles (Column A) and 600 – 36" tiles (Column J). Thus, 7,400 – 18" tiles (Column C) and 700 – 36" tiles (Column L) were available for sales during Period –1.

In actual fact, the special order was smaller than Mr. Marino had anticipated and total sales

Period	Month	A Number Produced	B Stock on Hand at Start of Period	C Total Available for Sale C = A + B	D Sales in Period	E Inventory Remaining at End of Period E = C − D (Minimum = 0)	F Inventory Carrying Cost $2 × E	G Number of Stock-Outs G = D − C if Greater Than 0	H Stock-Out Cost H = $20 × G	J Number Produced	K Stock on Hand at Start of Period	L Total Available for Sale L = J + K	M Sales in Period	N Inventory Remaining at End of Period N = L − M (Minimum 0)	O Inventory Carrying Cost $6 × N	P Number of Stock-Outs P = M − L if Greater Than 0	Q Stock-Out Cost Q = $60 × P	R Total Inventory Cost R = F + O	S Total Stock-Out Cost S = H + Q	T Overtime Cost $20,000 (if Used)	U Total Period Cost U = R + S + T	V Cumulative Total to Date
							18" Tiles						36" Tiles							Totals		
−1	Mar	7,000	400	7,400	6,000	1,400	2,800	0	0	600	100	700	800	0	0	100	6,000	2,800	6,000	20,000	28,800	(28,800)
0	Mar	2,000	1,400	3,400	1,400	2,000	4,000	0	0	1,200	0	1,200	500	700	4,200	0	0	8,200	0	0	8,200	(37,000)
1	Apr																					
2	Apr																					
3	May																					
4	May																					
5	Jun																					
6	Jun																					
7	Jul																					
8	Jul																					
9	Aug																					
10	Aug																					
11	Sep																					
12	Sep																					
Total																						

Exhibit 2

159

turned out to be 6,000 for the 18" tiles (Column D) and 800 for the 36" tiles (Column M). Because 18" inventory available for sale exceeded sales, Mr. Marino entered 1,400 in Column E to show there was inventory remaining at the end of the period, and then entered zero in Column G to show that there had been no stock-out of 18" tiles on hand at the end of the period. He then calculated the carrying cost in Column F ($2 × 1,400 = $2,800) and the stock-out cost in Column H ($20 × 0 = $0). Column H shows that no stock-out cost was incurred. Because demand for the 36" tiles (800) exceeded the total available for sale (700), a stock-out of 100 occurred and no tiles were left in inventory at the end of Period −1. To show this occurrence, zero was entered in Column N and 100 was entered in Column P while a stock-out cost of $6,000 was entered in Column Q ($60 × 100 = $6,000).

The total inventory carrying cost was entered in Column R ($2,800 + 0 = $2,800) and the total stock-out cost in Column S (0 + $6,000 = $6,000). $20,000 was entered in Column T because overtime was used. The total period cost was calculated to be $2,800 + $6,000 + $20,000 = $28,800. This amount was then entered in Column U and also Column V.

Lamson began Period 0 with 1,400 − 18" tiles (Column B) and zero 36" tiles on hand (Column K). These totals had been brought down from Columns E and N respectively of Period −1. At the beginning of Period 0, Mr. Marino elected to produce 2,000 − 18" tiles (Column A) and 1,200 − 36" tiles (Column J). No overtime was called for. Thus there were 3,400 − 18" tiles (Column C) and 1,200 − 36" tiles (Column L) available for sale in Period 0.

In Period 0, sales totalled 1,400 − 18" tiles (Column D) and 500 − 36" tiles (Column M). Thus the inventory remaining at the end of the period was 2,000 − 18" tiles (Column E) and 700 − 36" tiles (Column N). There were zero stock-outs (Columns G and P). Inventory carrying costs were computed to be $2 × 2,000 = $4,000 (Column F) and $6 × 70 = $4,200 (Column O). There were no stock-out costs

(Column H and Q) because stock-outs equalled zero in this period.

The total inventory carrying cost for Period 0 was $8,200 ($4,000 + $4,200). This amount was entered in Column R, while zero was entered in Column S since there had been no stock-outs in the period. There was no overtime used, and consequently a zero was entered in Column T. The Column U entry shows that the total period costs incurred were $8,200. The Column V entry was $28,800 + $8,200 = $37,000. Since your team did not incur these costs, we will wipe them off the slate and have you start with a zero cost at the beginning of Period 1 in Column V.

A FEW OPERATING RULES DURING THE GAME

1. The only production combinations your team may choose are those given in Exhibit 1.

2. If your team makes a calculation mistake, a penalty of $25,000 will be assessed and all figures will be corrected.

3. If your team is unable to reach a decision by the end called for by the instructor, it will automatically be decided that you produce 2,000−18" tiles and 1,200−36" tiles.

4. Normally, at the beginning of the game, each team will have approximately 10 minutes to make a decision. This time will decrease as the game progresses.

START OF GAME

The game proper starts in Period 1. At the beginning of the game there are 2,000 − 18" tiles on hand (brought down from Column E of Period 0) and 700 − 36" tiles on hand (brought down from Column N of Period 0). It is now up to each team to pick the production level most appropriate for Period 1 and thus start the playing of the game.

MARTIN TRAILERS LIMITED

Prepared by Professor Chris Piper

 Version: (A) 2001-06-01

In early July, Kim Martin was reviewing Martin Trailers' production performance. Although sales this year had grown by 40 per cent, Martin wondered what could be done to improve the management of operations.

MARKETING

Trailers were sold under both the Martin label and under the private labels of major customers such as department stores. Private label trailers were ordered in November for delivery in January through June. Also, in November a one-year sales forecast was prepared by Martin. Last year's orders are shown in Exhibit 1, according to the month in which shipment was requested. The selling season for the Martin brand began with a trailer show in early February, at which each Martin dealer estimated how many of each model trailer could be sold. Martin then prepared a schedule of the expected number of each trailer model that would be required from the plant each month. This schedule was given to the production manager.

MATERIALS MANAGEMENT

The purchasing agent was told in early December of the forecast made by Martin, and purchased enough parts to produce the total number of trailers estimated. The purchasing agent usually established a schedule for each supplier, requesting at least half the total order immediately with one or two later deliveries.

Each trailer was made from about 100 different parts that ranged from pieces of precut plywood to nuts and bolts. Materials constituted about two-thirds of Martin's manufacturing cost, while labor (at $20 per hour) and overhead accounted for 13 per cent and 20 per cent respectively. The longest intervals between order placement and receipt of goods were for painted steel and springs, each of which required eight to 10 weeks for delivery.

Last November, Martin hired a clerk to maintain a perpetual inventory of raw materials. The clerk was informed when shipments arrived, and entered the amounts in a control ledger. Production figures for each model of trailer were received once a week and used to calculate the numbers of each part that must have been used. These were then subtracted from the previous balances. Since this was a new procedure, and had proven to be inaccurate on several occasions, the purchasing agent tended to rely on requests from the production manager. Workers usually told the production manager when they were just about out of a part.

MANUFACTURING

Camping trailers were produced from December until the end of June. (Last year's camping trailer manufacturing results are shown in Exhibit 1.) The company closed for vacation in July, then reopened to produce a line of snowmobile trailers (using the same production facilities) until the end of November. The production manager attempted to meet the monthly forecast requirements established by Martin. An attempt was made to schedule trailers in lots of at least 100. If the warehouse supply became very low (five or six), more would schedule into production.

In January and February, the production manager kept a mental schedule for the following three weeks. Typically, parts were manufactured for the trailers to be assembled the following week. At the same time, the production manager determined which trailers were most urgently required for the

Trailer	Activity	Dec	Jan	Feb	Mar	Apr	May	Jun
T10	O	0	55	−29	34	61	122	14
	M	0	0	15	36	97	104	0
T12	O	0	28	−12	14	43	28	11
	M	0	0	87	0	42	25	1
T15	O	0	19	−5	13	15	41	12
	M	0	0	24	50	9	83	0
T15 MarkII & T20	O	0	40	−10	27	32	30	12
	M	0	0	27	50	0	94	0
T40	O	0	8	6	24	26	48	14
	M	0	0	0	0	0	56	39
T41	O	0	3	1	5	6	−1	2
	M	0	0	0	0	0	0	3
Martin Brand Totals	O	0	153	−49	117	183	268	65
	M	0	0	153	136	148	362	43
Mark IV	O	0	100	250	250	400	400	100
	M	5	127	131	132	171	481	203
Crown	O	0	25	25	50	100	100	0
	M	0	1	0	31	111	0	137
Regal	O	0	25	50	50	50	65	0
	M	5	0	44	17	100	50	23
Viceroy	O	0	25	0	25	10	0	0
	M	5	0	55	0	0	0	0
Quality	O	0	35	90	85	140	140	36
	M	0	0	12	232	97	87	0
Discount	O	0	40	100	105	165	200	0
	M	60	0	103	175	132	140	0
Private Brand Totals	O	0	250	515	565	865	905	136
	M	75	128	345	587	611	758	363
Grand Totals	O	0	403	466	682	1,048	1,173	201
	M	75	128	498	723	759	1,120	406
Workers		40	40	40	40	40	80[1]	80
Hours/Week/Worker		20[2]	40	40	60[3]	60	60	20[2]

Exhibit 1   Record of Trailers Ordered (O) and Manufactured (M)

1. Second shift was hired for the months of May and June.
2. Short work weeks were used at the beginning and end of the season.
3. Overtime was used during March, April and May.

second week ahead. If parts were not available for this model, another model was chosen. Priorities were influenced largely by the importance of the customer, i.e., the demands of the largest buyers were filled first. In May and June, the tentative schedule was shortened to only one week ahead. This schedule was often upset by late demands from dealers. If a rush order were received, the trailers could be manufactured in three or four weeks, if no purchases were necessary.

Parts shortages presented persistent problems and upset the production manager's schedules several times a year. When this happened, the production manager quickly scheduled a different model into production, rather than allow the workforce to become idle.

It was clear to Martin that there were major problems in the operation of the plant, but he wondered which were the most serious, and what should be done about them.

Illustrious Corporation

Prepared by Professor John Haywood-Farmer

   Version: (A) 2002-12-16

Nancy Barfield, production planner at Illustrious Corporation, a small assembly shop, was preparing the operating plan for the next 10 weeks as she did each Friday. One of the products she had to deal with almost every week was X500, a product assembled for a regular customer. Even though the customer gave Nancy a forecast of required shipments of X500 every two weeks, the forecasts frequently changed.

The manufacturing and assembly process for X500 began with part H590, which Illustrious bought from another local company. The H590s came with a number of holes. Illustrious first had to tap the holes on some of the H590s for mounting screws. Illustrious carried the tapped H590s as part P712. Just this last week Illustrious had returned a shipment of 900 H590s to its supplier because of poor quality. Nancy did not expect the shipment to be replaced until the following Monday, 10 days hence.

The P712 was then attached to a G418 to form part Q307. In a similar operation an untapped H590 was attached to a G418 to form L600, which Illustrious carried as a separate part number even though the only difference between it and Q307 was its untapped holes. Nancy knew inventory was tight on G418 because of a recently settled strike at the supplier's plant.

Illustrious workers next mounted an F416 on each Q307 to make the subassembly L477. Illustrious purchased the F416 in kit form; the kits included all the necessary mounting screws and accessories. X500s were formed by screwing two L600s onto one L477 in a final assembly operation.

Nancy reviewed the projected week-ending inventory levels for X500 and each of its components, the latest shipment forecast, and the standard lead times. The relevant figures were:

Part	X500	H590	P712	G418	Q307	L600	F416	L477
Inventory (units)	400	210	115	290	490	620	750	310
Lead time (weeks)	0	1	1	2	3	3	2	2

Week	Demand	Week	Demand	Week	Demand	Week	Demand
1	205	6	300	11	150	16	200
2	395	7	215	12	525	17	150
3	100	8	50	13	425	18	450
4	295	9	600	14	0	19	0
5	265	10	310	15	120	20	350

4

PROJECT MANAGEMENT

A major building block of world-class operations is the effective management of projects. Companies must identify and schedule project activities and then monitor their progress against strict time, cost, and performance objectives. Projects always have an element of uniqueness and require a specific combination of resources to address particular company- or customer-specific objectives. Not surprisingly, constraints are placed on both time and cost, requiring active, ongoing project monitoring. Finally, uncertainties, such as the risks of product development, competitor actions, or labor disruptions, can change the project objectives or resources. As a result, projects are usually complex and challenging to manage; they are also something that every manager will encounter, or be responsible for, in many different job roles throughout his or her career.

So what is a project? A project is an interrelated set of activities that has definite starting and ending points and that results in a unique outcome for a specific allocation of resources. The people involved with activities that collectively form a project may include company personnel, subcontractors, customers, suppliers, or a variety of other possible sources. In general, some of the activities that collectively make up a project can occur in parallel, whereas others must occur in a sequence. Each activity is characterized by a definite completion time.

The output of a project is not necessarily a physical product, such as the launch of a new consumer product; it also can be service related, such as a musical production, as is discussed in the H.M.S. Pinafore case. Thus, projects often cut across functional disciplines to bring together the skills of many people and organizations. Although each project is unique, the reality is that the steps planned for one project usually can be transferred to some degree to similar projects in the future.

The cases in this chapter explore the last of the three basic foundational blocks (see Figure 4.1). Project managers must plan and control people and other resources, often without the benefit of direct reporting relationships, to ensure that project objectives related to time, cost, and other specifications (e.g., quality) are met. This is a central concern for the information systems project described in the Waterloo Regional Police Services case.

However, regardless of his or her level of authority, a project manager must establish a plan that identifies the sequence of individual activities and the assignment of resources.

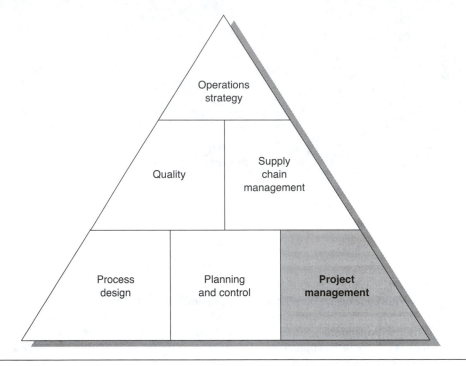

Figure 4.1   Project Management

Quite often, as the project develops, the manager is forced to reschedule activities or adjust cost estimates. Project management tools, such as the critical path method (CPM) described in the accompanying Note on Project Management Fundamentals, provide a quantitative approach to assess the impact of using more or fewer resources for particular activities or adjusting the sequence of activities on the overall project completion time. Moreover, these techniques are also extremely helpful to communicate the overall project plan to the many people involved in undertaking a typical project.

Note on Project Management Fundamentals

The basics of project management are described and applied to a simple tutorial problem. The steps for project management, as well as the calculation of the critical path using CPM, are presented.

Learning objectives: define project management concepts, construct a CPM diagram, and identify the critical path and project crashing.

Gadget Toy Company

Joe Huffman, a product development manager, must plan the launch of a new toy for the upcoming Christmas season. Huffman has estimated activity times, as well as the interrelationships between activities involving internal resources, training, equipment suppliers, and raw material purchases. Now, he must assess whether adjustments should be made and how to best meet the rapidly approaching project deadline.

Learning objectives: apply project management techniques, develop a project plan, use project management software, and reduce completion time.

H.M.S. PINAFORE

Francis Vanden Hoven, the student producer of a university-based stage show society, would like to use project planning techniques to improve the planning and execution of this season's performances, to be presented 4 months from now. Drawing on comments from committee members and personal judgment, Vanden Hoven must identify the tasks and their dependencies, develop the project plan, and identify key constraints. This service setting offers an important set of contrasts to more traditional project planning settings.

Learning objectives: project management in a service setting, identifying activities, and mapping precedence relationships.

CPSIM: THE CRITICAL PATH SIMULATOR (WINDOWS VERSION)

As a project manager overseeing the construction of an automated factory, you must complete a complex, 43-activity project in 107 days if penalties are to be avoided. This Windows-based simulation requires you to make effective trade-offs between the costs incurred by crashing (speeding up) activities and the financial penalties for late completion. For some tasks, unforeseen delays and early completion require timely replanning. CPSim maintains a current display of the project's CPM network, as well as the critical path(s) and activity slacks. Total time for the simulation is less than 60 minutes, and a site license is available.

Learning objectives: monitor project execution, adjust project plans to changing circumstances, estimate cost-time trade-offs, and reconcile multiple project objectives.

WATERLOO REGIONAL POLICE SERVICES: THE CIMS PROJECT

Chief Larry Gravill must decide whether to continue with the installation of the computer system or pursue other project alternatives. The Waterloo Regional Police Service, along with seven other police services, was 4 years into a project to collaborate and jointly invest resources in a project that would streamline many community response functions and, most important, information sharing between these police services. The project had already been under way for several years, and a number of major issues with the computer system vendor were still unresolved. Both time and money were now running short.

Learning objectives: resolve competing objectives in public-sector projects; examine project uncertainty, contingency planning, monitoring, and evaluation; and reconcile multiple project objectives.

MANAGEMENT QUESTIONS ADDRESSED IN PROJECT MANAGEMENT CHAPTER

1. When should project management tools be applied?
2. What is a PERT/CPM diagram, how is it constructed, and how is it used by managers to improve project management?

3. How are critical activities defined and identified? How do they need to be managed?

4. How should noncritical activities be dealt with?

5. What insights and value might other functional areas, such as marketing, finance, and human resources, gain from having joint input into the development of a project plan?

6. How is planning affected by changing project scope, performance objectives, cost, and time?

NOTE ON PROJECT MANAGEMENT FUNDAMENTALS

Prepared by Professors
Fraser Johnson and Robert Klassen

Copyright © 1998, Ivey Management Services   Version: (A) 1999-08-04

What do the following have in common: launch of a new car model, development of a new computer software package, and construction of an office tower? Each of these are examples of a project. Shorter product life cycles, the proliferation of product lines and the need to react quickly to dynamic market forces are but a few of the reasons why projects have become commonplace. For example, many organizations have turned to project management as a means of coordinating cross-functional activities.

This Note is designed to review the fundamental aspects of project management. In doing so, it covers the rudimentary project planning techniques and critical path analysis, and summarizes other basic issues that need attention when managing a complex project.

WHAT IS A PROJECT?

Projects are defined as a set of interrelated activities that are directed at achieving a particular goal or objective. In all cases, projects have a definitive starting and ending point. The output of a project is not necessarily a physical product, such as the launch of a new consumer product, but also can be service-related, such as a Broadway play. Although each project is unique, the reality is that the steps planned for one project usually can be transferred to similar projects in the future.

The activities that make up a project may involve company personnel, subcontractors, customers, suppliers, or a variety of other possible sources. In general, some of the activities that collectively make up a project can occur in parallel, while others must occur in a definite sequence. Each activity is characterized by a completion time.

Project management is then defined as the process of planning and controlling the resources that make up a project, with the objective of completing the project within specified time, cost and other performance parameters, like quality. Ultimately, a project manager must establish a plan that identifies the sequence of individual activities and the assignment of resources. Quite often, as the project develops, the manager is forced to re-schedule activities or adjust cost estimates. Project management techniques assist by providing a quantitative tool to assess the impact of using more or fewer resources for particular activities or adjusting the sequence of activity on overall project completion time.

PROJECT MANAGEMENT TECHNIQUES

In general, project management techniques are used by managers to help them plan, control, direct and re-plan resources for their projects. These techniques are also extremely helpful to communicate the overall project plan to the many people involved in undertaking a typical project.

PERT (program evaluation and review technique) and CPM (critical path method) are the two most common project management techniques. CPM was developed by J.E. Kelly, of Remington-Rand, and M.R. Walker, of DuPont, as a tool to assist with scheduling maintenance shut-downs of chemical plants. PERT was developed the following year for the U.S. Navy, to help manage the Polaris missile project. Originally, PERT was more flexible in dealing with variations in lead times, while CPM assumed that project activities could be estimated accurately. Today, however, differences between PERT and CPM techniques are relatively minor, and the two terms are often used interchangeably. The term PERT/CPM will be used here.

PERT/CPM techniques display project activities in a network diagram to help managers focus their attention on the sequence of events most crucial for project completion. In order to create a network diagram, the project must include activities that not only are clearly defined, but also must be carried out in a specific order (precedence relationships). In most situations, opportunities exist to re-order, compress or extend the activities with the objectives of revising the program budget or completion date.

Due to the large number of activities involved with many projects, computers are commonly used for analysis and provide answers to "what if" questions. A variety of relatively inexpensive software packages is available. These packages organize the project using a standard format based on the duration time of each activity and the sequence of activities.

THE PROJECT MANAGEMENT PROCESS

Project management using a network model can be separated into four steps:

- define the project
- identify activities, precedence relationships and time elements
- establish critical path
- make adjustments

1. Define the Project

Each project should have clearly defined beginning and ending points. It is up to the project manager to describe the project activities in terms that team members will easily comprehend. Consequently, a clear statement should be created, identifying the scope of the project, its major activities and their relationships, and the time unit in which the project will be monitored.

2. Identify Activities, Precedence Relationships and Time Elements

The project should then be broken down into "activities," which represent the individual tasks that the project team expects to coordinate. The activities will have precedence relationships; that is, the sequence of activities is constrained because certain activities must be completed before others can begin.

A difficult part of this step is establishing time estimates for each activity. In particular, at the beginning of the project, time estimates may be difficult to specify accurately. Experienced project managers, however, rely on a variety of sources to determine their initial time estimates, ranging from personal experience to formal engineering studies.

One easy method of organizing these data is to create a three-column list which includes the following: Activity, Activity Description, and Immediate Predecessor(s). Once organized, the activities can then be translated into diagrams that can take on any of several formats.

The Gantt chart, similar to a bar chart, depicts individual activities and the length of time required to complete each activity with a bar. The Gantt chart often organizes the sequence of activities by listing at the top those that must be completed first. Gantt charts allow a manager to quickly identify, in a visual way, the relative start and finish times of individual activities in a project plan.

However, while Gantt charts also can display relationships between activities for small projects, it becomes increasingly difficult to visualize these relationships as the number of activities in a project increases. Furthermore, it is also difficult to identify the critical path solely by relying on a Gantt chart.

To overcome these weaknesses, the PERT/CPM diagram shows the activities as a series of nodes on a network. An activity, shown as a node, is directly linked by an arrow to activities that immediately follow it and depend on its completion. This format makes the interrelationships between activities immediately apparent visually. However, because each activity is only represented by a node, the relative start and end dates for each are difficult to portray visually. In practice, both PERT/CPM and Gantt charts are widely used to plan and track projects.

3. Determine Critical Path

The critical path is defined as the sequence of activities which takes the longest time to complete. The critical path represents the minimum completion time of the project. A project can have more than one critical path; however, the completion time of each of these paths must be equal. Once the critical path is calculated, all activities can be divided into two general types:

- *critical* activities; and
- *non-critical* activities.

Critical activities directly impact the total project completion time; their delay immediately impacts the overall completion time of the entire project. In contrast, if non-critical activities are delayed or extended, the entire project may still be completed on schedule, depending on the degree of *slack* available with that activity. Total slack is defined as the maximum amount of time that an activity can begin late or be extended by, without delaying completion of the entire project. In general, the slack for any individual non-critical activity is *not* independent of the slack for other activities.

4. Make Adjustments

Most projects are constrained primarily by two factors: time and cost. Since improvements in project completion times often require additional resources at a premium cost, balancing the trade-offs between activity cost and overall project completion time is an important issue in the project management process. Additional activity cost can take many forms, including more personnel, expedited delivery, additional equipment, etc. Identification of critical and non-critical activities is central to managing these trade-offs.

Because critical activities directly impact the total project completion time, management decisions to delay or speed the completion of these activities are very important. If the overall project completion time is initially assessed to be too long or delays develop as the project proceeds, additional resources can be allocated to the critical activities to reduce their completion time, and ultimately, shorten the project completion time. Other options include expedited delivery and activity redesign.

All these actions to shorten an activity time are termed *crashing*. Activity crashing should only be directed at critical activities. However, it is very important to assess the overall project as individual activities are crashed. *As activities on the critical path are crashed, new critical paths may be added.* Consequently, managers might be forced to deal with several different critical paths before finalizing their project plan. If more than one path is critical, the activity times for several activities might need to be simultaneously crashed to reduce the total project completion time.

Another option to reduce project completion time is to re-sequence or *reorder the precedence relationships*. Obviously in a project such as a product launch, the ordering of some activities is constrained, e.g., with equipment installation preceding initial production. However, rather than necessarily having employee training also follow equipment installation, training might occur in parallel if a simulation could be used or a similar facility is available elsewhere.

In contrast, non-critical activities provide an opportunity for cost savings. Because these activity completion times do not directly impact overall project completion time, they can be extended if cost savings result. Slower modes of shipping, eliminating overtime, reducing peak usage of resources, etc. are possible cost-saving options. The maximum that any non-critical activity can be extended is given by its total slack. Like crashing, careful monitoring is necessary as each non-critical activity is extended, or non-critical activities will quickly become critical and potentially delay the entire project.

AN EXAMPLE

The following example illustrates the use of PERT/CPM techniques in a project. Bart plans to go skiing for his week-long holiday. He intends to leave the office immediately after completing a major presentation for senior management, which is expected to conclude at 12:00 noon on Friday. The trip from his office to his apartment usually takes 30 minutes.

Unfortunately, Bart has spent the last few days preparing for the presentation, and as a result, has not prepared for his vacation. After arriving home, Bart knows that he must wash his clothes. Ideally, he will do three loads of laundry, which he expects to take four hours. He knows that packing, which he anticipates will take 30 minutes, must wait until he has finished doing his laundry.

Bart also needs to go to the bank to withdraw some money and obtain travellers' cheques for the trip. He expects this activity to take one hour,

and this can take place at the same time his laundry is being done. Finally, Bart must pack the car and drive to airport; he expects both of these activities to take 30 minutes each. The check-in time for his flight is 5:00 p.m., and Bart knows that he cannot be late.

The list of activities that Bart must complete is provided in Table 1. Note that this table also identifies predecessor activities and estimated completion times.

A Gantt chart, outlining the activities together with their duration, start and finish times, is presented in Figure 1. Recall that an activity is a specific task which takes time and resources. This diagram immediately communicates the planned start and completion times for each activity and the overall project. The difficulty in using these data to manage Bart's activities is that they fail to show the relationships among the activities, the sequence of events constraining completion of the project (the critical path), and the slack times. In short, we know when the project starts and when it needs to be completed, but we cannot see how the activities are interrelated.

As an aid in analyzing the above information, it is useful to represent it schematically as an activity-on-node diagram. To do this, we adopt the convention of using the nodes (small squares) to represent activities and arrows to represent the necessary sequence in which they are performed. The PERT diagram for Bart's ski trip preparation is presented in Figure 2.

The network diagram shows the activities which must be performed before Bart leaves, their duration, as well as the sequence in which

Table 1 Bart's Ski Trip

Activity	Activity Name	Immediate Predecessor	Estimated Time (hours)
A	drive home	—	0.5
B	wash clothes	A	4.0
C	pack	B	0.5
D	go to bank	A	1.0
E	pack car	C, D	0.5
F	drive to airport	E	0.5

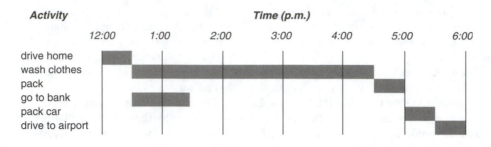

Figure 1   Gantt Chart for Bart's Ski Trip

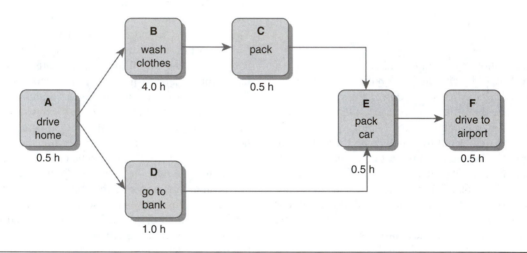

Figure 2   Ski Trip PERT Diagram

they must be performed. Specifically, note that both activities C and D must be completed before E can begin. The diagram typically includes the letter representing the activity inside each node, along with its activity time (duration). This format helps us to quickly calculate critical path, along with the planned activity start and finish times.

Now we can begin our analysis. First, we must establish the earliest possible time that each activity can begin and finish, termed the *Earliest Start* time (ES) and *Earliest Finish* time (EF), respectively. By convention, for the first activity, here A, we define its ES as zero, and

record this above and to the left of the node. The EF time is equal to the ES plus the activity duration time. This time is noted above and to the right of the activity. For activity A, the EF is 0.5 hours.

$$\text{Earliest Finish time (EF)} = \text{Earliest Start time (ES)} + \text{activity duration (d)}$$

Then, for each of the activities that follow this activity, their ES is equal to the EF of the preceding activity. Thus, the ES and EF for activity B are 0.5 and 4.5 hours, respectively; for activity D is 0.5 and 1.5 hours, respectively.

When two or more activities immediately precede an activity, such as E, the ES for that activity is the largest of all preceding EF times. For example, at activity E, the EF for activity C is 5.0 hours, while for activity D is 1.5 hours. Consequently, we take the greater of the two, and use 5.0 hours. The rationale is that we cannot begin the next activity until *all* of the preceding activities are complete.

We continue this way until we have calculated an ES and EF for each activity, as illustrated in Figure 3. The EF for the last activity, F, is 6.0 hours. This last figure is the total time to complete this project.

We now work backward through the diagram to establish the latest times that we can start and finish an activity, *without delaying the whole project*. These are termed the *Latest Start* (LS) time and *Latest Finish* (LF) time for each activity. The LF for the last activity, here F, is equal to the EF, and is recorded beside the EF, separated by a slash. The LS for F equals the LF minus the duration, here 5.5 hours. We record this figure beside the ES, separated by a slash. In general, the LS time is given by:

$$\text{Latest Start time (LS)} = \text{Latest Finish time (LF)} - \text{activity duration (d)}$$

For each preceding activity, the LF is equal to the LS of the next activity. Thus, for activity E, the LF is 5.5 hours and the LS is 5.0 hours.

If two or more activities follow an activity, such as activity A, we used the smallest LS time of those activities as the LF time of A. The rationale now is that we must finish the preceding activity by this time in order to avoid delaying all subsequent activities. Because the LS of event B is 0.5 hours and the LS of D is 4.0 hours, therefore, we use 0.5 hours as the LF for activity A. Figure 4 updates the network diagram with LS and LF data.

The final calculation is to identify the "slack" or "float" for each activity. Total slack is the maximum amount of time that an activity can begin late or be extended by, without delaying completion of the entire project. As stated

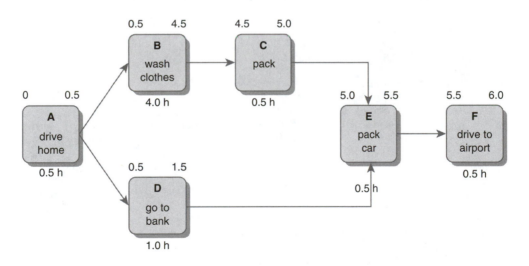

Figure 3   Ski Trip With Earliest Start and Earliest Finish Times

before, the slack time for an activity is *not* independent of the slack for other activities. Thus, it is *not* meaningful to add together the slack times of two or more activities.

$$Slack = LS - ES = LF - EF$$

Here the only activity with any slack is activity D, where it is (4.0 − 0.5) = 3.5 h.

Now, we find the *critical path*. It is the chain or chains of activities that have zero slack, which for the Ski Trip is A-B-C-E-F. If any of the critical activities are late, the completion of the entire project is delayed. Moreover, efforts to reduce the total project time first must be directed at the activities on the critical path.

The Benefits of Project Management Software

There are many different project management software packages available, the most popular being Microsoft Project (MS Project). Project management software simplifies the process of planning, organizing and controlling complex projects. It uses information about the project, such as activity

durations, start dates, available working time and completion dates/deadlines to build a model of the project that is being managed.

Using project management software offers several advantages. First, the software automatically organizes the activities based on the duration times and sequences identified in the data. The data will be organized into standard format, making it easy to share information. Generally, the project can be viewed in many different ways, e.g., Gantt charts, PERT/CPM diagrams, calendar-based views, task summary sheets, resource graphs and resource usage views. Each view gives a particular user a different way to examine the data, dependent largely on the type of analysis needed.

The flexibility of project management software systems allows the manager to ask "what if" questions easily and perform sensitivity analyses. Allocating resources at the planning stage can be a complicated process, characterized by vast amounts of data, leading to a seemingly endless number of possible alternatives. Project management software assists with the comparison and evaluation of proposed alternatives. For example, assumptions can be adjusted in order to assess trade-offs with respect to timing and cost.

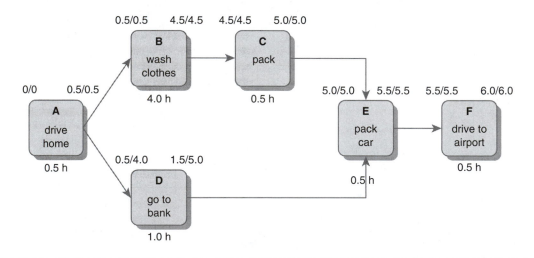

Figure 4   Ski Trip With Latest Start and Latest Finish Times

Different options also are available for levelling the demand placed on costly resources or for constraining the availability of other resources over the course of a project.

Finally, as a project is undertaken, project management software can be used to monitor the overall project schedule, note the achievement of key milestones, track the use of resources and generate progress reports. These capabilities allow managers to anticipate and respond to problems before they impact the schedule by replanning activities.

GADGET TOY COMPANY

Prepared by Fraser Johnson under the supervision of Professor Robert Klassen

Version: (A) 2002-10-11

Joe Huffman, project manager at Gadget Toy Company (Gadget), had just submitted a proposal for funding to the new product review committee. He recommended that Gadget introduce, through its retail distribution network, a new children's toy based on a popular cartoon character. Joe felt that if he could get the product out by Christmas, Gadget could take advantage of what he felt would be strong market demand. However, due to the volatility of the market for these types of games, Joe could not be certain that the product would have the same level of market acceptance the following year. It was now May 6, 1996, and Joe knew he would have to manage the timing of the project carefully to meet the delivery date of September 15th, just 19 weeks away.

Gadget's head office was in Kitchener, Ontario, where it also operated a manufacturing plant and distribution center. Whenever possible, Gadget preferred to manufacture its products in-house.

Joe expected feedback from the committee by the end of the week, at which time he would begin coordinating the launch of the project. Since Joe was an experienced project manager, he established a preliminary list of activities, as shown in Exhibit 1.

Based on his schedule, Joe felt he could start work on some activities immediately, such as finalizing the product design and placing an order for the equipment. However, many of the activities had to be performed sequentially. For example, he could not train the workers until the equipment was installed and the tools for the machine were completed. Similarly, he could not order the raw material until the engineering work was complete and the advertising plan was completed, since the advertising plan would influence colour selection.

Concerned about the delivery schedule, Joe investigated opportunities to cut the project time. After talking with the marketing manager, Peggy Pilon, Joe learned that he could reduce product advertising. Peggy anticipated a five per cent reduction in sales for each week of lost advertising. Furthermore, she indicated that Joe could not get away with less than six weeks of advertising for a new product of this nature.

Joe also spoke with Steve Jeffrey, the production manager at the tool shop. Steve offered to speed up the tool build by working weekends, for a cost of $5,000. Steve thought he could improve their delivery time by two weeks if Joe authorized the extra cost.

Activity	Description	Immediate Predecessor	Estimated Time (Weeks)
A	obtain funding approval	—	1
B	finalize engineering	A	1
C	deliver new equipment	A	8
D	build dies/tools	B	12
E	install equipment	C	1
F	train workers	D, E	1
G	de-bug process	F	1
H	establish advertising plan	A	1
I	finalize package and art work	H	2
J	advertise	H	12
K	raw material delivery	D, I	2
L	initial production run	G, K	3
M	ship product	J, L	1

Exhibit 1   Activities Needed for New Product Introduction

H.M.S. Pinafore

Prepared by Martin Stapleton and
Francis Vanden Hoven under the
supervision of Professor John Haywood-Farmer

Version: (A) 2001-05-02

On September 5, 1993, Francis Vanden Hoven, producer of the University of Western Ontario's (Western) Gilbert and Sullivan (G&S) Society, met with his assistant Deborah Carraro, the costume coordinator, Mona Bryden, and the artistic director, Elizabeth Van Doorne, to obtain their advice on how to plan for the performances of *H.M.S. Pinafore* which would take place from Thursday, January 13 to Saturday, January 22, 1994 (see Exhibit 1).

BACKGROUND

The University Students' Council (USC), the student governing body which represented Western's undergraduate students and funded projects from school fees, funded the G&S Society. The Society's mandate was to give students, faculty, alumni, and the greater community an opportunity to participate in and enjoy high quality theatre productions at affordable prices. Each year the G&S Society staged a single production.

From 1871 to 1889, during the Victorian age, the well-known English humorist and playwright William S. Gilbert teamed up with the English composer Arthur Sullivan to prepare witty operettas satirizing British society. The quality of both the lyrics and the music made these plays perennial favourites. Each year, Western's G&S Society staged one of the 13 famous operettas

August

Sun	Mon	Tue	Wed	Thu	Fri	Sat
1	2	3	4	5	6	7
8	9	10	11	12	13	14
15	16	17	18	19	20	21
22	23	24	25	26	27	28
29	30	31				

November

Sun	Mon	Tue	Wed	Thu	Fri	Sat
	1	2	3	4	5	6
7	8	9	10	11	12	13
14	15	16	17	18	19	20
21	22	23	24	25	26	27
28	29	30				

September

Sun	Mon	Tue	Wed	Thu	Fri	Sat
			1	2	3	4
5	6	7	8	9	10	11
12	13	14	15	16	17	18
19	20	21	22	23	24	25
26	27	28	29	30		

December

Sun	Mon	Tue	Wed	Thu	Fri	Sat
			1	2	3	4
5	6	7	8	9	10	11
12	13	14	15	16	17	18
19	20	21	22	23	24	25
26	27	28	29	30	31	

October

Sun	Mon	Tue	Wed	Thu	Fri	Sat
					1	2
3	4	5	6	7	8	9
10	11	12	13	14	15	16
17	18	19	20	21	22	23
24	25	26	27	28	29	30
31						

January

Sun	Mon	Tue	Wed	Thu	Fri	Sat
						1
2	3	4	5	6	7	8
9	10	11	12	13	14	15
16	17	18	19	20	21	22
23	24	25	26	27	28	29
30	31					

Exhibit 1   Calendar From August 1993 to January 1994

Designates a statutory holiday in Ontario.

on the Western campus in London, Ontario. The 1993/1994 season marked the Society's 40th year.

Francis and Deb had already made a number of key decisions: they had decided to stage *H.M.S. Pinafore,* one of the most popular of the operettas; they had set the ticket prices at $14 for adults, with a $2 reduction for students and seniors; they had decided to have a cast of 40; they had hired a musical director; and, in common with past practice, they planned to stage 10 evening and matinee performances in the 360-seat Talbot Theatre.

The Society operated under a budget set and administered by the USC. In 1992/1993 the total budget had been $28,000 and Francis believed that the 1993/1994 budget would have to be about the same. Although the Society hired some paid staff, particularly musicians, it relied extensively on volunteers in all areas of the production. Although most of the people involved were Western students, about 40 per cent of the cast and crew came from elsewhere in the community. Because the fixed costs such as honoraria, theatre shop fees, costumes, and radio and television advertisements totalled over $14,000, the producer had to be careful managing the variable operating costs.

THE PRODUCER'S JOB

The producer's job was to help the production staff to complete their assigned duties on time. Specifically, his or her duties included:

- along with the production's business manager, formulating a realistic budget to ensure that each department received its financial compensation and behaved in a financially responsible manner;
- assembling primary production and artistic staff;
- booking sufficient suitable rehearsal space for each audition and rehearsal;
- arranging for the rental or purchase of the words (scripts) and music (musical scores—a different one for each instrument) for the operetta;
- arranging for the sale of tickets;
- in conjunction with the production's advertising director, formulating and carrying out an advertising campaign;

- along with the show's production manager, gathering the secondary production staff and ensuring that they are informed of their duties and obligations; and,
- making a final report to the USC's theatre commissioner.

Thus, the producer had overall responsibility for all aspects of the show. The USC expected him or her to plan the show's major phases, delegate authority to several managers, provide moral support, and ensure that revenues and expenses met budgeted targets. The USC believed that the producer could achieve these ends by being available to all cast and crew, by holding regularly scheduled meetings of department heads and theatre staff, and by keeping the USC informed of all important production matters. Because there were no formal organization chart or lines of authority, control and reporting were more challenging, and open communication was critical throughout the pre-production, production, and post-production stages of the show.

The producer and his or her assistant were typically students who took the job for a single season. Francis Vanden Hoven was in his final year of Western's well-known, two-year honours business administration program. Although he had experience in theatre and was seeking a theatre career, this was his first experience as a producer.

THE MEETING

Francis knew that he would face some pressing issues in the near future. In order to become more familiar with what he was getting into, he invited Deb, Mona and Liz to help him plan for the upcoming weeks. They had had experience with similar roles in earlier years. Francis began the meeting:

Francis: Thanks everyone for meeting on a Sunday afternoon—and on a long weekend too. Deb, I know that you were part of the production last year. Can you give us any advice on how to run things this year?

Deb: Yes, there is plenty that you can learn from last year; we faced some major problems in a couple of areas that you'll have to think about. One was in getting the program completed—was that a headache! Before you do anything else, make sure you hire a publicity director! We can't run any ads without one. They are always tough to come by and it might take you two weeks to find a capable one. After that, you should start working early on the program. You have to get photographs taken of the cast and the crews, and collect biographies of everyone so they can be included in the program. It may take you four to five weeks to get them. Everyone keeps putting it off. After you've collected the information, you will have to enter it into a computer program. That will take a full day.

Francis: What about getting it printed?

Deb: Well that's not so bad. Once you've keyed in all the information, all you have to do is to deliver it on a diskette to the printer so she can complete it. It will take her about five days. This job might well cost you $3,500 after all the adjustments are made, so you want to make sure it is right before you go ahead. It all has to be ready by opening night. By the way, how is your budget coming?

Francis: It is almost done. What a job! I am going to present it to the USC for approval on Tuesday morning. Until they approve it, we can't do a thing. Don't we need the cast arranged before we work on the program?

Deb: Yes, of course we do! We have to nail down the names of everyone in the cast, crew and orchestra before the bios and pictures.

Liz: Of course all that stuff is important, Francis, but don't forget that what really carries this Society is what happens on stage! Now listen. What I am concerned about is getting our set designed and built. That will take six weeks and must be completed before the costume parade—that's when the cast members put on their costumes for the first time. Of course, you will have to hire the production crew before you begin designing or building. Some of them will do a lot of the construction. It might take four weeks to find them. Who really knows though? That is the price you pay when you rely on volunteers. We also need to train the production crew for their stage work. That might take 12 days. We should advertise in the student paper to attract volunteers. We could kill three birds with one stone by using the same ads for the publicity crew, the production crew and the cast. I think you can get advertising space for about $40 right now and it will probably take a week. You've hired a set designer, right Francis?

Francis: Well, not exactly. . . .

Liz: You haven't! All you producers seem to worry about is the bottom line. You have to have a set designer before you can design and build the set or train the stage crew. You should spend some time selecting your set designer, because a well designed set is critical for a high quality show. This shouldn't take you any longer than two weeks. We will also have to arrange to audition and choose the cast. We should be able to get through them in a couple of days—probably a Friday and Saturday—but we will have to advertise first and make sure we arrange a time and a place with a piano. We should try Talbot Theatre again but they may be busy so allow a week to get a place. What about the music, Francis?

Francis: Well, we have hired Chuck Baxter as musical director. He has had quite a bit of experience with G&S productions in the past, both as musical director and also in other roles. Once the USC approves the budget, he will recruit the orchestra members and arrange to get the sheet music. It will probably take him a week to recruit and a week to get the music.

Liz: Look, we have to have music before the cast starts rehearsals. I would like to rehearse on a regular basis for three hours each Sunday afternoon and Monday and Tuesday evenings every week for 12 weeks.

Don't forget about the Christmas exam and holiday period. Exams start on December 5, and run through to about the 22nd. The exact duration varies from student to student but when you have a cast of 40 you can essentially write off the whole period. Students are understandably reluctant to do much either during or just before exams. We also have some trouble in late October when many write mid-terms and essays. And, the university will be officially closed from December 23 to January 3. Even if our cast and crew is in London, we won't be able to get access to Talbot Theatre to practise or build the set during that time. And, that is just days before opening night. Will Chuck get the scores on time?

Francis: Let me check and get back to you. The orchestra will only rehearse for about four days though, so they won't need the music immediately.

Mona: Francis, Liz's sets and the cast are important but don't forget about my costumes! That's when my job begins. I will need some basic supplies and someone to help me out. After I collect the supplies and measure the cast, we can go ahead and order costumes from Toronto. The whole thing should take about a week, even allowing for delivery. However, just to be sure, I would like to have them here a week before we absolutely need them in case there are any problems. The total cost shouldn't exceed $6,500. Sometimes I can negotiate an extra 10 per cent discount.

Francis: What happens once the costumes arrive?

Mona: Then I will have to organize a costume parade to ensure that there are no problems before opening night. Invariably, some costumes will need to be altered. The costume parade and alterations will take about five days but shouldn't cost much—but it works best if the set is complete first so we can get a better idea of how the costumes are going to work. Right after the costume parade we can do our dress rehearsal. That is the first time when it all comes together.

We only have one dress rehearsal a day or maybe two before opening night. That is the first time that the orchestra and the cast actually work together. And, of course, the stage crew works that one too.

Deb: Oh yeah, and one last thing Francis. Don't forget about publicity—you wouldn't want to forget about selling tickets, would you? Once you've hired a publicity director, you can advertise and then select a crew to develop an advertising plan. It will take about four weeks in total. It shouldn't take more than about a week to develop a plan, but after that we should blitz all types of advertising media over about three weeks. It is important to take the time to hire capable crews—after all, they are volunteers and if they do a poor job, the whole production, and all of us, will suffer. It might take you up to four weeks or so, but it is probably worth it. Don't forget that your time is valuable too, though!

Francis: I am sure we have lots of time. But, if something goes wrong, can we speed up any of these activities if we have to? And, by how much? And, how much will it cost?

Deb: Well, Francis, we can probably speed up most of the things we have to do. You have to be careful though. Don't forget that we are dealing with volunteers here. They are committed but we don't pay them anything and they do have other responsibilities. If you push them too hard they might quit and there isn't much you can do about it. If that happens, especially at crucial times, we are toast.

Liz: Yeah, that's right Deb. But, there are some things we can do, especially on the activities we pay for. For example, if we spent more on advertising, we could attract more good candidates and shorten the time to find the crews by a couple of weeks. And, we could also get the printer to speed up by doing it on overtime. I think we might be able to get it done in only two days if we were prepared to spend an extra $750.

Mona: And, that costume place will do the same thing for an extra $100 per day. We could get them delivered in 48 hours if we paid for it. With our small budget, though, I wonder if it is wise to spend our money that way.

Francis: What about the set? It is one of our primary activities.

Deb: Well, we obviously couldn't get the time down to zero. But, by hiring an extra master builder we could probably knock a week off. Don't we pay about $80 per day for the master builder now?

Francis: Yes, that is what last year's budget was. What about rehearsals? Can we speed them up?

Liz: We could, but again we have to be careful. The orchestra isn't much of a problem. But, if we push the cast for more hours per week we will run into problems with cast members not having time to absorb the material and with rehearsals interfering with their other activities. We might lose some of them. And, if we cut down on the total time, we won't look as polished as I would like come opening night.

CONCLUSION

Francis summed up his feelings:

We want to have the most professional looking production we can for our money. We have certain standards we would like to keep, such as the glossy posters and radio and television ads.

But the true test will come in the music, singing, dancing and acting on opening night. A great opening night performance will generate the newspaper reviews and the word of mouth that will either make or break the run of the show. All the producer can do is set the stage and attempt to have everything flow in an organized fashion.

After I get the budget approved on Tuesday, I will need a schedule so that I can prioritize my time. Although many tasks can be performed at the same time, I have to know which ones are critical so I can focus on them. After all, I am a full-time student in a tough program and I can only be a part-time producer. Right now I am only concentrating on what needs to be done up to opening night. I will worry about the clean-up activities later. I will also need a more complete budget so I can make some of the tough financial decisions.

CPSIM: THE CRITICAL PATH SIMULATOR (WINDOWS VERSION)

Prepared by Professor Chris Piper

Version: (A) 2001-07-31

CPSIM OBJECTIVES

The objectives for the critical path simulator are to provide experience and develop insights in the following areas:

1. Interpreting the results of PERT/CPM analysis;
2. Rebalancing network activities in light of (un)favorable events as the simulated project unfolds;
3. Making trade-offs between activity times and activity costs; and
4. Making sequential decisions, where decisions that must be made in the present depend upon the decisions that will be made in the future.

PROJECT DESCRIPTION

The CPSim project involves the construction of an automated factory. The project is targeted for completion in 107 days, and a $5,000 per day penalty will be incurred if the project is not completed on time. State-of-the-art process controls are to be used, and some of the custom computer programming has yet to be completed. As project manager, your job is to adjust for any changes that occur, and position each activity time to accommodate future uncertainty so as to minimize the total cost of completing the project. The management task entails making effective trade-offs between the costs incurred by speeding up (crashing) activities, and those avoided by reducing the $5,000 per day penalty for late completion.

USING CPSIM

To begin the CPSim exercise, double click on the CPSim icon. CPSim initially displays a title screen. The simulator clock begins when you click the "Start CPSim" button.

Exhibit 1 describes each of the 43 activities that must be completed before the project is finished. Exhibit 2 shows the slowest time in which each activity can be completed and the corresponding activity cost. Subsequent columns of the table give the "crash" costs for reducing activity times by one or more days. The last column shows the shortest possible activity completion time. The simulator will not permit you to set durations outside these bounds.

As an example, consider activity 4, which takes a maximum of 13 days and costs $26,230 to complete in this time. Referring to Exhibit 2, we see that an additional $770 would be incurred to complete it in 12 days. Since this activity is on the only critical path, reducing it by one day will reduce project lateness to 15 days, thus saving $5,000 in late completion penalties, for a net saving of $4,230. Crashing activity 4 one additional day to 11 days would cost an extra $900, for a total crash cost of $1,670, and a total activity cost of $27,900. It may or may not save an additional $5,000 in delay penalties, depending on whether activity 4 continues to be on the only critical path after being reduced to 12 days. Similarly, slowing down an activity reduces costs. Thus, increasing activity 4 from its shortest time of nine days to 10 days would save $1,330, and result in an activity cost of $29,000.

During the exercise, you will be assisted by an on-screen representation of the project network. Exhibit 3 shows the project's starting condition. The network represents each activity with a rounded rectangle (node). The lines connecting activities show activity dependencies. Activities at the left end of lines must be completed before activities on the right end can begin. Solid red lines join activities on the critical path, while dashed green lines connect non-critical activities. Each activity's number appears at the top-left corner of the node. Inside the node are two numbers. The top number shows the current duration of the activity. The bottom number shows the current slack in the activity, followed by a lowercase "s" (for slack). On the outside right of the node are two buttons. The one on top that is marked with a plus, increases activity duration by one day each time it is clicked. The bottom button is marked with a minus to indicate that clicking it reduces activity duration by one day. "Tool tips" provide additional information based on the position of the mouse pointer. Note the $770 displayed under activity 4 in Exhibit 3.

When cell pointer is over:	The tool tip shows:
• Activity number	Activity description
• Activity duration	Minimum and maximum activity duration
• Activity slack	Earliest finish day (EF) of the activity
• Increase duration button	$ saving if duration increased by one day
• Decrease duration button	$ cost if duration reduced by one day

Each time that an activity's duration is changed the program reports the incremental cost or saving of the change. CPSim automatically calculates and displays the resulting critical path, as well as updating all of the activity slacks. The program also calculates project status, in terms of the number of days early or late, and computes the associated penalty cost. A project status display along the bottom of CPSim's screen reports

Activity	Description
1	Organization and staffing
2	Employee recruiting
3	Design study (inspection equipment)
4	Power source study
5	Computer systems design
6	Orientation of hourly employees
7	Report hourly employees available by skill level
8	Finalize factory layout
9	Methods study
10	Procure power equipment
11	Site modification
12	Equipment processing and delivery
13	Build prototype product (breadboard)
14	Test power equipment (concurrent with installation)
15	Preliminary model design
16	Control application software testing
17	Simulation testing
18	Inspect purchased equipment and prepare report
19	Install power equipment
20	Prepare report on preliminary model design
21	Set up for installation of safety equipment
22	Prepare test report on power equipment and software
23	Theoretical testing of preliminary model
24	Specification study
25	Install safety equipment
26	Develop product literature for customer
27	Perform trial run of breadboard components
28	Orientation of hourly employees on technical equipment
29	Customer on-site inspection
30	Translate preliminary model design
31	Review and approve specification study
32	Adjust power and safety equipment if necessary
33	Preliminary production of customer's prototype
34	Adapt components for volume production
35	Design control reports
36	Fabricate preliminary model
37	Perform stress-testing on preliminary fabricated model
38	Concurrent testing
39	Print and distribute the specification study
40	Perform trial run of power and safety equipment
41	Inspect and adjust customer prototype
42	Perform preliminary production run
43	Systems simulation

Exhibit 1   CPSim Activity Descriptions

project lateness or earliness, along with the penalty cost, activity cost and total cost.

Just to the right of the project status display is the project clock. The current day, and the hour of the day, is updated approximately four times a second. Time elapses continuously during the project, but in the interests of better planning, the simulator's clock moves ahead more slowly at the beginning of the project, and then moves faster as the project progresses.

A button labelled "Advance Date" is located to the immediate left of the project status display.

Activity	Most Days	Least Cost	1	2	3	4	5	6	7	8	9	10	11	12	13	Least Days
			Added Cost for Day Saved (Dots Indicate Infeasible Days)													
1	4	10,000	.	.	.	.	.	.	.	.	.	.	.	.	.	4
2	9	5,000	.	.	.	.	.	.	.	.	.	.	.	.	.	9
3	14	33,420	500	580	680	820	1000	1250	1600	.	.	.	.	.	.	7
4	13	26,230	770	900	1100	1330	.	.	.	.	.	.	.	.	.	9
5	33	184,840	2660	2820	.	.	.	.	.	.	.	.	.	.	.	31
6	21	35,710	290	310	400	390	440	500	570	660	770	.	.	.	.	12
7	3	4,830	1670	.	.	.	.	.	.	.	.	.	.	.	.	2
8	18	36,110	650	740	.	.	.	.	.	.	.	.	.	.	.	16
9	19	83,150	730	820	920	1040	1190	.	.	.	.	.	.	.	.	14
10	22	7,500	.	.	.	.	.	.	.	.	.	.	.	.	.	22
11	15	383,330	23810	27470	32050	37880	.	.	.	.	.	.	.	.	.	11
12	19	97,630	2920	3270	.	.	.	.	.	.	.	.	.	.	.	17
13	16	70,620	040	1190	1380	1600	1890	.	.	.	.	.	.	.	.	11
14	16	162,500	4160	4760	5500	6410	7570	9100	.	.	.	.	.	.	.	10
15	19	256,570	7310	8170	9200	10410	11910	13730	.	.	.	.	.	.	.	13
16	15	37,500	.	.	.	.	.	.	.	.	.	.	.	.	.	15
17	41	270,730	4270	4480	4730	4970	5260	5560	5880	6240	6630	7050	7530	8040	8630	28
18	3	4,830	1670	.	.	.	.	.	.	.	.	.	.	.	.	2
19	24	134,160	4530	4940	5410	5960	6570	7310	8170	9200	10410	.	.	.	.	15
20	1	1,500	.	.	.	.	.	.	.	.	.	.	.	.	.	1
21	3	20,000	.	.	.	.	.	.	.	.	.	.	.	.	.	3
22	5	7,000	1000	1660	.	.	.	.	.	.	.	.	.	.	.	3
23	21	69,040	460	500	550	620	700	790	.	.	.	.	.	.	.	15
24	18	63,330	780	890	1000	1140	1320	1540	1810	2190	2660	3340	.	.	.	8
25	21	61,420	580	630	700	780	.	.	.	.	.	.	.	.	.	17
26	22	71,810	330	360	390	440	490	550	630	710	.	.	.	.	.	14
27	23	103,040	590	650	720	780	880	980	1110	.	.	.	.	.	.	16
28	18	112,220	720	810	910	1050	1210	1410	1670	2000	2440	.	.	.	.	9
29	18	41,660	690	770	880	1000	1150	1350	1590	.	.	.	.	.	.	11
30	22	85,450	500	550	600	670	750	850	960	1090	1270	.	.	.	.	13
31	16	91,250	750	.	.	.	.	.	.	.	.	.	.	.	.	15
32	21	61,660	340	360	410	460	520	580	670	760	.	.	.	.	.	13
33	18	132,770	750	850	960	1090	.	.	.	.	.	.	.	.	.	14
34	17	95,000	620	710	810	930	1090	.	.	.	.	.	.	.	.	12
35	18	67,220	420	480	540	620	720	830	980	1190	1440	.	.	.	.	9
36	17	238,230	5520	6250	.	.	.	.	.	.	.	.	.	.	.	15
37	18	73,880	820	920	.	.	.	.	.	.	.	.	.	.	.	16
38	21	81,900	600	650	730	820	920	1040	1190	1380	1600	.	.	.	.	12
39	20	36,500	340	380	420	480	540	620	.	.	.	.	.	.	.	14
40	19	118,420	1020	1140	1290	1460	1670	1920	2240	.	.	.	.	.	.	12
41	22	82,720	1080	1200	1310	1460	1640	1840	2080	.	.	.	.	.	.	15
42	20	157,500	920	1020	1140	1290	.	.	.	.	.	.	.	.	.	16
43	22	71,360	540	600	650	730	820	.	.	.	.	.	.	.	.	17

Exhibit 2   CPSim Activity Durations and Costs

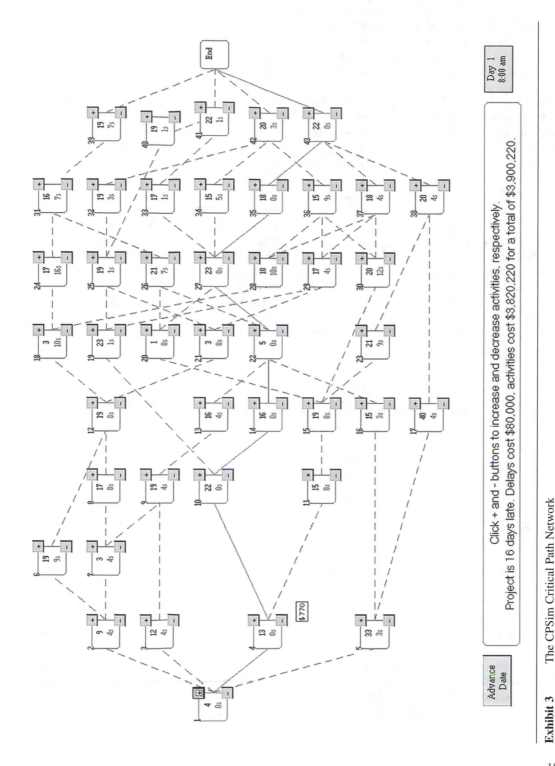

Day 1
8:00 am

Advance
Date

Exhibit 3 The CPSim Critical Path Network

185

Clicking on this button will move the project's clock to 12:00 p.m. of the day on which the next activity will be completed. Avoid using this button unless you are certain that the project cannot be improved upon.

Activities are completed as soon as their earliest finish times have passed. Actual activity durations are influenced by fate, however, so the project may be unavoidably accelerated or delayed. Once an activity's earliest finish time has passed, CPSim reports its actual completion time and the reason for any change from the planned duration. Since the duration of a completed activity cannot be changed, its duration change buttons are removed at this time.

When all activities have been completed, CPSim will confirm the project's completion, and report its final status. You will be given an opportunity to record your final results for subsequent discussion in class.

If you need to exit CPSim before finishing the exercise, use the usual program exit icon on the top, right-hand corner of the screen. Your results will not be representative of the project's final outcome if you quit, however, since some activities will not have been completed. As an alternative, consider using the Advance Date button to quickly run through the remaining days of the project.

ACKNOWLEDGEMENT

CPSim is adapted from an exercise called CAPERTSIM that was developed by North American Aviation, Inc., Autonetics Education and Training Department. CAPERTSIM was available from the IBM SHARE library, and was adapted by the Harvard Business School in 1974 and renamed PLANETS II. CPSim is based on the same project as the earlier exercises, but has been reprogrammed for the Microsoft Windows environment to provide the more common activity-on-node network representation, a graphic user interface, and an uninterruptible, continuous, real time project clock.

WATERLOO REGIONAL POLICE SERVICES: THE CIMS PROJECT

Prepared by Jane Movold under the supervision of Professors Deborah Compeau and Scott Schneberger

Version: (A) 2003-02-24

Chief Larry Gravill of the Waterloo Regional Police Service (WRPS)[1] in Cambridge, Ontario, Canada returned from lunch reluctantly. It was February 13, 2001, and today was not turning into a good day. On top of the usual challenges Gravill faced as manager of the police force, he knew that he was going to have to tackle the problem of the Common Information Management Systems (CIMS) project. CIMS was a four-year (and counting!) project of the WRPS and seven other police services organizations. WRPS and its partners had invested significant resources in this project over its life, yet there continued to be problems working with the principal contractor—Integrated Technologies Group (ITG). With the functional design specifications still under debate, Gravill had to decide whether to sign off on payment of the installment of $350,000 to ITG, or whether it was time for WRPS to cut its losses and move on to other options.

CAD	Computer Aided Dispatch (not to be confused with Computer Aided Design or Drafting)
CIMS	Common Information Management Systems project
CPIC	Canadian Police Information Centre—also the module of CIMS that links with the center in Ottawa
eCOPS	Enterprise Case and Occurrence Processing System—the system developed by Metro Toronto and IBM
FDS	Functional Design Specifications—the output of an analysis of needed system requirements—the FDS becomes the blueprint for developing the system modules
ITG	Integrated Technologies Group—the vendor
OPP	Ontario Provincial Police
PRIDE	Police Regionalized Information Data Entry System—a precursor to CIMS, built by five agencies in the Waterloo area—Larry Gravill was the leader of this project
RCMP	Royal Canadian Mounted Police
RFP	Request for Proposal
RMS	Records Management System—a component of CIMS
SOW	Statement of Work—a document that describes what a vendor will do to meet the system requirements as outlined in the Request for Proposal
UCR	Universal Crime Reporting
WRPS	Waterloo Regional Police Services

Exhibit 1   Listing of Acronyms

BACKGROUND ON THE WATERLOO REGIONAL POLICE SERVICES (WRPS)

The WRPS provided policing services to a population of 431,300 in the Regional Municipality of Waterloo, which was an area of 1,382 square kilometres (see Exhibit 2). Its mission communicated its commitment to a leadership role in crime prevention and law enforcement in a community partnership to improve safety and the quality of life for all people.

WRPS had 538 police officers, plus 178 support staff for a total of 716 employees. There were three major divisions within the service.

Division 1 encompassed the Kitchener and New Hamburg stations with 154 police officers and a support staff of eight. Division 2 was the Cambridge station with 112 police officers and seven support staff. Division 3 was the Waterloo and Elmira stations with 98 police officers and seven support staff, plus the headquarters location in Cambridge, Ontario, with 178 police officers and 156 support staff.

The 1999 annual report indicated that the WRPS had an annual net budget of $55.7 million, which was up 2.4 per cent from the previous year. Eighty-two per cent of the operating budget was allotted to salaries and benefits (see Exhibit 3).

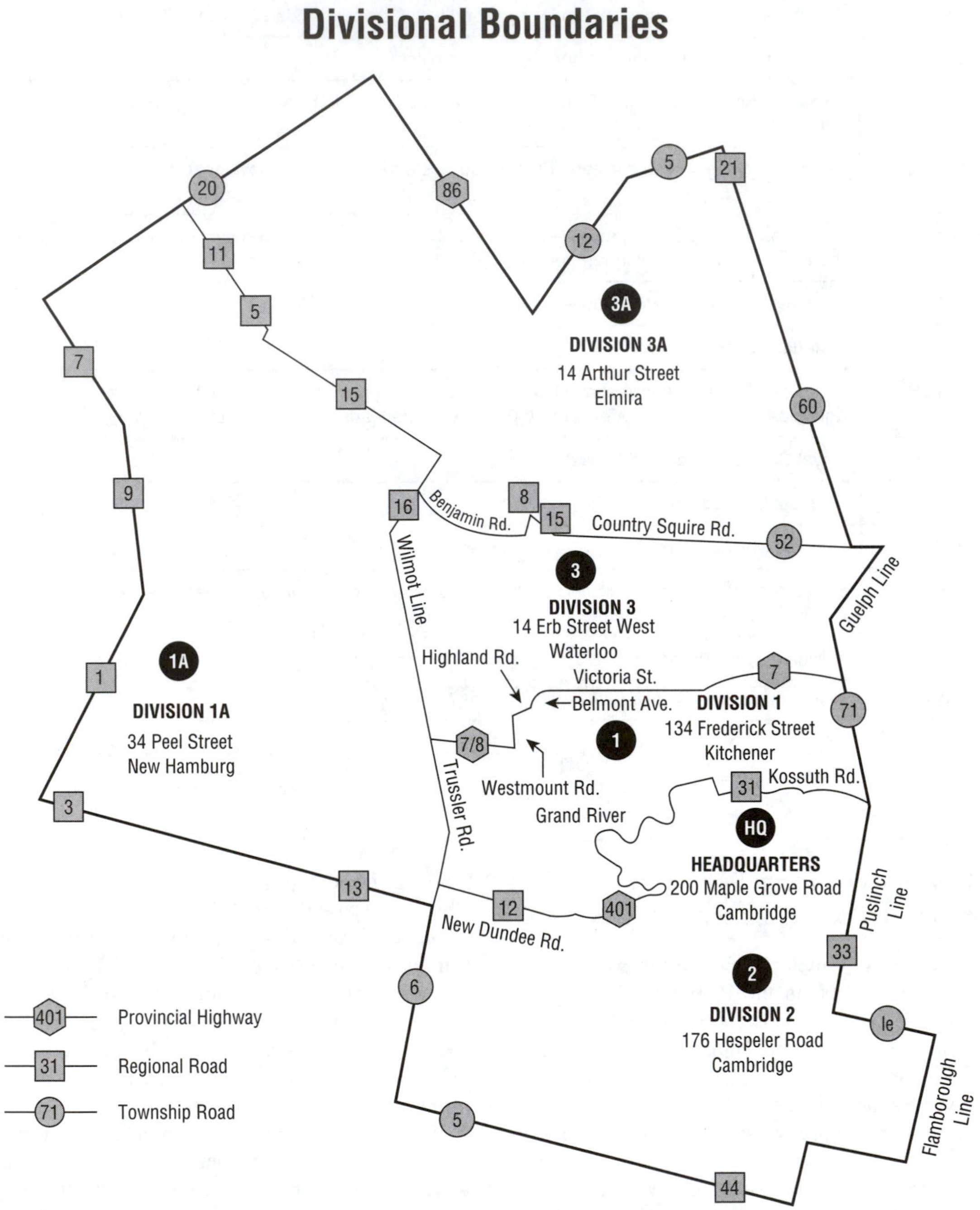

Divisional Boundaries

Exhibit 2   Map of the Area Served by Waterloo Regional Police Services

Source: 1999 WRPS Annual Report. Divisional pg. 6.

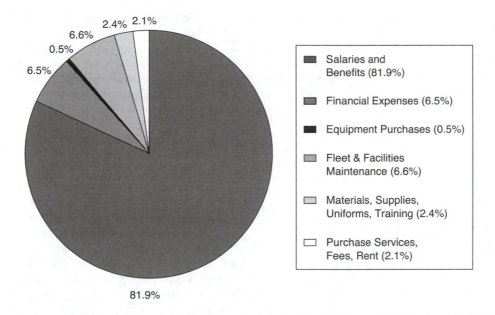

2.4% 2.1%
6.6%
0.5%
6.6%
6.5%

Salaries and
Benefits (81.9%)

Financial Expenses (6.5%)

Equipment Purchases (0.5%)

Fleet & Facilities
Maintenance (6.6%)

Materials, Supplies,
Uniforms, Training (2.4%)

Purchase Services,
Fees, Rent (2.1%)

81.9%

Exhibit 3   Operating Expenses

Total Budget: $55,765,062

Source: 1999 WRPS Annual Report.

POLICE CHIEF LARRY GRAVILL

Chief Gravill had been with the Waterloo Regional Police Service since 1973. He started his career performing patrol duties, and then accepted an assignment to the Police Traffic Branch—Motorcycle Patrol. He was seconded to the Ontario Police Commission for two years, from 1977 to 1979. Many special assignments followed, including project leader of the PRIDE[2] computer system; executive officer to the chief of police divisional commander—Waterloo division; superintendent of field operations and deputy chief of administration. He was also the recipient of the Police Exemplary Service Medal.

On October 1, 1992, Gravill was appointed chief of police of Waterloo Regional Police Service. He had also served as president of Ontario Association of Chiefs of Police from 1997 to 1998, and accepted the major responsibility of service as president of the Canadian Association of Chiefs of Police in 1999. In addition, Gravill was a member of the National Executive Institute Associates, a 400-plus member foundation affiliated with the United States Federal Bureau of Investigation.

An advocate of ongoing education, Gravill completed his undergraduate degree at Wilfrid Laurier University in Waterloo, Ontario. Later, he completed post-graduate programs at the F.B.I. National Academy and the University of Virginia, as well as executive development courses at the Canadian Police College, and the police management program at the Ontario Police College.

Chief Gravill had a long history of involvement with information systems. In 1981, he managed the implementation of the first police network to extend beyond the police services political and geographical boundaries (PRIDE). At that time, the Ontario Provincial Police (OPP) had a network, but it did not cross the organization's boundaries. Gravill's appreciation for the value of effective management information systems in implementing strategies for operational success continued throughout his career. This was evident in his description of the role of information systems (IS) in the police service:

> I have a vision for fully integrated systems accessible from mobile stations in the cruiser that would support improved crime analysis procedures for proactive action, and improved police services which support the facilitation of the community mobilization strategy where communities would be able to become knowledgeable and aware of their own safety or security issues, and would be better able to address these issues as a community successfully.

> This proactive approach is absolutely required for provision of improved police service. For example, in the Bernardo case,[3] if there had been more information sharing among the Police Services involved, Bernardo's criminal activity may have been discovered at an earlier stage. Information sharing is the key to identifying crime trends, allowing us to function proactively in an effective manner. To detect these trends, and to operate in an informed manner, system integration is required. We do not want to be in a position where we simply respond to calls for assistance. With the growing population in our area, we would need many additional resources to operate in this reactive manner. We want to use our resources fully and be able to identify problem areas before the situation escalates.

> The WRPS is a leader in the level of systems integration among police services, and intends to leverage this resource to provide premium service to the community.

CIMS PROJECT BACKGROUND

The Common Information Management Systems (CIMS) project was an extension and expansion of earlier police information systems projects, including PRIDE. This would be the third upgrade of the systems for WRPS.

CIMS was planned as a joint effort among 10 organizations: the Royal Canadian Mounted Police (RCMP), the Ontario Provincial Police (OPP), the Metropolitan Toronto Police, and the seven regional police services boards in the Golden Horseshoe area of Ontario—Waterloo (which also represented the PRIDE agencies of Stratford, Brantford and Guelph), Halton, Hamilton-Wentworth, Niagara, Durham, York, and Peel (see Exhibit 4).

The process began with about a year of background work with the involved agencies to establish the overall blueprint for the system. CIMS included five basic functions: computer aided dispatch, records management systems, mapping, mobile workstation environments, and the Canadian Police Information Centre (CPIC) module. Computer aided dispatch (CAD) was used to record calls and assign work to officers. The records management system (RMS) was the primary system for maintaining information on crimes and offenders. Mapping was the software that could generate maps for dispatchers to identify addresses more quickly to officers. The mobile workstation environment referred to the systems in the patrol cars. CPIC was the module that was to provide integration with the Canadian Police Information Centre—a federally operated, computer-based information system that provided national information on crime. Standardized information (following the Universal Crime Reporting guidelines) was shared between police forces through CPIC on a regular basis.

The CIMS project was key to providing the foundation for many operating efficiencies, further amalgamation of systems and service improvements in the Golden Horseshoe area. Chief Gravill observed:

> The CIMS project is important, as the objectives of this project provide the basis for effective information sharing among the regional police services. Systems integration and the information sharing it provides is key, as it will allow us to act in a more proactive manner and serve the community better. We will be in a better position to identify and facilitate the resolution of safety issues within communities before these issues become major problems, which typically result in calls for our assistance. Improved information sharing will result in improved police service to the community.

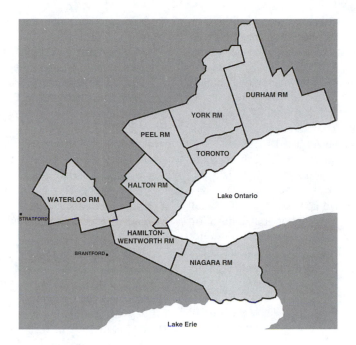

Exhibit 4   Map of the Golden Horseshoe Area

REQUEST FOR PROPOSAL (RFP) PROCESS

The RFP process for CIMS began in 1998. Unfortunately, the initial process did not succeed in identifying any vendors that could meet the stringent integration requirements of this proposed project design. All of the proposed statements of work (SOW) failed to meet the integration criteria established by the team.

The second RFP process took another year to complete. The integration requirements were made less stringent. Each of the 10 agencies involved in the process independently reviewed the response from the only vendor that submitted a proposal, indicating their ability to meet the requirements. This vendor was Integrated Technologies Group (ITG), based in the mid-Atlantic United States.

ITG had a solid score based on the statement of work, and appeared to be able to deliver the level of integration required. At this point, however, three of the original 10 agencies left the project. Metro Toronto and the OPP decided to leave the project in order to design and implement systems that would more closely meet their specific needs. The Metro Toronto region partnered with IBM to develop an Enterprise Case and Occurrence Processing System (eCOPS), which was featured in a Computerworld article in 2001.[4] The OPP contracted with Niche Technology Inc. (Niche) to provide implementation and integration of their management information systems.[5] Niche was a small family-owned business located in Winnipeg, Manitoba, which had entered the public safety systems arena through the success of their photo mug shot software.

The RCMP wanted to stay on board with the CIMS project, but could not, due to an operational policy that required any vendor to commit to a five-year support agreement regarding the product or service provided. ITG could not legally commit to this lengthy support contract; therefore, the RCMP was forced to exit the project. However, since they valued the objective of the CIMS project and wanted to stay involved, they assigned a full-time project manager to the CIMS project.

This left the group of seven regional police services on board[6] with the CIMS project to work toward the standard system platform and systems integration. The contract with ITG was signed by all parties on August 19, 1999.

In total, the contract was valued at approximately $16 million including hardware, software and systems integration. Each agency contributed a share determined based on the "total authorized strength" (or authorized number of police officers) in their respective regions. WRPS's share was about 17 per cent of the total. The major milestones in the project (and payment schedule) were:

1. initial signed agreement and delivery of performance bond (10 per cent of payment)

2. delivery implementation plan (five per cent)

3. delivery of draft functional system descriptions (10 per cent)

4. approval of functional design specifications for CAD and RMS (25 per cent)

5. functional design specification approval plus 30 days (10 per cent)

6. installation of application software (15 per cent)

7. completion by ITG of train the trainer program (five per cent)

8. completion of functional system testing (10 per cent)

9. completion of reliability testing/beneficial use (10 per cent)

Exhibit 5 shows the project timeline.

INTEGRATED TECHNOLOGIES GROUP—THE VENDOR

The vendor selected for the project was ITG. A leading provider of integrated public safety and criminal justice systems in the United States,

the company had more than 5,300 employees in 80 offices worldwide.

ITG primarily designed infrastructure and enterprise architectures, and sold itself as a customer-centric organization that realized that responsiveness and adaptability were key to meeting customer needs. In providing these solutions, ITG specialized in complete client/server, storage and network solutions. ITG believed that its global presence and many strategic partnerships[7] allowed it to offer the best solution to their customers. This meant that whether it was a single product or a complete product, services, maintenance or training solution, ITG was able to deliver the solution.

Until 1998, ITG had had a branch office in Newmarket, Ontario, but it was closed due to business requirements in the United States. Because the CIMS contract required a Canadian office, the company reopened an office in December of 1999 in Toronto, Ontario. As one of the team members observed:

> ITG opened a beautiful office in the third floor of a building by the Toronto airport. This office space would hold about 80 people. However, I have never seen more than three people there at any time I have visited the site. They need to bring more resources north of the border to work on a major project like CIMS. ITG was also awarded an e-commerce deal with police services in British Columbia and Halifax, so maybe this will encourage them to send some more people up here.

PROBLEMS SURFACE AS THE PROJECT BEGINS

When the CIMS core project team, which had representatives from all regional police services, began reviewing the detailed functional design specifications (FDS) with ITG, problems began to surface. This team met daily to ensure progress on the CIMS project was achieved. It became clear that the CIMS project team and the vendor did not agree on the interpretation of requirements.

ID	Task Name	Phase	Phase	Duration	Start	Finish	Responsible	Precedes
1	Implementation Plan Agreement			0 days	Mon 7/31/00	Mon 7/31/00		
2	**CIMS Program Implementation**			**555 days**	**Tue 5/30/00**	**Sat 9/14/02**		
3	CIMS Program Planning	Planning	0-Planning	372 days	Mon 7/31/00	Thu 2/21/02		
4	CIMS Implementation Plan	Planning	0-Planning	0 days	Mon 7/31/00	Mon 7/31/00		
7	CIMS Training Plan	Planning	0-Planning	185 days	Tue 5/15/01	Thu 2/21/02		
23	CIMS Acceptance Test Plan	Planning	0-Planning	25 days	Fri 12/08/00	Thu 1/25/01		
29	CIMS Data Conversion Plan	Planning	0-Planning	50 days	Mon 8/7/00	Mon 10/16/00		
36	Data Conversion Activities			165 days	Tue 10/17/00	Thu 6/28/01		
43	Data Entry Activities	Develop	0-Develop	85 days	Wed 2/21/01	Fri 6/22/01		
49	CIMS Site Preparation Plan	Planning	0-Planning	30 days	Tue 11/14/00	Thu 1/11/01		
55	CIMS Cutover Plan	Planning	0-Planning	30 days	Tue 10/23/01	Thu 12/6/01		
61	CIMS FUNCTIONAL DESIGN	Design	0-Design	169 days	Tue 5/30/00	Wed 2/14/01		
116	REMAINING CIMS SOFTWARE DEVELOPMENT	Develop	0-Develop	200 days	Mon 9/18/00	Tue 7/24/01		
135	CIMS HARDWARE PROCUREMENT	HDWR	0-HW	208 days	Mon 7/31/00	Tue 6/12/01		
158	**HALTON REGIONAL POLICE**	**HRPS**	**1-HRPS**	**306 days**	**Fri 1/12/01**	**Wed 4/17/02**		
159	System Integration and Installation	HRPS	1-HRPS	140 days	Fri 1/12/01	Tue 8/7/01	ITG	
179	Site Testing	HRPS	1-HRPS	139 days	Tue 3/13/01	Fri 9/28/01		
187	**TRAINING**	**HRPS**	**1-HRPS**	**135 days**	**Mon 7/30/01**	**Thu 2/21/02**		
188	System Admin Training			5 days	Mon 7/30/01	Fri 8/3/01		
191	Train-the-Trainers			30 days	Mon 10/1/01	Mon 11/12/01		
195	User Training			60 days	Tue 11/13/01	Thu 2/21/02		
199	Training Completed			0 days	Thu 2/21/02	Thu 2/21/02	CIMS	194, 198, 190
200	System Cutover			63 days	Fri 1/18/02	Wed 4/17/02		
215	Final Acceptance - HRPS			0 days	Wed 4/17/02	Wed 4/17/02	CIMS	
219	Hamilton Wentworth Regional Police Service	HWRPS	2-HWRPS	497 days	Tue 5/30/00	Thu 6/20/02		
274	Durham Regional Police Service	DRPS	3-DRPS	358 days	Fri 1/12/01	Thu 7/4/02		
336	York Regional Police Service	YRPS	4-YRPS	367 days	Fri 1/12/01	Thu 7/18/02		
398	PRIDE Agencies	PRIDE	5-PRIDE	386 days	Fri 1/12/01	Wed 8/14/02		
460	Niagara Regional Police Service	NRPS	6-NRPS	396 days	Fri 1/12/01	Wed 8/28/02		
522	Peel Regional Police Service	PRPS	7-PRPS	408 days	Fri 1/12/01	Sat 9/14/02		

Exhibit 5   Project Timeline

Source: Company files.

Staff Sergeant Al Stauch, a member of the core CIMS project team, explained:

> At one point we had 200 issues in dispute regarding the FDS with respect to the CAD module, 60 issues in the RMS, all of CPIC was an issue, and two issues in the mapping software. Canadianization of the software is the big issue, and is the major misunderstanding between them and us. We paid $200,000 for this Canadianization, and they did not understand what was required. They (ITG) should have understood the scope of Canadianization, as they implemented an upgrade for us in 1993/1994 for the PRIDE agencies, so they had first-hand knowledge of what would be required.
>
> Canadianization includes providing "a fully integrated CPIC interface," the integrated rollover from our RMS into our CPIC database. We maintain that this requires all of the software functionality to complete this task. ITG's position is that the Canadianization integration means only the specific hardware integration.
>
> In addition, there are issues around words used for various terms. For example, they should have known things like the word "juvenile" in their software must be replaced by the words "young person" for our use. They have done this type of work for us before. If we have any documents that come out of our system using the term "juvenile," we may actually have some litigation based on these reports. There are about seven of this type of word-change issues that need to be resolved. ITG's problem is that a lot of this functionality is hard coded into their system, and it will cost them some dollars to make these changes.
>
> This Canadianization requirement was likely not spelled out in enough detail in the RFP, but ITG should have been aware of the requirement as they were the vendor that actually conducted these same types of modifications for our existing PRIDE system. They should have known.

This dispute escalated into a complete communication breakdown during February 2000. By July 2000, when communications had not resumed, the project was in jeopardy. Thus, the project teams from each of the regions met with the vendor and the regional police chiefs in order to resolve the problems. With the strong support of the police chiefs backing the position of the project team, ITG stated it was in total agreement and wanted to make the project a success. As a result of this meeting, the CIMS project was resumed.

In September of 2000, the RCMP had to pull out their project manager, due to resource constraints and demands of their own system development. At that time, Al Rosenberg, one of the first proponents of the CIMS project, was brought on board.

Over the next several months, disagreement between the project teams and the vendor reignited, to the point where dispute over several key project deliverables became—for the second time—a major issue. By February 2001, many issues had been resolved, but a number of key issues were still outstanding. Stauch explained:

> This was a large list that we started with, but we resolved the bulk of them by discussing the integration requirements and making appropriate modifications. The remaining unresolved issues are now about 30 in number, and these revolve mostly around the Canadianization problem, which they can't seem to address or face up to.
>
> What it comes down to now is that there are some very specific requirements that, if resolved with ITG, would render all other issues irrelevant, and we could move forward without a problem.
>
> ITG thinks we are reading too much into the FDS that we included in the RFP, and that the deliverable they are to provide is not as integrated as we are assuming. But we are saying that they must provide this, as this is the objective of the project. We just spent three days in the United States with ITG's president and some vice-president's trying to resolve these issues on a face-to-face basis.
>
> The next level of discussion will go to the chiefs, and it will have to be sorted out there. When we sign off on the FDS, that is really committing to the project, so this has to be sorted out soon. ITG has not even started writing code yet, so they have not really assigned resources to this project. Our next installment shows our complete commitment to the project, and they are waiting for this sign-off and payment. This has to be resolved soon.

It is getting to the point where we are checking the FDS documents that ITG is sending us word for word to see what they have changed or revised. They used to send us the documents in MS Word format so we could use the document to compare function with previous versions of the same document. Now they are sending the documents in Adobe Acrobat format, which is a picture file, and we cannot compare these easily to previous versions. This is taking a lot of our time, but it looks like it is required. We are very careful not to stray from any agreed upon deliverable or time line with this vendor. We have worked weekends and evenings to review and turn around the documents they have sent us to meet a predetermined time line. We do not want them to have any reason to point the finger at us for any project delays. They are a very good vendor with a lot of expertise, but this is a big project with a lot riding on it, and it hasn't been easy. It must be done right.

CHIEF GRAVILL'S DILEMMA

As Sergeant Stauch indicated, the next phase of the project was due to start in February 2001 and required a major payment installment of $350,000 from the WRPS to ITG (a total payment of $2.1 million from all the agencies involved). With the go-live date of August 2002 fast approaching, Chief Gravill had to decide whether it was best for WRPS to abide by the contract terms with ITG and pay the $350,000 for ITG to continue working on this project, or whether to withdraw from the contract, possibly face litigation from the vendor, and evaluate other options such as searching for other vendors or beginning the RFP process all over again.

To further complicate the situation, the Hamilton-Wentworth Region, a CIMS project member, desperately required a new system, as theirs was becoming inoperable. This region was still operating on old Macintosh computer equipment in some cases, and they made it known that upgraded equipment and systems were urgently required. Therefore, for Hamilton to remain part of the CIMS project, the project go-live date could not be pushed out from August 2002. They simply could not afford delays. Pushing out the go-live date or delaying the next major phase of the project would risk Hamilton-Wentworth pulling out of the CIMS project completely to address their own needs. This would reduce the number of regions on board with the CIMS project to six, and the project would therefore be less effective, given the regional information sharing objectives.

In essence, Chief Gravill needed to evaluate the situation to ensure the WRPS would move ahead at this critical turning point in the CIMS project under the appropriate conditions, at the right time and with the right vendor. He knew that these and other elements of the CIMS equation were critical for project success. Faced with the pressure to sign off on the FDS, it was time to objectively analyse the CIMS project situation by identifying the key decision criteria at this point and determine how the WRPS should best more forward.

NOTES

1. For ease of reference, Exhibit 1 contains a listing of all acronyms used in this document.
2. PRIDE was the Police Regionalized Information Data Entry system. It was a joint initiative of WRPS and three other municipalities—Stratford, Brantford and Guelph.
3. Paul Bernardo committed at least 18 sexual assaults in Scarborough Ontario between 1987 and 1992. He was finally caught after the brutal assault and murder of two young girls in St. Catharines, ON. According to a government initiated review of the case, a key reason why Bernardo was not caught earlier was the inability of police forces to share information.
4. Lahey, L. (2001). "Ontario gets e-police." Computerworld, February 9, 2001.
5. The contract with Niche was signed in February 2001.
6. Waterloo Regional Police Service, Halton, Hamilton-Wentworth, Niagara, Durham, York and Peel.
7. The company had strategic partnerships with firms such as Hewlett-Packard, Cisco Systems, LexMark, Astor Technologies, EMC2, Veritas, Compaq, Oracle, and Sun Microsystems.

5

QUALITY

Quality has been an important concern ever since firms began producing goods or delivering services and managers realized the importance of meeting standards. Quality has emerged as one of the key dimensions of customer value; however, customers define quality in various ways, partly dependent on whether the customers are internal or external to the firm. In general, quality may be defined as meeting or exceeding the requirements, needs, and expectations of the customer—whether or not those needs have been articulated.

QUALITY DEFINED

It is widely accepted that quality represents an important attribute underlying customer value. Quality is often a difficult attribute to assess, and many consumers, when asked to identify quality, are likely to respond, "I know it when I see it." Managers need to understand the elements of quality, as perceived by the user, to assess whether a product or service is of high quality.

Garvin (1988) identified eight dimensions of quality:

- *Performance:* measurable primary characteristics of a product or service
- *Features:* added characteristics that enhance the appeal of a product or service
- *Conformance:* meeting specifications or industry standards
- *Reliability:* consistency of performance over time
- *Durability:* useful life of a product or service
- *Serviceability:* resolution of problems and complaints
- *Aesthetics:* the sensory characteristics of a product or service
- *Perceived quality:* subjective assessment of quality based on cues related to the product

To design and deliver quality, a company's products need not be rated high on each dimension. Manufacturers of food products, such as Noram Foods, might focus heavily on conformance, reliability, and aesthetics. In contrast, a diesel engine manufacturer, such as LongXi Machinery Works, could emphasize performance (i.e., power) and features relative to competitors. Thus, customers (and managers) must choose which dimensions of quality to emphasize, meaning that trade-offs between these dimensions might be necessary.

Not all of Garvin's (1988) eight dimensions of quality apply equally well to both goods and services. For services, which are often intangible in nature, it is also necessary to assess a number of process-based elements. Parasuraman, Zeithaml, and Berry (1988) posit five dimensions to service quality:

- *Reliability:* ability to perform the promised service dependably and accurately
- *Responsiveness:* willingness to help customers and provide prompt service
- *Assurance:* employees' knowledge, courtesy, and their ability to inspire trust and confidence
- *Empathy:* caring, individualized attention given to customers
- *Tangibles:* appearance of physical facilities, equipment, personnel, and written material

Assessing service quality, which is a critical task for managers and employees of Blue Mountain Resorts and Mutual Life of Canada, is primarily done through surveying customers on their expectations and perceptions of performance across various dimensions.

These definitions of quality have, as seen in the cases that follow, significant implications for the operational control and improvement of quality. Irrespective of how quality is defined in the manufacturing or service context, the strategic elements, practices, and tools necessary for the successful management of quality fall under the umbrella descriptor "total quality management."

QUALITY DELIVERED

Total quality management (TQM) requires the managing of the entire organization so that it excels in all dimensions of goods and services that are important to the customer. TQM represents a pragmatic and comprehensive system for managing quality. The "total" component of TQM emphasizes that performance excellence needs to exist throughout all the firm's operational activities: design, procurement, production, distribution, and service. Furthermore, involvement from all firm stakeholders—employees, suppliers, and customers— is critical to the TQM effort. Successful implementation of TQM transcends culture, as illustrated in the LongXi Machinery Works case, and requires customer focus, top management support, active involvement of all employees, continuous improvement and learning, business planning and performance measurement, management by fact, and collaborative relationships. Each of these contributes to the synergy required for effective TQM.

Many firms have achieved significant performance benefits—operationally, financially, or customer based—from implementing an effective TQM system. These benefits are the result of successfully deploying both the philosophical elements and generic tools of TQM. In the Noram Foods case, for example, you will have to address the philosophical implications to managing quality resulting from an analysis of statistical process control data.

Although quality may be an important priority for an organization's survival, it alone may not guarantee success. Indeed, managers recognize that there are both quantitative and qualitative costs for poor quality. Some of these quantitative and qualitative costs include scrap, rework, downtime, lost customers, and negative word of mouth. Implemented successfully, TQM provides managers with new strategic options. Given increased customer expectations on quality, cost, delivery, and flexibility, companies are challenged to design, produce, and deliver products and services better, faster, and cheaper. TQM represents an integrated approach to addressing such challenges.

Furthermore, TQM's emphasis on continuous improvement affects the efficiency and effectiveness of many operational practices, including those related to process design and planning and control. For example, manufacturers implementing just-in-time production as part of a broader supply chain management system are required to first achieve stable and capable production processes. TQM can be effectively employed to achieve the required stability and capability through the continual focus on identifying and eliminating predictable variability that results in waste. Most organizations that have implemented quality management have quickly recognized the importance of continuous improvement and that the rate of improvement achieved is as important as the resulting performance improvements. For these reasons, the management of quality represents an important component for achieving world-class operations (see Figure 5.1).

The cases in this quality management module generally involve the definition, control, and improvement of quality, for products or processes, in both service and manufacturing organizations. The module includes discussions of the costs of poor quality, statistical quality control, benchmarking, standards such as ISO 9000, quality guarantees, and operational options for improving quality.

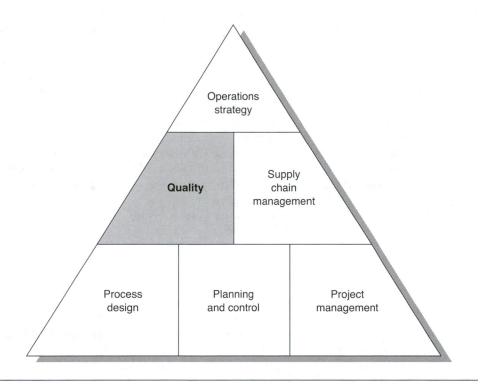

Figure 5.1   Quality Management

LongXi Machinery Works—Quality Improvement (A)

Zhang Lin, the assistant engineer in the Thermal Treatment Department of LongXi Machinery Works (Longxi), a state-owned enterprise in China, has received approval for the formation of a new quality control group to reduce the high defect rate of a critical part. This high defect rate had significant implications for Longxi's future development because it caused costly production delays and engine failures at a time when many industry players were fighting for survival. Lin must decide who will be directly involved in the quality control group, which data must be collected and analyzed, what is the cause of the problem, and which actions should be taken. Longxi's total quality concept is presented within the context of a specific quality problem. (Note: This case is the first of a three-part series that applies the principles and tools of TQM in a Chinese setting. This case can either be used independently or in combination with the (B) case, 9A98D002, and (C) case, 9A98D003, available from Ivey Publishing.)

Learning objectives: compare and contrast TQM concepts, frameworks, and tools, especially in an international setting; assess quality systems; and apply quality tools and improvement cycle.

Blue Mountain Resorts: The Service Quality Journey

Blue Mountain Resorts had been driving its business with a service quality program for several years, which the vice president of human resources, David Sinclair, was responsible for coordinating. With a new ski season under way and the critical Christmas season approaching, Sinclair wanted to continue progress of the program by introducing a new set of initiatives. He had recently gathered together a team of Blue Mountain Resort managers from a variety of different areas in the company to identify opportunities to improve service quality. The group provided three proposals that he felt warranted consideration. Sinclair would be expected to set the priorities for the coming year and recommend what action, if any, should be taken for each at the upcoming executive team meeting. He had to decide which programs made the most sense for immediate action and which ones required additional study and analysis. Each of the proposals affected different parts of the organization, so Sinclair also needed to be concerned about who else in the company should be involved in further evaluation and implementation.

Learning objectives: differentiate product and service quality, illustrate quality management in services, and examine the role of internal and external customers.

Noram Foods

Noram Foods, a major producer of consumer food products known for its high-quality brands, had recently experienced a period of declining profits when the Canadian economy suffered under conditions of high unemployment, high interest rates, and high inflation. The president of Noram Foods has expressed the need to exploit revenue-increasing and cost-reduction opportunities wherever possible. Pat Marsden, the plant manager for Noram Foods, was considering the impact of changing Noram's policy on package weight, as the weight control issue represented a major opportunity for reevaluation and increased performance. Marsden had to decide whether to recommend to Noram executives that company standards on package weight control be lowered to secure cost savings. Government regulations were more lenient than Noram's corporate standards, but a citation for weight violations might seriously affect its brand image with customers.

Learning objectives: understand statistical process control, contrast "voice of customer" and "voice of process" quality perspectives, and assess ethical trade-offs in operating decisions.

HILCREST AUTO

Mark Bailey, quality manager and business unit manager of the Small Parts Division of Hilcrest Auto, discovered that scrapped parts had been used in a shipment to a major customer. Although Hilcrest had experienced quality problems for some time, this shipment decision could have a potentially disastrous effect on the firm's future. Bailey must decide what action to take regarding the scrapped parts shipment and determine which among four options to choose to address quality issues. Each of these options would result in operational changes to the production facility for heating core tubing. However, some of the improvements required additional investments and expenditures. Bailey felt the need to ensure that strong quantitative support and a convincing qualitative rationale formed the basis for his decision.

Learning objectives: examine costs of quality, apply quality management tools for improvement, and implement quality-based changes in operational policies, procedures, and practices.

MUTUAL LIFE OF CANADA—THE GROUP CLIENT SERVICE GUARANTEE (A)

Alex Brown, the senior vice president and head of Mutual Life's group division, was trying to decide whether to proceed with a plan to guarantee his division's services as a task force had recommended. If the division decided to proceed, he would have to decide whether to accept the task force's suggestions on the design of the guarantee and answer a number of questions that they had left unanswered. Brown was currently considering three distinct service guarantee options and was faced with an urgent decision as the task force would expect that any service guarantee be implemented quickly. (Note: A sequel to this case bearing the same title, case 9A94D017, describes the guarantee and an issue that has arisen; this is available from Ivey Publishing.)

Learning objectives: design, assess, and implement service guarantees; understand operational and marketing implications for service quality; and evaluate informational requirements for quality management.

MANAGEMENT QUESTIONS ADDRESSED IN THE QUALITY CHAPTER

1. How is quality defined? What is the goal of total quality management (TQM)? Why is TQM important?

2. Who are the quality gurus? Compare and contrast the gurus in terms of how they defined quality and how quality was to be managed.

3. How does quality and the management of quality differ between manufacturing and service organizations?

4. What role should the customer play in the management of quality?

5. What tools and practices are commonly used in TQM? Describe the types of qualitative and quantitative tools and practices commonly employed in TQM and indicate under what circumstances they are likely to be effective or ineffective.

6. How should an organization's TQM efforts be assessed? What approaches are available for measuring quality?

7. What is required for successful TQM implementation? What are the challenges in implementing an effective TQM program?

8. Compare and contrast TQM with business process reengineering (BPR). What is required for successful BPR?

REFERENCES

Garvin, D. A. (1988). *Managing quality: The strategic and competitive edge.* New York: Free Press.
Parasuraman, A., Zeithaml, V. Z., & Berry, L. L. (1988). SERVQUAL: A multiple-item scale for measuring consumer perceptions of service quality. *Journal of Retailing (Spring),* pp. 12–40.

LONGXI MACHINERY WORKS—QUALITY IMPROVEMENT (A)

*Prepared by Larry Li
and Tom Gleave under the
supervision of Professor Rob Klassen*

Version: (A) 1998-05-04

As the end of September 1996 neared, Mr. Shi, Manager of the Quality Management Department at LongXi Machinery Works (Longxi) in Zhangzhou, China, was reviewing an application for the formation of a new quality control (QC) group. Mr. Lin, an assistant engineer in the Thermal Treatment Department, was proposing that this group focus on growing quality concerns with the production of a critical part, called the duo-gear shaft (DGS).[1] This part was used in Longxi's multi-cylinder diesel engines to transfer power between gears. If a DGS did not meet minimum performance standards, it could crack, and

then break, possibly resulting in complete seizure of the engine.

This was not the first time that quality concerns about this part had come to Shi's attention. He recalled recently receiving a report from the Inspection Department complaining about numerous quality problems originating in the Thermal Treatment Workshop. When similar problems had occurred several years ago, Longxi's engineers had been unable to determine the precise cause of the quality problems. At that time, after noticing a marked improvement in DGS quality following the rainy season, the engineers simply attributed the problem to the changing temperature and humidity in the plant.

While the DGS part itself was relatively small and inexpensive (RMB 15),[2] continued quality problems would have significant implications for Longxi's future business. Longxi's multi-cylinder engines were used in the agricultural sector, and there had been a growing number of customer complaints about losses in production time resulting from engine breakdowns. Since the beginning of the year, there had been 14 incidents related to failure of this part. Because special equipment was needed to fix any failure, Longxi was forced to cover the costs of sending a mechanic to replace the part, or in cases of severe damage, of replacing the engine completely at a cost of RMB 4,000.

While the Inspection Department identified most defective parts before their final assembly into engines, the high defect rate, 44 per cent in September, had resulted in costly delays to engine production at a time when industry players were competing fiercely with each other. After reviewing and approving Lin's application, Shi commented:

> Unfortunately, the number of reliable suppliers who could produce this part is extremely limited, and those that could possibly help us are already over-stretching their production capacity. I believe that purchasing from these suppliers would further aggravate our quality problem. Thus, Longxi has no choice—we must find a way to improve quality in-house. If we are not successful, we run the risk of jeopardizing our long term strategy, which calls for expanding our product sales both at home and abroad.

CHINA'S SMALL DIESEL ENGINE INDUSTRY

China's agricultural machinery sector, Longxi's primary market, had been experiencing profound change since 1978 when a series of economic reforms designed to boost China's overall farm output were introduced. The reforms provided farmers with incentives to exceed their traditional quotas and proved to be a considerable success as China's total agricultural output increased dramatically in the ensuing years. This led to increased buying power in the rural sector, resulting in a rising demand for low-cost, small to medium-sized diesel engines for use on small-scale agricultural units. Reform measures also had encouraged the development of larger cooperative farming efforts that benefit from greater economies of scale. Cooperative farms, in turn, translated into additional demand for larger model engines, thus encouraging manufacturers to offer a greater range of product options.

Sales of diesel-powered agricultural machinery and vehicles in China had grown by more than 10 per cent annually since 1985, and this growth rate was forecast to continue until at least the year 2000. This year, Longxi estimated that domestic manufacturers across this sector would combine to produce 1.91 million small tractors, 85,000 domestically produced medium to large tractors, 15,200 seeders and 23,600 threshers, along with a host of other agricultural machines, such as irrigation pumps and small transportation vehicles. Approximately 85 per cent of this equipment used single-cylinder diesel engines.

Four large manufacturers jointly accounted for approximately 45 per cent of China's production of single-cylinder engines. The remainder of the market was divided among several medium-sized (including Longxi) and numerous smaller firms. Over the past several years, industry consolidation and rationalization had reduced the number of medium-sized firms from the previous high of 30 to about 15. This trend was expected to continue over the next five years.

The principal strategy employed by most Chinese manufacturers was to compete on the basis of low cost production. For example, Chinese firms typically were able to produce engines at 25 per cent of the cost of their Japanese counterparts, who currently had the second largest single-cylinder diesel engine industry in the world. Recent investment had pushed the industry into a state of overcapacity for single-cylinder engines. Yet, many manufacturers continued to add capacity as they upgraded production technology to lower costs and improve quality. As a result, it was widely expected that a price war was imminent.

In contrast, the market for small multi-cylinder diesel engines was much more promising. Although sales levels were currently well below those of single-cylinder engines, customer demands for more power were being heard as efforts were made to further increase productivity in the agricultural sector. One factor was the formation of larger cooperative farms, with their drive for economies of scale. Another was the greater need for small transportation vehicles in the agricultural sector to move more products greater distances. Moreover, multi-cylinder engines also offered greater versatility, with a broader range of applications across both agricultural and other small machinery sectors. Because demand was growing faster than supply, manufacturers had been able to impose price increases on multi-cylinder engines.

COMPANY BACKGROUND

LongXi Machinery Works (Longxi) was a state-owned enterprise (SOE) located in Zhangzhou, Fujian, a southern coastal Chinese province situated across from Taiwan. The company was founded in 1957 as a result of the merger between a military machinery works from Sichuan province (in China's southwest interior) and an agricultural machinery plant owned by the city government of Zhangzhou.

Since its inception, Longxi had produced various single and multi-cylinder diesel engines primarily for the agricultural sector. These engines were typically used in the powertrains of four-wheel and three-wheel tractors, hand-held tractors, as well as related equipment such as tillers, seeders and threshers. They also were modified for use as irrigation pumps. These varying applications meant that the company serviced four primary customer groups: tractor manufacturers, ancillary equipment manufacturers, engine wholesalers and farmers who bought directly from the plant.

In the early years, Longxi produced only one model of single-cylinder, low-speed diesel engine. This model was primarily sold in the domestic market, although a small volume were exported to Africa, Latin America and Southeast Asia. In the 1970s, the plant shifted its focus toward the production of single-cylinder, high-speed engines which were sold both locally and in export markets. By the 1980s, the product line had further expanded to include several two- and three-cylinder models. It was during this period that Longxi began exporting its multi-cylinder products to the United States. In the last five years, the company had broadened its product line to include a series of four-cylinder, high-speed units.

At this time, Longxi's most popular multi-cylinder unit was the SL2100,[3] a two-cylinder model generating 28 horsepower (hp). Management felt that this particular engine was the key to future sales for several reasons. First, the primary market for these engines, 25–30 hp wheeled tractors, was expected to remain buoyant over the next several years. This engine also could be readily adapted for other agricultural equipment use, further increasing its market potential.

Second, the marketplace was increasingly viewing an older, multi-cylinder engine—model S295—as having insufficient power. The two-cylinder S295, produced by competitors, generated only 24 hp, was larger, and was of lower quality. This view was particularly prevalent in export markets like the U.S. Longxi's new model SL2100 recently had received favorable feedback from U.S. importers, and the company believed that there was strong potential for the SL2100 to replace the S295 throughout the industry.

Third, the SL2100 offered a wider range of uses outside the agricultural equipment sector than other single or two-cylinder models. For example, the SL2100 could be used in 0.8 ton and 1.5 ton front-end loaders, as well as 2.0 ton forklifts. This engine also could be easily adapted for electrical generators and small boat engines.

Management was confident that sales of this model would increase dramatically in 1997 to a projected total of 12,000 units. Company-wide, financial results for the year to date indicated that Longxi was on target to reach revenues of RMB

176 million in 1996, with an income of RMB 6.5 million in 1996. These figures were based on projected sales of 80,000 single-cylinder engines and 6,900 multi-cylinder engines in 1996.

Changchai: Longxi's Primary Competitor

Changchou Diesel Engine Works (Changchai) was the world's largest producer of single-cylinder diesel engines, a distinction it achieved in 1993, the same year its popular S195 model became ISO 9002 certified. The vast majority of its sales, 92 per cent, were destined for the domestic market, which was serviced through a network of 275 service centers located throughout 26 provinces. Changchai's engines also were increasingly being exported to the Southeast Asian countries of Indonesia, Vietnam and Thailand, where it was able to sell its products for a small premium. About 80 per cent of Changchai's sales were to tractor and agriculture equipment manufacturers, while distributors purchased the remainder.

The company had experienced significant growth in recent years. In 1995, the Changchai group of companies operated 33 separate engine production lines and had doubled its 1994 sales to reach RMB 2.16 billion. Profits jumped even more dramatically, more than four-fold, to RMB 208 million. Forecasted sales and profits for 1996 were RMB 3.0 billion and RMB 300 million, respectively.

This spectacular growth had been largely achieved through investing in a series of joint ventures. Since 1994, Changchai had acquired controlling interest in three small domestic diesel engine manufacturers which were incurring losses or operating at undercapacity. Changchai licensed its better known brand name to these companies in an effort to increase their sales. As a result, the company captured 23 per cent of the domestic market for single-cylinder engines in 1995 with sales of 1.2 million units, with output projected to rise to 1.8 million units in 1996. The corporate objective was to capture 30 per cent market share by 2000.

In contrast, Changchai sold only 3,000 multi-cylinder units in 1995, despite having capacity to produce 60,000 units. Current plans called for expanding R&D in this area and increasing the range of models offered. Management also had announced plans to double the capacity of their multi-cylinder production lines in the near future to meet anticipated market demand. Finally, two joint ventures with diesel engine component manufacturers had been established earlier in the year in a move to backward integrate and better control the supply of parts.

The capital necessary for all this expansion was raised through a series of share offerings, with the first, initial public offering occurring in 1994 for 20 million class "A" shares on the Shenzhen Stock Exchange. Then, earlier this month, 100 million class "B" shares, valued at US$ 90 million and accounting for about 30 per cent of the company's expanded capital base, were listed on the Shenzhen Stock Exchange. Immediately following this issue, Japan's Kubota Corporation, a high quality manufacturer of farming equipment, purchased US$ 25 million of the stock. This investment by Kubota was in anticipation of future cooperation between the two companies involving technology transfer and market access.

Changchai competed primarily on the basis of offering high quality products at prices similar to or less than most of their competitors, including Longxi. The firm's manufacturing strategy called for outsourcing all non-critical components while retaining control over the production of key items such as cylinder heads and engine blocks. By 1996, about 83 per cent of its component requirements were outsourced. New manufacturing technology was imported from Germany, U.S., Japan, Taiwan and France to improve quality and productivity.

PRODUCTION FACILITIES AT LONGXI

Like many other SOEs in China, the "Works" was split into two distinct areas, one for living, the other for production. The living area contained apartments for employees and their families, an employee club, entertainment center, hospital and canteen, all provided by Longxi. Employment had steadily declined from 2,300 at the beginning of this decade to the current level of approximately 1,880.

As employees entered the production area (Exhibit 1), they were greeted at the entrance by the company's two guiding slogans: "Love LongXi, Complete Contribution," and "Market, Management, Quality, Profit." Most of the facilities were built during the 1960s and 1970s, although several new engine assembly lines had been added more recently as the company had expanded its range of multi-cylinder products. Most recently, new technologies, such as group processing centers, had been acquired from Germany, Britain, Japan and Taiwan to help bolster both the company's component and machine manufacturing capabilities. These centers were capable of cutting, grinding and drilling engine parts and were especially valuable for rapidly developing and testing engine component prototypes. However, the operation of much of the older equipment still relied heavily on human judgment.

Warehouse

| material storage | sawing machines (6) | inspection office |

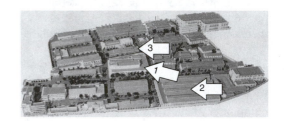

1 Warehouse
2 Machining Department
3 Heat Treating Department

Machining Department

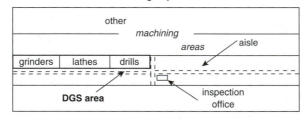

Thermal Treatment Department

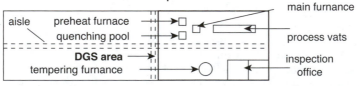

Exhibit 1   Plant Layout

Increased competition during the last decade had encouraged customers to demand greater value from engine producers, which in turn forced the industry to reduce production costs. In response, Longxi increasingly engaged in outsourcing or co-production of its engine components. By 1996, about 80 per cent of Longxi's engine components were manufactured externally. However, the company continued to maintain complete control over what it viewed as key components for its engines: cylinders, cylinder heads, and a number of component parts, including the DGS. Management had considered greater vertical integration, but one senior manager noted:

> We have discussed the possibility of vertically integrating with some of our domestic suppliers and buyers; however, our location remains a concern for them. There is only one railway line to Zhangzhou and it has proven to be severely inadequate and has caused us great difficulties in getting our products distributed and marketed.

The firm also had over 350 technical staff helping to manage its facilities, including 14 separate production lines. About 30 per cent of these employees had achieved the title of "Senior Engineer" from several different government ministries. This title was given to individuals with 15 or more years of technical work experience who had passed a rigorous examination set by the State.

Longxi's senior management team directed most of its efforts towards fulfilling the "Market, Management, Quality, Profit" credo. At the beginning of each year, the team established goals for marketing, production, profits and employee benefits. Action plans were also developed in the areas of technological improvement, quality improvement and new product introduction. The goals set by senior management required approval of the Employee Assembly (all the other permanent employees). These goals were translated into quotas which were distributed accordingly throughout the company. Every month, each department analyzed its actual versus planned performance. The senior management team reviewed the departmental results on a bi-annual basis, although issues concerning quality and production planning were discussed on a weekly basis.

The senior general manager at Longxi was Mr. Yang Bin Feng, the company's Managing Director. Mr. Yang began working at Longxi in 1981 after spending over 13 years in the defense and automobile manufacturing industries. In his early years with Longxi, Yang was a teacher in the company's training school before moving to the casting division where he was quickly promoted to Manager. Over the next ten years, he assumed increasing management responsibility for broader production and personnel concerns throughout the company. Finally, in 1991, he was promoted to the position of Managing Director.

As a managing director of a typical State-Owned Enterprise (SOE) in China, Mr. Yang thought that his role was different from his counterparts in the West.

> I have been looking for a point which balances the benefits to the country and the Works' own employees. I have to be an actor who is suitable for multiple roles. Devotion to both the country and company is very important for a managing director in China. To be frank, I do not think it would be difficult for me to get a comfortable, highly paid job in a foreign enterprise. I did not do so because I love the Works. I want to devote what I have to her. Our country is not rich; the spirit of devotion is the pillar for directors working in the state-owned enterprises in China.

Mr. Yang was currently active in the Communist Party of China and was the Vice President of the Fujian Entrepreneurs Association, the same body which had conferred upon him an award for entrepreneurial excellence. Unlike some other managing directors who had achieved similar success, he did not ask for a car from the Works for personal use.

When asked to assess Longxi's future, Yang stated:

> The challenge over the next few years will be upgrading our technology and quality processes. Unlike Changchai, our city government does not intend to let us go public, at least not at this time. This is because the Zhangzhou city government wishes that we maintain employment levels for

now. Instead, we may seek to obtain loans from banks for any investment or expansion project. Our borrowing will be in smaller increments over a longer period of time, rather than borrowing a large amount at any one time. By doing so, we will be able to repay our obligations. I expect that 70 per cent of this money will be used to improve our technological processes.

Development of Quality Management

Prior to 1978, the only formal mechanism for assessing quality at Longxi resided with the Inspection Department which examined components and engines after they were produced. This changed that summer, when managers at Longxi were invited to participate in a two-week Total Quality Management (TQM) training course given by China's Ministry of Machinery and Industry. During the previous spring, a senior director from the Ministry had spent three months in Japan learning the Japanese approach to TQM. Deeply impressed by his findings, the director persuaded the Ministry to sponsor a formalized TQM training program, to be taught by himself and given to selected state-owned enterprises (SOEs).

Longxi accepted the Ministry's invitation and sent its Managing Director, Inspection Department Manager and an Inspection Department engineer to attend the training course. Having been one of the first companies in China to receive TQM training, Longxi was mandated by the provincial government to provide similar training to other SOEs in Fujian province. The following year, Longxi established a Quality Management Department (QMD), which included three groups: Inspection, Measurement, and Management Groups. If defects were reported by the Inspection Group, the QMD was allowed to summon the heads of any other departments that it felt could assist in resolving the issue.

However, in 1981, Longxi's senior management concluded that QMD had weakened the inspection function. In practice, for the QMD to carry out its mandate to resolve quality issues, production lines often needed to be shut down.

The QMD was reluctant to intervene in this way, and typically allowed operations to continue despite conditions of substandard quality. In response, senior management separated the Inspection Group from the QMD. A name change accompanied this restructuring: QMD became known as the Office of TQM.

During the 1980s, the Office of TQM gradually developed plant-wide quality control systems for many of the company's production activities. In August 1986, the provincial government formally recognized Longxi for its achievements in quality management by awarding it the certificate of "Provincial Excellence in TQM." Since then, the company had been consistently viewed as having one of the strongest quality management teams in Fujian.

By the end of the 1980s, senior management realized that the growing Office of TQM was overloaded with responsibilities, and separated the Office into two parts: the Quality Management Department (QMD) and the Enterprise Management Office (EMO).

In its newest incarnation, the four people assigned to the QMD became responsible for:

- planning and administering all of Longxi's quality management activities, as well as ensuring that all State and company regulations were being adhered to properly;
- ongoing development of the company's quality assurance system, including the design and implementation of quality improvements;
- organizing all of QC group activities; and
- training of employees in quality management concepts and techniques.

As part of quality improvement efforts, the quality reward system was changed so that employees were rewarded according to product quality in their department. Employees started with 100 quality points each month, which was equivalent to 40 per cent of their base salary. Formerly, the reward system had been based on plant-wide quality performance. Now, if quality levels fell below standards in their department, all employees in that department lost quality points, resulting in a lower quality bonus. The number of points lost varied by the severity of the quality problem, although the number of points lost typically was quite small.

The "Method"

In 1994, Longxi put into place what later became viewed as one of the cornerstones of its overall approach to TQM: the development of an evolving manual entitled "Management Methods of Quality Improvement Activities," otherwise known as "The Method." The content of the "Method" was based on the structure of ISO 9000. Among the details included in the Method were guidelines governing the systematic change of working routines, rules for establishing quality improvement targets and implementation of brainstorming techniques. Instructions to govern activities such as harnessing employee enthusiasm for solving quality problems and incorporating customers' suggestions also were included.

In addition, the Method described the procedures for designing and using QC groups as a means for achieving quality improvements. Since that time, QC groups had become an increasingly popular means for resolving quality issues at Longxi. All QC group activities within the plant came under the direct responsibility of the QMD, including the registration of QC groups, verification of quality issues, establishment of rules governing group activities, provision of general guidance and inspection of group results.

The QMD also was responsible for recognizing the input of individual group members and communicating their contributions to others. For example, if a QC group developed a notable quality improvement, the QMD would ask the Employee Assembly to confer the title of "Excellent Employee" on their champions and display their pictures on the wall at the main entrance to the plant. These people received diplomas which were presented to them by the company's senior executives at the annual Employee Assembly. If the results of a group's activities were of great significance, the QMD would recommend that the QC group present

their findings to the appropriate city, provincial or central government authorities.

In sum, management felt that this approach to quality had proven very successful. Throughout the 1990s the company received several awards from both the Provincial and State governments. These awards included the following:

- 1993 Provincial QC Excellence Award for stabilizing the engine painting process;
- 1994 Provincial QC Excellence Award for improved technology and new product;
- 1995 Ministry of Industry QC Excellence Award for improving the tidiness of single-cylinder engines; and
- 1996 Ministry of Industry QC Excellence Award for increasing first-test pass rates for running engines.

Notwithstanding these quality-related achievements, senior management realized that further efforts were needed before the company would become a true world-class competitor. While many employees understood the need for quality and how TQM could be applied to their working environments, many others did not. Technical support continued to be inadequate for many employees, particularly production line workers. For example, several workshops did not schedule technicians who were capable of providing support during the night shift. Furthermore, flaws in some operating procedures continued to contribute to the plant's quality troubles. All of this meant that further employee development, hands-on supervision and operating process refinements were required throughout many areas of the plant.

Views of TQM at Longxi

Since being promoted to Managing Director, Mr. Yang had received direct exposure to Western management ideas and approaches which were of potential benefit to the company. In 1992, he attended a four-week training course in New York which focused on the principles of general management. Later, in 1994, he and 200 other managers from mainland China attended a general management training program in Hong Kong where he received instruction in marketing, finance and quality management.

In terms of his personal role in the development of TQM at Longxi, Yang offered the following:

> When it comes to TQM, I see myself as a strategic decision maker. It is my view that a good senior manager needs to be a good negotiator and an arbitrator. I do not have time to become involved in the smaller details of TQM, but I do wish to provide guidance and counselling when it is needed.

Other senior managers noted that Yang had adopted a more democratic approach than his predecessors, with responsibility being placed at lower levels in the firm and the use of teams for QC groups. As a result, more workers became directly involved in quality improvement efforts. These efforts bore fruit in 1995 as two single-cylinder models were among the first products to be awarded the designation of Prestigious Products in Fujian province.

Reflecting upon Longxi's past accomplishments, and the future role that quality improvements would play in achieving the firm's objectives, Yang stated:

> There are three achievements which have contributed to Longxi's record of quality improvement over the past 10 years for which we can be especially proud. The first is the company's quality methods manual [The Method]. This manual has become "the Bible" of quality management at Longxi. The second has to do with our training system. We have trained our workers to understand both the concepts of quality management, as well as the skills they need to do their jobs properly. The third achievement is that we have established an effective reward system which is based on a combination of spiritual and material rewards.

Prior to submitting his application for the DGS QC Group to Mr. Shi in the QMD, Mr. Lin Zhang had participated in one other QC group project. Lin had received his Bachelor's degree in Thermal Treatment from the University of Fuzhou in 1992, the same year he started his career at Longxi and joined the Communist Party. Work on this project, like other QC groups at Longxi, required the use of employees' spare time. In explaining his motivation for wanting to develop the DGS project group, Lin remarked:

> The primary reason that I wanted to participate in this QC group was not because of money. Instead, QC group projects give me a chance to apply what I learned in school. Other types of projects do not allow me to refresh my knowledge so thoroughly.
>
> Another reason is the knowledge I expect to receive from other people. Sometimes, when I have encountered problems in the past and have run out of possible solutions, I have taken the chance to ask other more experienced people for their ideas. Their insightful opinions have helped, and they have become big brothers to me. However, many of them have been promoted and given many administrative responsibilities, which I believe does not make full use of their technical expertise.

On the issue of top management involvement in TQM, Lin suggested that:

> Top management should be more involved in QC group activities. They should require reports from the plant's middle level management detailing QC group actions. This would ensure that the QC groups get more support. From my point of view, a plant is an army at peace time. It should have strict orders to keep production and other activities in order. Without strict control systems, we can expect problems to keep recurring.
>
> Recurring problems are related to our reward system. A good reward system should keep pace with our QC group activities. Sometimes a problem recurs simply because people made the same mistakes again. These people were not motivated enough to do a good job. So, as time passes, they go back to their old tricks. Technical personnel also need to be motivated. The reason why we have failed to solve some problems sooner is because technical personnel have failed to foresee the problem, or else they simply tried to avoid addressing the problem. These people need to be motivated to attend training seminars and work towards their potential.

ISO 9000 Certification

Unlike Changchai, Longxi had not yet received ISO 9000 certification for any of its products. However, the ISO process formed the basis for the Method. On achieving certification, Lin offered the following view:

There are two reasons why I don't think that we need to have such a certificate at this point of time. First, it is costly. An ISO 9000 certificate requires renewal each year. This just tells me that they [ISO] want people to spend money repeatedly for the same thing. The second, and most important reason, is that ISO 9000 has lost its credibility with me. I know that there are some plants which have ISO 9000, yet their products have much lower quality than ours. How did they get the certificate?

There are many quality control systems in the world these days. They are all very good. The key is not which system a plant has chosen to adopt, but whether it can produce quality products. Our products are superior to other plants in terms of quality. Our plant's environment and working stations are cleaner and our workers work harder, too. That is what matters.

Mr. Yang further elaborated,

With respect to ISO 9000, we are actually practising it, but have not got the certificate yet. What is more, renewing this certification on an annual basis takes a significant amount of time and money. However, the certificate is becoming a powerful marketing weapon. With our expansion into the international market, we will seek to achieve certification by 1998 or 1999.

THE DUO-GEAR SHAFT (DGS)

The duo-gear shaft (DGS) was one of the critical parts used in the production of two-cylinder diesel engines (Exhibit 2). This part was assembled into the Gear Housing Assembly (Exhibit 3), which coordinated the functions of other assemblies and transferred power from the engine to the drive train. Because quantities were considered small, Longxi had decided against purchasing sophisticated equipment which would have automated DGS production.

Production involved four basic sets of operations across three different departments: raw material preparation, followed by machining, heat treatment, and then final machining (Exhibit 1). Based on demand forecasts, the Production Department initiated the production of DGS parts by scheduling the movement of raw steel rods from storage in the warehouse to sawing machines, located in the same building. Overhead cranes moved a maximum of three rods, each measuring 6m by 58mm, to one of several sawing machines that cut the rods into short, 46mm lengths. While six sawing machines were available, usually only a maximum of three were used simultaneously to prepare the raw material for this part.

Quality Inspection

Approximately 130 inspectors were responsible for scrutinizing quality throughout the Works. In raw material preparation, as with other production steps, an inspector periodically performed three types of Professional Inspections during the sawing operation: Initial Inspection; Patrol Inspection; and Completion Inspection. After the first unit of each batch (i.e., 125 parts at the sawing operation) was produced, the inspector would perform an Initial Inspection to confirm that the unit conformed to specifications. For cutting, the inspector would confirm that the shafts were made of the proper grade of steel, HB45, and the dimensions were correct. After granting approval, the inspector would give a plate of Initial Inspection to the sawing machine operator. Without this plate hanging at an operator's position, further production could not proceed.

During the remaining production of that batch, typically twice per shift, the inspector would return to conduct a Patrol Inspection to ensure that production was continuing according to specifications. Finally, when the batch of parts had moved through all the required operations in a department, such as Machining or Thermal Treatment Departments, described next, an inspector conducted a Completion

Front View

Section A-A

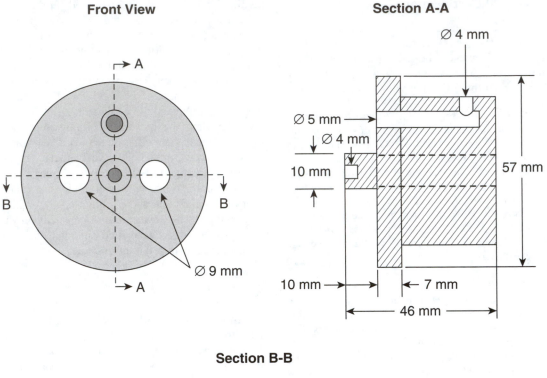

Section B-B

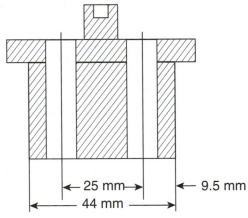

Exhibit 2   Duo-Gear Shaft (DGS)

Inspection. This final inspection was necessary to authorize the release of the batch to the next department.

Workers also were responsible for ensuring high quality production. During the sawing operation, as with other operations, workers were told to inspect the quality of their own production, termed Self Inspection. In addition, workers examined the quality of parts received from upstream operations, called Mutual Inspection, to confirm that they continued to work on good parts. For raw material preparation, Mutual

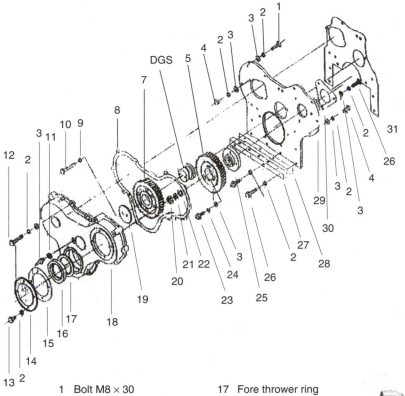

SL2100

1	Bolt M8 × 30	17	Fore thrower ring
2	Spring washer 8	18	Timing gear housing
3	Washer 8	19	Idle gear retainer
4	Bolt M8 × 22	20	Nut M12
5	Injection pump timing gear	21	Spring washer 12
6	Duo Gear Shaft (DGS)	22	Washer 12
7	Idle gear	23	Bolt M8 × 25
8	Gear housing gasket	24	Spring washer 8
9	Idle gear bolt	25	Connecting plate
10	Washer	26	Bolt M8 × 40
11	Pointer	27	Sealing clamp
12	Bolt M8 × 55	28	Sealing clamp gasket
13	Bolt M8 × 16	29	Suspension plate
14	Front cover	30	Injection pump gasket
15	Front cover gasket	31	Suspension plate gasket
16	Oil sealing GS60 × 80 × 12		

Exhibit 3   SL2100 Diesel Engine and Gear Housing Assembly

Inspections relied on visually checking the parts. Finally, the worker was responsible for notifying the inspector to conduct other necessary inspections (such as Initial Inspection and Completion Inspection).

Machining Department

After the sawing operation for an entire batch of parts was completed, a person responsible for materials handling would load the parts onto a small cart for transit to the Machining Department, about 200m away (Exhibit 1). Upon arrival there, the raw parts were stacked beside one of three lathes and the operator for that lathe signed a material receipt. Each operator could produce up to 350 DGS parts per month, in addition to other production assignments, and only a single shift was currently scheduled.

The operation at the lathe involved cutting the steel rod into three different diameters along its cylindrical axis. As with sawing, inspectors performed an Initial Inspection after the first part was completed for each new batch. Later, an inspector would return for a Patrol Inspection, when a few parts would be inspected at random. Because this area of the plant was quite cramped and noisy with equipment and operators, each operator stacked completed parts on top of his tool box, which measured 80cm by 60cm by 120cm high.

Once this step of production was completed, the materials handler again moved the batch of DGS parts on a hand cart to the next operation, drilling. Here, two 9mm holes, parallel to the cylindrical axis were drilled completely through the part. In addition, several other holes were drilled partway into the part. Following drilling, the batch of parts was moved by the materials handler to Final Inspection. If approved, the materials handler moved that batch of parts to the Thermal Treatment Department, about 250 meters away (Exhibit 1).

Thermal Treatment Department

Heat treatment was needed for many steel parts to develop the proper hardness after the cutting and drilling operations. In addition, an anti-rust coating was applied. Unlike the Machining Department, the Thermal Treatment Department had been built fairly recently, in the early 1980s. To reduce the presence of toxic fumes, which were generated as surface contaminants such as oil vaporize, fume hoods and exhaust fans had been installed. However, the fumes were not completely captured, and workers were urged to wear both mouth masks and gloves, although many refrained from doing so because the temperature inside the plant often exceeded 36C in summer.

Three workers were assigned to work on DGS parts during each of two daily shifts. Because of heat and fumes, they rotated among the different positions. The first operator used steel wire to string together four DGS parts through the 9mm holes. This worker would then place four of these strings (16 parts) using a 130cm steel hook into a well-shaped electrical furnace, called a Preheat Furnace. This furnace preheated the DGS parts to 200 to 300C for 10 minutes. The Preheat Furnace, which was not covered, was maintained at approximately 300C, and the worker was expected to use his judgment, based on visual cues and overall time, to determine when the parts were at the proper temperature.

When the parts finished preheating, the worker would use the steel hook to transfer the 16 parts to the larger Main Furnace. Like the Preheat Furnace, this furnace had a well-shaped interior measuring $30 \times 35 \times 35$cm deep and no cover. Because smoke was produced by residual traces of oil on the parts, a fume-hood had been installed above the furnace to exhaust the gases outside the building.

After placing the preheated DGS parts in the Main Furnace, the operator would push a button at a nearby station that started and controlled the heating cycle of the furnace. Engineering specified that the DGS parts be heated to 850C. Data on the heating times and cycles of the Main Furnace were automatically recorded on chart recorders, which were changed each shift. Current operating practice required that the operator hold the parts during the entire heating cycle.

Following the heating cycle, the worker removed the DGS parts from the Main Furnace and quenched them by plunging them into an adjacent vat of water. The temperature rapidly dropped to 200 to 300C. This process was monitored visually and required careful experienced observation. If the DGS was removed from the water too soon, it became too soft; if it was removed too late, it became brittle.

The worker then used a steel hook to place the 16 parts into a heavy iron basket sitting nearby on the concrete floor. Within 10 minutes, an overhead crane transferred the iron basket into a larger Tempering Furnace for a further two-hour tempering process. The purpose of tempering was to stabilize the part's material structure and lower internal stresses, thereby reducing the chances of cracks and premature failure. This furnace, located 10 meters away, also was electrically controlled and had a cover to reduce energy losses. The crane would remove the cover, place the basket of parts inside, possibly remove another basket of parts from Tempering, and then replace the cover.

After removal from the Tempering Furnace, the overhead crane moved the basket of parts to a series of process vats. First, the parts were washed. Following washing, a worker removed the steel wires from the bundles of parts and an inspector tested the hardness of the steel of these parts. If approved, a worker placed the parts back into the basket and used a small electrical crane to dip the parts into a hot alkalized water cabin for three to 10 minutes. The alkali bath removed any remaining traces of contaminants from the surface of the parts.

Next, a hot acid bath, again for three to 10 minutes, prepared the parts for subsequent coating with a thin anti-oxidant to prevent rust. Then the basket was dipped into a hot, specially formulated anti-oxidant liquid for 35 to 45 minutes. After this, the parts were again washed in a water bath and coated with oil by dipping them in a nearby oil vat. Finally, the semi-finished parts were placed on a drying rack to await Completion Inspection. The hardness of each part was measured using a specifically designed instrument, while the thickness of the anti-rust layer was inspected visually. If approved, a materials handler stacked the parts for return to the Machining Department for a final grinding operation.

Return to Machining Department

After returning the parts to this department, the grinding machine operator signed for their receipt. Two shifts were used for grinding, usually with one operator per shift. One surface of each part was ground to ensure precise alignment of the DGS with the Idle Gear in the final assembly of the Gear Housing Assembly.

As before, Initial Inspections were performed after the first part was complete, with Patrol Inspections occurring in both shifts. Finally, the finished product was sent to the Machining Department's inspection station for the final Completion Inspection. Once approved, the DGS parts were forwarded to a finished products warehouse where an administrator stacked them and assistants would coat each DGS, one by one, with oil as further anti-rust treatment.

QC GROUP 96020

Following review by Mr. Shi of the application, Zhang Lin was elated to receive rapid approval to establish a new QC group, license number 96020. At the same time, Lin realized that much work needed to be done. Lin's previous QC group experience had taught him that an important first step for ensuring group effectiveness was selecting the right people to be involved in the process.

First, he solicited support from people working in the Metallurgical Division to have access to their experience. In particular, he believed that much of the DGS problem(s) was related to the metallurgical techniques being used in the plant. Lin approached and tried to recruit the best available people.

In addition, he followed the accepted Chinese practice that required subordinates to invite the manager of their respective department to become the head of the QC group. For example, while Mr. Chen, Manager of the Thermal Treatment Department, did not necessarily have the strongest background with respect to metallurgy, he was nevertheless invited to provide the leadership role to this group. Chen's role became one of coordinating the activities of group members, as well as monitoring and communicating the progress of the process. In total, the QC group had six members, including Lin.

QC Member	Title	QC Training	Years at Longxi
Chen K.F.	Manager, Thermal Treatment	60 hours	27
Lin Zhang	Assistant Engineer	60 hours	4
Chen X.N.	Line Worker	48 hours	18
Chen C.S.	Line Worker	48 hours	9
Chen Q.Y.	Assistant Engineer	60 hours	5
Chen P.Y.	Engineer	80 hours	28

All of the older members of QC Group 96020 had gained experience at Longxi by working in a variety of departments over the years. The two youngest employees, Lin and Q.Y. Chen, had worked exclusively for the thermal treatment department. They, along with P.Y. Chen, were the only members who possessed specialized, university-level training in thermal treatment.

As the group members prepared to tackle the project, P.Y. Chen stated:

Our success will depend on whether or not we attack the correct problem. To do so, we need to be diligent and careful when collecting data. Honesty is also required when it comes time for drawing conclusions. If the problem is due to people not fulfilling their responsibilities, we need to point this out. We should not be afraid of embarrassing anyone.

This view matched that of Mr. Yang, Longxi's Managing Director, who was pushing people toward "Fact Management" rather than the traditional "Relationship Management," termed *guanxi,* where each individual tries to "save face."

THE NEXT STEPS

With the membership of the QC group established, the process of gathering and analyzing data could begin in earnest. Ultimately, Lin knew that this group needed to recommend credible improvements that would fix this recurring problem.

NOTES

1. Also translated as idle gear shaft.
2. In 1996, the Renminbi (RMB) exchange rate was about US $1.00 = 8.30 RMB.
3. Chinese small diesel engine model numbers were consistent between firms. For example, 2100 designates a two-cylinder engine, with piston diameter of 100 mm. A single-cylinder engine with piston diameter of 95 mm is designated by 195.

BLUE MOUNTAIN RESORTS: THE SERVICE QUALITY JOURNEY

Prepared by Mark Sheppard under the supervision of Professor P. Fraser Johnson

Version: (B) 2002-10-18

Dave Sinclair, vice-president of human resources at Blue Mountain Resort, was considering his options concerning the company's service quality program. It was Thursday December 2, 1999,

and a light snow was falling outside. Since 1991, Blue Mountain Resorts had been driving its business with a service quality program, which he was responsible for coordinating. With the

1999–2000 ski season now underway and the critical Christmas period approaching, he wanted to continue progress of the program by introducing a new set of initiatives.

Dave had recently gathered together a team of 25 Blue Mountain Resort managers, from a variety of different areas in the company, to identify opportunities to improve service quality. They had provided Dave with a number of specific proposals that he felt warranted consideration. On the following Monday, Dave would be reviewing his plans for the service quality program at the executive team meeting. In preparation for the meeting, Dave wanted to evaluate the proposals and decide on a course of action.

THE CANADIAN SKI AND SNOWBOARD INDUSTRY

There were a total of two million skiers and snowboarders in Canada in 1999. The total number of skier and snowboarder visits to Canadian resorts in the 1998–1999 season was 17.3 million, up 12 per cent from the previous season. British Columbia and Alberta captured approximately half of the market, with popular resorts in Whistler and Banff, followed by Quebec with approximately 30 per cent, and Ontario with most of the balance.

A number of factors influenced decisions regarding which resorts skiers visited, namely location, cost, quality of the runs, speed and capacity of lifts and amenities. Ticket prices could vary according to a number of factors, such as ski conditions, time of year, time of day and day of week.

BLUE MOUNTAIN RESORTS

The Greater Toronto Area (GTA) was home to an estimated 400,000 active skiers and snowboarders. Although Ontario had approximately 60 private and public resorts available for skiing and snowboarding, the Toronto market was served primarily by five public resorts: Blue Mountain, Talisman, Horseshoe Valley, Mount St. Louis/ Moonstone, and Snow Valley.

Blue Mountain Resort (BMR), located 135 kilometres north of Toronto, was one of Ontario's most popular ski resorts, with 18 percent of the Ontario skier and snowboarder visits in 1998–1999. Situated near the town of Collingwood, BMR was founded in 1941 by the Czechoslovakian born Jozo Weider.

BMR had expanded and modernized as the sport gained popularity. In the 1980s, the company added a year round four star resort hotel and conference centre, a condominium development and the Monterra Golf course.

By 1999 BMR was a four season resort. However, winter sports, skiing and snowboarding, were still its dominant activities, accounting for approximately 65 per cent of total revenues. The ski hill offered 251 acres of ski-able terrain with a vertical drop of 721 feet and an additional 50 acres was available for future trail development. BMR had fifteen lifts to service the area and the longest run was four thousand feet, approximately 1.2 kilometres. The terrain broke down to 17 per cent beginner, 42 per cent intermediate, and 41 per cent advanced. Special facilities, to accommodate snowboarders, had been introduced, keeping up with the trends in the industry. For night skiing, BMR had 11 trails on 88 acres under lights. In general, Blue Mountain was regarded as having a good variety of skiing and snowboarding facilities, which tended to attract large crowds. Exhibit 1 provides a map of BMR.

In the 1998–1999 season, BMR hosted 415,920 skier visits, the second highest in the company's history. During the previous three years attendance in skier visits at BMR had been 358,000 in 1997–1998, 368,000 in 1996–1997, and 416,000 in 1995–1996. Approximately 60 per cent of the skiers at Blue Mountain came from the GTA, while the balance came from other parts of Ontario and United States. BMR's average lift ticket price was approximately $24 and the expected average total revenue per person per visit for the coming season was approximately $40, which included revenue generated by the other operations on site.

Blue Mountain offered over 15 different ski and snowboard package options, but the three

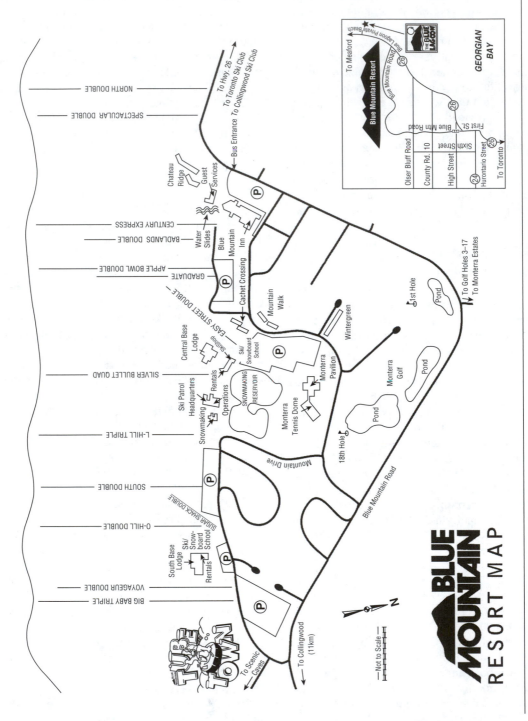

Exhibit 1   Map of Blue Mountain Resorts

most popular price packages—the weekend individual or "walk-ups," midweek individual and the full season pass—made up 54 per cent of lift ticket sales. Group tickets made up 12 per cent of ticket sales. Destination ticket holders comprised of the three day package ski ticket, and the one week pass made up one per cent of sales. BMR catered to a wide range of skiers— 20 per cent were beginner to novice, 40 per cent were intermediate, and the balance were advanced to expert. The company estimated that intermediate level skiers and snowboarders typically came to the resort an average of 4.1 times per year, while advanced and expert level customers came an average of 6.7 and 9.4 times per year respectively.

INTRAWEST INVESTMENT IN BMR

In 1999 Blue Mountain Resorts was the largest family operated ski resort in Canada. Gordon Canning, president and chief executive officer of BMR, was the son-in-law of the founder, Jozo Weider. Gordon joined the company in 1971, and became president in 1978. On January 14th, 1999, BMR announced that it would sell a 50 per cent interest in the company to Intrawest Corporation. Intrawest, headquartered in Vancouver, British Columbia, was a leading developer and operator of village centered resorts across North America. The company owned ten properties, including Whistler/ Blackcomb, North America's most popular mountain resort.

In conjunction with its investment in BMR, Intrawest also purchased 16 acres of developable real estate lands at the base of the BMR resort, with plans for a village development. This expansion would include approximately 1,000 condo-hotel units, 200 townhouse units and 100,000 square feet of commercial space. Intrawest announced plans to develop a four season pedestrian village, complete with quality restaurants, shopping and nightlife similar to Intrawest's village at Tremblant. Gordon Canning commented on the Intrawest investment in BMR:

Our business plan called for continued capital investments to maintain our growth. We are no longer just a ski hill—Blue Mountain is a four season resort with golfing, waterslides, tennis, beach and meeting facilities. We felt that to capitalize on the opportunities we needed a strategic partner that could help provide financing and management expertise. Overall, we expect a $585 million investment to develop an authentic Victorian style Ontario village at the Blue Mountain. This will include walkways and parklands to enhance the four season aspect of the resort throughout the village.

A primary attraction of BMR to Intrawest was the existence of an experienced management team. Consequently, Gordon Canning and his management team remained in place following the Intrawest investment. Exhibit 2 provides a corporate organization chart.

BMR OPERATIONS

BMR operations included facilities and guest services, the ski hill, golf course and summer recreation facilities. BMR employed a year round staff of 200, and hired an additional 750 winter seasonal employees and 250 summer seasonal employees. Dave Sinclair commented on the managing staff:

Despite the growth in our summer business, our operations are still quite seasonal. We hire a lot of seasonal employees who require orientation and training. With an annual payroll of over $10 million, our staff costs are a large part of our expense. However, we still have to be respectful of our employee needs and carefully plan staffing levels and remain flexible where possible if the weather doesn't cooperate.

Facilities and Guest Services

For many customers initial contact with BMR came through its call center. Dave Sinclair described the call center operations:

We have 16 people working in the call center during peak periods, with 10 people at any one time. In terms of average calls per day, they handle

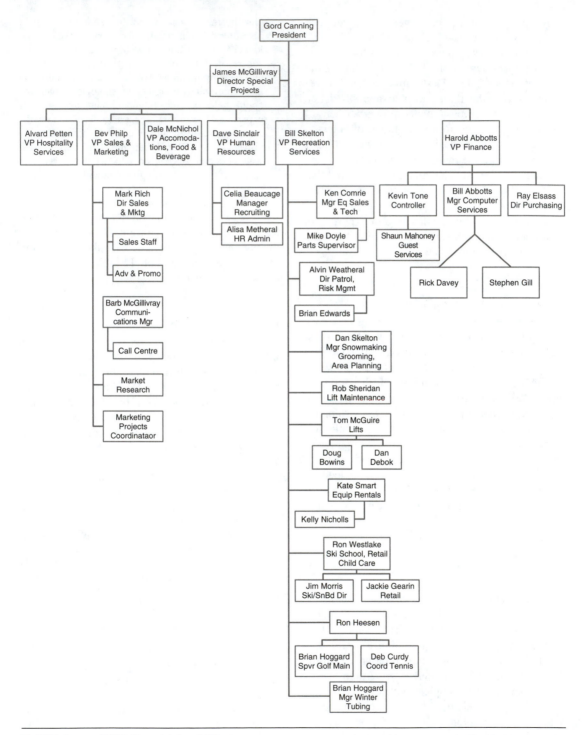

Exhibit 2   BMR Organizational Chart

anywhere from a high in January and February of 950, to a low in April of 230. Our professionally trained call center operators can answer questions about the resort, reserve accommodations, give directions, book golf tee times, and sell a variety of programs available at the resort.

There were eight different food service facilities at the resort that included a wide range of restaurants, from food court style cafeteria to fine dining. BMR conference facilities had capacity to handle conferences and large meetings for a total of up to 5,600 people, and in 1998–1999 Blue Mountain hosted 19,000 people in 350 different conferences and large meetings. Although these facilities operated year round, the peak period was between September/October and May/June.

Winter guests at BMR could shop at the three retail stores located on the resort. The retail shops were located at the two Base Lodge locations and hotel. The main lodge held a shop that offered a full line of ski fashions, accessories, and logo items. The South Base Lodge carried a smaller selection of fashions.

A daycare facility was open daily from 9:00 to 4:30 during the ski season, and could accommodate children from 15 months to five years of age. Weekend programs were available for children from ages six to 12 on weekends and holidays. In addition, BMR operated an eight week Tiny Tykes program at the South Base Lodge.

Ski rental and repair shops were in two locations. The Central Base lodge had 1,000 pairs of skis and 250 snowboards available for rental, while an additional 600 pairs of skis were available for rent at the South Base lodge. These shops also handled repairs for customers.

Finally, BMR also offered a number of other miscellaneous services to its guests, such as a chalet rental location service to provide assistance finding seasonal accommodation.

Ski Hill Operations

Hill grooming and snowmaking played an important part in BMR's operations. Dave Sinclair explained:

We estimate that our ski hill has the capacity to handle 7,500 skiers comfortably during any particular day, while night skiing handles an additional 3,000. Since we can't control the weather, hill grooming and snowmaking help us get maximum utilization of the hill. Each night the trails are groomed with special machines with hydraulic attachments. We have about 12 people working in snowmaking, and another eight in the hill grooming operations.

BMR offered a wide variety of services to skiers and snowboarders. Among the most important was the ski school, located at the Central and South Base Lodges. It employed 180 ski and snowboarding professionals, which made it one of the largest ski and snowboarding schools in the country.

A number of systems were in place to help skiers. Electronic message centers that were located at all chair lifts displayed which lifts were operating and the current waiting time at each. Fourteen mountain guide volunteers were available to greet bus groups, answer questions and give guidance on the slopes and in the base lodges. There were 15 full time and 15 part time ski patrollers plus an additional 75 volunteers who promoted safe skiing and snowboarding, and provided first aid assistance. There were also 10 staff dedicated to the Badlands Terrain Park, and another 25 staff assigned to the snow tube area.

Golf Course and Summer Recreation Facilities

BMR had been moving steadily into a four season resort since 1977 when the Great Slide Ride was built for summer sledding down the mountain. By 1999 BMR had 225 part time seasonal staff working in its summer recreation facilities, which included the Monterra Golf Course, tennis, outdoor pools and water park complex. The Monterra Pavilion, opened in 1990, was the focal point of BMR's summer recreation activities. It included the Monterra Bar and Grill, pro shop, condominium check-in center, conference facilities, and outdoor pool and whirlpool.

BMR SERVICE QUALITY PROGRAM

In spring 1991 David Sinclair was hired as BMR's first director of human resources. Dave had extensive experience as a human resource manager in a large consumer products company, and he commented on the situation in 1991 when he joined BMR:

Blue Mountain enjoyed very good times during the 1980s. However, the focus had been revenue growth and facility expansion. Although the company had been profitable, it began to develop a reputation for long line-ups and poor service. Blue Mountain competed based on our location, expecting skiers to show up every season.

Gordon Canning decided to survey the employees in 1990, and the results indicated problems with morale. Consequently, a consulting company was hired to conduct a series of seminars that focused on communication, team performance, and improving supervision techniques. The issues that came up during the course of the meetings indicated employee concerns about a number of issues ranging from working conditions to frustration concerning service quality levels.

When I arrived, one of the first requests that I made was for a management training program aimed at improving service at the resort. From my perspective, a major problem was one of poor service that was affecting employee morale and job performance—it costs us five times as much to attract a new customer as it does to retain an existing one. However, it was evident that our service quality problems were not going to be an easy fix—it would involve a complicated process and a long-term commitment from senior management.

I then began looking into organizations that might be able to help us and eventually contacted a consultant at a firm called Achieve International, who agreed to help us. We started the process with an executive retreat, which included the six people who made up the senior management team: Gordon Canning, president; Harold Abbotts, vice-president of finance; Beverly Philp, vice-president of marketing; Bill Skelton, vice-president of recreation services; Dale McNichol, vice-president of accommodations, food and beverage; and myself. Throughout the two day workshop we considered the future vision of the company, focusing on our vision for the organization and values that we considered critical for creating a supportive corporate culture. The people from Achieve International provided some very persuasive data concerning the advantages of service oriented culture and the potential benefits to the company, its employees and our customers. At the end of the two day session they left us at a decision point. We considered the individual and corporate costs to beginning a service quality journey. As the change was perceived to be significant, it was, for some, not an easy decision.

We reconvened to decide what, if anything, we should do next. At that point we made the commitment to develop a service quality philosophy, and we adopted Achieve International's book, *Firing on All Cylinders,* as our service quality bible. We also developed a vision statement—"To be the best resort in Canada at exceeding customer expectations"; a value statement—"caring, trusting and committed"; and a method—the three rings of perceived quality: basic service or product, support, and enhanced service (see Exhibit 3). We subscribe to the same basic vision, values and method today in spirit, although the words have changed slightly in order to be consistent with our new partner, Intrawest.

Part of the commitment involved designating a service quality coordinator, a role that became part of my job description. I was to spend half my time on human resource activities and the other half as the service quality coordinator. As part of my new responsibilities, I went on a one-week training retreat to learn Achieve International's quality philosophy. Interestingly, I found that all other firms represented were in manufacturing industries. It was during this training that I developed a rough draft for a two year plan, which identified our priorities, methods and goals. This plan was based on Achieve International's implementation framework (Exhibit 4).

At the start of the service quality program Gordon Canning made the following comments regarding the opportunities of improved service quality for BMR and its employees:

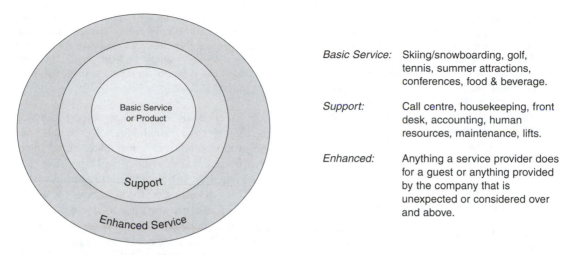

Basic Service: Skiing/snowboarding, golf, tennis, summer attractions, conferences, food & beverage.

Support: Call centre, housekeeping, front desk, accounting, human resources, maintenance, lifts.

Enhanced: Anything a service provider does for a guest or anything provided by the company that is unexpected or considered over and above.

Exhibit 3   The Three Rings of Service

Source: Achieve Group Inc.

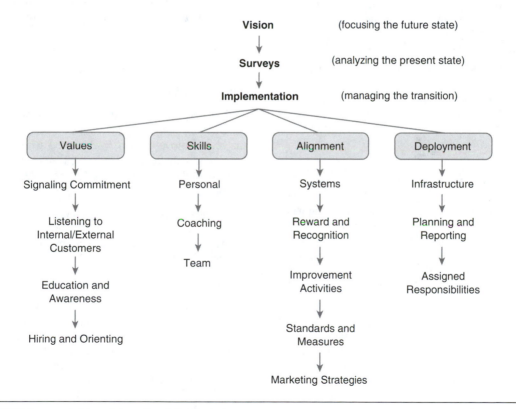

Exhibit 4   Achieve International Framework

Source: Achieve International.

The world is experiencing a service revolution. An organization must continuously improve just to keep up with the competition. Our challenge is to be better than others at exceeding customer expectations. Today the most important capital investment we can make is in our people. It is essential that Blue Mountain Resorts provide a level of service which sets it apart. This may be the most important thing the resort will do in the nineties—a decade when companies will rise, or fall, on their level of customer service.[1]

Early Service Quality Initiatives

The service quality program was introduced in the fall of 1991, in time for the 1991–1992 ski season. The program resulted in several changes at the company. Management felt that they had been too focused on external services, and that the term "customer" needed to be re-defined. Consequently, as part of the service quality vision statement, customers were defined as internal and external, in order to recognize the importance of satisfying the needs of internal stakeholders.

Although BMR had been collecting customer data for several years, the new service quality program forced management to act on the information. Dave Sinclair explained:

> We needed a place to start so we used the bench-marking question on our customer survey— "How does Blue Mountain's service compare to other Canadian resorts?" Customers were given three alternatives: better, same or worse. We focused attention on the "better" category and set targets to steadily improve our rating. If we hit our targets, then employees received an incentive bonus that represented about $50 for a seasonal employee and $200 for a full-time staff member. In 1991–1992 19.6 per cent of our customers classified us as better, in 1992–1993 our rating increased to 30 per cent and it reached 41 per cent in the 1993–1994 season. Meantime, customers that classified us as worse than other Canadian resorts fell from 16.5 per cent to three per cent over the same period.

> Initially we were looking for exposure with our employees and simple method of communicating performance. Eventually we reached a ceiling with respect to our ratings and by about 1996 we changed our approach. In the early years, however, it worked well for us.

In 1993 BMR changed its hiring practice with the objective of matching job demands with employee capabilities. A more structured inter-view process was developed and front line staff were invited to participate in some hiring activi-ties. This was intended to build better teams in allowing those participating to decide on their future team members.

Finally, the management team prepared annual service quality reports. BMR published 10,000 reports each year to communicate to both the employees and to stakeholders what Blue Moun-tain's commitment to service quality entailed. The reports showcased improvement initiatives and recognized the many successful service quality initiatives coordinated by the employees.

The Move to Enhanced Service

The results of the first year of service-quality program encouraged management to consider how they could move quickly to enhanced service, the outer ring in the model (see Exhibit 3). Dave com-mented on the strategy adopted for the 1993–1994 season:

> We felt that we weren't doing enough to "wow" the customer—that service quality meant impressing the customer by exceeding their expectations. We began to focus on enhanced service and ignored the fundamental aspects of good operations neces-sary for high levels of quality service.

> Let me give you an example. At the Christmas hol-iday season we staffed up to put people on the hill to handle complaints and to answer questions from guests. We also put people on the hill to provide services to our guests that they might not expect— we had staff on the hill handing out hors d'oeuvres on silver platters and others were handing out hot chocolate drinks.

This was all nice except we still weren't able to manage the basic levels of service that our customers were expecting. For example, we estimate that we lost over 1,000 calls in our call center in March that year and customers unfamiliar with our location had difficulties finding our resort because of poor signage. We were trying to achieve high levels of service without adequate processes and systems.

The result was a difficult season, from a financial perspective, as our labor costs shot up. This was an important lesson, and it made us reconsider our concept of service quality and reevaluate our approach.

Process Teams

Concerned that service improvement efforts had ignored many of the fundamental aspects of process management and control, Dave Sinclair turned to Achieve International for assistance. Dave commented on what happened:

They helped us learn how process management techniques commonly used in the manufacturing sector could be applied to our service business. As a result, we shifted our approach to continuous improvement, supported by cross-functional teams using data analysis and planning techniques. Our process improvement teams identified failure points in our processes, looking for the root causes of the problem, then making recommendations for corrective action. We called these productivity initiatives and developed a formal process for each team to follow.

A number of process teams were organized in the 1994–1995 season, in areas such as the call center, check-in, purchasing and signage. The teams had cross-functional representation and spent about four hours per week on the project. Each team used a standard process as identified in Exhibit 5. Each team used a number of different problem solving and analysis techniques, such as Pareto charts, brainstorming and process flow mapping. Dave Sinclair described the results of one productivity initiative, the call center:

We used to treat the call center as an order desk, but in 1994, as part of our service quality program, conducted a study of call center activities. The end result was an initial investment of $100,000 for infrastructure followed by another $575,000 in new technology in December 1997 for a new telecommunications platform, in addition to a new management approach at the center. We provided formal training programs for our call center staff,

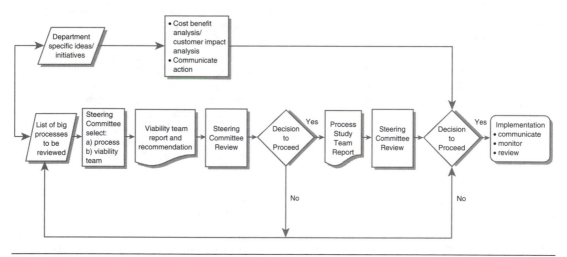

Exhibit 5   The Project Review Process

set performance targets and started using the call center to help manage revenues. For example, on the performance measurement side, we aim for 80 per cent of our calls to be answered within 20 seconds, and we monitor the rate that calls are abandoned. We are now using yield management techniques in the call center to offer variable pricing structures for bookings in an effort to better manage revenues, and the call center is set up for one-stop shopping. They handle anything from bookings for accommodations, to tee off times, to BBQ rentals.

A move was also made to improve communications between management and staff. Employees were invited to join Gordon Canning over lunch. This provided an opportunity for Gordon and the staff to discuss a wide range of issues in an informal setting.

Finally, in the 1994–1995 season the company decided to abandon its incentive program based on percentage of customers classifying Blue Mountain's service as better than other Canadian resorts. By the summer of 1994 its rating had hit 50 per cent, and management felt that it would be difficult to consistently achieve a better rating. Consequently, a new measure was established—the percentage of customers that ranked staff friendliness as a 10 on a ten-point scale. In 1994–1995, 17.2 per cent of customers gave BMR staff ratings of 10 on the staff friendliness question. The company set targets to increase their rating in this area, starting with an objective of 18 per cent for the 1995–1996 season. Management expected to steadily increase the targets each year, and had set an objective of 24 per cent for the 1998–1999 season.

The SWOP Program

"SWOP" was the strengths, weaknesses, opportunities and proposals program that Dave Sinclair had initiated several months prior to continue the improvement of customer service. In June 1999, Dave had organized five teams of five BMR managers and staff from different functional areas. Each team was asked to identify specific areas where they felt an opportunity existed for BMR to improve its service quality and to submit a one- or two-page SWOP proposal describing the issues to be resolved and to provide specific recommendations. A total of twenty-five separate proposals were submitted from the five teams.

Once the reports were completed, several were presented to the executive management team and acted on immediately and others were discounted as not being feasible. However, Dave identified three proposals that he felt required careful consideration: customer flow, speed of service and information technology. Dave selected these proposals because he believed that they offered significant opportunities to improve service quality at BMR.

1. Customer Flow

Problems familiarizing guests with the resort area and its services had become increasingly difficult as BMR expanded. This had in turn created problems particularly for first time guests, who sometimes became frustrated because they were unable to find a particular service or because they had been misdirected to the wrong line. Deb Lynch, manager of the Monterra Bar and Grill, described the problem:

> Having people find the resort easily isn't the only customer logistics issue. Obviously our regular customers are familiar with our services and they know the best way to navigate through the resort. However, customers less familiar with Blue Mountain need help understanding everything from where to park to where they can find the ski and snowboard rentals. Guests have a lot of specific questions as well, such as: Are there lockers? Is the terrain right for my ability? Is there child-care? Can I get my skis repaired? Where will I meet my tour bus?
>
> One big problem is parking. Apparently many of our guests aren't familiar with the parking areas because we have to tow cars from restricted areas, which causes obvious problems.

Another problem is that sometimes people are sent from one line to another and then to a third. For example, a guest might start at the south base lodge information desk where they are directed to administrative guest services and then get redirected to hotel front desk activities. Also, sometimes guests looking for rentals are sent from administration to the rentals desk at Central Base Lodge, only to discover that they are out of stock.

As the resort has expanded, problems associated with customer flow have become more pronounced. Obviously Intrawest plans to grow our facilities, so if anything this problem is going to get worse.

Right now we have approximately 14 mountain guides on the hills to answer questions. However, these people are only able to address the needs of guests after they are out on the mountain. The SWOP team felt that we should get to our customers earlier and identified a number of possible solutions. We could hire three attendants at a cost of approximately $9.50 per hour to work in the parking lot to address customer questions and coordinate parking.[2] However, they also identified a number of other alternatives including using an internal Web site, call center, hotel condo TV channel, walk-up information booths, drive-through information booths, an FM radio station or computer terminal kiosks.

2. Speed of Service

The second major recommendation was to improve speed of customer service. Weekends and holidays could cause problems at the resort as the number of guests approached the resort's capacity. The result was long line-ups, which guests equated as poor service. The SWOP team saw this as an area of frustration for the staff and an opportunity to improve customer service and made six recommendations that they felt would improve speed of service:

- Better forecasting in order to predict changes in business activity;
- Improved communication between departments;
- Provide fast and accurate information to staff;

- Train staff to be more flexible to adopt new approaches to their work;
- Adopt self-service information technology applications for guests;
- Schedule staffing levels based on a scientific examination of staff capacity to process customers.

Although BMR had made substantial improvements over recent years to shorten customer waiting times, Dave Sinclair agreed that speed of service represented a potential area for improvement and made the following observations:

BMR guests are increasingly concerned with the speed of service, especially as families make up a large portion of the target market. There are a great number of line-ups that guests work though for services and products. These range from wait time on the phone to get information, to waiting in line to check into their room, to waiting in line to pick-up equipment—all before they even get on the hill. We feel that the acceptable time for the lift line is ten minutes. If we consider the times that guests spend in consecutive queues for complementary services, then we are exceeding this limit by a great deal.

Recently we had one of our most successful weekends in history. A storm system dumped fresh snow on Friday night and Saturday opened up with beautiful sunshine. We had stuff happening on the hill, including three major suppliers doing demonstrations. Additionally, it was the American Presidents' Day long weekend—they love our dollar. So we had a big turnout. The place was jumping, but it was to the point where we were overwhelmed. The parking lot was jammed; there were crowds at the lifts, at the cafeterias, at the bars, at the rentals. On the one hand everyone seemed willing to pay the price, but we exceeded our comfortable carrying capacity. We knew we'd not met expectations of some guests.

3. Information System

BMR's information system consisted of several independent databases and operating systems. For example, vendor information, invoices and other purchasing data, tee time info, and conference center guest history were in the AS/400 system. Payroll, hotel guest history, ski and snowboard revenue, and call center data was held on the Novell system. Finally, rental revenue, golf and tennis memberships, ticketing sales, skier visits and other retail information were on stand-alone systems. Dave Sinclair described how the SWOP team saw the problem:

> Our information system had grown up with the company. We added capacity and features as we needed new capabilities. However, we never worried about system integration. The team felt that staff needed the capability to access information on a common system. For example, the call center could benefit from customer purchase history when processing information requests or booking a reservation. Staff at the information desk would benefit from tracking ski and snowboard rental bookings so to understand if equipment is available when responding to guest inquiries. An online information system would allow managers to make appropriate changes one time and provide access to all staff as needed—from telephone sales reps, front desk clerks, and conference sales and service personnel. Right now all of our information is on hard copies, so staff sometimes have to sift through different binders to find what they need. Unfortunately the information is sometimes inaccurate or badly outdated. With an online information system it could be checked for accuracy and updated on a regular basis.

> I can see where such a system could be very expensive. Installing a PC on each call center desk, for example, would cost approximately $50,000. We would also have substantial costs for setting up the intranet system and database, not to mention the costs of installing the infrastructure and cabling.

> The team proposed that we should hire a graduate level co-op student on site for approximately five months to help us get our information systems organized. They expected that such a person might cost $600 to $800 per week, and he or she could investigate and document the databases and our current reporting requirements, and identify a long-term plan and budget. For example, evaluate the appropriateness of our Crystal Reports program over the long term and evaluate the viability of establishing an Intranet system.

CURRENT SITUATION

As Dave considered the three proposals before him, he knew that he would be asked for his recommendations on Monday. Although each had its merits, he recognized that Gordon Canning would expect him to set priorities for the coming year and recommend what action, if any, should be taken for each. Dave felt that he had to decide which programs made the most sense for immediate action and which ones required additional study and analysis. If there were a need for additional information, Dave needed to identify what information was still required and how long it would take to get it. Furthermore, each of the proposals affected different parts of the organization, and Dave needed to be concerned about who else in the company should be involved in both further evaluation and implementation. Finally, Dave also recognized that he had to consider the investment that Intrawest would make in the resort and how his recommendations might fit with the aggressive expansion plans for Blue Mountain.

NOTES

1. Source: Ontario Skills Development Office, 1993 promotional publication.

2. Labour cost based on $8.00 per hour plus 18 per cent for benefits.

Noram Foods

Prepared by Professor M. R. Leenders
and John Walsh based on research
by Professors Forsyth and Wood

Version: (A) 2003-07-15

Pat Marsden, plant manager for Noram Foods (Noram) of Toronto, Ontario, was considering the impact of changing Noram's policy on package weight. Pat knew this was a matter of overall concern for the corporation. Before raising the possibility of a change in policy with the company's executive committee, Pat wished to have a clearer picture of the options available and the implications of any change in policy. Pat was particularly concerned about the capability of the plant to hold tolerances on weights.

COMPANY BACKGROUND

Noram Foods was a major producer of a variety of consumer food products, including baby foods, cereals, and a variety of canned products. Noram Canada was part of Noram International which had plants in 12 different countries. The head office of Noram International was located in New York. Head office control was primarily financial, as part of Noram's success was based on giving its international units a large amount of local autonomy. Moreover, food tended to be subject to specific and different legislation in each country in which Noram produced its products. Noram Foods had existed in Canada for over 80 years and its brands were extensively advertised. Even though management had frequently been pressured to do custom packaging or produce "no-name" products, it had steadfastly refused to get involved in either. Management believed that exclusive concentration on the production of high-quality branded products was in the corporation's best interest.

Noram Foods in Canada had an enviable record of sound financial performance. Recently, however, the president had called for special vigilance by all managers to look for opportunities to increase revenues or reduce costs. Pat Marsden believed the weight control issue represented a major opportunity for re-evaluation and increased performance.

Policy on Weight Control

Pat's concern was with the company's current policy on weight control, which read:

> At least 95 per cent of all packaged net weights shipped will be above the stated net weight.

Pat believed this policy could result in too high a proportion of overweight packages at substantial cost to Noram, and had therefore requested a meeting with Noram's packaging engineer, Joe Turner. Joe was the recognized expert in the company on statistical quality control, and filling and weighing equipment. In discussing the current policy with Joe, Pat said:

> I know that Noram has had this policy for many years and that during this period Noram has never been cited for putting out underweight products. A lot of things have happened over the years, however. For example, today's weighing technology is a heck of a lot better than it used to be. I think we could save a bundle if we took a more realistic look at our policy. The last time I brought this issue up at an executive meeting was about 10 years ago. At that time, the vice president of marketing was completely opposed to any changes. I can still remember how upset she was. She said:

The consequences of underweight product reaching the public could be disastrous for this company. We have a fantastic reputation to protect and I don't want to run any risk that we will lose something that took decades to build and on which we have spent tens of millions of advertising and promotion dollars. If you're proposing that we start playing statistical games with the government and the consumer, I don't want any part of it.

Pat continued:

Nevertheless, especially in today's economic climate, we would be remiss if we didn't at least look at any major opportunity at cost reduction. Before I propose anything to the executive committee, however, I want to be sure I'm on safe ground. I want to be absolutely sure, for example, that I do not propose anything we're not capable of doing in this plant.

Joe Turner replied:

Pat, I think I know what you're saying, but it is more than just a matter of statistics and technology in filling and weighing. From time to time, I've had discussions with our marketing people about this whole area. They keep insisting that if we ever get caught with underweight packages, it will be seen by consumers as just as serious as a citation of unsanitary conditions. It is a topic where a lot of corporate psychology is involved. We see ourselves as real corporate winners in the food field. Our current policies on sanitation, weight control, package design, and a host of other areas all reflect that winning attitude. In that kind of environment, how much of a risk should this company take? Also, as you can well appreciate, our wide product diversity makes it difficult to apply the same weight policy to everything we do. Even now, on some products, we have substantially less than five per cent of our packages underweight, just to make sure we run no chance of running below the government permitted tolerances.

Both Joe and Pat agreed that raising the issue of weight control without getting down to specifics was going to be meaningless. They, therefore, agreed to concentrate on a specific product line, pre-cooked baby cereals, to see what options might be available and what impact any change in policy might possibly have. Pat and Joe decided they would go and have a good look at the pre-cooked baby cereal package line.

FILLING OPERATIONS

Weight and Volume Standards

Noram used a variety of filling equipment in its plant. For some less popular products, or products with unusual physical characteristics, some older equipment was used. Almost all of the larger-volume product lines were produced on sophisticated modern, high-speed filling equipment that was developed especially for the types of products Noram manufactured. An interesting design trade-off on filling equipment involved speed of fill versus tolerance holding ability on weight or volume. Obviously, a greater filling speed resulted in a higher capacity of the equipment and a lower labor cost per unit produced. On the other hand, a lower filling speed afforded better weight and volume control, resulting in a package weight and volume closer to specifications. Overweight packages resulted in higher material costs for Noram, but underweight packages might result in adverse consumer reactions or government citation.

For many products, Noram not only had weight standards, but also volume standards. "Settling" of product in a package after filling was always a concern, as Noram managers believed consumers might be upset if on opening a box or bag they found a substantial empty space at the top of the package. Special vibrators were attached to the filling equipment to encourage settling before packaging closure. Particle size and weight also affected filling rates and weight and volume control. For example, a granola-type cereal, with particles ranging in weight from one-half gram to seven grams and particle size up to about a cubic centimetre, was much more difficult to control than pre-cooked baby rice cereal in which unit size and weight were small and uniform.

Operation for Pre-Cooked Baby Cereals

For pre-cooked baby cereals, the filling operation was performed on a double line consisting of nine pieces of equipment (see Exhibit 1). The parallel lines were designed to optimize staffing, since one operator could attend to two pieces of equipment at the same time. The first unit in each

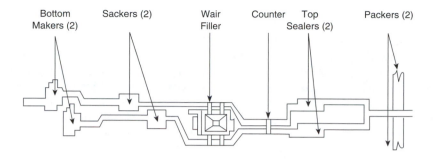

Exhibit 1   The Pre-Cooked Baby Cereal Line

line, a bottom maker, formed the pre-made carton and sealed the carton bottom. The sacker, second in line, formed the wax-paper liner and inserted it into the carton, completing the package. From the sacker, the carton was moved to the Wair filler, which measured out by weight the cereal content and inserted it into the waiting carton. From the filler, the carton was moved to the top sealer for final closure, and then to the packer.

The crew consisted of five operators. One tended the bottom makers and sackers, making sure that each unit was kept supplied with raw materials like flat cartons and wax paper. The second operator looked after the Wair filler, while the third operator packed the completed cartons into cases at the end of the line. Another operator, trained in line machine operation and minor maintenance, was responsible for effective operation of the whole line. The fifth acted as a spare operator who could temporarily relieve any of the other operators and also assist in maintenance. The top sealer glue supply tended to be touchy and had to be watched carefully. A considerable amount of the spare operator's time was spent on the two top sealers. This operator also rotated with the other line personnel. The work arrangement allowed for job rotation each half hour.

The Wair Filler Operation

The net weight filler consisted of four separately-operated filler heads fed from a food bin located on the floor above the filler room. The capacity of the Wair filler was placed at about 100 cartons of 454-gram pre-cooked baby cereal per

minute by the machine's manufacturer. This amounted to a filling speed of about 25 cartons per filling head per minute. The capacity of the other machines on the lines was in balance with the filler capacity. Actual experience with the equipment showed that daily effective capacity ran at about 85 per cent for the seven and a half hour shift the equipment operated.

The Wair filler operator was primarily concerned with package weight control. This job consisted of taking full cartons from each head (four cartons from one of the four heads every 10 minutes), pouring their contents into a plastic container, and weighing the cereal to determine the actual net weight. The operator recorded the weight for each head on a control chart ($\bar{x}$ and R chart) and noted its position between the control limits. If the point fell outside of the specified limits, the operator adjusted the questionable filler head. If the filler had continued out of control after the adjustment, the operator summoned the operator in charge of the line who decided on further action.

Typically, the machine was allowed to continue if the condition was one of overweight. However, an underweight situation was cause for the operation to be stopped.

During the normal course of the line operation, the filler machine operator had control over the in-feed of cereal weight (variable high-low adjustment), food agitators (to maintain cereal consistency, prevent lumping and make room in the carton for the required net weight), vibrators (to make the food settle in the carton), and the stop-start controls for the line. Each of the four heads on the Wair operated independently of the others and could be adjusted without affecting the operation of the other heads. By operating the Wair with a split heads setup, at least part of the line could continue to operate at all times except under severe breakdown conditions.

Efficiency

When Joe and Pat observed the filling operation, they noted everything was running smoothly. The line was running pre-cooked baby cereal and seemed to be meeting its daily production goal of about 38,000 cartons. Since the rice cereal was the most popular of the pre-cooked baby cereals, and since the 454-gram size was the most popular package weight, approximately 60 days a year were scheduled for this package size and cereal alone. The remainder of the year, the machine produced a variety of package sizes in rice, soya, barley, oats, and mixed pre-cooked baby cereals. Pat believed that the cost of 454 grams of pre-cooked baby cereal was about one dollar. This was a fully allocated cost, including an appropriate share of overhead in the various processing departments prior to filling, as well as a share of general plant overhead.

The equipment in the baby cereal area was about three years old and had operated well since its original installation. When Pat asked Joe what new technology was coming along on the horizon, to replace it, Joe replied:

> As you know, Pat, the technology in measuring and weighing and packing equipment is changing all the time. They are always trying to increase speed and accuracy. However, the costs are going up substantially as well. I'm not aware of anything at the moment that would make it worthwhile for us to pull out this line now and substitute it with something better. It may well be that in another year or so, somebody may have some new equipment that's attractive enough for us to take a good look at. Frankly, compared to some of the older equipment in other parts of our plant, the performance of these two lines and this particular filler is quite astounding. We really have no problem staying within a plus or minus one per cent range on weight control in this department, which, considering the speeds we're running at, is outstanding performance.

Joe moved to the Wair filler and asked the operator to show Pat the weight control charts. Pat noted that the equipment was consistently running within the control limits specified. (See Exhibit 2 for a typical Wair filler plot.) Joe also selected at random one of the sheets summarizing the previous day's operations (see Exhibit 3). It summarized both the day's performance for one of the filling heads, as well as the month's to date statistics for the same head. Pat asked Joe to make a copy of this and also to bring the latest government regulations on weight control. The government had issued regulations on acceptable tolerances, and Pat wanted to be absolutely sure that they had the latest information available on consumer packaged goods.

LEGISLATION

Joe returned to Pat's office later in the day. He brought with him, not only a copy of the Wair filler chart that Pat had requested, but also copies of the consumer packaging and labelling act and various amendments and information brochures provided by the Department of Consumer and Corporate Affairs of Canada. Joe said:

> Pat, I've gone through all of this government material. As you can appreciate, the primary reason for its existence is to protect the consumer from misrepresentation by the manufacturer of consumer packaged products. I have underlined here a few specific points which deal with the net weight issue you're trying to raise.
>
> *7(3): where a declaration of net quantity shows the purported net quantity of the pre-packaged product to which it is applied, that declaration shall be deemed not to be a false or misleading representation of the net quantity if the pre-packaged product is, subject to the prescribed tolerance, not less than the declared net quantity of the pre-packaged product and the declaration otherwise meets the requirements of this Act and the regulations.*
>
> Tolerances
>
> *39. (1) For the purposes of Schedule 1, "catch weight product" means a product that because of its nature cannot normally be portioned to a predetermined quantity and is, as a result, usually sold in packages of varying quantity.*

(Text continues on page 237)

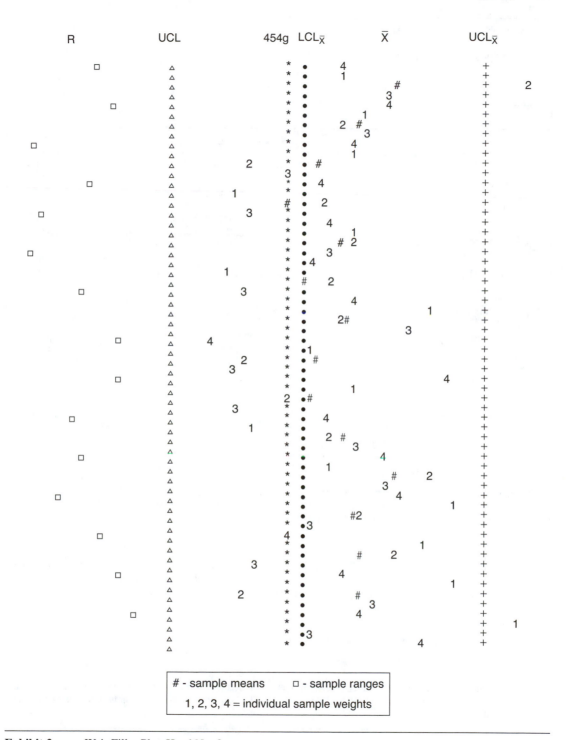

Exhibit 2   Wair Filler Plot, Head No. 3

Product	Pre-Cooked Baby Food
Package Weight	454 g
Head	#3
Capability	1.65 g

	Month to Date	Day
Mean weight ($\bar{x}$)	456.609	457.064
Mean range (R)	3.124	3.876
$UCL_R = D_4R$	7.129	8.845
$LCL_R = D_3R$	0	0
Std. Dev. = S = R/D_2	1.517	1.882
5% Control = 1.645S	2.496	3.097
A_2R	2.277	2.826
$UCL_{\bar{x}} = x + A_2R$	458.886	459.890
$LCL_{\bar{x}} = x - A_2R$	454.332	454.238
Sample size	630	45
Adjusted sample size	622	45
# Light	119	8
Total lightweight	257.516	20.520
% Light	4.783%	4.444%
Total overweight	6,749.944	572.040
Mean overweight	2.713	3.178
Mean % overweight	0.598%	0.700%
Percentage variability	8.046%	−14.089%

A NOTE ON CONTROL CHART CALCULATIONS

Date, Product, Package Weight, Head

Each day summary tables of operations for the Wair Filler were prepared. On any given day there might be several summaries for each head as package weights or products changed. This summary refers to the previous day's run of 454-gram Pre-cooked Baby Cereal through #3 head.

Capability

This is the standard deviation determined by Noram management which under the filling conditions relevant to this product, speed, particle size, Wair manufacturer specifications, etc., should be achieved in meeting the company policy that: "95 per cent of all packaged net weights shipped will be above the stated net weight."

Mean Range

The average of the ranges in the samples taken for the period is called the mean range.

Std. Dev.

This is the sample standard deviation. Theoretically, it is calculated as the square root of the sum of the squared deviations of n observations from the mean divided by n−1. The bigger the standard deviation, the more "spread out" the distribution about the mean.

Exhibit 3   Wair Filler Operating Results   *(Continued)*

$$S = \sqrt{\frac{\sum(Y - \bar{y})}{n - 1}}$$

In Noram's case, S is calculated from the mean range instead of from the individual observations. Dividing the Mean Range by the factor D_2 (from Table A at the end of this Exhibit) provides a very close approximation of the population standard deviation. Table A shows D_2 to be 2.059 for subgroups of four, so for the month to date:

$$\text{Std. Dev.} = S = R/D_2 = 3.124/2.059 = 1.517$$

UCL$_R$

The upper control limit on the range is calculated as D_4 times the mean range. D_4 equals 2.282 for a sample of n = 4 (see Table A). For the month to date:

$$\text{UCL}_R = D_4 R = 2.282 \times 3.124 = 7.129$$

LCL$_R$

The lower control limit on the range is calculated as $D_3 \times$ mean range. Since D_3 is equal to zero for a sample of four, the lower control limit on the range is also zero.

Operators use the upper and lower control limits on the range to monitor the filling operation.

5% Control

This setting ensures that 95 per cent of the packages are filled with 454 grams or more.

To assure ourselves that 95 per cent of the observations will exceed a certain mean value, we first note that 50 per cent will be at or above the mean. Thus, we need only determine the number of standard deviations below the mean that are needed to account for the remaining 95 per cent minus 50 per cent = 45 per cent of the observations. Do this by locating 0.4500 in the body of Table B and read off 1.645. For the month to date:

$$5\% \text{ Control} = 1.645 \times 1.517 = 2.496$$

A$_2$R

The 3-sigma control limits on the mean are based on $A_2 R$. For samples of four packages Table A shows that A_2 is 0.729. For the month to date:

$$A_2 R = 0.729 \times 3.124 = 2.277$$

UCL$_{\bar{x}}$

The upper control limit on the mean is calculated as mean weight plus $A_2 R$. For the month to date:

$$\text{UCL}_{\bar{x}} = 456.609 + 2.277 = 458.886$$

LCL$_{\bar{x}}$

The lower control limit on the mean is calculated as mean weight minus $A_2 R$. For the month to date:

$$\text{LCL}_{\bar{x}} = 456.609 - 2.277 = 454.322$$

Sample Size

This is the unadjusted size. Each sample consists of four packages. Thus, the 630 samples reported for the month to date represent 2,520 individual packages.

Exhibit 3   Wair Filler Operating Results   *(Continued)*

Adjusted Sample Size

The adjusted sample discards "wild" samples. We can think of two kinds of "causes" for package weight variation. There are statistical variations which we can regard as normal fluctuations around a mean and which arise from acceptable operating characteristics of the equipment, and there are assignable variations where the variation from target is a result of some malfunction. If a blockage occurs, for example, and produces a half-filled package in a sample, this would be termed "wild" by Noram and the sample would be discarded for computational purposes. The reasoning here is that Noram wishes to track statistical variation and not malfunctions. In the event of a wild sample being detected, operators would remove affected packages. A total of eight such samples were omitted from the adjusted sample for the month to date. The 622 samples reported for the month to date represent 2,488 packages.

Light

This is the number of packages in the samples under the net weight of 454 grams. For example, if, in one of the samples of four packages, one of the packages was less than 454 grams, this would count as one light package. For the month to date 119 such packages have been recorded.

Total Light Weight

This is the amount in grams of underweight in the light packages. For example, if a light package has been detected in a sample, weighing in at 451 grams, this would be recorded as three grams of light weight. The total light weight associated with the 119 light packages for the month to date is 257.516 grams.

% Light

This is the percentage of packages in the adjusted sample under the net weight. It is calculated as # light divided by the number of packages in the adjusted sample size and expressed as a percentage. Thus, for the month to date:

$$\% \text{ Light} = 119/2,488 = 4.783\%$$

Total Overweight

This is the total weight in grams in excess of the net weight requirements. Each package that weighed in excess of 454 grams would contribute to the total overweight.

Mean Overweight

This is the total overweight divided by the number of packages in the adjusted sample size. Noram does not deduct the number of light packages from the adjusted sample size in computing mean overweight. Thus, for the month to date:

$$\text{Mean Overweight} = 6,749.944/2,488 = 2.713g$$

Mean % Overweight

This is the mean overweight divided by the package weight and expressed as a percentage. Thus, for the month to date:

$$\text{Mean \% Overweight} = 2.713/454 = 0.598\%$$

Percentage Variability

This can be interpreted as a measure of Wair Filler performance against "standard." It is calculated as capability minus std. dev. and expressed as a percentage of capability. A positive figure indicates performance better than standard, while a negative result suggests worse. Thus, for the month to date:

$$\text{Percentage Variability} = (1.650 - 1.517)/1.650 = 8.061\%$$

Exhibit 3   Wair Filler Operating Results   *(Continued)*

**Table A: Factors for Determining the
3-Sigma Control Limits for X̄ and R Charts**

Number of Observations in Subgroup	Factor for X̄ Chart	Factors for R Chart		
		Std. Dev.	LCL_R	UCL_R
n	A_2	D_2	D_3	D_4
2	1.880	1.128	0	3.267
3	1.023	1.693	0	2.575
4	0.729	2.059	0	2.282
5	0.577	2.326	0	2.115
6	0.483	2.534	0	2.004
7	0.419	2.704	0.076	1.924
8	0.373	2.847	0.136	1.864
9	0.337	2.970	0.184	1.816
10	0.308	3.078	0.223	1.777

Exhibit 3   Wair Filler Operating Results   *(Continued)*

Source: Adapted from J. R. Evans and W. M. Lindsay, *The Management and Control of Quality,* Second Edition. West, 1993. Appendix B, page 661.

(2) Subject to subsection (3), the amount set out in column II of an item of the appropriate Part of Schedule 1 is the tolerance prescribed for the purposes of subsection 7(3) of the Act for the net quantity set out in column I of that item.

(3) Where the net quantity of a prepackaged product referred to in Part I, II, III, IV, V, or VI of Schedule 1 is declared by weight or volume and that net quantity is not set out in column I of that Part, the tolerance prescribed for the purposes of subsection 7(3) of the Act for that net quantity is an amount based upon linear interpolation between the appropriate tolerances[1] appearing in column II of that Part.

Inspection

40. (1) Where an inspector wishes to inspect any lot, shipment, proposed shipment or identifiable quantity of prepackaged products all purporting to contain the same net quantity or product (hereinafter referred to as a "lot") to determine whether the lot meets the requirements of the Act and these Regulations respecting the declaration of net quantity and where, in his opinion, it is impractical or undesirable to inspect all the separate prepackaged products in the lot, he may inspect the lot by selecting and examining a sample of the lot.

THE DECISION

Pat thanked Joe for his work and concluded:

Joe, why don't both of us think this whole situation out for a week or so and then get together on it again. I want to be thoroughly familiar with this whole situation before I look at any options or propose any changes. I like the idea of concentrating first at the pre-cooked cereal line, because it is a steady seller and it is an area we appear to have under reasonable control. I know we can't stop there, but it is a good place to start.

NOTE

1. Excerpt from Consumer Packaging and Labelling Act, Consumer Packaging and Labelling Regulations amendment, P.C. 1975-479 4 March 1975. See Exhibit 4 for Schedule 1.

Table B: Areas Under the Normal Curve

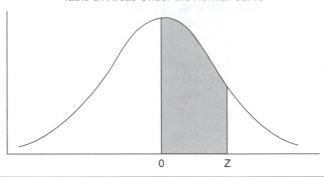

z	0.00	0.01	0.02	0.03	0.04	0.05	0.06	0.07	0.08	0.09
0.0	0.0000	0.0040	0.0080	0.0120	0.0160	0.0199	0.0239	0.0279	0.0319	0.0359
0.1	0.0398	0.0438	0.0478	0.0517	0.0557	0.0596	0.0636	0.0675	0.0714	0.0753
0.2	0.0793	0.0832	0.0871	0.0910	0.0948	0.0987	0.1026	0.1064	0.1103	0.1141
0.3	0.1179	0.1217	0.1255	0.1293	0.1331	0.1368	0.1406	0.1443	0.1480	0.1517
0.4	0.1554	0.1591	0.1628	0.1664	0.1700	0.1736	0.1772	0.1808	0.1844	0.1879
0.5	0.1915	0.1950	0.1985	0.2019	0.2054	0.2088	0.2123	0.2157	0.2190	0.2224
0.6	0.2257	0.2291	0.2324	0.2357	0.2389	0.2422	0.2454	0.2486	0.2517	0.2549
0.7	0.2580	0.2611	0.2642	0.2673	0.2704	0.2734	0.2764	0.2794	0.2823	0.2852
0.8	0.2881	0.2910	0.2939	0.2967	0.2995	0.3023	0.3051	0.3078	0.3106	0.3133
0.9	0.3159	0.3186	0.3212	0.3238	0.3264	0.3289	0.3315	0.3340	0.3365	0.3389
1.0	0.3413	0.3438	0.3461	0.3485	0.3508	0.3531	0.3554	0.3577	0.3599	0.3621
1.1	0.3643	0.3665	0.3686	0.3708	0.3729	0.3749	0.3770	0.3790	0.3810	0.3830
1.2	0.3849	0.3869	0.3888	0.3907	0.3925	0.3944	0.3962	0.3980	0.3997	0.4015
1.3	0.4032	0.4049	0.4066	0.4082	0.4099	0.4115	0.4131	0.4147	0.4162	0.4177
1.4	0.4192	0.4207	0.4222	0.4236	0.4251	0.4265	0.4279	0.4292	0.4306	0.4319
1.5	0.4332	0.4345	0.4357	0.4370	0.4382	0.4394	0.4406	0.4418	0.4429	0.4441
1.6	0.4452	0.4463	0.4474	0.4484	0.4495	0.4505	0.4515	0.4525	0.4535	0.4545
1.7	0.4554	0.4564	0.4573	0.4582	0.4591	0.4599	0.4608	0.4616	0.4625	0.4633
1.8	0.4641	0.4649	0.4656	0.4664	0.4671	0.4678	0.4686	0.4693	0.4699	0.4706
1.9	0.4713	0.4719	0.4726	0.4732	0.4738	0.4744	0.4750	0.4756	0.4761	0.4767
2.0	0.4772	0.4778	0.4783	0.4788	0.4793	0.4798	0.4803	0.4808	0.4812	0.4817
2.1	0.4821	0.4826	0.4830	0.4834	0.4838	0.4842	0.4846	0.4850	0.4854	0.4857
2.2	0.4861	0.4864	0.4868	0.4871	0.4875	0.4878	0.4881	0.4884	0.4887	0.4890
2.3	0.4893	0.4896	0.4898	0.4901	0.4904	0.4906	0.4909	0.4911	0.4913	0.4916
2.4	0.4918	0.4920	0.4922	0.4925	0.4927	0.4929	0.4931	0.4932	0.4934	0.4936
2.5	0.4938	0.4940	0.4941	0.4943	0.4945	0.4946	0.4948	0.4949	0.4951	0.4952
2.6	0.4953	0.4955	0.4956	0.4957	0.4959	0.4960	0.4961	0.4962	0.4963	0.4964
2.7	0.4965	0.4966	0.4967	0.4968	0.4969	0.4970	0.4971	0.4972	0.4973	0.4974
2.8	0.4974	0.4975	0.4976	0.4977	0.4977	0.4978	0.4979	0.4979	0.4980	0.4981
2.9	0.4981	0.4982	0.4982	0.4983	0.4984	0.4984	0.4985	0.4985	0.4986	0.4986
3.0	0.4987	0.4987	0.4987	0.4988	0.4988	0.4989	0.4989	0.4989	0.4990	0.4990

Exhibit 3 Wair Filler Operating Results

Source: Op cit Appendix A, page 660.

Item	Column I Declared Weight	Column II Tolerances
1	1 g*	0.16 g
2	1.5 g	0.20 g
3	2 g	0.25 g
4	3 g	0.32 g
5	4 g	0.38 g
6	5 g	0.44 g
7	6 g	0.50 g
8	8 g	0.59 g
9	10 g	0.68 g
10	15 g	0.88 g
11	20 g	1.05 g
12	30 g	1.36 g
13	40 g	1.63 g
14	50 g	1.87 g
15	60 g	2.1 g
16	80 g	2.5 g
17	100 g	2.9 g
18	150 g	3.8 g
19	200 g	4.5 g
20	300 g	5.8 g
21	400 g	7.0 g
22	500 g	8.0 g
23	600 g	9.0 g
24	800 g	11.0 g
25	1 kg**	12.5 g
26	1.5 kg	16.0 g
27	2 kg	19.4 g
28	3 kg	25.0 g
29	4 kg	30.0 g
30	5 kg	34.0 g
31	6 kg	39.0 g
32	8 kg	46.0 g
33	10 kg	53.0 g
34	15 kg	68.0 g
35	20 kg	80.0 g
36	over 20 kg	0.4% of declared weight

Exhibit 4   Declaration of Net Quantity by Metric Units of Weight on Products Other Than Catch Weight Products

*g = grams

**kg = kilograms

(1) Excerpt from *Consumer Packaging and Labelling Act,* Consumer Packaging and Labelling Regulations Amendment, Schedule 1, Part III, P.C. 1975-479, 4 March 1975.

HILCREST AUTO

*Prepared by Carlie Bell under
the supervision of Elizabeth M. A. Grasby*

Version: (B) 2003-09-09

Late one afternoon in March 2000, Mark Bailey returned from an emergency out-of-town meeting to discover that scrapped parts had been used in a shipment to one of Hilcrest Auto's major customers. Although the company had been experiencing quality problems for some time, this shipment decision could have disastrous effects on the future of the firm. Bailey, quality manager and business unit manager of the Small Parts Division of Hilcrest Auto (Hilcrest), had to decide what action, if any, he should take regarding the scrapped parts shipment. As well, he would have to determine which of four options to choose to address the quality issues as soon as possible: buying a second bending machine, adding a third shift, continuing as is with more overtime production, and/or requesting a change to the contract to allow more variance in the specifications of the part.

THE AUTOMOTIVE INDUSTRY IN NORTH AMERICA

The automotive supply industry consisted of companies competing for contracts to produce parts for automobile assemblers dominated by Ford, GM and Daimler-Chrysler, known as the "big three" automotive assembly companies, and/or the Tier One and Tier Two[1] manufacturers of automotive parts in North America. In 1999, GM held 33.26 per cent of the North American automobile market, Ford had captured 26.38 per cent, and Daimler-Chrysler held 18.67 per cent.

North American automobile sales recorded a banner year in 1999, and PriceWaterhouse-Cooper's AUTOFACTS had forecast that North American car and truck production would rise from 53.18 million cars and trucks produced in 1999 to 54.06 million produced in 2000. Although North America would continue to be the largest production region with a 30.55 per cent share of global production in 2000, this figure would represent a drop of 1.12 percentage points from 1999 as foreign manufacturers (Mazda, Honda, Volkswagen) increased their global market share.[2]

The Office for the Study of Automotive Transportation at the University of Michigan forecasted that while the amount of product design and engineering occurring in North America by international automakers would increase from 15 per cent in 1999 to 30 per cent by 2009,[3] domestic manufacturers would source an increasing percentage of parts from outside North America. Therefore, as the global industry continued to experience growth, North American parts manufacturers were under intense pressure to remain competitive by improving quality and at the same time by decreasing costs.

The industry experienced some seasonality in response to plant shutdowns, often occurring in December, July and August. The number of competitors in the industry had decreased since Hilcrest first entered the market, and those that remained were dependent upon winning contracts to supply the "big three" to ensure continued success. To win a contract, suppliers submitted a bid and attempted to prove themselves more reliable, more capable, and more cost effective than other bidders. It was an intense process, and the "big three" had the power to demand additional cost-cutting measures and service requirements that would affect the profitability of the smaller suppliers. Additionally, the "big three" demanded loyalty from their suppliers. As a result, GM,

Ford and Daimler-Chrysler often received unique parts and had total control over their suppliers, such that it was impossible for a supplier to sell to the other members of the "big three."

HILCREST AUTO COMPANY BACKGROUND

Michael Hill opened Hilcrest Auto in the early seventies in Hamilton, Ontario, an industrial city located at the western end of Lake Ontario, along the Niagara Escarpment. Hilcrest produced steel tubing components that were used in the assembly of numerous automotive units. Hill chose this location because of its proximity to major transportation routes between other manufacturing cities in Ontario and the United States. This site ensured that Hilcrest had easy access to the steel required to produce steel tubing and to the shipping routes to its customers, many of whom were located within the southwestern Ontario region. By 1998, the majority of Hamilton's population of approximately 500,000 was employed in heavy industries such as iron, steel, and machinery.

The business grew slowly but steadily over the years and Hill passed the business to his son, Dennis, in the late 1980s. Dennis had earned an engineering degree at The University of Western Ontario and a master's degree in business (MBA) from the Richard Ivey School of Business. Carl Wilson, Hill's son-in-law, was offered the role of vice-president and material control manager for Hilcrest. Carl had no formal business education, but was excited to be offered a role in the family business, and accepted the role enthusiastically. Under Dennis and Carl's leadership, Hilcrest earned its QS9000[4] certification, and by March 2000, Hilcrest's annual sales topped $30,000,000 and the company employed over 160 non-unionized employees.

MARK BAILEY AND THE SMALL PARTS DIVISION OF HILCREST AUTO

Upon graduating with a B.Sc. in mechanical engineering from The University of Western Ontario and later obtaining an MBA degree, Bailey worked as a quality control manager for several firms before joining Hilcrest in 1998. As the quality manager and business unit manager of the Small Parts Division of Hilcrest, Bailey was responsible for the manufacture of tubing used in the production of heater cores for vehicles.[5] All vehicles with heating systems needed heater cores, and many companies competed to supply the market with the tubing for these heater core units. Hilcrest won a three-year contract to supply a major Tier One company with the tubing, at $1.05 per heater core tube, in 1999. Weekly demand by the major Tier One customer ranged from 17,000 to 20,000 units, and forecasted demand for the year 2001 was expected to increase to 35,000 units per week. The quality problems Hilcrest had been experiencing were threatening Hilcrest's contract with this customer, who demanded that the tubing be "free, perfect, and yesterday."

TUBING PRODUCTION

The heater core tubing production process was not complex. One operator (who earned $12 per hour for 50 weeks each year) was needed to ensure that the process ran smoothly. Pre-cut steel tubing, supplied by a United States supplier at a cost of $0.93 per piece, was manually loaded into a pressing machine that rounded both ends of the tube in about seven seconds. The operator then unloaded the rounded tubes into bins. Since the pressing machine was also used to produce another unrelated part, 30,000 units of rounded tubes were kept in inventory at all times. Once a bin was full of rounded tubes, the operator loaded the bin into a custom-designed bending machine where the tubing was bent into a zigzag shape to fit into the heater core. This step took 13 seconds per tube. The bent tubing was then washed for about one minute in batches of about 1,000 pieces to remove any oil or grime that had contaminated the tube. Finally, the heater core tube was ready for shipping to the customer.

The production process normally operated two eight-hour shifts each day, five days a week, and produced between 1,000 and 2,000 finished heater core tubes per shift. Lately, the production of 1,300 units on a shift was considered "a good day." When production fell behind demand, Hilcrest used voluntary overtime to increase output. Workers were paid time-and-a-half on Saturday and double-time on Sunday, with Sunday shifts difficult to staff. Overtime shifts were often unproductive because if the operator experienced trouble with the machinery or was concerned about the quality of parts, no support personnel was available to assist the unskilled operator, and production was usually halted as a result.

Machine Problems

The bending machine was a chief concern within the process. The bender was required to operate continuously in order to meet demand, leaving no time for scheduled preventive maintenance. Maintenance could not be performed during the night because no supervisory or maintenance staff were available. As a result, equipment failures requiring maintenance would cause an unscheduled downtime of up to three or four shifts. To avoid this unscheduled downtime, the machine required a proper overhaul that could take up to a week and had to be done offsite. This overhaul had not been performed, however, because the machine could not produce enough inventory to meet the contractual obligations while the overhaul was being performed.

In addition, because of the lack of maintenance, the bending machine often slightly squeezed the rounded ends of the tubes as it bent the tubing. Hilcrest performed only infrequent checks on this particular feature, but were aware that the ends of the tubing did not meet the exact specifications of the contract because of this machine error. Bailey believed this slight distortion of the tubing ends in no way affected the safety or function of either the tubing or the completed heater cores; however, the fact remained that the shipped parts to the customer were not always "up to spec."

The Returned Shipment

Hilcrest had sent this Tier One customer slightly "out-of-round" tubing for quite some time, but recently this customer had performed a quality check on 8,000 heater core tubes received and phoned Bailey to inform him that the tubing did not meet specifications and, therefore, would be returned. Bailey authorized the return of the shipment, and desperately began to try to sort out the in-house situation to ensure that the next shipment met contract specifications.

Inconveniently, Bailey was forced to attend another major company emergency out of town. Upon his return a few days later, Bailey was horrified to discover that the returned parts were no longer in the holding area. In response to Bailey's inquiry, Carl Wilson stated that due to the plant's inability to hastily produce 8,000 perfect units, and because the customer had never noticed the distortion before, he had instructed the shipping department to re-package the returned order and re-send it to the customer.

Since the customer had already received the "new" shipment, had obviously not inspected the units, and was using the parts in the assembly of the heater core units, Bailey was unsure what to do. He was certain that informing the customer of the error now would be costly to Hilcrest because once the tubing had been installed into the heater cores, the entire heater core unit would have to be scrapped if any component was deemed to be defective. In addition to the replacement tubing costs, Hilcrest would have to pay the Tier One customer $60 per heater core (as written in the contract). Bailey did not know if he could save Hilcrest's relationship with this customer if he did report the "error" to the customer.

Changing the Process

Given this most recent event, Bailey was more determined than ever to fix the capacity and quality issues within the heater core tubing department. He was considering several options. It appeared that the purchase of a second bending machine would successfully address the volume constraint and improve the quality of the finished product. However, the custom-designed bending machine would cost $70,000 and, combined with the old machine, the new duo-machine process would require another operator. The addition of a second bending machine would not affect any of the other stations on the line. Bailey knew he would have to justify these expenses to Dennis and Carl. Further, since the new bender would take up to four months to arrive, Bailey was going to have to make some interim changes to production quality and output.

To improve in-house quality immediately, Bailey could add two more steps to the production process. After the tubing was bent, it could pass through a re-work station where the distorted ends of the tubing would be re-shaped into proper rounds in less than seven seconds per tube. Once re-shaped, the tubes would pass through a 100 per cent gauge inspection station where the ends of the tubes would be automatically measured to ensure they had been re-worked to the required specifications. The gauge inspection would take virtually no time at all. This new process would result in the rejection of five per cent of the finished tubes, which would be totally scrapped. Because the current single operator would be unable to keep up with the new process, an additional (full-time) employee would have to be hired to ensure that production was not hindered further. Bailey would need to assess whether these new steps should be continued after the new bender arrived.

Bailey also considered approaching the engineers of the final customer—one of the three major automakers—to re-evaluate and re-test the heater core units with the intent to approve a contractual print change allowing Hilcrest a wider range of acceptable variance in the shape of the round tube ends. It was the Big Three automakers that ultimately dictated the specifications for the heater core units. Bailey was concerned, however, that this request would negatively impact Hilcrest's reputation and hinder potential future contracts with other Tier One companies, especially since Hilcrest had won

this contract by stating it could produce the necessary quality and quantity of parts.

To increase output, Bailey was considering either the implementation of a mandatory overtime policy or the addition of a new third shift. He was concerned about the effect mandatory overtime might have on employee morale and productivity, but it could be a more cost-effective way to produce tubing than adding another full-time shift. If a third shift were added, in addition to hiring new tubing operators, maintenance and other support personnel would have to be available to assist the operators and to ensure that the additional shift was equally productive.

DECISION

Bailey knew he had little time to make some major decisions. He questioned how he could justify the purchase of a new bending machine to management. He wondered how to most effectively and efficiently improve the quality and output of the heater core tubing operation while waiting for the new machine's arrival. Should any short-term changes made to the production process be continued once the new bender was operational? Right now, he had to decide what to do about the "out-of-round" parts re-sent to the customer.

Bailey believed that making long-term changes to improve quality and output was the right move for Hilcrest; it was a good step toward growth and would help the company remain competitive within this industry. However, he also knew that he would have to present a strong case to Dennis Hill and Carl Wilson when seeking approval for additional investments and expenditures. Bailey wanted to ensure that he had both strong quantitative support and a convincing qualitative rationale to make the necessary changes to the heater core tubing production facility.

NOTES

1. Tier One suppliers manufacture most of their products and ship them to automotive assembly plants. Tier Two suppliers, in turn, supply Tier One companies

with some of the parts required (parts the Tier One companies either do not want to or are unable to manufacture) in the finished goods shipped to the automotive assembly plants.

2. Automotive market information: Dale Jewett, Automotive Industries: Industry Statistics, January, 2000. http://www.findarticles.com/cf_atinds/m3012/1_180/59035633/pl/article.jhtml (August 16, 2001).

3. University of Michigan News and Information Services, Auto Industry Will Be Challenged by Technology, Regulations and Global Competition" April 3, 2000. http://www.umich.edu/~newsinfo/Releases/2000/Apr00/r040300a.html (August 16, 2001).

4. QS9000 is the set of fundamental quality requirements established primarily by Chrysler, Ford and General Motors to reduce the confusion and cost that came from having different quality standards which suppliers had to meet. Derived from ISO9001, the international standards for manufacturing quality, QS9000 includes requirements and measurables specific to the automotive industry.

5. The heater core is a smaller version of the radiator that is used to keep your toes warm when it's cold outside. It is mounted under the dashboard. Some of the hot coolant is routed through this little radiator by more hoses. A small electric fan is also mounted there especially for the purpose of directing the heat inside the car. The principle is exactly the same as the one used in the radiator for your engine, except that the heat is released inside the car instead of outside. (Source: IndiaMART Network, http://www/auto/indiamart.com/auto-part/autopart-html, May 31, 2001.)

MUTUAL LIFE OF CANADA—THE GROUP CLIENT SERVICE GUARANTEE (A)

Prepared by Janet DeSilva under the supervision of Professor John Haywood-Farmer

Version: (A) 2002-12-11

In August 1992, Alex Brown, senior vice-president of Mutual Life of Canada's Group Division, was preparing for the meeting of the Group Division Quality Council the next day. One item on the agenda was the decision on the group client service guarantee. For four months the Service Guarantee Working Group, reporting to Mr. Brown, had been investigating the possibility of the division guaranteeing some of its services. The working group had now prepared its final report which, although recommending that the division proceed with a service guarantee, raised a number of questions and left a major design decision unanswered. Mr. Brown now had to decide if he should endorse the group's recommendations. Mr. Brown believed that no Canadian insurance company had yet issued a service guarantee, although he thought that one company in the United States had.

Although the opportunity looked attractive, he knew that the stakes were high.

THE MUTUAL GROUP

The Mutual Group, one of Canada's largest insurers (over $20 billion in total assets under administration), was the marketing name of a financial services organization led by Mutual Life Assurance Company of Canada (Mutual Life). The company's headquarters were in Waterloo, Ontario, approximately 100 kilometres west of Toronto. It operated from offices and agencies across Canada and the northern United States. The Mutual Group, which began in 1868 with the incorporation of Canada's first mutual life insurance company (The Ontario Mutual Life Assurance Company), comprised a number of financial services companies offering a wide range of insurance, employee group benefit, investment, and trust company products and services. Exhibit 1 lists the companies of The Mutual Group, all of which were subsidiaries of Mutual Life. In addition, Mutual Life had four divisions (Individual, Group, Investment, and Corporate), each headed by a senior or executive vice-president.

Because Mutual Life was a mutual organization, clients buying participating life insurance became owners of the firm, entitling them to vote

---

1. The Mutual Life Assurance Company of Canada (Mutual Life of Canada). Products and services include life and health insurance, annuities, registered retirement income funds (RRIFs), registered retirement savings plans (RRSPs), life income funds (LIFs), pensions, commercial mortgages, real estate financing, and corporate lending offered to both individuals and groups.

2. Mutual Diversico Limited. Administrator of The Mutual Group of Funds (mutual funds); responsible for processing of purchase, redemption and exchange orders, distributions, and service to unit holders.

3. Mutual Investco Inc. Distributes and markets The Mutual Group of Funds (mutual funds); registered with the 12 Securities Administrators (regulatory authorities) across Canada; Investco agents are all dual-licensed as life insurance agents of Mutual Life of Canada.

4. Mutual Asset Management Ltd. Once regulatory approval is granted, Mutual Asset Management Ltd. will manage Mutual Life of Canada's stock and marketable bond portfolios and provide investment management services for The Mutual Group of Funds.

5. R.D.C. Property Services Limited. Manages revenue-producing real estate properties.

6. Mississauga Executive Enterprises Limited. Fifty owned by Mutual Life of Canada; real estate development.

7. Mu-Cana Investment Counselling Ltd. Investment management services for pension funds and other taxable and non-taxable assets, for Canadian corporations, unions, universities, foundations, and individuals.

8. Mu-Cana Data Services Ltd. Microfiche services for Mutual Life of Canada and client companies in the Kitchener-Waterloo area.

9. The Mutual Trust Company. Federally chartered trust company located in Toronto; gathers deposits through the marketing network of Mutual Life of Canada; invests primarily in residential mortgages.

10. Mutual Securities Inc. Member of the Investment Dealers of Canada; carries on investment banking activities principally related to mortgages and real estate offerings.

11. The Mutual Group (U.S.), Inc. An operating company responsible for strategic planning and investment management.

12. TMG Life Insurance Company

   The Mutual Group (U.S.)/Employee Benefits. Based in Brookfield, Wisconsin; serves the small group marketplace with health, life, short- and long-term disability, stop loss and dental insurance; and offers flexible benefits and managed care health services.

   The Mutual Group (U.S.)/Personal Financial Services. Based in Fargo, North Dakota; specializes in the sale of individual life insurance and annuities.

Exhibit 1   The Composition of the Mutual Group

Source: Mutual Life of Canada Annual Report.

at the annual meeting and also to share in the firm's financial success. Although mutual companies were not obliged to pay dividends which reflected this ownership, in 1990 Mutual Life broke with tradition, becoming the first mutual insurance company to pay participating policy holders an ownership dividend (it totalled $30 million). Historically, such companies had applied earned surpluses as "participating dividends" to reduce future premiums. Mutual Life was committed to both participating dividends as well as triennial ownership dividends.

MUTUAL LIFE OF CANADA—GROUP DIVISION

Mutual Life's Group Division, headed by Alex Brown, had several departments led by vice-presidents. It specialized in employee group benefit programs such as life, health, rehabilitation, and pension products. Exhibit 2 gives some data comparing the 1991 performance of 20 of Canada's leading group insurers. Overall, Mutual Life had the fourth largest group premium income. An industry publication claimed that the industry was very competitive.[1] The largest companies were growing at a rate above the industry average; in 1991 the five largest firms had increased their collective market share by 2.4 per cent over 1990. The Group Division was finding 1992 to be particularly challenging from a bottom-line perspective.

The division served approximately 1.35 million Canadians in 9,600 groups, many of which had been Mutual Life clients for decades. Groups with life and health plans represented 56 per cent of the total; groups with pension plans represented the remaining 44 per cent. The division segmented groups as small (up to 50 lives insured), medium (50 to 500 lives), or large (over 500 lives). Like its competitors, the division offered its largest clients many special services including assignment of group policyholder service officers to manage the relationship. Unlike smaller insurance companies which tended to specialize by benefit and group size, the division

offered a broad range of products to a full spectrum of groups.

The division's mission was to be a leader in the group life, health, and pension markets in terms of its products, the quality of service it provided, and the degree of innovation it brought to the marketplace. The division prided itself on being in touch with clients and their needs. It believed that it was the only company in the industry that routinely measured speed of settlement and payment accuracy. Mutual Life client surveys showed that the division was number one in the eyes of customers. Audits showed that it was considerably better than the 99 per cent industry standard for accuracy. The division had a high degree of confidence in its ability to deliver.

The division offered benefit programs in two categories: life and health benefits and pension plans. Exhibit 3 gives some details of typical coverage. Annually, the division estimated its costs for the next year in three categories: claims (using, for example, actuarial tables), services claimed (using, for example, semiprivate hospital room rates, dental fee guides), and administration (e.g., for processing claims, premiums, accepting contributions, generating tax and employee statements, investing deposits, and handling enquiries). Employers typically paid life and health fees; employers or employees usually paid pension fees, either directly or as adjusted investment returns on contributions.

Many groups designed their own plans, typically with the help of an advisor: the group decided what coverage it wanted and then sought bids and possibly presentations from potential insurers. Exhibit 4 shows a typical request from a benefits consultant for a sales presentation; on July 31, the client awarded Mutual Life this contract, worth $6 million per year. Although price was the dominant criterion in choosing an insurer, others were also important: the structure of costs, the continued financial viability of the organization, their systems capabilities, special value-added services (such as individualized statements and special seminars), interpersonal relationships, etc. Insurers based their proposals on their estimates of initial and on-going costs.

(Text continues on page 250)

Exhibit 2 — Data on Canada's Top 20 Group Insurers (for the year ending December 31, 1991)[1]

Company	Group Life Premiums	Group Pension		Administrative Services Only	Group Health Premiums	Total Business	Market Share
		Premium Cash Flow	Pension Assets				
Confederation Life	$143 (10.4%)	$561	$5,440	$434 (18.1%)	$315 (2.9%)	$1,452 (27.7%)	11.0%
Great West Life	146 (0.1%)	324	3,479	455 (17.2%)	501 (3.6%)	1,448 (−4.5%)	11.0%
Sun Life	201 (11.2%)	597	3,453	190 (18.4%)	422 (6.8%)	1,418 (12.1%)	10.8%
Mutual Life	79 (−5.1%)	470	3,948	252 (52.0%)	262 (1.5%)	1,076 (9.8%)	8.2%
Canada Life	144 (−11.6%)	343	5,299	119 (31.8%)	208 (26.5%)	814 (5.1%)	6.2%
London Life	90 (3.2%)	254	1,973	100 (18.2%)	312 (1.4%)	756 (10.6%)	5.7%
Standard Life	23 (4.1%)	464	3,227	21 (35.6%)	87 (47.6%)	596 (37.7%)	4.6%
Metropolitan Life	93 (5.4%)	103	1,147	174 (11.3%)	142 (−11.4%)	513 (−16.7%)	3.9%
Aetna Canada	56 (0.6%)	116	717	177 (18.6%)	124 (−7.1%)	473 (4.1%)	3.6%
Manulife Financial	31 (−3.4%)	248	2,583		170 (3.2%)	453 (10.2%)	3.4%
North American Life	65 (17.0%)	194	1,395	98 (8.2%)	150 (30.2%)	412 (28.8%)	3.1%
Prudential Insurance	56 (10.0%)	60	109	135 (−12.5%)	169 (28.0%)	390 (35.9%)	3.0%
Ontario Blue Cross					225 (9.2%)	360 (−0.1%)	2.7%
Crown Life	37 (−5.0%)	101	847	25 (−38.4%)	112 (−1.7%)	274 (−10.1%)	2.1%
Maritime Life	29 (5.1%)	73	336	75 (12.7%)	96 (−0.4%)	273 (3.5%)	2.1%
Industrial Alliance Life	22 (9.3%)	185	1,247			268 (27.5%)	2.0%
Laurentian/Imperial	38 (52.6%)	115	1,083		106 (15.7%)	268 (−6.1%)	2.0%
SSQ D'Assurance	30 (−1.6%)	24	173	32 (5.3%)	180 (11.7%)	266 (19.8%)	2.0%
Prudential Assurance		228	1,661			228 (37.6%)	1.7%
Green Shield				158 (10.4%)		201 (13.0%)	1.5%
Sample Totals	**$1,283 (3.8%)**	**$4,460**	**$38,117**	**$2,445 (16.3%)**	**$3,581 (7.0%)**	**$11,939 (11.2%)**	**(90.6%)**
Industry Totals[2]	**$1,427 (6.9%)**	**$4,621**	**$39,340**	**$2,661 (14.5%)**	**$4,312 (7.2%)**	**$13,178 (6.3%)**	**(100.0%)**

Source: Benefits Canada, July–August, 1992, pp. 32–35.

1. Financial numbers are in millions of dollars; numbers in parentheses are the percentage increases from 1990; blanks indicate unavailable information.

2. Numbers do not add to the totals shown because of data from other coverage categories not included in the table and 23 smaller firms in the survey.

Group Life and Health Programs

Life	typically a multiple of salary (e.g., two years)
Accidental death	lump sums paid in the event of accidental death; reduced amounts and dismemberment for dismemberment
Extended health	includes items such as drug reimbursement, vision, hospital (e.g., upgrade to semi-private), supplementary care (e.g., wheelchairs, nursing care)
Dental	includes semi-annual check-up and cleaning, non-orthodontic dental treatment
Short-term disability	salary coverage for periods up to 17 weeks
Long-term disability	salary coverage for periods exceeding 17 weeks

Group Pension Plans

Registered Retirement Savings Plans (RRSP)

Registered Pension Plans (RPP)

Deferred Profit Sharing Plans (DPSP)

Exhibit 3 Typical Types of Group Coverage

Source: Company files.

July 10, 1992

Based on our analysis of the proposals submitted to the client on its Canadian Group Benefit Program and the findings and recommendations presented to the client's Canadian companies, we are pleased to advise that three companies have been selected to participate in finalist presentations. The client's Human Resource Council will receive presentations as identified below. A representative of our company will attend to facilitate the discussions.

Date, Place, and Time

The presentations will be held on July 29, 1992 at the company's offices. Directions from Toronto are attached. The presentations will be 1½ hours each, including 30 to 45 minutes for questions and discussion. The times have been scheduled as follows, as previously confirmed by telephone.

Competitor A	9:00 a.m.
Mutual Life	10:30 a.m.
Competitor B	1:30 p.m.

Insurance Company Representatives

It is expected that each competing insurer will have a presentation team of four representatives which may be comprised as follows:

1. The Ontario group representative who will be directly responsible for the client's Ontario-based companies and have on-going responsibility for the overall account;

2. The Quebec group representative who will be directly responsible for the client's Quebec-based companies;

3. A disability claims specialist or manager who can describe the facilities, philosophies, techniques, procedures, and special advantages or skills which your company applies in the successful management of disability claims and rehabilitation efforts;

4. One or two other representative(s) chosen at your discretion, who you believe would best round out your presentation team. However, the client has requested that all those in attendance have an on-going role in servicing or managing the client's account, and thus be accessible to the client's companies in the future.

Exhibit 4 A Benefits Consultant's Recent Request for a Competitive Sales Presentation[1] *(Continued)*

In advance of the meeting, please supply a list, identifying the individuals who will represent your company, including their job titles and roles. Also, please request any audio-visual equipment you require for your presentation, in writing, no later than July 20, 1992.

Presentation Format and Priorities

As mentioned, the presentations will be 1½ hours long. Your formal presentation should allow time for an informal discussion and/or question period of 30 to 45 minutes. To assist you in preparing your presentation, the client has identified the following priorities and areas of particular interest that you should address in the course of your overall presentation:

Disability Claims Management Facilities, including:

- a profile of the resource group that makes up your disability management team and an outline of your claims management process and techniques;
- the measure of success achieved by your company through rehabilitation efforts, expressed in terms of the cost/benefit ratio of rehabilitation expenses versus claims/reserve reductions;
- a brief (*quantitative*) account of a recent disability management success story;
- highlights of any other special attributes of your company's philosophies and claims control approach, which you believe contribute to the success of your disability management efforts.

Customer Service Support Systems, including:

- *online transfer of data* for eligibility purposes;
- *electronic claims validation* (EDI), including any special features or safeguards of "automated drug card" programs;
- direct (*electronic*) *deposit of claims* payments to employees' bank accounts, including eligibility of benefits arrangements.

Employer/Employee Claims Inquiry Programs, including:

- *online claims inquiry* programs;
- *telephone inquiry systems,* including voice interactive programs, 800 numbers, extended service hours, etc.

Plan Administration Issues, including:

- a detailed description of your capability and systems support of flexible spending accounts, including your handling of resulting tax reporting requirements (*identify existing flexible spending accounts under your administration*);
- financial concessions accruing to the client if your company fails to meet performance standards for claims turn around, documentation delivery and financial reporting, as outlined in the specifications;
- advanced statistical claims reporting that facilitates more effective claims analysis and financial forecasting, specifically addressing:
  - drug analysis by therapeutic grouping
  - brand-name versus generic drug identification
  - availability of claims data in electronic format, which can be manipulated to obtain custom reports, i.e., question and answer format

Value-Added Client Services, including:

- *customer driven value-added services,* introduced in response to client requests;
- *pro-actively created value-added services,* developed as a result of internal company initiatives.

In describing your commitment to value-added services, rank your organization in terms of its response to new or emerging benefit developments, issues, and products and provide copies of plan sponsor directed information material such as newsletters, etc., and provide sample copies.

Exhibit 4   A Benefits Consultant's Recent Request for a Competitive Sales Presentation[1]

Source: Company files.

1. The actual letter identified the client, Mutual Life's two competitors, and the benefits consultant. It also included complete directions on how to get to the client's office.

Because of the uniqueness of each plan and the complexity of the decision-making process, it was difficult to compare insurers. Groups almost always used the services of brokers or specialist benefits consultants. Although contracts were usually for one year, insurers expected them to be renewed; indeed, because of a contract's initial costs, insurers often would not see profits for several years. The insurer reset rates and contract terms annually on the basis of experience. The group might decide to take the business to the market to test the viability of the new terms.

The typical process worked as follows. A member of a group plan received dental service and subsequently paid the dentist. The plan member and the dentist completed a form which the plan member then sent to Mutual Life, possibly after the group administrator had checked it. Mutual Life checked to make sure that the claimant was covered, that the dental procedures performed were included in the group plan, and that the dentist's fee was within accepted guidelines. The company then reimbursed the plan member. In some cases Mutual Life paid the dentist directly. Increasingly, the dentist transferred the information electronically to Mutual Life.

TOTAL QUALITY MANAGEMENT AT THE MUTUAL GROUP

Although Mutual Life had considered itself to be a provider of top quality service for decades, it first incorporated the principles of quality service into its mission statement in a formal way in 1990. It believed that one of a financial services organization's key objectives was to focus on client needs. Its stated vision was: "To be the best in the financial markets we serve." One of the organization's goals was to be recognized by its clients as a provider of excellent value and service. The company developed specific programs and initiatives to ensure that quality service became part of every staff member's work habits.

The company established Quality Councils in every division and offered special leadership and quality management training to ensure that every member of the organization had the knowledge and support needed to meet or exceed client needs. Mutual Life actively sought feedback from clients using devices such as questionnaires and focus groups. It viewed feedback as vital because it enabled the organization to solve problems and develop better processes to deliver services important to its clients.

The growing focus on quality service during the late 1980s led employers to demand more from the administrators of their benefit programs. In the United States several large companies had negotiated performance-based contracts, including penalty clauses, with their benefit plan administrators with reported savings of three to 10 per cent of paid claims.[2] These contracts focused on maintaining specific standards and making improvements in claims processing, payments, clerical work, and pricing. The portion of employers negotiating such contracts rose steadily from six per cent for those with fewer than 500 employees to 57 per cent for those with over 40,000 employees. The items covered in the contracts varied: turnaround time, 92 per cent of contracts; financial error rate, 64 per cent; administrative error rate, 66 per cent; percentage of benefits paid in error, 41 per cent. The most popular form of penalty was a cash payment (78 per cent).

DEVELOPMENT OF A SERVICE GUARANTEE AT MUTUAL LIFE

In early 1992, the concept of guaranteeing policyholders' satisfaction was raised at one of the regular meetings of the Group Division's seven-person Quality Service Council, whose membership included vice-presidents. The idea of guaranteeing service had originally occurred to Mr. Brown when he had seen an advertisement from a shipping company that, in essence, said: "If we don't deliver, you don't pay." Mr. Brown thought: "Why couldn't we do something like that?" The Council subsequently discussed the notion but reached no conclusions because it remained quite divided on the merits and feasibility of a service guarantee. Subsequently, the Council decided to refer the concept for detailed study to a working group responsible to Mr. Brown. It wanted the working group to represent the whole division, to be small enough to be effective, to represent opinions that were strong, but different, and to be composed of staff who would be affected by a guarantee—marketing people, line area managers, and actuaries.

In late April Mr. Brown chose eight staff for the working group, and appointed the company's quality service officer, Maureen Long, who was also a Council member, as the chairperson. He explained that the concept was to guarantee policyholders' satisfaction or "your money refunded." In his words: "Because our errors increase our clients' costs, we should reimburse them."

Mr. Brown outlined one possible approach to the working group: survey policyholders just before their anniversary dates to determine satisfaction levels and reduce plan expenses for the following year by one to 10 per cent depending on the degree of dissatisfaction, with no questions asked, and indicate that a company manager would follow up to investigate the reasons for dissatisfaction.

Mr. Brown asked the working group to determine if there were overwhelming reasons not to proceed, and if not, how the Group Division could put the service guarantee concept into action. In his memorandum to the group he cited some potential advantages of a service guarantee:

- provide an opportunity to gain a competitive edge by being the first Canadian company to add this feature;
- send a message to people, both inside and outside the company, that Mutual Life was serious about quality service; and,
- open the door to more feedback from clients.

He asked the working group to report by late May.

The working group met for two or three days during May, produced a report in early June, and met with the Quality Council in mid-June to review progress. The Council agreed that the working group had not yet finished the job. Subsequently, the working group performed

additional analysis and met twice. Now, the working group's final report was complete.

THE WORKING GROUP'S REPORT[3]

The working group did not find the task easy. Their meetings generated what they called "considerable fiery debate." As they commented:

> A performance guarantee is really not a very difficult concept, except for the few million details. And it was those few million details that generated much debate over the course of our meetings.

Objectives

The working group recognized that a service guarantee would differentiate the division by visibly demonstrating its commitment to service and leadership in the Canadian marketplace. Their report commented that visibility would help distinguish Mutual Life from all the other companies which claimed to be committed to, and providing, high quality service. Mutual Life considered that it already was a good provider of service and that a guarantee would allow it to do more than just talk about it. The working group also recognized that a service guarantee would help the division develop a stronger, more aggressive, and innovative image in the marketplace.

Principles

The group identified the following principles as being important in guarantee design:

1. Clients should see the guarantee as being simple and uncomplicated. A simple "money back guarantee" would lose all of its sizzle if it was layered with conditions that the client had to meet before making a claim.

2. Although the division could always make its guarantee better over time, once it launched the guarantee, it could not revoke it—at least not without considerable market damage. The working group wanted the guarantee to stretch the division, but not unrealistically—there had

to be a good chance of success. They wanted the division to be capable of meeting the needs of at least 95 per cent of its clients.

3. The division wanted an opportunity for clients to tell it why they were dissatisfied so the division could learn and improve.

4. The cost of the guarantee should come from the bottom line rather than be recovered from clients through higher administrative fees. The working group believed that because the guarantee would bring the division new business, keep business on the books longer, and help reduce expenses through process improvement, the division should view its cost as an investment to help reach these objectives.

Options

The working group considered several options, including the following:

1. The division would guarantee to meet certain specified standards for turnaround time, accuracy, responsiveness, and courteousness, expressed as 100 per cent achievement within X days; if the client believed that the division had not met the guarantee, the division would pay, no questions asked.

The working group believed that although Option 1 would make the strongest statement to clients, it would also be the most difficult for the division to live up to. Once the division guaranteed 100 per cent performance, it could not later back off to 90 per cent without suffering significant market damage. The working group agreed that, although all clients wanted good performance on the proposed measures, the real issue was how much they valued these features compared to others such as cost and flexibility.

The group believed that the division was already close to meeting the proposed standards. However, committing to perform at the stated level consistently was another matter. Would the company be prepared to add the needed space and human resources? Would staff be prepared to work shifts of variable length to match fluctuating work volumes? Would support areas in the rest of the company, such as mail services,

computer systems, and translation, function well enough?

The group realized that, although the division would not always be able to meet the standards, if it met them 97 to 99 per cent of the time, many clients would not make a claim.

2. The division would guarantee client satisfaction, and would provide guidelines for what to expect for turnaround time, accuracy, responsiveness, and courteousness, expressed as, for example, 85 per cent achievement within Y days. It would also state that, although the division expected to be able to meet or exceed the stated standards, the guarantee was not built around meeting them; if the client was not satisfied with the division's performance on these dimensions, the division would pay, no questions asked.

The attractive features of Option 2 were that it would require neither the large initial investment of Option 1, nor immediate adherence to the standards. However, the working group recognized that this option also had some potential problems:

- The service guidelines might be for items that clients did not value.
- This option might not have an impact on clients.
- Any advantage it offered might not be sustainable.

3. The division would guarantee client satisfaction. If the division's efforts did not satisfy the client, the division would pay, no questions asked.

The working group described this option as the most wide open. Because clients would have to initiate claims against the guarantee, the division would get important information concerning what clients valued. On the other hand, there was the potential that this option could flood the division with relatively minor items; for example, some clients might want duplicate copies of forms, or request that multiple copies be mailed to different addresses. Although Option 3 allowed the division an attempt to resolve the problem, it might decide not to support the changes needed to implement the correction. How would the division deal with a similar claim the next year? Would this option really add value?

The working group was unable to choose among the options without input from senior management on several questions:

- How serious is the division about this?
- How big a splash does the division want to make in the marketplace?
- How difficult does the division want to make it for competitors to copy it?
- Is the division prepared to make a service guarantee its primary focus and defer or eliminate other initiatives?

The Amount and Structure of Payment

The working group decided to abandon two proposals: paying claimants a percentage of administrative expenses paid, and paying them a percentage of premiums paid. They rejected the first because many clients did not readily know how much they paid in administrative expenses, and the second because the very small (single digit) percentages involved would not have much impact. However, this second method would be much more visible to clients. In the end, the working group decided to recommend a flat rate per member. The working group recommended that for clients with several plans, payment be limited to the number of members covered in the section making the claim.

The working group decided that the launch of the guarantee should focus on the fact of the division's preparedness to refund administrative expenses, rather than concentrate on the details of how it calculated those expenses. In their words: "We do not want the details to detract from the impact of our message." The division would explain details to clients when they made a claim.

Payment of the Guarantee

The working group recommended that the division immediately issue a cheque for the full amount of the refund payable to the plan sponsor. An alternative was to issue a credit against future expenses or assess it against a plan deficit. The group also recommended that the division be prepared to make the cheque payable to a chosen charity, or to allocate refunds directly to members should the client be unable to accept a refund. These variations would require some changes to the division's internal processes and record keeping. For clients with multiple plans, the working group believed that it was preferable to make payment through the client's main administrative section so that the client was aware that one of its sections was making a claim. Should the plan sponsor demand a different route, the division should at least inform the client's main section.

Collecting Feedback From Clients

The working group believed that collecting feedback regularly from clients would represent an excellent opportunity for the division, whether or not it proceeded with a service guarantee. They recommended that the division formally ask clients to evaluate the division annually at renewal time. They also recommended that clients be sent a short, informal comment card each month to encourage them to send in their comments—both good and bad—only some of which might be related to guaranteed items. The working group advised that the cards be distributed with monthly statements; clients that did not receive monthly statements would be given a number of cards in advance so that they could submit comments with their regular mailings to the division.

The working group recognized that the division would face the critical challenge of having to deal with the comments in a timely, effective manner. They recommended that sufficient staff at a junior management level be allocated to this task. These staff would be responsible for resolving the issues raised; this would most likely involve coordinating the activities of line managers. Because client concerns entered the division at many points, it was difficult to determine how many comments the division received now; making it easier for clients to comment should increase the number of enquiries. Centralizing responsibility for responding to comments would give the division a better overall feel for client concerns and ensure that dealing with client concerns would become a priority. It would be important for the client contact person to act first and inform others second. Although it would be important to keep front line sales and service workers informed, waiting to ensure that representatives were involved before responding to a client concern would unacceptably reduce responsiveness.

The working group recommended that the division develop a simple online tracking system to capture data on client comments and the action taken to resolve them. If used wisely, such a data base could both keep field staff informed efficiently and allow better client management. They recognized that they had to do more analysis of a tracking system, particularly as it affected other data systems within the division.

Launch Date

The working group established September 1992 as a target for launch with the guarantee being announced and effective immediately. They chose this date because competition for clients with January renewal dates was high in the fourth quarter.

Preparation for Launch

The working group recognized that the division would have to be ready prior to launch, especially if it chose Option 1. They believed that it would be unfair and very stressful to expect managers to react to new standards without prior warning. However, they also realized that the division wanted no public discussion of the guarantee until shortly before implementation. The working group recommended that the division talk to the managers most affected about the new standards and level of service towards which it wished to work without revealing that they were tied to a guarantee. In September, when the division hoped to meet the standards, it could go the extra step of announcing that it was prepared to guarantee its performance.

The working group acknowledged that communication to staff at all levels would be a critical factor for success. They recommended that any communication be done in person, not in writing. It was important to communicate that: the division believed it was a good service provider; it wanted to continue to improve; the guarantee initiative would demonstrate to its clients its commitment to quality service; and the guarantee would help to focus the division's improvement efforts on items clients valued most (through client feedback). It would be important that the division's devotion of time, money, systems, and people to the guarantee be visible to staff.

The working group believed that the division should inform management staff first, followed shortly by non-management staff. Regarding announcing the guarantee to Group and Claims offices, the working group suggested that a video with a message from Mr. Brown, supported by written material, would be appropriate.

The working group decided that representatives should receive two weeks' advance notice and promotional material to give them time to notify their market sources.

The pre-launch preparation would have to include internal services, such as translation, computer systems, and mail services. This option would require early involvement, support, and commitment. Regardless of the option chosen, the division would have to ensure that internal services did not make changes that might affect the Group Division without prior discussion.

The working group decided that Mr. Brown should inform clients of the guarantee by letter. They suggested that the division inform potential clients, using such media as newspaper advertising or industry magazines.

Finally, the working group recognized a need for follow-up communication to increase the division's profile for its work on this initiative and to capture positive staff reaction. They suggested using existing company newsletters for this purpose.

Financial Impact

The working group projected the financial impact of a number of scenarios. However, they had no idea what the actual claim rate or the claim amount would be.

Measuring Effectiveness

The working group concluded that although no one measure would be definitive, the division should measure several items to gauge the guarantee's effectiveness. Although the working group identified these items, they recognized that they would not be easy to measure and that it would be even more difficult to establish cause and effect relationships between their values and the service guarantee. The working group proposed that the division could measure performance using surveys, and feedback (both solicited and unsolicited) from sales staff and business sources. They also pointed out the need for good measures of the division's processes to allow it to identify and correct problems before they became issues to clients. The identified items were:

1. The retention of the division's block of business compared to pre-guarantee levels and industry averages.

2. Staff awareness and demonstrated commitment to quality service.

3. Market response to the division's delivery of quality service.

4. Client satisfaction.

5. The effect of the guarantee in generating new business.

6. The direct cost of the guarantee.

7. The benefits realized from improved processes and services.

8. The division's responsiveness in fixing concerns raised by clients.

9. The effectiveness of advance warning controls in identifying and correcting problems before they became issues for clients.

Uncontrollable Factors

Guaranteeing service was a big move. Although the division could take action on several fronts to support the guarantee, many other factors, which could affect service or client perceptions about service, remained outside its control. These included:

1. Communication between offices could fail—for example, through postal strikes, or failure of equipment or services.

2. Legislation could add to Mutual Life's administrative load and/or change its environment. For example, when the government introduced its registered retirement savings plan (RRSP) home buyers' loan plan, Mutual Life's requirements increased, affecting the company's ability to complete RRSP withdrawals within its stated time frame.

3. Actions taken by agents and other divisions and offices within The Mutual Group could affect client satisfaction because clients did not differentiate among the various arms of Mutual Life.

Problems

In its report, the working group identified a number of questions or potential problems. They were concerned whether the message to staff should be an objective or a by-product of the guarantee. If a message to staff were the objective, was a service guarantee the right way to do it?

Second, the working group pointed out that, no matter how well the division performed, some clients might abuse a guarantee. How large would this group be? How much might they cost? What should the division do about them?

A final issue concerning client feedback had to do with clients that did not fit well with the division. How should the division deal with such clients?

CONCLUSION

Although the working group had recommended that the division proceed with the notion of a service guarantee, they left several questions unresolved. Should the division guarantee its service? If so, what should the details of the guarantee be? If not, what would happen if one or more of the division's competitors successfully introduced a guarantee? Mr. Brown now had to decide whether to accept the working group's main recommendation, and, if so, what changes he should make to the proposal and how he should answer the unresolved issues. The decision was not an easy one for him:

A guarantee is really a leap of faith. I don't think anyone can really tell in advance exactly what will happen. The guarantee could be seen as a blank cheque and going with one is essentially an irreversible decision. Once we offer one, it will be almost impossible to step back from it, or even to make significant changes. But, if we don't offer one, how else can we continue to demonstrate our commitment to service and differentiate ourselves?

NOTES

1. J. Charles, "Sea of Shove," Benefits Canada, 10 (7), 32–35, July–August 1992.

2. N. Connors, "Employees Are Demanding More From Their Claims Administrators," Business and Health, 10 (5), 70–73, April, 1992; and, "Data Watch: Tackling Claims Administration Expenses," Business and Health, 10 (5), 18–19, April, 1992.

3. This section presents edited extracts from the report, not the report in its entirety.

6

SUPPLY CHAIN MANAGEMENT

Every organization, whether a manufacturer or service provider, is required to execute or manage a number of distinct "upstream" and "downstream" operational activities critical to the delivery of products and services that customers value. Upstream operational activities include purchasing and inbound logistics, whereas downstream operational activities include outbound logistics and service. However, most firms lack the necessary resources and competencies to successfully perform each of these important activities on their own. This has required that managers look beyond their organization's "four walls" to their supply chain and consider how suppliers and customers could be used to create the type of value required for long-term sustainable advantage. A supply chain is the set of value-adding activities spanning multiple organizations that connects a firm's suppliers to the firm's customers (see Figure 6.1).

According to The Global Supply Chain Forum, supply chain management "is the integration of key business processes from end user through original suppliers that provides products, services, and information that add value for customers" (Cooper, Lambert, & Pagh, 1997, p. 2). Supply chain management focuses on the efficient flows of material, information, and capital that integrate tiers of material suppliers, service providers, and customers to minimize systemwide costs while simultaneously satisfying service level requirements.

Despite the fact that supply chain systems' activities—communication, inventory management, warehousing, transportation, and facilities location—have been ongoing operational concerns since the start of commercial activity, only recently has there been widespread recognition of the strategic importance in effectively managing these activities. The emergence of supply chain management as an important operations consideration has largely been driven by shrinking product life cycles and more intense competition found in many industries. In the Daikin Industries case, for example, you will need to reconsider the current configuration of Daikin's supply chain, given some of these external pressures.

In theory, effective supply chain management enhances coordination and communication among the different members of the entire supply chain or distribution channel. Improvements in coordination and communication, in turn, lead to more efficient materials management among supply chain partners, with total system inventory reduced, cycle

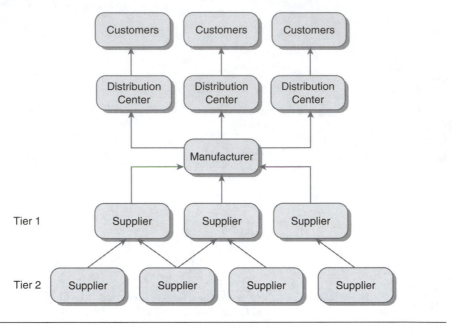

Figure 6.1   The Supply Chain

times shortened, and greater delivery flexibility and response. Indeed, many of the under-lying principles and applications of "lean systems," which are operating systems designed to create efficient processes through adopting a total systems perspective, are required for effective supply chain management. Hence, supply chain management is an important formative building block for world-class operations (see Figure 6.2). The Dabbawallahs of Mumbai, for example, developed a unique service network that has garnered them international recognition as being exemplars of supply chain management.

In practice, however, many firms struggle with the implementation of supply chain man-agement due to difficulties in establishing adequate partner relationships, processes, and controls. The utilization of information systems such as Electronic Data Interchange, bar coding, satellite tracking, and data warehouses have improved management data forms and functions required for supply chain coordination. However, alliance management is still required to ensure that supply chain partners are both able and willing to communicate with each other, as you will encounter in the International Decorative Glass and Spin Master Toys cases. Implementing an effective supply chain management system requires managers to address a myriad of operational, organizational, financial, and marketing concerns.

The cases in this supply chain chapter cover both design and execution issues. Supply chain *design* focuses on the strategic management of infrastructure—plants, production processes, distribution centers, transportation modes and lanes, and so on—that is used to satisfy customer demands. Supply chain *execution* focuses on the tactical management of operational issues—inventory policies and deployment, manufacturing and transportation schedules, performance measurement, and so forth—important for coordination and com-munication. These execution issues are the focus, for example, of the Ladner Building Products case.

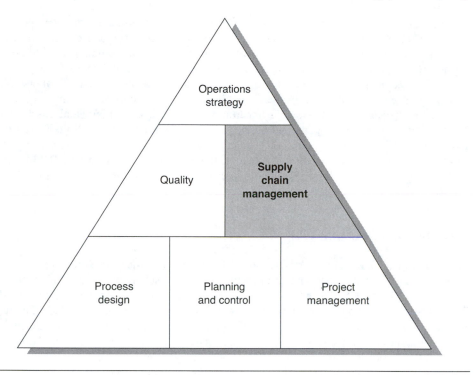

Figure 6.2   Supply Chain Management

INTERNATIONAL DECORATIVE GLASS

International Decorative Glass (IDG) is a small manufacturer of glass panels that are inserted into exterior steel doors. Although their primary market is in the United States, most of IDG's manufacturing is done in China through a joint venture arrangement. In response to rapidly growing customer demand, Frank Lattimer, the vice-president of operations, is considering the expansion of either their Chinese or Canadian manufacturing operations. Alternatively, he has been approached by a supplier to form a new joint venture manufacturing operation in Vietnam. Lattimer must weigh financial, political, and infrastructural considerations, in addition to any signal that would be sent to their current Chinese partners.

Learning objectives: discussion of production sourcing (domestic and offshore), evaluation of international network of suppliers, and strategic and operational implications of joint ventures.

SPIN MASTER TOYS (A): FINDING A MANUFACTURER FOR E-CHARGERS

Spin Master Toys was a Canadian manufacturer of toys ready to produce its latest product, E-Charger, an electrically powered model airplane. Alex Perez, the operations manager, had to decide which supplier should design and manufacture this new product. The timeframe from design to delivery was very short, requiring an accelerated development schedule. The company had a short list of two potential companies, both located in the major toy-manufacturing district of southern China, near Hong Kong. Perez had to develop the appropriate criteria for this decision and evaluate the two suppliers. With relatively little information and already behind schedule, the company must make its decision in the face of considerable uncertainty. (Note: The supplemental cases "Spin Master Toys (B): A New E-Chargers Supplier?" [case 9B01D002] and "Spin Master (C): Keeping the E-Chargers' Wings On" [case 9B01D003] follow the progress and the challenges in the production of the E-Charger; these are available from Ivey Publishing.)

Learning objectives: discussion of supplier selection and development; evaluation of supply chain risks.

Dabbawallahs of Mumbai (A)

In November 2003, Raghunath Medge, president of the Nutan Mumbai Tiffin Box Suppliers Charity Trust (the Trust), had just returned to his office in suburban Mumbai after meeting with Britain's Prince Charles, who was on an official visit to India's commercial capital. The Trust was the managing organization of the dabbawallah meal delivery network. The dabbawallahs' service was cited internationally by management scholars and industry executives as an exemplar in supply chain and service management. The service had acquired a reputation for its reliable delivery in Mumbai. However, many observers now expressed concerns over the future viability of the dabbawallahs' service, given the difficulty in duplicating its delivery network elsewhere, the emergence of other lunch competitors in Mumbai, and an array of environmental changes affecting both its customers and the workforce. (Note: A follow-up titled "Dabbawallahs of Mumbai (B)" [case 9B04D013] describes various options for growing the dabbawallahs' service; this is available from Ivey Publishing.)

Learning objectives: assess supply chain network configurations, evaluate the role of information in supply chain execution, and illustrate tactical issues of transit points and cross-docking.

Daikin Industries

Toshinari Oka, president of Daikin Industries Residential Air Conditioning Shiga factory, was confronted by the prospects of an unseasonably cold summer, at a time when the Shiga Factory had large quantities of its products in inventory in anticipation of strong summer sales. Oka was concerned not only about pending losses in the current year but also about the factory's long-term survival. Daikin was caught in a stagnant market in which it was increasingly difficult to build shares through product differentiation. The Shiga factory had been forced to use large inventories to cope with uncertain demand and a long, unwieldy supply chain. Oka must decide, among possible options considered, whether to reduce the number of models, build a lower cost factory outside Japan, or exit the business.

Learning objectives: examine lead times and customer responsiveness; understand the operations-marketing interface in supply chain management.

GROCERY GATEWAY: CUSTOMER DELIVERY OPERATIONS

As Canada's largest direct online grocer, Grocery Gateway provided home delivery to approximately 125,000 customers in the Greater Toronto area, which covered a territory of approximately 3,200 square kilometers. Grocery Gateway's management staff was concerned that the company had met only 67% of its target of making four deliveries per hour. Consequently, Dominique Van Voorhis, the vice president of industrial engineering and operations, had been asked to make some recommendations aimed at improving delivery operations. These recommendations would be presented at Grocery Gateway's next weekly management meeting. A number of options were worth considering. Van Voorhis's job was to pinpoint those options and assess how each one might affect the company's existing operation. The final choice would have to reflect and maintain Grocery Gateway's focus on low cost and high service.

Learning objectives: examine logistics systems, discuss supply chain issues in B2C e-commerce, and evaluate the role of information technology in supply chain management.

LADNER BUILDING PRODUCTS

Gordon Stephens, a logistics analyst at Ladner Building Products (Ladner), a large, national distributor of building materials, has been asked by his boss to prepare a report analyzing the company's logistics practices. Management is particularly concerned about the high cost of servicing customer deliveries. Ladner competed in an industry that distributed many commodity and commodity-like products. Stephens recognized that the building materials distribution industry was fragmented, with Ladner being one of the few companies with a national distribution network in the Canadian market, and knew that materials distributors that competed on the basis of price/cost would need to operate efficient logistics systems.

Learning objectives: examine logistics systems, policies (e.g., freight costs and sales mix), and practices; understand the role of decentralized organizational structures in supply chain management; and achieve congruence between marketing and logistics activities.

CANADIAN PHARMACEUTICAL DISTRIBUTION NETWORK

With revenues of more than U.S.$1 billion, UPS Logistics Group was a wholly owned subsidiary of United Parcel Service, which offered a full range of supply chain services in North America, Europe, Asia, and Latin America. UPS Logistics was responsible for distribution in eastern Canada for the Canadian Pharmaceutical Distribution Network, an association of pharmaceutical manufacturers that jointly distribute products to hospital pharmacies. Members of this association are unhappy with the current performance of the supply chain and have asked Peter Bromley, the newly appointed UPS Logistics general manager for operations, to establish a set of key performance indicators for the network's distribution operations. Bromley must determine how the logistics would be measured before setting specific improvement targets.

Learning objectives: evaluate performance issues in logistics and supply chain management, discuss implications of continuous improvement in supply chain management, and discuss third-party logistics.

MANAGEMENT QUESTIONS ADDRESSED IN SUPPLY CHAIN MANAGEMENT CHAPTER

1. What is supply chain management? Why is successful supply chain management strategically important for organizations?

2. Supply chain management is recognized as an important cross-functional business concern. Please describe the impact of supply chain management for the following functions: distribution/purchasing, finance and accounting, information systems, marketing, and operations management.

3. What is required for effective supply chain management? Examine the roles and responsibilities of each member of a supply chain and discuss the challenges in managing the product and information flows between the members.

4. Compare and contrast supply chain design and supply chain execution. How are supply chain design and execution effectiveness measured?

5. What impact do information technologies have on the management of supply chain activities? Describe how information technologies are deployed in supply chains.

6. What efficiency and responsiveness dynamics exist in most supply chains? How are those dynamics to be managed?

7. What is the service supply chain? How does it differ from manufacturing supply chains?

8. What is outsourcing? Under what circumstances should firms outsource?

REFERENCE

Cooper, M. C., Lambert, D. M., & Pagh, J. D. (1997). Supply chain management: More than a new name for logistics. *International Journal of Logistics Management, 8*(1), 1–14.

INTERNATIONAL DECORATIVE GLASS

*Prepared by Jim Barker
under the supervision of Professors
Robert Klassen and Paul Beamish*

Version: (A) 2002-11-11

In June 1996, Delta, British Columbia, remained overcast and rainy. Frank Lattimer, vice-president operations of International Decorative Glass (IDG), mused that it really didn't matter, as there would be little time for golf this year. Rapidly increasing demand for decorative glass panels by steel door manufacturers in the United States, IDG's primary market, had its two production facilities in Delta and Shuenyi, China scrambling to keep up.

Lattimer had been asked to develop a recommendation for capacity expansion for consideration by the board of directors. The board had emphasized the need to move quickly as sales were increasing faster than IDG's ability to meet them. Although either existing plant could be expanded, IDG also had recently been approached about considering further off-shore sourcing in the rapidly developing country of Vietnam. Frank knew that any decision would have significant ramifications for the company's long-term positioning and ability to meet its ambitious goals for growth.

THE INDUSTRY

Decorative glass panels typically are inserted into residential steel doors, and were increasingly being used by builders and home renovators to add architectural interest and a customized appearance to doorways (Exhibit 1). Growth in the industry was being fuelled by the general trend away from wooden exterior doors to steel doors. Forestry restrictions, lumber prices, energy efficiency and increasing criminal activity all contributed to the growing demand for retrofitting wood doors with steel replacements, often with decorative glass panels. In addition, the lower price of steel doors relative to the traditional wood door, with wholesale prices starting as low as Cdn$300, further eroded market share in new home construction. Decorative glass was now being incorporated into 10 per cent of new home construction.

The total North American sales for decorative glass panels was conservatively estimated at $2 billion in 1995 (all figures are reported in Canadian dollars), and the market showed signs of continued strong growth. Industry experts predicted that annual sales could reach $4.5 billion in the United States alone, within five years. Canada's weighting of the North American market was disproportionately high, at 15 per cent, reflecting the somewhat earlier development of the market there for these panels. By 1996, panels were found in approximately 85 per cent of steel doors in Western Canadian homes.

Exhibit 1   Sample of Decorative Glass Panel Applications

Manufacturers in Canada tended to be more vertically integrated than their U.S. counterparts, with plants fabricating both the steel door and the decorative panel. Locally, British Columbia's supply capacity grew well past the sustainable growth rate during the late 1980s and early 1990s as new market entrants scrambled to ramp up production capability to capitalize on the residential construction boom. The result was steadily eroding margins, followed quickly by industry consolidation, with high cost producers closing or being absorbed by more competitive operations. In spite of these changes, Canadian industry continued to be characterized by oversupply, underutilized capacity and commodity pricing. Lattimer had recently completed a basic competitive assessment of several key Canadian competitors as part of IDG's business plan (Exhibit 2).

By contrast, U.S. manufacturers of decorative glass panels acted as original equipment manufacturers (OEMs) for large residential steel door fabricators and retail chains. The industry was quite fragmented, with the largest three producers in the United States each having less than six per cent of the total market. Unfortunately, information on these producers was limited (Exhibit 3). Manufacturers ship panels to predetermined central warehousing and assembly points where their panels are fitted into the steel doors and distributed by the door fabricators through their retail channels. In general, the U.S. marketplace demanded high quality, fast service and increasingly, low price.

At this time, the United States, unlike Canada, was rapidly growing and underserved. In addition, Canadian manufacturers generally were about three years ahead of their U.S. counterparts in product functionality and design and, thus, able to develop strategic partnerships with steel door manufacturers. An undervalued currency also provided Canadian suppliers, such as IDG, with an initial competitive advantage. Combined, these factors created a significant market opportunity for any Canadian supplier who could meet rigorous quality standards and maintain a high level of customer responsiveness to design customized panels.

Early attempts by Canadian firms to develop their export sales quickly revealed that a customer would pay only so much for quality, service and product differentiation, and price was becoming an increasingly important driver in the purchase decision. In response, manufacturers on both sides of the border began to source production of the glass panels at lower cost to facilities located abroad. Because labor represented a large portion of cost of goods sold,

production was increasingly being moved to countries with low labor costs, such as Mexico, Thailand and China. At this time, only a few Canadian manufacturers had been able to address all of these challenges successfully.

PRODUCTION OF DECORATIVE GLASS PANELS

The production process for decorative glass panels was quite standardized, with little variation among firms and plants. As might be expected with a product that until recently was considered a "craft," the process was very labor intensive, with the equivalent of up to two person-days required for each panel. Production equipment was generally quite flexible, and could be purchased from several suppliers.

Decorative glass panels consist of multiple glass panes of different sizes, colors and grades assembled between soldered brass rods to form a decorative picture. The production of the panels used a multistep process that cut and formed the glass and brass components, and assembled the parts into sealed decorative glass units that could withstand the harsh exposure needed for exterior doors.

The manufacturing process began with the cutting of raw glass sheets of various colors and finishes into pieces of the precise shape and size needed for the final design. Some of these pieces were then bevelled to give a more attractive final appearance. The specialized cutting and bevelling of the glass pieces were the most capital intensive steps in the production process.

In a separate area, brass rods were cut and shaped into segments that ultimately serve to hold and separate the glass pieces. The correct set of glass pieces and brass rods were grouped into panel-specific "kits." These kits were assembled and soldered into predetermined patterns that formed semifinished panels. Several cleaning and touch-up steps followed.

Next, clear solid glass panes were added to each side of the inlay, creating a "sandwich" that protected the more delicate decorative inlay.

Company	Accent	JCX Glass	Roseview
Target Market	Small regional distributors.	Anyone who calls.	Small regional distributors.
Supply	Custom—None Volume—Langley, B.C. and Tacoma, WA	Custom—None Volume—New Westminster, B.C. Georgia Buy from China	Custom—None Volume—Surrey, B.C.
Positioning	Good Quality.	Copy designs of others.	Design Leader. Lower Quality.
Cost Base	– Two locations, 38,000 sq. ft. – Heavy overheads. – Non-union. – Small orders, but purchase materials in volume. – Thus very high raw material & finished goods inventory. – Efficient production system.	– Two locations, 105,000 sq. ft. – Heavy overheads. – One year left on collective agreement. – Volume purchase. – Finished goods inventory of $3.2 million. – Efficient production system.	– One location, 38,000 sq. ft. – Heavy overheads. – Non-union. – High raw material costs. – Finished goods inventory of $1.6 million.
Sales (est. 1995)	$11 million Down, some of their lowest months.	$14 million Up 39 per cent.	$3 million Down.
Warranty	One year.	10 years.	One year.
CAD	Yes.	No.	No.
MRP	Some implementation.	Some implementation.	No.
Reputation/Customer Relations	Very good in Pacific Northwest with the "old boys" network.	Generally poor, can let the customer down.	Generally poor, always lets customer down.
Management	Good, but have lost their spark and desire.	Aggressive, but weak in the middle management.	Generally weak.

Exhibit 2   Summary of Major Canadian Competitors

Company	Spanner Door	Western Design	Billings	New England Glass
Target Market	National (U.S.)	National (U.S.)	National (U.S.)	Eastern (U.S.)
Positioning	Good quality. Simple, high volume panels.	Broad product line.	Broad product line; focus on high volume commodities, although some lower volume panels.	Fast delivery, high quality.
Supply	Good operations in Mexico, with long-term commitment.	Plants in Mexico and Thailand.	No offshore production.	High cost producer. Focus on automation.
Est. 1995 Sales	$120 million	$85 million	$60 million	$25 million
Reputation/ Customer Relations		Extensive distribution system.	Product line is narrower than IDG.	Strong, dependable supplier.
Management		Three top managers have left recently.		

Exhibit 3   Summary of Major U.S. Competitors

Swizzle, a sealant material, was added around the edge to insulate and protect the panel from water damage. The panel was then put through an automated sealing machine, washed and inserted into a frame. Finally, the finished panel was labelled and packaged for shipment. These operations typically were performed in small batches of panels.

THE COMPANY

Located near Vancouver, British Columbia, IDG was founded in 1984 by Michael Jeffrey, decorative glass designer and entrepreneur. Initially, the company started as an integrated manufacturer of steel doors and decorative glass panels, and IDG enjoyed modest prosperity through the 1980s as the housing market boomed in that province. During this period, numerous firms entered the market, hoping to share in the prosperity of the industry. As real estate development slowed and even stagnated in the early 1990s, and the competitive basis shifted to cost, Jeffrey realized that the company was losing money in their manufacturing of steel doors. He felt that IDG could significantly enhance profitability by concentrating exclusively on decorative glass panels.

Jeffrey also recognized the need for a senior operations and business development person to make the operations more competitive in that market. Lattimer was hired in 1991 with the mandate to grow the international market, to improve cost efficiency, to set up a fully integrated management information system, and to create a corporate structure and culture that would support continued expansion. To meet these objectives, contacts and sales were further developed with several U.S. steel door manufacturers, the largest being Midwest. Lattimer also gained concessions in wage rates and flexibility in staffing requirements during collective bargaining with the union. Finally, a management information system, including materials requirements planning (MRP), was installed and brought on line to improve access to timely information and to raise customer responsiveness.

Historically, IDG's sales had been driven by custom orders for the glass panels. However, with recent efforts to increase sales volume, an increasing number of higher volume orders were being pursued, although often at much lower margins. In spite of labor concessions, high wage rates and limited flexibility continued to make IDG's plant in Delta increasingly less cost competitive. To reduce production costs, Lattimer was forced to explore alternative, off-shore sources of production.

CENTURY GLASS

In January 1995, IDG began sourcing some of its high volume, low skill production through a strategic partnership with Century Glass, located in Shuenyi, approximately an hour's drive outside of Beijing, China. This manufacturing facility was developed solely to meet the production needs of IDG, although the actual plant was owned and operated by the father of a former employee, Jianwei (Jerry) Lo. Lo had returned to China to set up the joint venture with IDG.

When IDG first arrived, the Shuenyi facility was little more than a deserted warehouse, situated across the highway from the village of 2,000 people where Lo had been born. The Lo family was well respected in the area, even though they came from modest means relative to Canadian standards. There was no electricity, telephone or plumbing in the village, and fresh water was unavailable.

With minimal infrastructure in place, power requirements, communication and capital equipment challenges all needed to be addressed. Co-generation power supplies and inverters were supplied by IDG; satellite and cellular phones were used until Century received a land line (faxes were sent from Beijing in the interim). Basic

production equipment needed to cut glass sheets and brass rods were sourced locally; however, one large panel sealing machine was imported from Korea. Practically everything else at the facility was built by the local workforce. Approximately one-third of the workers lived in four-person dormitory rooms located on the premises, and the production plant also included space for the workers to grow their own food in the courtyard.

Family ties of the Los facilitated the shipment of goods, as Chinese bureaucracy was legendary. Jerry's uncle was the police chief of the local district and, thus, extremely well connected politically; IDG benefited from the association. The movement of raw materials into China and finished goods out of China, via Tientsin to the Gulf of Chihli, was expedited through Jerry's uncle.

Because of differences in proximity to the market and cost structure, the Chinese production facility concentrated on producing high volume, low cost glass panels for IDG. These panels were then shipped in bulk to the Delta production facility for final processing, followed by packaging and shipment to U.S. or Canadian customers. The additional processing in Canada resulted in a change in product classification under the North American Free Trade Agreement (NAFTA), which allowed the finished product to be imported duty-free into the U.S. market. (By contrast, if complete, sealed panels were imported directly from China into the United States, a 60 per cent duty would apply.)

For some customers, the standardized panels produced at Shuenyi were modified and further assembled at Delta to form larger, more complex, customized panels. By necessity, these arrangements required a long lead time, currently 18 to 20 weeks (Exhibit 4), well above that of the Delta plant, where lead times averaged one month.

Initial start-up problems in 1995 centered on logistics and quality. Rather than allow IDG's reputation for excellent customer service to suffer by missing delivery dates, orders of panels were, at times, air freighted to Delta from China, at an extra cost of $250,000 in

Raw materials ordered and received for shipment	2–4 weeks
Components in transit to China facility	5 weeks
Raw materials conversion to WIP and semi-finished goods	4 weeks
Sub-assemblies shipped to Canada	5 weeks
Final assembly completed at Delta, B.C. facility	2 weeks
Finished goods shipped to customer	½ week
Total Time	**18–20 weeks**

Exhibit 4   Order Cycle Time for Production at Shuenyi Plant

the first year. These problems were gradually overcome as typical production lead times were reduced to their current levels. Low yields and high waste/breakage also plagued the start-up. However, as the skill levels of the local workforce improved, yields increased dramatically. By mid-1996, finished panel yields consistently surpassed 99 per cent, although in-process breakage and other losses remained a problem.

Current Status

By June 1996, Century Glass produced 80 per cent of IDG's panels, representing 60 per cent of revenues. The remaining somewhat more specialized, lower volume panels were produced by 70 employees in the Delta plant. The Century plant was operating close to capacity, with approximately 100 employees producing 8,000 panels per month. Dorms were overcrowded and people were elbow-to-elbow in the manufacturing area.

The joint venture agreement specified that IDG purchase all materials, own all inventories, and specify all finished product standards. The production arrangement with Century stipulated a fixed charge per employee and a variable cost per finished panel. Specifically, IDG paid $140 per employee, per month. In addition, IDG also paid Century a product transfer price of $4 for each panel that met IDG's rigorous

quality standards for finished panels. Employment levels could be varied as needed to match sales volumes. Employees worked seven, eight-hour days per week, every week. This was high by Chinese standards, where the five- or six-day work week was more common.

By comparison, in Canada, unionized employees received $9.75 per hour, per 40-hour work week. Combined, these differences in labor translated into a significant cost advantage for Shuenyi, without accounting for the operational advantages of increased labor flexibility. Relative product costs are illustrated in Exhibit 5.

Labor savings were offset to some degree by a higher working capital investment necessary to finance larger inventories and longer payment cycles. For example, inventory turnover at Century Glass was only two turns per year in 1995, whereas Delta averaged six. In addition, banks refused to finance or factor raw material and work-in-process (WIP) inventories located in, or in transit to or from, China as the risk of recouping funds in the case of insolvency was considered too high. This risk varied by country. Some developing countries, such as Mexico, were viewed as less risky, while others, such as India, offered government guarantees for export-oriented manufacturers.

The Lo family was anxious to keep 100 per cent of IDG's business at their facility. However, Lattimer was very concerned about having only

		Production Location	
Product		Shuenyi	Delta
#677, Oval–San Marino			
Materials		95.19	92.97
Labor		6.61	69.44
Freight		7.82	1.25
Total direct costs		**$109.62**	**$163.66**
#936, 22" × 36" panel			
Materials		44.27	44.27
Labor		3.18	40.27
Freight		7.08	1.25
Total direct costs		**$54.53**	**$85.79**
#445, 7½" × 18½" panel			
Materials		15.51	15.51
Labor		1.10	10.13
Freight		1.08	0.50
Total direct costs		**$17.69**	**$26.14**

Exhibit 5   Typical Production Costs

a single supplier in China, where political risks were perceived to be significant for such a large portion of their production. For example, the repatriation of Hong Kong in 1997 and adverse trade tensions and possible trade restrictions between China, the United States and Canada all indicated that a move to establish another production source might have strategic and operational merits.

FINANCIAL RESULTS

IDG's revenue growth had been impressive since 1990, increasing from $2.6 million to $5.4 million for fiscal 1995. Financial results for the last two years are summarized in Exhibits 6 and 7. Revenues were projected to reach $10.5 million this year, with 95 per cent of sales being made in the United States. As noted earlier, margins had eroded during the early 1990s as residential construction slowed and competition increased. Sales levels had risen significantly in 1995 as

new production capacity became available at Shuenyi. However, profitability fell as a result of poor initial yields and air freight shipment costs at this new plant. Looking forward, Lattimer expected margins to increase as productivity further improved in Shuenyi.

Both Jeffrey and Lattimer strongly felt that the market for strong growth by IDG was there. IDG had already been turning away business as they struggled to meet existing customer commitments from their two production facilities. Current plans called for revenue growth to $30 million by the year 2000. Critical to achieving these long-term results was an increase in production capacity to match the forecasted sales volumes.

This aggressive growth necessitated access to additional capital to finance investment in new capacity and additional working capital. In August 1995, IDG approached a venture capital firm, Working Opportunity Fund, for $2 million of equity financing. The structure of the investment was negotiated, due diligence conducted,

	1995	1994
Sales	$5,404	$3,634
Cost of sales	4,365	2,610
Gross profit	**1,039**	**1,024**
Expenses		
administration and marketing	388	413
travel and promotion	97	44
rent and assessment	120	138
amortization of debt	48	55
bank charges and interest	141	48
interest on long-term debt	18	17
other expenses	182	258
subtotal	**994**	**973**
Income (loss) from operations	45	51
Other income	28	—
Income (loss) before taxes	**73**	**51**
Income taxes		
current	24	—
deferred	(6)	11
Net income (loss) for the year	**$55**	**$40**

Exhibit 6   Income Statement for International Decorative Glass as of September 30 (all figures reported as $000s)

and the deal finalized in November of that year. In addition, IDG paid down its line-of-credit from the bank by financing its inventory in China with a guarantee from Canada's Export Development Corporation. This effectively reduced IDG's investment in working capital and made the sourcing of manufacturing to Asian facilities increasingly attractive. Combined, these additional sources of capital enabled IDG to increase its operating flexibility, and further develop its presence in the U.S. market.

CAPACITY EXPANSION

Lattimer had narrowed the options for expansion of production to three alternatives. Expansion was possible at either existing plant. In addition, another strategic partnership could be developed in another low labor-cost country, similar to IDG's earlier decision to expand into China.

After exploring options in other developing nations with low labor costs, Lattimer, in consultation with senior management, had narrowed the candidate list of countries to one: Vietnam. This country offered a critical advantage in Lattimer's mind over other developing nations: a potential local partner, Dan Kim. Kim's firm currently supplied raw glass to IDG, and Kim had approached Lattimer about establishing a manufacturing joint venture.

Expansion in Delta

At this time, company-wide capacity could be doubled by investing a relatively modest amount of capital, $30,000, in the Delta plant. Labor costs would rise based on existing wage levels. Given the close proximity of this plant to the U.S. market, the existing production planning system could be further leveraged and customer responsiveness further improved.

	1995	1994
Current		
cash	1	2
accounts receivable	1,513	474
income taxes recoverable	15	22
inventories	1,422	988
prepaid expenses	54	28
	3,005	1,514
Capital assets	233	296
	3,238	**1,810**
Current		
bank loans	1,435	593
accounts payable	886	482
income taxes payable	17	—
current portion of long-term debt	32	39
	2,370	**1,114**
Long-term debt	152	177
Deferred income taxes	13	20
Due to (from) affiliated company	522	372
	3,057	**1,683**
Share capital	0.1	0.1
Contributed surplus	45	45
Retained earnings	136	82
	$3,238	**$1,810**

Exhibit 7   Balance Sheet for International Decorative Glass as of September 30 (all figures reported as $000s)

Expansion in Shuenyi

Because production at the Shuenyi plant was already very tight, any expansion would involve a significant increase of middle management and support staff and an expanded production planning system, mirroring the earlier MRP investment made in Delta. Existing arrangements for labor would be maintained, where IDG would pay a flat monthly fee per person, plus a variable rate per panel.

Although some of the existing production equipment still had excess capacity, additional equipment would be needed. In total, an estimated capital investment of $30,000 would be needed in new cutting equipment to double company-wide capacity. Incremental manufacturing overhead costs would be approximately $150,000 per year. Direct labor costs would increase proportionately with production volumes. These costs did not include either a desperately needed new building or additional inventory carrying charges. Timing for ramp-up to this volume level would be approximately six to eight months.

The most significant concerns with expansion at Shuenyi were related to further dependence on a single supplier and issues related to political risks associated with production in China. Trade uncertainties between China and the United States also aggravated long-term planning efforts. Management was apprehensive that existing tensions could escalate over any, or all, of repatriation of Hong Kong in 1997, intellectual property rights (software piracy and patents), dissident protests, strained relations with Taiwan and a general trade imbalance.

Smaller manufacturers that supply the U.S. market, like IDG, inadvertently have been punished by short-term high tariffs, customs delays and other non-tariff barriers. Although quite unlikely now, the worst case scenario would be a ban on importation from China. Unfortunately, because of the general income levels in China and construction norms, there was little local market for IDG's products at this time, although it did look promising in the longer term.

Foreign Operations in Vietnam

Vietnam had only recently begun to exhibit the economic growth characteristic of other countries in Asia-Pacific. Like many developing countries, infrastructure at this time was terribly inadequate. Lattimer estimated that development was at least five years behind China, and conditions were even more challenging than those first faced by IDG when they established their joint venture in China.

In recent years, Vietnam had been plagued by internal political problems, and foreign investors were apprehensive to invest. This situation now was beginning to change, as the United States had moved to reestablish diplomatic relations with the Socialist Republic of Vietnam in 1995. In turn, this thawing of the political climate had encouraged foreign investment which had grown rapidly as a result. Vietnam also had a strategic location for re-export to other markets in Asia.

Although a Communist state, the central government had instituted the beginnings of "Doi Moi" or "open door" policy as early as 1986. The objectives of Doi Moi were to develop export-oriented production capabilities that create jobs and generate foreign currency, to develop import substitutes, to stimulate production using natural resources, to acquire foreign technology and to strengthen Vietnam's infrastructure. Incentives

offered included: the option to establish wholly-owned foreign subsidiaries; favorable corporate income tax and tax holidays; waivers on import/export duties; and full repatriation of profits and capital.

With 75 million citizens and a labor force of 32 million, Vietnam had the second lowest wage rate in the Pacific Rim. Only about 11 per cent of the working population was employed in manufacturing, another 19 per cent in the service sector, and the remainder in agriculture. Inflation was high, at 14 per cent in 1995, partially because of the devaluation of the "new dong" as the government had allowed the currency to float in world markets for the first time. The primary industries of Vietnam included food processing, textiles, machinery, mining, cement, chemical fertilizers, tires, oil and glass. Vietnamese companies already supplied some of the standard glass and bevelled glass components used by IDG.

Generally, the labor force was energetic, disciplined and hard working, although unemployment remained high, at 20 per cent. English and French were widely spoken but literacy was relatively low, at 88 per cent. Unfortunately, basic human rights and freedoms had received little attention. There was widespread conflict between local and central governing bodies, extensive corruption and exhaustive bureaucracy at both levels.

Production of Decorative Glass Panels in Vietnam

The State Committee for Cooperation and Investment (SCCI) identified seven areas of the Vietnam economy where foreign investment would receive preferential tax treatment. Of particular relevance to IDG, labor-intensive manufacturing was one such area. The SCCI would assist the new venture in whatever way they could, typically through the development of contacts with customers and suppliers, as well as guiding the investor through the government bureaucracy that approved any business venture.

The Vietnamese government also had legislated five approaches for establishing a business venture in the country. Of the five, the international business community and the government widely favored the joint venture approach. Under this approach, a foreign firm such as IDG would sign a contract with one or more Vietnamese parties to create a new legal entity with limited liability. Foreign capital had to constitute at least 30 per cent of the new entity's total capital. A foreign investor could then leverage the local partner's contacts, knowledge of the local market, and access to land and resources.

The Vietnamese had a saying: "*Nhap gia tuy tuc*," which means "When you come into a new country, you have to follow the culture." Clearly, identification of a strong local partner would be critical for meeting the cultural norms in Vietnam and ensuring the success of any investment by IDG; this had been a major obstacle for many other foreign firms.

Lattimer saw many parallels with the earlier joint venture into China. That investment had succeeded largely as a result of IDG's strategic partnership with Century Glass and the Lo family. IDG had been able to limit their investment risk to supplying capital equipment for the facility and inventories. By contrast, other decorative glass suppliers operating in China were paying higher costs, and making larger investments in plant and infrastructure. The partnership with Century also had provided IDG with additional political clout and allowed them to bypass much of the Chinese bureaucracy.

One obvious choice for a local partner was IDG's beveled glass supplier, managed by Dan Kim. Kim operated a glass plant in Da Nang, which was well under capacity, and had an oversupply of qualified labor. Kim had approached both IDG and government authorities and essentially paved the way for IDG to begin joint venture operations within a six- to 12-month time frame. Labor and product transfer prices were likely to be significantly lower than either the Delta or Shuenyi plants, with these costs being approximately half those of Shuenyi. Additional overhead costs were estimated at $50,000 annually. Finally, a significant investment would be needed in new equipment to reach the same, company-wide production volume possible with the other options (Exhibit 8). Lattimer wondered whether he might be able to extract more favorable terms for any joint venture relationship, such as shifting responsibilities for financing inventories to Kim.

The Decision

As Lattimer was putting together his proposal for the board, he reflected on a conversation he had with Jerry Lo last month. Lo had indicated that Century would soon expect their piecework compensation to increase from $4 to $7 per finished panel. While seemingly a small fraction of total production costs, Lattimer worried that further requests for increases would follow unless other alternatives were developed. He also was only too aware that with up to $1 million invested in inventory at Century at any given time, IDG was in a very precarious position. Single sourcing had given Century a level of bargaining power that might limit IDG's future options and cost competitiveness.

Lo had become agitated as Lattimer described IDG's exploration of additional manufacture sourcing arrangements, but had to agree it made sense from IDG's perspective. Lattimer reassured Lo that IDG wanted to add capacity, not replace it. This discussion had reinforced the need to delicately handle IDG's existing relationships. Any recommendation for locating new production capacity would have to take into account the skilled Canadian workforce, Century Glass and the Lo family, and Dan Kim's offer for an expanded relationship in Vietnam.

Production Equipment	Cost
Electrical back-up generator	$13
Air compressor	2
Glass equipment	
two-shape cutter (pneumatic, from Korea)	7
shape cutter (CNC, from Canada)	110
glass washer	60
Brass equipment	
roll-former	55
roll-forming dies	22
circle rollers (large and small)	5
saws (4)/blades/sharpeners	4
Bevelling equipment	
straight-line beveller	125
curved bevelling machines (12)	30
Miscellaneous equipment	
small forklift	7
pallet jack	2
computer, fax, etc.	3
hand tools, tables, etc.	5
Total capital equipment	**$449**

Exhibit 8   Production Equipment Required for Start-Up in Vietnam (all figures reported as $000s)

SPIN MASTER TOYS (A): FINDING A MANUFACTURER FOR E-CHARGERS

Prepared by Ken Mark under the supervision of Professor John Haywood-Farmer

In mid-July 1999, Alex Perez, operations manager of Spin Master Toys of Toronto, Ontario, was trying to decide from which supplier to purchase the design and production of the company's latest toy, an electrically powered airplane named E-Chargers. He had investigated a number of potential suppliers in southern China and had settled on two finalists, Wah Shing Electronics Co. Ltd. (Wah Shing) and Wai Lung Plastics Mfy. Ltd. (Wai Lung).

With the anticipated date for the launch of this product just a few short months away, Perez had to make his choice quickly.

SPIN MASTER TOYS

In April 1994, Anton Rabie, Ronnen Harary and Ben Varadi graduated from The University of Western Ontario, Rabie and Varadi from the Ivey

Business School and Harary from political science. The three decided to forgo opportunities in the corporate world and strike out on their own. They were soon making Earth Buddy, a nylon stocking filled with sawdust and grass seed moulded into a head. After immersion in water, the grass seed would sprout to give the head a crop of grass—hair. Although Earth Buddy was clearly a fad item, the company managed to sell 1.5 million of them in just six months, making it one of the most popular gift items that year.

In February 1995, the company followed this success with the launch of Spin Master Devil Sticks, which consisted of two hand-held sticks used to manipulate a third. This product also became a resounding success. Eventually the company incorporated Spin Master into its name. The company's principals believed they had achieved their success through avant-garde, grassroots marketing savvy and a two-tier distribution network, which covered both the major and independent retail segments in North America.

In the following three years, Spin Master Toys produced an array of relatively low-technology, high-margin toys for the Canadian market. The product list included:

- Spin-A-Blo   spinning toys
- Radical Reptiles   foam reptiles attached to a metal leash
- Top-No-Sis   spinning board
- My First Kite   a starter kite for children
- Grow-Things   water-absorbent play animals

Although Spin Master Toys achieved notable success with these fad items, none reached the unit sales that Earth Buddy had produced. Following its success with Spin Master Devil Sticks, Spin Master Toys spent six months moving from being project-focused to building relationships with retailers, investors and creating a research and development department.

At a major 1996 toy show, two inventors approached Rabie and Harary, and many other toy companies with the concept for a compressed-air-powered toy plane. Their initial design was a plastic soft drink bottle with wings attached.

Rabie and Harary and the major toy companies rejected the idea as being too ambitious. However, the inventors were persistent, and after the original prototype had been revised several times, Spin Master Toys decided to purchase the rights to the concept. After a frustrating two years and $500,000 in development, Spin Master Toys rolled out its Air Hogs line of compressed-air-powered planes, and, with outside engineering expertise, proceeded to manufacture them in China. The company used an innovative marketing campaign to generate a groundswell of excitement. Air Hogs became a top-selling toy for the 1998 North American Christmas season and was hailed by *Popular Science* as one of the 100 greatest inventions of the year, creating, as it did, a new category—compressed-air-powered planes. Spin Master Toys had to double production of Air Hogs just to keep up with demand, which was increased by the product shortage in the first few months after the initial shipments.

Following the success of Air Hogs, Spin Master Toys decided to develop a line of toys driven by compressed air. It subsequently launched a compressed-air-powered water rocket called the Vector, a car named the Road Ripper, and two new compressed-air-powered product-flanking planes, the V-Wing Avenger and the Renegade.

With over 50 people working in its Toronto head office, and a recently opened office in Hong Kong staffed by two project managers, Spin Master Toys was enjoying rapid expansion through its combination of speed to market and innovative marketing. Revenue had grown from nearly $525,000 in 1994 to a projected $45.8 million in 1999, earning it the 10th spot on the Profit 100 Canada's Fastest-Growing Companies list.

THE TOY INDUSTRY

The toy market included both hard and soft goods, as well as combinations. Hard goods included plastic and metal toys—water guns, construction toys, action figures, etc. Soft goods included plush toys, fabrics and dolls. Either hard or soft toys increasingly used embedded electronic components as differentiators.

Southern China in and near Hong Kong accounted for a large percentage of the world's toy manufacturing industry; many manufacturers there had over 50 years of toy-making experience. Beginning with low-technology plastic and metal toys in the early years, toy makers in the area had developed sophisticated design, engineering and manufacturing skills. Such factors could be important. Perez, who used to work for a large toy company, remembered a competitor that sourced from Thailand because production costs were slightly lower. Despite this advantage, the project was a dismal failure, in part because of the lack of toy-making expertise in that country.

Aside from experience, the Hong Kong market had English-speaking workers, a western-style banking system, easy access to low-cost production facilities and workers in China, an entrepreneurial spirit and major port facilities. Deciding to source toys from this region was relatively easy.

E-Chargers

E-Chargers were Spin Master Toy's next foray into the powered toy airplane market. Unlike the traditional toy airplane powered by a stretched rubber band, gasoline engine, or compressed air, E-Chargers were driven by electricity. The product came in two parts: a battery pack holding four AA dry cell batteries and a plastic foam airplane containing a small capacitor[1] connected to an electric motor. By inserting the battery pack into a special port on the airplane, the user both started the electric motor driving the plane's propeller and charged the capacitor. The user then disconnected the plane from the battery pack and launched it into the air. Spin Master Toys touted E-Chargers as being capable of flights of up to 90 metres and as "high performing, easy-to-use rechargeable planes that come with their own chargers—kids just have to let them charge for 10 seconds and then let them fly." In the company's view, the product line allowed it to extend

the magic of real flight to children as young as five—younger than the user of Air Hogs. To encourage users to collect E-Chargers, the company planned to produce six different styles and promised high performance at a low price.

Spin Master Toys had sold the E-Chargers concept to retailers who subsequently placed endcap[2] orders for a December 7, 1999, delivery date to meet the spring planogram[3] shelving period. This was the first time that Spin Master Toys would ship products for a planogram. In the past, the company had been able to obtain special shelf space only because of its products' uniqueness. The main advantage in shipping to a set deadline was the guarantee of shelf space. Spin Master Toys now had to design and make the E-Chargers in time to meet the order date.

Preliminary E-Charger Production Estimates

Working back from December 7, 1999, Perez developed a somewhat accelerated schedule that would allow delivery of the E-Chargers plane. Exhibit 1 shows the development schedule, delay in any step of which would make the project late.

Rough Engineering Model

This stage involved the engineering work needed to craft a design to meet the desired specifications provided by the manufacturer. These specifications included, for example, that the toy would be capable of high-speed production while maintaining acceptable finished-product quality, that it was within the weight and size required, and that any electronic components involved would function within tolerances provided. Although design work normally took about eight weeks, Spin Master Toys allowed less than three weeks for E-Chargers; the design work would have to be completed no later than the middle of June.

On June 22, K-Development of Erie, Pennsylvania, the company to which Spin Master Toys had contracted the development engineering, transferred the completed engineering

Item# 40004
Item Name: E-Chargers Flying Machines (6 styles)
Pack: 12
Target FOB HK (US$) 1.75
FOB HK (US$)
Landed Cost (Estimated in US$)

Spin Master Toys Engineer: Alex

Project Manager: Tammy

Date: June 30, 1999

Description	Responsible	Planned	Current
Quote package	Alex	July 1	
• General product profile	Tammy	June 23	June 30
• Product electronic schematics	Tammy	June 25	July 2
• Preliminary parts drawings	Tammy	June 25	July 2
• Assembly—exploded view drawings	Tammy	June 25	July 2
• Bill of materials/parts list	Tammy	June 25	July 2
• Rough engineering model	Tammy	June 15	June 22
Vendor preliminary quotes	Alex	July 10	July 17
• Final vendor decision	Ronnen	July 11	
• 1st engineering model	Tammy	July 1	
• 2nd engineering model	Tammy	July 3	
• 3rd engineering model	Tammy	July 5	
Final design release	Alex	July 1	
• Model ready (propeller)	Factory	July 10	
• Decision on gear	Factory	July 10	
• Recommend foam type	Factory	July 19	
• Approval on foam type	Alex	July 20	
• Samples of the motor and capacitor	Factory	July 22	
• Plastic housing evaluation	Alex	July 27	
• Verify motor specification is compatible with Mabuchi	Factory	July 31	
• Plastic housing resubmission	Factory	July 31	
Models available	Factory	July 22	
Approved product quote (purchase order, material authorization release)	Tammy/Ronnen	July 26	
Tooling purchase order for airplane	James	July 22	
Tooling purchasing order release (all others)	James	August 4	
Tool start (35 days leadtime)	Factory	August 4	
1st test shot	Factory	September 8	
1st engineering pilot	Factory	September 18	
Sales samples ready (from 1st shot)	Factory	September 23	
2nd test shot	Factory	September 28	
2nd engineering pilot	Factory	October 3	
Final shot	Factory	October 8	

Exhibit 1   Projected Development Schedule and Current Progress   *(Continued)*

Description	Responsible	Planned	Current
Final engineering pilot	Factory	October 14	
Production pilot	Factory	October 21	
Production pilot tests completed	Factory	October 29	
Final production pilot approval	Ronnen	November 2	
Final quote approval	Ronnen	November 2	
Production start	**Factory**	**November 22**	
1st on-board shipment	Factory	November 28	
Packaging timeline			
English film and disk send to Hong Kong	Selene	July 20	
Packaging approval (7 days)	Tammy	July 27	
English package arrival (3 weeks)	Factory	August 17	
Bilingual package disk to Hong Kong	Selene	August 3	
Bilingual package approval in Hong Kong	Willy	August 10	
Bilingual package arrival	Factory	August 31	
TV commercial sample (quantity)			
TV commercial sample (date)			
Estimated sales forecast	Jennifer	July 17	
Consigned materials		**N/A**	
Motor and capacitor			
Material authorization or purchase order	Heather/James	August 3	

Ramp-Up Schedule		Date	Produce	Cumulative	Changes
First week:	Day 1	November 8	50	50	
	Day 2	November 9	50	100	Ramp-up
	Day 3	November 10	100	200	not yet
	Day 4	November 11	150	350	confirmed
	Day 5	November 12	250	600	
	Day 6	November 13	400	1,000	
First on-board shipment		November 15	600	1,600	
Second week		November 22	9,000	10,600	
Third week		November 29	12,000	22,600	
Fourth week		December 6	18,000	40,600	
Fifth and subsequent weeks			18,000		

Exhibit 1   Projected Development Schedule and Current Progress

Source: Company files.

designs to Reh Kemper, a prototype designer based in Chicago, Illinois. Reh Kemper completed its work on July 2. According to Perez's timeline, the project was already a week behind schedule for the start of production.

Engineering Models

After one week of examination, study and discussion of the prototype, Perez and his]team approved it and issued a "Final Design Release." Spin Master Toys then returned it to K-Development, which had five days to improve the rough engineering model and produce three initial prototypes to ensure that the design was engineered correctly to the specified tolerances. This preliminary work showed that the weight of the plane would be of great concern. Initial tests showed that to achieve the expected flight times, E-Chargers had to weigh 17 grams. Once the third engineering model was ready, Perez released it to vendors, requesting preliminary quotes within five days.

Tooling

From this stage on, all work would be performed at the factory, with regular updates sent to Perez by phone or fax. The tool start involved creating the moulds and other tooling required to produce the toy in mass quantity. Plastic parts such as those used in E-Chargers were normally made by injection moulding in which a molten plastic was injected into the carefully machined cavity inside a two-piece block of metal (the mould). After applying pressure and cooling, the mould was opened to remove the part. In practice, moulders might use large moulds capable of making several parts simultaneously. This crucial step usually took four weeks; the time required was usually factored into the design component. Perez estimated that Spin Master Toys would need the first test samples by September 8.

Engineering Pilots

The next step was testing the moulds and other tools, ideally with two engineering pilots.

At least one engineering pilot had to be performed before the next stage, as it was almost inevitable that the moulds would need some adjustments. A factory would count on three weeks to run both engineering pilots. The first and second engineering pilots and the shots from them had to be completed by October 8.

Final Engineering Pilot

In this two-week process, the final moulds and other tools were finished. To have the product ready for the production pilot date of October 21, this step had to be completed in one week.

Production Pilot

This step tested whether the moulds and other tools would withstand high-speed production while delivering product within the required tolerances. The production pilot tests and the final quote had to be approved by November 22.

Production Start

In the case of E-Chargers, Perez estimated that production would have to start at least two weeks before the shipping date to allow production of enough units to meet retailer demand. Thus, production would have to start on November 22 to just make the December 7 ship date.

SPIN MASTER TOYS' CONTRACT MANUFACTURERS

In the past, Spin Master Toys had obtained its products from various Chinese manufacturers. Because of the large differences between its previous toys, the company had treated each product separately. Consequently, Spin Master Toys had gained considerable experience with several suppliers, as each toy had been manufactured by a different factory. Spin Master Toys believed that its product closest in design to E-Chargers was Air Hogs. In May 1999, while working on Water Rocket, one of its second generation compressed-air-powered toys, Spin Master Toys had visited Kin Seng Ltd., the Air Hogs manufacturer. During a factory tour, Spin Master Toys discovered that the Kin-Seng factory was at capacity. Because of the tightness of its E-Chargers schedule, Spin Master Toys decided not to consider Kin Seng as a potential supplier.

Spin Master Toys thus searched for an alternative manufacturer, eventually creating a short list of two, Wai Lung and Wah Shing.

WAI LUNG

In early 1999, Harary had been introduced to the owner of privately owned Wai Lung Manufacturing Co. Harary believed that Spin Master Toys would receive more attention from an owner-operated factory than from a subsidiary of a public corporation. Reassuring Harary that he would provide personal attention to this project, Eric Lee, Wai Lung's owner seemed eager to strike a deal with Spin Master Toys. Harary subsequently initiated a toy project, Flick Trix Finger Bikes, with Wai Lung. Finger Bikes were miniature die-cast replicas of brand-name BMX bikes with fully functional parts. Already in a rushed situation, Harary had asked Wai Lung if it could engineer the Finger Bikes, produce and ship them in six weeks—it normally took other manufacturers six to 10 weeks to perform these tasks. With Finger Bikes already engineered by Reh Kemper, Spin Master Toys would rely on Wai Lung's staff to beat a competitor to the market. Working at a break-neck pace, Wai Lung had been able not only to build the tools in the allotted time, but also to increase production very quickly with little lead time. Although Wai Lung had initially built tools to support a production rate of 10,000 bikes a day, once it was evident that demand was strong, the company was able to build additional tools in four weeks versus the previous six weeks, boosting Finger Bikes production to 40,000 bikes a day.

Not only had Wai Lung come through for Spin Master Toys, but it went on to produce a high quality toy and increased production more steeply than Harary had thought possible. Perez expressed his thoughts:

> Wai Lung is highly committed and has put us at the top of its priority list. During our early experience with Finger Bikes, they returned calls promptly and answered all questions during the critical production period.
>
> Wai Lung's performance with Finger Bikes allowed us to beat a major competitor to the market. This prompted our competitor to drop the project in mid-design. We should look at Wai Lung as a supplier for E-Chargers because of our positive experience with them. However, their engineering workforce is fairly small and they haven't produced toys with electronic components. They have focused on die-casting and plastic action figures. E-Chargers have to be designed and produced to much more stringent tolerances than die-cast or plastic toys. To put it bluntly, flying toys would take a paradigm shift in Wai Lung's engineering expertise.
>
> We did plan to use a vendor survey report, but we don't have any engineering expertise at our Hong Kong office. And, in Canada, our manufacturing team includes me and Ronnen—with this in mind, I wonder if we can gather this information for Wai Lung and Wah Shing in time. We are already behind schedule as it stands.

Harary returned to visit Wai Lung in May 1999 and, while walking through the factory, estimated by observation that Wai Lung was at 40 per cent of capacity. He also found out that Wai Lung had excess capacity to utilize because it had just lost a significant portion of its business during a disagreement with a large toy company. Harary was impressed by its size: it had 2,000 workers in its 100,000 square-foot factory in Shenzhen, about a one-hour journey by train and car from Hong Kong. Typical toy factories in this area averaged about 600 workers. He casually asked the owner of Wai Lung for a quick overview of the projects currently in progress. Wai Lung was working on plastic play sets and action figures for Hasbro. Another company with which Wai Lung had a contract had gone bankrupt. Pressing further on a different subject, Harary got the sense that Wai Lung would not begin many projects in the near future.

Lee, 48, had always been very accommodating to Harary and considered himself to be a self-made man, building up a successful factory. Still hungry to grow his business, he had recently hired three engineers. He was willing to extend favorable credit terms to Spin Master Toys, allowing for Finger Bikes production to commence with a simple wire transfer of funds versus a more formal letter of credit. Otherwise, a letter of credit from the bank, along with the requisite documentation, meant that up to 30 per cent of the total invoice amount needed to be securely transferred before the start of production. Once production was started, payments would immediately be taken out of cash flow. With a wire transfer, however, funds would be wired to the supplier's bank account 21 days after the goods were shipped.

WAH SHING

Wah Shing was a subsidiary of a Hong Kong public toy manufacturer. It was a company with annual revenues of US$40 million (the average Hong Kong toy company with product line similar to Wah Shing's earned about US$30 million in revenues per year). While at his previous employer, Perez had worked with Wah Shing. Wah Shing had been one of the suppliers of choice for major toy companies such as Tiger and Hasbro which needed electronic toys. These companies wanted to maintain their track record of successful electronic toy engineering development and manufacture in the electronic hand-held, feature electronic plush, radio control and IR interactive categories, including toys such as "Shotgun and Skidzo," "Furby," "Laser Light Tennis" and "Galactic Battle."

Wah Shing employed 3,500 people in its 100,000-square-foot factory, counting six engineers on its staff. Although Harary had toured the factory, during his visit, he had been unable to meet the owner, who was travelling. By observation, Harary estimated that Wah Shing was at 70 to 80 per cent of capacity at its Chinese factory, which was located five hours away from Hong Kong. Perez expressed his thoughts:

> Before coming to Spin Master, I worked for a major toy company and got some experience with Wah Shing. Their upper and lower management are very committed. They are a non-hierarchial, action-oriented company. I have a personal friendship with the general manager.
>
> In my experience, Wah Shing provides products on time and within quality specifications. But it has been four years since my last contact. During a visit a few weeks ago, I found out that the lower management had been changed. Also, there seemed to be less communication between upper and lower management than there used to be. However, they still have a good reputation in electronic toys and their costs are comparable to similar companies.
>
> Ronnen, who was with me on the tour, noted that they had put their North American account manager in charge of the tour. Ronnen is used to dealing directly with factory owners and wonders if we could expect the same commitment as we have had with our previous projects.

RONNEN HARARY'S CHOICE

Harary discussed the decision he faced:

> We believe that retail sales for toy airplanes will peak from March to mid-May, after which water toys will dominate. For E-Chargers, we've been fortunate to have secured a sizeable amount of shelf space in retail stores for this period and also have been awarded several large feature endcap orders! To meet this demand, we have to have 20,000 units ready to ship by December 1999 as shown in this schedule [see Exhibit 1]. On top of the fact that the retailers need time to move our product through their distribution system, we've heard that a major competitor, a large toy company, is also working on the same E-Chargers concept. We have to beat them to market at all costs because, in this industry, it is hard to overcome the first mover advantage. While we would like to have

a five- to six-month design-to-delivery window, we have four months, max.

But we also have to consider the tight tolerances we require. Our initial work revealed that we have to be very careful to balance weight shaving and structural integrity. Ideally, an E-Charger should weigh 17 grams. An increase of only one gram decreases the flying time by 15 seconds. Just painting the plane adds enough weight to affect the performance significantly. According to our preliminary tests, the plane will weigh 18 grams, and we have to work tremendously hard to reduce that figure. At 18.5 grams, this thing won't even fly.

We have to find a supplier who can deliver on engineering expertise. Not many manufacturers in Hong Kong had experience with flying toys and, to add to the complexity of this project, we are using materials that are not commonly available.

This is an unprecedented toy requiring design work for the engine and to accommodate the capacitor, not to mention the separate battery box. Our rough design calls for about 50 different parts! How should we compare the quality of work between the Wai Lung and Wah Shing factories? Although both have done projects for us in the past, this product is totally new. Price might play a factor in the decision, but it will not override our most pressing concern of getting to market quickly.

A concern is the quality of the suppliers' sources of raw materials and prefabricated components, most of which are based in mainland China. A large number of small- and mid-sized competitors vie for the world toy business—no one factory controls a significant portion of toy manufacturing. Clients like us have to be extra careful, because machinery and worker training in mainland China are generally inferior to those in Hong Kong.

We should consider many factors in making this decision: reputation, capacity, quality levels, capability in engineering, the capability of the factories' Chinese suppliers, speed to market, costs, tooling time needed (critical in this project), attention to

your company. In the past, due to our small size and limited engineering expertise, we prioritized a close working relationship with the owner of the factory in question. Because the owner took a personal interest in our projects, it reassured us that our needs would be top priority, and he would do whatever it took to produce results. With E-Chargers, I still strongly believe that this is necessary to ensure we meet the December 7 deadline. A personal relationship is key. What could make that difficult is the fact that the owners of these private toy manufacturers, like many in Hong Kong, all seem to have several businesses going on at once.

We are very pressed. We might not have enough time to do proper due diligence on Wai Lung or Wah Shing. We just got these quotes from each of them [see Exhibits 2 and 3]. Although we would like to have more time to qualify more suppliers in the Hong Kong area, we simply can't afford the time. We need engineering development work to start almost immediately! We need a factory to develop the wings and fuselage for E-Chargers, the rest of the 50 parts, prototype moulds, then sample shots for our inspection. We do not have the luxury of extra time. We're not even sure what our competitors are up to. Which factory should we choose?

NOTES

1. A capacitor is an electronic device used to store charge—in essence it is like a rechargeable battery. It consists of an arrangement of conductors, separated by an insulator.

2. Endcaps are the attractive, highly visible end spaces on shopping aisles. Executives of Spin Master Toys expected that an E-Chargers endcap order from a large retail customer would result in sales of about 150,000 units.

3. Retailers took three weeks after Christmas to clear out old stock and put in new toys for the spring period. The layout of toys by aisle and shelf, known as a planogram, was determined in advance.

Quotation Submission Form (Summary)
Spin Master Toys

Attention:	Ronnen Harary
Item:	4004
Description:	E-Chargers
Reference:	Quotation Submission
From:	Wai Lung Plastics Mfy., Ltd

Description	Cost in HK$ per 1,000 Toys[1]
1. Plastic	$540.50
2. Other parts	4,670.00
3. Packaging	3,620.00
4. Shipping carton	295.00
Total material cost	**$9,125.50**
Total labor cost	**$2,380.00**
Total materials plus labor	**$11,505.50**
Overhead and markup @ 16% (of materials and labor)	$1,840.88
Scrap allowance @ 1.5% (of materials)	136.88
Capacitor handling charge @ 3% (of capacitor cost)	150.74
Motor handling charge @ 3% (of motor cost)	197.12
Total	**$13,831.12**
Transportation FCL,[2] Hong Kong, FOB[3] Hong Kong, 40-foot FCL container	$487.00
Total	**$14,318.12**
Transportation LCL,[4] Hong Kong, FOB Hong Kong, 40-foot LCL container	$1,607.50
Total	**$15,438.62[5]**

Exhibit 2   Quote From Wai Lung Plastics Mfy., Ltd.

Source: Company files.

1. The Hong Kong dollar was pegged against the United States dollar at the rate of HK$7.75 = US$1. In July 1999, a Canadian dollar was worth about HK$5.21.
2. FCL: Full container load.
3. FOB: Free on board. In essence, the location signifies the point at which the customer takes ownership, and thus financial responsibility.
4. LCL: Less than container load.
5. This price does not include the capacitor or the motor.

To: Alex Perez
From: John Yi
Subject: E-Flyer Quote: Ref "0" vs. Mattel

Cost Summary Sheet

Product Name: E-Flyer

Item	Cost Description	FCL (HK$)	LCL (HK$)
1	Electronic parts (includes motor and capacitor)	15.7998	15.7998
2	Plastic material	0.2396	0.2396
3	Metal parts	0.8976	0.8976
4	Packaging material	2.5805	2.5805
5	Miscellaneous	4.2534	4.2534
6	Bonding	0.0000	0.0000
7	Labor cost	0.8000	0.8000
8	Decoration cost	0.0000	0.0000
9	Injection cost	0.5313	0.5313
10	Overhead and markup	3.3523	3.3523
11	Transportation	0.2914	1.0238
	Ex-factory price FOB Hong Kong	**28.7459**	**29.4783**

Exhibit 3   Quote From Wah Shing Electronics Co., Ltd.

Source: Company files.

DABBAWALLAHS OF MUMBAI (A)

Prepared by Ramasastry Chandrasekhar
under the supervision of Professor Larry Menor

Version: (A) 2004-10-12

INTRODUCTION

On November 7, 2003, Raghunath Medge, president of the Nutan Mumbai Tiffin Box Suppliers Charity Trust (the Trust), had just returned to his office in suburban Mumbai after meeting with Britain's Prince Charles who was on an official visit to India's commercial capital.

The Trust was the managing organization of the dabbawallah meal delivery network (see Exhibit 1). The dabbawallahs' service, often referred to as tiffinwallahs outside of Mumbai, was cited internationally by management scholars and industry executives as an exemplar of supply chain and service management. The service had acquired a reputation for its delivery

Dabba was a generic, colloquial term used explicitly in Mumbai to describe any cylindrical box. In the context of meal delivery service, a dabba was an aluminum box carried by its handle like a tin of paint. Each dabba housed three to four interlocking steel containers and was held together by a collapsible metallic wire handle. Each of these containers accommodated an individual food item found in a typical midday lunch.

Wallah was a label for a tradesperson in a particular profession. For example, a paperwallah was an individual who delivered newspapers. Taken together, a *dabbawallah* was a courier who picked up a lunch-full dabba from a client's home in the morning, left it outside of the client's workplace for pick-up, retrieved the empty dabba after the lunch was consumed and returned the empty dabba to the client's home in the evening.

This is a special pushcart that holds 150 dabbas. It takes between three to four dabbawallahs to maneuver this pushcart.

Exhibit 1   Dabbawallahs of Mumbai

Source: Company files.

reliability in Mumbai. International interest in the dabbawallahs was largely due to a 1998 article published in *Forbes:*[1]

> Mumbai's "tiffinwallahs" have achieved a level of service to which Western businesses can only aspire. "Efficient organization" is not the first thought that comes to mind in India, but when the profit motive is given free rein, anything is possible. To appreciate Indian efficiency at its best, watch the tiffinwallahs at work.

Documentaries on the dabbawallahs were produced by the *BBC, MTV* and *ZEE TV,* and their delivery performance earned them recognition in the *Guinness Book of World Records* and *Ripley's Believe It or Not!*

Medge, who had personally demonstrated to Prince Charles how the dabbawallah meal delivery system worked, was himself in the spotlight of late. He had recently been invited by the Confederation of Indian Industry to speak to its members at a leadership summit in a special module titled "Leading Without Suits and Ties." He was also approached by human resource executives and asked to present seminars on team building. Additionally, he was asked by corporations, such as Siemens India, to make a presentation to their employees on the dabbawallahs' working practices. Finally, he was also regularly sought by the print and television media within and outside of India.

Medge had begun to see a pattern in his interactions with these diverse audiences. The questions he was asked were, by and large, predictable. Typical queries revolved around the dabbawallahs' workforce, customers and strategy:

- How do the dabbawallahs find recruits?
- How can an incentive system based on "equal pay for all" work?
- Do the dabbawallahs know their clients?
- How does the dabbawallah system ensure that the individual links in the delivery network do not break down?
- How is the Trust dealing with the issue of growth?
- How is the Trust coping with dabbawallah competitors?
- The world around you is changing but the dabbawallahs have not changed; why not?

The question that Medge was asked most often—and which amused him the most—was: Is there a future for the dabbawallahs? Based on his own personal experience over the last three decades, Medge had developed a standard response to this particular question.

HISTORY OF THE DABBAWALLAHS

The dabbawallah service had begun informally in 1890 in Mumbai. According to Medge:

> A Parsi banker working in Ballard Pier employed a young man, who came down from the Poona district to fetch his lunch every day. Business picked up through referrals and soon our pioneer dabba-carrying entrepreneur had to call for more helping hands from his village. Such was the origin of the dabbawallahs.

> However trivial the task may sound, it is of vital importance since havoc is caused if the client had to skip his home-cooked food or worse, carry the dabba himself in the ever so crowded Mumbai trains during the rush hour!

By the early 20th century, people from all parts of India were migrating to Mumbai in large numbers. Once they found a source of livelihood and settled down, they wanted home-cooked food at their workplaces. Home-cooked food had a comfort level for various reasons. First, the food was prepared in the ambience of a domestic kitchen, with recipes that were tried and tested, and that resulted in familiar fare. Second, home-cooked food was comparatively inexpensive. The dabbawallahs were initially charging two annas per month per dabba for their delivery service.[2]

Working independently and in small groups for decades, the dabbawallahs had united in 1954 to put together a rudimentary co-operative. This umbrella organization was officially registered in 1956 as a charitable trust under the name Nutan Mumbai Tiffin Box Suppliers Charity Trust. At that time, some of the dabbawallahs employed delivery boys to carry their dabbas and transport them along their routes on bicycles and pushcarts.

These dabbawallahs would collect the fees from their clients every month and pay the boys whatever they could negotiate with them. This changed in 1983 when the Trust adopted an owner-partner system. Under this new system, the practice of subcontracting was dispensed with and dabbawallahs started to receive equal earnings. The delivery boys' system was converted into an apprenticeship system wherein new recruits were trained for at least two to three years on a fixed remuneration before they became full-time dabbawallahs.

By 2003, more than 5,000 dabbawallahs worked under the aegis of the Trust. Together they delivered about 175,000 lunches daily in Mumbai (see Exhibit 2). They served a total area that covered approximately 75 kilometres (km) of public transport. The dabbawallah business generated approximately Rs380 million per annum. Given the two-way route for each dabba, the number of deliveries worked out to more than 350,000 per day. Despite the sheer number of daily deliveries, the failure rate reported by the media numbered one in two months, or one in every 15 million deliveries.

The Nutan Mumbai
Tiffin Box Suppliers Charity Trust

The Trust was responsible for managing the overall meal delivery system. It worked in close co-ordination with the Mumbai Tiffin Box Suppliers' Association, a forum that provided opportunities for social interactions among the dabbawallahs, and the Dakkhan Mavle Sahakari Patpedhi, a credit union that catered to the financial needs of individual dabbawallahs by providing personal loans. Given its charitable trust status, the Trust was also involved in community initiatives by providing free food and accommodation to low-income families at some pilgrimage centres.

The Trust had a three-tier structure: Executive Committee, mukadams and dabbawallahs (see Exhibit 3). Under this structure, the basic operating unit was the team. Each team, which comprised between five and eight dabbawallahs, was

Year	Number of Dabbawallahs	Number of Customers
1900	58	1,445
1905	75	1,965
1910	142	4,120
1915	204	6,504
1920	321	9,675
1925	407	12,140
1930	695	22,865
1935	1,024	34,230
1940	1,206	42,340
1945	1,715	64,240
1950	2,106	82,000
1955	2,552	105,120
1960	3,216	140,000
1965	4,406	198,100
1970	4,605	176,040
1975	4,904	215,000
1980	5,511	275,075
1985	5,524	190,645
1990	5,102	130,860
1995	5,180	142,260
2000	5,164	165,670
2003	5,142	175,040

Exhibit 2   Dabbawallahs and Customers
Source: R. Medge.

headed by a mukadam. Having risen from the ranks of the dabbawallahs, a mukadam's primary daily responsibility involved the sorting of the dabbas. However, as team leader, the mukadam performed several administrative tasks that included maintaining records of client payments, arbitrating disputes between dabbawallahs and customers, and apprentice training. The

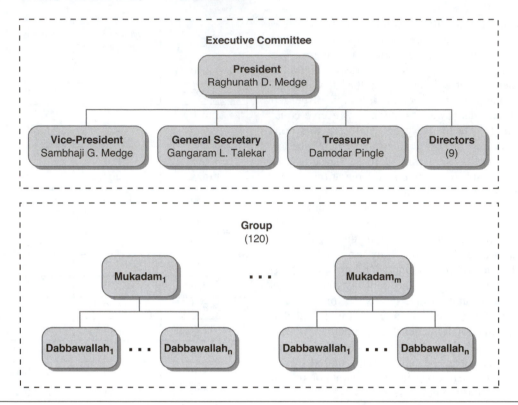

Exhibit 3   The Nutan Mumbai Tiffin Box Suppliers Charity Trust's Organizational Structure

m: # of mukadams in a group

n: # of dabbawallahs in a team

Source: R. Medge.

mukadam was also in charge of acquiring new clients for the team and managing customer satisfaction. New customers purchased their dabba from the dabbawallahs when service was commenced. Dabbas were typically replaced, at cost to the customer, once every two years.

Seven to eight mukadams typically aggregated their efforts and constituted a profit centre; each profit centre was referred to as a "group." There were about 120 groups in total. While each group was managed autonomously, its members stepped in without hesitation to help other groups in dealing with emergencies such as dabbawallah absenteeism. Monthly group maintenance costs totalled Rs35,000, covering the maintenance of the bicycles, pushcarts and

wooden boxes the dabbawallahs used in their daily deliveries.

The 13 members of the Executive Committee, which were elected by the general body every five years, co-ordinated the activities of the various groups. The Committee, which undertook all major decisions for the Trust and worked on the principles specified in the Co-operative Societies Act, met on the 15th of each month. Operational issues typically dominated each meeting's agenda. Examples of such issues included disputes with the Mumbai city railways over dabbawallahs not carrying their monthly passes or the ID issued to them by the Trust, and with the city police when dabbawallahs parked their pushcarts or bicycles where parking was not permitted. Annually, there were few reports of lost or stolen dabbas. In such instances, clients were reimbursed by the individual dabbawallah or given a free dabba.

Dabbawallah Profile

The dabbawallahs were a homogenous group in many ways. Its members, traditionally male, hailed from the same geographical region— known as Mavla—located east of the Sahyadri (Western Ghats) near Pune, and they spoke the same language (Marathi). They shared similar customs and traditions, such as gathering together for a week every April for a festival in their hometown. They wore the same dress, a loose white dhoti shirt, cotton pajamas and their trademark white oval cap.

All of these combined to form a distinct local identity for the dabbawallahs. They were easily recognized even in the busiest of locations. Pedestrians and commuters yielded to the dabbawallahs in order not to interfere with their service delivery. Seemingly always in a rush, the dabbawallahs were known for their reliability and work ethic. They ascribed to the traditional Indian belief that "work is worship." Averaging 55 years in age, dabbawallahs were typically lean, agile, active and physically fit. While the minimum level of education of a dabbawallah was grade seven, most never got past grade eight schooling.

Each dabbawallah earned a monthly income between Rs5,000 and Rs6,000. Out of this income, each dabbawallah was responsible for paying:

1. Rs120 for the monthly railway pass that allowed for unlimited access to Mumbai's railways;

2. Rs60 for the maintenance of the bicycle or the pushcart (which were owned by the group or profit centre); and

3. the compulsory monthly contribution of Rs15 to the Trust.

"It is a good earning for a semi-literate by Indian standards," observed Medge.

Each new recruit would undergo an apprenticeship for two years on a fixed remuneration of Rs2,000 per month. Each apprentice was then required to purchase a delivery route before being admitted as a dabbawallah. The price for the route was fixed as a ratio of the average monthly earnings of the group at 1:7. For instance, most groups' monthly earnings were approximately Rs140,000, so the apprentice was expected to deposit Rs20,000 for a delivery route. This money went to the Shared Capital of the Trust and would be returned to the dabbawallah upon retirement. Once admitted, the dabbawallah was guaranteed a monthly income and a job for life.

Dabbawallah Meal Distribution Network

The dabbawallah meal distribution network was characterized by a combination of a "baton relay system" in which dabbas were handed off between dabbawallahs at various points in the delivery process and a "hub and spokes" system in which the sorting of dabbas was done at specific railway locations from where individual spokes branched out for distribution. There was no local historical model on which this distribution network was designed. All design decisions were driven by the singular purpose of delivering a dabba in time for the customer's lunch. The delivery processes had largely remained unchanged since their inception even though the environment of service delivery had changed. For example, the delivery system did not rely on the use of computers. According to Medge:

> If we were to use computers, we would be out of business. It is not because we do not know how to use computers but the system itself is not amenable to the use of technology in whatever form.

The only major change in the dabbawallahs' delivery model was the fine-tuning of the coding system in 1966. The number of customers using the delivery service had continued to grow, and without some form of common identification that all dabbawallahs could follow, the sorting process at the hubs was likely to become overly time-consuming. Medge observed:

> We decided to decentralize the coding at the level of groups and each group was free to develop its own coding system based on simple and easily identifiable numbers and signs. In time, each group gradually developed its own distinctive color code—from a spectrum of combinations of the seven primary colors—serving as the first line of identification for any dabbawallah.

The workday for a dabbawallah started with the first delivery pick-up at 8:30 a.m. (see Exhibit 4). Leaving their Mumbai home, most of the time by bicycle, the dabbawallahs arrived punctually to the minute at the doorstep of each collection point, although they might not be wearing a watch. The collection point would typically be the client's home. Customers were aware of their responsibilities in the delivery process. Each knew that if the dabba was not ready for pick-up, the dabbawallah simply moved on; the dabbawallah did not wait. Each dabbawallah was personally responsible for the daily delivery of 30 to 35 dabbas. Dabbawallahs found that number to be usually manageable in terms of personal memory and physical handling capacity.

As each dabba was picked up, it was hitched to the handle or the back-carrier of a bicycle. Sometimes it was placed on a wheeled wooden trolley pushcart. Once the pick-up route was covered and all the dabbas were finally collected,

8:25 a.m.	The dabba is filled with lunch at the client's kitchen and kept outside the door of the residence.
8:30 a.m.	The dabbawallah arrives, picks up the dabba and moves on knocking at the door only if the dabba is not seen. Under normal circumstances there is no interaction with any member of the client's household.
8:38 a.m.	The dabba is placed on the bicycle or pushcart together with dabbas collected from other customers.
9:20 a.m.	Bicycles and pushcarts drawn by individual dabbawallahs arrive from various collection centres to the suburban railway station.
9:30 a.m.	The sorting operation begins with dabbas sorted according to destinations and placed in cartages that are specific to each destination. The cartages come in two standard sizes, accommodating 24 and 48 dabbas each.
9:41 a.m.	The suburban train arrives. The cartages, normally numbering five to six, are loaded into the special compartment located next to the driver's cabin.
10:21 a.m.	The train arrives at one of the major hubs. The cartages are unloaded and bundled with those arriving from other collection centres. They are resorted according to destinations.
11:05 a.m.	Cartages are loaded into the suburban train for onward journey to the final destination terminals.
11:45 a.m.	The suburban train reaches the terminal station. Cartages are unloaded and dabbas are re-sorted, now according to specific delivery routes.
12:10 p.m.	Dabbas are placed in destination-specific cartages and hitched typically on to bicycles or pushcarts for delivery to individual clients.
12:30 p.m.	The dabba is delivered at the doorstep of the client's workplace.

The delivery process is reversed in the afternoon. The empty dabba is picked up between 1:15 p.m. and 2:00 p.m. for its return to the client's home early that evening (e.g. by 5:30 p.m.).

Exhibit 4   Sample Morning Journey of a Dabba

they were transported to the nearest of 68 suburban railway stations the dabbawallahs used. It was at this station that a second set of dabbawallahs, already positioned on the platforms, took over. They sorted the dabbas according to destinations and placed them in destination-specific wooden cartages. The cartages came in two standard sizes, accommodating 24 and 48 dabbas each. As the train arrived, at two-minute intervals, the cartages were placed in a specially designated cargo carriage on the train located next to the driver's cabin. The loading had to be completed in 30 seconds, the time for which the train halted at each station. The cartages, accompanied by one or two dabbawallahs, were now ready to be transported to various hubs and destination terminals in Mumbai.

The hub was essentially a mid-point station in the suburban railway network where trains converged before branching out to other parts of the city. Dadar, Bandra, Andheri and Kurla were the four major hubs for the dabbawallahs' meal distribution network (see Exhibit 5). As epicentres that had to be passed through while moving from one end of the city to the other, the hubs were crucial links in the delivery system. They were also places where delivery errors could take place. That was why each of the hubs was actively managed by the mukadams, who stepped in to co-ordinate the sorting operation at each hub. As trains kept arriving in rapid succession, it became imperative to orchestrate three activities—sorting, loading and unloading—simultaneously. Doing so was a challenge during Mumbai's rush hour when thousands of commuters were also getting on or off each train. Given the tight time schedule for Mumbai's railways, the dabbawallahs had to complete their tasks quickly and precisely.

From these hubs, the sorted dabbas spoked out to various destinations—including the terminal stations of the city railway—where a third set of dabbawallahs was waiting to take over. The dabbas were off-loaded at various terminals and re-sorted, depending now upon specific customer location information, such as the street, building and the floor. The dabbas were then handed over to the fourth set of handlers, individual

dabbawallahs, who were assigned to specific delivery routes in Mumbai city. Placing the dabbas on pushcarts or bicycles, or in some cases carried by hand or in crates on top of their heads (a full crate of dabbas could weigh up to 100 kilograms), the dabbawallahs delivered the home-cooked lunches to the designated recipient by 12:30 p.m.

An hour or two later, the empty dabbas—dropped off by the satiated client at the same spot used for dabba pick-up—were collected to be routed backwards on their return journey. In short, each dabba was picked up at the source by one dabbawallah for transport to the railway terminal, sorted and loaded by a second dabbawallah, unloaded and re-sorted at the hub or destination station by a third dabbawallah and delivered by a fourth dabbawallah to the home from which the dabba was picked up earlier in the day. The exact combination of dabbawallahs used each day varied with the volume and density of traffic, but it remained the same on the return route.

Since each dabba traveled through four sets of hands each day, it was important to identify and monitor the dabbas while in transit. This was done through a system of codes painted on the top of each dabba's exterior (see Exhibit 6). The originating station and the destination station were the primary codes. They were crucial for the sorting operations that took place at each of the hubs, and they were normally identified by alphabets that any sorter could recognize. The other encoded data included the apartment, floor, building and street the dabba originated from and was to be delivered to. The codes included symbols (e.g. dashes, dots, etc.), alphabets, numbers and other forms of notation which likely made little sense outside of the dabbawallah community, but which the dabbawallahs recognized and understood instantly. The movement of the dabbas was monitored solely through these codes and client names were not utilized. Pulling one dabba aside, Medge explained:

The codes "K-BO-10–19/A/15" on top of this dabba mean the following: K was the dabbawallah who picked it up; BO meant Borivali, the area from

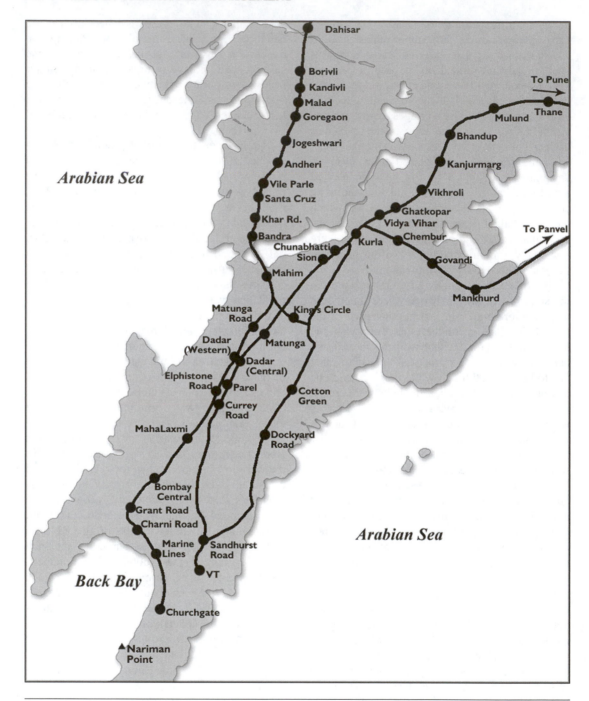

Exhibit 5   Mumbai City's Suburban Rail Network

Coding Key:*

VP   Code for the residential location (e.g. Vile Parle, a suburb of Mumbai)
9 VS 12 Code for dabbawallahs to use at the destination location where:

    9   is the code for dabbawallahs at the destination station
    VS is the code for the building name
    12 is the code for the floor number

E Code for dabbawallahs at the residential railway station
3 Code for destination railway station (e.g. Nariman Point)

* Codes are painted on the top of each dabba in distinct group colors.

Exhibit 6   Sample Dabbawallah Delivery Codes

Source: R. Medge.

where the dabba was collected; 10 referred to the Nariman Point area, the destination; 19/A/15 referred to the 19th building; A was the dabbawallah who delivered it; and 15 was the floor of the building where the customer's workplace was located.

DABBAWALLAHS' OPERATING ENVIRONMENT

For many decades, the labor-intensive textile mills in Mumbai made the single largest contribution to the overall pool of dabbawallah customers. While the customer composition had recently changed to include school children, the basic customer profile had remained unchanged. The majority of dabbawallah customers comprised the Indian middle class of fixed income earners. Approximately 4,000 dabbawallahs daily served workforce clients. Given the larger geographic spread of these clients from their homes, dabbawallahs typically employed bicycles, pushcarts and the Mumbai railways to make these deliveries. Servicing school children, on the other hand, did not require the use of the railway system as most were located close to their residences. Despite the shorter distances for delivery, the dabbawallahs charged more for these deliveries since school lunch timings and their pick-ups varied.

Dabbawallahs had three primary lunch competitors: fast-food chains, restaurants and roadside vendors. Kamat and Udupi were chains of both fast-food counters and restaurants located throughout Mumbai, catering to the lunch hour needs of their customers. These local chains were in direct competition with global chains, such as McDonalds, which entered the Mumbai market in 1997. Specialty food stalls, sans frills, serving local favorites provided another lunch option for Mumbai's workforce, as did roadside vendors offering fast and efficient service and a varied lunch fare. Lastly, some Mumbai companies—for tax shelter purposes—offered their workers lunch coupons that were redeemable at select food outlets known as "Ticket Restaurants."

In Medge's view, the growing presence of these lunch competitors did not meaningfully impact the dabbawallahs' business. He observed:

> Dabbawallahs have a niche of their own. We do not see any of them as competitors. They prepare food, but we are not in the business of preparing food. We do not manufacture; we only deliver. There is no other meal delivery service in Mumbai. We work in a unique operating space where we have a monopoly.

Several factors worked in the Trust's favor. First, people in Mumbai, given a choice, seemed to prefer home-cooked food. Those who were already using the dabbawallah service were not inclined to switch to other providers as lunch hour routines were habit forming. Second, and perhaps most important, was the cost of home-cooked lunches. Home-cooked food delivered by a dabbawallah almost always cost far less than having lunch at a food counter or a restaurant. For instance, at Nariman Point, Mumbai's central downtown location, a vegetarian lunch, served in a steel plate called a thali, purchased at a restaurant would cost Rs120. Further, a combination of snacks that passed off for lunch at a fast-food counter would cost about Rs30, while similar fare from a roadside vendor would cost Rs18. All these options required that customers leave their workplace to eat food whose quality was not assured. A lunch delivered by a dabbawallah from a catering establishment would cost an average of Rs20

(including Rs5 for delivery). A home-cooked lunch delivered by the dabbawallah would cost the home-owner about Rs8, with the majority of that cost paid for the dabbawallah delivery.

Some of the smaller courier firms, known in Mumbai as angadias, were viewed in the local media as potential threats to the dabbawallahs in terms of their ability to develop a parallel delivery service. Medge was doubtful about this potential threat as "an angadia would require an army of couriers to handle the meal delivery business." Mobilizing and motivating the requisite workforce would likely prove challenging for angadias, many of whom were mom-and-pop businesses that lacked the resources and skills to manage a substantially larger business demand.

Larger courier firms operating in Mumbai, such as Blue Dart, DHL and FedEx, were not interested in pursuing a service similar to that offered by the dabbawallahs, given the unique requirements of this type of delivery and their concerns about the inability to extend this service beyond Mumbai.

FOUNDATIONS FOR THE SUCCESS OF THE DABBAWALLAH SERVICE

Observers generally agreed that there were five distinct reasons for the success of the dabbawallahs.

Low-Cost Delivery

Clients typically paid between Rs150 and Rs200 per month for delivery, depending upon the route and the geographical distance traveled by the dabbawallah. According to Medge:

> If a courier company were to be involved in this business, it would be charging at least Rs20 per transaction for a box weighing 1.5 kilograms. But we charge far less—between Rs4 and Rs5 per transaction—even while ensuring that every dabbawallah makes enough money for a living.

The prices charged to the customer were fixed at the discretion of the group. There were two broad considerations in determining the price. First, the pick-up location was considered. For example, the delivery charges for large residential complexes and apartment buildings were lower because of the concentration of customers that allowed for delivery pick-up economies. Less populated areas typically meant fewer customers and longer pick-up/delivery times for the dabbawallahs, and therefore, the prices to service those areas were higher. The second consideration was time. For customers who could not deliver dabbas by the stipulated pick-up time, their charges were higher by up to 25 per cent. If the pick-up time was too close to the lunch hour, requiring an expedited delivery service, the charges were double. Medge observed:

> We see future potential for revenue enhancement with such premium pricing. Indeed, customers with special needs and requests have gone up by 25 per cent, from about 20,000 to about 25,000, in 2002 alone.

Client service charges were generally increased across the board once every two years by about 15 per cent. This increase usually coincided with a major development, such as an increase in railway fares by the government.

Delivery Reliability

The service reliability of dabbawallahs was rooted in the following factors. First, dabbawallahs considered themselves as entrepreneurs, not employees. That explained why, for instance, they had never gone on strike. They worked six days a week, taking a break for five days in April every year to attend an annual village festival en masse. Second, they were not governed by a hierarchy that defined working relationships in terms of a boss and subordinates. Everyone worked as part of a team with a common goal that had to be achieved every working day: No customer should go without food. Third, they lived and worked in clans. All apprentices were recruited through referrals from relatives and friends migrating to Mumbai from the same geographical region. It ensured that there was no dilution

of service culture or erosion of the basics. Fourth, each dabbawallah was solely responsible for the delivery for his 30 to 35 clients. While others may fill in occasionally, he generally maintained total control over his route.

Decentralization

The group structure allowed for independent operations. Each group maintained its own records of revenue and expenditure, serviced its own pool of customers, and managed its own system of billing, collection and expenditure allocation. Each group was also responsible for generating and distributing the monthly revenue among its members, resolving disputes on its own and acquiring new customers entirely independent of the Trust. In fact, the Trust had distanced itself completely from the day-to-day activities of each group. It had no centralized records of group clients or the dabbawallahs' and mukadams' incomes and expenses. The Trust's Executive Committee dealt only with those matters that the mukadams deemed necessary for discussion at the monthly meeting. Decentralization had been instrumental to building cohesion within each group, and operational autonomy helped to provide focus on delivery effectiveness and improvement.

Perceived Equality

Given the design of the delivery service, not every dabbawallah was required to put in equal time and effort. Yet each dabbawallah in the group earned equal remuneration. As such, senior dabbawallahs earned the same monthly income as dabbawallahs with less experience and tenure. According to Medge:

> The dabbawallah system has its own checks and balances because of the large component of physical labor which is integral to effective service delivery. For example, a senior dabbawallah undertook only those tasks, like sorting at a hub, which required co-ordination. Tasks involving legwork, like collection, loading, unloading and delivery, were done by the younger workforce. This system was a leveler. It helped forge equal relationships among the dabbawallahs.

Suburban Railway Network

Mumbai's longitudinal-based geography provided a great deal of latitude in logistics management because the movement of dabbas towards the various north to south destination points remained largely unhindered. This helped in reducing the amount of food spoilage during delivery. The dabbawallahs made extensive use of Mumbai's suburban railway network. Indeed, one popular saying in Mumbai was: "If the local train is the lifeline of the city, then the dabbawallahs are the foodline." It was only on days when the suburban railways grounded to a halt, such as the once or twice a year that monsoons flooded the tracks, that dabbas were not delivered. However, few recipients of the dabbas reached their workplaces when the railway system was not working. The railways provided the most convenient and economical mode of transport for the dabbas. On average, a dabbawallah covered 70 km to 80 km in two-and-a-half hours by train; on bicycle, dabbawallahs covered much less territory.

RAGHUNATH MEDGE AND THE FUTURE OF THE DABBAWALLAHS

Medge was an independent businessman in his own right, running a profitable operation known as the Tiffin Box Suppliers & School Bus Service. All dabbawallahs were allowed to pursue a business outside the delivery system as long as it did not interfere with their delivery activities. "But this is an exhausting and demanding job, and it is only after one becomes a mukadam that one has some free time," said Medge. Medge, now in his late 40s, had worked his way through the Trust's organizational structure and was currently serving his second three-year term as president. He also served as secretary of the Dakkhan Mavle Sahakari Patpedhi Credit Union. Medge's father, himself a dabbawallah for four decades, also had served as a previous president of the Trust.

Observers of the service generally cited three broad issues as potentially affecting the future of the dabbawallahs.

Shrinking Customer Base and Customer Loyalty

The number of dabbawallah clients peaked at around 275,000 in 1980. The closure of several textile mills during the 1980s explained much of the subsequent decline in customers as thousands of mill workers lost their jobs. The number of customers shrank gradually to less than half by the end of the decade, forcing dabbawallahs to tap new customer segments, such as delivering to school children or delivering lunches produced by caterers.

Targeting new customers was a task that was left to individual groups and the mukadams, as there was no co-ordinated effort at the level of the Trust aimed at new customer acquisition. According to Medge:

> We have a great deal of decentralization in this business and each group is free to pursue new customers, depending upon its ability to mobilize resources and to cope with demands of servicing new customers. There is no interference from the Trust and no pressure of any kind on any of the dabbawallahs to get new customers. We do not want to stretch our human resources to a point where our delivery system faces the risk of a breakdown, leading to a loss of reputation built assiduously over decades.

The delivery system had built-in mechanisms that allowed for accommodating fluctuations in demand (e.g., customers going on annual vacations or schools being closed during summer). Clients were required to pay for the full month if a dabba was to be delivered for more than seven days in a month. Every customer paid on time, usually immediately upon being presented with the monthly invoice, and there was no credit for services not rendered (see Exhibit 7). More than 3,000 of the current dabbawallah clients had stayed with the service for more than two decades.

।। श्री ज्ञानेश्वर प्रसन्न ।।

M : 98194 77199 / 98691 52163
O : 2682 1897

मुकादम : **रघुनाथ धों. मेदगे**
रोहिदास स. आढाव

१) लक्ष्मण गव्हाणे २) सुनिल मेदगे ३) आहीलू आढाव
४) मारुती यादव ५) एकनाथ बधाले ६) सचिन ढोकळे
७) बबन कदम ८) एकनाथ बच्चे ९) किसन चौधरी

३, रघुनाथ पाठकचाळ, सहार रोड, विजय नगर सोसायटी समोर,
संभाजी नगर, अंधेरी (पूर्व), मुंबई - ४०० ०६९.

दिनांक ——————————————— माहे ———————————

भोजनाचा डबा नेणे आणण्याचा हिशेब रु. ————————————

वसुल करणाऱ्याची सही ————————————————

✦ Notice ✦

1) One months Salary is Diwali Bonus. 2) Please do not pay without Bill. 3) Please do not keep silver or stainless steel utensils in carriers. 4) If carries are lost only value will be paid in the monthly payment of half. 5) We are not responsible for carries lost in your office. 6) Delivery will depend as per train timings. 7) If train are late for 1-30 Hours of more than carrier will be return as it. 8) If any have any complaint about our servants Please let us know by post. 9) Please look carrier having single supporters hence are will not be held responsible for damage of the lunch. 10) Payment to be made in full even carrier fails to carry for 8 to 10 days in a month 11) If carriers lost we pay half from my only.

The Marathi text at the top of the invoice specifies the name of the specific dabbawallah servicing the delivery route, the nine other dabbawallahs in his team and the mukadam overseeing this team's efforts (e.g., Raghunath Medge in this instance).

Exhibit 7   Sample Dabbawallah Invoice
Source: R. Medge.

Lifestyle Changes

As double-income families became the norm in Mumbai and the demand for convenience foods rose, the time that might be spent cooking at home became a precious commodity for most. As a result, what constituted home-cooked or convenience food was likely to change over time, as new lunch items were becoming available on grocery shelves (e.g. microwavable food). In Medge's view:

> These changes are superficial and will not affect the core of our business, because at the end of the day, everyone prefers home-cooked food to all other foods. It is that innate preference that has been the basis of our survival so far. It will continue to be so in the future.

Workforce Management

While each dabbawallah worked as an owner-entrepreneur, there were workforce management issues that currently needed to be addressed at the operational level. For example, some dabbawallahs had been in the business for more than four generations, and they were finding it difficult to get their children interested in following in their footsteps. Some of the dabbawallahs themselves seemed to prefer different careers for their children mainly because of the large component of physical labor involved in the job. To Medge, however:

> For every current generation member of our families in Mumbai who fancies an office job, there are many others from our villages willing to join us as apprentices with hopes of becoming a mukadam.

While recognition of individual effort through monetary rewards was generally considered to have a positive and demonstrative impact on general work performance, the dabbawallah system had no provision for such individual rewards. Excellence was normally expected from every dabbawallah every day. There were three broad service expectations mukadams had for each dabbawallah: timely delivery to the client, courteous attitude and behavior towards the customer, and understanding the special needs, if any, of each customer. Dabbawallahs were expected to avoid drinking alcohol during business hours, to always wear their white cap on the job and to carry their identity cards. There were two measures of service performance actively monitored at the individual dabbawallah level: the number of customer complaints and the number of encounters with the authorities. There were no financial incentives for achieving excellence on either measure. For Medge:

> Excellence is a state of mind that every dabbawallah automatically gets conditioned to, once he is part of the system. While we do not offer extra incentives, we offer little disincentives. In particular, we do not fire anyone.

CONCLUSION

Medge was scheduled to address the faculty and students of the Indian Institute of Management in Lucknow in early January 2004 on how the dabbawallah meal distribution network worked. He was aware that this audience would be interested in the learning that the dabbawallahs could provide to improve supply chain—and service—design and execution. He was also aware that it was likely that most of the audience would have concerns about the future of the dabbawallahs. Since he anticipated being asked about that concern, Medge already knew what he was going to say in response:

> The dabbawallah is a Mumbai institution that has survived for over a century now. It will survive for the next century and beyond. There will of course be a churning of customers. But children will continue to go to school, people will continue to go to work, everyone feels hungry at lunch hour and, if given a choice, everyone wants to have home-cooked food delivered personally to them. Dabbawallahs facilitate that choice. We will continue to be there as long as people exercise that choice. We will continue to be there because no one can provide the kind of error-free service that we provide.

NOTES

1. Subrata N. Chakravarty and Nazneen Karmali, "Fast Food," *Forbes Global,* October 8, 1998.

2. 16 annas comprised one rupee (Rs) at that time. The anna was replaced by the paise in 1960, and 100 paise comprised Rs1. As of November 2003, Cdn$ = Rs31.40.

DAIKIN INDUSTRIES

Prepared by Tetsu Imigi under the supervision of Professor Chris J. Piper

Version: (A) 2004-08-31

Early in June, 1998, Mr. Toshinari Oka, recently appointed president of the Shiga Factory,[1] paused to reflect on the gloomy news. The long-term weather forecast pointed towards an unseasonably cold summer, when the Shiga Factory had large quantities of finished goods inventory in anticipation of strong sales. Mr. Oka's concerns were not just for the current year, however, but also for the factory's long-term survival. He thought, "We may not be able to stay in this business."

Summer temperatures had a major impact on the total sales of residential air conditioners, and the business was only marginally profitable. Mr. Oka knew that he would need to make major changes if he wished to become more competitive and improve profitability. The question was, "How?"

THE RESIDENTIAL AIR CONDITIONING MARKET

Competition for domestic market share in Japan was fierce. There were over 10 players, including Matsushita, Mitsubishi, Hitachi, Sharp, Sanyo and Fujitsu General. Fortunately, Japan's complex retail distribution systems, together with strict environmental and energy-saving laws, had so far deterred overseas players based in Korea and China. Of Daikin's domestic competitors, Matsushita was the leader with over 20,000 exclusive nationwide retailers operating under the Panasonic and National banners. Daikin and most of the other competitors, on the other hand, sold through non-exclusive appliance and home entertainment dealers who carried products from several competing manufacturers.

Industry demand in recent years had been static. Historically, new housing had been the primary source of growth, but Japan's lengthy recession had greatly reduced housing starts. As a result, industry players aimed most of their efforts at increasing their share of replacement sales. Residential air conditioners typically lasted 10 to 12 years before being replaced. Competition was intense and profit margins were slim as players strived to increase their sales in a near-zero growth market by taking market share from their competitors. In spite of its best efforts, however, Daikin's market share hovered in the nine per cent range (see Exhibit 1).

Typically, consumers in Japan bought an air conditioner for each room in their house or apartment, so homes often had three or four installed. The typical set-up consisted of two components. A refrigeration unit was mounted outside the dwelling in a place where it did not block the light or the view through the windows, and where its coils could exchange heat with

Manufacturer	Market Share (%)
Matsushita	18.0
Mitsubishi Electric	15.0
Toshiba	11.0
Hitachi	10.5
Sanyo	10.0
Daikin	9.0
Others	26.5

Exhibit 1   Market Shares in the 1997 Season (October 1996 to September 1997)

Source: Company files.

Total industry unit sales: 7,154,000

the outside air (see Exhibit 2). The exterior unit was connected by coolant lines to an interior unit that contained a heat exchanger. The latter was frequently mounted on a wall or ceiling so that it did not take up living space.[2]

Exhibit 3 shows a typical product and its room location. Products were priced from about ¥80,000[3] for basic low-powered models, to almost ¥250,000 for high-powered products that, in addition to cooling the air in the room, heated it during the winter, as well dehumidifying, freshening and cleaning the air.

Residential air conditioners in Japan were common enough to be considered commodities. Most manufacturers tried to differentiate their products by including value-added features such as on-off timers, energy-savers and

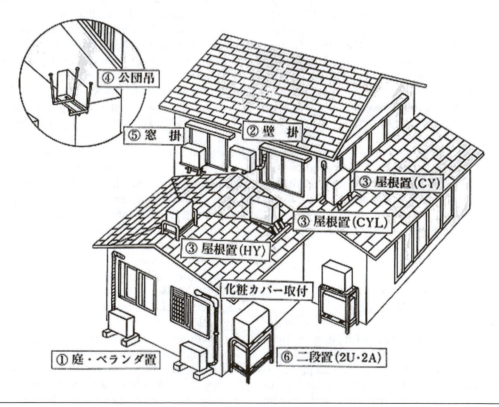

Exhibit 2   Alternative Mounting of Outside Air Conditioning Units
Source: Company files.

Daikin Interior Unit

Exhibit 3   A Typical Interior Unit Mounted Above-Window

Source: http://global.daikin.com/global/our_product/index.html July 22, 2004.

---

noise-minimizers. Although they hoped to avoid direct price competition, features tended to be quickly matched by the competition. Product quality was comparable across brands and was not considered a significant factor in brand choice. Similarly, a manufacturer's installed base was not a factor when customers selected replacement units, since the cost of installing a new brand was no more than replacing an existing brand.

For these reasons, air conditioners were mostly chosen according to installed price and the amount of cooling required. During periods of extreme heat, however, customers also wanted their air conditioners to be installed quickly, so speed of delivery and installation were significant competitive factors. If their first choice could not be installed within three or four days, they would switch to a competing brand or store. Independent dealers, which accounted for all of Daikin's sales, avoided the risk of lost sales by recommending only those products that were either in stock or could be obtained from their regional warehouse within three days.

SUPPLY CHAIN

Daikin had the widest product line-up in the industry. There were about 600 combinations of options, which included several cooling capacities, inside mounting types (wall versus ceiling, and built-in versus surface-mounting), outside mounting types (roof, ground, wall, etc.), and functionalities (cool-only, or cool-and-heat). Because product designs changed every year, a determined effort was made to avoid carrying goods produced in one year over to the next. Seasonal peaks and troughs could be anticipated, but their exact timing and magnitude could not, since they depended on the precise days on which extremely high levels of heat and humidity occurred. Consequently, there were large fluctuations in weekly demand. And, of course, it was never easy to predict in advance whether the coming summer would be extremely hot. The extent of the annual variations in seasonality is shown in Exhibit 4. The graph displays cumulative weekly demand as a percentage of the annual totals for four consecutive

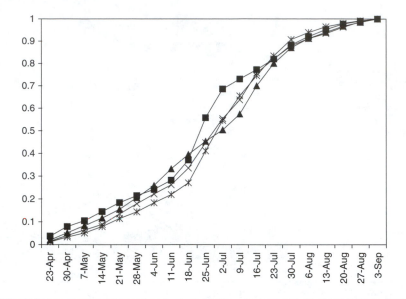

Exhibit 4   Cumulative Demand in Each Week as a Percentage of Annual Total Demand
Source: Company files.

years. By the end of May 1998, Daikin had sold about 180,000 units. The annual demand for Daikin's products tended to vary by about plus or minus 15 per cent.

Sales Companies

Daikin served the domestic market through 21 regional sales companies. Each sales company handled the needs of the retailers in its geographic region. The sales companies, which did not carry inventory, relied on the factory to carry sufficient inventory to support the orders they received. Generally, the sales companies would not be aware of retailer inventory at either the store or warehouse level.

The sales companies provided the factory with forecasts of dealer requirements based on experience and discussions with the retail organizations' buyers. Actual retailer orders were an important input to demand forecasts, but a manufacturing manager said, "Because the sales companies are afraid of stock-outs, they often withhold the actual level of dealer orders from the factory, and do not provide precise forecasts."

The Shiga Factory called the forecasts "pre-purchase orders" (pre-POs). Pre-POs could be cancelled by the sales companies at any time up to one month before the requested delivery date. At that point, the pre-POs automatically became firm purchase orders (POs) that the sales companies were obliged to sell. In normal years, the pre-POs and POs received by the first day of June were sufficient to fill the factory's capacity for all of June and July.

Shiga Factory Warehouse

Products were shipped by truckload from the factory[4] directly to retailers' warehouses nationwide once a week. This provided economical transportation quantities for Shiga, since each warehouse would be ordering for many of its stores. Deliveries took one to two days. During the peak season, additional mid-week deliveries were made in response to urgent orders from retailer warehouses.

Retailer Warehouse and Store Operation

The retailers were mostly chains that maintained their own regional warehouses. The retailers' warehouses would ship consolidated loads of an assortment of merchandise (air conditioners, TVs, refrigerators, etc.) to their stores, so that they also had economical transportation quantities. Shipments were timed to arrive at the stores at the start of the weekends when most air conditioners were sold. It took a day or two for the retailer warehouses to pick and move the required merchandise to the stores.

The individual retail stores did not have much space, so they would only stock what they expected to sell over the weekend, plus a safety margin. With potential demand for 600 different Daikin product variations, however, it was difficult to carry anything more than the most frequently requested options. Therefore, the stores relied on rapid order fulfillment from their regional warehouses.

MANUFACTURING

The Shiga factory was established for mass production of residential room air conditioners in Kusatsu City, Shiga prefecture, in 1970. The factory was located 20 miles from Daikin's corporate headquarters in Osaka, Japan. The 276,000 square-metre factory was Daikin's only production base for home room air conditioners.

About 670 thousand units were produced for domestic consumption in 1997. An additional 15 thousand units were exported.

The Assembly Lines

The manufacturing process was predominantly light assembly. There were approximately 100 components in each product. About 20 components were varied to produce the 600 different product combinations, while 80 components were common across most models. All the components that might be required at a particular work station were positioned behind the assembly workers. Defects occasionally occurred when workers installed the wrong component after an option change.

Assembly was divided between interior and exterior units. The components for the indoor units consisted of a plastic outer cover, a steel inner frame and a heat exchanger. These components were produced on four automated lines before merging into the final assembly line (see Exhibit 5). Purchased parts, including tubing, fan motors and fans were installed by line workers. After assembly, functional checks were performed by sensor machines. Products that passed inspection were packaged at a final stage.

The components for the outdoor units consisted of parts that were also mostly produced automatically. Refrigerant tubing was automatically checked for leakage before being merged with the other items on the final line. The main component installed on the final line was the compressor, which compresses and circulates refrigerant through the system. It took 138 minutes for each unit to flow through the entire assembly process.

HUMAN RESOURCES

Shiga Factory had about 330 permanent employees who worked year-round. Daikin attempted to closely follow seasonal demand by employing over 600 temporary workers at the peak. Long-term relationships were formed with many of the temporary workers. They returned, year after year, under contracts that promised them a minimum number of hours during the peak season, but they allowed Daikin to specify when the hours were to be worked.

To compensate for the work's unpredictability, hourly pay was slightly more than the wages that were paid to full-time, permanent workers. Permanent workers had an unbalanced schedule that also helped address the seasonal peaks. Permanent employees worked 50 hours or more per week in the peak and only 30 hours during

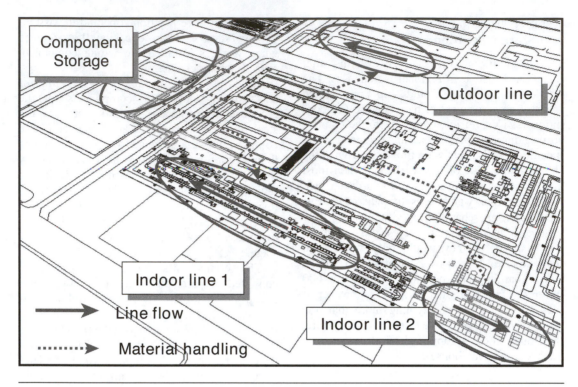

Exhibit 5   Shiga Factory Assembly Line
Source: Company files.

the off-peak. The extra help and the extra summer work hours allowed Daikin to staff three eight-hour shifts for six days a week during the peak.

The system worked well since it provided the factory with experienced workers who had to be paid only when they were needed. In return for their service, temporary workers were given first consideration for full-time employment when the factory required more permanent workers.

Production Planning

The factory's capacity requirements were accumulated by requested pre-PO delivery date and prioritized according to date received. The factory did not accept orders for delivery during weeks in which it had already filled its capacity. When orders were refused, the sales

companies attempted to convince retailers to accept a different—usually later—delivery date, but retailers usually declined, opting for another supplier. Orders were frequently lost because the factory was unable to promise delivery in the requested week. Hence, the sales companies' forecasts tended to err on the side of optimism.

Production plans and employment schedules at the Shiga factory were updated once a month, based on the pre-POs received. The factory made from 50 to 70 different product variants each day, following a mixed model production strategy. The factory maintained centralized control over all finished goods inventory. Highly seasonal demands forced the factory to carry large inventories. The monthly average finished goods inventory amounted to 86 days in the 1997 fiscal year (April 1997 to March 1998).

Purchasing and Research and Development

The factory was also responsible for research and development (R&D) and purchasing. A wholly owned Daikin subsidiary supplied electronics components and pipe assemblies. The suppliers of heat converters, copper and aluminum components frequently collaborated with the factory in technology development. Supplier relationships were based on close interactions within the Daikin Group, and, where cross-share holdings did not exist, long-term associations were maintained with outside suppliers.

These arrangements provided the factory with reliable deliveries of high-quality inputs at the lowest cost consistent with reasonable returns on supplier investments. Materials were ordered from suppliers once a month based on the production plan. The longest component lead time was three months, but most items were received and processed through the factory eight to 10 days after being ordered.

Material cost, at 85 per cent of the cost of goods sold, dominated the typical product cost. Direct labor accounted for six per cent, while overhead added the remaining nine per cent. Mr. Oka reflected back on the cost reduction efforts that the factory had made to date. "We have achieved a cost reduction of ¥50 billion over the last three years, but it is still not enough to surpass our competitors."

OPERATIONS IN CHINA

Many Japanese manufacturing companies considered China to be a strategic location for producing products for export to Japan and North America. China was also an attractive domestic market due to China's extremely large and mostly underserviced population. Labor costs for line workers in China were about five per cent of their counterparts in Japan, making production in China especially attractive for labor-intensive assembly operations like Daikin's.

There would also be opportunities to reduce the costs of material purchased in China due to suppliers' low labor rates. While competitors, such as Matsushita, had residential air conditioner plants in China, Daikin did not. It did, however, have some manufacturing presence in China (see Exhibit 6).

Mr. Oka wondered about the implications of moving production from Japan to China. If it did move, Daikin's relationships with its 21 sales companies, 91 suppliers, and even the consumers who purchased its products, could change. For example, what would be the effect of the longer supply chain?[5] Who would take care of the logistics from the factory to the port in China, from there to the port in Osaka and then on to Shiga Factory? Would the sales companies insist on opening their own warehouses? Would acceptable input materials be available in China? If not, would Daikin's suppliers be willing to move to China, or would Daikin be forced to import its

Division	Products	Application
Shanghai Daikin Air Conditioning	Commercial air conditioning	Commercial sales in China
Xi'an Daikin Qian'an Compressor	Compressors	Large commercial air conditioners
Hui Zhou Daikin Suns Air Conditioning	Water chilling units	Shipping container refrigeration
Daikin Fluoro Coatings Shanghai	Fluorocarbon resin coatings	Refrigerators and freezers

Exhibit 6   Daikin Manufacturing in China

Source: Company files.

materials from Japan? Would consumers perceive the quality of "Made in China" products to be lower? It seemed that the competitive advantages and disadvantages of producing offshore needed more thought.

THE DECISION

In addition to current efforts to forecast demand fluctuations, Mr. Oka was considering the following alternatives to the status quo.

Product Consolidation

Consolidation of the 600 product variants would surely help the factory reduce inventory and improve operational efficiency, However, Mr. Oka was unsure how the sales companies, and ultimately the customers, would respond to the consolidation, given the fact that Daikin's market share was under downward pressure and that providing maximum choice was an explicit sales strategy.

Build a Factory Outside Japan

Another possibility would be to build a new factory in China or Malaysia to take advantage of the lower labor costs. This could allow a stronger emphasis on competitive prices. It was not clear how the move would affect Daikin's relationships with its suppliers and sales companies. The move of the manufacturing base would mean that the employees in the affected areas at Shiga Factory would have to be laid off. The company had a policy of no lay-offs, which it was reluctant to abandon. A few could probably be transferred to other Daikin factories in Japan. Other stakeholders might also be affected, so the costs and benefits of this option needed to be thought out carefully.

Exit the Business

While Mr. Oka did not give it much thought, now might be the right time to simply exit the business and divest itself of its assets.

RECOMMENDATIONS TO THE BOARD

Mr. Oka wondered whether there were other alternatives that might help Daikin gain a competitive advantage. While mindful of the rapidly approaching peak season, Mr. Oka was more concerned about long-term survival. Mr. Oka knew that procrastination would diminish the chances of staying in business, much less of growing the business. He also knew that whatever changes he made, he must think of their ramifications for employees, suppliers, retailers and, most importantly, consumers. He had only two weeks until the board meeting at which he would be presenting his recommendations.

NOTES

1. Mr. Oka was a member of Daikin's board of directors, and managing director of residential air conditioning production prior to assuming direct responsibility for the Shiga Factory.

2. Window air conditioners and whole house air conditioning systems were much less common in Japan than they were in North America.

3. ¥1,000 = US$7.17, June 1, 1998.

4. Several of Daikin's competitors maintained warehouses at their sales companies, whereas Daikin held all of its air conditioner inventory at the Shiga Factory.

5. Sourcing from China would add about five days to Daikin's lead time. Some competitors were already operating supply chain times that were five days shorter than Daikin's.

GROCERY GATEWAY: CUSTOMER DELIVERY OPERATIONS

Prepared by Professor P. Fraser Johnson

Dominique Van Voorhis, vice-president of industrial engineering and operations systems for Grocery Gateway, was analyzing the October 2001 monthly report for the company's delivery operations at its Downsview, Ontario, customer fulfilment centre. Although the company was targeting four stops per hour on area (SPHOA) for its drivers, it had been able to achieve only 2.7 stops per hour in the month. It was November 10, and Al Sellery, Grocery Gateway's chief executive officer (CEO), and Claude Germain, the chief operating officer, had asked Dominique to make recommendations aimed at improving delivery operations at the weekly management meeting seven days hence.

GROCERY GATEWAY

Founded in 1997 by Bill Di Nardo, Grocery Gateway was Canada's largest direct online grocer in November 2001, with approximately 125,000 registered customers. Online shoppers could select from 6,500 items at the grocerygateway.com Web site, including dry goods, health and beauty products, meat, fresh produce, frozen foods, wine and beer. Products were priced competitively with grocery retailers, although customers were expected to place minimum orders of $60 and pay an $8 delivery fee. Orders could be altered until about 14 hours prior to delivery.

Grocery Gateway provided its service to residents of the Greater Toronto area (GTA), the largest urban centre in Canada. The company serviced an area of approximately 3,200 square kilometres, with a population of approximately seven million people (see Exhibit 1 for a map of the GTA). On a typical day during the peak period between November and April, Grocery Gateway would receive approximately 1,500 orders with an average value of $135. Sales volumes were subject to some seasonality with orders declining by approximately 50 per cent of peak levels in the summertime. Furthermore, order sizes could fluctuate from 30 to 90 items.

The company offered 90-minute delivery windows from 6:30 a.m. to 10:30 p.m. and orders were delivered directly to the customer's door. Claude Germain commented on Grocery Gateway's strategy:

> We focus on low-cost, high service logistics execution in one market. Some people focus on technology, others on merchandising, but right from the get-go we focused on logistics execution. We wanted to get it right and have the lowest cost capability with the best service we could provide.[1]

In May 2000, Grocery Gateway secured $33 million in second-phase venture capital funding, bringing to $70 million the total private sector financing raised by the company. During its first two years of operation, management had focused on growth and brand awareness. The current business plan called for continued aggressive growth, with a target of 5,000 orders per day within three years. Meanwhile, a primary focus of management was to become cash flow positive in 2001 on a variable cost basis.

CUSTOMER FULFILMENT CENTRE

In May 2001, Grocery Gateway relocated from its original 6,225 square metre customer

Exhibit 1   Greater Toronto Area

fulfilment centre in Mississauga to a new facility in Downsview, north of Toronto (see Exhibit 1). Claude Germain commented on the new facility:

> There are two core capabilities within our business model, broken case picking and direct delivery. Our aim is to have the low-cost position. We have optimized our facility only for broken case and for a pick-per-sku profile of close to a ratio of 1:1. This is the profile of e-commerce orders.
>
> Our new plant is 26,000 square metres at a cost of $15 million. At the design stage, we clearly determined what we wanted to execute against, from a throughput, cost position and capability perspective. We then studied business models out

there and took pieces that seem to fit. Next, we segmented our design into nine segments—a three-by-three matrix that has A, B, C movers on one axis and three temperature zones (ambient, cooler and freezer) on the other. We then tried to fit the best design and technology into each and played with integration issues to arrive at a balance blend that would meet our objectives.[2]

Approximately 275 people worked in Grocery Gateway's customer fulfilment centre. Grocery Gateway's systems integrated a variety of technology solutions, built around five main systems that were used to generate and execute orders. The Web-order processing system was developed in-house.

Orders from the Web were downloaded into the resources in motion system (RIMMS) and the warehouse management system (WMS) twice daily. RIMMS was a dynamic route optimizer solution from Descartes Systems. It provided route delivery schedules generated from algorithms that took into account delivery windows, drive time, time of day, road type and other factors. The WMS was tied to an order processing system (OPS) and a warehouse control system (WCS). The OPS managed the execution of the order picking tasks, handled initiation of the totes and made decisions regarding when an order should be picked to arrive at the truck on time. The WCS was customized software that controlled the movement of totes on the conveyor lines, assisted with fixed-position scanners that read the identity of each tote, much like a licence plate, and directed them accordingly.

For A items, which were the fastest moving skus, employees walked the aisles and picked items directly into totes as instructed by the EASYpick pick-to-light system. The pick lights were mounted on the eight-foot flow racking that held the inventory. In contrast, a batch picking strategy was used for the slower moving B and C items. An entire wave's worth of B and C items were picked simultaneously using radio frequency scanners. Batch picking required deconsolidation, where products were separated into individual orders. During this process, totes were lined up behind lights at the deconsolidation station, where a pick-to-light system instructed employees to place items in appropriate totes. When an order was completed, or the tote was "cubed out," the totes were sent to a print-and-apply station where man-readable labels containing route, stop and address information were applied.

DELIVERY OPERATIONS

Grocery Gateway drivers called 10 minutes before arriving to ensure that customers were available. Unlike other e-tailers, customers paid at the door, not over the Internet. Delivery staff were equipped with remote point-of-sale terminals for debit or credit card transactions.

Grocery Gateway had approximately 100 drivers and a delivery fleet of 55 trucks capable of handling a total of 125 totes filled with dry goods, cold produce and frozen items. Claude Germain described the strategy underlying Grocery Gateway's delivery operations:

> We have optimized around small-order drop-offs. Our average tote-per-order is four to five. Large drops-offs that could benefit from being palletized do not fit our model. Indeed, our trucks are custom designed and resemble UPS trucks—but with three temperature zones.[3]

When Grocery Gateway first started in 1997, drivers would schedule routes manually, which took each driver approximately 30 to 45 minutes per shift. In January 2000, the company purchased RIMMS route optimization software from Descartes. The RIMMS software established the most cost-effective delivery routes based on parameters such as dwell time at the door, vehicle speed and internal vehicle capacity utilization (number of totes). The system provided drivers with specific directions and maps for their routes.

Delivery window capacity management was handled by the Web order processing system. When the software recognized that no additional deliveries could be made within a given time frame, the window was closed.

On average, the driver took 15 minutes for set-up time, 30 minutes for stem time (driving to delivery area), 30 minutes for return to the customer fulfilment centre and 15 minutes for close-out. This left an average of 6.5 hours available for deliveries. Management estimated that the variable cost of a vehicle and driver was approximately $30 per hour.

PERFORMANCE OBJECTIVES

Two key objectives for Grocery Gateway's delivery operations group were to achieve four SPHOA and reduce delivery windows to 30 minutes. In preparation for the meeting the following week, Dominique established what he considered a reasonable breakdown on driver delivery time:

1. Nine minutes of contact time per customer:
    *   Two minutes to park, prepare invoices, identify totes
    *   Two minutes to unload and get to the door
    *   Four minutes with customer—unloading, receiving payment
    *   One minute to return to vehicle
2. Six minutes of drive time per customer:
    *   Average speed in residential areas of 15 kilometres per hour, including starting, stopping, etc.

In preparation for the meeting, Dominique collected information on the most recent week's delivery activity (see Exhibit 2). In October, Grocery Gateway delivery operations achieved 2.7 stops per hour on area (SPHOA), which measured from the beginning of the first stop to the end of the last stop and did not include drive time to and from the delivery area.

Dominique felt that there were a number of alternatives worth considering. First, he could keep the trucks on the road longer by extending driver shifts. However, to execute such a plan he would need a plan to replenish the trucks as well as ensure the high level of service the GGI customer base had become accustomed to. A second option was to approach Descartes, who provided the RIMMS route optimization software, to expand the licensing arrangement to include a new feature that analysed route profitability and to determine the desirability of delivery in particular time slots. Dominique expected this would cost approximately $250,000. A third option was to suggest an increase in the delivery charge. Dominique felt that Grocery Gateway's customers were attracted to the convenience, and charging a slightly higher delivery charge might be a good trade-off compared to decreasing customer service levels.

As Dominique examined the data, he recognized that he still had a week to get ready for the meeting. However, he knew that he must present a thorough plan, one that was consistent with the overall strategy of the company.

NOTES

1. Source: "Pick Pack Pro," Materials Management & Distribution, vol. 46, no. 10, October 2001, p. 35.

2. Source: "An Interview with Grocery Gateway," Logistics Quarterly, vol. 7, no. 2, 2001, p. 30.

3. Source: Ibid., p. 30.

Coverage Area	% Volume	Sun.	Mon.	Tue.	Wed.	Thu.	Fri.	Sat.	Total	% Growth Over Prev. Week
Burlington	1.9	15	27	18	15	27	39	9	150	5.5
Oakville	3.0	21	45	30	21	39	63	15	234	10.2
Mississauga	10.1	96	135	126	84	93	204	48	786	8.3
Brampton	3.6	30	48	51	24	54	66	9	282	6.0
Georgetown	0.5	3	9	0	3	6	12	6	39	23.8
Etobicoke	4.0	30	63	45	36	54	66	18	312	15.2
North York	25.2	81	405	324	240	312	414	195	1,971	8.0
Toronto	34.9	330	465	426	324	390	504	291	2,730	11.0
Scarborough	3.0	18	48	24	27	45	57	15	234	3.2
Pickering/Ajax	2.1	18	36	18	21	21	36	12	162	2.5
Vaughan	3.0	24	39	27	27	33	69	15	234	10.1
Richmond Hill	3.9	33	78	33	30	48	66	15	303	5.0
Newmarket/Aurora	4.9	51	66	57	36	63	66	42	381	13.0
Total	**100.0**	**750**	**1,464**	**1,179**	**888**	**1,185**	**1,662**	**690**	**7,818**	**9.4**

Exhibit 2   Orders per Day

311

LADNER BUILDING PRODUCTS

Prepared by Professor P. Fraser Johnson

     Version: (A) 1999-04-07

Gordon Stephens, logistics analyst for Ladner Building Products (Ladner), a building materials distributor located in Montreal, Quebec, had been asked by Doug Turner, vice president, logistics and materials management, to prepare a report analysing the company's logistics practices. Doug was especially interested in where changes could be made to reduce costs, improve company performance, or accomplish both simultaneously:

> We spend a lot of money on logistics at Ladner— especially in the distribution end of our business. Right now I am not at all satisfied that our area is performing as well as it could. Our delivery performance is getting better, but we still have a ways to go. What troubles me most, however, is that our costs are too high. I'm not sure if we should simply charge more for customer deliveries or take another approach.

It was Monday, August 24, 1998 and Gordon knew Doug did not want a report that simply summarized Ladner's logistics costs—he was expecting Gordon to offer specific recommendations on how to address the problems uncovered. Although Doug wasn't expecting the report for another two weeks, Gordon felt that he would easily need all of that time to analyse the information that he had collected over the past few days and to gather any additional data he might need.

THE BUILDING MATERIALS INDUSTRY

Product Segments

The Canadian building materials industry comprised three main product segments: commodities, industrial, and allied products. The domestic forest products industry provided a competitive supply base for commodity products, including lumber and plywood. Prices for these products were based on commodity exchanges, such as the Chicago Board of Trade and the Winnipeg Commodity Exchange.

Some industrial products, such as hardwood plywoods and particleboard, were essentially commodities. However, others, such as formica counter tops, were manufactured goods with well-established pricing structures. Canadian building materials distributors typically used domestic suppliers as their main source of supply for industrial products.

Allied products included hardware, fasteners and exterior and interior home repair and maintenance items. Typically, only about half of the allied products sold by Canadian building materials distributors were sourced domestically. U.S. companies supplied products for approximately 40 percent of this market segment, while the remaining 10 percent were purchased from offshore suppliers. Building materials distributors were usually able to negotiate pricing arrangements with allied products suppliers that fixed prices for a one-year period.

Customer Groups

Building materials distribution companies in Canada served two main customer groups: dealers and industrial. Dealers included large buying groups and retail chains. The buying group segment, such as Home Hardware, represented independent retailers that combined purchases in an effort to lower acquisition costs and gain access to a wider range of products. Large retail chains included companies such as The Home Depot and Wal-Mart.

There was a wide variety of firms in the industrial segment, including prefab home construction companies, boat and recreational vehicle manufacturers, and cabinet and furniture manufacturers. Most companies in this segment had one manufacturing location.

Dealers and industrial customers typically made purchases from each of the three main product segments. Demand was mostly seasonal, with approximately two-thirds of sales occurring between May and November.

Competition within the building products distribution industry was fierce and margins were low. Operating margins, representing the difference between product acquisition costs and customer purchase prices, averaged 10.5 percent. Most firms competed on a regional basis, with some specializing in a narrow product segment, thereby creating a market that was fragmented both geographically and by product lines. No single firm had a dominant position in the marketplace, and Ladner was one of the few national firms in the Canadian building material industry. Its market share was estimated at four to five percent.

LADNER BUILDING PRODUCTS

Company Operations

Ladner began operations in 1986 for the purposes of selling and distributing products for a large forest product company. Initially, Ladner's product line was limited to the products manufactured by its parent company, such as plywood sheets and wood panels. In 1989, new management was hired as part of an effort to improve Ladner's financial performance and expand its market presence. As a result, Ladner's product base grew dramatically to include a broader range of building product materials, particularly in the allied and industrial product segments.

In August 1998, Ladner had 15 distribution centers, located across Canada. The company's distribution network was divided into five regions: British Columbia, Prairies, Ontario, Quebec and Atlantic. Each region was headed by a general manager, who had profit and loss accountability for the region. Ladner had a total of 385 employees in its distribution centers and 35 staff in the Montreal, Quebec head office. Exhibit 1 provides a corporate organization chart.

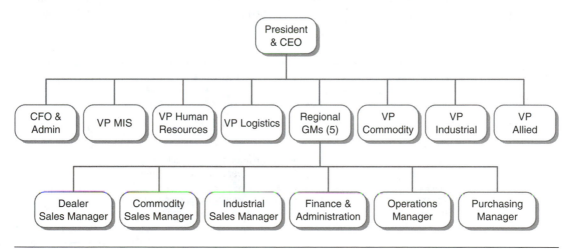

Exhibit 1   Organization Structure

Ladner had sales of $495 million in 1997, with an operating loss of $1.9 million. Although the general economic climate had been strong in Canada, the company had generated losses in each of its last four years.

Ladner offered over 15,000 brand name and private label products. Although Ladner's shareholder was still its largest supplier, the company had a supplier base of approximately 500 organizations. Company products were grouped into seven categories: commodity, industrial, exterior, interior decor, fasteners, storage and shelving and security products. Exhibit 2 provides examples of each product group.

Each region carried approximately 3,000 stock keeping units (SKUs). However, because of differences among the regions, only three percent of the company's SKUs were common across all five regions.

The company had three product vice presidents: commodity, industrial and allied. The product vice presidents were responsible for sourcing, promotions and negotiating supplier contracts. The regions placed orders and scheduled deliveries on the basis of these contracts.

The sales mix among product groups varied substantially. For example, commodity products represented 40 percent of annual dollar volume and 10 percent of Ladner's SKUs, while industrial products accounted for 20 percent of the annual dollar volume and 30 percent of the SKUs.

Customer Base

Ladner served 5,120 customers and 8,525 customer shipping locations. A single customer could have several shipping locations, each with different requirements in terms of products, delivery and volume. These differences made it difficult to establish minimum order sizes, even for large, national retail chains. Both customer orders and deliveries were made on the basis of the individual shipping locations, with very few customers requiring deliveries to central distribution centers.

The company dealt with approximately 20 buying groups and 1,000 large retailers, which accounted for $365 million in sales and 4,360 shipping locations. Customers in the dealer segment used their purchasing power to negotiate volume discounts that averaged one percent.

Sales to the 4,100 firms in the industrial segment varied substantially—some were among Ladner's largest customers, while others were quite small. Most customers in this segment had only one shipping location per customer.

Ladner's regional industrial and dealer sales groups handled requirements for their respective customer segments, with the exception of commodity products. Regional sales groups had both inside and outside sales representatives. The inside sales staff processed customer orders placed over the telephone or by fax, while the outside sales representatives met with customers

Product Category	Examples
Commodity Products	plywood, oriented strandboard, lumber
Industrial Products	formica, particleboard, hardwood plywood
Allied Products	
Exterior	vinyl siding, vinyl fencing, asphalt shingles
Interior decor	mouldings, spindles, columns, wall paneling
Fasteners	nails, screws
Storage and shelving	wood shelving, wire shelving, closet organizers
Security	door locks, dead-bolts, door knobs

Exhibit 2   Product Categories

to solicit new orders, address customer complaints and collect information on market activities.

Prices for commodity products were based on published prices in international commodity exchanges and were, therefore, managed differently from other sales activities. It was not unusual for a Ladner commodity trader to be on the phone with both the supplier and customer negotiating the purchase and selling prices simultaneously. Margins for commodity products ranged from seven to nine percent.

Industrial and allied products had higher margins than commodities. Margins for industrial products ranged from 12 to 15 percent, while allied products were 12 to 28 percent. Generally, products with higher volumes had lower margins.

Large orders for commodity, industrial and allied products could be shipped directly from Ladner's suppliers, bypassing its distribution centers. These "direct mill" shipments were full-truck-load (FTL), and freight was paid by the customer. In 1997, total sales from direct mill shipments amounted to $130 million. Margins on these shipments were usually four percent lower than those shipped from a distribution center.

Doug Turner wondered if the company could do a better job managing the diversity of Ladner's customers and products:

Should we set some parameters regarding our customer base? Maybe we should not accept certain small orders, and send some customers to The Home Depot, which is better at handling small orders. Right now we give too much flexibility to our sales people, who like to get on the phone and play "dial-a-deal." The difficulty is that the sales staff gets evaluated on the basis of product gross margins, which ignores the costs of handling, storage and transportation.

Regional Operations

Ladner's decentralized organization structure provided a great deal of authority to the five regional general managers and their staff (see Exhibit 1). Regional management was given flexibility when negotiating arrangements with customers and establishing distribution policies based on the competitive climate within each region.

Each region had an operations manager, a small purchasing staff, product sales managers and a financial manager, all of whom reported to the regional general manager (see Exhibit 1). The sales staff negotiated the terms of customer orders, including pricing and delivery. The regional operations manager had responsibility for inventory control, warehouse operations and outbound transportation. As part of Ladner's financial planning process, operations managers negotiated annual operating budgets in these three areas and were held accountable for their performance. Budgets were typically based on historical performance and adjusted based on expected changes to regional sales.

The regional purchasing manager was responsible for arranging supplier deliveries, including inbound transportation. The purchasing managers worked off the national contracts negotiated at head office, with the exception of certain unique, small volume requirements for their region.

The regional sales department established delivery charges when negotiating customer orders. Sales representatives could rebate all or part of the delivery charge to customers, depending on circumstances. Rebates could be made for any number of reasons, including high volume orders, promotions or simply because of price pressures.

Logistics and Materials Management

Doug Turner headed Ladner's logistics and materials department. He joined Ladner in 1990 in a newly created position in charge of company-wide logistics activities. Doug had extensive experience in transportation and logistics before joining Ladner.

Doug reported to the president and CEO, Ken Jacobs. Ken had joined Ladner in January 1997 from a large industrial manufacturer, located in Ontario, and had extensive experience in product marketing. Ken was hired with a mandate to turn around Ladner's poor financial performance.

Responsibility for logistics activities at Ladner was shared among several members of the organization. The corporate logistics staff consisted of Doug, Gordon and Bill Jenkins, the transportation manager. Gordon had been with the company for about a year. He had experience with a major consulting firm before returning to school to complete his MBA, and he joined Ladner immediately after graduation.

Doug's head office group was responsible for establishing logistics-related performance objectives, guidelines and policies for the regions, and assisting with their implementation. For example, Doug worked with Ken Jacobs to develop target customer service levels of 95 percent for the company, as measured by line fill rates (LFR).[1] It was up to Doug to work with the regional general managers and their staff to achieve this objective.

THE DISTRIBUTION SYSTEM

Customer Deliveries

Freight charges tended to reflect the industry pricing practices within each region. Consequently, differences existed between regions regarding customer freight policies. Doug had asked Gordon to focus on the Ontario Region when preparing his report. He was particularly interested in this region since it represented 40 percent of total company freight costs.

The Ontario Region had sales of $117 million in 1997, including $28 million in direct mill orders. The balance of the region's sales was handled through one of its four distribution centers. In Ontario, Ladner delivered 91.5 percent of its sales from its distribution centers, charging customers a flat rate of 1.5 percent of sales for delivery fee. According to the region's financial report, Gordon determined that the Ontario Region delivered 81,346 orders from its distribution centers in 1997, and rebated $418,000 in customer delivery charges that year.

Ladner did not have its own truck fleet, but contracted with three regional carriers to handle deliveries for different geographic regions of the province. The Ontario Region classified its deliveries into two groups: local and rural. Both local and rural shipments were handled by highway transport tractor-trailer units with a capacity of 72,000 pounds. Because some of Ladner's products were heavy, trucks that were properly loaded would typically reach the maximum weight before running out of available space.

Gordon knew that in Ontario, carriers were paid $34 per hour and $0.37 per kilometre for local runs, while costs for rural runs were $17 per drop and $0.87 per kilometre. Gordon had collected one fairly typical example of a local run (see Exhibit 3) and another typical example of a rural run (see Exhibit 4). In 1997, the Ontario Region paid $2.827 million to its carriers for customer deliveries.

Pick-Up Orders

Some of Ladner's customers preferred to pick up their orders rather than use the company's delivery system. During 1997, 8.5 percent of distribution center sales in the Ontario region were pick-up orders, representing a total of 11,224 orders during that year.

Ladner did not have many policies regarding pick-up orders, other than payment conditions. Established customers were able to negotiate appropriate credit limits and charge their orders. Other customers were expected to pay at the distribution center with cash or a cheque.

ADDITIONAL CONSIDERATIONS

Gordon felt that Ladner's transportation volume allowed it to negotiate competitive freight rates. Since logistics, including transportation, were a significant expense to Ladner, Gordon understood why Ken Jacobs had identified logistics and materials management as a critical area in his efforts to improve the company's financial performance.

Activity	Invoice Number	Weight[1]	Km.	Time[2]	Sales	Customer Charge	Total Cost
Load			0	2.0	$0	$0	$68.00
Drop #1	35061	14,399	8	2.25	1,120.46	0	79.46
	35069				457.64	0	
Drop #2	34243	795	40	1.25	287.20	4.31	57.30
Drop #3	33673	467	25	1.0	286.08	4.29	43.25
Drop #4	34920	132	15	0.75	525.60	7.88	31.05
Drop #5	34977	215	4	0.75	64.50	0.97	26.98
Drop #6	33617	4,425	4	0.75	960.00	14.40	26.98
	35104				806.40	12.10	
Drop #7	35085	15,322	10	0.75	4,778.28	71.67	29.20
Return			51	1.5		0	69.87
Total		**35,755**	**157**	**11.0**	**$9,286.16**	**$115.62**	**$432.09**

Exhibit 3   Example of One Local Run for One Ontario Regional Distribution Center

1. lbs.

2. hours

Activity	Invoice Number	Weight[1]	Km.	Time[2]	Sales	Customer Charge	Total Cost
Load			0	1.25	$0	$0	$0
Drop #1	35974	5,040	31	1.5	1,680.00	25.20	43.97
Drop #2	36069	744	67	1.75	616.80	9.25	75.29
	34834				218.42	3.28	
	36202				92.55	1.39	
Drop #3	36354	216	27	1.0	153.00	2.29	40.49
Drop #4	35497	8,884	37	1.25	1,519.00	0	49.19
	35738				34.10	0.51	
Drop #5	35876	368	17	0.5	153.09	2.30	31.79
	35766				112.80	1.69	
Drop #6	36383	1,366	8	0.75	509.74	7.65	23.96
Drop #7	31266	5	13	0.5	143.27	2.15	28.31
Drop #8	34941	3,888	4	0.5	658.80	9.88	20.48
Drop # 9	31202	1,385	23	0.75	2,595.84	38.94	37.01
	35376				364.82	5.47	
Drop #10	36007	10	42	1.0	80.80	1.21	53.54
Return			160	2.75			139.20
Total		**21,906**	**429**	**13.5**	**$8,933.03**	**$111.21**	**$543.23**

Exhibit 4   Example of One Rural Run for One Ontario Regional Distribution Center

1. lbs.

2. hours

Gordon knew that a couple of years earlier Ladner moved its freight cost charged to customers from one to 1.5 percent of sales. There had been strong market resistance, particularly from the dealers in Ontario. Some of them even went as far as to boycott Ladner. However, eventually most of Ladner's competitors followed.

As Gordon sat down to review the information, he recognized that it was important to consider how his recommendations might affect other activities in the company such as marketing and sales, regional operations and purchasing. Since Ken Jacobs was a strong proponent of the decentralized structure of the company, Gordon knew that he should be prepared to address the concerns raised by other members of the organization when recommending changes to Ladner's logistics practices. He wondered if he should collect additional information and of what kind to bolster potential changes that he might recommend.

NOTE

1. $LFR = \dfrac{number\ of\ lines\ filled}{number\ of\ lines\ ordered}$

CANADIAN PHARMACEUTICAL DISTRIBUTION NETWORK

Prepared by Professor P. Fraser Johnson

 Version: (A) 2002-03-15

Peter Bromley, the newly appointed general manager of operations for UPS Logistics Group Canada Limited (UPS Logistics), sat in front of his laptop in his office in Oakville, Ontario, preparing for the meeting on Friday, August 10th with the operations committee for The Canadian Pharmaceutical Distribution Network (CPDN). UPS Logistics managed CPDN's product distribution activities for Eastern Canada, and Terry Rooney, CPDN's president, was concerned that the current performance measurement system did not provide him with value-added information. It was late Wednesday afternoon and Peter needed to establish a set of key performance indicators for CPDN's distribution operations to review at the meeting.

CPDN

CPDN was an association of pharmaceutical manufacturers that jointly provided distribution of their products to Canadian hospital pharmacies. Five years earlier, several large pharmaceutical companies recognized two important trends in the market. First, hospitals were largely organized into buying groups and were aggressively seeking cost reductions from their suppliers. Second, distributors were taking an increasing portion of the hospital pharmacy market share, separating the pharmaceutical manufacturers from their traditional customers, the hospital pharmacist and doctor.

To address these challenges, a small group of pharmaceutical manufacturers decided to establish a source of consolidated supply owned and operated by the pharmaceutical companies. After a successful pilot test, CPDN was founded, supported by an initiative of Astra Pharma Inc., Bristol-Myers-Squibb Canada and Glaxo Wellcome Inc. These three companies were the shareholders of CPDN, while approximately 24 other pharmaceutical companies joined as associates. The pharmaceutical companies that used

CPDN's services (e.g., shareholders and associates) were collectively referred to as "members."

CPDN provided integrated order management and distribution services to its members—providing a single point of contact for the hospital pharmacy managers. For convenience to the hospitals, orders were placed through an integrated catalogue and consolidated into a single invoice. This approach eliminated the need for hospital pharmacists to deal with multiple suppliers, allowed customers to make a single payment and provided a single location for product returns. CPDN processed payments to the pharmaceutical manufacturers and administered the product return activities. The individual pharmaceutical companies owned inventories maintained in the CPDN warehouse. The CPDN members paid an annual fee and also paid their share of the monthly distribution costs.

CPDN supplied approximately $300 million of pharmaceutical products to Canadian hospitals each year, which represented approximately 30 per cent of the market. Terry Rooney, CPDN's president, had a small staff that was responsible for hospital and member relationship management. Product distribution—including the order desk, warehousing, inventory control, picking and packing, transportation and accounts receivable management—was outsourced. Medis Health and Pharmaceutical Services Inc. handled distribution in Western Canada, while UPS Logistics was responsible for Eastern Canada. Shipping volumes were approximately 25,000 lines per month in Western Canada and 30,000 lines per month in Eastern Canada. While approximately 550 hospitals across Canada ordered pharmaceutical products from CPDN each month, these customers could order directly from the pharmaceutical manufacturers if they desired.

UPS LOGISTICS SERVICES

With revenues over US$1 billion, UPS Logistics Group was a wholly owned subsidiary of United Parcel Service, which offered a full range of supply chain services in North America, Europe, Asia and Latin America. Peter Bromley had responsibility for four UPS Logistics facilities in Ontario, including the CPDN warehouse.

UPS Logistics handled CPDN distribution activities from a 35,000 square foot warehouse in Oakville, Ontario. Approximately 18,000 square feet of the warehouse was dedicated to providing logistics services for CPDN. Orders could be placed by customers by phone, fax, e-mail or an Internet Web site, and the order desk processed approximately 6,000 orders per month, including backorders. Order picking and packing was scheduled for the 3 p.m. to 11 p.m. shift, to allow for order receiving and replenishment during the day shift. CPDN committed to its customers that all orders received by 4:30 p.m. would be shipped same day, and most deliveries arrived at the customer the next day. All orders were shipped through a national courier company and were accompanied with an invoice.

UPS was responsible for managing CPDN accounts receivable. Although normal payment terms were net 30 days, some hospitals stretched these terms a bit. According to its contract with CPDN, UPS Logistics paid the pharmaceutical manufacturers for all products 45 days after shipment.

THE PERFORMANCE MEASUREMENT SYSTEM

Peter Bromley had just recently been appointed general manager of operations, and addressing problems with CPDN was his first major challenge. Historically, the site manager at the CPDN warehouse reported three performance indicators monthly: inventory accuracy, on-time shipments and receiving turnaround time. Inventory accuracy was based on a percentage of the dollar value of inventory on hand as verified by a physical count versus inventory on record; on-time shipments were measured by the number of same-day shipments as a percentage of the total; and receiving turnaround time was based on the number of shipments received and stocked in 24 hours as a percentage of the total shipments received from the pharmaceutical manufacturers. Each of these measures was "qualified," taking into account conditions controllable by UPS Logistics only. For example, if an inventory adjustment was required as a result of factors caused by the manufacturer, such as incorrect labeling, the performance measure would be modified accordingly. Past performance levels had been very good, and typically approached 100 per cent performance.

This issue of performance measurement was raised by Terry Rooney, who indicated to Peter that some customers were complaining of late shipments while the pharmaceutical companies were concerned about inventory record discrepancies and delays in processing shipments at the warehouse. Terry commented that:

I have too many unhappy customers and members. Last month we had about 2,000 lines backordered and 1,000 orders not shipped on time. As a result, some of the hospitals are getting upset and ordering directly from the manufacturers. Meanwhile, we have problems with inventory discrepancies between the warehouse and our members.

Terry demanded that Peter look into the situation and present his recommendations to the Operations Committee, which was made up of approximately 12 representatives from member companies. Both Terry and Peter decided that an appropriate starting point was to establish a set of key performance indicators, agreed upon by both UPS Logistics and the CPDN Operations Committee. Once the measures were finalized, both men felt they could then proceed to setting improvement plans and targets. Peter described his objective:

There was a credibility gap. We saw our performance as pretty good, but Terry and the pharmaceutical manufacturers were not happy with our performance at all. Furthermore, we couldn't agree on where the problem areas were, how well we were doing in these areas and what levels

represented acceptable performance. We needed to develop a performance measurement package that would provide value-added information to the supply chain partners and provide the basis for corrective action.

CONSIDERING HIS OPTIONS

As Peter sat down to work on his presentation, he knew that his training as a chartered accountant would come in handy. One problem that he would need to address was the conflicting interests of the stakeholders. Terry Rooney, interested in expanding CPDN's market share with Canadian hospitals, would be interested in service levels. The manufacturers, however, were keenly interested in receiving times, inventory management and fulfillment practices. For his part, Peter did not want to be held accountable for problems caused by CPDN, the manufacturers or the hospitals. For example, since the manufacturers owned the inventory and were responsible for replenishment and forecasting, some stock-outs in the past had been caused by product unavailability.

When creating the performance measurement indicators, Peter knew that he needed to address three issues. First, CPDN and UPS Logistics kept all information for individual members confidential, even to the Operations Committee, in order to address concerns regarding collusive trade practices. Second, Peter wanted to clearly define what was being measured and how the performance measures were to be calculated. He felt it was important to hold the various parties—CPDN, the pharmaceutical manufacturers and UPS Logistics—accountable for their performance. Consequently, the metrics had to clearly distinguish between UPS controllable performance indicators and performance measurers controllable by other supply chain stakeholders. Finally, he wanted to focus on a maximum of a dozen indicators and highlight four or five of these as the most critical.

7

OPERATIONS STRATEGY

Over the past several decades, a growing number of managers at all levels of the organization have recognized that successfully managed operations require as much focus on strategic considerations as on tactical concerns such as process design and planning and control. Operations strategy, whether applied in a manufacturing or services context, refers to the pattern of operating decisions and investments used to implement an organization's corporate strategy and to create customer value. Organizations typically make substantial investments in resources and activities with the intent of developing distinct operational capabilities. As you observed from the Industrie Pininfarina case (see Chapter 1), a substantial financial and operational investment was likely required if Pininfarina was to accept the Mitsubishi offer to manufacture a sport utility vehicle. It is critical that managers undertake appropriate, coherent investments in operational structure ("hard" issues) and infrastructure ("soft" issues) based on market opportunities and the requirements of other functional areas.

COMPETING THROUGH OPERATIONS

Generally, there are two basic ways that organizations can leverage operations to yield a competitive advantage (Hayes & Upton, 1998). First, a firm can adopt an operations strategy that offers a competitive advantage along one or more dimensions of customer value that have been largely overlooked by competitors. This may involve, as discussed in the Blinds To Go case, operating in new locations or offering a different means of delivery. This is referred to as a *positioning* or differentiating strategy.

Second, managers can develop a tightly integrated system of supporting values, skills, technologies, supplier or customer relationships, and approaches to human resources that are neither easily copied nor transferable to other organizations. As a result, the firm *executes* a given strategy more effectively than its competitors through the better design and deployment of its operations systems. Each of the cases in this chapter addresses how organizations—whether in a manufacturing or services, or domestic or international, context—can competitively "attack" others or "defend" themselves through implementing an effective operations strategy.

Organizations compete operationally on a number of distinct dimensions. These dimensions include *flexibility* in modifying production mix, volumes, and processes; *delivery* timeliness and reliability; *quality* performance (e.g., conformance, reliability, durability, etc.); and *cost*. These dimensions could represent both competitive priorities (i.e., intended strengths) or competitive capabilities (i.e., realized strengths) and, depending on the specific operational context, order qualifiers or order winners. *Order qualifiers* are the dimensions used for screening products and services for purchase consideration, whereas *order winners* are dimensions used to actually differentiate products and services between firms, resulting in a purchase.

Although organizations have traditionally focused primarily on competing on cost or quality, many have recently recognized the importance of being competitive on all or multiple operational dimensions, as is the situation with ASIMCO International Casting Company. They have also recognized that operational processes, policies, and practices may vary depending on what strategic priority is pursued.

ELEMENTS OF OPERATIONS STRATEGY

Developing an operations strategy requires managers to make a number of operational decisions. These decisions encompass an array of complementary issues that typically include the management of capacity, facilities, process technology and equipment, vertical integration and materials systems, human resources, quality, production control, performance measurement, and organizational design. Collectively, these operational decisions must be aligned with those of other internal business functions and with the requirements dictated by the external business environment. Overall, an effective operations strategy should contribute to the competitiveness of the firm or enhance the competitive advantage that management is seeking.

Implementing an operations strategy requires a focus not only on the content of operating decisions but also on the process employed in making those decisions. An audit of the firm's operating capabilities, largely built on the processes and systems reviewed in early chapters, are typically carried out as part of the overall strategic planning process. However, organizations differ in terms of the specific intent and role operations strategy plays in the strategic planning effort. Hayes and Wheelwright (1984) have provided an insightful classification scheme highlighting these differences. An organization's operations strategy can be classified as follows:

- *Stage 1 (internally neutral):* Operations strategy seeks to minimize the negative contribution of operations to the business.
- *Stage 2 (externally neutral):* Operations strategy allows for the firm to meet and match industry norms.
- *Stage 3 (internally supportive):* Operations strategy aligns with business strategy through more systematic and longer term consideration of operations issues.
- *Stage 4 (externally supportive):* Operations strategy contributes to a world-class organization where operations is viewed as an important competitive weapon for the firm.

Managers need to realize that operations effectiveness not only serves to reinforce a company's existing competitive position but also is inherently difficult to imitate as operating processes, systems, and strategies need to be carefully configured and aligned. The Mitel Semiconductor and Atlanta Symphony Orchestra cases, in particular, highlight some of these operational configuration and alignment issues in manufacturing and services, respectively. Organizations that truly compete through operations-based strategies are constantly examining their competitive environment for new opportunities and potential threats.

WORLD-CLASS OPERATIONS REVISITED

Managers in organizations possessing world-class operations believe that, to compete effectively, they must develop value-added processes that produce and deliver high-quality, low-cost products and services on time, with shortened cycle times and greater levels of responsiveness. As a result, these organizations have systematically and dynamically orchestrated their operational efforts to be aligned with their competitive priorities and environmental demands. By definition, a world-class operation is one that demonstrates best practices in manufacturing or service delivery. World-class operations adopt and use best practices, and they pursue operating strategies that allow them to maximize their competitiveness.

The cases in this operations strategy chapter build on and, in most cases, integrate operational processes and systems issues discussed in the earlier chapters (see Figure 7.1). These cases illustrate decisions that span traditional operating issues such as capacity, plant location, process design and improvement, and factory focus. In addition, emerging relevant issues such as international operations, manufacturing and service integration, and environmental management are raised. The cases depict the operating issues and challenges for Stage 1 to Stage 4 organizations in both the manufacturing and services context.

BUTLER METAL PRODUCTS: FOCUSING THE FACTORY

Tom Peppiatt, the newly appointed general manager of Butler Metal Products, a medium-sized supplier of stampings to the North American automotive industry, was considering changes to his firm's shop floor organization. About two years earlier, his predecessor had switched from a traditional functional hierarchy to focused factories. Although the changes were accompanied by 35% reductions in inventories, throughput times, and defect rates, there was concern that they would not be enough to ensure Butler's survival in the economically stressed automotive industry. The focused factories were struggling with conflicting demands for shared equipment and human resources. Did the factories need to be refocused, left alone, or reverted back to the old organization?

Learning objectives: examine factory focus, illustrate operational strategic choices and their alignment, and evaluate operational turnaround.

MITEL SEMICONDUCTOR

Kirk Mandy, the vice president and general manager of Mitel's semiconductor division, is faced with a rapidly growing market for the company's business communication chips but has limited capacity at the semiconductor plant. There is little industry capacity to outsource production; that which is available can only be secured through substantial up-front investment. With current capacity unable to meet demand and traditional suppliers concentrating on their most important customers, Mandy must determine how to

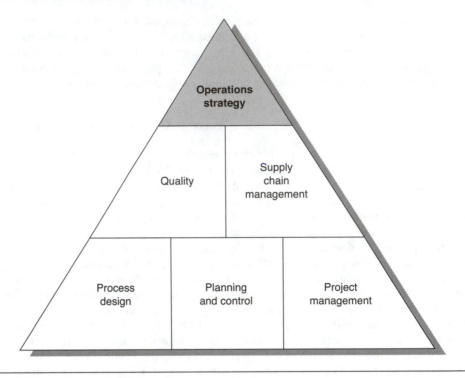

Figure 7.1   Operations Strategy

pursue the growing market and how to secure additional capacity. Options include modifications to the current facility, construction of a new facility, or the acquisition of a plant from another company.

Learning objectives: illustrate strategic importance of capacity decisions and integrate marketing and operations decisions in manufacturing.

ELECTROSTEEL CASTINGS LIMITED

Electrosteel Castings Limited, based in India, had been the largest domestic manufacturer of iron pipes for more than four decades. Although it had achieved solid growth in recent years, the market was under increasing pressure as overall growth slowed and new competitors entered the market. Anil Das, the chief executive officer, believed that international expansion was critical to future growth and would also provide additional currency for further investment in new process technologies. After extensive study, management had narrowed the options to Europe or Southeast Asia. Given limited resources, Electrosteel could only enter one market, with either a new marketing office or a new manufacturing plant. Building an overseas plant was particularly attractive, as it would effectively translate into Electrosteel being considered a local competitor in that market, reducing costs and improving customer service. In recent weeks, the need for a decision had increased significantly, as management had become aware of foreign competitors investigating similar international expansion options. (Note: A video highlighting the manufacturing process of the iron pipes is available from Ivey Publishing, product 7B02D016.)

Learning objectives: examine international production strategies, develop multisite operations and international plant networks, and create operational designs for world-class competitiveness.

BLINDS TO GO: INVADING THE SUNSHINE STATE

Blinds To Go (BTG), a Montreal-headquartered producer of made-to-order window coverings, had made the decision to enter the Florida market by opening eight retail stores. As a result of this decision, Rintaro Kawai, the senior vice president (SVP) of operations for BTG, was faced with the dilemma of deciding if and when an assembly plant should be built to support these and future Florida retail stores. The most recent plant, built in Lakewood, New Jersey, had experienced operational problems during its start-up, resulting in the eventual replacement of most of the supervisory staff and a significant portion of the plant employees. This led to additional start-up costs and customer service problems. Faced with this expansion into Florida, the SVP set about devising an operating plan that would achieve the goals of the Florida expansion without the growing pains of past efforts. As the stores were to be opened in 6 months, a plan would have to be finalized soon.

Learning objectives: integrate manufacturing and services, design a service factory, examine mass customization, and discuss challenges of production plant start-up.

ASIMCO INTERNATIONAL CASTING COMPANY (A)

ASIMCO International Casting Company, a joint venture between ASIMCO and Caterpillar, had recently finished several major projects designed to upgrade the manufacturing capabilities in its foundry. The plant was now under significant pressure to increase revenue and had received an invitation to bid on a new customer order. Although this order might provide the ideal opportunity to further upgrade its process technology and capabilities, significant challenges were presented by several critical product characteristics. Alternatively, the plant's limited resources could focus on meeting the internal needs of one of its partners. Caterpillar was expected to authorize test runs of two new products soon; however, the annual production volumes were very uncertain.

Learning objectives: align product and process requirements, discuss new product start-up and improvement of operating capabilities, and assess innovation risks.

THE ATLANTA SYMPHONY ORCHESTRA

The Atlanta Symphony Orchestra (ASO), conducted by its newly appointed music director, performed a rarely heard composition. The musical performance was, by all accounts, superb. Although most in the audience cheered the performance, a few of the audience members stormed out of the concert hall. These audience members were largely reacting to the high-tech mixed-media show designed by a well-known artist that accompanied the performance. This performance was one of the Atlanta Symphony Orchestra's recent occasional and innovative breaks from concert tradition. John Sparrow, the vice president and general manager of the ASO, recognized that opportunities existed onstage and offstage for broadening and enriching the orchestra's services and the concert experiences of its audience to facilitate growth. Sparrow was examining ways to enhance the ASO's service offerings and improve service delivery.

Learning objectives: contrast operational approaches to innovation, design and deliver effective service encounters, and integrate operations and marketing decisions in services.

NAVISTAR: ENVIRONMENTAL MANAGEMENT (A)

Dan Uszynski, the environmental coordinator at the Chatham Assembly Plant of Navistar International Corporation, must develop a total waste management program that addresses both corporate waste reduction objectives and regulatory requirements. A plantwide waste audit had just been completed by an outside contractor in response to the introduction of provincial legislation, referred to as 3R Regulations. Uszynski must assess the competitive implications of different alternatives, design the program, decide which materials will be recycled, identify who will be involved in implementation, and take into account the reaction of different stakeholder groups. (Note: A sequel to this case, titled "Navistar: Environmental Management (B)" [case 9A96D001], is available from Ivey Publishing.)

Learning objectives: integrate environmental issues and operations; analyze corporate and plant environmental policies, programs, and practices; and examine reverse logistics.

INDIAN OIL CORPORATION LIMITED—THE MATHURA REFINERY

In March 2002, Rakesh Verma, the general manager of Mathura Refinery, had to respond to new national legislation that mandated the production of new, cleaner burning fuels. Although these fuels would reduce vehicular emissions in the country, there was the possibility of increased local emissions from the refinery from the new processes used to produce these fuels. Effluent and oily sludge emissions also demanded management attention. Verma recognized that Mathura Refinery had unique constraints because of its close proximity to the Taj Mahal. Any future expansion of the refinery's capacity would be contingent on its ability to reduce sulfur dioxide emissions and address public expectations.

Learning objectives: management of operating risk and examination of stakeholder analysis and implications for operations.

MANAGEMENT QUESTIONS ADDRESSED IN OPERATIONS STRATEGY CHAPTER

1. What is an operations strategy? What is the role of operations strategy? How are operations strategies developed?

2. What constitutes an effective or ineffective operations strategy? Describe "offensive" and "defensive" approaches for managing a firm's operations.

3. How can firms compete operationally? Describe the concepts of competitive priorities, competitive capabilities, order winners, and order qualifiers.

4. Define the concept of *world-class operations*. What is required for the operational design and execution of world-class organizations? Please give examples of world-class operations and describe what makes these organizations world class.

5. What is the value of operational focus? How can an organization focus itself operationally?

6. What dynamics exist in the management of operations strategy? Examine the challenges these dynamics create for managing operations strategy.

7. What are the strategic challenges in managing operations internationally?

REFERENCES

Hayes, R. H., & Upton, D. M. (1998). Operations-based strategy. *California Management Review, 40*(4), 8–25.
Hayes, R. H., & Wheelwright, S. C. (1984). *Restoring our competitive edge.* New York: John Wiley.

BUTLER METAL PRODUCTS: FOCUSING THE FACTORY

Prepared by Wendy Osborne under the supervision of Professor Chris Piper

Version: (A) 2002-03-22

In November 1991, Tom Peppiatt was contemplating changes to Butler Metal Products' focused factories. Tom had just been transferred from his position as vice-president of finance of Butler's parent company, BMG Canada, and appointed as Butler's general manager. Twenty-two months earlier, Tom's predecessor had replaced Butler's traditional functional hierarchy with a focused factory concept. Although throughput times, inventories and defect rates had each decreased by more than 35 per cent, Tom was concerned that the changes would not be enough to ensure Butler's survival in the economically stressed automotive sector.

BUTLER METAL PRODUCTS

Butler manufactured automotive stampings and assemblies for North American car companies. Butler and BMG shared premises in Cambridge, Ontario. Butler supplied about 100 end-products on a just-in-time (JIT) basis to 19 customer locations. Exhibit 1 shows three automotive products that are representative of its stamping and assembly activities.

Butler made a pre-tax profit (before deducting charges for the corporate office) of $0.6 million on sales of $75.8 million during the 10 months ending March 31, 1990, and lost $1.7 million on sales of $72.9 million during the fiscal year ending March 31, 1991. In November 1991, Butler had approximately 300 hourly and 70 salaried employees.

The Manufacturing Process

Butler's major raw material was coils of steel which it received on a JIT basis. The manufacturing process began when the operators loaded the coils onto presses that straightened the steel and punched out ("blanked") the basic form of the part. Butler had eight blanking presses ranging from 250 to 800 tons. The parts then moved to one of 44 forming presses (ranging from 55 to 2,600 tons) which bent ("formed") them into their final shape and pierced additional holes. The larger presses required special foundations

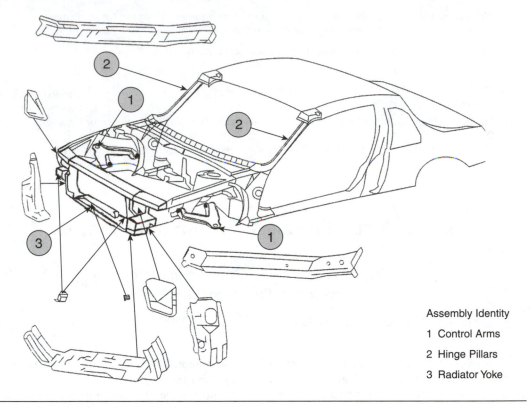

Assembly Identity

1 Control Arms

2 Hinge Pillars

3 Radiator Yoke

Exhibit 1   Car Parts and Assemblies Made by Butler

that made moving them expensive. A manager commented:

> Large presses are like houses—each has its own foundation. Just as you couldn't move a house onto another house's foundation, you can't move a machine onto another machine's foundation. You have to re-cut floors and pour concrete. It would cost about $100,000 to dismantle a 1,000 ton press, pour a foundation and reassemble it. It costs $10,000 to $15,000 to move a smaller (< 250-ton) press.

After being formed into their final shape, the parts moved to assembly. Butler had 10 robotic welding stations dedicated to high volume parts, plus 18 multipurpose welders. The company subcontracted other work such as heat treating and painting. The plant was divided into seven areas for reference purposes, which are lettered A through G on Exhibit 2. In general, material flowed from top to bottom.

BUTLER'S ORGANIZATION STRUCTURE BEFORE FEBRUARY 1990

Before February 1990, Butler had a functional organization structure (see Exhibit 3). Hourly employees, who were members of the Canadian Auto Workers Union (CAW), worked on one of two shifts. The A-shift operated five eight-hour day-shifts per week and the B-shift operated four 10-hour evening-shifts per week. Some maintenance and tool room activities were done in the six hours between the end of the evening shift and the start of the day shift.

As can be seen from Exhibit 3, no technical personnel reported to the plant manager. Moreover, the interaction between management, technical personnel, and people on the shop floor, was limited. One of the supervisors described the lack of communication:

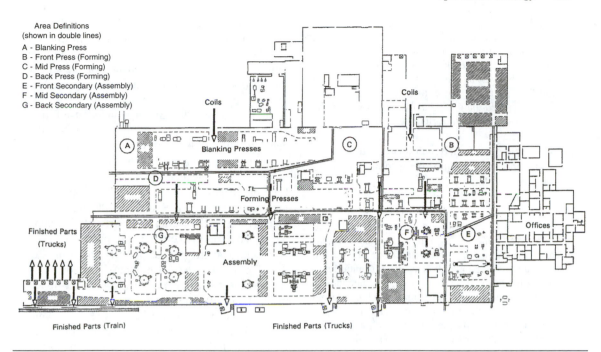

Exhibit 2   Plant Layout and Work Flow

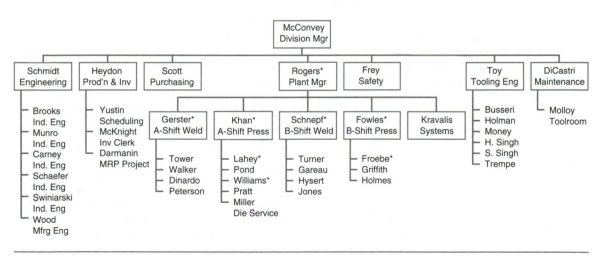

Exhibit 3   Functional Structure Before February 1990

*Left organization after this.

I came in one night to work the B-shift and there was this new machine. The engineers had built it, tested it, and then left it in my area with a note left on it saying: "Use this to run [the customer's] parts." That was it. I'm sure they spent lots of time figuring out the best way to use it, but that's all I got. I assumed the green buttons meant go and the red ones stop, and got it running.

The number of hourly workers required in the plant depended on the jobs being run. One of the supervisors explained:

With presses, the number of people required depends on the type of die and the number installed in a press. One die in a press making one part requires one person. Four dies in one press could need up to four people. It also depends on through-put. If the press isn't a bottleneck, and the job isn't a rush, instead of two people removing parts from a press, just one can do it but takes slightly longer. The number of people required to do welding depends on the type of job too. One product has a manual welding line with four people doing manual welds. Another has a robot doing the welding with one person checking and doing touch-up welds.

Butler paid incentive rates to the forming press and welder operators. Blanking press operators, who did their own setups, were paid a flat rate. Supervisors were responsible for equipment utilization and efficiencies in their area. To keep these measures high, they preferred to run the largest possible batches. Occasionally, supervisors authorised short setup jobs to be run in anticipation of future requirements.

Under Butler's functional organization, it was impossible for customers to determine who was responsible for their products. No one at Butler was responsible for ensuring customer satisfaction.

FOCUSED FACTORIES

In the late 1980s the North American auto makers instituted plans to certify their suppliers' commitment to continuous improvement in the areas of management, quality, cost, delivery and technology. For example, General Motors'

Targets for Excellence (TFE) was a formal program that was aimed at motivating its suppliers to adopt company-wide continuous improvement processes focusing on customer satisfaction. To meet this challenge, Butler had to become more customer focused.

In February 1990 Butler divided itself into six focused factories. Exhibit 4 illustrates the new structure. Three of the focused factories made parts for General Motors (GM). These were for the so-called "W-cars" (the Chevrolet Lumina, Buick Regal, Cutlass Supreme). The factories were called "Rad Yoke," "Control Arm" and "Hinge Pillar" after the parts of the same name. The fourth factory made parts for GM's K-Truck. The fifth made products for Chrysler and Tecumseh. The sixth focused factory was responsible for the blanking presses, and made products for all other customers.

The focused factory managers (FFMs) were responsible for providing customer liaison. Each FFM reported to the group factory manager. Welding stations and presses that were dedicated to specific products became the responsibility of the appropriate FFM. Butler provided dedicated support for the FFMs by dividing its industrial engineers, tooling engineers, schedulers, and skilled trades (such as electricians) among the factories.

With the change to focused factories, the divisional manager became the general manager. The human resources manager and controller who had previously reported to BMG's vice president of finance, now reported to the general manager. The quality control manager, who had also reported to BMG, now reported to the Group Factory Manager.

BMG management believed that the focused factories were more responsive to the customers' needs and provided their employees with a customer and product focus to their work. The assignment of technical personnel directly to the factories broke down functional barriers and improved responsiveness to problems on the shop floor. Butler credited its focused factories for improved customer measures, and its successful completion of GM's Target for Excellence (TFE) audit.

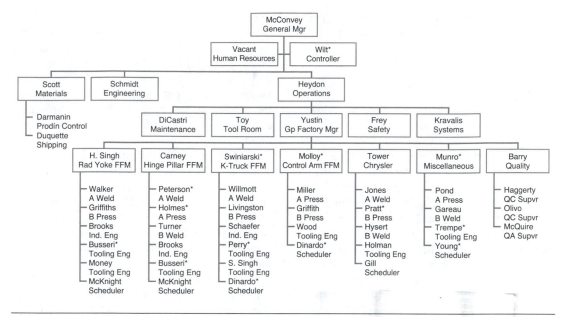

Exhibit 4   Focused Factories From February 1990 Until March 1991

*Left organization after this.

Quarterly Review

Early in 1991 management reviewed the performance of its focused factories, and concluded that, although customer responsiveness had improved, further progress was required. The FFMs were seen to be a major problem. All were young, with about five years work experience, and had no management training. They were having difficulties in the areas of planning, budgeting, delegation, communication, and dealing with difficult people. One FFM described his situation:

> We were told we could run everything now, but we didn't know what to do. We became FFMs in February and had to prepare budgets for the new fiscal year starting April 1. None of us had ever done a budget before and we weren't given any help. Butler started using a new MRP-based scheduling system at about this time. I had to teach myself how to use it at the same time as I was learning to run my factory. We tried to find each other's strengths and help each other out. However, we still had conflicts.

The FFMs had different backgrounds: one had worked on the floor and knew the union contract, one had worked for maintenance and was familiar with the skilled trades, one was a tooling engineer who had experience with tooling, and three were industrial engineers who knew the cost structure of the product. Although the FFMs tried to help each other out, they had too many crises to deal with in their individual areas.

Technical services were another problem. The production supervisors were not skilled trades people, yet they were supervising people doing jobs the supervisors had never done. The Maintenance, Toolroom and Engineering service groups still existed, but they had lost most of their people to the focused factories. As a consequence they did not provide assistance to the FFMs because "they had their own people." The maintenance manager was responsible for the maintenance budget, but the FFMs were charging to it.

The factories also had problems sharing equipment. Sometimes more than one focused factory made heavy use of a particular press.

Although each press supervisor reported to only one FFM, the other FFMs whose products shared his press also made demands on him.

Refinement: Three Factories

During 1990, when the economy slowed down and entered a recession, the automotive sector was hard hit. The car companies made fewer cars, and therefore ordered fewer parts from Butler. Butler responded by reducing its hourly employees from over 500 to about 300.

In March 1991, Butler consolidated Rad Yoke, Control Arm and Hinge Pillar into a single focused factory, and merged Chrysler/Tecumseh with Miscellaneous. The three factories that remained shared the indirect labor and split the costs roughly evenly. At the same time, the operations manager moved his office to the shop floor to increase his accessibility and to provide additional support to the FFMs. The number of levels of management was reduced by eliminating the position of group factory manager. Skilled trades were re-centralized under the maintenance manager. The quality function was given more visibility by having the quality manager report directly to the general manager. Exhibit 5 summarizes the revised organization.

Two months later, the general manager left.

Despite the factory consolidations, equipment-sharing problems persisted. Each FFM was supposed to be responsible for the equipment used to make his product. In reality, there were substantial overlaps. Exhibit 6 shows the extent of equipment-sharing between focused factories.

The biggest problem with equipment-sharing was the large blanking presses, which were worth several hundred thousand dollars. The two

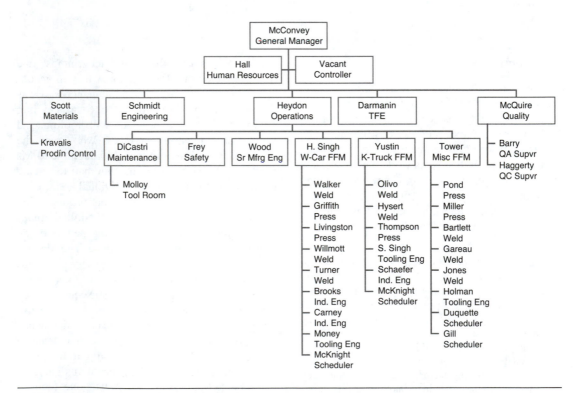

Exhibit 5   Revised Focused Factories After March 1991

Focused Factory: W-Car

Back Press Area (D)
  8 presses from 150–2000 tons
    1 800-ton dedicated to Miscellaneous
  2 3-press work stations
  2 nut welders

Back Secondary Area (G)
  6 robotic welding stations
  2 stud welders

Focused Factory: K-Truck

Mid Press Area (C)
  7 presses from 150-2600 tons
    3 dedicated to Miscellaneous
      (600, 450, and 175 tons)
    1 dedicated to W-Car (150 tons)
  1 2-press work station dedicated to W-Car

Mid Secondary Area (F)
  4 robotic welding stations
  1 welder
  1 nut welder

Focused Factory: Miscellaneous

Blanking Press Area (A)
  8 presses from 250–800 tons
    4 shared between W-Car and Miscellaneous
    2 shared between K-Truck and Miscellaneous
    1 dedicated to W-Car (400 tons)

Front Secondary Area (E)
  4 welders
    1 dedicated to W-Car
  3 welding stations
  1 55-ton press shared between W-Car and
    Miscellaneous
  1 drill press

Front Press Area (B)
  11 presses from 150–1000 tons
    1 dedicated to W-Car (1000 tons)
    1 shared between W-Car and Miscellaneous
  3 press work stations (one consisting of
    3 presses, one with 2 presses and 2 nut welders)
    1 shared between W-Car and Miscellaneous
      (consisting of two 600-ton presses)

Exhibit 6   Equipment Assigned to Focused Factories[1]

1. Unless otherwise noted, equipment is dedicated to the focused factory's parts. The letters in brackets after each area refer to the labels on the plant layout in Exhibit 2.

biggest bottlenecks were a 700-ton and an 800-ton press. Exhibit 7 provides a representative schedule for these two machines. Although every Butler product started here, the supervisor reported only to the Miscellaneous FFM. Exhibit 8 provides sample employee assignments for four consecutive weeks. The numbers were lower during the first two weeks because a major customer temporarily closed a plant.

Mike Tower, the Miscellaneous FFM described some of the equipment-sharing problems that arose:

The equipment-sharing problem is mostly a people problem. For example, one press in the W-Car

focused factory is dedicated to making Miscellaneous parts. If the press supervisor needs people for a W-Car job he will borrow them from the press that is assigned to my parts because he is not measured on its output.

Sometimes I can't get a press to do my jobs because it's being staffed by another focused factory. For example, the biggest press in the shop runs parts almost exclusively for K-Truck, our highest dollar-value product. It is also scheduled to run two shifts every two weeks to make a part for me on a much smaller contract. My supervisor goes over to the press and says, "I'm entitled to use this press now" and they say, "No, you can't have it." What am I supposed to say to my customers?

If a supervisor needs more people to complete a job he tries to borrow them from another factory. When a job goes down, if the supervisor can't find another job in his area, he puts the operator on clean-up. If another focused factory's supervisor asks if he can borrow the operator the answer is usually no, because the supervisor is afraid that if he gives the guy up he won't be able to get him back when he needs him. The attitude is, "I am measured on my department and I don't care about yours."

700-Ton Blanking Press

Part	Factory Supplied	Time (hours) Set-Up	Time (hours) Run	Number of Operators	Order Quantity	Start Day	End Day
A	K-Truck	3.0	0.00114	1	16,000	6	8
B	K-Truck	3.0	0.00083	1	13,600	7	9
C	Miscellaneous	2.5	0.00080	1	4,000	8	9
D	Miscellaneous	3.0	0.00086	1	4,250	8	9
A	K-Truck	3.0	0.00114	1	8,200	9	13
E	W-Car	2.0	0.00081	1			

(Part E was not required in this week.)

800-Ton Blanking Press

Part	Factory Supplied	Time (hours) Set-Up	Time (hours) Run	Number of Operators	Order Quantity	Start Day	End Day
F	W-Car	2.0	0.00135	2	12,495	1	9
G[2]	Miscellaneous	1.5	0.00125	1	16,960	2	6
H	Miscellaneous	1.5	0.00062	2	6,000	6	7
I	Miscellaneous	1.5	0.00062	2	6,000	7	8
J	Miscellaneous	1.5	0.00125	3	3,000	7	8
K	Miscellaneous	1.5	0.00125	3	3,000	7	8
L	Miscellaneous	3.0	0.00125	2	2,800	7	8
M	W-Car	9.0	0.00072	2	15,000	8	9
N	W-Car	3.0	0.00072	2			

(Part N was not scheduled in this week.)

Exhibit 7   Representative Weekly Capacity Load at Two Bottleneck Blanking Presses (Schedule Issued on Tuesday, Day 7[1])

1. The schedule is shown as being issued on day 7 to be consistent with the start of part F on Wednesday, six calendar days earlier. Days 4 and 5 were on the weekend, when most of the plant was closed.

2. Part G should have been completed on Monday (day 6). It is now one day late.

Production	Week 1 Shift A	Week 1 Shift B	Week 1 Total	Week 2 Shift A	Week 2 Shift B	Week 2 Total	Week 3 Shift A	Week 3 Shift B	Week 3 Total	Week 4 Shift A	Week 4 Shift B	Week 4 Total
Hinge Pillar (W)	7	0	7	7	0	7	10	4	14	10	4	14
Back Press (W)	20	0	20	20	0	20	25	25	50	25	25	50
A. Pillar (W)	2	0	2	2	0	2	1	0	1	1	0	1
Rad Yoke (W)	8	0	8	8	0	8	12	8	20	12	8	20
Middle Press (K)	14	10	24	14	10	24	16	12	28	18	14	32
K-Truck (K)	17	13	30	17	13	30	12	11	23	12	11	23
MIG Weld (K)	6	4	10	6	4	10	4	4	8	4	4	8
Blanking Press (M)	8	4	12	8	4	12	9	5	14	10	8	18
Front Press (M)	15	0	15	15	0	15	14	7	21	14	7	21
Front Secondary (M)	10	4	14	10	4	14	10	4	14	10	4	14
Service (S)	5	1	6	5	1	6	4	3	7	4	3	7
Lift Truck (S)	8	3	11	8	3	11	8	7	15	8	7	15
Total Production	**120**	**39**	**159**	**120**	**39**	**159**	**125**	**90**	**215**	**128**	**95**	**223**
Non-Production												
Senior Shipper (P)	1	0	1	1	0	1	1	0	1	1	0	1
Receiving (P)	3	0	3	3	0	3	3	0	3	3	0	3
Stock Room (P)	1	1	2	1	1	2	1	1	2	1	1	2
Yard Truck (P)	1	1	2	1	1	2	1	1	2	1	1	2
Shipping Lift Truck (P)	2	0	2	2	0	2	2	1	3	2	1	3
Shipping Clerk (P)	1	0	1	1	0	1	1	0	1	1	0	1
Truck (P)	1	0	1	1	0	1	1	0	1	1	0	1
Inspection (Q)	6	3	9	6	3	9	7	5	12	7	5	12
Quality Assurance (Q)	4	0	4	4	0	4	4	0	4	4	0	4
Rework (Q)	3	0	3	3	0	3	3	0	3	3	0	3
Union	2	1	3	2	1	3	2	1	3	2	1	3
Total Non-Production	**25**	**6**	**31**	**25**	**6**	**31**	**26**	**9**	**35**	**26**	**9**	**35**
Total Workers	145	45	190	145	45	190	151	99	250	154	104	258
Allowance for (5%)	8	2	10	8	2	10	8	5	13	8	5	13
Grand Total	**153**	**47**	**200**	**153**	**47**	**200**	**159**	**104**	**263**	**162**	**109**	**271**

Exhibit 8   Representative Personnel Assignments[1]

1. Production workers are assigned to the focused factory indicated in brackets: (W) W-Car, (K) K-Truck, (M) Miscellaneous or (S) shared between focused factories. Non-production workers are assigned to: (P) Production Control or (Q) Quality.

TOM PEPPIATT TAKES OVER

In November 1991, BMG's president, Jim Robinson, announced that Tom Peppiatt would be the new general manager of Butler Metal Products. Peppiatt, an accountant, had been with Butler for 15 years. He described how he became GM:

After the previous general manager left in June, we began a search to find a replacement and Jim and I filled in as general manager part time. In the meantime, sales were going way down. In August, it was time to start negotiating a contract with the union. The human resources manager had left in 1990. We had hired Monica Hall in February 1991, and we realized she would need support negotiating the contract. The only person who had been at the table before was me—I had been at every union-company negotiation. I stepped in to help Monica and got a good feel for what was going on.

In mid-September, on a Monday morning, Jim and I had a meeting scheduled. I had come to the realization that the company didn't need a general manager with technical expertise, it needed someone who could add the human element and that person was me. I went into the meeting to tell this to Jim, only to find out that Jim had come to the same decision. Once the union negotiations had been completed, I became general manager.

Peppiatt described his style of management:

I have always shared information with my people. Sometimes I got into trouble for showing them forecasted financial information that was considered to be confidential. In my opinion, that's the only way to manage. If people don't have access to the same information that management does, how can you expect them to buy into the need for change?

He summarized his concerns with Butler's focused factories as they were currently constituted:

Focused factories added more levels of management between the general manager and the people on the floor. I was concerned about this at the time and mentioned it to our previous general manager. The first change to the focused factory concept went away from a well-defined focused factory, but eliminated one level of management. To me this wasn't enough. People make this place run. The way we make money is how we use our people.

Focused factories tried to segregate resources. Our type of work does not lend itself to this. We have multi-use equipment. Our key to profitability is the management of people. The people management was poor in the focused factories. Each FFM was staffing equipment to his needs—one could be laying people off when the other was recalling people.

The B-shift had traditionally been the better shift at this company and usually did outstanding work. Lately they had become the black sheep, and

their output had dropped substantially. This happened because focused factories focused on the A-shift. Previously there had been superintendents in charge of each shift. Now, no one was in charge of the B-shift; the highest level of management was the area supervisors, who were left on their own.

The union had a terrible attitude. I saw it when I was at the negotiating table in the summer of 1991. The focused factories had dehumanized the working environment and treated people as pieces of equipment.

Butler went into the focused factories without providing any training for the people. The company put young inexperienced people into positions of authority without training, and as a result, experienced some failures.

The costs of direct labor and overhead were going way up. Rumors were rampant: the company was being sold, going bankrupt, Jim was quitting, I was quitting, etc.

When the company went to the focused factory structure it tried to create profit centres in each factory, a situation which created enormous allocation problems. We evaluated the FFMs on profits, but they had no control over sales, material, overhead or service costs.

TOM PEPPIATT'S CHALLENGE

Butler's sales had dropped 33 per cent in the two years prior to Peppiatt becoming general manager. The outlook for the domestic automotive sector was not promising. Total sales were declining and foreign auto makers were making increasing inroads into the North American car market. Butler's customers were forecasting permanently decreased market shares and unit volumes. Moreover, in return for concessions from the United Auto Workers union, the car companies in the United States had guaranteed the union certain employment levels. To fulfil their promises car manufacturers were actively considering internal sourcing of parts currently made by outside suppliers like Butler. Thus,

Butler not only faced declining order quantities for the parts it made, but also risked losing some parts altogether if its customers decided to make rather than buy.

Butler needed to find additional customers to maintain sales. Butler was attempting to obtain orders from the North American-based Japanese auto makers. Sales to these "transplants" would be slow in coming, however, because Japanese managers preferred to buy parts from suppliers with which they had established long-term relationships.

To stay in business the company had to improve performance and quality and reduce costs. The internal problems with the focused factories were limiting Butler's ability to compete. Peppiatt had to get everyone in the company working together to serve the existing customers and develop new ones. He wondered what he should do.

MITEL SEMICONDUCTOR

Prepared by Gavin Liddy
under the supervision of Professors
Mark Vandenbosch and David Large

Version: (A) 1999-08-12

It was late on a Friday afternoon in September 1995 as Kirk J. Mandy, vice president and general manager of Mitel's Semiconductor Division, sat back in his chair and stared out over the vast Mitel Campus in Kanata, Ontario. He had just finished reading the Semiconductor Division Investment options for FY 1996 through 2001, and sighed as he pondered his upcoming meeting with Mitel's president and CEO, Dr. John B. Millard. Given the production challenges and opportunities facing Mitel Semiconductor over the next five years, Kirk knew that Dr. Millard would expect a firm recommendation on which option to table at Mitel's October 15th board meeting. Having analysed each option thoroughly, Kirk realized that it was decision time, and leaned forward to ask his assistant, Jill Seymour, to schedule a meeting with the directors of Mitel Semiconductor. As he left his office that day, Kirk pledged to enjoy himself over the next two days because it was likely to be his last free weekend for a couple of months.

SEMICONDUCTORS

Semiconductors had become so important to the modern economy that it was now difficult to envision life before they existed. Semiconductors, initially developed in the 1960s, were used to make the integrated circuits (chips) that formed the backbone of all electronic devices. Consumer electronics, automobiles, aeroplanes, space travel, appliances and many other products depended on semiconductors to perform even the most basic operations. Computers, medical equipment, entertainment, telecom, datacom and whole industrial sectors had been developed or restructured as a result of the introduction of the semiconductor. Even those industrial or service sectors that did not directly contain or service semiconductors could not be competitive without the semiconductor-based production, automation and management equipment that was used to create, manufacture, and deliver products or services. According to several sources, worldwide semiconductor sales were expected to reach

US$140 billion by 1996. Longer-term estimates showed sales growth in excess of US$300 billion by the turn of the century and a market of US$1 trillion in ten to twelve years.[1]

The word semiconductor actually referred to the polysilicon material used to make integrated circuits. The polysilicon was made by purifying and crystallizing (growing) sand, which was then shaped through circular molds to form solid cylinders of various diameters. These cylinders were then cut into 0.44mm thick wafers and polished to provide a base onto which a circuit could be etched. Using an analogy comparing an integrated circuit to a road map, the basic building block of an integrated circuit was the transistor or street. In the same way that many streets form a neighbourhood, transistors were combined in accordance with the integrated circuit design to construct logical devices, for example, a memory cell. Numerous logical devices were then combined to form the city or DIE, which was an unpackaged integrated circuit or chip. Depending on the complexity of the integrated circuit, a single fabricated silicon wafer could contain thousands of chips and the transistor count on a single DIE could be as high as six million.

Integrated circuits were manufactured in a three-stage process:

1. *Masking.* In the first step, the circuit design was converted into a series of thin film "masks" which allowed the circuit pattern to be etched onto the wafer one layer at a time.

2. *FAB.* In the fabrication stage, the wafers were coated with very thin layers of insulators. A mask was then placed over the wafer and was used to control the exposure of the insulating layers to ultraviolet light, electron beams, or x-rays which etched the wafer to form the desired patterns. This process might be repeated 10 to 15 times until the entire integrated circuit was etched onto the wafer. Once the etching process was complete, the wafers were "doped" to induce electronic flow. The wafer now contained several thousand integrated circuits or DIE.

3. *Test and Probe.* The wafers were tested, bad DIE were marked and the wafers were cut into individual unfinished chips and sorted for assembly. Each DIE was then glued or soldered to a lead frame, wires were attached, and the whole unit was sealed to protect the DIE. The packaged integrated circuit or chip was then retested.

In summary, the semiconductor process converted sand into silicon wafers, then fabricated and tested the integrated circuit producing thousands of chips from each wafer.[2]

In 1995, two important technological trends were affecting semiconductor manufacturers:

1. *Wafer Size.* Within the semiconductor industry wafers were made in three diameters: 100mm; 150mm; 200mm; and several semiconductor companies expected to have 300mm wafer lines running by 1998. Wafer diameter determined the capacity of the foundry making the chips because the larger the wafer, the greater the surface area from which chips could be made. For example, the area of a 200mm wafer was 1.77 times greater than that of a 150mm wafer.

2. *Line Width.* Line width referred to the actual width of the transistors on the integrated circuit. Line widths varied from 9 microns (m) to today's leading edge technology of 0.35m. The fundamental reason for moving to lower line width technology was to achieve lower DIE costs. In most cases a manufacturer moving to the next generation technology was able to double the number of DIE per wafer for an increased cost of between 25 and 33 per cent. From the integrated circuit user's perspective, smaller line width improved chip performance by increasing the operating speed and lowering the voltage.

MITEL

History

Mitel's two founding members, Michael Cowpland and Terry Matthews, incorporated and organized the corporation in 1971 ("Mitel" is generally understood to be an acronym for Mike and Terry's Lawnmowers).

Investing $20,000 of their own money and another $100,000 from partners, Mitel launched its first product in 1973: a device that allowed companies to use touch-tone phones without replacing existing lines designed for rotary phones. This product was quickly followed by a PBX system that was cheap and reliable due to a special chip Mitel had designed. The early years at Mitel were characterized by brash entrepreneurial spirit and technological innovation. Mitel lore suggested that, when the company was a four-man operation, Cowpland and Matthews wanted to convince a potential customer that the company was bigger than it actually was so they tacked up Mitel signs in their leased building and convinced other tenants to pose as Mitel employees.

By 1977, the company had sold more than 50,000 touch-tone converters, had offices in more than a dozen countries, had doubled sales for each of the last five years and was employing more than 200 people. Key to Mitel's success was the in-house-designed semiconductor-based PBX. PBX sales based on these newer chips led to explosive growth throughout the seventies. Mitel went public in 1980 and started to develop a new switching system, the SX-2000, capable of handling up to 10,000 lines.

By 1982, Mitel was one of the world's five fastest growing companies with more than 4,000 employees and more than $200 million in sales. The success didn't last forever, and as kind as the seventies were to Mitel, the exact opposite would be true of the eighties. The wheels came off in 1983 when the U.S. government broke up AT&T's monopoly and Mitel lost 25 per cent of its PBX market within two months. Development of the SX-2000 fell behind schedule, and as a result,

IBM withdrew from a potential deal and dealt instead with a major competitor. Mitel's share of the PBX market dropped from 11 to 9.9 per cent while the overall market grew by 23 per cent. In 1986 British Telecom (BT) purchased 51 per cent of Mitel for $322 million and Cowpland resigned his position as chairman.

Despite having cleared an accumulated debt of $260 million, BT was unable to turn the company around or break the trend of almost continuous losses. BT put the company on the block in 1991 and it wasn't until June 1992 that Schroder Ventures purchased 51 per cent of Mitel for $60 million. At a purchase price of $1.40 a share, this represented a significant reduction from its peak trading value of slightly over $40 in 1983. The company soon stabilized with the emergence of a new product line, certainty of ownership and new management. Posting its last loss in 1992, the company's sales and earnings have climbed steadily from $363 and $(5.7) million to $589 and $42 million, respectively, for fiscal year (FY) 94/95. More importantly for Schroder, Mitel's share price climbed to $7.50 by the end of the first quarter of FY 95/96.[3] Exhibits 1 and 2 present detailed financial statements.

The Corporation

Mitel developed, manufactured and sold electronic communications products and semiconductors. Mitel's product lines were divided into three principal types: customer premise equipment (CPE), semiconductors, and other communication products.

Sales for the three product lines are shown below:

Table A Sales in Millions of Dollars (FY ending)

	Mar. 31, 1995		Mar. 25, 1994		Mar. 26, 1993	
Customer Premise Equipment	458.5	78%	381.4	77%	336.8	80%
Semiconductors	87.7	15%	71.0	14%	51.5	12%
Other	42.6	7%	44.0	9%	35.1	8%
Total	588.8	100%	496.4	100%	423.4	100%

Assets	31-Mar-95	25-Mar-94
Current Assets		
Cash/Cash Equivalents	$141.3	$101.1
Accounts Receivable	$128.5	$102.7
Inventory	$70.8	$78.5
Prepaid Expenses	$4.5	$3.8
	$345.1	$286.1
Fixed Assets	$81.5	$78.8
Other Assets	$12.4	$11.5
	$439.0	**$376.4**
Liabilities & Shareholders' Equity		
Current Liabilities		
Accounts Payable	$95.0	$85.9
Income & Other Taxes Payable	$9.2	$9.2
Deferred Revenues	$23.8	$12.9
Current Portion of LTD	$9.0	$3.9
	$137.0	$111.9
Long-Term Debt (LTD)	$34.5	$27.8
Deferred Income Taxes	$4.5	$5.0
	$176.0	$144.7
Shareholders' Equity		
Capital Stock	$188.3	$190.1
Contributed Surplus	$32.4	$32.5
Retained Earnings	$31.7	$3.4
Translation Account	$10.6	$5.7
	$263.0	$231.7
	$439.0	**$376.4**

Exhibit 1 Mitel Corporation Consolidated Balance Sheets (Cdn$ millions)

Mitel manufactured its products in Canada, the United States and the United Kingdom. The company purchased parts and components for assembly of its products from numerous suppliers worldwide. As of March 31, 1995, Mitel employed 3,561 employees, approximately 49 per cent located in Canada, 24 per cent located in the United States, 26 per cent located in the United Kingdom and one per cent throughout other worldwide locations.[4]

MITEL SEMICONDUCTOR

Mitel Semiconductor had been designing, manufacturing and marketing integrated circuits

for almost twenty years. As a division of Mitel Corporation, Mitel Semiconductor counted on the other divisions for approximately eight per cent of its annual sales. Mitel Semiconductor employed more than 500 people in various manufacturing and sales organizations throughout the world. As a division, Mitel Semiconductor was expected to be largely self-financing for capital investments.

Products

Mitel Semiconductor competed in a fairly small segment of the semiconductor industry—business communications—which generated just under $1 billion in semiconductor purchases.

	31-Mar-95	*25-Mar-94*	*26-Mar-93*
Revenues			
Products	$521.7	$436.4	$367.2
Service	$67.1	$60.0	$56.2
	$588.8	$496.4	$423.4
Cost of Sales			
Products	$275.5	$238.6	$201.5
Service	$42.5	$34.4	$33.4
	$318.0	$273.0	$234.9
Gross Margin	$270.8	$223.4	$188.5
Expenses			
Selling & Admin	$184.1	$149.6	$133.2
R&D	$41.9	$34.2	$35.0
Amortization	$16.5	$17.6	$21.3
	$242.5	$201.4	$189.5
Operating Income	$28.3	$22.0	$(1.0)
Interest			
Income	$5.7	$4.1	$2.8
Expense	$(1.2)	$(1.0)	$(0.6)
	$4.5	$3.1	$2.2
Income Before Taxes	$32.8	$25.1	$1.2
Income Tax Expense	$1.0	$4.4	$(1.4)
Net Income	$31.8	$20.7	$2.6

Exhibit 2   Mitel Corporation Consolidated Income Statements (Cdn$ millions)

This segment represented slightly less than 0.5 per cent of the entire semiconductor market but was expected to have a compound average growth rate of almost 18 per cent over the next five years (Exhibit 3a). Mitel Semiconductors' market share within this segment was slightly more than seven per cent and management wanted to see their share of the market double by the turn of the century.

The division had two main integrated circuit product lines: (1) Analog Line cards: essential components of modern communications equipment because they converted analog signals to digital and vice-versa; and (2) Telecom and Networking Components: the switching, transport and shaping products which were key to the PBX and telecom solutions offered by major telecommunication companies. Sales of these two product groups totalled $77.7 million in FY 94/95 (Exhibit 3b). The other $10 million in revenues were generated through the Mitel Semiconductor design services and Custom Wafer Foundry products.

Customers

The four principal markets for Mitel Semiconductor products were:

- customer premises and network communication equipment manufacturers,
- PBX manufacturers,
- central office networks and high speed network providers,
- wireless and CTI product makers.

Market	Product	FY 94/95 $M	FY 95/96 $M	FY 96/97 $M	FY 97/98 $M	FY 98/99 $M	FY 99/00 $M	Market CAGR
Telecom & Networks	Switching	$62	$74	$88	$105	$125	$149	19%
	Transport	$70	$80	$92	$106	$122	$140	15%
	Shaping	$13	$13	$16	$19	$22	$27	20%
	Total	$145	$167	$196	$230	$269	$316	17%
Analog Line Cards	SLICs	$395	$454	$522	$600	$690	$794	15%
	COICs	$53	$60	$70	$80	$92	$106	15%
	DAAs	$87	$104	$125	$150	$180	$216	20%
	CODECs	$260	$313	$375	$450	$540	$648	20%
	TELE	$44	$54	$68	$85	$106	$133	25%
	Total	$838	$985	$1,159	$1,365	$1,608	$1,896	18%
	Grand Total	$981	$1,153	$1,369	$1,637	$1,906	$2,260	18%

Exhibit 3a   Projected Growth Business Communications Semiconductor Segment

Market	Product	FY 94/95 Mkt Size ($M)	FY 94/95 Mitel Share (%)	FY 94/95 Mitel Sales ($M)	Mitel CAGR	FY 99/00 Projected Mitel Sales
Telecom & Networks	Switching	$62	30%	$18.6	21%	$48.3
	Transport	$70	35%	$24.3	15%	$49.0
	Shaping	$13	25%	$3.3	27%	$10.7
	Total	$145		$46.2		$108.0
Analog Line Cards	SLICs	$395	2%	$7.9	20%	$19.6
	COICs	$53	15%	$7.9	20%	$19.6
	DAAs	$87	2%	$1.7	70%	$24.7
	CODECs	$260	2%	$5.2	25%	$15.9
	TELE	$44	20%	$8.7	40%	$46.8
	Total	$838		$31.4		$126.6
	Grand Total	$981		$77.7	25%	$234.6

Exhibit 3b   Projected Growth by Product

The latter was a niche market that supported the telephone, data communications, and CTI manufacturers within the business communication sector. It was anticipated that this market would be an increasingly important sub-market in the future as the integration of the telephone and computer continued.

Mitel customers were a diverse group of over 300 companies in the business communications sector. Sales were well diversified throughout the world making Mitel less susceptible to the business cycles within specific geographic regions. Mitel's fundamental sales strategy was to serve developing countries' needs for a basic telephone infrastructure. This was viewed as a key infra-structure requirement in many countries; thus a continuing demand was anticipated in the primary markets which used Mitel's chips. In addition, Mitel's more recent products met the requirements of multimedia applications like e-mail and the Internet, leaving management confident that demand for their products would remain strong for the next five years.

Mitel's product mix and rate of new product development meant that, on average, the revenue generated per wafer remained constant. This trend was expected to continue over the foreseeable future.

Channels

About 70 per cent of Mitel Semiconductor sales were sold through manufacturer's representatives (MRs) and distributors. The MRs were managed directly by the Mitel sales force and operated worldwide. They worked on a commission basis and were responsible for generating contacts and introducing customers to the latest Mitel Semiconductor products. The MRs suggested how a particular chip might improve a customer's existing products or how it might be used in a product that was currently under design. If a customer decided to purchase one of Mitel Semiconductor's products, contact was normally established with one of the distributors suggested by the MRs. The primary function of distributors was not sales, but delivery and after-sales service of finished goods, as well as credit management. The remaining 30 per cent of revenue was generated through sales directly with the end customer.

Competition

Like the rest of the semiconductor industry, the business communication segment was characterized by rapid technological change and the frequent introduction of newer, more complex and more powerful products. Competition was based on design and quality of the products, price and service. Competition within the business communications segment of the semiconductor market was global and very intense. Major players included Dallas Semiconductor, PMC-Sierra, Brooktree, Motorola, National Semiconductor, California Micro Devices, Hewlett Packard, Siemens, Rockwell and Lucent.

Finances

As shown in the table below, revenues rose substantially over the four-year period due to rapid growth in the semiconductor industry and the success of Mitel's products within the business communications sector.

With a combined annual growth rate of almost 30 per cent and an increasing share of annual corporate revenues, the division became an engine of growth for Mitel Corporation. As a division, the operating performance of the business unit was incorporated in the financial statements of Mitel Corporation; however, the following financial information is available (these figures have been disguised to protect company confidential information):

1. Cost of Goods Sold for FY 94/95 was 50 per cent;

2. Total other expenses for FY 94/95 were 30 per cent; and

3. Operating Income for FY 94/95 was 20 per cent.

It was Mitel policy that, over the long term, all business units should finance their own growth.

Table B   Sales in Millions of Dollars (FY ending)

	Mar. 31, 1995	*Mar. 25, 1994*	*Mar. 26, 1993*	*Mar. 27, 1992*
Annual Sales	$77.7	$63.0	$51.5	$37.0

The senior management team was debt-averse due to lessons learned during the period of poor profitability in the eighties; thus, funds for any capital investments would likely be limited to the cash and cash equivalents found within the corporation's assets. Mitel used a cost of capital of 15 per cent when comparing investment opportunities.

Production

In 1995, production of Mitel Semiconductor integrated circuits was split between two locations in Canada: Kanata, Ontario and Bromont, Quebec. Chip design was performed by R&D staff at the Kanata location. Once the circuit design was complete, the masking was contracted out to a local company under the control of the R&D staff. The completed masks were then forwarded to the Wafer Foundry in Bromont. Bromont occupied a 73,000-square foot plant that worked with 100mm/9–1.2 micron wafer technology and performed the entire FAB portion of the integrated circuit manufacturing process. The chips were then returned to Kanata for test and shipment to distributors or directly to the customer.

The capacity of the entire operation was 100 lot starts per week, the equivalent of 112,000, 100mm wafers annually. Mitel Semiconductor demand based on FY 94/95 sales was the equivalent of 90,000, 100 mm wafers. The primary limit on current capacity was the size of the Bromont Foundry and the 100mm technology employed there. The operations at Kanata could be expanded relatively easily for a low fixed investment and the mask contractor had virtually unlimited capacity but Bromont's effective capacity was fixed and, without substantial capital investment, could not be increased beyond its current level.

Mitel Semiconductor sourced its wafers from a large European supplier. Unfortunately, the supplier had just indicated that it would soon start converting to a larger wafer size to meet the demand of other more important customers. Another concern was that Bromont could be faced with similar problems in terms of 100mm

plant equipment. Most equipment manufacturers no longer produced 100mm equipment, and obtaining spare parts and servicing existing equipment were becoming more difficult. In addition to manufacturing its own integrated circuits, Mitel Semiconductor had also contracted out the production of integrated circuits from external suppliers, primarily from an East Asian firm. Unfortunately, this firm recently announced that it would no longer be able to provide Mitel Semiconductor capacity past June 1996.

ALTERNATIVES

Kirk found himself in the unenviable position of trying to balance the various opposing challenges facing the semiconductor business unit. On the one hand, growth within the business communications segment was rising at more than 17 per cent annually and Mitel's growth was almost 50 per cent higher than the industry level. On the other hand, his supply of 100mm wafers was threatened, equipment maintenance was under pressure, and his traditional contract supplier of additional capacity would not be available in nine months. Kirk also knew that Mitel Semiconductors' true value-added was its customer-focused applications engineering group. It was in this environment that Kirk and his manager of the Bromont Foundry, Francois Cordeau, developed the following alternatives for enhancing production capacity (October 1, 1995 start date for all options).

Status Quo

This option meant that Bromont would be kept on 100mm wafers. For $10 million, Mitel could upgrade its current equipment and license 0.8m technology from its current supplier. The upgrade could be accomplished in eight months without a plant shutdown and would increase annual 100mm wafer capacity by 44,800. It really wasn't a "do nothing" option because the reduced supply of 100mm wafers meant that an alternative supply of wafers would have to be found or developed in-house. Kirk felt that finding another supplier would present the highest risk with respect to this option and was probably not possible. Developing an in-house wafer-growing capability was an alternative but would cost $40 to $50 million. Other 100mm equipment could be purchased for low cost from other FABs switching to larger wafers and perhaps Mitel could train its own technicians to maintain the equipment.

Of course, this option could not meet the increased demand for very long, but by maintaining low production costs and, provided Mitel could obtain a supply of wafers, profitability might be sustained for the near future.

Convert Bromont to Larger Wafers

Mitel could convert Bromont to larger wafers; 150mm, 200mm, or 300mm were all options. A conversion to any new wafer size had the added advantage of allowing the division to convert to smaller line width for relatively low cost because they would already be making production equipment changes and installing more advanced clean rooms. While the 300mm wafer would increase capacity substantially, Kirk was concerned with immature technology and the high price, over $250 million for a conversion to 112,000, 300mm wafers.

A conversion to 112,000, 200mm wafers would also increase capacity significantly, so much so that the Director of Logistics and Finance, Bob Wild, questioned whether or not they could sell the additional integrated circuits. Cost was also a major factor with estimates all hovering around the $150 million mark. They would not be able to use any of their current equipment and Kirk was also concerned that the supply situation would be critical because so many other 200mm FABs were under construction. Although it would take four years to plan, build and get the foundry operational, the larger wafers would extend the useful life of the plant substantially.

A conversion to 112,000, 150mm wafers could be accomplished for $35 to $40 million. This would also increase capacity significantly

but without a plant shutdown and the conversion could be completed in as little as two years. The major risk with this option was the use of 150mm wafers. At the time, supply was plentiful and cheap but, despite reassurances from potential suppliers, including Mitel's current supplier, Kirk was concerned that it would not be long before 150mm wafers would suffer the same fate as the 100mm wafers. This would mean another expensive conversion at some future date.

Contract Out Fabrication

In theory, this was an attractive option because Mitel Semiconductor could increase its capacity with no investment. The deal with its supplier increased the cost per wafer to $600 but provided welcome relief when it could not meet demand peaks or customer deadlines for critical deliveries. Fixed costs would also rise by $1 million annually because of the additional engineers needed to manage the supplier(s). The major risk with this option, securing supply, was illustrated through Mitel's experience with its current supplier and clearly indicated a worldwide capacity problem. An initial search for alternative foundries was unsuccessful and a report from the Fabless Semiconductor Association indicated that capacity utilization was at an all-time record high of 90 per cent. Bob expressed concern that the assumption that this option would require no investment might not stand up to reality given the experience of other companies who made large up-front payments to secure capacity. Kirk also noted that increasing the cost per wafer to $600 would cut significantly into Mitel's gross margins.

Secure External Capacity Through Acquisition

The last option under consideration was to acquire another chip maker. This was not a serious consideration until Kirk visited a small FAB in Jarfalla, Sweden. Owned by the large engineering firm, ABB, the plant was for sale and initial observations led Kirk and Bob to conclude that its products could be integrated nicely into the Mitel

Semiconductor line. Although primarily an R&D facility, it was producing 20,000, 100mm wafers annually and could be brought up to 48,000 wafers with minor production changes in about twelve months. The financials looked good and consultations with ABB indicated that the plant could be purchased for $45 to $50 million. This option also provided security of supply for customers.

However, there were some drawbacks. Although he had no specific concerns with respect to the ABB option, Kirk knew that changing the orientation of an R&D organization to one of production was tough and that dealing with a completely different culture could also present other challenges. An article in *Business Week* commenting on the high failure rate of foreign acquisitions confirmed these risks. To make any acquisition work he would need to send a key player from his own organization but demands at the time precluded this. He would also be purchasing a market of 20,000 wafers; therefore, until production was increased beyond the 20,000 mark, he wouldn't get any capacity relief for Bromont.

THE DECISION

Which option would be the most appropriate for Mitel Semiconductor? What could it afford? What option would meet expected demand? What option would provide the best return? Which option would be the least risky? Could Mitel implement a combination of options? Kirk knew that these, and many other questions, would have to be answered before he could make a recommendation to the CEO.

NOTES

1. Integrated Circuit Engineering (ICE) report: Cost effective IC manufacturing 1995. Vladdi Catto, TI Chief Economist, Electronic Buyers' News, 7 Aug. 1995.

2. http://supersite.net: The Semiconductor Story.

3. R. Voyer & P. Ryan, The New Innovators, p. 169–185.

4. 10K Mitel, FY 1995.

ELECTROSTEEL CASTINGS LIMITED

Prepared by Nitish Bahl under the supervision of Professor Robert Klassen

Version: (A) 2004-12-07

On June 30, 2001, Anil Das, chief executive officer at Electrosteel Castings, headquartered in Calcutta, India, received a call from the company's Singapore sales office. A Vietnamese firm, Construction Machinery Corporation (CMC), wanted an update on Electrosteel's possible decision to invest in Vietnam.

Electrosteel had been India's largest manufacturer of ductile iron pipes (DIP) and cast iron pipes (CIP) for over four decades. Its growth had been solid in recent years, largely driven by new infrastructural projects in the domestic market. However, this market was expected to come under increasing pressure as foreign competitors were pushing aggressively to enter the Indian market. International expansion would offer a strong opportunity for continued growth, with the added benefit of providing additional hard currency for further investment in new production technologies.

At a minimum, management wanted to at least double international volumes over the next three years. After extensive study, Das had narrowed the options to either a new marketing office or new manufacturing facility in one of two particular markets: Europe and Southeast Asia. Building an overseas plant was particularly attractive, as it would effectively translate into Electrosteel being considered a local competitor in that market, yielding lower costs and reduced import duties.

To assess Southeast Asia, Electrosteel had approached CMC five months ago to explore the costs of constructing a new plant in Vietnam (see Exhibit 1). This location offered a strong base to serve the domestic Vietnamese market, as well as the surrounding region of rapidly developing economies—each with great need for basic infrastructure. However, Das was not convinced that this location was ideal. Expansion into Europe also was very attractive, where a new plant could be built in France. In recent weeks, the urgency for a decision had increased dramatically as Das became increasingly aware that foreign competitors were also investigating similar expansion options—including India.

ELECTROSTEEL IN INDIA

During the 1990s, India had achieved strong annual economic growth rates exceeding five per cent. As one of the largest democracies in the world with a population of one billion, the country had an intricate political web, which

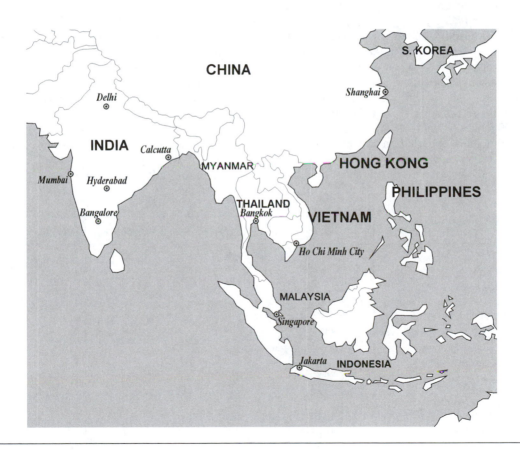

Exhibit 1   Map of Southeast Asia

affected many aspects of business. India had adopted policies that protected local industry, and that combined with both a complicated government bureaucracy, complex duties, and convoluted tax structures made it difficult for multinationals to conduct business there. However, in 1991, the government started a liberalization program aimed at reducing these barriers, partly driven by India's membership in the World Trade Organization (WTO). Since that time, low progress had been made, partly held back by politically linked labor unions.

Electrosteel was the largest manufacturer of DIP and CIP in India and had been producing pipes since 1965. Given its long history in the domestic market, local protectionism for the steel industry had fostered Electrosteel's growth. Overall production reached 231,000 tonnes for CIP and DIP last year, generating revenues of US$124 million and contributing to cash reserves of about US$50 million (see Exhibit 2). The company was listed on the stock exchanges in Mumbai and Calcutta.

Export sales of DIP in 2001 represented a small proportion of total production, at 25,000 tonnes, which was down slightly from the 30,000 tonnes exported in the previous year. These sales were primarily directed at Asia, including Bangladesh, Nepal and Sri Lanka.

Unfortunately, newer markets in this region, such as Singapore, Hong Kong, Brunei, Malaysia and Vietnam, had proven difficult and slow to develop. In addition, Electrosteel exported small quantities to customers in the Middle East, including Syria, Lebanon, Kuwait, Oman, Ethiopia and Qatar. The export department in Calcutta, as well as branch sales offices in Singapore and Lebanon, served these markets. Das believed that Electrosteel could be transformed from a domestic supplier into a strong international competitor:

> We aim to be world class—committed to customer satisfaction and demonstrating strong leadership in design and manufacturing.

CHARACTERISTICS OF IRON PIPE

National and local governments, as well as private sector utilities, routinely used large iron pipe to supply basic infrastructural needs such as water and sewage systems. Historically, CIP had been favored for its relatively low cost and durability. Since 1965, DIP had been increasingly used, particularly in developed countries, because the metal pipe was less brittle, which translated directly into easier handling and

	1998	1999	2000	2001
Revenues	$81	$99	$120	$124
expenses	62	74	87	97
Gross profit	19	25	33	27
less: interest, depreciation & tax	9	11	13	13
Net profit	$10	$14	$20	$14
Production (000's tonnes)				
ductile iron pipe (DIP)				
capacity	90	100	100	130
production	80	90	95	110
cast iron pipe (CIP)				
capacity	126	150	165	165
production	120	120	120	121

Exhibit 2 Historical Operating Statistics, Year Ending March 31 (in US$ millions)

installation. Moreover, during subsequent use, the enhanced ductility reduced breakage and leakage. As a result, DIP was expected to last 70 years versus 40 years for CIP and was therefore priced about 20 per cent higher.

DIP also faced competition from other materials, such as plastic (PVC), mild steel, asbestos, and pre-stressed concrete. Pipes of these materials were generally cheaper than DIP, but had several disadvantages. First, a shorter life span was typical, ranging from 15 to 20 years for PVC and mild steel pipe, respectively. Second, the quality of water flowing through pipes of these other materials tended to deteriorate more quickly. Water quality was compromised as leakages developed and contaminants from the surrounding soil entered the pipe.

ELECTROSTEEL'S OPERATIONS

Ductile Iron Pipe Manufacturing Process

The manufacturing process used molten iron as a raw material, drawn where possible from a blast furnace (Exhibit 3). Magnesium was added to improve metallurgical properties. Pipe was then cast using sophisticated centrifugal casting machines. A rotating metal, water-cooled mold used centrifugal force to create a hollow pipe, thereby eliminating the need for a central core. This operation employed highly specialized, automated equipment with computerized controls.

After centrifugal casting, the iron pipe was heated to between 1,000 C and 1,400 C

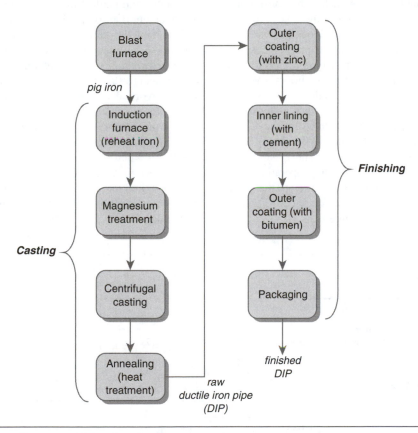

Exhibit 3   Overview of Manufacturing Process

(depending on the metallurgical properties of the pipe) and then gradually cooled in an annealing furnace to relieve internal metal stresses. The specific temperature and cooling rate had to be precisely monitored in order to ensure a high quality, durable finished product. This annealed pipe was termed *raw* DIP.

Raw DIP was then coated and lined on a finishing line to meet specific standards, which varied based on intended use and other customer requirements. An external coating of zinc improved resistance to rust, with its thickness conforming to the previously mentioned, widely recognized international standards. An internal cement lining improved the flow of water through the pipes, prevented the ductile iron from coming in contact with the water and provided an acceptable pH value for drinking water. Again, a centrifugal process was used to create a smooth cement finish, with the thickness being determined by international standards.

Finally, a second external coating, now of bitumen, was added to further protect both the zinc coating and the underlying ductile iron. After a drying time of about 10 hours, the pipe could be packaged and shipped.

Finished DIP had to withstand specific hydrostatic test pressures dictated by the widely accepted, international standards, such as British or International Standards. These standards ensured compliance for jointing, operating pressure and types of fluid flowing through the pipe.

Sandeep Sengupta, senior manager of quality and development, commented,

In contrast to CIP, manufacturing DIP is like producing art, as it requires expertise at each stage. The proper chemical composition must be developed in the molten metal, process temperatures must be closely monitored and controlled, and the casting machine requires training and judgment. Both expertise and effective systems are essential to producing consistent metallurgical properties and surface finishes that meet customer expectations.

Plant Operations

Although Electrosteel had been producing CIP for decades, its first plant to manufacture DIP was built in 1994. The DIP production facility was located in Kardah, near Calcutta, India. Setting up the plant in Calcutta offered the advantage of using the infrastructure of the existing CIP plant and the services of trained staff. Being close to corporate headquarters in Calcutta also simplified management control and engineering support.

Much of the new equipment for the casting and finishing operations was manufactured in India. However, German technical knowledge was critical to starting up this plant. German consultants worked with skilled in-house personnel, including design engineers and civil contractors. The plant layout was developed to minimize handling and throughput times, with straight-line flows wherever possible. While many of the raw materials were sourced locally, some were imported, including metallurgical coke, zinc and bitumen, as well as some of the alloying metals (see Exhibit 4).

	Process Stage		
	Casting	Finishing	Total
Raw Materials			
• imported	15	8	23
• domestic	60	7	67
Labor	3	7	10
Total	78	22	100

Exhibit 4   Cost Structure for DIP Manufacturing (in percentages)

The plant had recently been accredited with ISO 9002 certification and the product was licensed to carry the British Standards Institution (BSI) Kitemark, an important, international product certification widely recognized by customers.

By 2001, the Kardah plant had DIP production capacity of 130,000 tonnes annually, and supplied 15 standard pipe sizes ranging from 80 to 1,000 millimetres (mm) in diameter. Three different pipe joints (i.e., shape of the end of the pipe) were also offered. CIP also was manufactured here, as well as in another plant in Elavur, with a total capacity of 165,000 tonnes per year (see Exhibit 2). In 2002, management planned to increase Electrosteel's installed worldwide capacity for raw DIP. However, the best location—either in India or abroad—for new casting and finishing capacity remained a difficult decision.

Capital Investment for DIP

Because the basic process was structured into two stages—casting and finishing—investment was generally assessed separately for each stage. Capital investment for a casting operation including annealing was very high, and was only feasible in large increments. Based on recent experience, each incremental addition of 50,000 tonnes per year to casting capacity was expected to cost about US$40 million.

In contrast, investment for a finishing line, which included both external coating and internal lining, required a much smaller investment. This line also could be separated geographically from casting. By installing finishing capacity overseas, the finished DIP was considered local production for purposes of tendering. Separating the two stages also reduced transportation costs by about 10 per cent, which was the weight of the coating and lining. Expected costs of constructing a finishing line are provided in Exhibit 5.

Over the last few years, Electrosteel had made annual investments of approximately US$2 million to expand finishing capacity and upgrade process technology for DIP. While minimum functionality was still determined by conformance

Description	Annual Capacity (tonnes)		
	10,000	30,000	50,000
Civil/Construction			
Utilities	$70	$110	$130
Civil structure	30	43	50
Overhead cranes	35	35	35
Gantries & trolleys	40	55	65
Finishing Line Equipment			
Chamfering equipment	40	40	40
Cement lining equipment	390	600	700
Zinc coating equipment	80	100	150
Bitumen coating	150	800	900
Packaging			
Stenciling & bundling	30	45	55
Packaging	10	10	20
Tools for inspection	25	35	35
TOTAL	**$900**	**$1,873**	**$2,180**

Exhibit 5   Estimated Capital Cost of Finishing Line: Three Possible Capacities (in US$000s)

with international standards, technological upgrades in the lining and coating operations improved product quality (i.e., appearance, metallurgical properties, and uniform thickness of coatings and linings), and reduced costs by about 10 per cent. Reject rates also dropped to less than five per cent over this period—comparable to larger global competitors.

Initially, a blast furnace was not built, and pig iron (a form of processed raw iron used as an input to casting) was purchased on the open market. A blast furnace soon followed in 1996 with further investment of US$20 million. This backward integration provided better control over the quality of molten iron, which in turn improved the quality of the finished product.

Combined, product and process improvements in DIP had been credited with significantly improving customer acceptance and increasing sales in countries as diverse as Singapore, Malaysia, Brunei, Korea, Kuwait, Saudi Arabia and England. Bryan Tong, a senior manager at Singardo Trading, a Singaporean customer, commented, "The manufacturing facility is truly world-class. The final product is at par with those of any global manufacturer."

DOMESTIC MARKET FOR DIP

Demand

The domestic market was spread across 28 different states in India, with the state-level governments being the primary buyers to improve infrastructure. This market for DIP had been growing at between five per cent to 10 per cent annually over the last four years as international agencies increased funding for water supply projects in India.

Unfortunately, the growth experienced in the late 1990s was not expected to continue. Current estimates strongly indicated that these agencies were significantly reducing support over the next few years. With less international funding, state governments were forced to rely on a cash-strapped central government, which translated into much lower funding for infrastructural projects. As a result, overall demand for DIP was expected to remain at roughly the current level with greater year-to-year variation.

The manufacturing and delivery of iron pipe (both DIP and CIP) was undertaken only after the government had placed a firm order. The peak buying period tended to occur in the first quarter of the calendar (January to March), coinciding with the state and central governments fiscal year-end. Demand then usually fell by a third in the much slower second quarter.

The steel market, including DIP, was protected by an import tariff of 25 per cent of landed price. Partly as a result, domestic prices for DIP were about 15 per cent higher than international prices (before duty). India's participation in the WTO suggested that these restrictions were likely to be phased out, although the timeframe was somewhat flexible and uncertain because of strong lobbying for delays by the local steel industry.

Competition

Electrosteel was a well-established brand in India and maintained an extensive local network of agents and a team of sales professionals. In 2001, Electrosteel supplied over 90 per cent and 60 per cent of the domestic demand for DIP and CIP, respectively. A new domestic competitor had recently started manufacturing DIP in 2001, and currently held about half the remaining DIP market share, while imports accounted for the remainder.

Manufacturers around the world had been very secretive about specific technologies related to DIP production. Several manufacturing operations, such as casting, zinc coating and cement lining, had proven difficult to duplicate. Moreover, skilled employees were difficult to recruit, as Electrosteel's employees were very loyal and reluctant to join this new start-up. As a result, this new competitor found it very challenging to initiate and ramp up production. Das estimated that Electrosteel had approximately two years before this competitor would present a serious threat. Once the competitor was fully functional, Das expected much stronger price competition in the domestic market.

The size of the Indian market, both now as well as in the longer term, presented an attractive opportunity to international manufacturers such as France's St. Gobain Group (see Exhibit 6). Rumors were circulating that this firm, along with others, was contemplating entry into the Indian market in the near future. Any reduction in import duties would only offer a further incentive for their aggressive entry.

GLOBAL OPPORTUNITIES

The markets in Asia were rapidly expanding, as many developing countries were moving aggressively to develop their infrastructure. Here, much of the funding came from international organizations such as the World Bank, the Asian Development Bank, and the Organization for Economic Cooperation and Development (OECD). In contrast, the emphasis in developed countries such as Europe was to maintain their

---

St. Gobain Group (France)

- Global leaders in DIP and fittings
- Installed annual capacity of two million tonnes annually, with much of that capacity in Europe, where they were market leaders
- Manufacturing throughout Europe, and in Brazil, China, South Africa, and Saudi Arabia, each with casting and finishing
- Extensive range of products, including a wide range of pipe joints

Kubota Corporation (Japan)

- Estimated capacity of about 800,000 tonnes per year
- Producer of high quality pipe allowing a slight premium in price

Kurimoto Pipes (Japan)

- Smaller manufacturer with a strong presence in Asia
- Capacity of about 80,000 tonnes per year
- High quality of finish for lining and coating

Tyco Pipes (Australia)

- Installed capacity of about 70,000 tonnes per year
- Due to cyclical demand in Australia, they were able to offer attractive discounts, when the Australian demand was low

Xinxin Pipes (China)

- Growing competitive threat with a current installed capacity of about 250,000 tonnes per year
- Currently export to many markets served by Electrosteel
- Estimated cost of production was lower than Electrosteel

Korean Cast Iron Pipes (KCIP) (Korea)

- With capacity of about 150,000 tonnes per year, was the largest manufacturer in Korea
- Very competitive in Asian markets, as attractive discounts were offered in the absence of a strong domestic market

---

Exhibit 6   Summary of Major Competitors

existing system with the steady replacement of older pipelines.

A number of developing countries such as Singapore, Vietnam, Cambodia and Brunei did not have local manufacturers of DIP and were forced to import. For those countries with local production, either duties might be imposed to protect local manufacturers (e.g., India) or unique local standards might be enacted. Specific national standards could include improved coatings, such as epoxy or polyurethane coated pipes, different pipe sizes or a different thickness of coatings, linings or pipe walls. DIP manufacturers could respond to these unique standards by developing a specific product—an expensive six- to 12-month process typically costing about $500,000.

Manufacturers exporting pipe also had to deal with the logistics of handling a very large and heavy product. Thus, it was not surprising that smaller diameter pipes, up to 200 mm, were favored for export business, where the weight-to-volume ratio was higher. Smaller pipe was exported in 20-foot containers; larger diameters were stacked directly on the ship (i.e., break-bulk). This meant that adequate port facilities and handling equipment were required in close proximity to the customer to receive imported pipe.

Prices for DIP in the international market were about US$600 per tonne, with smaller pipes (i.e., 80 and 150 mm) commanding a five to 10 per cent premium because of their greater manufacturing complexity. (In general, manufacturing costs for large-scale, international firms were roughly 80 to 85 per cent of the international price.) Transportation, port handling charges and insurance typically added another 10 per cent to the delivered price, plus any applicable import duties.

Global Competition

In general, large-scale manufacturers tended to increase their export volumes when the local market was unable to absorb the installed production capacity. As a result, several competitors at any given time were usually willing to sell their products at a discounted price in order to maintain minimum production levels at their plants. A survey by senior management of the primary competitors highlighted six of particular importance, based in France, Korea, Japan, Australia and China (see Exhibit 6).

Regardless of the competitor or market, raw DIP was not available; manufacturers offered only finished DIP. This allowed the producers to retain direct contact with the end-customer (e.g., government agency) and capture additional margin. Customers also favored this arrangement. If a quality problem developed, liability and responsibility for correcting the issue could be clearly assigned.

Electrosteel's International Expansion

After a series of planning sessions, the manufacturing and export departments had concluded that Electrosteel should target a total export volume of approximately 60,000 tonnes per year, based on current domestic demand and an expansion of production capacity. As a result, Das had formalized a corporate objective of ramping up international volumes by 10,000 tonnes per year. While many locations were possible, a detailed and thorough analysis by management had narrowed the candidate list to two specific countries: Vietnam and France.

EXPANSION INTO VIETNAM

Vietnam was the second largest country in Southeast Asia with a population of 78 million. As the socialist state had become increasingly liberalized over the last decade, foreign investment had begun to reshape the major cities of Hanoi, Ho Chi Minh City, Da Nang and Hai Phong. Most Vietnamese companies were owned and controlled by the government, although private ownership was increasingly encouraged. English was also becoming accepted as the language of business.

Economic growth since liberalization had been strong, but recent decreases in foreign direct investment (FDI) had slowed growth to about four per cent annually. Yet, the country continued to lack proper infrastructure in most areas. For example, transportation was challenging, with inadequate port facilities and poor roads that slowed the movement of heavy equipment.

Water supply and sewage systems faced similar shortcomings and needed urgent investment. Moreover, these projects targeted only the water supply in major centres, leaving an estimated 80 per cent of the country with water that did not meet basic drinking standards. There also were no functioning wastewater treatment plants in the country. Adding further to the challenge, a number of national agencies and provincial water companies had overlapping responsibility combined with a weak administration structure. As a result, the political system was very bureaucratic and difficult to penetrate.

These water supply projects had been funded by international agencies such as the World Bank and Asia Development Bank. These agencies offered open tenders, which allowed a local supplier a premium of 15 per cent over international prices. Other projects had been funded by country-specific development agencies from countries including France, Denmark, Finland and Japan. This dependency on foreign agencies for funding was expected to continue into the foreseeable future.

Since 1997, water-related infrastructure projects totaling US$1,210 million had been undertaken, utilizing approximately 130,000 tonnes of DIP. Four DIP manufacturers, none with a local manufacturing plant, had strong sales in Vietnam: St. Gobain, Kubota, Xinxin, and KCIP (estimated, cumulative sales volumes over the previous four-year period are noted in Exhibit 7). Management estimated that a similar amount of CIP had been used, all of which was produced by a local firm. In addition, low-cost pipe of other materials was imported.

Electrosteel's Options

Up to this point, Electrosteel had exported only small quantities of DIP to the Vietnamese market, totalling about 900 tonnes of pipe for two projects. Several options were available to establish a stronger presence here, including opening a branch sales office or building a new manufacturing facility. (In contrast, establishing a manufacturing plant in nearby Singapore or Hong Kong was prohibitively expensive, given the combined high cost of land and labor.) A sales office would cost about US$120,000 annually, with minimal start-up costs. If Electrosteel decided to build a plant, at least two configurations were possible. First, both a casting operation

	Vietnam	Singapore	Hong Kong	Malaysia
St. Gobain Group	20,000	15,000	25,000	2,000
Kubota Corp.	15,000	60,000	35,000	15,000
Kurimoto Pipes	—	16,000	10,000	—
Tyco Pipes	—	15,000	35,000	—
Xinxin	30,000	—	25,000	—
KCIP	25,000	—	15,000	—
Electrosteel	900	30,000	4,000	8,000
Others	40,000	—	—	130,000*
Total	**130,900**	**136,000**	**149,000**	**155,000**

Exhibit 7   Competitor Analysis for Selected Southeast Asian Markets Four-Year Cumulative Market Volume for DIP (1997 to 2000) (in tonnes)

*A local firm accounts for the majority of this market.

and a finishing line could be installed to provide integrated, local production. Pig iron, the primary input, would be purchased on the open market. In addition to being considered a local supplier, cost savings would be possible by avoiding the transportation of DIP from India to Vietnam equal to approximately 10 per cent of the market price.

Second, foreign investment could be reduced by simply installing a finishing line, with any necessary casting capacity added to the Kardah plant in India. Raw DIP would then be shipped from the Kardah plant to Vietnam, where it would be externally coated and internally lined in the new plant. However, transporation savings would be much less than the first configurations as raw DIP accounted for 90 per cent of the weight of finished DIP. Initial market research indicated that if an estimated 10 per cent cost advantage were achieved, relative to foreign competitors, sales of about 10,000 tonnes per year should be possible.

Plant configuration could be structured either as a wholly owned subsidiary or as part of a joint venture arrangement with a local Vietnamese partner. Unfortunately, the earlier record of foreign manufacturers in Vietnam had been poor, with little success. The Vietnamese government offered a further incentive to Electrosteel: a credit loan of US$3.1 million. This loan was to be allocated to an Indian manufacturer to encourage new investment and would be used by CMC, a contractor based in Hanoi, for construction. CMC also offered to purchase DIP from Electrosteel as needed for other projects on a contractual basis.

Das reflected:

> Vietnam is a fast growing market. The growth potential is huge, but the lack of infrastructure and resources creates many new challenges for Electrosteel. The opportunity to be the first local manufacturer of DIP in Vietnam is very attractive.

EXPANSION INTO EUROPE

Unlike much of Asia, which promised strong growth, the European market as a whole was stable, with annual demand of between 700,000 and 800,000 tonnes of DIP. France and Germany represented the largest markets because of the preference by their local utilities for DIP (see Exhibit 8). The fastest growing market was Spain. However, demand in some other countries was falling; for example, demand in the United Kingdom had fallen by 50 per cent over the last decade.

While each market was controlled by specific government regulations and subject to particular pricing structures, a manufacturer located in any European Union country was considered a local supplier for all other EU countries. DIP for this market also was produced to common European standards. Collectively, government regulations, approval processes and buyer preferences favored local suppliers, allowing an average 12 per cent price premium over international prices.

Electrosteel's Options

Europe was very attractive because of the large, stable business environment with fewer political and bureaucratic problems. In contrast to developing countries, DIP was a well-established and accepted material for public infrastructure in Europe. Developing countries tended to favor lower cost pipe alternatives because their tightly constrained funds could be stretched to service more people. Finally, unlike Vietnam, project funding was not limited to foreign development agencies but instead came from a variety of domestic sources.

In the past, Electrosteel had been able to build a small presence in Europe by sending executives as needed from head office to address particular sales requirements. Unfortunately, the large geographic area of the European market made it difficult to effectively expand and service this customer base from India.

Das and his senior management team had focused on France as the principle location. France had the largest market (see Exhibit 8), which allowed for greater local contact with potential local customers and also minimized transportation costs. Manufacturing process

	France	Germany	United Kingdom	Spain	Italy	Total
St. Gobain Group	220,000	—	—	60,000	65,000	345,000
Stanton Pipes*	—	—	40,000	—	—	40,000
Halburghutte*	—	150,000	—	—	—	150,000
Tiroler Röhren-und Metallwerke AG (Austria)	—	40,000	—	—	—	40,000
Buderus Guss GmbH (Germany)	—	50,000	20,000	—	—	70,000
Others	30,000	—	5,000	5,000	80,000	120,000
Total	**250,000**	**240,000**	**65,000**	**65,000**	**145,000**	**765,000**
Electrosteel's potential**	14,000	3,000	3,000	2,000	3,000	30,000

Exhibit 8 Competitor Analysis for Selected European Markets Market Volume for DIP in 2000 (in tonnes)

Note: All these firms also actively exported elsewhere in the world.

*Part of the St. Gobain Group.

**Based on management's extensive discussions with local distributors and customers.

technology was also very advanced here. One senior manager expressed the opinion:

> Europe is a diverse market and the home of the largest global manufacturer of DIP. Entering Europe with our own manufacturing operations would move us onto St. Gobain's home turf. In doing so, we might be able to establish Electrosteel as a serious global competitor.

The expansion options in Europe were similar to those being considered for Vietnam. A branch sales office could be opened, for US$400,000. Alternatively, Electrosteel could build a new manufacturing plant, with both casting and finishing operations, or just a finishing line. If the finishing line was located close to a French seaport, transportation and handling costs from India would be reduced, as well as potentially facilitating shipment of finished goods to other markets in Europe.

As with Vietnam, it was difficult to accurately forecast the sales volumes that Electrosteel might achieve. However, potential agents in several countries indicated that, by focusing on niche segments where clients were hesitant to

deal with larger incumbent firms, Electrosteel could expect to build significant volume. Based on these lengthy discussions, Das projected that Electrosteel could reasonably achieve an annual volume of 30,000 tonnes.

Expanding operations in France presented several significant challenges. First, there was the issue of operating cost. French labor was about 10 times more expensive than that in India or Vietnam. Second, the French language presented a challenge for Electrosteel's managers. Third, the strong presence of St. Gobain Group complicated any decision, and a joint venture was very unlikely. Das was unsure how this global leader would react.

MOVING FORWARD

Das realized that Electrosteel was at a significant crossroad. He was convinced that the current approach of corporate sales executives servicing foreign markets offered very limited potential. Instead, international sales would be appreciably increased only with a significant investment in a particular foreign market. The remaining question, given the firm's limited resources, was where to concentrate that investment and how to implement any decision. Both

Europe and Vietnam appeared attractive for different reasons. Das believed that now was the time to act—before he was forced to react to aggressive competitors.

BLINDS TO GO: INVADING THE SUNSHINE STATE

Prepared by Ken Mark under the supervision of Professor Larry Menor

Version: (A) 2002-02-25

INTRODUCTION

Blinds To Go (BTG), a Montreal-headquartered producer of made-to-order window coverings, had decided to enter the Florida market by opening eight retail stores beginning in January 2001. As a result of this decision, Rintaro Kawai, the senior vice-president of operations for BTG, was faced with the dilemma of deciding if and when an assembly plant should be built to support these and future Florida retail stores. The most recent plant that was built, Lakewood, New Jersey, had experienced operational problems during its start-up, resulting in the eventual replacement of most of the supervisory staff and a significant portion of the plant's employees. This disruption had led to additional start-up costs and customer service problems. Faced with this expansion into Florida, Kawai set about devising an operating plan that would achieve the goals of the Florida expansion without the growing pains of past efforts. As it was already June 2000, Kawai's plan would have to be finalized soon.

BLINDS TO GO

Operating out of its head office in Montreal, Canada, BTG counted 120 retail locations in eight

Northeastern states and in Ontario and Quebec as of June 2000. Revenues had quintupled to over US$100 million during the past 20 months, and with two fully operational manufacturing plants, BTG had come a long way from its humble beginnings.

Growing up in the Côte-des-Neiges district in Montreal, David Shiller, the patriarch of the Shiller family, started in business in 1954 by selling bedding products from the trunk of his family's Chevrolet. Opening his own store one year later, the elder Shiller started to sell carpets, floor coverings, draperies and fabrics. When Stephen Shiller joined the business in the mid-70s, he convinced his father to focus on selling blinds. Operating out of "Au Bon Marché," as it was known in Quebec, the Shillers started making blinds out of a small factory in the back of the store. By cutting delivery time to a few days, they found themselves with a winning concept, given that this was a huge improvement from the six to eight weeks that other manufacturers promised. Au Bon Marché soon became the number one location for blinds in Quebec. Over time, in that original store, they were able to deliver custom-made blinds to customers in about an hour.

Early on, the Shillers noticed that other retailers in the all window coverings (AWC) industry relied on a three-tiered distribution system—retail outlet, fabricator and manufacturer. As the AWC industry was already mature, it was slow to change and was experiencing slow growth. It was not uncommon for customers to wait six to eight weeks for customized blinds if they did not like the selection of stock blinds in the store. Customized blinds were sold at a higher price to consumers, but they were made to order entirely by local or regional fabricators. Stock blinds were usually manufactured in the Far East because of the lower cost of operations. By manufacturing in Asia, these manufacturers enjoyed cost savings in exchange for standardization. The customer who bought stock blinds was then limited to prefabricated blinds within that retailer's inventory. The AWC market was a multibillion-dollar industry, and there were few catalysts for change in the three-tiered distribution system.

The Shillers saw an opportunity to offer customized blinds and opted to manufacture their blinds in the same city, reasoning that customers would be eager to purchase customized blinds that could be delivered within a significantly shorter window.

Stephen explained,

We fed them [customers] food, kept them busy while they waited for their blinds to be ready. Our first factory was literally next to the store and we offered our one hour delivery guarantee, which kept our customers happy.

Our St. Leonard, Quebec, store, the prototype for the current Blinds To Go stores, opened in 1991. Prior to that, people used to drive up to 100 miles to come to our stores. But since the recession in the early 1990s, we found that they tend to refurbish one room at a time. Shortly thereafter, we opened a store in Laval.

We had renamed the new stores "Le Marché Du Store," not wanting to cannibalize sales from our original store. But what we found was that sales increased in Le Marché Du Store without affecting the others, leading us to conclude that people, if given a choice, would shop closer to home.

At that point, in early '94, we realized what a hot concept we had on our hands—our sales were

higher for each consecutive store opened, and none of our competitors could replicate our model [see Exhibit 1]. They were either manufacturers or retailers; none were both. None could hope to deliver the 48-hour turnaround we promised, had our unique sales model, which is commission-based, or had our attention to customer needs.

BLINDS TO GO NORTH AMERICAN SALES GROWTH

In 1995, the Shillers had studied the North American market opportunity and proceeded to open stores in Albany, New York. An introduction to Harvard Private Capital (HPC) led them to discussions with this investment arm of Harvard University. HPC looked at 600 companies a year, but invested in only about a dozen of them.

I recommended to my father that we take a leap of faith. We were a private company, making more money than we could intelligently spend. If we went with HPC, we would not take money out; we would reinvest it so that eventually, we could take the company public. HPC never put pressure on us to grow. It was equally important for them to see my vision to build a great company. We want to grow, but in a way that is sustainable and improves the company, not growth for growth's sake.

The focus was now on North American expansion (see Exhibit 2). To prepare for this growth, the Shillers hired on Nkere Udofia, formerly the managing director at Harvard Private Capital, as vice-chairman of Blinds To Go, entrusting him with the responsibility of helping direct the expansion.

Not long after the first group of stores were opened in the northeastern United States, Blinds To Go soon built its Lakewood, New Jersey, plant to supply and service them. Construction of the 100,000-square-foot facility was completed in early 1998, and employment at the plant was expected to reach 500 in two years as the company expanded in the American northeast.

BLINDS TO GO™ HAS REDEFINED WINDOW COVERING INDUSTRY...

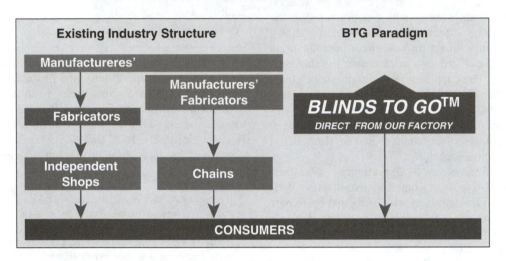

Exhibit 1 Blinds To Go Model

Source: Company records—Nkere Udofia's Harvard Business School presentation.

THE ALL WINDOW COVERING MARKET

The Sullivan Marketing Group, a market research and consulting organization that specializes in business planning for building materials and decorative products, projected that industry sales of all variants of blinds would amount to US$2 billion market in 2000, with individual sales at 56 million units (see Exhibit 3). Retailer gross margins varied from 20 to 28 per cent for distributed products, to 42 to 55 per cent for private-label blinds. There were many retailers of blinds and manufacturers of blinds (see Exhibit 4). A newly emerging segment, the retail fabricator segment, of which BTG was one of the key players, accounted for

about 12 per cent of the AWC market, and was growing at least nine per cent per year, four times the expected market growth for the AWC market as a whole.

It was inevitable that consumer demand in the retail fabricator segment was also driven, in part, by the success of BTG and its service concept. Sensing that the time was right, BTG senior management devised a strategy to grow quickly in the North American market. To add a greater sense of urgency to their plans, BTG's senior management announced to employees that they would take BTG public in the next few years if key performance objectives were met and the public markets were receptive. Their next phase of expansion was the Florida market.

Total Blinds To Go

	1994 (not BTG)	1995	1996	1997	1998	1999	2000*
Number of stores		28	36	69	87	97	120
SKUs per order**					2.5 to 3	2.5 to 3	2.5 to 3
Returns based on measurement, errors, freight damages***					3.5%	4.0%	4.0%
Returns based on plant defects***					3.5%	8.0%	6.0%
Number of store employees					300	440	500
Average order turnaround time in hours (Montreal/Lakewood)						60/72	48/72

Montreal and Lakewood Plants

	1997	1998	1999	2000
Production volume: Montreal, orders per week	5,000	16,500	19,200	24,600
Production volume: Lakewood, orders per week			4,800	14,500
Number of plant employees (Montreal)	110	200	350	400
Number of plant employees (Lakewood)			120	250

Exhibit 2   Manufacturing Statistics

*Early 2000 average estimates.

**A stock keeping unit refers to one single unit of blinds.

***% of total sales.

THE BLINDS TO GO FABRICATING PROCESS

Custom blinds in the AWC market were in demand because home windows differed widely in size and shape, and homeowners sought blinds in different shapes and colors to match the décor of their rooms. As a result, BTG offered over 20,000 different combinations of types, styles, colors and features of blinds (not including the virtually limitless combinations of window dimensions) (see Exhibit 5 and 6). This complexity made it infeasible to manufacture blinds in advance of actually receiving a customer's specifications. Each order had to go through several basic steps whereby the headrail was chosen, cut and assembled, the slats were arranged, threading holes cut in the slats, hanging hardware installed, then quality tested. Furthermore, there were differences in manufacturing between types of blinds. For example, roller shades took significantly less time to assemble than wooden blinds.

In both plants, each product group type (wood, verticals, horizontals, specialty shades)

(Text continues on page 366)

Growth at one to two per cent per year, about the same as the growth in the number of U.S. households

Company	Horizontals				Vertical Totals	Pleated Shades			All Other Total	Grand Total
	Metal	Vinyl	Wood	Total		Cellular	Single	Total		
Hunter Douglas	112	8	80	200	75	198	19	217	94	586
Newell	123	24	37	184	90	62	13	75	—	349
Springs	75	10	55	140	60	54	13	67	1	268
Comfortex	—	—	12	12	—	30	8	38	8	58
Novo	—	—	—	—	49	—	—	—	—	49
Jencraft	—	25	—	25	20	—	—	—	—	45
Achim Importing	—	21	—	21	5	—	—	—	—	26
Kenney	—	8	—	8	14	—	—	—	—	22
Lewis Hyman	—	10	—	10	6	—	—	—	—	16
Total Identified	310	106	184	600	319	344	53	397	103	1,419
All Others	201	18	117	436	167	38	4	42	5	650
Grand Total	511	224	391	1,036	486	382	57	439	108	2,069

Exhibit 3 Projected Year 2000 All Window Covering Unit Sales, North American Market; Manufacturer Shipments of AWC by Product Type ($ million at fabricator/wholesale level)

Source: Sullivan Marketing Group.

Top Four Retail Fabricators

Company	Blinds To Go	3-Day Blinds	House of Blinds	Next Day Blinds
Sales (US$ million)	100	110	23	23
Number of U.S. stores	50	170	25	25
Number of employees	500	850	200	120
Private label as percentage	100	65	75	60
Average store size (sq. ft.)	4,000	2,000	2,500	2,000
Company status	Private + Harvard P.C.	Privately held	Privately held	Privately held
Base	Montreal, Quebec	Anaheim, California	Southfield, Michigan	Washington, D.C.
Competitive point	• 100% Private label • Funded by Harvard Private Capital • Strategy is to create a superstore for blinds and shades.	Opening larger, more upscale versions = 5 to 7 thousand sq. ft. stores. Both hard and soft window treatments will be sold. Five to 6 large format stores opened in 1997, more expected in 2000.	New HOB stores will be 6,000 sq. ft., feature a more showroom setting. Product assortment will extend to include soft window coverings and a planned line of custom beddings to co-ordinate with fabric window treatments. Shop-at-home service available.	Offers a shop-at-home service but is not a significant part of their business. Expected to expand past 30 stores in 2000.

Top Four Manufacturing Competitors

Company	Hunter-Douglas	Newell	Springs	Comfortex
Sales (US$ million)	586	349	268	58
Growth rate (%)	1–2	1–2	1–2	1–2
Competitive point	Strategy is to grow the market and enhance its market share by offering a fully integrated line of fashion and color co-ordinated AWC, and by developing innovative proprietary window covering products mainly for the upscale markets.	Leveraging the brand names of acquired companies while enhancing financial performance through cost reduction, centralization, and improvement of manufacturing processes and efficiencies.	Renewing effort to penetrate chain retailers leveraging AWC sales off its base of drapery hardware and other home textile accounts—all toward corporate end of being a leader in marketing of products to the home.	Developing retail fabricator base to serve as outlet for its innovative cellular and wood alloy shades and blinds. Recent acquisition of Verosol will provide platform for development of wholesale business.

Exhibit 4 Comparison of Blinds To Go and Indirect Competitors

Source: Sullivan Marketing Group 1997.

			Blinds To Go—2000—Sample Stock Keeping Units						% of Total Sales
	$0 to $24	$25 to $39	$40 to $59	$60 to $74	$75 to $89	$90 to $99	$100 to $119	$120+	FY 2000
Pleated Shades	n/a	Capricorn	Dante	Firenze	Marseille	Duopleat	Catania	Medley	10%
Cellular Shades	n/a	Capricorn	Masquerade	Venice	Liliana	Duopleat	Corfu	Matinee	15%
Wood Blinds	n/a	n/a	n/a	n/a	n/a	Natura	Tango	Laredo	15%
Speciality Shades	Yes	Yes	Yes	Yes	Yes	Yes	Yes	Yes	15%
Horizonal Blinds	Camino	Avanti	Mini	Mini GC	Micro GC	Aluminium	n/a	Laminated	20%
Roller Shades	Deluxe	Moire	Solarvue	Mallorca	Portofino	n/a	n/a	n/a	5%
Vertical Blinds	Premiere	Decorama	Diego	Aruba	Berber	Ascot	Chamonix	n/a	15%
Stock and/or Other	Yes	n/a	n/a	n/a	n/a	n/a	n/a	n/a	5%

Exhibit 5   Average Retail Prices for Blinds To Go Products

Source: Blinds To Go company records.

For an average blind size of 36" × 48", average retail price per order = CDN$226.

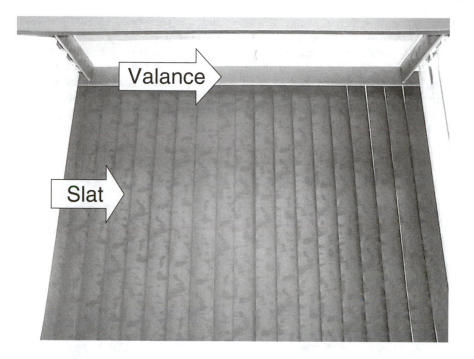

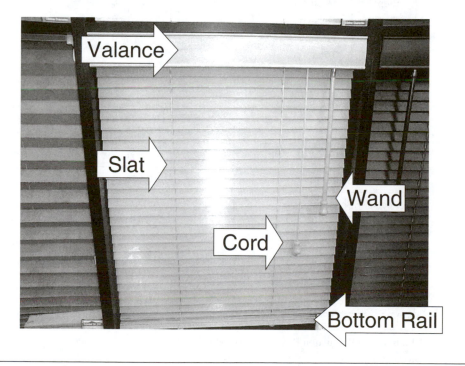

Exhibit 6   What Is a Blind?

Source: Blinds To Go company records.

had its own manufacturing department and each section employed from 40 to 50 people working at approximately 10 different stations. Work-in-process materials were shuttled between these stations using metal wheeled "buggies" that could hold up to 50 blinds at once. The workers within each station filled each buggy and then maneuvered it to the next station. Manufacturing blinds began with the selection of the head rail and slats. This was a process called "picking,"

and was performed by two people on opposite ends of the production floor. Next, slits were cut in the slats to allow for cord routing, and then the valance was matched to the head rail and the slats. Then, the head rail was assembled, painted or stained. The blinds or shades were then moved to a finishing station where they were hoisted on a rail and checked for defects and order correctness. Last, each blinds order was boxed in cardboard and shipped (see Exhibit 7).[1]

	Process for a Set of Wood Blinds	Time (minutes)
Step 1	Picking	8.2
Step 2	Slats Cutting	4.1
Step 3	Valance	3.9
Step 4	Head Rail Cutting	2.3
Step 5	Head Rail Assembly	6.4
Step 6	Painting	7.8
Step 7	Machining	14.8
Step 8	Finishing	13.6
Step 9	Packing	4.8
	Total	**65.9**

Average Total Times per Product	Time (hours)
Stock Cut	0.276
Pleated Shades	0.631
Cellular Shades	0.576
Specialty Shades	1.799
Horizontal Blinds	0.751
Roller Shades	0.470
Wooden Blinds	1.100
Vertical Blinds	0.330

Exhibit 7 Blinds To Go Production Process for Wood Blinds*

Source: Blinds To Go company records.

*The manufacturing process was slightly different for each type of blind.

As each order was slightly different from the next, care had to be taken to adhere to the unique requirements of each set of blinds. The fabrication process was very manual, and while people were trained to use the most effective method known to their supervisors, human error and poor training did lead to manufacturing errors and customer returns.

Denis Farley, the Montreal plant manager, stated,

> All our blinds are custom orders—we have to wait for them before we can begin making them. We'll know only the exact orders when they arrive. Although we can forecast the aggregate number of orders each week, we can never predict exactly what the customer will order because there are so many combinations of size, color and material available for him or her. We have over 5,000 SKUs of raw material from which to make a blind. We've set our production departments up by forecast—and our goal is to deliver finished blinds within 48 hours. The real issue is how do you train people quickly to learn how to make blinds consistently and efficiently as we continue to grow?

SALES AND SERVICE AT BLINDS TO GO STORES

The BTG selling process involved a high level of interaction with the customer, which translated into high levels of service expectations. At the retail stores, the emphasis on customer satisfaction and sale closure led to a higher volume of orders relative to their retail competition. Outlined in the Blinds To Go University Manual (training program for new sales staff) were the following four operating guidelines:

- Service and Satisfy Every Customer
- Never Lose a Sale
- Make the Customer Feel Special
- Bring the Manager Into Every Sale to Give the Customer "Old Fashioned Service"

Sales people were trained to bond with a customer through a personal greeting before asking questions about what the customer was looking for. The purpose of the next few minutes of interchange between store employee and customer was to understand the customer's primary concerns and work towards a sale by resolving those issues. Thus, the process for selling at the BTG store included the following:

- Bonding—greeting the customer and welcoming them to the store, then determining their needs by asking them open-ended questions.
- Select Product—working with the customer to find the product for their needs, addressing any objections as they come up.
- Present Price and Close the Sale—reaffirm the factory-direct price and lifetime guarantee.
- Deduct a Coupon—verify and approve coupon if customer has one.
- Introduce Customers to Managers—walk through the order with the manager and have manager greet customer.

Given that BTG's company mantra was "No customer should walk out without buying a set of blinds" and fueled by its commission-based selling culture, stores generally enjoyed an average of over US$1 million in sales per year. Orders were sent to the factory on an hourly basis, and up to 40,000 blinds per week could be processed at both manufacturing locations. Occasionally, errors would be made in customer orders due to a mistake in the selection of the correct SKU, measurement, measurement confirmation, measurement reversal, or not accounting for particularities (when working with fabric or pleats) (see Exhibit 8). If an order was incorrect for any reason, the returns process ensured that the error was corrected. The blinds were tagged and a replacement or a modified order was expected from the factory within 48 hours.

THE MONTREAL PLANT

Outgrowing its location above the original "Au Bon Marché" store in the early 1990s, a Montreal factory was built and opened in 1995 not far from Montreal's '76 Olympic Stadium. Initially serving BTG's Canadian stores, the factory soon began serving BTG's northeastern

After Sales Service Procedure

1. Hang and inspect the blind or shade with the customer

2. Review original order to determine what went wrong
   - Did customer change his/her mind?
   - Was product misordered?
   - Was product quality to blame?
   - Determine who is at fault—BTG or the customer

3. Next steps
   - Send blind or shade back to the factory*
   - Offer blind or shade at a discount
   - Offer store credit or refund

Exhibit 8   Blinds To Go Returns and Repair Process

*The salesperson had the option of reordering a new set of blinds instead of sending the blinds back to the factory, but this practice was discouraged.

U.S. stores. Running on a single extended shift of between eight to 10 hours, it handled well over 20,000 orders per week, including units processed for repairs. Blinds manufacturing was a labor-intensive operation, and skills for blinds-making were passed on to trainees through personal training from supervisors and experienced employees. BTG was in the process of creating a standard manual for its workforce, but up until now, it had relied on each supervisor's and experienced employee's specific skills to train new workers.

The labor-intensive nature of manufacturing led to differences between product group teams. It was not uncommon to see the wooden blinds section approaching its manufacturing process in a slightly different manner from the PVC blinds section. Since the Montreal factory had been in place for the longest time, it enjoyed the experience of workers who had started with BTG from its inception. New employees were trained during the first four weeks by an existing worker, who usually was a group leader, and who knew all the techniques to make blinds consistently and efficiently. Given the experience base, the Montreal plant could add new employees without a significant decrease in performance. Because of the high productivity

of the Montreal plant, at one point, some production from the Lakewood plant was shifted to Montreal while Lakewood's start-up issues were being resolved.

THE LAKEWOOD PLANT

During its first expansion phase into the United States, BTG built a plant to service its first group of stores. One of the key components of BTG's expansion was its over US$30 million manufacturing plant in Lakewood, New Jersey. Built in 1998 to eventually supply 70 to 80 stores, it started with 250 workers in the plant, expecting that number to double by the end of 2000. BTG located the new plant in an industrial park in Lakewood due to a combination of proximity to its U.S. stores, incentives offered by the city and state and the area's relatively high unemployment rate. However, unemployment had dropped by half by the time the plant opened. Thus, from the beginning, it was difficult to find qualified workers for this manufacturing facility.

During its start-up phase, problems with defects from the Lakewood plant arose rapidly. At first, the Lakewood plant employees were overwhelmed by the complexity of the manufacturing process, and a rapid rise in orders triggered a spike in the defect rate to over 10 per cent of orders in late 1998. Senior management at BTG quickly moved to remedy the problems by temporarily transferring workers from Montreal to train the staff on production procedures. Even with the influx of experience, the situation did not improve immediately, and the bulk of the new U.S. orders were shifted to the Montreal plant, which then experimented with a second shift. Finding that the second shift was not as productive as the first, BTG reverted to having one shift as soon as Lakewood came back online. A year after opening, Alfredo Fuentes, a veteran production manager from the Montreal plant, was brought in as plant manager of Lakewood. Kawai commented,

> It took two years to get Lakewood up to the efficiency of Montreal and we probably spent US$4 million in training costs and lost productivity. We had US$2 million in training grants and we spent twice that amount. And that does not include the cost of defects and additional transportation from Montreal. Knowing what we know today, we'd do it differently. We started Lakewood by having three or four people come to Montreal to train for a month—now, we'd send down 20 to 30 seasoned people to actually open the plant. We trained approximately 200 plant employees who did not stick around so we had to train another 200. We did one department at a time and didn't handle repairs in Lakewood for over a year. Thus, the salespeople were allowed to reorder a blind for a customer if they felt that it would take longer to repair one. When this happened, we had to absorb the cost of the returned blind.

> We learned a lot from the Lakewood experience and have now developed a bunch of people that we can use to open a new plant. Still, opening up in Florida will take up to one year and US$2 million of training cost to get to acceptable efficiency and quality.

Kawai had learned from the mistakes his predecessor made with Lakewood: he would not promote people before they were ready; he would have explicit standards and hold employees accountable to their objectives; and he would manage people through the training period, treating it like an apprenticeship period. He continued, "We cannot lower our standards even in a tight labor market." Since its opening, Lakewood had gone from 200 to 150, and now was approaching 250 plant employees. "What we're doing is different from what everyone else is doing," added Udofia. "Hiring somebody who doesn't come in and learn the business and who doesn't share our service objective is a huge mistake."

One interesting finding was that the most successful U.S. expansion store was located next to the Lakewood manufacturing facility. The store encouraged its customers to pay a visit to the plant, and sales employees themselves were known to make frequent trips to check on the status of orders. The rate of defects for the Lakewood retail facility was substantially lower than at other stores in the United States. Kawai wondered if his manufacturing team could draw any insights from this example.

The Lakewood production problems began to improve as the workers gained more experience, but productivity at Lakewood lagged behind that of Montreal for almost two years. For instance, direct and indirect labor were higher when compared to Montreal standards. BTG senior management attributed this discrepancy to the relatively new plant culture and thought that it would not be an issue in the following years.

Another issue that Kawai was grappling with involved scheduling shifts to better balance production with demand. Reflecting on the two production plants, Kawai noted,

> A lot of our volume comes from weekend sales. We've played with different models, but have not made a decision yet. We might work 10 hours on Monday, 10 hours on Tuesday, etc. Or we may go to a "4 + 3" schedule—four days at 10 hours per shift, then three days at nine hours per shift with a different team. There are obvious implications on labor and management supervision.

THE FLORIDA DECISION

BTG's plan was to expand its stores across North America while it still held the lead and had the momentum. There was talk of an initial public offering in the plans for 2001, putting even more pressure on senior management to improve the Lakewood plant and begin the Florida expansion (see Exhibit 9). Florida had an estimated blinds market size of US$400 million to US$500 million, enough to support at least 40 or 50 BTG stores.

Kawai outlined,

The question for Florida is this: How do we configure our manufacturing activities to best serve this Florida expansion? Our Montreal plant operations are fairly stable. Our Lakewood plant is recovering as well [see Exhibit 10]. There are going to be Florida stores starting this coming January, and we need to supply and service them.

Kawai wanted to avoid the troubles that BTG had experienced with the start-up of the Lakewood plant, and he sat down to ponder his options. "Do I build a new plant, as everyone seems to think we should do? If so, when? Or, should I just build a distribution and service centre? Or perhaps there is another, more creative solution.

NOTE

1. The manufacturing process for some types of blinds, such as fabric blinds and roller shades, differed from this description.

Type	Full-Scale*	Shell**	New Jersey
Building	$9	$3	$9
	100,000 sq. ft.	30,000 sq. ft.	100,000 sq. ft.
Leaseholds	$5	$2	$5
Inventory	$6	$2	$6
Equipment	$8	$2	$8
Personnel	400	60	250
Training Costs	$2	$1	$4
Transportation	N/A	Ship from MTL***	N/A
Total	$30	$10	$32

Exhibit 9   Blinds To Go Florida Expansion Resource Requirements (US$ millions)

Source: Blinds To Go company records.

*Full Scale = Full Production Factory.

**Shell = Distribution Centre to handle returns and repairs.

***Plant-to-plant trucking costs from the Montreal plant to the Florida plant were $1,200 per full container load (the cost was the same in both directions). Each container load could handle the requirements of 30 to 40 stores. In addition to plant-to-plant trucks, there would be local trucks that would deliver blinds from the Florida plant to the Florida stores also at a cost of $1,200 per truck. All in all, the local truck fees would cost about US$1.2 million per year to service Florida.

Montreal (2000)

Size: 110,000 sq. ft.

Employees: 400

As Percentage of Manufacturing Cost*

Product	Direct Materials	Direct Labor	Indirect Labor	Delivery	Other
Pleated Shades	60%	13.7%	6.3%	5.5%	14.5%
Cellular Shades	63%	11.7%	5.4%	4.7%	15.2%
Wooden Blinds	66%	18.8%	4.6%	4.0%	6.6%

Lakewood (2000)

Size: 100,000 sq. ft.

Employees: 250

As Percentage of Manufacturing Cost*

Product	Direct Materials	Direct Labor	Indirect Labor	Delivery	Other
Pleated Shades	55%	19.1%	11.5%	5.0%	9.4%
Cellular Shades	56%	16.1%	9.7%	4.2%	14.0%
Wooden Blinds	60%	23.8%	8.9%	3.2%	4.1%

Exhibit 10   Blinds To Go Montreal and Lakewood Plant Statistics

Source: Blinds To Go company records.

*Retail gross margins were 45 per cent.

ASIMCO INTERNATIONAL CASTING COMPANY (A)

*Prepared by Sophia Liu under the
supervision of Professor Robert D. Klassen*

Version: (A) 2004-04-06

After a heated debate, Ron Martin, general manager of ASIMCO International Casting Company (AICC), returned to his office from a product meeting to review an inviting offer to bid on new business. Mr. Tadayi, general manager of SAME, a new potential customer, had offered glowing praise after his three-hour tour of AICC's operations. "I'm a foundry man, and this is one of the best foundries I have visited. In many ways this plant is as good as those in Japan. We are willing to discuss a long-term supply contract with you."

AICC's sales director had observed, "This is a golden opportunity to dramatically build our sales and reputation." In response, the operations director quickly countered, "But the product doesn't fit our process and equipment. SAME's 4G6 gasoline engine block is very different from our current diesel engine castings, and I don't think our people are ready for that yet."

It was September 1998, and AICC, a Chinese joint venture between ASIMCO and Caterpillar, had recently finished several major projects designed to upgrade its operations. Martin was now feeling significant pressure to increase revenue as the Chinese plant was operating far below capacity. But was SAME the right customer for AICC? This order might also provide the ideal opportunity to change the molding process to a new, higher quality technology. Or should the plant's limited engineering resources be focused on meeting the needs of Caterpillar? Martin expected Caterpillar to soon authorize test runs of two new products, although the annual production volumes were very uncertain.

FOUNDRY INDUSTRY IN CHINA

Iron castings, whereby a metal object is obtained from molten metal that solidified in a mold, were used in a wide array of market applications. In China, the industry was both large and diverse, with many small operations to service local needs. In 1997, there were approximately 22,000 foundries producing a total of 12 million tonnes of castings annually. (Comparable figures for the United States were 3,000 foundries producing about 14.5 million tonnes.) Because of the shortage of investment capital, many foundries used older technologies that were labor-intensive and delivered marginal quality.

A major market for the foundry industry was the automotive and transportation sector. For example, castings represented about 45 per cent of an automobile by weight, with the most technologically complex castings being the engine block and the engine head. Most of the foundries supplying this sector were subsidiaries of large automotive groups, termed *captive* foundries; these foundries shipped most of their castings to other business units in the same auto group. Transfer prices were typically at or below cost, with the parent company subsidizing any foundry losses.

One such auto group, First Auto Works (FAW), was based in Changchun, in northern China. Its 43 subsidiaries employed more than 100,000 people and produced a wide range of parts, components and vehicles. In an effort to improve overall efficiency, FAW had started to outsource non-critical parts. While engine manufacturing was still viewed as critical and had been retained in-house, some industry analysts expected that even these foundry operations would soon be separated out to encourage competition on quality and price.

FAW's five foundries had a total capacity of 208,000 tonnes annually, although current shipments were estimated to be only 140,000 tonnes (overcapacity was common throughout the industry). The products of these foundries were generally simpler in design and of lower quality than castings produced in leading foundries in Japan and the United States. Unfortunately, FAW did not have either the equipment or technical competence (i.e., the engineering or production worker capabilities) to produce newer, more complicated block and head castings. To address these shortcomings, the foundries were gradually being upgraded to improve quality.

In contrast to many captive foundries, Komatsu Changzhou Foundry (KCF) was a major foundry in China that had benefited from foreign investment of RMB250 million.[1] In 1998, KCF had the capacity to produce 24,000 tonnes of castings, although it too was reported to be operating at less than 50 per cent of capacity. Among its many products, KCF produced an engine casting that approached the complexity and quality demanded for SAME's 4G6 engine block.

Foundries capable of producing such engine castings required substantial capital investment and usually took two to three years to build and start up operations, with key equipment for sophisticated casting operations being imported from Germany and Japan. Operations were also very labor-intensive, and worker training was a substantial undertaking, often requiring six or more months.

To protect the industry, the Chinese government historically had imposed high duties on imported parts. These duties were expected to fall from 30 per cent to 10 per cent by 2005. But cost was not the only challenge. Evolving environmental standards were forcing domestic manufacturers to introduce new engine designs that reduced emissions and improved fuel economy. Naturally, these engines were much more complex to cast than their predecessors. It was clear that if Chinese foundries were unable to produce new designs quickly, the complex engine castings would continue to be imported from elsewhere in the world.

ENGINE BLOCK MANUFACTURING

Design of Engine Blocks

Medium- and heavy-duty trucks and tractors favored diesel engines, while passenger cars and vans typically used gasoline engines. Gasoline engine blocks tended to be much smaller, often weighing less than 100 kilograms, versus 150 kilograms or more for a diesel engine block (see Exhibit 1). These basic design differences translated into much more demanding technical requirements, in such areas as metal strength and dimensional tolerances, for gasoline engine blocks.

The tighter specifications were reflected in market prices and manufacturing challenges. The market price for high-quality *diesel* engine block castings averaged at RMB8,000 per tonne, with a range of RMB6,000 to RMB9,000 (industry practice was to quote prices by weight, not pieces). The greater complexity of the *gasoline* engine blocks tended to inflate scrap rates, which translated in price premiums of 40 per cent to 50 per cent. Finally, head castings were priced on

average about 25 per cent higher than the comparable engine block.

Basic Foundry Processes

Foundry operations for engine block production comprised several basic steps (see Exhibit 2).

1. A set of three-dimensional shapes was produced in the core-making operation. These shapes, termed cores, were largely made of sand with a resin additive, and subsequently formed the inner surfaces and voids of a casting. Depending on the casting design, basic cores could be assembled into more complex shapes (e.g., piston cylinders). New core machines could be added or removed to accommodate changes in demand or to configure new products.

2. In a parallel operation, molds were created that would later form the outer surface of the finished casting. Molds were formed using one of two technologies: green sand process or cold core capsule process (see Molding Process Technology). The mold was transferred to a large metal frame, called a flask, which was used to move the mold through the remainder of the foundry process. A molding line was designed to accommodate a particular size of flask, and dozens of flasks were placed on a molding line. This line was always viewed as the heart of the foundry operations and required the largest proportion of capital investment.

To improve efficiency, molds could be designed to create multiple copies of the same casting, with the number being limited by the molding technology and the relative sizes of the casting and flask. For example, several castings of a gasoline engine block or a single casting of a diesel engine block might be produced in the same flask on a molding line.

Suppliers of molding equipment had become quite specialized because of significant product and process differences between diesel and gasoline engine blocks. DISA, a Japanese firm, was a frequent supplier of equipment for casting gasoline engine blocks, whereas German suppliers,

SAME's 4G6 Gasoline Engine Block (60 kg.)

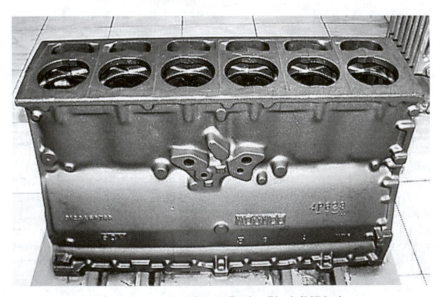

Caterpillar's 3306 Diesel Engine Block (267 kg.)

Exhibit 1   Diesel and Gasoline Engine Blocks

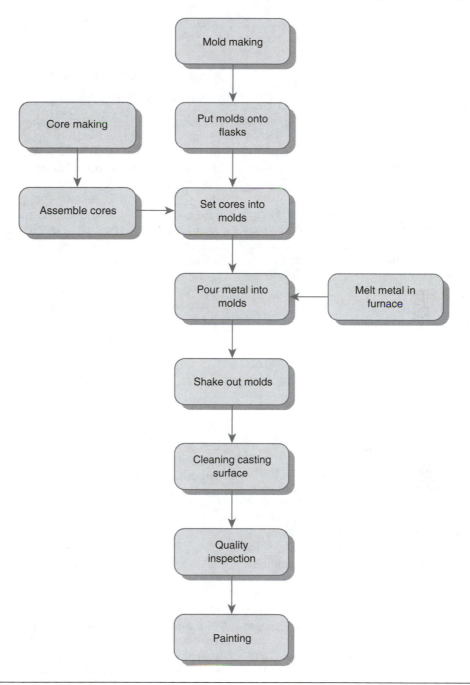

Exhibit 2   Foundry Process for Engine Blocks

such as Kunkel Wagner, provided equipment that was better suited for large, heavy diesel engine blocks. Diesel and gasoline engine blocks were typically produced in separate foundries, or if in the same foundry, in separate molding lines.

3. Assembled cores were transferred from core-making operations and inserted in molds (see Exhibit 3). Next, molten metal was poured into the assembled molds. The raw material for iron castings was prepared by mixing and melting together different grades of raw iron, foundry scrap, steel scrap, ferroalloys and other metals. Finally, the solidified castings were extracted from the molds, cleaned, inspected and painted before shipment to customers. Because of the size and weight of the filled molds, little inventory was possible between the molding line and downstream operations.

Manufacturing Challenges

Product quality and operational efficiency depended to a significant degree on three major factors: product complexity, labor skill and process design. As the complexity of the casting increased, more cores were needed to create the necessary product features and voids, which also tended to increase the likelihood of quality problems.

The foundry process was very labor-intensive, especially in the core assembly and the cleaning of the casting surface. In core assembly, workers bolted together a dozen or more cores, and then placed the assembled cores into molds. While skilled workers could do this with a reasonable degree of accuracy, new workers used additional tools to check the positioning of the cores. In developed countries with high labor costs, such as Japan, foundries might use capital-intensive, automatic core assembly machines to reduce labor costs and lower defects.

During assembly, workers also checked for broken cores. Again, judgment was needed, as some broken cores could be used successfully for castings, while others, depending on the nature of the defect, would cause a problem. Changing a broken core required additional rework and slowed operations. Finally, process technologies could be used to improve the quality of castings and raise productivity.

Molding Process Technology

Green Sand Technology

Green sand molding was the traditional foundry technology, whereby the mold was formed from a mixture of silicon sand, bentonite clay and coal. The mixture was packed around a pattern, and then compressed into the required shape using high pressure. The pattern was then removed, and its imprint became the mold cavity into which the molten metal was poured. The mold was then transferred to the flask to be moved through the rest of the foundry operations.

This method required highly skilled production workers, particularly when the cores were set and assembled into the molds prior to adding the molten metal. Any deviation from specifications in the placement of the cores resulted in dimensional defects, which could not be detected until final inspection. Dimension defects varied dramatically, ranging from as high as 20 per cent to 50 per cent in new foundries, to as low as five per cent or less for basic castings at foundries in developed countries with highly skilled workers and mature processes, such as that at Mitsubishi Japan. In China, variable costs for materials, labor and utilities collectively amounted to about half the market price.

Cold Core Capsule Technology

Instead of using green sand to form the exterior surface of the casting, a resin capsule could be employed. Capsules were very similar to cores—formed of sand and resin, and produced on core machines. However, the capsules were cured using sulfur dioxide to create a strong smooth surface. Green sand was then used around the edges of the mold only to position the capsules. Because both sand and capsules were now required, fewer castings were possible in molds that produced multiple copies (see Exhibit 4).

Given the greater strength of the capsules relative to green sand molds, cold core capsule

Cores are set before the mold is closed

Exhibit 3   Core Placement in Molds on Molding Line

technology made it easier for workers to set and assemble cores accurately. Thus, while fewer castings per mold reduced productivity, this technology produced castings with a better surface quality and tighter dimensional accuracy. Both the initial and long-term scrap rates were expected to be about half of those from a green sand process, particularly for more complex castings. As a result, modern foundries favored this method for high quality, complex castings.

Obtaining a domestic supply of resin for both cores and capsules had proven problematic for Chinese firms, and foundries were forced to import resin from the United States. In 1998, one of the world's largest suppliers of resin had

begun to explore options for building a resin plant in China. However, this supplier had indicated that its decision was contingent on a large foundry, such as AICC, adopting the cold core capsule technology for a high-volume casting—something that no foundry had yet done.

Variable costs were approximately 30 per cent higher for this process technology, relative to green sand technology, largely driven by the extra labor and resin needed to produce the capsules. However, this cost difference did not take into account scrap rates. Little could be recycled from scrapped castings produced by either process, with the exception of the cast metal (i.e., materials from Melting) (see Exhibit 5).

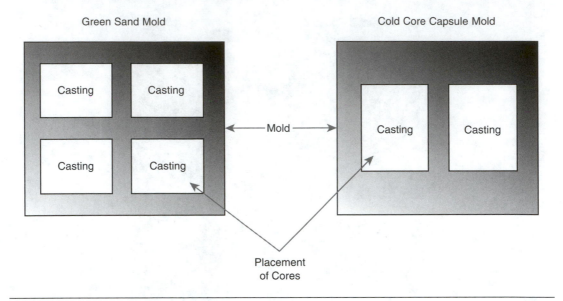

Green Sand Mold | Cold Core Capsule Mold

Casting | Casting

Casting | Casting

←— Mold —→

Casting | Casting

Placement
of Cores

Exhibit 4   Mold Technology and Casting Placement

	Green Sand	*Cold Core Capsule*
Materials:		
Core making	34	62
Molding	4	5
Melting	30	30
Cleaning	11	12
Labor	10	10
Utilities	11	11
Total	**100**	**130**

Exhibit 5   Comparison of Production Costs for Molding Technologies (percentage of total variable costs)

Note: Variable costs represented about half the market price for engine castings using green sand technology. Total variable costs were 30% higher if cold core capsule technology was used.

AICC JOINT VENTURE

The government had built a military manufacturing base in the 1970s in the central mountainous area of Shanxi Province. Eight scattered factories, collectively managed by CITIC Machining and Manufacturing Inc. (CMMI), were built to produce tanks and military trucks. One of the factories, Factory 5419, was a foundry designed to produce medium to large iron and steel castings for tanks and diesel engines. Unfortunately, the factory now operated at very low volumes with a workforce of 2,800 people. Worker skills were limited; however, much less training was needed than for a new workforce. The foundry also had a shortage of skilled engineers capable of directing a new product introduction and ramp-up. While engineers were being actively recruited, it had proven difficult to attract and retain qualified people to work and live in this remote mountainous area.

ASIMCO Technologies

Headquartered in Beijing, China, ASIMCO Technologies was formed in 1994 with total investment of US$300 million to create a leading components manufacturer in China. The strategy was to acquire majority positions in existing suppliers and then add capital, management and technology to bring the acquired companies up to global standards for quality and service. By 1998, ASIMCO was China's third largest auto parts supplier, with 17 plants and 36 sales offices throughout China.

Management was first introduced to Factory 5419 in 1996 and spent six months evaluating the facility and its potential. However, ASIMCO had little specific experience with foundry operations, and the facility clearly needed investment in both advanced technology and better management techniques. The project was presented to Caterpillar, who had been searching for an opportunity to enter a Chinese joint venture.

Caterpillar

A U.S. Fortune 500 company, Caterpillar was recognized for the advanced design of diesel engines and components, including castings. Engine sales generated about a quarter of the firm's total revenue, second only to earth-moving machinery. A company-owned foundry in the United States produced most of the castings for the critical components in Caterpillar's diesel engines.

As one of the major engine producers in the world, management wanted to establish a presence in China to improve access and gain market information, as well as to develop experience with local operations. This market was expected to grow dramatically over the coming years. A joint venture foundry was seen by Caterpillar as a test before any further expansion into China, and could serve as a backup source of supply for critical castings.

Ron Martin, who led the Caterpillar team in their search for a foundry joint venture partner in China, explained the rationale behind the investment decision:

> Caterpillar did not seek to establish a wholly-owned foundry primarily because local partners could bring access to the market and knowledge of operating in the unique Chinese environment. An established manufacturing operation also was expected to shorten the start-up time because a skilled work force was already in place, which is very critical for a foundry. We visited several potential partners with manufacturing bases in larger cities such as Beijing, Dalian and Guangzhou. However, concerns about possible environmental regulations for foundries in larger cities forced us to search for other sites.

What attracted these investors most was the German molding line. Purchased in the late 1970s, it had seldom been used since. Unfortunately, despite its almost new condition, significant investment was needed to enable the production of higher quality castings. To encourage investment, CMMI significantly discounted the value of the molding line, other equipment, buildings and land.

Based on these factors, ASIMCO, Caterpillar and CMMI established a joint venture, with the agreement signed in February 1997. ASIMCO was the largest contributor of capital, and this foundry represented one of its largest investments. Initially called the Shanxi International Casting Company, the name was later changed to ASIMCO International Casting Company (AICC). The nature of the joint venture also dictated that this would not be a captive foundry. In addition to potentially supplying Caterpillar, the plant would also target the growing market in China for more complex engine castings.

FOUNDRY INVESTMENT

A start-up team, including three people from the foundry operations of Caterpillar (U.S.), three from ASIMCO and seven from AICC, started working on redesign and planning, termed technical reform. This began even before the joint venture contract was approved by the government. Hank Sun, the engineering manager from ASIMCO, observed:

> In many ways, technical reform was more difficult and complicated than building a new facility. Several foundry experts who worked in the Caterpillar foundry brought unique techniques and process designs, and we had to incorporate those into the existing equipment and building. Unfortunately, some equipment, although still functional, had to be scrapped because it did not fit the redesigned process; some buildings also had to be demolished.
>
> Yet, we could not simply copy Caterpillar's process design. The molding line was more technically advanced in the U.S., and raw materials like scrap steel were of higher, more consistent quality. Most importantly, workers and engineers in Caterpillar's foundry were more experienced and capable. We tried to simplify AICC's process to match local engineering and worker skills.

Once the plan was finalized, equipment selection and design of the building renovation was started. AICC selected major manufacturing equipment from the world's best suppliers, putting the most advanced industrial technology into China to date. Approximately 60 per cent of the equipment was purchased domestically, which helped to limit the capital investment to about RMB275 million.

In addition to capital investment, Caterpillar made a five-year commitment to provide technical and management assistance. The general manager, director of technical reform, director of operations and a number of other experts were brought from Caterpillar foundry operations in the United States to oversee the technical reform project and manage daily operations.

Production Ramp-Up

Production began even as new investment continued. Quality of the incoming raw materials was particularly critical, and Caterpillar's specifications were adopted for the supply of metal. An experienced metallurgist from Caterpillar U.S. was assigned to visit potential suppliers to evaluate the production process and quality control system.

The molding line was designed for medium-sized engine blocks and heads. Each flask, measuring 1.2 m × 1 m × 0.45 m, was designed to carry the mold that supported a total casting weight of 150 to 300 kilograms. The molding line was expected to run at 60 molds per hour during the first year, with a further ramp-up to 70 molds per hour by 2000.

The line restarted production in June 1998, but unfortunately, was down 70 per cent of the time for repairs and maintenance. Engineers then predicted that downtime should fall to 25 per cent over the next year. Current workforce availability allowed for either two 10-hour shifts or three 8-hour shifts over a five-day workweek.

Although technical reform was less than half finished, small production volumes were started in mid-1998. Ron Martin explained such a strategy:

> We used existing patterns to make the YC6105 engine block, which was an old and relatively simple casting. This product had been in production for a Chinese engine company prior to upgrading the foundry operations. While manufacturing during equipment installation and building renovation can create problems, these conflicts can be minimized through good scheduling. We expected that it would take at least six months to train our workers, and we wanted them to get ready for more complex work in the near future.
>
> To convince potential customers to contract with us, we must sell the factory first, and the best presentation is a running factory. North American customers simply would not sign a long-term contract until they are convinced that AICC is capable of producing high quality castings.

New Market Opportunities

AICC's primary target markets were domestic and foreign engine manufacturers, who would be likely to pay a premium for high-quality products yet would benefit from lower labor costs. Early efforts resulted in several potential Chinese and North American customers requesting a quotation to produce an *existing* engine block casting already manufactured in another foundry.

To prepare a bid, the foundry would estimate production costs based on a customer-supplied product design, which helped to determine the material, process and quality characteristics. Tighter specifications tended to generate higher scrap rates, which in turn had to be captured in the price quotation. The foundry also paid all development costs related to any new casting; these costs could range from RMB75,000 to more than RMB750,000 (see Exhibit 6). By September 1998, AICC had identified a number of potential customers and products (see Exhibit 7).

In contrast, long-term contracts for *new* high-volume engine block castings were negotiated only with established foundries that had a strong reputation for quality and delivery. Both the manufacturer and foundry committed considerable time, money and energy to develop castings for new engines. For these reasons, engine manufacturers would initially target one supplier, which would typically maintain the supply contract throughout the life of the engine, and later possibly add another foundry as a supplier as the product matured.

Caterpillar's 3306 Engine Block and Head

Caterpillar had been purchasing castings for engine components from its captive foundry in the United States, as well as non-captive foundries in Brazil and Mexico. As an investor to AICC, Caterpillar anticipated purchasing castings equivalent to about 30 per cent of AICC's capacity. However, contracts were not assured, as AICC still had to compete against other potential suppliers on quality, price and

Process design	Based on the casting design drawings provided by the customer and the manufacturing equipment required, product engineers design the production process. Initial process design takes about one month.
Pattern design and building	Metal patterns are needed for core making and assembling. Typically, engine manufacturers pay and own the tooling, but foundries work with tooling suppliers to design and build patterns. It takes three to six months to build a pattern. A set of complicated high-quality patterns for gasoline engine block would cost US$1 million if made in America, or RMB2 million if made in China.
Sample production & process adjustment	Engineers arrange and monitor to produce sample castings using the new pattern and process. During the process, engineers record the quality variations and adjust process, before making more samples. It takes two to 12 months before qualified samples are made. The length of the sample process largely depends on engineering experience and operation capability.
Sample validation	10 to 100 pieces of samples are sent to engine manufactures to verify quality. Metal strength and dimensions are key quality specifications. Engine manufacturers assemble castings with other parts of the engine and run the engine for up to 1,000 hours for quality and durability test. Sample validation takes two to three months.
Small batch production	If samples pass all quality tests, the foundry will arrange small batch production to test if the production process is under control. Each batch varies from 50 to 200 pieces.
Mass production	Process will be finalized and mass production starts after small batch production succeeds.

Exhibit 6   New Product Introduction

Exhibit 7 AICC Five-Year Sales Forecast

#	Casting Product	Potential Customer	Degree of Confidence for Order**	Weight (kg. per piece)	Molding (pieces per mold)	1999 pieces	1999 tonnes	2000 pieces	2000 tonnes	2001 pieces	2001 tonnes	2002 pieces	2002 tonnes	2003 pieces	2003 tonnes
1	YC 6105 block	Yuchai China	1	180	1	16,400	2,950	20,000	3,600	20,000	3,600	15,000	2,700	15,000	2,700
2	YC 6112 block	Yuchai China	1	262	1	600	160	4,000	1,050	10,000	2,620	15,000	3,930	15,000	3,930
3	YC 6112 head	Yuchai China	1	83	1	—	—	3,500	290	10,000	830	15,000	1,250	15,000	1,250
4	SAME 4G6 block	SAME China	2	60	2 or 4*	12,000	720	24,000	1,440	80,000	4,800	100,000	6,000	130,000	7,800
5	CAT 3306 4P0623 block	Caterpillar U.S.	2	267	1	2,600	690	22,500	6,010	19,700	5,260	20,000	5,340	20,000	5,340
6	CAT 3306 7C3906 head	Caterpillar U.S.	2	106	1	100	10	20,000	2,120	22,000	2,330	20,000	2,120	20,000	2,120
7	CAT D88N4674 head	Caterpillar U.S.	3	115	1	—	—	2,000	230	2,000	230	3,000	350	3,000	350
8	CAT 9G9982 case	Caterpillar U.S.	3	265	1	—	—	1,000	270	2,000	530	3,000	800	3,000	800
9	CAT 3304 7N5454 block	Caterpillar U.S.	3	196	1	—	—	2,000	390	1,300	250	1,500	290	3,000	590
10	CAT 3304 7C3906 head	Caterpillar U.S.	3	75	1	—	—	2,500	190	1,700	130	2,000	150	3,000	230
11	CAT 3208 9N3758 block	Caterpillar U.S.	3	213	1	—	—	2,300	490	2,100	450	2,500	530	2,500	530
12	CAT 3208 2W7165 head	Caterpillar U.S.	3	65	1	—	—	1,200	80	2,000	130	2,500	160	2,500	160
13	LB3201041 block	Liberhare China	4	205	1	25	5	3,000	620	4,000	820	4,000	820	5,000	1,030
14	LB3201042 block	Liberhare China	4	287	1	25	7	3,000	860	4,000	1,150	4,000	1,150	5,000	1,440
15	LB3021286 case	Liberhare China	4	125	1	25	3	3,000	380	4,000	500	4,000	500	5,000	630
16	NC X6110 block	Nanchang China	4	225	1	—	—	1,500	340	3,000	680	5,000	1,130	5,000	1,130
17	NC X6110 head	Nanchang China	4	30	1	—	—	1,500	50	3,000	90	5,000	150	5,000	150
18	BJ 6-Cylinder block	Chrysler China	4	85	1	—	—	—	—	2,000	170	5,000	430	8,000	680
19	BJ 6-Cylinder head	Chrysler China	4	20	1	—	—	—	—	2,000	40	5,000	100	8,000	160
20	Perkin 660 block	Perkins China†	3	167	1	—	—	—	—	10,000	1,670	10,000	1,670	20,000	3,340
21	Perkins 440 block	Perkins China†	3	121	1	—	—	—	—	10,000	1,210	10,000	1,210	20,000	2,420
22	CAT 3116 block	Caterpillar U.S.	3	205	1	—	—	—	—	20,000	4,100	30,000	6,150	30,000	6,150
	Total potential volume (annual)					31,775	4,545	117,000	18,410	234,800	31,590	281,500	36,930	343,000	42,930

*Two pieces per mold for cold core capsule versus four pieces per mold for green sand technology.

**Rated from 1 = confirmed to 4 = very uncertain. If an order was confirmed, it was expected to continue for all years shown.

†Perkins had been purchased by Caterpillar in early 1998.

delivery. In 1998, AICC received a request for quotation from Caterpillar for two castings produced in the United States and Mexico: the 3306 engine block and the 3306 head. AICC's quotation of RMB2,200 for the engine block and RMB1,100 for the head was based on the prices charged by the Mexican supplier.

The engine block and heads would use the same green sand molding technology that was employed by the U.S. and Mexico foundries. Because of the size of the castings, only a single piece (i.e., one block or one head) could be cast in each mold. Preliminary engineering estimates indicated that an engine block would require about 72 minutes per tonne of production time from a core machine; an engine head would require about 130 minutes per tonne.

If the bid was accepted, AICC would proceed with detailed process design and start-up, which was expected to take at least 12 months. AICC would assign the only two senior product engineers to manage this start-up process because of the importance of this customer; more junior staff simply did not have sufficient experience. Once production commenced, Caterpillar U.S. would approve the products and process for mass production. However, annual volumes were very uncertain, as most production might still remain in North American foundries. While marketing estimates exceeded 7,000 tonnes annually by 2000, volumes might vary from as little as 1,000 tonnes up to 8,000 tonnes per year.

Mitsubishi's SAME 4G6 Engine Block

The 4G6 engine was a mature design used in jeeps and light buses. The 4G6 engine block was relatively light in weight, with tight specifications for both the metal strength and dimensional accuracy. The engine was currently produced using green sand technology in Japan for the Japanese market. The Japanese foundry had an excess annual capacity of 50,000 castings. Despite the excess capacity, Mitsubishi had entered a new joint venture, SAME, to produce this engine in China for the Chinese market.

Production from SAME's plant was expected to commence in early 1999, and ultimately, the plant was to assemble up to 150,000 gasoline engines, all of the 4G6 design. In order to test the new assembly line, SAME planned to import key components from Japan to simplify start-up. However, higher labor and utility costs in Japan, combined with shipping costs and import duties, suggested that imported engine blocks were likely to be at least twice the price of those potentially supplied by a Chinese foundry.

A major task for SAME's purchasing department was to source local suppliers. Potential suppliers for the engine block casting included FAW, KCF and AICC. The volume of engine sales in the Chinese market varied considerably from month to month, with sales in March to May being the highest, sometimes amounting to 50 per cent of annual sales. Engine manufacturers typically give suppliers a three-month rolling forecast for the monthly demand.

As AICC product engineers developed a preliminary process design for the bid, it became clear that the choice of molding process technology was a major issue. The green sand and cold core capsule processes required different patterns, and changing the process at a later point would require significant additional investment. If green sand molding was used, four engine block castings could be produced in each mold. Producing this large number in one mold was only feasible because the 4G6 engine block was about one-quarter of the size of diesel engine blocks such as the Caterpillar's 3306.

Alternatively, using the cold core capsule technology for the 4G6 would offer definite advantages in terms of quality. This technology, if adopted, would be its first application in China. However, because the capsules required additional space in the mold, only two castings could be produced per mold. The core machines would also have to produce capsules as well as cores, which would require about 276 minutes per tonne of production (twice that for green sand molding). If necessary, core machines could be purchased for approximately RMB1.2 million to supplement the six core machines currently installed.

GOING FORWARD

Martin faced several critical decisions. Should AICC continue to aggressively pursue both the Caterpillar and Mitsubishi orders? His basic concerns centered on plant capacity, process design and organizational capabilities. It was not clear how the two could be managed simultaneously, and if AICC aggressively pursued only one, which one?

In terms of the capacity, Martin was feeling intense pressure to ramp up both revenue and production volumes to justify the recently completed capital investments. It was not clear that dropping either potential order would be well-received by the joint venture partners. Unfortunately, the small production volumes had generated only very limited data on which to estimate costs.

Martin was also very concerned about how capable the molding process and people were to quality demands of any new orders. The inherent quality advantages of the cold core capsule process technology might smooth start-up and offer other strategic benefits. Producing the Mitsubishi 4G6 casting might provide the perfect opportunity to learn about this new technology.

Organizationally, there was a critical shortage of engineering resources. Only two experienced senior product engineers were capable of leading new product start-up. Until now, Martin had planned to assign them to lead the two Caterpillar products. He was not confident that these engineers could address the needs of SAME too. While the Caterpillar's U.S. foundry was willing to provide technical support when needed for any new production, the U.S. foundry did not produce a small engine block similar to the 4G6. If AICC experienced problems during start-up, how would they be overcome?

NOTE

1. RMB1 = US$0.12.

THE ATLANTA SYMPHONY ORCHESTRA

Prepared by Jorge Colazo under the supervision of Professor Larry J. Menor

Version: (A) 2004-12-07

INTRODUCTION

In November 2001, the Atlanta Symphony Orchestra (ASO), conducted by its newly appointed music director Robert Spano, performed the rarely heard *A Sea Symphony* by the English composer Ralph Vaughan Williams. The musical performance of *A Sea Symphony,* with lyrics taken from poems contained in Walt Whitman's *Leaves of Grass,* was by all accounts superb. While most members of the audience cheered the performance, a few stormed out of the concert hall, largely in reaction to the high-tech mixed media show designed by Polish video artist Piotr Szyhalski that accompanied the ASO's performance. Szyhalski's black and white video, shown on a single jumbo screen situated behind the orchestra, depicted for some a story all its own. The images of women cutting cloth, banners waving and clocks spinning seemed to be connected only subtly to Whitman's text and Vaughan Williams' music. This performance of *A Sea Symphony* was one of the ASO's recent occasional and innovative breaks from concert tradition. By adding visual complements to selected concerts and increasing interactions between the musicians on stage and the audience, the ASO was in the midst of broadening its orchestral concert experience. The ASO's performance innovations were the result of a partnership between the artistic stakeholders and the community.

The enhancement of the ASO's concert experience also extended beyond the performance stage. John Sparrow, vice-president and general manager of the ASO since October 2000, was in the midst of reviewing an incentive program intended to encourage the current group of symphony hall ushers to be more service oriented. For example, if an usher overheard an ASO patron talking about finding a place to eat after the concert, Sparrow hoped the usher would be able to approach that patron and say, "I could not help overhearing your need for a place to eat after tonight's performance, so here are a couple of nearby restaurants that we recommend." Sparrow recognized that opportunities existed onstage and offstage for enriching the ASO's services and the concert experiences of its audience.

History of the
Atlanta Symphony Orchestra

The ASO was founded in 1945 as a youth ensemble. The orchestra grew into a semi-professional adult orchestra, then to a professional orchestra in 1947. The orchestra currently employed 95 musicians who were complemented by the ASO Chorus and the Atlanta Symphony Youth Orchestra. The ASO's music directors, conductors who had wide-ranging authority over artistic issues from setting the tempo of a musical performance to the hiring and firing of players (within the contract constraints for unionized orchestras), included Henry Sopkin (1945–1966), Robert Shaw (1967–1987), Yoel Levi (1988–2000) and Robert Spano (2001 to present). ASO musicians were full-time professionals who performed over 200 concerts annually. Many of these musicians, who started with a base salary of $70,000, also engaged in musical instruction as well.[1]

Over the past 30 years, the orchestra had performed at the Woodruff Arts Center's Symphony Hall (WAC), a 1,765-seat concert hall situated in downtown Atlanta. Atlanta, with a population exceeding three million, was the largest metropolitan area in the southeastern United States and represented almost 40 per cent of Georgia's population. The ASO also regularly performed at several local venues including the Chastain Park Amphitheater, the summer home for the ASO, and other civic and regional venues. While the ASO's music director, like that of other orchestras, oversaw artistic quality and musical performances, there were other individuals involved in the administrative management of the organization (see Exhibit 1).

The ASO, unlike the American "Big Five" orchestras, had toured infrequently.[2] Its first European tour, under the direction of Robert Shaw, took place in 1988. The second European tour in 1991, under the baton of Yoel Levi, involved presenting concerts in 16 different cities including London, Paris and Vienna. Subsequent financial challenges led to the decision to defer touring from the mid- to late 1990s in order to facilitate the orchestra's economic growth.

The ASO was the most recognized and active of the orchestras that were based in Georgia (see Exhibit 2). Several of the other Atlanta-based orchestras were non-professional (e.g., Atlanta Community Symphony Orchestra and the Emory Symphony Orchestra) and presented a limited number of performances annually. The ASO's 2001–2002 annual operating budget of $25 million made it the largest performing arts organization in the southeastern United States. However, its endowment, which surpassed $70 million in fiscal year ending (FYE) 2001, generally used to support expenditures with interest and dividend income and to cover budget deficits, was still comparatively small for a major U.S. orchestra. Typically, an orchestra's artistic quality could be quickly assessed based upon the size of that institution's annual operating budget, while its financial soundness was based on the size of its endowment (see Exhibit 3).

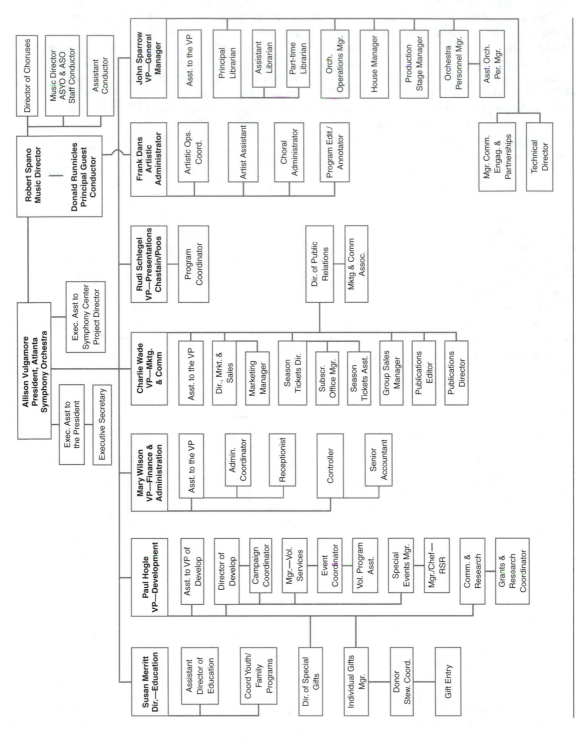

Exhibit 1   Atlanta Symphony Orchestra Organizational Structure

Source: ASO files.

(Continued)

Selected Administrative Job Descriptions

President

Responsible for managing the human and financial resources of the orchestra. Also responsible and accountable for all operations aspects of the organization, and implementing the policies set by the board of directors. The president is selected by and reports to the orchestra's board of directors through the board president. His/her artistic counterpart is the music director.

Vice-President—General Manager

Responsible for ensuring that the scheduling and production of all orchestra events (concerts, rehearsals, tours and special events) run smoothly, effectively and in a financially responsible manner. This individual functions as a liaison between the orchestra and the rest of the administrative staff.

Vice-President—Marketing and Communications

Responsible for planning, supervising, administering and evaluating programs that meet/exceed attendance and ticket revenue goals and maximize the visibility of the orchestra. This individual plans and manages public relations (e.g., press, program books), advertising, season subscription and renewal campaigns, audience research, new subscriber activities and merchandising.

Vice-President—Finance and Administration

Responsible for the business and financial operations of the organization (e.g., financial planning, control and reporting). The chief financial officer is also responsible for preparation of the annual operating budget and financial projections, monthly financial statements, banking relations and the administration of payroll, employee benefits and personnel policies.

Vice-President—Development

Responsible for the development, management, implementation and evaluation of fund-raising (e.g., annual campaign, sponsorship, endowment and planned giving programs). This individual is also responsible for making grant applications to federal, state and local government agencies providing arts funding, and researching and applying to private foundations and corporations providing arts grants.

Director—Education

Responsible for designing, developing, administering and evaluating all education and outreach programs (e.g., supervision of all volunteers and staff involved in delivering any aspect of these programs). He/she represents the orchestra to other arts, education and civic institutions to promote constructive working partnerships in the community.

Exhibit 1   Atlanta Symphony Orchestra Organizational Structure

Source: Adapted from American Symphony Orchestra League "Administrative Job Descriptions—The Orchestral Association."

The majority of the ASO's concerts, taking place at the WAC, revolved around playing standard classical music compositions performed with world-renowned soloists and, on occasion, under the baton of guest conductors. The scope and quality of the ASO's musical activities and offerings over the past three decades had firmly established the orchestra's reputation, and it enjoyed a strong regional appeal. The ASO was the only North American orchestra to have ever performed at a United States presidential inaugural concert and at Olympic opening and closing ceremonies (see Exhibit 4).

(Text continues on page 391)

Orchestra	City	Number of Musicians	Number of Concerts per Season	Annual Operating Budget Classification	Annual Guest Artist & Guest Conductor Fees Classification
Albany Symphony Orchestra	Albany	80	15	$260,000–$1,050,000	$20,000–$75,000
Atlanta Community Symphony Orchestra	Atlanta	65	5	< $35,000	$1,500–$3,500
Orchestra Atlanta	Roswell	55	6	$100,000–$150,000	$7,000–$20,000
Atlanta Pops Orchestra	Atlanta	55	45–55	$100,000–$150,000	—
Atlanta Symphony Orchestra	Atlanta	95	200+	> $10,000,000	> $1,000,000
Atlanta Symphony Youth Orchestra	Atlanta	120	5	$35,000–$100,000	< $1,500
Augusta Symphony Orchestra	Augusta	80	31	$260,000–$1,050,000	$20,000–$75,000
Coastal Symphony of Georgia	St. Simon's Island	45–50	5	$35,000–$100,000	$1,500–$3,500
Cobb Symphony Orchestra	Marietta	75	7	$150,000–$260,000	$3,500–$7,000
Columbus Symphony Orchestra	Columbus	85	16	$260,000–$1,050,000	$20,000–$75,000
DeKalb Symphony Orchestra	Tucker	88	14	$100,000–$150,000	$7,000–$20,000
Emory Symphony Orchestra	Atlanta	85	4	< $35,000	< $1,500
Gainesville Symphony Orchestra	Gainesville	72	4	$150,000–$260,000	< $1,500
Georgia State University Symphony	Atlanta	80	8	< $35,000	$7,000–$20,000
La Grange Symphony Orchestra	La Grange	42–55	11	$150,000–$260,000	$3,500–$7,000
Macon Symphony Orchestra	Macon	75	26	$260,000–$1,050,000	$7,000–$20,000
Rome Symphony Orchestra	Rome	65	6	$35,000–$100,000	< $1,500
Savannah Symphony Orchestra	Savannah	85	75	$1,050,000–$3,600,000	$75,000–$300,000
Valdosta Symphony Orchestra	Valdosta	75	20	$260,000–$1,050,000	$20,000–$75,000

Exhibit 2 Symphony Orchestras in Georgia

Source: Musical America Directory.

Orchestras With Annual Operating Budgets of $10,000,000 and Above

- Los Angeles Philharmonic*#
- Pacific Symphony Orchestra (CA)
- San Francisco Symphony*
- Colorado Symphony Orchestra
- National Symphony Orchestra (DC)
- Florida Philharmonic Orchestra
- Atlanta Symphony Orchestra
- Chicago Symphony Orchestra*#
- Indianapolis Symphony Orchestra
- Baltimore Symphony Orchestra
- Boston Symphony Orchestra*#
- Detroit Symphony Orchestra
- Minnesota Orchestra*
- The Saint Paul Chamber Orchestra (MN)
- Saint Louis Symphony Orchestra
- New Jersey Symphony Orchestra

- Buffalo Philharmonic Orchestra
- New York Philharmonic*
- Cincinnati Symphony Orchestra*
- The Cleveland Orchestra*
- Columbus Symphony Orchestra (OH)
- Oregon Symphony
- The Philadelphia Orchestra*
- Pittsburgh Symphony Orchestra*
- Dallas Symphony Orchestra
- Houston Symphony
- Utah Symphony & Opera
- Seattle Symphony
- Milwaukee Symphony Orchestra
- Orchestre Symphonique de Montreal
- The Toronto Symphony Orchestra

* Among top 10 in annual operating budgets in 2001.
\# Annual operating budget exceeding $50 million in 2001.

Orchestras With Annual Operating Budgets of $3,600,000 to $10,000,000

- Alabama Symphony Orchestra
- The Phoenix Symphony
- Tucson Symphony Orchestra
- San Diego Symphony
- The Florida Orchestra
- Jacksonville Symphony Orchestra (FL)
- Naples Philharmonic Orchestra (FL)
- Honolulu Symphony Orchestra
- Fort Wayne Philharmonic Orchestra (IN)
- The Louisville Orchestra
- Louisiana Philharmonic Orchestra
- Grand Rapids Symphony
- Kansas City Symphony
- Omaha Symphony Orchestra
- New Mexico Symphony Orchestra
- Rochester Philharmonic Orchestra

- Syracuse Symphony Orchestra
- Charlotte Symphony
- North Carolina Symphony
- Toledo Symphony Orchestra
- The Nashville Symphony
- Fort Worth Symphony Orchestra
- San Antonio Symphony
- Richmond Symphony (VA)
- Virginia Symphony Orchestra
- Calgary Philharmonic Orchestra
- Edmonton Symphony Orchestra
- National Arts Centre Orchestra
- Orchestre Symphonique de Québec
- Vancouver Symphony
- Winnipeg Symphony Orchestra

Exhibit 3   Major and Regional North American Symphony Orchestras

Source: Musical America Directory.

Time	Event
September 20, 1945	Corporate charter granted to Atlanta Youth Symphony
January 26, 1947	First performance under the name the Atlanta Symphony Orchestra (ASO)
1950–51	All ASO members are professional musicians
February 2, 1962	First ASO Pops concert
October 19, 1967	Robert Shaw conducts first concert as ASO music director
September 24, 1970	Debut of ASO Chorus
March 4, 1971	First ASO performance in Carnegie Hall
June 1974	ASO begins summer concerts at Chastain Park
1976	ASO wins ASCAP Award, the first of four, for adventuresome programming of American Music
1976	ASO's first commercial recording, *Nativity*, released
January 18, 1977	ASO and Chorus perform at Inaugural Concert in Washington for President-elect Jimmy Carter
October 1978	ASO tour of western United States
1979	Release of ASO's first Telarc recording
February 1986	ASO recording of Berlioz's *Requiem* wins four Grammy Awards
March 1988	ASO's first European tour
June 1988	Nationwide syndication of ASO concerts begins on a network of public radio stations
August–September 1988	Robert Shaw steps down as music director and is named music director emeritus; Yoel Levi conducts first concert as ASO music director
February 1991	ASO recording of choral works is the fifth ASO recording in six years to win a Grammy Award
October 1991	ASO's second European tour
July–August 1996	ASO plays in Opening and Closing Ceremonies of the Centennial Olympic Games in Atlanta; ASO and Atlanta Symphony Youth Orchestra perform in eight concerts of the Olympic Arts Festival/Cultural Olympiad
1997	ASO initiates $40 million endowment campaign, the largest ever for a performing arts organization in the Southeast (campaign completed in October 2000)
1999	Arthur Blank Family Foundation commits $15 million gift for new concert hall
February 2000	Appointment of Robert Spano as music director designate and Donald Runnicles as principal guest conductor designate
September 15, 2001	Robert Spano conducts first concert as ASO music director

Exhibit 4   ASO Artistic and Musical Event Timeline

Source: ASO files.

MUSICAL ACTIVITIES AND OFFERINGS

The ASO's performances each year reached nearly half a million people through its various concert series and diverse initiatives in music education and outreach. In addition to its Master Season—Classical Concerts subscription series, the orchestra performed more popular and current music to a variety of audiences through pops and family concerts (see Exhibit 5). Additionally, it offered a full summer schedule including classical and pop music and free outdoor concerts. Noteworthy musical offerings included:

- Master Season—Classical Concerts: Twenty-four three-performance concerts of traditional and contemporary classical repertoire performed from September through May at the

WAC. Performances were given to an estimated audience of 90,000 annually.

- Classic Chastain: Approximately 30 concerts offered through a relationship with the City of Atlanta each June through August. The musical performance featured a mixture of musical styles (e.g., rhythm and blues, country, pop and classical) often accompanied by the ASO. These performances reached an estimated audience of 150,000 annually.

- Holiday Concerts: Approximately 17 concerts centred around the Christmas and New Year season. Holiday standards such as *Messiah* and Strauss family waltzes, polkas and popular Broadway medleys were performed. Attendance for these performances was approximately 22,000 annually.

- Free Outdoor Concerts: The ASO annually performed at various locations in Metropolitan Atlanta. Partial funding for these concerts came

Concert Series	Number of Concerts (2001)#	Single/[Series] Ticket Prices (2001)	Ticket Sale % of Total (2001)	Subscription Sales (% Series Sales)		Average % of Paid House	
				2000	2001	2000	2001
Master Season— Classical Season	72	$19–$57 [$99–$273]*	26.8	71.3	71.4	70.0	71.9
Classic Chastain	30	$33–$73	52.8	54.1	50.4	64.0	69.2
Coffee/New Mornings	4	$16–$32 [$76–$108]	0.6	64.1	64.6	53.1	44.0
Champagne/SunTrust Pops	12	$21–$57 [$111–$276]	5.5	57.3	58.3	83.1	80.9
Family	8	$15–$20 [$44–$61]	1.6	71.0	76.7	87.0	91.6
Holiday	17	$12–$100	6.3	—	—	77.4	75.1
Special Events	4	$26–$57	2.2	—	—	83.7	74.7
Other**	46	—	4.2	—	—	—	—

Exhibit 5   ASO Musical Offerings

Source: ASO files.

#Date indicates fiscal year ending.

*Series ticket prices for six concerts.

**These concerts included Saturdays/Casual Classics/ASO to Go, Symphony Street/Young People's Concerts/Atlanta Symphony Youth Orchestra, and Summer concerts.

through grants from the City of Atlanta and Fulton County, with the remainder supplemented from the ASO's operating budget. These performances reached more than 25,000 annually.

In addition, the ASO was actively involved in a number of community-based projects. These included offering annual King Celebration concerts honoring the legacy of Dr. Martin Luther King, Jr., participation in the National Black Arts Festival (joining in 1994 to sponsor a competition for new compositions by African-American composers), and concerts given in collaboration with local churches. In 1995, the ASO embarked on the "Building Bridges to the Community" initiative in metropolitan Atlanta. Programs associated with this initiative included the Atlanta Symphony Youth Orchestra, which was created in 1945, an auditioned and professionally coached organization for high-school age musicians; a Talent Development Program where young minority players were coached and mentored by ASO musicians; and young people's concerts in the Discover, Next Generation, and Symphony Street series.

The ASO launched a number of outreach partnerships through a program titled Partners in Performance (PNP). The program involved taking the orchestra's musicians, individually or in groups, to school children who would not normally meet professional musicians. The program utilized recordings and educational materials along with interactive presentations, master classes and coaching in providing these musical education opportunities. Overall, more than 50,000 youngsters were annually exposed to the ASO. Orchestral players regularly volunteered their time for these activities and joined ASO administrators and community leaders in developing and implementing the mission and activities of the PNP program.

In 2001, the ASO was one of the few remaining North American symphony orchestras actively recording; many of the major classical recording companies found the cost of recording in North America prohibitive. The orchestra began recording for the Cleveland-based Telarc

label in 1979, with which it had recorded over 70 records of a wide-ranging repertoire of choral and orchestral works. These recordings garnered the ASO much praise, winning an Audio Excellence Award, Gramophone and Ovation Magazine Awards, and 18 Grammy Awards. The ASO recorded *A Sea Symphony* in conjunction with the November 2001 concerts.

FINANCIAL AND ARTISTIC TROUBLES

From the cutting of staff at Florida's Jacksonville Symphony Orchestra and New York's Rochester Philharmonic Orchestra to the bankruptcy and restructuring of the San Diego Symphony, many regional orchestras were experiencing financial crises by the fall of 2001. Larger, more established major orchestras such as the Pittsburgh Symphony Orchestra, St. Louis Symphony and Toronto Symphony were also on the brink of bankruptcy and asking their musicians to take pay cuts and possibly shorten their performing season. Especially troubling were financial concerns for the Big Five. The Chicago Symphony, long a model of financial solvency, was projecting several years of deficits for the first time in almost two decades. Despite its $59 million budget and $168 million endowment, the Chicago Symphony wound up with a deficit of about $1.3 million in 2001. The Cleveland Orchestra and The Philadelphia Orchestra also faced similar looming deficits.

Several reasons for the financial troubles of many symphony orchestras included:

- Shrinking endowments and funding;
- Competition for the entertainment dollar;
- Declining and aging audiences;
- Decreasing emphasis on musical education;
- Geographic spread away from city and metropolitan centres; and
- Adversarial relations between musicians and management because of conflicting priorities.

Related to these troubles was the artistic concern that symphony orchestras were simply repositories for performing only the core classical repertoire. Orchestras generally were not known for their innovative or novel musical offerings. To some, the symphony orchestra as an art form had become less relevant in society. Relevancy was especially important given that most orchestras faced one further reality beyond their control: society appeared to be moving at an increasingly faster pace and time was a precious commodity. Given that the typical classical orchestral concert lasted two hours, attending a live symphony orchestra concert might become a less prominent activity for present and potential patrons.

The financial troubles facing symphony orchestras—primarily budget deficits and diminishing endowments—and their underlying causes were not new. In 1988, Thomas Morris, managing director of the Cleveland Orchestra, criticized orchestras for their "fundamental lack of leadership, governance, and strategic focus. Better artistic planning, a consistent approach to programming and repertoire, and strong boards are the keys to revitalizing orchestras."[3]

The ASO was not immune to the troubles that many other orchestras faced. Much of the past decade represented a period of turmoil for the ASO. Among the troubles faced were a 10-week musicians' strike in 1996; the death of its long-time music director Robert Shaw, who was a charismatic leader integral to the development of both the orchestra and ASO chorus; strained relations within the orchestra and between its supporters over the departure of Yoel Levi; and a seven-figure budget deficit. All this resulted in morale being at an all-time low by the end of the 1990s. Financially, the orchestra—guided by the need for fiscal discipline—operated at a modest surplus in FYE 2001 with total revenues exceeding $24 million. Total ticket sales for the 2000–2001 season were just under $10 million with subscription sales accounting for just over 50 per cent of the total ticket sales. While the orchestra offered both fixed and flexible subscription package options, only 10 per cent of subscribers to the Master Season (i.e., the "great patrons") attended 12 or more of the different concert programs offered each season.

The orchestra operated under the financial strategy of balancing its annual operating budget and utilizing what surplus was available. It created a special fund of banked, restricted money that allowed for some artistic freedom to pursue unique musical opportunities as they arose. Overall, the primary financial concern for management was to have an adequate resource foundation for all the ASO's music programming commitments. Towards that end, the orchestra had recently completed a $40 million endowment campaign. Additionally, Atlanta-based businesses such as Delta Airlines and SunTrust Bank sponsored the Master Season and Pops concerts, respectively.

In addition to these financial troubles, one critical challenge the ASO faced was the need to increase its presence within the Atlanta community. According to Robert Spano:

> Here's this great orchestra, here's this very vital, thriving, growing, exciting city, and the two have nothing to do with each other. There's a total disconnect. We're not getting audiences.
>
> That's a challenge that fascinates me. How do you get this credible, viable artistic institution to mean something to the community in which it lives? Because if it doesn't, it's going to die.[4]

As a means to raise awareness, for example, fans attending Atlanta Braves baseball home games were treated to a between-inning video of the ASO and Spano performing the famous conclusion to Gioacchino Rossini's *William Tell Overture* (i.e., the Lone Ranger theme) while the stadium grounds crew quickly refreshed the baseball infield.

THE LONG-RANGE PLAN AND CREATIVE PARTNERSHIP

In the fall of 1997, ASO musicians, board, staff and volunteers undertook a new initiative to address the turmoil then surrounding the orchestra. Specifically, a planning process was undertaken involving extensive interviews, focus groups and other data-gathering activities with members of the ASO family. The result of the two-year process included a new mission statement, vision and three-year strategy for the ASO.

Emanating from the ASO's Long Range Plan (LRP) (see Exhibit 6) was a revised mission statement that read:

The Atlanta Symphony Orchestra and its affiliated members are committed to build on our foundation of artistic excellence. We unite in our desire to serve and to expand our audience through innovative programming, broader venues and increased educational opportunities while balancing artistic growth with financial soundness. We share a heritage of passion for the music. We embrace our responsibility to be a vigorous part of the cultural fabric of our community and to strive to reach national and international audiences.

The objective of the ASO's Long Range Plan was to provide the long-range directions and goals that would guide all proposed actions. Further, it was meant to provide a context for both the orchestra's Three Year Strategy and for continued artistic and financial planning over the coming years. The plan's directions and goals are detailed below.

1. Invest in the Music

- Display artistic leadership and creativity.
- Improve the ASO instrument: hall, musicians, programming.
- Capitalize on unique assets of ASO chorus and youth orchestra.

2. Engage and Significantly Grow the Audience

- Engage our audiences and enhance the classical concert experience.
- Develop and offer a summer classical program to engage current audiences and attract new audiences.
- Pursue an enhanced role at Chastain and return all parks concerts to Piedmont Park.
- Significantly increase and strengthen marketing efforts.

3. Serve Our Evolving Community

- Expand outreach to new audiences; enhance diverse community partnerships.
- Provide educational programs for ASO audiences, both adults and young people, that enhance their enjoyment, appreciation, and understanding of the musical arts and inspire the community to attend ASO concerts regularly.

  Engage professional support, build bridges between ASO education offerings, utilize technology and enhance participatory value for attendees, funders and partners.

- Enhance membership value of the Atlanta Symphony Associates and increase involvement in outreach.

4. Develop and Maintain a Strong Organizational, Technical and Financial Infrastructure

- Significantly increase and expand development efforts.
- Leverage technology and staff development for ASO success.
- Strengthen the ASO's organizational and governance systems, with the goal of clarifying roles and responsibilities and enhancing communication.
  - Strengthen our understanding of roles and responsibilities.
  - Develop evaluation procedures.
  - Build strong communications, well supported by systems and personnel.

Exhibit 6 The ASO's Long Range Plan
Source: ASO files.

This vision was intended to provide a snapshot of the organization in the future, and to articulate the way the organization would look and act in the future to carry out its mission. The vision's main points were to:

- Grow artistic excellence and nurture creativity;
- Serve multi-faceted communities in Atlanta and the southeastern United States;
- Achieve financial strength and soundness; and
- Galvanize the organization and build infrastructure capacity.

A three-year strategy was developed that would be the driving force for the ASO planning process. This strategy focused on putting the organization into the most advantageous position for success and fulfilment of its mission and vision. The three-year strategy revolved around three aims:

- Focus on vision;
- Increase ASO exposure; and
- Increase and leverage revenues.

The LRP was not designed solely to improve the ASO's economic model. Rather, the LRP was initiated to also improve the orchestra's management model.

The 125 participants in the LRP process—individuals representing the community, local businesses, volunteers and the orchestra's board, musicians and staff—were unified by the desire to position the ASO above the orchestral crowd. A critical component in achieving this objective was the creation of a new culture of collaboration. This culture of "creative partnership," which also translated into a sense of ownership and responsibility by the orchestra stakeholders, became the guiding principle at the ASO. The belief was that a creative partnership dictated that collaboration must occur in order to achieve broad institutional ownership of initiatives. Only with the process-focused implementation of these collaborative initiatives would the ASO be successful. The orchestra arranged an annual retreat each September, involving a group of participants similar to that

employed in the LRP process, for strategic—financial and artistic—planning and assessment purposes.

A critical component to achieving the objectives of the LRP involved embarking on a campaign of innovation intended to ensure the ASO's highly distinctive artistic identity and musical offerings. Concurrent to this ASO campaign was the selection of a new music director and principal guest conductor, along with the building of a new performance venue.

Search for a New Music Director

By the late 1990s, many of the major North American orchestras, including those in Boston, Cleveland, New York and Philadelphia, were searching for new music directors. The ASO found itself included in this mix as the orchestra's board decided in 1998 not to renew Yoel Levi's contract as music director. Allison Vulgamore, president of the Atlanta Symphony Orchestra since 1993, noted that:

> About 200 people—board, staff, chorus members and musicians—came together in 1998 in order to discuss how to bring the organization back together, post strike, and determine what we were looking for in a music director. Fourteen task forces were created, one of which became the music director search committee.

According to Vulgamore, that search committee's charge was simple. A new music director was needed who would foster creativity in musical programming. Unlike many of the other previously mentioned orchestras who were looking for conductors largely with a European background and/or years of success in leading major orchestras, the ASO chose Robert Spano as its music director. Spano, music director of the Brooklyn Philharmonic, was one of the few American orchestra leaders who had earned an international reputation as an innovative and adventurous programmer and orchestra builder. In describing the ASO's choice, Vulgamore remarked:

It was clear that we needed to expand our performing repertoire. We desired some experimentation, going so far as not caring just how wild that might be. Thinking wild might result in something interesting.

Proof of this experimentation was found in the ASO's "war room," where much of the important concert programming decisions were made. Programming decisions, normally taking place two to three years in advance and finalized by February of the preceding music season, were perennial problems for most orchestras, since issues such as the marketability of a program were weighed against financial considerations and concerns over artistic integrity (see Exhibit 7). The ASO developed and employed a predictive programming model, premised on considerations of sound budget management and artistic growth, to create its lineup of concerts for the 2001–2002 Master Season. The goal of this programming approach, given the constraints of the operating budget, would be to create a portfolio of concert programs that could be characterized in terms of an A, B, C, or D classification scheme (see Exhibit 8). Given Spano's desire to perform new or seldom heard classical music in addition to the traditional and oft performed masterpieces, novel concerts—like the one containing *A Sea Symphony*—had to be balanced with more traditional and recognizable concert programs. This desire to perform classical music that would be novel to both the musicians and audience was offset by the need to figure out what would sell.

Based on our collective desire to sell more tickets and move forward artistically, we must find ways to bring in audiences with winner programs/artists and very carefully give them something at the same time that they didn't expect but really liked. Here are three points that are critical to moving us toward our goal.

1. Build Trust and Loyalty to New Leadership

- Approachability both on and off stage
- Convey excitement and enthusiasm for music
- Demonstrate a real desire to listen and engage audience
- Strategic introduction to community at large

2. Programming

- Scheduling strategically based on what we know and what we will learn
- Connection between audience and stage is critical
- Embed new works around more popular pieces or as themes within current subscription packages
- Still must always give the audience plenty of what they want

3. Concert Format

- Audience yearns for greater sense of connection to the stage
- Short enthusiastic comments from stage are well received
- Video enhancement has great potential
- Greater use of lighting and other visual enhancements a plus

Connecting to audience + concert enhancement leads to trust & loyalty leads to bigger audience and opportunity for more adventurous programming.

Exhibit 7   The Road to Strong Sales and Artistic Adventure
Source: Charlie Wade, ASO files.

Inputs to the ASO's predictive programming model included consideration of:

a) composer and piece of music,
b) guest artists,
c) solo instrument type,
d) time of year,
e) performance fees and costs, and
f) what is being performed elsewhere.

Individuals involved in programming included the ASO's music director, principal guest conductor, president, vice-president general manager, vice-president marketing and communications and artistic administrator.

Program Category (attendance in %)	Number of Programs (2001–2002)	Sample Program From Master Season (2001–2002)*
A—90 to 100	3	January 10, 12, 13 (2002) [100%] Beethoven: *Two Romances* Beethoven: *Symphony No. 8* Brahms: *Symphony No. 3* Itzhak Perlman, conductor and violin
B—80 to 89	4	November 15, 16, 18 (2001) [83.1%] Rossini/Respighi: *La Boutique fantastique* Vivaldi: *The Four Seasons* Robert Spano, conductor Gil Shaham, violin
C—70 to 79	7	April 25, 26, 27 (2002) [75%] Wagner: *Die Walküre—Act III* Donald Runnicles, conductor Christine Brewer, soprano James Morris, bass
D—60 to 69	7	November 8, 9, 10 (2001) [68.7%] Debussy: *Nocturnes* Vaughan Williams: *A Sea Symphony* Robert Spano, conductor Christine Goerke, soprano Brett Polegato, baritone ASO Chorus

Exhibit 8   ASO's Predictive Programming Model

Source: ASO files.

*Average percentage of paid house per concert in brackets.

ASO musicians were actively involved with the music director selection in an effort to stay true to the organization's commitment towards keeping lines of communication open. Jun-Ching Lin, assistant concert master and one of the five musicians on the 11-member search committee, summarized the process:

> We put together a wish list of the qualities we wanted in a music director, and the word "collaboration" kept coming up. It was the first time in my 12 years here that I felt the board and management could hear what the musicians were saying. For me, personally, that was worth the entire two and a half years of the search process.[5]

New Performance Venue

The ASO embarked in 1999 on a plan to construct a new performing arts centre. The musicians and management felt the ASO would not be able to achieve its future artistic growth goals at the WAC; as the orchestra's needs grew, the WAC was no longer able to provide the acoustical instrument the orchestra required. The new Symphony Center would be built on three acres at the corner of 14th and Peachtree streets, one block south of the present Woodruff Arts Center campus. The close proximity of the new venue was necessary in order to maintain the ASO's connection with the other residents of the Woodruff Arts Center, such as the Alliance Theatre Company, Atlanta College of Art, High Museum of Art, and the 14th Street Playhouse.

The proposed plan was to build a new home for the orchestra, at an estimated cost of $240 million, by fall 2008. This plan would accomplish many things. Besides offering a 2,000 seat auditorium that would be an acoustically superb home with cutting-edge technology, plans for the multi-purpose arts centre also included educational and administrative facilities, along with restaurants and cafés.

In 2001, the ASO and Houston-based developer Hines announced a six-year development plan to build two residential towers next to the new Symphony Center on 6.2 acres at Peachtree and 14th streets. The first tower, projected to open by 2005 at a cost between $110 and $125 million, would have 250 to 300 residential units. Retail components would add an additional estimated cost of $5 million. The second tower, expected to be completed in 2007 at a cost between $120 and $160 million, would include 100 to 125 residential units and 100 to 225 hotel rooms. In order to fund construction of the new hall, the ASO engaged in a massive capital campaign led by Home Depot co-founder Arthur Blank; the early goal was for $200 million to be raised from private individuals, foundations and government.

Estimates prepared by Ernst & Young of the economic impact of the new hall indicated that the proposed Symphony Center project would generate more than $2.1 billion in the state through the year 2017. The ASO contribution alone was estimated at $1.7 billion over the 17-year period from 2000 to 2017.

The ASO worked with the community in planning the new Symphony Center. In describing the project, Vulgamore remarked:

> The "wow" factor was an important consideration. We want a home that is not only monumentally beautiful, but also welcoming. Of course, the acoustical properties of the new hall are extremely important and should drive most of the architectural and aesthetic decisions. We want the new home of the ASO to be a landmark.

A SEA SYMPHONY

In 2000, a member of the ASO Chorus suggested that the ASO perform Ralph Vaughan Williams' 1910 composition titled *A Sea Symphony*. Recognizing an opportunity to put the LRP into action, ASO administrators undertook an experiment that would mix the traditional symphony performance with technology. The ASO commissioned, at a final cost of $35,000, visual art from Polish video artist Piotr Szyhalski to accompany the performance of the symphony.

This rarely performed symphony was composed to evoke the sea as a metaphor for the inexplicable vastness of the cosmos, for mankind's tiny place within it, for the restlessness of life, and for man's ultimate fate—death. Near the end of the 70-minute ASO performance of this symphony, the jumbo screen positioned above the stage displayed a rapid flash of faces augmented by spinning gears and cogs. Above the faces appeared Orwellian double-speak slogans, such as "There is no escape / for you / strong thoughts / fill you / and confidence / you smile!"

The ASO's premier performance on November 8, 2001 immediately drew some heated reaction. One patron, displaying atypical concert hall behavior, shouted "Boo the bastards!" as he left his seat in mid-concert. In all, over a dozen of the audience members expressed opinions about the performance to Michael Granados, ASO season ticket manager. Granados commented:

> We received different reactions. One patron suggested that we should have had medical professionals assess the video to make sure it would not cause epileptic seizures. A different person indicated that the video was fabulous art but a distraction to the music. It appeared that people either hated or loved the video. In the end, the symphony orchestra was not passé that Thursday night. The performance clearly affected concertgoers.

One ASO subscriber e-mailed the local newspaper, *The Atlanta Journal-Constitution* (AJC), the following message:

> I did not go to this performance of such beautiful music to be depressed and upset—an emotional state solely caused by that awful video.

ASO administrators actively observed audience reaction. According to Charlie Wade, the ASO's vice-president, marketing and communications:

> Negative feedback from some of the audience may not be what we want to hear, but at least it provides us with useful information on patron perceptions.

The fact that people offered such feedback indicates that they love and care for the ASO's art form. That is a very useful thing.

The AJC newspaper critic who reviewed the performance concluded:

> As a companion to the music, Szyhalski's images seemed banal, dreary once the novelty wore off, and certainly beside the point while the music was playing. . . .

> What was inescapable about Thursday evening was the seismic effect Spano is having on the ASO and its audience. Like it or not, we're on the leading edge of the 21st-century symphony orchestra. It's a rather fun place to be.[6]

The ASO administration viewed the *A Sea Symphony* experiment as an attempt to enhance the concert hall experience in the hope of increasing the orchestra's long-term relevance. Another example of the ASO's innovative efforts was the videotaping of interviews with active American composers whose works were being performed by the orchestra for the first time. One of these interviews was played to the audience prior to the playing of Christopher Theofanidis' composition titled *Rainbow Body,* which proceeded without incident. Another of these interviews was scheduled for display prior to the ASO premier of Jennifer Higdon's work titled *Blue Cathedral* the following May. According to Vulgamore:

> A concern commonly voiced is that orchestras are living in the past and are not connected to the present. The ASO is one orchestra that wants to change that. Doing so may require that we continue to stretch the boundary of performance standards and experiment through calculated risk. Clearly, we have to progress wisely as we go. Perhaps mistakes will be made along the way, but that is a potential outcome that comes with not being afraid to think about trying anything. No other orchestra is doing as much as we are this season to accomplish staying alive and in tune.

Other orchestras had occasionally tinkered with their musical offerings. The New York Philharmonic in the early 1970s offered "rug concerts" in which auditorium seats were removed so that patrons could sit on small carpets and listen to contemporary music. The audience would then debate the music's merits with the musicians. Another one-time trial in combining visuals to music included The Philadelphia Orchestra's 1998 performance of Messiaen's *Turangalila-Symphonie* with color slides of birds and erotic Indian art.

While there was no intention of mixing extra-musical activities into every concert, the ASO administration had already decided on another ASO-commissioned video to accompany a performance of Ravel's *Ma mère l'Oye* (Mother Goose Suite) in the spring of 2003. A subscriber wrote to the ASO after seeing the *A Sea Symphony* performance that:

> We have been subscribers for more than 30 years. We see you offering a variety of novelty items at persons who don't care much for traditional offerings. You may attract some of them but they will never stay. Meanwhile, you are alienating the faithful. If the music can't stand on its own, the gimmicks will never save it. If there is a next time, we will walk out.

DEMYSTIFYING THE CONCERT EXPERIENCE

John Sparrow, along with an increasing number of individuals familiar—or associated—with the orchestra, viewed the ASO as a major U.S. orchestra aspiring towards strengthening its national recognition. As far as Sparrow was concerned, the greatest challenge he faced was not one of justifying the ASO's existence, but demystifying the concertgoers' experience. It was important to get people to experience the ASO in the right way. Given the quality of the orchestra's performances, Sparrow felt the music would stand on its own. Yet, further broadening and enhancing the ASO's services and experiences was an ongoing concern. In addition to deciding how to address the reaction to the *A Sea Symphony* performance, Sparrow noted:

> I would love it if all patrons walked out of an ASO concert with the feeling of having had a great musical experience in which they were comforted, well attended to, and had all their needs met. The ASO should be able to provide a service as seamless as that offered at Nordstrom, and with the consistency found at Wal-Mart.

NOTES

1. All monetary figures in U.S. dollars.

2. The "Big Five" traditionally referred to the Boston Symphony Orchestra, Chicago Symphony Orchestra, The Cleveland Orchestra, New York Philharmonic and The Philadelphia Orchestra. These orchestras, widely recognized for their artistic quality, regularly engaged in domestic and international touring and recording with world-renowned conductors. Additionally, these orchestras possessed large annual operating budgets and endowments, the basis for financial stability, which allowed for the offering of a range of musical activities. Generally, the quality and reputation of orchestras was a general indicator of the artistic vitality in the community and a source of civic pride.

3. Thomas Morris, "Is the Orchestra Dead? A Context for Good Health," *McBride Lecture,* Case Western Reserve University, Cleveland, September 27, 1988.

4. "The Atlanta Symphony Gets a Jolt of Energy," *New York Times,* December 16, 2001.

5. "The Atlanta Symphony Gets a Jolt of Energy," *New York Times,* December 16, 2001.

6. "Shouting Fan Can't Disrupt ASO Concert," *The Atlanta Journal-Constitution,* November 9, 2001.

Navistar: Environmental Management (A)

*Prepared by Fraser Johnson under the
supervision of Professor Robert Klassen*

Dan Uszynski, environmental co-ordinator at the Navistar International Corporation truck assembly plant in Chatham, Ontario, reviewed the results of the plant-wide waste audit conducted in August 1994, and contemplated which steps he should take next. It was now November 1994, and he knew that senior management was expecting a recommendation from him for a solid waste management program for the plant.

Navistar International Corporation

On August 13, 1902, a merger of the McCormick Harvesting Machine Company, Deering Harvester Company, Milwaukee Harvester Company, Plano Manufacturing Company, and Warder, Bushnell & Glessner formed the International Harvester Company. At that time, the company was primarily involved in the production of farm machinery. The first truck rolled off the assembly line at the Chatham plant in 1922, and a total of 217 trucks were built at the plant that year. A new plant was constructed in 1948 to replace the old Chatham Wagon Works facility.

International Harvester Company continued to manufacture both trucks and agricultural equipment until 1985, when the agricultural equipment division was sold to Tenneco Inc.'s J.I. Case Company as part of a restructuring plan. In January 1986, International Harvester Company changed its name to Navistar International Corporation (Navistar), while still maintaining the International brand name for its trucks.

In 1994, Navistar manufactured and marketed the International brand medium and heavy trucks, school bus chassis and mid-range diesel engines for North American and selected export markets.

The company operated eight manufacturing facilities and two technical centres, employing more than 14,900 people worldwide. Revenues for fiscal 1994 were $5.3 billion. A summary of Navistar's financial results is provided in Exhibit 1.

Navistar led the North American market in sales of medium and heavy trucks for 14 consecutive years. The company's products, parts and services were sold through a network of 951 dealer outlets in the United States and Canada, and 92 distributors in 77 other countries. Navistar also provided financing for its customers, dealers and distributors through Navistar Financial Corporation.

Navistar's premium conventional and severe service trucks were produced at the Chatham plant, while its regular conventional and cabover trucks were manufactured and assembled at the company's assembly plant in Springfield, Ohio. Exhibit 2 illustrates the 9400 premium conventional "Eagle" sleeper truck built in the Chatham plant. The plant first began producing Navistar's premium line in 1983.

The heavy truck market in the United States and Canada was expected to be 205,000 units in 1994, an increase of 23 percentage points from the 166,400 units sold in 1993. Major competitors in this segment included Ford, Freightliner, Mack PACCAR (maker of the Kenworth and Peterbilt brands) and Volvo/GM.

Chatham Plant
Truck Assembly Operations

The Chatham plant, which had been expanded and modernized over the years, occupied a 790,000

	1992	*1993*	*1994*
Total Sales and Revenues	$3,897	$4,721	$5,337
Income Before Taxes	(145)	(441)	158
Income Tax Benefit (Expense)	(2)	168	(56)
Net Income (Loss) From Operations	(147)	(273)	102
Loss From Discontinued Operations	(65)	—	(20)
Accounting Policy Adjustments	—	(228)	—
Net Income (Loss)	(212)	(501)	82
Cash Flow From Operations	(27)	35	154
Net Income per Common Share	(9.55)	(15.19)	0.72
Total Assets		5,060	5,056
Liabilities Other Than Debt		2,911	3,021
Debt		1,374	1,218
Shareowner's Equity		775	817

Exhibit 1   Summary Financial Results as of Fiscal 1994* (millions of U.S. Dollars, except per share data)

Source: Annual Report for the Year 1994.

*Fiscal year end is October 31.

Exhibit 2   Premium Conventional Truck

Source: Chatham Assembly Plant 1995 Fact Sheet.

square foot assembly operation situated on 80 acres of property, and employed 2,082 people. The plant operated a 5,059 foot assembly line. Truck assembly operations started in the frame assembly department and progressed through chassis paint and chassis assembly. Components, such as rear axles, transmissions and engines, were assembled into the trucks as they passed through the initial stages of the chassis assembly department. Cabs and hoods were assembled onto the trucks at chassis assembly. Cabs were delivered to the paint prep department, then moved through the paint department, sleeper trim, cab trim #2 and cab trim. Prior to shipping, each truck was sent to the tune and test department.

Hourly workers at the plant were represented by the Canadian Automotive Workers (CAW) Local 127, and earned approximately $23 per hour. As on many assembly lines, workers had specific work assignments which were timed to support smooth line flow. The clerical office employees were represented by CAW Local 35. Truck production was 14,532 units in 1993 and was expected to climb to 18,000 units in this year. Currently, the production line was operating with two shifts, five days each week. Production of the premium conventional line represented approximately 90 per cent of the production at the plant. A plant layout is provided in Exhibit 3.

The trucks were offered with a range of styling and features and each was customized to meet customer specifications. The sleeper cabs for long-distance truckers could include features such as televisions and microwave ovens in a variety of layouts. The average cost of a premium conventional Eagle ranged between $120,000 and $150,000, depending on features, and sometimes reached as high as $200,000.

Approximately 850 suppliers with 1,430 shipping points provided the over 13,000 different parts that were assembled into each truck. The company issued orders to its suppliers via electronic data interchange (EDI), specifying both delivery schedules and quantities. Navistar dictated shipping and packaging requirements for each part, and attempted to use returnable containers whenever possible. Because of a variety of factors, many of Navistar's suppliers used non-returnable, or cardboard, packaging. A shortage of returnable containers and compatibility with the method of transportation were identified as the most common reasons for using non-returnable packaging.

Environmental Management Activities at Navistar

Navistar issued its first environmental, health and safety report for fiscal 1994. This report highlighted company-wide activities in the area of environmental management and health and safety, and also set an agenda for future environmental and health and safety activities for the company. Included in the report was the Navistar Environmental Protection Policy, which is provided in Exhibit 4.

The company maintained an environmental staff to monitor and implement environmental programs and to provide training to company employees. The corporate environmental staff reported to the vice-president, quality management and technology, who reported to the president & CEO. The board of directors of Navistar, which had approved the Environmental Protection Policy and Management Program, was regularly informed about environmental performance. Navistar conducted ongoing planning to ensure that capital and operating expenditures needed to comply with environmental, regulatory and company policy requirements were identified and funded.

During October 1994, Navistar formalized its Environmental Executive Committee, reporting to the Audit Committee of the Board of Directors. The five member committee, which included both the CEO and the chief financial officer, had essentially been in place for the previous six years, and was responsible for the following areas:

1. Monitoring and evaluating the company's compliance with environmental requirements.

2. Assuring that environmental considerations became an integral part of all business plans and that adequate resources existed to support Navistar's Environmental Management Program.

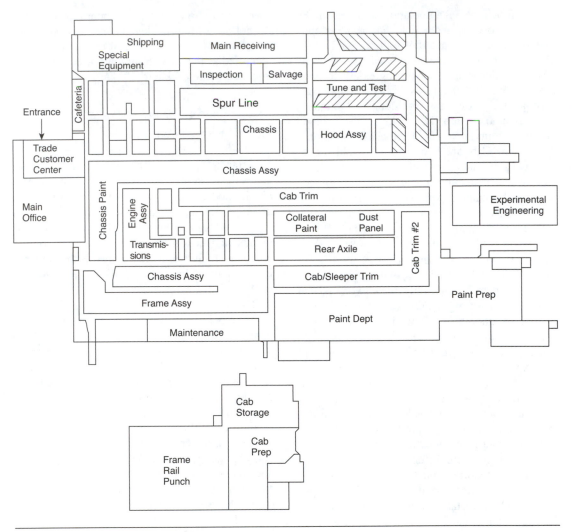

Exhibit 3   Chatham Plant Layout

Source: Chatham Assembly Plant 1995 Fact Sheet.

3. Reviewing environmental disclosures in the annual report 10-K and other shareholder reports as required by the Securities and Exchange Commission.

4. Developing and communicating corporate positions on significant environmental programs, issues, legislation and participation in voluntary environmental programs sponsored by government agencies.

5. Developing and recommending for approval by the board of directors any changes to Navistar's Environmental Protection Policy and Management Program.

As part of Navistar's Environmental Management Program, environmental procedures were developed for implementation, as appropriate, at all company locations. The Environmental

---

POLICY AND PROGRAMS

NAVISTAR ENVIRONMENTAL PROTECTION POLICY

Navistar is committed to adhering to high standards of environmental quality and to providing a workplace that protects the health and safety of our employees and the communities surrounding our facilities. To carry out these commitments, in a technically sound and cost-effective manner, it is the policy of Navistar to:

- Conduct all operations in compliance with all applicable environmental laws and regulations.

- Design, construct and operate our facilities in a manner that protects the health and safety of our employees, individuals in the neighboring communities and the environment.

- Implement programs for self-monitoring, assessing and reporting to ensure compliance and continuous improvement in the pursuit of our environmental goals.

- Exercise innovation in our manufacturing processes and our end products to minimize or prevent the generation of waste and the discharge of contaminants into the environment.

- Ensure, through management support and training, that employees understand and accept responsibility for incorporating environmental quality in their conduct of business.

- Work with all levels of government toward the development and implementation of equitable and effective environmental laws, rules, regulations and policies.

- Establish and maintain operating policies, procedures and programs to implement our corporate environmental protection policy.

Exhibit 4   Policy and Programs

Protection Policy, together with the Environmental Management Program and corporate procedures, were designed to ensure that company-wide environmental programs were carried out in a technically sound and cost effective manner, and complied with applicable government regulations.

Navistar institutionalized its pollution prevention activities under the GREEN Program: Get Reductions of Environmental Emissions at Navistar. Under this program, Navistar's senior environmental and health and safety managers were responsible for establishing overall goals for waste and emissions reductions. Each facility, however, was given autonomy to develop site-specific approaches for accomplishing program goals.

In its 1994 environmental health and safety report, Navistar set pollution prevention goals for 1996. These included a goal of a 20 per cent reduction in the generation and disposal of solid waste. Each plant was expected to contribute to

the achievement of this goal and progress was reviewed annually.

GREEN Program activities also generated bottom-line benefits. Navistar estimated that between 1992 and 1994, it saved more than $15.7 million by reducing raw material and waste disposal costs. A range of projects was underway, targeting pollution prevention and minimization, and recycling and treatment. For example, Navistar had implemented recycling programs for cardboard, wood pallets and other packaging materials at each of its manufacturing sites.

Environmental Activities at the Chatham Plant

Environmental management at the Chatham plant was the responsibility of Dan Uszynski, the environmental co-ordinator. Dan came to the Chatham Plant in 1992 as the New Ideas Program co-ordinator, a position which gave him responsibility for plant cost reduction activities. He then became the environmental co-ordinator in March 1994, and reported to the environmental, health and safety manager. Dan did not have any direct reports.

This plant had been successful in developing an in-house environmental management program, which focused on compliance with government-mandated hazardous waste disposal requirements. Although developing recycling programs for non-hazardous materials had not been a priority, the plant was recycling several types of waste materials. The plant recycled 87 per cent of its paper waste (most office paper and cardboard packaging), and 50 per cent of its scrap wood waste (all wooden pallets). Steel scrap was also segregated and sold to a local scrap dealer.

In 1993 the plant received a Certificate of Achievement from Environment Canada, which recognized the plant's "outstanding achievements and dedication in the protection and restoration of the environment, particularly in the treatment of paint systems waste, as well as overall recycling efforts." Early in 1994, this plant also received an award of merit from the Ontario Ministry of Environment and Energy.

Ontario 3R Regulations

The natural environment had received a great deal of regulatory attention in the Province of Ontario over the last five years. Ontario Regulations 101–105/94, called "3R Regulations," were enacted on March 3, 1994. They consisted of five separate regulations designed to encourage municipalities, business and industry to design, develop and implement programs which would reduce the amount of solid waste materials generated and directed to landfill sites. The stated objective was to eliminate 50 per cent of landfill-directed solid waste by the year 2000 through the implementation of programs designed to reduce, reuse and recycle.

The 3R Regulations did not include fines or penalties for noncompliance. The legislation represented a set of guidelines for municipalities, business and industry to establish programs to support sustainable development. However, a number of industry officials believed that stronger legislation was inevitable.

According to the 3R Regulations, manufacturing operations were required to conduct a waste audit by September 1994, which included the following:

- The amount, nature and composition of the waste generated at the plant.
- The manner by which the waste was produced, including management decisions and policies that related to the production of waste.
- The way in which the waste was managed.

In order to comply with the intent of the 3R Regulations, companies were required to develop a waste reduction work plan which outlined activities designed to reduce, reuse or recycle. The work plan was to include: who will implement each part of the plan; timing of implementation; and expected results. Management was required by law to update the work plan annually, using the following principles:

- Reduction was the first objective.
- If reduction was not possible, then reuse was the next objective.
- If reduction and reuse were not possible, then recycling was the final objective.

The regulation also stipulated that specific wastes had to be separated in the plant. Plants were required to account for aluminum, cardboard, fine paper, glass, newsprint, high density polyethylene (jugs, pails, crates, totes and drums), low density polyethylene (film), expanded polystyrene (foam), polystyrene (trays, reels and spools), and steel.

Chatham Plant Waste Audit

Navistar categorized waste into four streams:

1. *Solid Waste:* Non-hazardous, solid waste, including materials sent to landfills or recycled. The plant generated approximately 9,800 tons

each year, over 60 per cent of which was generated in the trim and chassis assembly operations. Of this total, approximately 5,340 tons was recycled, with the remainder being sent to landfill.

2. *Liquid Industrial Waste:* Non-hazardous, liquid wastes, including pit water and sludge. The plant generated approximately 1,127 tons of this waste annually, most of which was removed from pits in the paint department.

3. *Oil Recycling:* All recycled oil and oil water from pits and totes. Approximately 18 tons of this waste was generated annually at the plant.

4. *Hazardous Waste:* Any hazardous waste, including lab packs, drums, emergency response spills, paint purge solvent recycling system and cyclonic solvent parts/gun cleaners. The plant generated 14 tons of hazardous waste annually.

Dan Uszynski was surprised to find that, according to the budget, the Chatham plant spent $603,000 during fiscal 1994 on waste disposal. Disposal of liquid industrial waste consumed the largest portion of the budget, at approximately 50 per cent. Solid waste disposal was also a significant portion, at an estimated 42 per cent. Hazardous waste and oil recycling represented seven per cent and one per cent, respectively. These figures were for payments to a variety of suppliers, and excluded internal costs, such as the one employee per shift dedicated to collection of the solid waste.

In order to comply with the 3R Regulations, Dan contracted with Browning-Ferris Industries (BFI), a large waste management company, to conduct a waste audit in August 1994. This audit involved a complete analysis of all plant waste generated over a five-day period. To support this audit, all non-hazardous solid waste was directed to a central location on the plant premises where the material could be either sorted and categorized or removed for sorting at a BFI facility. Exhibit 5 provides a summary of the waste audit, with a breakdown of waste generated by waste category and generation point, for the plant's solid non-hazardous waste stream.

DEVELOPING A SOLID WASTE MANAGEMENT PROGRAM

As Dan examined the waste audit he wondered what his next step should be. Although he felt the need to consider all four waste streams, the objective of the 3R Regulations focused on solid waste. Dan also believed that significant opportunities for recycling were available in the solid waste stream, and a plant-wide recycling plan would be the best route to meet waste reduction goals.

Dan believed that establishing a budget and identifying the required resources was critical. The existing arrangement for the cardboard or scrap wood wastes which were currently recycled was revenue-neutral (processor charged no fee and returned no revenue). If his waste management program involved further commitment to recycling, this arrangement would be discontinued. Instead, the plant could recover some of the costs through lower landfill expenses and revenues from recycled materials sold to dealers. Although the market price for recycled materials fluctuated monthly, several companies provided a rough estimate of potential recovery values (Exhibit 6).

Dan believed that he had at least two alternatives. First, he could contract with a waste management company to sort plant waste at a centralized depot, located on the plant premises or at a third-party site. Under this alternative, solid waste collection in the plant would continue unchanged; however, once collected, the solid waste would go to a depot for sorting and processing. This sorting would obviously be a labour intensive process, and Dan expected that Navistar would have to pay approximately $75 per ton for external sorting, handling and transportation for all materials.

A clear advantage of this alternative was that it would have a minimal impact on plant operations and would not require the unionized work force to change their routine. However, Dan was concerned about the implications of not having a plan that dealt with the source of the waste. Contracting with a waste management company to collect and segregate the material would not

A. Breakdown by Waste Category

Waste Category	% Total Weight
Cardboard/Paper	47.2%
Scrap Wood	27.0%
General Waste	19.3%
Plastic	4.1%
Metal (excluding scrap steel and aluminum)	2.2%
Glass	0.2%
Styrene	0.1%

B. Breakdown by Generation Point

Generation Point	% Total Weight
Administration & Cafeteria	1.1%
Material	2.3%
Paint	9.0%
Maintenance	6.5%
Frame	12.6%
Special Equipment	2.7%
Tune & Test	4.1%
Trim	39.5%
Quality	0.4%
Chassis	20.7%
Miscellaneous	1.2%

Exhibit 5   Waste Audit Results, Solid Non-hazardous Waste Generation

Source: BFI Waste Audit of the Chatham plant.

assist in the identification of opportunities for source reduction or reuse.

A second alternative was to install recycling stations throughout the plant. Each station would consist of multiple containers—the number depends on the variety of materials recycled—with each container labeled to hold a specific waste, such as glass or paper. The estimated cost of each station was approximately $250. Although it was unclear exactly how many stations would be required, the waste audit identified approximately 1,000 waste containers throughout the facility. Dan suspected that, if properly organized, a recycling station would be

Waste Category	Recovery Value ($/ton)	Processing, Handling & Transportation Fee ($/ton)	
		Externally Separated	Internally Separated
Cardboard/Paper	$105	$75	$52
Scrap Wood (pallets)	$65	$75	$52
Scrap Wood (other)	$50	$75	$110
Plastic	$60	$75	$52
Metal (excluding scrap steel)	$40	$75	$71
Glass	$35	$75	$52
Styrene	$60	$75	$52
General Waste	none	$75 + current disposal cost ($56.50)	current disposal cost ($56.50)

Exhibit 6   Material Recovery Values & Processing Costs

Source: Estimates by local waste firms.

required for every 2,500 square feet of plant space.

Under this alternative, the segregated solid wastes would be removed to a processing station located in the plant where the material would subsequently be sold to or disposed of by outside firms. Dan estimated that four additional employees, two per shift, would be needed to collect the recyclable materials and operate the processing station, in addition to current staff, if all solid waste materials were recycled. Dan also realized that he would have to hire a full-time employee to co-ordinate plant recycling activities, at a cost of approximately $50,000 annually. Finally, external processing, handling and transportation fees would reduce the direct revenue from the recycled materials by a substantial amount (last column of Exhibit 6).

Although Dan thought that this alternative might provide greater control over waste disposal activities, it would require full co-operation from all plant employees as well as a training program. Because employee work assignments were based on completing specific assembly line operations,

new recycling efforts would add to the workers' tasks and complicate assembly operations. Dan wondered how much support and co-operation he would receive for such a program.

Finally, Dan recognized that he would require the support of corporate and plant management. Corporate management would want to ensure that Dan complied with corporate policies and procedures, including the 20 per cent waste reduction target established as part of the GREEN Program. Plant management would be very concerned about the impact on plant operations and profitability.

Although compliance with the 3R Regulations had been the initial driver for the waste audit and waste reduction work plan, Dan recognized that there may be an opportunity not only to comply with government objectives to eliminate 50 per cent of waste but also to provide legitimate cost savings and position the Chatham plant in an environmental leadership role within the Navistar organization. He knew that both plant management and the corporate environmental staff were anxious to see his plan, and he wondered what steps he should take next.

INDIAN OIL CORPORATION LIMITED—THE MATHURA REFINERY

Prepared by Manish Kumar
under the supervision of Professors
P. Fraser Johnson and Robert Klassen

Version: (A) 2003-12-18

On March 11, 2002, Rakesh Verma, general manager of Mathura Refinery (Mathura), Indian Oil Corporation Limited, India, emerged from the office of the executive director, S.K. Mishra. New national legislation had mandated the industry to produce cleaner-burning fuels. While cleaner-burning fuels would reduce vehicular emissions in the country, there was the possibility of increased local emissions from the refinery from the new processes used to produce these fuels, a situation that Mishra wanted to avoid. Effluent and oily sludge emissions also demanded management attention.

Verma recognized that Mathura Refinery had unique constraints because of its location. Close proximity to a great architectural wonder of the world, the Taj Mahal, and other prominent archeological and ecological landmarks ensured constant public and legal scrutiny of the refinery's environmental performance. Also, being the largest refinery serving the northwest—India's biggest market—meant constant operational pressure to process and deliver products year-round. While other refineries were expanding capacity to address increasing demand, Mathura's capacity was currently capped at eight million metric tonnes per year. Any future expansion of the refinery's capacity would be contingent on its ability to reduce sulfur dioxide (SO_2) emissions and address public expectations.

Verma knew that addressing all of these issues simultaneously, while difficult, was critical. He was expected to present his recommendations next month, and begin implementation later in the year.

THE TAJ MAHAL AND BHARATPUR BIRD SANCTUARY

Northwestern India was home to two of the country's most significant national treasures, the Taj Mahal and the Bharatpur Bird Sanctuary. Located at the city of Agra in the state of Uttar Pradesh, India, the Taj Mahal was one of the most beautiful masterpieces of architecture in the world. Agra, situated about 200 kilometres (km) south of New Delhi, was the capital of the Mughals, the Muslim Emperors who ruled Northern India between the 16th and 19th centuries. It was Shah Jehan who ordered the building of the Taj Mahal in 1630, to honor his wife, Arjumand Banu, who later became known as Mumtaz Mahal, *the Distinguished of the Palace*. The Taj Mahal, a World Heritage Monument, was considered one of the world's most photographed buildings. More than two million tourists visited the Taj Mahal each year.

The Bharatpur Bird Sanctuary was located in the Indian northwestern state of Rajasthan, about 190 km from the national capital of New Delhi and between two of India's most historic cities, Agra and Jaipur. Bharatpur hosted close to 380 species of birds in a 29 square km stretch, approximately 10 square km of which comprised marshes and bogs. The remainder of the area comprised scrublands, grasslands and more than 44,000 trees that have been used for nesting by birds each year. In 1985, Bharatpur was deemed a World Heritage Site.

Indian Oil Corporation Limited

Incorporated in 1959, the Indian Oil Corporation Limited (IOCL) was the largest commercial undertaking in India, engaged in the business of refining, transporting and marketing of petroleum products throughout the country. IOCL was a state-owned enterprise with an objective to build national oil security and competence in the oil refining and marketing business. In 2001, it was ranked 226 in the *Fortune* Global 500 ranking of the world's largest industrial and service companies, and was the only Indian company listed. Among the petroleum refining companies, it was ranked at 19th place by profits and 22nd by sales.[1]

IOCL had a divisional organizational structure. The four divisions, each headed by a director who reported to the chairman, were the pipeline, refineries, marketing, and research and development divisions. In April 2002, IOCL owned seven of the country's 18 refineries, with a combined capacity of 38 million metric tonnes per annum. IOCL had the country's largest network of pipelines, with a combined length of 6,523 km and a capacity of 43.45 million tonnes per annum. With sales of 47.17 million tonnes in fiscal year 2001/02, IOCL held more than 53 per cent of the petroleum products market share in India. Its extensive network of more than 22,000 sales points were backed by 182 bulk storage points and 78 Indane[2] bottling plants. In the fiscal year 2001/02, IOCL had a turnover of Rs 1,149 billion,[3] the net profit was Rs29 billion.

Environmental performance at IOCL had always been regarded by management as a critical component of managing business operations, as reflected in the corporate mission statement (see Exhibit 1). IOCL management believed it had high standards for safety, protecting human health and maintaining close harmony with the ecosystem.

Industry Deregulation

The oil industry in India had operated under the government-controlled Administered Price Mechanism[4] for petroleum products since 1976. The Administered Price Mechanism ensured a fixed level of profitability for the oil companies, and also ensured products used by the economically weaker sections of the population (e.g., kerosene), or for public transport and the agricultural sector (e.g., diesel fuel), were protected from the volatility of international markets.

This regulated structure began to change after a strategic planning group established by the government in 1995 recommended the complete deregulation of India's oil industry by April 2002 and the adoption of market determined pricing. As a result, many companies developed expansion plans as part of its strategy to respond to this newly deregulated marketplace. For example, Reliance's refinery at Jamnagar—a competitor—was rumored

---

To achieve international standards of excellence in petroleum refining, marketing and transportation with concern for customer satisfaction.

To create a modern technology base for self-reliance, growth and development of the business.

To contribute to the national economy by providing adequate return on investment and by setting high standard of leadership in productivity and total quality.

To foster a culture of participation and innovation for employee growth and contribution.

To help enrich quality of life of the community and preserve ecological balance and national heritage.

Exhibit 1   Indian Oil's Corporate Mission
Source: Annual report, 2001.

to have increased its capacity by 80 per cent, to 27 million metric tonnes per annum, in anticipation of market competition and an effort to capture economies of scale. IOCL's Panipat refinery also had plans to double its capacity to 12 million metric tonnes per year.

With many refinery expansions and new refineries under construction, the supply of petroleum products had outstripped the demand. As a result, the industry had started to focus on improving refinery margins by driving down costs in an effort to improve profitability.

THE OIL REFINING PROCESS

Oil refineries process crude oil, a compound that has multiple boiling points, through several heating, distillation and catalytic reaction operations to yield a wide variety of products (see Exhibit 2). These products generally fall into three broad product fractions: light distillates (e.g., gases and naphtha), middle distillates (e.g., motor spirits[5] and kerosene) and heavy distillates (e.g., black oils and tars).

In a typical refinery, crude oil from storage tanks was heated and desalted. The desalted crude oil was then distilled in the atmospheric distillation unit to produce light and middle distillates, along with a residue stream that was further processed. Next, this residue was heated and further processed in a vacuum distillation unit to produce distillate products, as well as an intermediate feedstock for the fluid catalytic cracking, visbreaker, and bitumen units. This fluid catalytic cracking unit chemically treated the feedstock to yield more light and middle distillates. In contrast, the visbreaker unit used

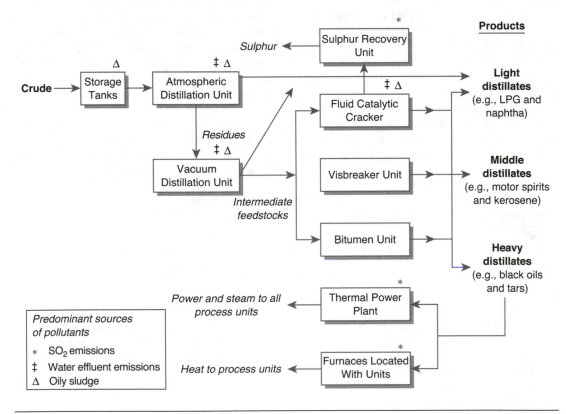

Exhibit 2   Typical Simplified Refinery Process

thermal treatment to yield heavy distillates. Finally, the bitumen unit oxidized residues using compressed oxygen and nitrogen to produce heavy, tar-like products.

Product margins were highest with light and medium distillates, and refinery operations generally tried to maximize their yields. At Mathura Refinery, the overall distillate yield hovered at about 74 per cent, with the remaining heavy distillates being sold as is or used internally. Internal consumption, at five to 10 per cent, was used to heat the furnaces of various units, and to generate power and steam in the refinery's thermal power plant.

The exhaust gases from process operations contained significant amounts of hydrogen sulfide gas (H_2S), a precursor to acid rain that reacts with air to form sulfur dioxide (SO_2). These sulfur compounds were one component of crude oil, with the term "sweet" applied to crude with relatively low levels of sulfur, and "sour" applied to high-sulfur crude. Sweet crudes commanded a price premium of US$4 to US$15 per tonne, relative to sour crudes. It was estimated that if only sweet crude were used in a refinery similar to Mathura Refinery's size and configuration in 2002, the SO_2 emissions would be around 250 kilograms per hour (kg/h). However, certain products, such as bitumen, could not be produced in this situation.

To minimize atmospheric emissions, exhaust gases from operations were fed to a sulfur recovery unit, where the H_2S was converted through oxidation to solid lumps of sulfur. In 2002, the internal combustion of fuel at many refineries such as that at Mathura remained one of the largest sources of SO_2 emissions; another source was a small percentage that escaped the sulfur recovery unit.

MATHURA REFINERY

The densely populated northwestern region of India constituted a major portion of the vast and fertile Indo-Gangetic plains, south of the Himalayas. During the late 1960s, this region witnessed an industrial and agricultural expansion.

The annual rate of growth in demand for petroleum products was estimated at 18 to 25 per cent, and the scale and pace of development was hampered by the lack of refining capacity in the region. Furthermore, logistics constraints limited the ability to import petroleum products into the northwest. Consequently, government planners began to examine the feasibility of setting up a refinery as part of the northwest region's long-term economic development plan.

The central planners had decided to establish the refinery close to the consumption centres in the northwest, as opposed to locating the refinery at the source of the crude oil. After extensive study by IOCL, four sites were shortlisted. In June 1972, based on various technical and commercial criteria, such as close proximity to the national capital region of Delhi and access to major rail and road networks, it was decided to set up the refinery between Delhi and Agra, at Mathura. Mathura was a prominent historical city on the banks of the river Yamuna and believed to be the birthplace of Hindu deity Lord Krishna (see Exhibit 3). The refinery site was 150 km south of Delhi and 50 km northwest of Agra on connecting National Highway 2.

In October 1972, the foundation stone for northwest refinery project at Mathura was laid by Indira Gandhi, prime minister of India. The design engineering contemplated a refinery of conventional design. Although there were no industrial environmental laws and legislation at the time of the detailed feasibility report, IOCL had chosen contemporary technologies for the refinery project; many of these were the cleanest from an environmental standpoint. At that time, the government and IOCL were eager to get the refinery project underway and optimistically believed that the Mathura Refinery would be operational within six years.

Early Environmental Objections to Setting Up a Refinery at Mathura

With the announcement of building a refinery at Mathura, environmental concerns started to be voiced for the first time. Environmental activists

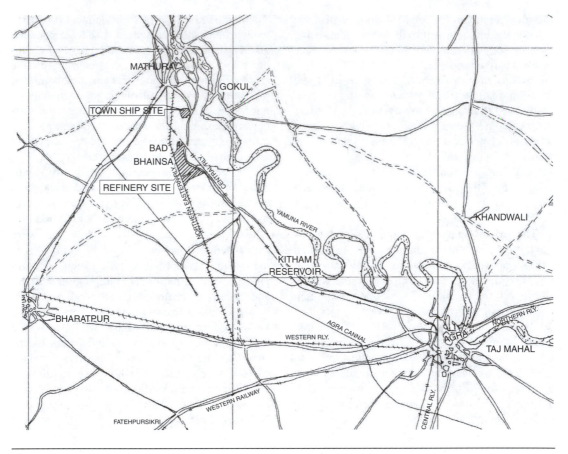

Exhibit 3   Location of Mathura Refinery, Agra, Bharatpur and Air-Monitoring Stations

Source: Company files.

believed that the emissions from the refinery would have a negative impact on the air quality of the surrounding area, which included both the Taj Mahal and Bharatpur Bird Sanctuary. They argued that the refinery emissions, in particular sulfur dioxide (SO_2) and nitrogen oxide (NO) would increase acid rain formation, which in turn would damage the delicate exterior marble surface and beauty of the Taj Mahal. They also argued that the increased air pollution due would have a detrimental effect on the migratory patterns of the birds coming to Bharatpur Bird Sanctuary. Not surprisingly, these concerns received national and international attention, and

both IOCL and government of India took the concerns very seriously.

India's First Environmental Impact Assessment Study

In response, in July 1974, the Dr. Varadarajan Committee was organized to conduct India's first Environmental Impact Assessment (EIA) study with a mandate to advise IOCL on necessary pollution control measures. The committee submitted its final report in August 1978 and found that the existing SO_2 level around Taj Mahal was unacceptably high, at 35 to

40 micrograms per cubic metre. The committee believed that this situation presented serious long-term problems for the region.

However, the committee endorsed the construction of the new refinery at Mathura under certain conditions:

1. the closure of two thermal power plants based at Agra;

2. the conversion of rail traffic from coal to diesel and the closure of the coal engine-marshaling yard;

3. the prohibiting of new pollution-causing operations from locating in the region of the Taj Mahal; and

4. the relocation of an existing iron foundry.

The Central Board for the Prevention and Control of Water Pollution[6] estimated a 50 per cent reduction of sulfur dioxide emissions would result if these recommendations were followed.

The Taj Trapezium Zone

In 1979, Professor M.G.K. Menon headed a high-powered committee to implement the recommendations from the Dr. Varadarajan Committee and proposed the concept of the Taj Trapezium Zone (TTZ). The TTZ, a trapezoidal area of 10,400 square km, was scientifically designed, based on the wind speeds and the existing knowledge of the spread of air pollutants. This area contained important cultural sites in Agra (in addition to Taj Mahal and the Bharatpur Bird Sanctuary). It was decided to relocate some polluting industries out of the TTZ, and forbid the construction of new polluting operations in future. The ambient air quality standard around the TTZ, even in 2002, was the strictest in the world (see Exhibit 4).

Commissioning of Mathura Refinery

The Mathura Refinery was finally commissioned in January 1982, with a capacity of six million tonnes per annum. At the time of commissioning, it was the only refinery supporting the northwest region of India.

The refinery continued to be under scrutiny for any possible impact on the Taj Mahal and the environment, despite the evidence of the various scientific studies. A public interest litigation (PIL) was filed against Mathura Refinery and others, in the Supreme Court of India in 1984, challenging the refinery's negative impact on the region. Although preliminary hearing for the case took place in September 1984, it was about a decade later, in September 1993, that the case came up for regular hearing in the Supreme Court.

ENVIRONMENTAL MANAGEMENT AT MATHURA REFINERY

IOCL had become very conscious of the Mathura Refinery project's controversial image and strove to demonstrate a strong commitment to the environment and the protection of the national heritages by adopting measures based on environmental impact assessment studies and expert committees. Management realized that the choice of process technologies and operating practices at the Mathura Refinery would be driven to a significant degree by environmental considerations.

Design Revisions

In 1982, the Mathura Refinery was commissioned using pollution control measures that were unprecedented in Indian industry at that time, to ensure that minimal effluents were discharged in the atmosphere (i.e., the air, the land and the water).

Air Emissions

A limit of 1,000 kg/h for SO_2 emissions was established for the refinery in the late 1970s. This level was believed to have an insignificant impact on the local environment, as the refinery's emissions were expected to contribute only about one to two micrograms per cubic metre of SO_2 in Agra, relative to the prevailing annual

Country	SO₂ Concentration Standard, Microgram/Cubic Metre (maximum)			
	Annual	24 Hourly	3 Hourly	1 Hourly
• India				
Industrial	80	120	—	—
Residential, rural and others	60	80	—	—
Sensitive (Taj Trapezium)	**15**	**30**	—	—
• USA, Federal				
Primary	80	365	—	—
Secondary	—	—	1300	—
California (US)	—	143	—	715
• Japan	—	107	—	267
• Canada	30	150	—	450
• Switzerland	30	100	—	100 (half hourly, 50 percentile)
Minimum SO₂ Ambient Air Concentrations in the World				
• Contribution from natural resources				3
• Concentration at places far away from pollution sources				
– Rain Forest Panama				2.86
– Antarctica				1.4–4.3

Exhibit 4   Ambient Air Quality Standard of TTZ and Comparison

Source: Expert committee report (chaired by Dr. Varadarajan), April 1995, Vol. I, pp. 45–47.

Note: All values are $\mu g/m^3$ of air.

average concentration of 15 to 20 micrograms per cubic meter. The impact on Bharatpur was expected to be much lower, in the order of 0.3 microgram per cubic meter.

Half of the refinery feed was to be low-sulfur, sweet crude. This facilitated the production of low-sulfur petroleum products, and resulted in lower SO_2 emissions from internal processes. To further reduce sulfur emissions, the design of refinery's power plant was changed in the late 1970s from coal to low-sulfur fuel oil to minimize the emissions of particulate matter and SO_2.

The sulfur recovery units at Mathura were 94 per cent efficient, the maximum possible at the time of commissioning. Moreover, the refinery design called for two sulfur recovery units for removal of sulfurous compounds from gases.

At all times, one unit was to be operational and the other standby. A standby sulfur recovery unit was unprecedented in the oil industry.

For better dispersal of SO_2 and other air emissions, the designs of the stacks for all main furnaces had been changed from stacks of 40 metres in height to concrete stacks of 80 metres. The thermal power plant chimney was made an unprecedented 116 metres high. Continuous ambient air-monitoring stations also were built in four locations: three in the direction of the Taj Mahal, at Farah, Keetham and Sikandra, and one at Bharatpur, in close vicinity of the bird sanctuary (see Exhibit 3). Monitoring at the refinery sites was started in March 1980, which provided the baseline air environment parametres of the region (see Exhibit 5).

Air-Monitoring Station	Distance From Refinery	Year of Commissioning	1981	1982	1994	2000
A. Towards Agra	45 km (Agra city)					
1. Farah	8 km	December 1981	4.8	1.7	7.5	7.2
2. Keetham	23 km	April 1981	3.0	1.0	5.0	4.5
3. Sikandra	35 km	September 1980	7.2	2.1	7.5	7.3
B. Towards Bharatpur	35 km					
1. Bharatpur	29 km (Bharatpur city)	June 1981	5.0	2.5	6.9	4.5

Exhibit 5 SO_2—Annual Average Concentration at Air-Monitoring Stations

Source: Mathura Refinery application for Indira Gandhi Paryavaran Puruskar, 1997.

Notes:

- Mathura Refinery commissioned in 1982.
- Maximum permissible for TTZ: 15 micrograms per cubic metre.

Effluent Emissions

A state-of-the-art, physical, chemical, biological and tertiary treatment plant for the refinery effluent water was also designed. The facility consisted of oil-recovering facilities and five polishing ponds, which provided natural retention and treatment of the effluent before discharge.

Early Progress in Environmental Management (1982 to 1996)

Air Emissions

Although the initial SO_2 emission limit was set at 1,000 kg/h, the Mathura Refinery had always operated well below this, typically at about 600 kg/h. The air-monitoring station data also indicated that the Mathura Refinery had an insignificant impact on the air quality in the areas of the Taj Mahal and the TTZ (see Exhibit 5).

In 1988, the refinery capacity was expanded from six to 7.5 million metric tonnes per annum. At that time, the main atmospheric column was reconfigured, and as a result, the SO_2 emissions from the refinery increased. Simultaneously, the permissible SO_2 emission limit was lowered to

700 kg/h for the winter period. The refinery responded by adopting energy conservation and operational improvement controls to keep the SO_2 emissions to approximately 500 kg/h, despite the increase in capacity (see Exhibit 6).

As a result, the SO_2 emissions of Mathura refinery continued to be comparable to other international oil refineries of similar size and complexity (see Exhibit 7). Efforts in energy conservation had also paid off. At commissioning, the Mathura refinery had been using nearly 10 per cent of its production for internal processes. By 1996, this fell to approximately six per cent, which yielded fuel savings of approximately 32,000 tonnes per annum (along with corresponding reductions in SO_2 emissions).

Effluent Emissions

When commissioned, the Mathura Refinery developed an area of 18,000 square meters around its polishing ponds as an ecological park. The ecological park served as a bio-indicator, as well as providing a home for migratory birds. Research by the Bombay Natural History Society in 1995 documented the presence of nearly 100 species of birds in the park.

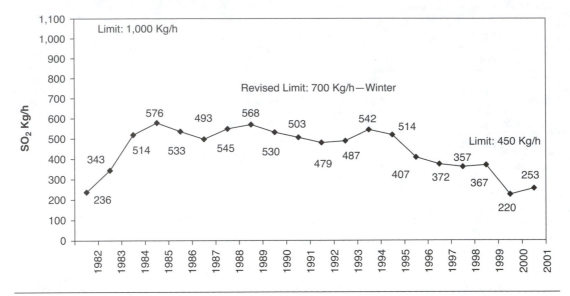

Exhibit 6   Average SO₂ Emissions From Mathura Refinery

Source: Mathura Refinery.

Notes:

• Annual averages are reported for Mathura Refinery.

• Approved limits are based on real time, not average emissions.

Parameter	KOC Japan	Imperial Oil Canada	Montreal Refinery	BP Oil Scotland	Mathura Refinery in 1997–98
Crude capacity (thousand barrels per day)	180	176	120	190	170
Fuel quality— furnace oil—sulfur	0.16%	1 to 3%	2%	1.5%	0.3%
SO₂ emission (kg/h)	210	510 to 750	775	1,600	372

Exhibit 7   Comparison of Sulfur Dioxide (SO₂) Emissions

Source: Mathura Refinery applications for Indira Gandhi Paryavaran Puruskar, 1997.

The effluent was treated to the Minimal National Standards and international standards (see Exhibit 8). To ascertain the suitability of final effluent for agriculture, the refinery started an experimental farming project in collaboration with Aligarh Muslim University in 1986. The 10-year study concluded that final effluent met the irrigation quality criteria and indicated an improved crop yield by around 18 per cent.

Sunil Gupta, chief manager, summarized IOCL's strategy during this time: "IOCL has had

Parameters	US	Canada	Singapore	India MINAS	Mathura Refinery		
					1994	1995	2001
pH	—	—	—	>6–8.5<	7.7	7.7	7.7
Oil	10	10	13.5	10	4	5	5.9
Biological oxygen demand (BOD)	30	—	50	15	7	8	5
Phenol	0.18	0.20	0.70	1	0.02	0.05	0.05
Sulphide	0.17	—	0.70	0.50	Nil	Nil	0.12
Total suspended solids (TSS)	30	15	50	20	17.2	19.3	14
Effluent discharge (m³/t of crude processed)	—	—	—	0.70	0.20	0.21	0.26

Exhibit 8   Comparison of Quality of Treated Effluent From Mathura Refinery

Source: Mathura Refinery applications for Indira Gandhi Paryavaran Puruskar, 1997 and Golden Peacock Award, 2002.

Notes:

- All values are in parts per million (ppm), except pH and effluent discharge.
- MINAS = Minimum National Standard.

a bias for progressively introducing advanced technologies and cleaner processes in its operations. This has largely been done to make our operations environment friendly in terms of both processes as well as products."

ISO Certification and Environmental Performance (1996 to 2002)

In 1995, despite the refinery's strong environmental performance, management was concerned that the PIL still represented a potentially serious problem. The PIL was now being heard in the Supreme Court, after being dormant for about a decade, and it heightened public concerns on Mathura's environmental performance. It became clear that a suitable environmental strategy was needed to address these public concerns.

During this time, the International Organization for Standardization (ISO) was developing a standard for certifying environmental management systems, ISO 14001, which was closely modeled on the earlier British standard, BS

7750. Released in 1996, certification required that a company or site comply with regulations, publicly communicate environmental policies and demonstrate continuous improvement—subject to repeated external, third-party audits. Given Mathura Refinery's earlier certification of its quality management system in 1994 under ISO 9002, management believed that environmental management certification would help improve public perception and offer a tool to monitor continued progress.

As one step in the ISO 14001 certification, environment policies and programs for the next five-year period were developed. These were then shared with all stakeholders, including the general public. A team of internal auditors also was put in place. In July 1996, Mathura Refinery earned the distinction of being the first refinery in Asia and the third in the world with the ISO 14001 certification.

H.P. Singh, general manager of safety & environment protection, who reported to the executive director, commented:

Environmental management, along with safety and health, at IOCL are business imperatives for sustainable growth in global competitive scenario. Our environmental management system has provided a structured framework for balancing and integrating economic and environmental interests. It provided a platform for identifying and reducing environmental impacts continuously. It also has offered a structured forum for monitoring and control by the top management.

For example, one of the environmental objectives was the reduction of overall SO_2 emissions by 40 per cent from 1995 to 2000. Meanwhile, in 1999, the SO_2 limit was revised downward from 1,000 and 700 kg/h in summer and winter, respectively, to a year-round limit of 450 kg/h. If this new lower limit had been exceeded, the refinery would have to be shut down or crude processing reduced until the emissions were brought under the limit.

In reality, the refinery's SO_2 emissions decreased from 514 kg/h in 1995, to 357 kg/h in 1998, to 220 kg/h in 2000 (see Exhibit 6). We reduced our emissions, despite the increase in our crude capacity from 7.5 to eight million tonnes per annum, by introducing cleaner technologies and optimizing processes.

A number of other environmental initiatives were also undertaken as part of ISO 14001 certification process (see Exhibit 9). By 2001, these programs also had met or exceeded their original targets.

New Environmental Pressures

Under the government's Auto Fuel Policy, most recently amended in 2000, cleaner burning fuels were to become a new standard for the industry. These standards specified the production of ultra low-sulfur diesel (which reduced sulfur content from 0.05 to 0.035 per cent), and motor spirits with lower levels of benzene and other aromatics. This standard was to be introduced first in the national capital region Delhi and the Taj Mahal Trapezium. Over the longer term, all fuels produced in India were to meet this standard. Consequently, the Mathura Refinery was

expected to implement the policy directive first, by early 2005, ahead of other refineries that would follow suit as they approached their respective roll-out dates.

Additional processing was required to meet these cleaner fuel standards. New secondary units at Mathura Refinery were to be integrated within the existing process to maximize the utilization of existing infrastructure and keep costs down. The new units were to be located downstream of the Fluid Catalytic Cracker (see Exhibit 2), and were expected to be fully operational by September 2004.

While these new secondary units did not increase crude capacity, the greatest immediate concern was the expected increase in air and water effluent emissions that would result. For air emissions, the refinery was currently operating well below 350 kg/h of SO_2. (Changes in crude oil feedstock and operating conditions resulted in variation in both the annual average and hourly SO_2 emissions.) Unfortunately, the commissioning of the secondary units was predicted to increase SO_2 emissions by approximately 70 kg/h as more sulfur was recovered from diesel and motor spirits.

Similar problems were expected with water effluent. Although the refinery operated significantly lower than the prescribed effluent limits of 0.7 m^3 per tonne of crude processed, the new units would increase the effluent load per tonne of crude processed from the current level of 0.26 to 0.37 m^3 per tonne of crude processed.

Although the Taj Mahal issue had drawn public attention primarily on the SO_2 emission, the refinery was committed to a broad spectrum of environmental protection and improvement. The challenge was to develop and implement an environmental management strategy that would keep air emissions, effluents and solid wastes near their current levels, despite the commissioning of new secondary units.

Air Emissions

At least two alternatives were possible to reduce potential SO_2 emissions. First, Rakesh

Environmental Targets (five years)	Actual Cost (approx.)	Results	Benefits
Reduction of overall SO$_2$ emission by 40% from the 1995 level.	Rs9,400 million	60% reduction achieved by 1999–2000	SO$_2$ emission reduced to 220 kg/h from 514 kg/h with use of cleaner technologies. The cleaner technologies included use of natural gas (started in 1996), for power generation and internal process furnaces and hydrocracker unit (in November 1999). Improved sulfur recovery unit with 99 per cent efficiency (started in August 1999). Improvement in quality and yields and boosting of middle- and high-end distillates, which are higher margin products.
To plant at least 50,000 trees in Agra-Mathura region.	Rs3.6 million	Planted 125,000 by end of 2001	Creation of a pollution sink and greenery.
To reduce energy consumption level to 110 MBTU/BBL/NRGF during next five years.	Rs4,000 million	Target 12% reduction achieved by end of 2001	Cost savings on account of lower energy bill being paid to external source and reduction in fuel oil used for internal generation of power. Lower SO$_2$ emissions.
To reduce consumption of raw water by 10% of the 1995–96 level.	Rs0.5 million	15% reduction achieved by 2001	Conservation of natural resource.
Disposal of total oily sludge, chemical sludge and hospital waste in such a manner to protect soil & ground water from contamination.	Rs7.6 million	3,000 m^3 total capacity PVC-lined concrete pit built by 1999	Centralized, safe disposal of hazardous waste. Avoids contamination of soil and water and recovery of oil. Segregation of wastes made possible recycle and reuse.
Reduction of fugitive emission by 10 per cent over the estimated level of 1998–99 by 2000–2001.	Rs2 million	7% reduction achieved by 2002	Cost savings because of lower fuel loss. Improved ambient air environment in refinery leading to improved occupational work conditions.
To take steps to minimize environmental effects associated with identified top 3 risks in refining activities.	Operational changes	Continuous exercise	Preventive measures to reduce top risks of refinery operations. Confidence building among population living in surrounding areas of refinery.
To educate 200 truck drivers per year on road safety hazards in transportation of petroleum products.	Rs0.1 million	Target achieved	General awareness, improved performance of truck drivers and public relations.

Exhibit 9   Five-Year Environmental Programs and Targets in 1996

could recommend investment in pollution control technology, such as higher efficiency sulfur-recovery equipment. Second, investments might be possible in process modifications in existing operations to reduce energy consumption. Lower energy consumption reduced the use of fuel for internal power generation, which in turn reduced the release of SO_2.

The first alternative, pollution control technology, involved the installation of a tail gas treatment unit that would treat the air emissions from the entire refinery. This clean technology was to be licensed, and was expected to boost the efficiencies of existing sulfur recovery units from their current level of 99 per cent to 99.9 per cent. The tail gas treatment unit and allied facility was estimated to cost Rs1,000 million, and additional Rs0.35 million per annum to operate and maintain. The facility could be operational in 18 months.

As a second alternative, Rakesh believed that there were also opportunities for further reductions in internal energy consumption. Fuel, equivalent to about six per cent of the crude, was being used in the thermal power plant and various process furnaces. These operations represented the largest sources of SO_2 emissions from the refinery. The Process Department had already undertaken a number of initiatives to reduce energy consumption—many of which required relatively little investment. However, other alternatives that would require much larger investment promised substantial reductions. Options included further optimization of the atmospheric distillation unit, installation of new coalescers and re-insulation of steam headers. Collectively, these changes required a capital investment of Rs950 million, with an estimated reduction in fuel consumption of 30,000 tonnes[7] annually. Implementation of those changes must be done during a refinery shutdown; the next one was planned for early 2004.

Unfortunately, the reduction in SO_2 emissions from reduced fuel consumption would not fully offset the increase from new secondary units. As a result, the net refinery emissions would increase after commissioning of new secondary units, to between 350 kg/h and 360 kg/h of SO_2.

A further benefit of investment in reduced energy consumption was a predicted improvement in a distillate yield of approximately 0.8 per cent. This translated into additional revenue of approximately Rs645 million.

Effluent Emissions

Rakesh also had identified two options for the water effluent. As with air emissions, new investment in pollution control technology to augment the existing effluent treatment plant could improve the removal and recovery of contaminants. Alternatively, process modifications might reduce the need for fresh water, thereby ensuring that the final effluent remained near the current levels.

First, further investment in the existing effluent treatment plant could increase its volume by 100 m³/h, to a total capacity of 750 m³/h. While this would cost Rs150 million, it would be possible to target the final quality of treated effluent to 50 per cent to 60 per cent more stringent than the minimal national standards, thus significantly improving the quality of final effluent as compared to the current level. Further, an estimated cost of Rs0.45 million would be required annually for operating and maintaining the new treatment facilities. The increase in capacity would take about 15 months to complete.

A second alternative was to try to reduce the intake of fresh water by an equivalent amount. This could be achieved by adding an additional process unit to purify waste water, such that recycled water could be used in the cooling tower and other areas of the refinery. This alternative would require a lower investment of Rs80 million, and take 10 months to implement. However, this option resulted in a poorer quality water effluent being discharged from the effluent treatment plant; for example, the emissions of oils and total suspended solids might increase by 10 per cent.

Oily Sludge

Like other refineries, the Mathura Refinery faced a challenge with managing its oily sludge, much of which separated from the crude oil while in storage. General industry practices included confinement of sludge, or incineration, or disposal by a third party. Given the sensitive location of the Mathura Refinery, incineration and nearby disposal were not attractive, and the safe confinement of oily sludge on-site had been the only viable option identified to date. However, management recognized that this only deferred treatment. At this time, the oily sludge from the refinery was being confined in a PVC-lined pit, completed in 1999 at a cost of Rs7.6 million, which was designed to accommodate sludge generated up to year 2008.

Rakesh was excited about a new technology being jointly developed by Tata Energy Research Institute and IOCL. The technology relied on oil-eating bacterial strains for the bioremediation of oily sludge and oil-contaminated soil. Successful field trials suggested that this technology had the potential to be a permanent solution for oily sludge treatment, although further development and investment was necessary to bring it to sufficient commercial scale to treat all of the refinery's oily sludge.

Commercial scale development required an investment of at least Rs1 million. Unfortunately, as with any new technology, the risk of failure was very real, despite the success of the field trial. Current estimates placed the probability of success at 80 per cent. If successful, little additional investment would be needed at Mathura; however, annual operating costs were predicted to be Rs0.15 million. The field trial success had drawn the attention of many other firms interested in its use, and Rakesh wondered if IOCL should be prepared to share its technology or charge a licensing fee for its use.

MOVING FORWARD

Rakesh knew that the Mathura Refinery needed an environmental strategy to address air, water and waste concerns, while also supporting IOCL's corporate strategy. While some might suggest that no immediate action was necessary as the new secondary units came online—given Mathura's strong environmental performance relative to government regulations—Rakesh was concerned about public perception and other possible risks. Undertaking any major new initiative would be closely scrutinized, as the refinery continued to wrestle with the implications of industry deregulation in India.

NOTES

1. 2001–2002 Annual Report of Indian Oil Corporation Limited, p. A-3.
2. IOCL's brand for bottled Liquefied Petroleum Gas, which is commonly used for cooking purposes.
3. Cdn$1 = approximately 31 Indian Rupees (Rs).
4. Administered Price Mechanism: A retention price concept, under which the oil marketing companies and the pipelines were compensated for operating costs and assured a return of 12 per cent after tax on net worth.
5. Generally termed gasoline in North America.
6. Control of Urban Pollution Series CUPS/7/1981–8, "Inventory & Assessment of Pollution Emission."
7. Rs10,000 per tonne.

About the Editors

Robert D. Klassen is an Associate Professor of Operations Management and Hydro One Faculty Fellow in Environmental Management at the Richard Ivey School of Business, The University of Western Ontario. Prior to joining Ivey, he worked as an environmental engineer in the steel industry, following earlier experience in the consumer products and petroleum sectors. He earned his doctorate from the University of North Carolina at Chapel Hill.

Since joining Ivey in 1995, Dr. Klassen has enjoyed interacting with students at all levels, including undergraduate, MBA, executive MBA, and doctoral students. He has developed and delivered courses in operations management, operations strategy, service management, management of technology, and, most recently, sustainable development. He has also written more than 20 cases for use with students to bridge between research and teaching, concept and application, theory and practice.

His research interests focus on exploring the challenges for and linkages between manufacturing and the natural environment, linked to both innovation and supply chain management. His research has been published in *Management Science, Journal of Operations Management, Academy of Management Journal,* and *Decision Sciences,* among others. He currently serves as an Associate Editor for the *Journal of Operations Management,* is a Departmental Senior Editor for *Production and Operations Management,* and is on the editorial review boards for several journals.

Larry J. Menor is an Assistant Professor of Operations Management and J. J. Wettlaufer Faculty Fellow at the Richard Ivey School of Business, The University of Western Ontario. He earned his doctorate from the University of North Carolina at Chapel Hill. He has taught undergraduate, MBA, and doctoral students in operations management and service management courses. He has written cases that span a number of operations and service topics such as supply chain management and service strategy.

Dr. Menor's research interests focus largely on strategic issues related to the management of services. He has focused a majority of his effort on understanding how organizations design and develop new services. His research has been published in *Manufacturing & Service Operations Management, Journal of Operations Management,* and *Production and Operations Management,* among others. He currently serves as a Departmental Senior Editor for *Production and Operations Management* and is on the editorial review boards for *Manufacturing & Service Operations Management* and *Decision Sciences.*